THE EMPIRE OF EQUUS

Chapman's zebra

Mongolian wild horse

Nubian wild ass

Domestic horse
(Thoroughbred)

Kulan or chigetai

Grévy's zebra

DPW

Some representatives of the genus *Equus* and its six existing subgenera: *Equus,*
Hemionus, Asinus, Dolichohippus, Hippotigris, and the new subgenus *Quag-*
goides proposed herein by the author. Not shown is *Hippotigris* (the mountain
zebra). In the center is the head of the Thoroughbred "Man o' War."
All figures 1/20 natural size.

THE EMPIRE OF EQUUS

David P. Willoughby

South Brunswick and New York
A. S. Barnes and Company
London: Thomas Yoseloff Ltd.

A. S. Barnes and Co., Inc.
Cranbury, New Jersey 08512

Thomas Yoseloff Ltd
108 New Bond Street
London W1Y OQX, England

Library of Congress Cataloging in Publication Data

Willoughby, David P
    The empire of Equus.

    Bibliography: p.
    1. Equus. 2. Horses. I. Title.
QL737.U62W54   599'.725   72-5180
ISBN 0-498-01047-3

PRINTED IN THE UNITED STATES OF AMERICA

There is no doubt that horses
will exist as long as the human
race, and that is well, for we
still have so much to find out
about them.

C. WILLIAM BEEBE (1877–1962).

Contents

Illustrations		8
Tables		15
Preface		17
1	Nomenclature of the Horse	21
2	Origin, Evolution, and Zoological Position of the Horse	28
3	The Immediate Ancestors of the Domestic Horse	44
4	Growth and Physical Structure of the Horse	49
5	The Equine Skull and Teeth	67
6	The Horse's Existing Perissodactyl Relatives (Tapirs and Rhinoceroses)	80
7	The Horse in History and Art	106
8	Przevalsky's Horse, the South-Russian Tarpan, and the Ancestral "Forest Horse"	128
9	Some Representative Breeds of Light and Medium-Heavy Domestic Horses	152
10	The Draft Horse and Its Derivation	230
11	Life History, Physiology, Intelligence, and Physical Powers of the Horse	247
12	Coat Coloration in the Domestic Horse	299
13	The Domestic Ass and Its Wild Ancestors	306
14	The "Half-Asses" (Hemionids) of Mongolia, India, and the Near East	316
15	Zebras and the Quagga	334
16	The Mule and Other Equine Hybrids	390
17	Anomalies of Size and Development in the Domestic Horse	400
	Appendix	410
	Selected Bibliography	446
	Index	463

NOTE: Since a considerable amount of "overlapping" of subject-matter occurs in this book, readers are advised to use the Index to locate such subjects as are dealt with in more than one place.

Illustrations

FRONTISPIECE.

FIGURE   1.   Mounted skeleton of *Eohippus* found in Wyoming in 1931 29
2.   Restoration of the probable appearance in life of *Eohippus* 29
3.   Changes in the skeleton from *Eohippus* to the modern horse 31
4.   Comparative body sizes of the horse and various ancestral forms .. 32
5.   Family tree, simplified, of the horse and its presumed ancestors .. 34
6.   Relative sizes and proportions of the skull from *Eohippus* to *Equus* 36
7.   Changes in the skull and feet from *Eohippus* to the modern horse 38
8.   Geologic range and geographic distribution of the Equidae 39
9.   Points of the horse (external anatomy) 41
10.   External parts and regions of the equine body 42
11.   Skeleton of the horse 50
12.   Skeleton of a man in four-footed posture 51
13.   Mare and foal 52
14.   Proportions of the body in a newborn Arabian foal 55
15.   Skolma and her foal, Shah 56
16.   Relative growth of the horse as compared with various other animals 57
17.   Growth in length of the limb bones in the Arabian horse 58
18.   Dimensions to be taken of the equine pelvis 59
19.   Comparison of the pelves of a Shetland pony and a domestic ass .. 61
20.   Figure 16 represented diagramatically 62
21.   Classification of the Equidae according to hoof proportions 62
22.   Cross-sections through the hoofs of an Arab horse and a domestic ass 63
23.   Relationship of the outer hoof to the coffin bone in various Equidae 65
24.   Growth of the skull in basilar length in the domestic horse 68
25.   Dimensions standardized for the equine skull 70
26.   Eruption times and appearance of incisor teeth at various ages 72
27.   Slant of the incisor teeth as an indication of age 72
28.   Skull of a two-year-old colt, showing growth of teeth 74
29.   Skull of a five-year-old horse, showing incisor and grinding teeth
in *situ* 75
30.   Schematic representation of tooth wear in the domestic horse 76
31.   Molar teeth of horse, mule, and domestic ass, compared 77
32.   Dental series in two different subgenera of *Equus* 78
33.   Family tree of the *Perissodactyla* (horses, tapirs, rhinoceroses, and
their fossil ancestors 81

8

34. Brazilian tapir 83
35. Malay tapirs in their native haunts 84
36. Brazilian tapir and infant young 85
37. Jaguar attacking a tapir 86
38. Bones of the right fore feet in the horse, the tapir, and the
    rhinoceros 88
39. Comparison of the feet of a horse, a tapir, and a dog 89
40. Skull of Javan rhinoceros 90
41. Great Indian rhinoceros 90
42. Drawing of Indian rhinoceros by Albrecht Dürer 91
43. Drawing of Javan rhinoceros by F. Smit 93
44. Drawing of Sumatran rhinoceros by H. Dixon 94
45. Female black rhinoceros and young 95
46. Head of black rhinoceros 97
47. Foot outlines of horse and black rhinoceros 97
48. Head outlines of a black and a white rhinoceros 99
49. Body outlines of a black and a white rhinoceros 99
50. Front view of white rhinoceros 102
51. White rhinoceros size—compared with man 103
52. Distribution of the two races of the white rhinoceros 104
53. Horses as depicted in prehistoric art 107
54. Wild horses falling over a cliff at Solutré, France 108
55. Head of an Assyrian horse 109
56. Bas-relief showing King Assurbanipal on horseback spearing a lion 110
57. An ancient Egyptian horse and rider 111
58. Egyptian two-horse light war chariot 112
59. Greek youth holding a horse 113
60. The Horse of Selene, a modernized interpretation 114
61. Amazon and Greek horse 115
62. A four-horse chariot race in Rome 117
63. An Indian scout and his horse 119
64. Napoleon and his war-horse Marengo 120
65. George Washington and his horse Lexington 122
66. Breeds of horses derived from the Light Horse type 123
67. Breeds of horses derived from the Heavy Horse type 124
68. "Fighting Stallions", by Anna Hyatt Huntington 125
69. "Female Centaur", by Anna Hyatt Huntington 125
70. Statuette of Arabian horse and rider 126
71. "White horse frightened by lion", by George Stubbs 126
72. Diana and her four-horse team 126
73. "Man controlling trade", by Michael Lantz 127
74. Map showing distribution of Przevalsky's horse and the kulan 129
75. Przevalsky's horse, Persian onager, kiang, and Nubian wild ass,
    compared 130
76. Mare and foal of Przevalsky's horse 132
77. Herd of Przevalsky's horses in New York Zoological Park 133

78. Przevalsky's stallion in winter coat 134
79. Drawing from life of a tarpan filly 136
80. The tarpan, as pictured by Friedrich Specht 138
81. Scythian horsemen training a wild horse 139
82. A herd of "back-bred" tarpans in the Munich Zoo 141
83. The South Russian tarpan, for comparison with Przevalsky's horse .. 144
84. Przevalsky's horse, for comparison with the South Russian tarpan .. 145
85. Restoration of Abel's horse (*E. caballus abeli*) 149
86. Scale drawing, with dimensions, of desert-bred Arab horse 153
87. Head of Arab horse in normal and "classic" attitudes 155
88. Heads of an adult and a newborn Arab horse, for comparison 156
89. "Horse of the desert", in native surroundings 157
90. "Arab and horse", by Adolph Schreyer 159
91. The "Darley Arabian", by George Ford Morris 160
92. Chestnut stallion, Sahm 161
93. Heads of stallion Rifage and mare 163
94. The "Godolphin Arabian", by George Ford Morris 166
95. Eclipse, by George Stubbs 167
96. Scale drawing, with dimensions, of typical Thoroughbred stallion .. 169
97. Hanover and Doncaster, Thoroughbreds 170
98. Seabiscuit 172
99. Whirlaway 173
100. George Wilkes, a noted early-day trotter 174
101. Scale drawing, with dimensions, of a typical Standardbred stallion .. 176
102. Harness and rigging for a trotter 178
103. Harness and rigging for a pacer 178
104. Descent of Hambletonian 10 from the Darley Arabian, et al 179
105. Watson Hanover, a famous trotter 180
106. Billy Direct, holder of the one-mile pacing record (1:55) from
       1938 to 1969 ..:....................................... 181
107. Greyhound, holder of the one-mile trotting record (1:55¼) from
       1938 to 1966 182
108. Greyhound, trotting under the saddle 182
109. Statue of Justin Morgan, by F. G. R. Roth 184
110. Justin Morgan, by George Ford Morris 184
111. Ethan Allen, the first trotter to beat 2:30 for the mile 185
112. Champion Quarter Horse, Paul A. 186
113. Quarter Horse Bloodlines, a genealogical chart 189
114. Champion Criollo stallion, Coriaci 190
115. Head of typical Criollo horse 191
116. A *gaucho* and his Criollo mount 192
117. Head of Lipizzan stallion 193
118. Pluto XX, a Lipizzan "high-school" performing horse 194
119. A Lipizzan horse performing the spectacular *capriole* 195
120. Celtic pony stallion 198
121. Fjord or Western Norwegian pony 200

122. Highland pony stallion 201
123. Head of Shetland pony 202
124. Shetland pony stallion 202
125. Half-wild (feral) Hungarian horses 204
126. Head of a gaited saddle horse 206
127. A champion five-gaited saddle horse 207
128. A "leopard-spotted" horse 211
129. Cleveland bay horse 213
130. German coach horse 213
131. French coach horse 227
132. Two European tarpan stallions, by F. Jung 228
133. Scale drawing, showing body proportions, of a typical draft stallion 231
134. Inclinations of the limb bones in the genus *Equus* 234
135. Percheron stallion "Victor" 236
136. Head of Percheron stallion Don Juan 237
137. Calypso, an ideal type Percheron stallion 238
138. Percheron mare Nerva 238
139. Eight-horse hitch of Percherons from the W. K. Kellogg Institute .. 239
140. Blond-maned Belgian stallion 240
141. Strathore Guard 29109, a Grand Champion Clydesdale stallion .. 241
142. Gallant Prince, a Grand Champion Shire stallion 242
143. Beau Boy, a many-times champion Suffolk stallion 244
144. A herd of feral horses in Oregon 249
145. Some of the principal muscles of the horse 253
146. Brain weight vs. body weight in the Equidae 258
147. Ten phases of the action of a horse in full gallop 260
148. Foot tracks of a horse in various gaits 261
149. "Equine freedom"—a study in arrested motion 263
150. Sprinting time, in relation to distance, for man, greyhound, and
      horse 264
151. Actual running speeds, at given distances, of man, greyhound, and
      horse 265
152. The start of a race between a Quarter Horse, a greyhound, and
      a man 266
153. Miss Princess (Woven Web) setting a Quarter Horse world
      record for 440 yards 267
154. Seabiscuit in action 270
155. A "triple dead-heat" at the Aqueduct Race Track 271
156. World trotting records, 1871–1969 276
157. Location of the center of gravity in the horse 284
158. Horse and rider making a high jump. 285
159. Successive stages of a high jump 287
160. "Greatheart" making a high-jump record 288
161. Arabian stallion, Mustafir, in rearing position 289
162. Rock and Tom, Belgian geldings, pulling 3900 pounds 292
163. Rock and Tom's 3900-pound pull converted to a rolling load 293

164. A circus horse being reared upright 295
165. "Bronco-busting" at a Western rodeo 296
166. Laurent Franco and partners in his equestrian act, *Les Forces d'Hercule* 297
167. Head markings in the domestic horse 302
168. Leg markings in the domestic horse 304
169. Sicilian donkey 307
170. Two donkeys on a street in Naples, Italy 309
171. "Old and young", a study of donkey heads by Benno Adam 310
172. Nubian wild ass in the New York Zoological Park 312
173. A mounted group of the Somali wild ass 313
174: Kulan, or chigetai 317
175. Kulans in their native habitat 318
176. Hunting the kulan—a drawing by August Specht 319
177. Kiang in the London Zoo 322
178. Plaque showing a team of onagers in ancient Mesopotamia 324
179. Coin showing a chariot race with onagers (?) in ancient Greece .. 325
180. Persian onager in the New York Zoological Park 325
181. Indian onager, or ghorkhar 327
182. Head of ghorkhar 328
183. Syrian onagers being captured in ancient Mesopotamia 330
184. Skull of a male hemippus, or Syrian onager 332
185. Grant's zebras, after a sketch by Walter Wilwerding 335
186. Four distinct types of zebras 336
187. Map showing the geographical distribution of the zebras 338
188. Early engraving of an Abyssinian, or Grévy's, zebra 339
189. A Grévy's zebra in the San Diego Zoo 340
190. Head of a Grévy's zebra 341
191. Rear view of a Grévy's zebra, showing stripe pattern 342
192. A female Grévy's zebra in the New York Zoological Park 343
193. A diorama of Grévy's zebras 344
194. Early engraving of a mountain zebra, by George Edwards 345
195. A Cape mountain zebra in the New York Zoological Park 346
196. Hartmann's subspecies of the mountain zebra 347
197. Coat patterns of Burchell's zebra and mountain zebra 348
198. Patterns of croup-striping in three subgenera of zebras 349
199. A pair of true Burchell's zebras formerly in the London Zoo 353
200. Examples of coat-striping in the subspecies *E. burchelli burchelli* .. 356
201. Examples of coat-striping in the subspecies *E. burchelli antiquorum* 357
202. Examples of coat-striping in the subspecies *E. burchelli böhmi* 359
203. Selous's zebra. A mounted specimen in the Chicago Natural History Museum 360
204. Chapman's zebras in Kruger National Park 362
205. A Chapman's zebra in the Los Angeles Zoo 363
206. A Chapman's zebra in the San Diego Zoo 364

207. A Chapman's zebra in the San Diego Zoo 366
208. Head of Chapman's zebra, front view 367
209. Chapman's zebra, rear view 368
210. Chapman's zebras at a drinking-place in the wild 369
211. "No two alike"—a herd of Chapman's zebras in Kruger National
     Park 370
212. Burchell's zebras broken to harness, a drawing by F. W. Frohawk .. 371
213. Edwards's quagga, after a lithograph made in 1751 373
214. Daniell's quagga, from the author's *African Scenery* (1805) 373
215. A photograph from life of the female quagga in the London Zoo 374
216. Another photograph of the female London Zoo quagga 374
217. The stuffed skin of the male quagga that lived in the London Zoo,
     1858–1864 376
218. Mounted quagga foal in the South African Museum, Cape Town .. 377
219. Mounted quagga specimen in the Senckenburg Museum, Frankfurt,
     Germany 378
220. Skull (probably) of the female quagga of the London Zoo (1851–
     1872) 379
221. Skull of the male quagga of the London Zoo (1858–1864) 380
222. Skull of a male quagga in the Academy of Natural Sciences,
     Philadelphia 383
223. Mrs. M. H. Hayes riding a mountain zebra 384
224. Comparison of the limb-bone proportions of *E. occidentalis* with
     of *E. burchelli* and *E. quagga* 387
225. Sixth century B.C. statuette of a mule 391
226. Plaque showing a pack-mule used by King Assurbanipal of Assyria 392
227. Mules drawing a cart in Seville; a painting by Alex. Wagner 394
228. A Poitou mule, "Brunette" 395
229. Foal of a mountain zebra and Somali wild ass cross, and its mother 396
230. Hybrid offspring of a Grévy's zebra and a jennet 397
231. Hybrid zebra-horse, or zebrule 398
232. Giant and dwarf farm animals, after an engraving by H. Leutemann 401
233. "Lubber", a 6 ft. 8 in. high draft horse 402
234. "Brooklyn Supreme", probably the heaviest though not the tallest
     horse on record 403
235. The largest horse and smallest pony compared 405
236. Arabella Matilda 827, a miniature donkey jennet 406
237. A six-mule hitch of miniature mules 407
238. "Oregon Wonder", a horse with a 10-foot mane and tail 408
239. A horse with "rocking-chair" hoofs 409
240. Diagram to indicate the principal external measurements of the
     horse 412
241. Body outline, with proportions, of a typical Shetland pony stallion.. 414
242. Body outline, with proportions, of a typical Przevalsky's horse
     stallion 415

243. Body outline, with proportions, of a typical kulan or chigetai stallion 416
244. Body outline, with proportions, of a typical domestic jackass 417
245. Body outline, with proportions, of a typical Grévy's zebra stallion .. 418
246. Body outline, with proportions, of a typical mountain zebra stallion 419
247. Body outline, with proportions, of a typical Chapman's zebra stallion 420
248. Body outline, with proportions, of a typical Western quagga (*E. occidentalis*) 421
249. Hypothetical family tree of the genus *Equus* 437
250. Body weight in relation to carpus width in various hoofed mammals 441
251. The giant hornless rhinoceros, *Baluchitherium*, compared with a present-day great Indian rhinoceros 444

Tables

1. Comparative measurements of a typical male newborn and a typical adult Arab horse 54
2. The "Occipital Index" in various examples of the genus Equus 69
3. Eruption time of the teeth in the domestic horse 73
4. External differences between the South Russian tarpan and Przevalsky's horse 146
5. Comparative measurements of six champion trotting stallions and 11 Roadsters 175
6. Measurements of Orloff trotters 180
7. Heights and weights of some well-known Quarter Horses 187
8. Average measurements of Quarter Horse stallions and mares at 5 years of age 188
9. Average measurements of 95 purebred Criollo stallions and mares 191
10. Average measurements of 207 Lipizzan horses 196
11. Shoulder height and typical coloration in various breeds of ponies 197
12. Average measurements of purebred Shetland ponies 200
13. Height, weight, and body-build in various breeds of horses 205
14. Breeds or races of the domestic horse, listed geographically 208
15. Characteristics of some leading breeds of light horses in the United States .. 214
16. Brief descriptions of lesser-known breeds of light horses and ponies in the United States and elsewhere 215
17. Measurements of the typical draft horse 232
18. Typical inclinations of the limb bones in Light and Heavy horses 233
19. Factors for estimating the optimum bodyweights of horses 235
20. Some of the principal muscles of the horse 254
21. Intelligence in relation to adult age/gestation length 257
22. World records over various distances for Thoroughbreds 269
23. Reduction factors for rating horse-racing records 272
24. World records over various distances for trotting horses 275
25. World records over various distances for pacing horses 276
26. Pulling power in relation to bodyweight in draft horses 291
27. Distribution of white markings on the feet of 2000 domestic horses 304
28. Synonymy of terms for zebras of the Burchell's species 354
29. External differences between the Cape mountain zebra and Burchell's zebra .. 361
30. Typical proportions of the body and limbs in various examples of Equidae .. 413
31. Mean lengths of the limb bones in various examples of Equidae 424–425
32. Limb-bone ratios (indices) derived from Table 30 426–427

33. Cranial and dental measurements of equine specimens measured by the
      author 428–429
34. Basilar length of the skull 431
35. Postcranial skeletons of equine specimens measured by the author 434–435
36. Area, volume, and bodyweight in various hoofed mammals 441
37. Supporting area of the foot in several graviportal mammals 443

Preface

If, as someone has said, the literature of a subject is an index of the subject's popularity, the Horse ranks high in public favor, since to date, in numerous languages throughout the civilized world, more than five thousand volumes* have been published dealing with this time-honored servant and companion of man. Therefore, in adding to this vast literature the present volume, the author feels that no apology need be offered. In view, however, of the many branches of the subject, it will be appropriate to state the aims and scope of the present work, and its limitations.

First, this book is not intended to deal with *all* the breeds of the domestic horse—even, say, the fifty better-known breeds—in thorough detail. Secondly, it contains no advice either on veterinary practice or on horsemanship. Rather, it is primarily a treatise from the point of view of *natural history* on the various living species of the horse tribe: wild as well as domestic; and, so far as present knowledge permits, on their origin, distribution, characteristics, and relationships. Thus designed, and despite its limitations, it is hoped that *The Empire of Equus*** will appeal to a large circle of readers, both popular and scientific—in short, to hippophiles (horse-lovers) throughout the world.

A certain amount of the zoological background of the present work dates back over twenty years to material which was then assembled for a proposed book on the same subject to be authored jointly by Dr. Chester Stock, late Professor of Paleontology at the Institute of Technology, and the present writer. When Dr. Stock died in December 1950, the writer was left with this material, which included many fine photographs for which permission for reproduction had been obtained. For this reason, most of the following acknowledgments concern individuals or organizations who cooperated with Dr. Stock and the writer during that former period. It is to be emphasized, however, that the entire text of the present volume is new; and it has been updated so far as this has been possible or practicable. Happily, most of the natural history of the horse is a relatively unchanging subject. What it requires is knowledgable elucidation rather than periodic updating.

Necessarily a book of this nature and scope reflects the work of many previous investigators as well as that of the present author. Therefore, to all who have preceded

---

* As this estimate was made some years ago, the number of works today could well be *twice* this figure.

** Pronounced e'kwus, the Latin name for horse. (Equidae, however—the Latin name for the horse family—is pronounced ek' wa de.)

him in this well-trodden field, and whose contributions are referred to throughout the text, the author extends his thanks. However, for any and all misstatements or errors, the author alone assumes full responsibility.

To the many persons whose generous assistance and cooperation have helped make this book a reality, grateful acknowledgment is here made. Especially helpful have been the following persons, many of whom were contacted during the early stages of the author's investigations: Wayne Dinsmore, then Secretary of the Horse and Mule Association of America; Ellis McFarland, Secretary-Treasurer of the Percheron Horse Association of America; Bowman A. Brown, Manager, *The Harness Horse;* A. A. Cederwald, Secretary-Treasurer of the American Remount Association; C. E. Howell, former manager of the W. K. Kellogg Arabian Horse Ranch at Pomona, California; A. MacKay Smith, authority on the Cleveland Bay horse; Helen Michaelis, Secretary of the American Quarter Horse Association; S. R. Speelman, Associate Animal Husbandman of the Bureau of Animal Industry; Dr. Remington Kellogg, then Curator of the Division of Mammals, United States National Museum; Dr. John Eric Hill, Assistant Curator of the Department of Mammals, American Museum of Natural History; Dr. D. Dilwyn John, Department of Osteology, British Museum; Dr. D. A. Hooijer, Rijksmuseum van Natuurlijke Historie, Leiden, Holland; the late Dr. Angel Cabrera, Museo de la Plata, Argentina; and the late Tromp van Diggelen, Cape Town, South Africa. I am grateful also to officials of the Los Angeles County Museum of Natural History, who have generously permitted me to reproduce here a number of illustrations that I made originally for their own publications.

Finally, I extend my thanks to the Publishers, who, by sparing neither care nor expense, have carried through in the fullest degree the hopes and plans of the author.

David P. Willoughby

Laguna Beach, California

THE EMPIRE OF EQUUS

1
Nomenclature of the Horse

Although the familiar terms, horse and mare, are used to distinguish a male and a female animal of this kind, the name "horse" is used also as a general term for both sexes of *Equus caballus*. The latter is the "scientific" (Latin) name that was assigned in 1758 to the domesticated horse of Europe by the Swedish systematist, Carolus Linnaeus (he Latinized even his own name, from Carl von Linné).

To the reader who is unfamiliar with the "scientific," or technical, system of classification established by Linnaeus, it may be explained that under this system *all* animals (also plants) are identified by two names, the first being the name of the *genus* to which the animal belongs, and the second the same of the *species*. A genus is a division or category of classification *between* a family and a species. Occasionally a third name is used to indicate a *subspecies*, variety, or geographic race of the species. For example, the full scientific name of the Mongolian wild horse is *Equus caballus przewalskii*. Here, however, the third name refers not to a geographic locality, but to the *name of the person* (Nikolai Mikhailovich Przevalski, a Russian explorer) after whom the subspecies was named. The use in this manner either of a personal or a locality name is common zoological practice.

Thus, in any modern language, among those familiar with the Linnaean system of classification, the Latin name *Equus caballus* is known to refer to the horse, while the third name—in this case *przewalskii*—indicates that the animal is sufficiently different from the common or domestic horse to be regarded as a *subspecies* or variety. It should be noted that the generic name (in this case, *Equus*) is always capitalized, while the specific name (here, *caballus*), as well as the subspecific name, is written or printed in lower case italics.

As to the origin of the name "horse," that appears to be lost in antiquity. In Latin the classical name is *equus*** and the vulgar name *caballus*.** Another Latin name is *jumentum*, from which comes the French *jument* (mare). In Greek the name is *hippos;* in Anglo-Saxon it is *hors*. In Old German the name was *hros;* in modern German it is *Ross* or *Pferd*, in Friesian (Holland) *hars* or *hors*, in Dutch *paard*, in Old Saxon and Icelandic *hross*, in Swedish *hast*, in Danish *hëst*, in Italian *rozza*, in Spanish *caballo*,

---

* This would appear to be a common Indo-European term, in sound if not in spelling, since in Sanskrit it is *acvas*, in Irish *ech*, in Welsh *eb*, in Gaulish *epona*, etc.

** The word *caballus* comes from the horse's hollow hoof mark (*a cavo pede*) because, in walking, the sole of the foot leaves a hollow imprint that differs from the tracks of other animals.

in Russian *loschad,* in Polish *kon,* in Hungarian *honfoglalo,* and in French *cheval.* From the latter have come the words *chevalier, chivalry, chivalrous;* while from the Latin *caballus* have come *cavalier* (a horseman, or knight), *cavalry* (a body of horsemen), and *cavalcade* (a parade of persons on horseback). Other Latin words pertaining to the horse are *equinus* and *equus,* from which are derived our words *equine,* meaning horselike; *equitation* and *equestrian,* pertaining to horsemanship and to a horseback rider, respectively; *equerry,* an officer having charge of the horses of a prince or nobleman; and *equidae,* meaning the horse family.

In that large Asiatic area between China and Siberia known as Mongolia, the people of which have been horsemen from the earliest historic times, the domestic horse is known as *morin,* and the wild horse (*Equus caballus przewalskii*) as *taki.* The Hindustanian word for horse is *kuda* or *huda.* The word among the Malayans, some 2000 miles to the southeast, is exactly the same. This would seem to prove that the early Malayan tribesmen who introduced the horse into that region became familiar with the animal through the Hindus.

The name horse, according to one source, is descended, through the Old German *hros,* from the Sanscrit (sacred Hindu) word *hrēsh,* meaning to neigh, so that the name means "the neighing animal." A more generally accepted explanation, however, is that the name has come to us from the Anglo-Saxon word *hors,* which signifies swiftness; and it is possibly connected with the Latin *currere* (whence our word *courier*), to run.* Thus derived, the name horse means "the swift-running animal." In ancient Iran (Persia) the horse was named *aspa,* from the old Aryan root *ac* or *ak* (to go rapidly). According to Duerst, with reference to the primitive Iranian, "Just as he saw his swift horse cover long distances in a short time, he saw the sun go over the immense vault of heaven in a short time, So he called the sun, in his Avesta, by the name of 'aurvat-aspa' . . . the swift-horsed."

At least two series of names for the horse derive from the Greek words *hippos* and *kaballos.* From *hippos* have come many compound words, among them *hippopotamus,* meaning "river-horse"; *hippocampus,* meaning "sea-horse"; *hippodrome,* meaning "horse-course" (or race-course for horses and chariots); *hippotigris,* meaning "tiger-horse," and used by the Greeks and Romans to designate the zebra; *hippology,* the study of the horse; and such names for fossil horses as *hipparion,* meaning "pony," *hippidium,* "being like a horse," and various names ending in *hippus,* such as *merychippus* ("a ruminating horse"). From the Greek *kaballos* came the Latin *caballus,* the Italian *cavallo,* the Spanish *caballo,* and the French *cheval.* The Dutch name for the horse, *paard,* was used by the early Cape Colonists to denote the mountain zebra, which they called *wilde paard.* Curiously, the quagga, which was a more horselike animal in every way, they called *wilde esel* (wild ass).

Even certain present-day personal names have their origin in ancient names for the horse. The masculine name Philip, for example, is a shortened form of the Greek *Philippos* (*philos,* "loving," plus *hippos,* "horse"), meaning "a lover of horses." The corresponding feminine name is *Philippa.* The familiar word *hobby,* meaning an absorbing pastime or interest, is taken from *hobbyhorse,* which in turn comes from the Middle English word *hoby,* "an ambling pony." The common name *Dobbin,* for a workhorse, is from the personal name Dobbin, from Robin, diminutive of Robert. The name

---

* Concisely, William Beebe has put it: "The most reasonable derivation of the word *horse* is by way of the Old Teutonic *horso,* via the pre-Teutonic *kurso,* to the root *kurs* of the Latin *currere,* to run." [1]

"Jockey," applied to the rider of a racehorse, comes from the Scotch word *Jockie,* a diminutive of Jock, or Jack, a nickname for John.

As with other well-known domesticated animals, there are also many names to designate the two sexes and the young of the horse. The commonly used name of the uncastrated adult male, *stallion,* means "the horse at stall;" that is, one kept for breeding. This is derived from the Low Latin *stallum* (a stall), the Old High German *stal* (a stable), and the Old French *estallon.* It corresponds to the Modern French *étalon* and the Italian *stallone.* The Modern German equivalent is *hengst.* A stallion is also sometimes called an "entire." A castrated male horse is known as a *gelding* (from the Icelandic *geldr,* meaning barren). A *ridgel,* or *ridgeling,* is a horse half-castrated or with only one descended testicle. The word *stud* is sometimes used as a synonym for stallion, but more often is used to denote a collection of horses and mares for breeding, also the stable or place where they are kept. Originally, however, this word (from the Anglo-Saxon *stōd* meant a drove of wild horses. From *stod* came also the Anglo-Saxon *stēda,* and from this the English word *steed,* meaning especially a war horse, or one used for occasions of state or display; the term is now largely restricted to literary or poetic use. Another name for a war horse is the familiar term *charger.*

A stallion that is also a father or male parent is called a *sire;* and when a foal (see below) is of important lineage, as in the case of certain racehorses, we say that the foal was sired by his male parent. A sire's sire is a *grandsire,* and so on. A *tail male* is the sire line, or top line in a pedigree, back to the original sire.

Mare, the named used for a female over four years of age (or younger, if bred to a stallion), is derived, through the Scottish *mear* and the Middle English *mere,* from the Anglo-Saxon *mere* or *myre,* meaning simply a female horse. When the female is also a mother, it is customarily called a *dam* (French; from the Latin *domina,* feminine of *dominus,* master). A broodmare is one kept exclusively for breeding. A female parent's mother is called a *granddam,* or a second dam. The term *distaff side* means the female line or bottom line in a pedigree, back to the tap root. A *yeld mare* is one that has not borne a foal during the season; a barren mare.

A young horse of either sex may be called a *suckling* but is more generally referred to as a *foal* (from the Middle English *fole,* from the Anglo-Saxon *fola*) until it reaches the weaning age (about five to six months), when it is called a *weanling.* Beyond this age, if the sex is known, a young entire (uncastrated) male should be called a *colt,* and a young female a *filly.* These terms apply until the animal has reached the adult stage, or four or five years of age. Thereafter the erstwhile colt is called a *horse,* and the filly a *mare.* To designate both the age and the sex of an immature animal, it is quite proper to use the terms *filly foal, suckling colt, yearling filly,* etc. A racehorse, by the way, is regarded as being one year old on the first day of January following its birth, and its subsequent official "birthdays" are as of January 1. A *weanling* is a foal which has been weaned but has not yet passed a January 1.

Incidentally, the name *colt* (a word of Anglo-Saxon derivation) may be applied to a young male donkey, a zebra, or a camel, as well as to a young male horse. The name *filly* is derived from the Old Norse *fylia* and the Anglo-Saxon *fola,* and means distinctively a female foal or a young mare. Equivalent to the Anglo-Saxon *fola* are the Latin *pullus* and the Greek *polos,* all referring to a young horse of either sex. The sons and daughters of a stallion are known as his *get* (not his gets). The progeny, or offspring, of a mare are usually called her *produce.*

The English name *pony*—the term generally applied to a horse 13 hands (52 inches) or less in height—was at an earlier time spelled *powny.* The name is derived, probably through the Old French *poulenet* (diminutive of *poulain,* colt) and the Lower Latin *pullanus,* from the aforementioned Latin *pullus,* meaning a young animal. "Pony" is also connected with the Greek *polos,* or foal, and ultimately with the English foal. Thus, it would seem that the name pony was at first applied incorrectly, as an equivalent of the name foal, in the belief that *all* small horses were necessarily immature. "Cob" is a name correctly applicable to a strong, thickset, short-legged horse of medium size (13½ to 15 hands high).

A *palfrey* is a saddle horse for the road, or for state occasions, as distinguished from a war horse (from the French *palefroi,* from the Lower Latin *palafredus,* an extra post horse).

A *Thoroughbred* (the word being usually capitalized) is a horse especially bred and trained for racing under the saddle, and whose ancestry or pedigree can be traced back in all lines, without interruption, to forebears registered in the *General Stud Book.* Hence, in point of having a clear, unmixed ancestry, the Thoroughbred may be regarded as *purebred.* A horse, or other pedigreed animal, designated by the latter term, however, is not necessarily a Thoroughbred, and the two terms should not be used interchangeably. The term "Thoroughbred" is completely designative, and it is superfluous to say "Thoroughbred horse." The term "purebred" is customarily applied to horses, other than Thoroughbreds, which are free of alien blood, and which are registered, or are eligible to registry, in the record book of the breed to which they belong.

A *grade,* or halfbred, horse is one resulting from a mating in which one parent is a Thoroughbred or purebred and the other is of unknown or mixed ancestry. It is said that more than 90 percent of the horses in the United States can be so designated. The term *crossbred* is used in reference to the breeding of a horse whose sire and dam are of different, but known, breeds. If a cross involves two different *species* rather than breeds, the resulting offspring is known as a *hybrid,* and the practice as *hybridization.*

As an instance of the extent to which the meaning of a word may change through use, there is the word *nag,* which today commonly refers to an old, no-good, broken-down horse. Yet this name, which derives from the Dutch *negge* (after the Anglo-Saxon *knegan,* to neigh), originally mean a small horse, or a pony. Other disparaging names for a tired, worn-out, useless horse are "plug" and "jade." The latter word is probably a variant of the North English dialectal *yaud* and the Scottish *yade, yad,* or *yaud,* pertaining to a work horse, especially a mare. These terms come, in turn, from the Old Norse, *jalda,* a mare, which is of English origin. "Tit" is a name applied to a small or inferior horse; often a good little or young horse. In France, a small horse, or cob, especially one used to pack or courier service in the army, is commonly called a *bidet.* In early days, a *pad,* or *pad-nag,* was a horse ridden with a pad in place of a saddle, and often referred to as an "ambling pad."

A *jennet* (or *genet*) is a small Spanish horse, the name coming from the native term *ginete,* signifying nag. *Ginete,* in turn, was probably derived from *Zenãta,* a Barbary tribe, with whose horses the Spanish horses were crossed. In the United States, the term "jennet" denotes a female ass.

In China and Thailand (Siam), curiously, the native name for the horse is *ma,* pronounced just like our abbreviation of the word Mother.

Several centuries ago, in Europe, there was a great deal of discussion about an imaginary animal believed to have been produced by crossing a bull with a mare or jennet, or a horse or jackass with a cow. The name given to this hypothetical creature was *jumart,* or *jumar.* The name appeared suddenly in zoological literature in the middle of the sixteenth century, and the existence of the animal was given credence by many eminent scholars of the period. As a result, widespread belief in the animal persisted for more than 200 years. One of the first (about 1774) to doubt the existence of the jumart was the French naturalist Buffon. Others were the physiologist Albrecht von Haller and the German naturalist J. F. Blumenbach. It was not, however, until 1803 that the jumart was conclusively proved to be a myth. In that year Leopold M. Caldani, an Italian anatomist, showed that there was no authentic case of the impregnation of a mare by a bull or of a cow by a stallion. The so-called jumarts were really small hinnies or mules. The word "jumart" was perhaps a corruption of the French word *jument,* meaning mare (from the Latin *jumentum,* horse).

Names for the Western Horse

The vocabulary of the Western horseman abounds in picturesque terms, derived mainly from the Mexican or Spanish, describing the Western horse. The name *mustang* is said to have come from the Spanish *mesteño,* a group of stockraisers. Horses that escaped from a range controlled by a mesta and ran wild were called *mesteños,* the suffix *eño* meaning "pertaining to" or "belonging to." Thus the name mustang signified a *feral,* rather than a true wild, horse; that is, a horse which, through having strayed and become ownerless, had largely reverted to the natural or wild state. The man who chased the *mesteños* was called a *mesteñero,* or "mustanger." A drove, or band, of mustangs was known as a *manada.* Among the Indians, an outcast stallion was called by a name which meant "dog soldier"; and the white settlers adopted the same name referring to such rogue horses. In South America, the typical cow-horse is called *criollo* (Spanish) or *criolo* (Portuguese), meaning "native," the name being a diminutive of the Spanish *criado* (servant). A *remuda* (Spanish) is a relay of horses, from which are chosen those to be ridden for the day.

The name *bronco* (or *broncho*) also comes from the Spanish, and means "rough," "wild," "unruly." This name was applied particularly to individual range horses (descended from the mustang breed) which possessed more than the usual amount of wildness and fighting ability. And, as is well known, the cowboys who attempt to "break" these bucking, fighting, outlaw horses of unsavory reputation are called "bronco busters." Such "bronco busting" is still to be seen in the annual rodeos held in the Western states. Another name for a cowboy is "buckaroo." This is a corruption of the Spanish (or Mexican) word *vaquero,* "a cowboy or herdsman," from *vaca,* "a cow."

In the Northwest, a cow-horse, or cow-pony, is sometimes referred to as a *cayuse.* This name was first applied to Indian ponies that had been brought, probably from Mexico through California, into the Northwest and developed by the Cayuse (ki-uś) tribe of Indians living in Oregon. Indeed, it would appear that the cayuse is one of the very few characteristically Indian horses to have been purposely bred by them. Nowadays the horses bred and trained especially for "cowboy" work on the large cattle ranches of the West are generally grouped under the term "stock horses."

It should be pointed out that the Spanish names for the feral horses of the plains came into use only after such names had been introduced by Spanish-speaking cattlemen, about 1820–30. Earlier, the large herds of horses on the prairies were commonly referred to as "wild horses." Various places in which these horses had been particularly numerous are still known by such picturesque names as "Wild Horse Desert" (Texas); "Wild Horse Draw" and "Wild Horse Creek" (Kansas); "Bronco" (Texas); and so on. In fact, in the state of Texas alone there are twenty-seven places named

"Mustang Creek;" various "Horse Hollows;" and one town named "Wild Horse."

A present-day range horse of mustang descent, if straggly, underfed, and of poor physical condition, is generally called a *broomtail* or *fuzztail*. Sometimes the name used is *bangtail*; however, the original bangtail was a range *steer* whose tail had been "banged." In roundups, it was customary to snip the tuft of the steer's tail so that the animal would not be counted a second time. Thus, such a snip-tailed steer became a "bangtail." In the owyhee badlands of Eastern Oregon—one of the last strongholds of "wild" horses in the West—the horses are (or were) known interchangeably as *oreanas, slick ears,* or *broomtails.*

The pinto, so popular among the Indians, is a horse of mottled color, the name coming from the Spanish word *pintado,* meaning "painted." In cowboy vernacular, such a horse is often called, simply, a "paint." More specifically, if the markings of a pinto horse are white and black, the animal is to be called a *piebald;* and if white and any color other than black—such as bay, brown, or chestnut—a *skewbald.* The word *bald,* by the way, comes from a Middle English word meaning "a white-faced horse." Hence, the name piebald is particularly applicable to a horse that is not only of black and white mottling generally, but which has also a white face. Another name for a pinto or spotted horse is a *calico.*

The Spanish language is abundant in terms for designating the exact color characteristics of a horse. The vocabulary was already extensive in Old Spain, but the *vaqueros* (cowboys) of Spanish America added to it. A list of some of the principal Mexican terms used to denote peculiarities of color and markings, together with the English equivalents of the terms, was brought out in a book by W. A. Whatley in 1940.

Certain colorations distinguish several breeds, or types, of horses now being developed and popularized in the West. The name of that beautiful horse, the *Palomino,* is, according to one definition, taken from the more correct Spanish word, *palomilla,* meaning, among other things, "a cream-colored horse with white mane and tail." In Mexico, Palominos were once known as "Isabellas," because of the circumstance that Queen Isabella II of Spain (who ruled from 1833 to 1868) used horses of this type to draw her royal coach. Palominos with cream or white spots or patches are called "Palomino-Pintados."

The name *Appaloosa* designates a type of Western stock horse of localized spotted coloration. It is a corruption of the name, Palouse, of the region in Central Idaho and Eastern Washington where these horses were originally developed (from mustang stock) by the Nez Perce Indians. Another type of spotted horse, often (though not invariably) having more extensive markings than the Appaloosa, is the *Colorado Ranger.* This horse is being bred primarily, however, for cow-horse utility, and the coloration is of secondary importance. The name albino is self-descriptive; although it has been only recently that a strain of American Albino horses has been developed. In this connection, it is doubtful whether a true albino horse exists. Those so-called are simply individuals approximating the condition generally, but having pink skin and colored eyes.

Even the *voice* of the horse is interpreted differently by the peoples of different nations. Whereas we (and other English-speaking people) say "neigh," the French interpret the sound as "en-nee," the Germans as "ee-ha-ha," the Spanish as "ha-ee-ee," the Russians as "pr-r-r," and the Japanese as "heen."

When Jonathan Swift wrote his satirical romance, *Gulliver's Travels,* he gave to the horsepeople in his story the name "Houyhnhnms," a word ingeniously intended to express a horse's neigh or whinny. Perhaps this was Swift's subtle way of injecting a few "horse-laughs" into his story!

Although, strictly speaking, the name "horse" belongs only to the domesticated and wild or extinct members of the species *Equus caballus,* the term is often used by zoologists in a more inclusive sense. From this broader point of view one may speak not only, for example, of the Arab horse, the Morgan horse, or the draft horse, but may include with these familiar domestic forms such wild species as zebras and the Asiatic hemionids or "half-asses," looking upon them all as "horses." A less confusing procedure, however, is to call all forms other than *E. caballus* "members of the horse family."

On the other hand, one may refer conveniently to certain early ancestors of the present-day horse as "three-toed horses," even though such ancestral animals were far more dissimilar zoologically from *Equus caballus* than are today's zebras and wild asses.

When Linnaeus in 1758 named the "typical" horse *Equus caballus,* he took as its representative the Norse horse, or pony, of Scandinavia (see Fig. 121). Hence, in considering or evaluating other domestic breeds, or wild species of *Equus caballus,* it is well to bear in mind the distinguishing characters of Linnaeus's "Norse horse," which today is more generally called Norwegian Fjord-horse (see p. 198).

Note and Reference

1. Charles William Beebe, *Horses and Men, Bull. New York Zool. Soc.* 43, no. 6, (November-December 1940) : 186.

2
Origin, Evolution, and Zoological Position of the Horse

The earliest known ancestors of the horse family flourished about 55 million years ago during the geological epoch known as the Eocene ("dawn of the recent"). These "dawn horses," as they have romantically been called, were, however, so small in size and different in structure that had not larger, intermediate forms of horselike affinity been found in a geological or evolutionary sequence, the original or primeval animals would hardly have been recognized as ancestors of the horse as we know it today.

The remains of "dawn horses" have been found in Eocene deposits both in the United States and in England. Actually, those in England were discovered first (in 1838, in the London Clay of Herne Bay, Kent), and were studied and named in 1839 by the eminent British paleontologist, Sir Richard Owen. To the remains, Owen gave the name *Hyracotherium,* on the supposition that the little animals were related to the hyrax (or cony, of the Bible). *Hyracotherium* stood only about 12 inches high at the shoulder, thus having been about the size of a fox. It had three toes on the hind feet and four on the front. The terminal toe bones gave evidence of having been encased in tiny hoofs. "Splints," or vestigial toes, existed on each foot, indicating that still-earlier ancestors had possessed four (possibly five) toes on the hind feet and five (the basic number for most mammals) on the front.*

Eohippus, the remains of which have been found (the first in 1867) in Eocene rocks in Wyoming, New Mexico, Colorado, and Utah, may have been slightly larger on the average than its European contemporary, *Hyracotherium,* although there were probably many different species of each animal, with corresponding ranges in size (13 or more species of *Eohippus* alone have been catalogued.) The carefully restored specimen at the California Institute of Technology (Fig. 1), from which the writer made the external reconstruction shown in Fig. 2, stood nearly 14 inches high at the shoulder. The weight of the animal in life would have been about 12 pounds.

In both *Hyracotherium* and *Eohippus* the neck, head, and limbs were all relatively shorter than in the modern horse. The back was noticeably arched, and the general appearance of the animal in life must have been much more like that of a small

---

* It is generally believed that the common ancestor of all the *Perissodactyla* (odd-toed ungulates) was a small, five-toed member of the group called *Condylarthra,* which originated in the Paleocene and Late Cretaceous (see Fig. 33).

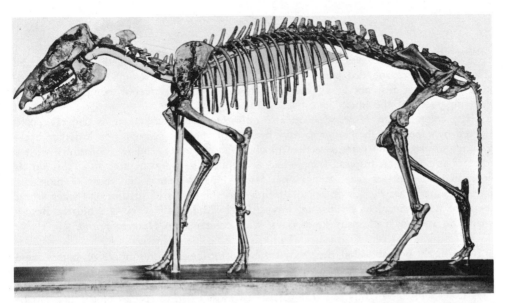

Fig. 1 Skeleton of Eohippus, found in 1931 in the Big Horn Basin, northeastern Wyoming, and mounted by William Otto of the Department of Paleontology of the California Institute of Technology. × 0.18 natural size. From this mount was made the drawing shown in Fig. 2.

Fig. 2 Eohippus, the "dawn horse," from a restoration by the author of its probable appearance in life.

carnivore, especially a civet, than like a horse. The teeth, which were short-crowned and covered with low, rounded knobs of enamel, without cement, resembled those of monkeys or of pigs, but not at all the long-crowned, cement-covered, complex-patterned grinding teeth of the horse.

The coloration of *Hyracotherium* and *Eohippus,* while unknown, is generally considered by experts in the matter to have been light spots or splotches on a darker background, similar to the pattern seen in newborn tapirs today, and in conformity with a forest habitat. That tropical, jungle-like surroundings were natural to *Eohippus* is deduced from the fact that among some of its remains were found those of monkeys. It is presumed that the "dawn horses" frequented the banks of streams and lakes where they fed upon succulent shrubs and leaves. Reginald Innes Pocock, a scholarly British writer on mammals of many kinds, says, with reference to *Hyracotherium:*

> It is highly probable that the many-toed, shorter-legged forerunners of horses were to a varying extent plantigrade and adapted to locomotion on soft soil, and walked on a large pad behind the middle toe of the feet, just as tapirs and rhinoceroses do. A useless vestige of this pad still persists in most existing species of the horse tribe as the 'ergot,' a small area of thick, horny, naked skin on the back of the fetlock.[1]

The several accompanying illustrations show the generally accepted course of evolution from *Eohippus* to *Equus.* Fig. 3 shows the changes in size and proportions of the body, skull, feet, teeth, and pelvis that occurred during the 55 million years between *Eohippus* and *Equus.* In Fig. 4 are illustrated the respective body-sizes of five successive generic forms, while in Fig. 5 these forms, interspersed between a number of other ancestral types, appear in relation to their respective geological epochs and a time scale. On this simplified family tree it will be observed that at least a half-dozen of the "stems" end in what have been called "blind alleys of evolution." That is, the present-day subgenera of the horse family have had as immediate ancestors only certain forms which in their evolutionary course had reached the Middle Pliocene on the stem shown.*

Fig. 6 illustrates in exact scale, for comparison, the skulls of six ancestors of *Equus,* along with the skull of a modern domestic horse.

Fig. 7 shows, in addition to skulls, the evolution in the hoofs and foot-bones of the ancestors of the horse, leading to *Equus.* (The longer of the two feet in each series is the hind foot.)

Fig. 8 shows twenty genera ranging from *Hyracotherium* to *Equus,* along with their distribution geographically as well as geologically. (On this chart the title, *Equidae,* is used in an unconventionally broad sense, as including *all* genera of horse-like perissodactyl, or "odd-toed," animals. Incidentally, the term "odd-toed" refers,

---

* It should be pointed out, though, that at the time the writer drew up this chart he had accepted *Astrohippus* as an ancestor of *Equus,* in conformity with the general belief on this point by American paleontologists. However, the writer's own subsequent analysis of the proportions of the limb bones in *Astrohippus* showed clearly that this form had no affinity with *E. caballus.* If any existing subgenus of *Equus* could be descended from *Astrohippus,* it would be *Heminous,* not *Equus;* but even in relation to *Hemionus* the dwarf-sized *Astrohippus* presents so many marked divergences in its skeletal proportioning as to make any relationship with the existing hemionids highly unlikely.

As is shown in the elaborate family tree in the Appendix (Fig. 249), it would seem that all forms of living Equidae, including *E. caballus,* have descended from one or more forms of *Pliohippus. Plesippus,* as is shown, was the probable ancestor, not of *E. caballus,* but of various zebra-like forms.

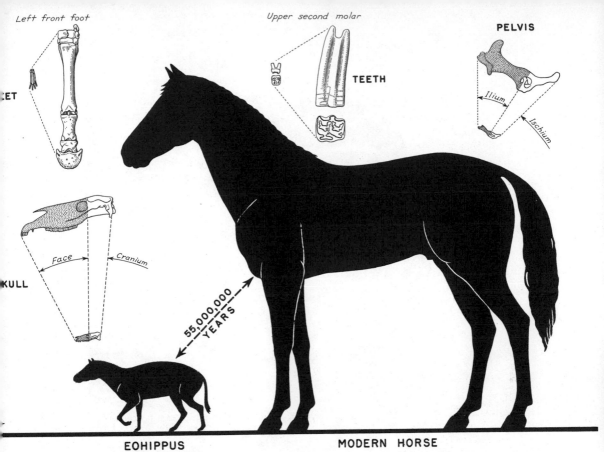

Left front foot

Upper second molar

TEETH

PELVIS

Ilium

Ischium

FEET

Face

Cranium

SKULL

55,000,000 YEARS

EOHIPPUS

MODERN HORSE

Fig. 3 Evolution of the skull, feet, teeth, pelvis, and general body size from *Eohippus* to *Equus*.

not to any *peculiarity* in the toes, but to their *odd number,* which characteristically is one, three, or five.)

Changes in climate, terrain, and vegetation during the approximately 50 million years between *Eohippus* and *Equus* brought such structural changes as enabled the species at any given time to escape their enemies, find sufficient food, and contribute to the evolution of their kind through natural selection and the "survival of the fittest."* The progressive development of greater body size, longer limbs, and specialized grinding teeth, along with the unique transition from three or four toes (and hoofs) to a single enlarged one, indicates the changes in the environment that must have taken place during this long period. Lush jungle vegetation gave way to temperate-zone forests, and then to treeless plains and hard ground. These environmental changes, in turn, brought a need for greater running speed and endurance in order to outdistance attacking carnivores.

By Pliocene time, the general proportions of the skull, body, and limbs had become essentially the same as those of the modern horse. In all the species of *Plio-hippus* the outer toes had become atrophied splints, and by mid-Pliocene time the first one-toed "horses" made their appearance. From *Pliohippus* have come (see the family tree in the Appendix) not only today's true (caballine) horses, but also the

---

* Which, more correctly, as was pointed out by H. G. Wells, should be "survival of the *fitter.*"

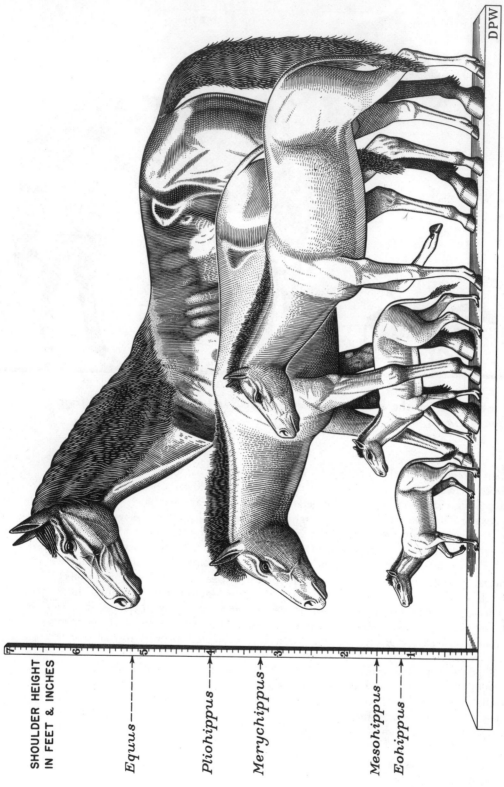

SHOULDER HEIGHT
IN FEET & INCHES

Equus

Pliohippus

Merychippus

Mesohippus
Eohippus

DPW

Fig. 4 Comparative body sizes of the horse and various ancestral forms. No attempt has been made to show the coat-pattern of the earlier forms, which were probably spotted, dappled, or striped.

five other subgeneric groups represented by three types of zebras, the domestic and wild asses, and the hemionids or so-called "half-asses." As is also shown by the family tree, numerous other descendants of *Pliohippus* died out before reaching post-glacial time, although three forms in Mexico and two in South America almost made it. So, too, died out the large, quagga-like form named *Equus* (*Quaggoides*) *occidentalis,* the so-called "tar-pit horse" of Rancho La Brea, of which the writer has made a definitive study and which will be described later in this book.

By Pleistocene (Ice Age) time, *Equus,* or the horse and its relatives as we know them today, had come into full bloom. From this period the skeletal remains of at least twenty different forms of the true horse, *Equus caballus,* have been studied and subspecies names given to them. Most of these subspecies were massive, heavy-built horses, resembling the present-day draft breeds but with relatively longer legs, while a few presented a contrast in being of the slender build of a racehorse. As to the horses and other equine forms present in North America during the Pleistocene, the indications are that some forms at least came to America from Eurasia, following a route which at the time included a land passage over Bering Strait. There is evidence also that a reversal of this immigration took place both in the case of horses and of various zebra-like species, which originated in America and migrated to Asia, Europe, and Africa. That is, there were probably many back-and-forth migrations both westward and eastward during the approximately one-million-year duration* of the Ice Age.[2]

So far as the present volume is concerned, the emphasis is on the existing or recently extinct subgenera, species, subspecies, and domestic breeds of the genus *Equus.* Fossil species are mentioned only where they have close affinity with existing forms. The classification of the latter forms as followed by the writer is as below. Following the scientific (Latin) name of each form is (1) the name of the author who first described the animal; (2) the year in which the description was published; (3) the *common* name of the animal; and (4) the typical locality (or locus of the type specimen). The classification followed herein—with the exception of the new subgenus *Quaggoides* proposed by the author—follows the two prime groupings (A and B) adopted by Bourdelle and Lavocat.[3]

GENUS *Equus* Linnaeus, 1758

A. Equidae with unmarked (or very incompletely striped) coats; a mid-dorsal stripe in all wild forms and in certain breeds of domestic horses; sometimes a shoulder stripe; sometimes zebra markings on limbs:
  1. Subgenus *Equus*** (H. Smith, 1841)
     a. *Equus caballus caballus* C. Linnaeus, 1758 (domestic horse) Norway.
     b. *E. caballus przewalskii* M. Poliakov, 1881 (Przevalsky's horse; Mongolian wild horse) Desert of Dzungaria, in the western Gobi.
     c. *E. caballus gmelini* O. Antonius, 1912 (tarpan; South Russian tarpan) Steppes of Ukrainia. Now extinct except for "back-bred" zoo specimens.
  2. Subgenus *Hemionus* (P. Pallas, 1775)
     a. *Equus hemionus hemionus* R. Lydekker, 1904 (kulan; kulon; chigetai; dziggetai) The Altai, in western Mongolia.

---

* The latest determination is "somewhat greater than" 800,000 years.

** Since the genus also is *Equus,* to avoid confusion the writer prefers the name *Caballus* for Subgenus 1.

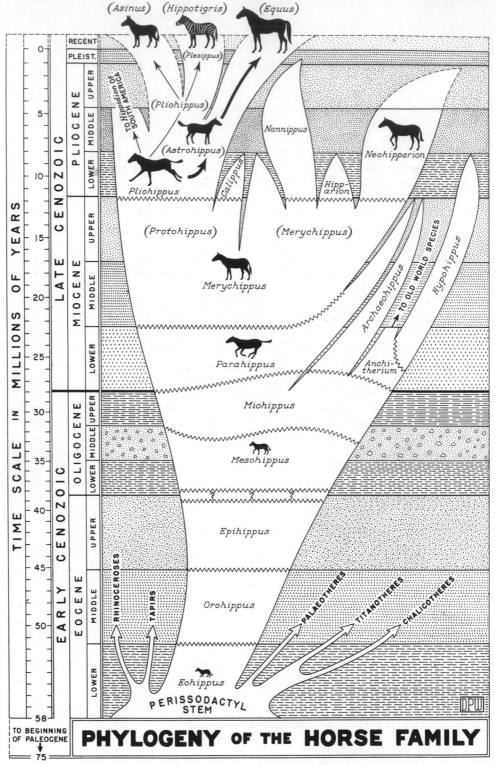

Fig. 5 Family tree, simplified, of the horse and its presumed ancestors. (See also the more detailed phylogenetic diagram in the Appendix.)

b. *Equus hemionus kiang* W. Moorcroft, 1842 (kiang) The Ladakh range, in the western Himalayas (elev. 13,000–16,000 ft.)

c. *E. hemionus onager* P. Boddaert, 1784 (Persian onager) Kasbin, N.W. Iran.

d. *E. hemionus khur* R. Lesson, 1827 (Indian onager; ghor-khar) Kach.

e. *E. hemippus* I. Geoffroy St. Hilaire, 1855 (hemippus; Syrian onager) Syria. Now extinct.

*3. Subgenus *Asinus* (J. E. Gray, 1825)

    a. *Equus asinus asinus* C. Linnaeus, 1766 (domestic ass; donkey; jack; burro) Southern Asia.

    b. *E. asinus africanus* L. Fitzinger, 1857 (Nubian wild ass) Eastern Sudan.

    c. *E. asinus somaliensis* T. Noack, 1884 (Somali wild ass) Somaliland, district of Berbera.

B. Equidae with striped coats:

  4. Subgenus *Dolichohippus* (E. Heller, 1912)

    a. *Equus grévyi* E. Oustalet, 1882 (Grévy's zebra) Abyssinia.

  5. Subgenus *Hippotigris* (H. Smith, 1841)

    a. *Equus zebra zebra* C. Linnaeus, 1758 (mountain zebra; Cape mountain zebra) certain mountain ranges in the south or southeast districts of Cape Colony (formerly included Southwest Africa also).

    b. *E. zebra hartmannae* P. Matschie, 1898 (Hartmann's zebra) between the Hoanib and Unilab rivers, Southwest Africa.

  6. Subgenus *Quaggoides,* subgen. nov. (D. P. Willoughby, 1966)

    a. *Equus burchelli burchelli* J. Gray, 1825 (Burchell's zebra; Dauw; Bonte-quagga) Plains of Cape Colony, south of the Orange River.

    b. *E. burchelli böhmi* P. Matschie, 1892 (Böhm's zebra; including Grant' zebra) Pangani, on the east coast of Tanganyika near the Kenya border.

    c. *E. burchelli selousi* R. Pocock, 1897 (Selous's zebra) Mashonaland and possibly eastward into Mozambique south of the Zambesi River.

    d. *E. burchelli antiquorum* H. Smith, 1841 (Damaraland zebra; Chapman's zebra) Southwest Africa, northern part; including Benguella district of Angola.

    e. *E. quagga quagga* J. Gmelin, 1788 (quagga; Cape quagga) Now extinct; formerly the plains of Cape Colony south of the Orange River.

    f. *E. occidentalis occidentalis* J. Leidy, 1865 (Western quagga) found in fossilized form in the tar-pits of Rancho La Brea, Los Angeles, California.

The above list comprises only those equine forms described or reviewed in the present volume, and which can with some confidence be classified subgenerically. The number of named fossil species and subspecies of *Equus* NOT considered here is very large, possibly as many as a hundred forms. For readers interested in the classification and descriptions of the numerous Pleistocene species and subspecies of *Equus,* the technical papers on the subject by the following authors in particular should be consulted: Rütimeyer, 1863; Kovalevsky, 1873; Burmeister, 1875; Woldrich, 1882; Cope, 1887; Ameghino, 1889; Pavlow, 1890; Wüst, 1900; Gidley, 1901; Duerst, 1908; Soergel, 1911; Sefve, 1912; Antonius, 1912b, 1913a, 1919, 1926, 1929a; Hay, 1913, 1914, 1915, 1917; von Reichenau, 1915; Matthew, 1015a; Merriam, 1916; Schwarz, 1922, 1927; Abel, 1928; Stehlin, 1929; Stirton, 1940, 1942; Cooke, 1950; Azzaroli, 1966; and Willoughby, 1966.

---

* In order to deal with the *domestic* forms of Equidae consecutively, Subgenus 3 (which includes the domestic ass) is presented hereafter in the text *before* Subgenus 2.

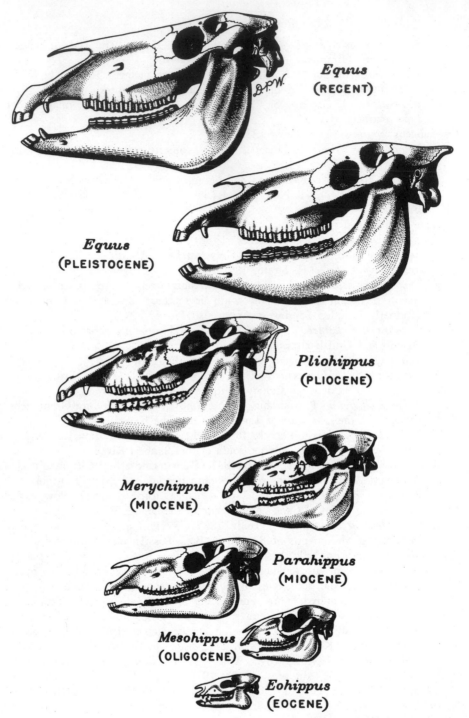

Equus
(RECENT)

Equus
(PLEISTOCENE)

Pliohippus
(PLIOCENE)

Merychippus
(MIOCENE)

Parahippus
(MIOCENE)

Mesohippus
(OLIGOCENE)

Eohippus
(EOCENE)

Fig. 6 Relative sizes and proportions of the skull from *Eohippus* to *Equus*. All figures $\times$ 1/8 natural size.

Systematically expressed, the zoological classification of the common or domestic horse is as follows:

KINGDOM *Animalia* (animals in general)

SUBKINGDOM *Vertebrata*

PHYLUM *Chordata* (animals with backbones)

CLASS *Mammalia* (warm-blooded animals that give milk to their young)

SUBCLASS *Theria* (mammals that bring forth living young)

INFRACLASS *Eutheria* (placental mammals. Excludes monotremes and most marsupials)

COHORT *Ferungulata* (carnivores and hoofed mammals)

SUPERORDER *Mesaxonia* (in which the leg is in line with the middle toe)

ORDER *Perissodactyla* (odd-toed, non-ruminating, hoofed mammals, comprising the horse, tapir, and rhinoceros)

SUBORDER *Hippomorpha* ⎱ of which the members of the horse family
SUPERFAMILY *Equoidea* ⎰ are the sole surviving representatives

FAMILY *Equidae* (the Perissodactyla, exclusive of the tapir and the rhinoceros)

SUBFAMILY *Equus* ⎱
GENUS *Equus* ⎰ horses, zebras, asses, and hemionids

SUBGENUS *Equus* (true or caballine* equidae)

SPECIES *Equus caballus* (existing or recently extinct forms include only the domestic horse, Przevalsky's horse, and the tarpan)

SUBSPECIES *Equus caballus caballus* (the domestic horse in all its breeds)

The various existing members of the horse family (horses, zebras, asses, and hemionids) have these distinguishing limb-bone and dental characters in common:

The digits, or toes, consist of a single functional one in each foot, the digit III or cannon-bone; while the lateral digits II and IV are represented by the splints (or splint-bones) alone. Hence, horses and their kin walk upon the terminal bone of the third digit only, this bone being encased during life in a large, solid hoof. To draw an analogy, in a human being this would be equivalent to walking, not just on the two middle fingertips (or toetips), but on the *nails* of these digits! In horses, what corresponds to the human wrist is called "knee"; and what corresponds to the human heel is called "hock"; and both these joints are located high off the ground, giving to the horse its distinctively long limbs (see Fig. 9) and running ability. In true horses the hoofs are roundish, sometimes fully circular; while in the zebras, asses, and hemionids they are elongate or oval-shaped (see Fig. 23).

In all these animals the upper incisor (cutting) teeth number three on each side, each tooth being chisel-shaped and slightly concave on the distal (tongue) side. The canine teeth are developed only in males, and are separated by a short space from the outer incisors and by a longer space, called *diastema,* from the first premolars. The premolars in the upper jaw usually number three on each side, but occasionally include a very small additional one, PM^1, present at the front end of the tooth-row. In the lower jaw the number of teeth is the same, with the exception that PM_1 occurs only rarely. The premolars in each tooth-row are normally three in number (PM^2, PM^3, and PM^4), as are also the molars (M^1, M^2, and M^3). Thus the tooth formula for males is normally 6 incisors, 2 canines, and 12 grinding teeth in each jaw, making a total of 40 teeth; while the number in females, which lack canines, is 36. The relationships of these various teeth are shown clearly in Figs. 28 and 29.

---

* By *caballine* is meant typical horses (those characterized by having broad hoofs and low, broad pelves), as contrasted with the narrow-hoofed, narrow-hipped zebras, asses, and the so-called Asiatic "half-asses" or hemionids.

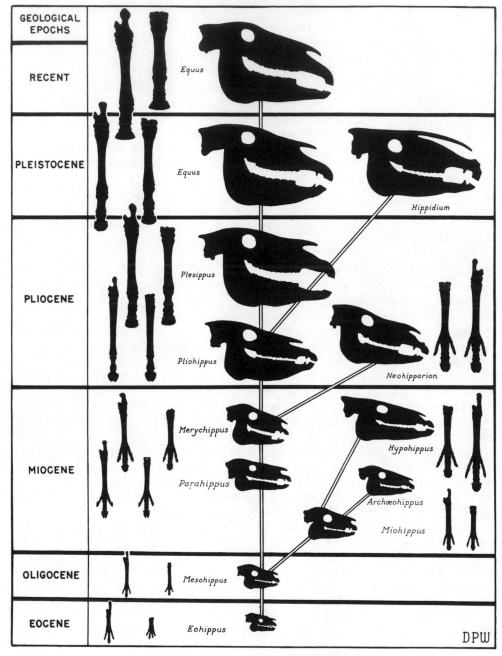

Fig. 7 Diagram showing some of the principal changes in skull and feet of the horse in its evolutionary history through geologic time.

The premolar and molar teeth have high (vertically long) crowns, which gradually push upward (or, in the upper jaw, downward) as they wear with use. At one time it was believed (and is still occasionally asserted) that the long-crowned teeth of horses grew continuously throughout life, but now it is known that these teeth reach their full length at four or five years of age. The continuous elevation of the occlusal (chewing) surfaces of the teeth is caused by regular *bone growth* at the bottom of the alveoli (tooth-sockets), which pushes the teeth outward and reduces the depths of the sockets. The crown of each tooth thus shortens with wear until the abraded surface reaches the neck of the teeth.[4]

The limbs of equine animals are clearly adapted for swift running over hard ground; and the teeth for cropping and masticating the coarse grasses and other herbage of the open plains comprising these animals' natural habitat. Foals are capable of rapid running within a few hours after birth. Horses and their relatives are gregarious, and they breed once in about every two years, normally giving birth to a single foal at a time. Mares have two nipples, located on the lower abdomen. The winter coats of horses grow in the fall, beginning about September, and are shed in the spring, when they are replaced by short summer coats. The truly wild species and subspecies assigned to the genus *Equus,* consisting of horses, zebras, asses, and hemionids, are today found only in Asia and Africa.

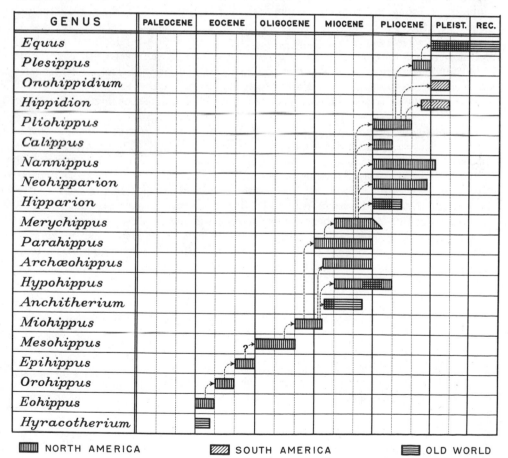

Fig. 8 Geologic range and geographic distribution of the *Equidae.*

Further to the foregoing general description of the existing Equidae, the following particulars apply specifically to the domestic horse (inclusive of its numerous varieties and breeds):

While the sexes are much alike in general appearance, males (stallions) are slightly taller, heavier-boned, thicker-bodied, and generally larger than females (mares). The necks, in particular, of stallions are visibly thicker than those of mares, while the width of hips may be slightly less. The greater docility of gelded males, and the circumstance that one stallion can serve 80–100 mares has led to the practice of castrating almost all yearling males (colts) except racehorses. A gelding loses neither strength nor speed, but may to some extent lose endurance; and he does not have the thick, high-crested neck of the stallion. As to the size and proportions of a horse's body, they vary according to breed, especially as to whether the individual is of "light horse" type or heavy draft build. (The specific physical measurements and proportions of representative forms of horses, zebras, asses, and hemionids are given in Chapter 18). Coat color, which varies greatly, is discussed in Chapter 12. Growth and development are dealt with in Chapter 4. In the latter chapter and in Chapter 5 are discussed various details of anatomy, dentition, and skeletal structure.

Taking the Norwegian horse (specifically, the Fjord pony* of western Norway, shown in Fig. 115) as a valid representative of the type of domestic horse familiar to Linnaeus, a listing of its principal physical characteristics would show these points (some of which are in marked contrast to those of wild forms of *Equus caballus*): head and ears relatively small; mane long and pendant, with a forelock; tail-tuft long and more or less fully haired to the root; general coloration dun (yellowish bay), with a dark mid-dorsal stripe running from tail to forelock through the mane; legs below knees and hocks usually dark; hoofs (especially those on the forelegs) broad and rounded; chestnuts small and usually on all four legs; number of lumbar vertebrae usually 6.

Paleontologists, when comparing fossil equids with living species, generally prefer to use the skeletal elements of wild equines rather than domestic horses, on the premise that the domestic animals have been appreciably altered by artificial selection and breeding. However, Otto Antonius, a Viennese authority on the subject, points out that "Perhaps no animal, except the camel, shows so little change of the skull due to domestication as does the equid type."[5] To this statement the writer would add that the proportions of the limb bones, also, in domestic horses show surprisingly little differentiation from those of Pleistocene species. In fact, the modern Arabian horse— with the exception of its enlarged hoofs—presents in the relative lengths of its limb bones proportions almost identical to those which express the average of the entire genus *Equus*.

---

* Various sources, including Webster's New International Dictionary, define the term "pony" loosely as a horse not over 56 or 57 inches in height, although the so-called polo pony, which is a type rather than a breed, may range up to 64 inches! The broncos, mustangs, and cayuses (Indian ponies) of the western United States are sometimes called ponies regardless of size. In Germany, where an effort has been made to be systematic in the matter, the term "pony" is restricted to horses not over 120 cm (47¼ inches) in withers (shoulder) height, while those that measure between 121 cm (47.6 inches) and 147.3 cm (58 inches) are known as *kleine Pferden* ("little horses").

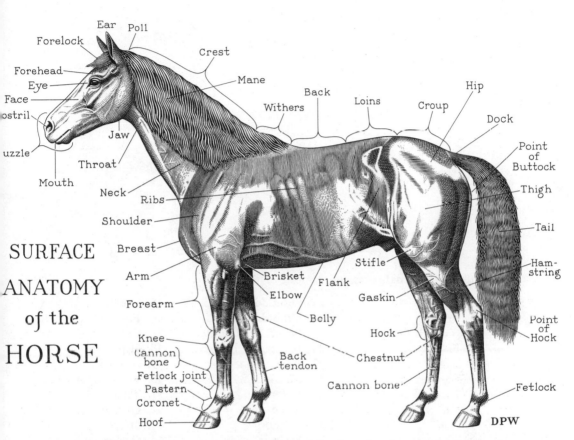

Ear — Poll
Forelock — Crest
Forehead — Mane
Eye — Back
Face — Hip
ostril — Withers — Loins — Croup
uzzle — Jaw — Dock
Throat — Point of Buttock
Mouth — Thigh
Neck — Ribs — Tail
Shoulder — Ham-string
Breast — Stifle
Arm — Brisket — Flank — Gaskin
Forearm — Elbow — Belly — Point of Hock
Knee — Hock
Cannon bone — Chestnut
Fetlock joint — Back tendon — Cannon bone
Pastern — Fetlock
Coronet
Hoof — DPW

SURFACE ANATOMY of the HORSE

Fig. 9 Points of the horse (Thoroughbred). The lengthening of the limbs in the modern horse has been brought about chiefly through a lengthening of the metapodials (long bones of the fore and hind feet). Thus, what is called the "knee" in the horse is what corresponds to the *wrist* in man; and what is called the "hock," the *heel*.

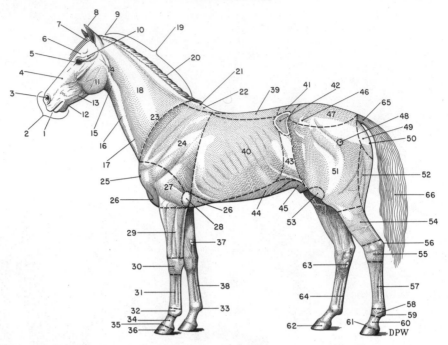

Fig. 10 External parts and regions of the horse.

1. Mouth	23. Shoulderbed	45. Sheath
2. Muzzle	24. Shoulder	46. Point of hip
3. Nostril	25. Point of shoulder	47. Croup
4. Face	26. Breast, or brisket	48. Hip joint
5. Eye	27. Arm	49. Buttock
6. Forehead	28. Elbow	50. Point of buttock
7. Forelock	29. Forearm	51. Thigh
8. Ear	30. Knee	52. Quarter
9. Poll	31. Cannon	53. Stifle
10. Temple	32. Fetlock joint	54. Gaskin
11. Cheek	33. Fetlock	55. Hock
12. Chin groove	34. Pastern	56. Point of hock
13. Lower jaw	35. Coronet	57. Cannon
14. Parotid region	36. Hoof	58. Fetlock joint
15. Throat-latch	37. Chestnut	59. Fetlock
16. Windpipe	38. Back tendon	60. Pastern
17. Jugular groove	39. Back	61. Coronet
18. Neck	40. Ribs	62. Hoof
19. Crest	41. Loin	63. Chestnut
20. Mane	42. Coupling	64. Back tendon
21. Point of withers	43. Flank	65. Dock
22. Withers	44. Belly	66. Tail

Notes and References

1. In: *Harmsworth Natural History* (London: Carmelite House, 1910), vol. 2, p. 786.

2. D. B. Ericson, M. Ewing, and G. Wollin, "Pliocene-Pleistocene Boundary in Deep-Sea Sediments," *Science* 139, no. 3556 (February 22, 1963): 727–37. (These authors state that the transition from Pliocene to Pleistocene is clearly defined by *changes in remains of planktonic organisms;* that the transition was abrupt; and that it marks the onset of the first Ice Age of the Pleistocene. The transition, or beginning of the Pleistocene, occurred *"not less than 800,000 years"* ago, and probably somewhat earlier than that.)

3. E. Bourdelle, and R. Lavocat, in *Traite de Zoologie* 17, part 1 (1955): 1066. (General treatise on the existing Equidae.)

4. The Russian paleontologist, W. Kovalevsky, in 1873 expressed the belief that the hypsodont (long-crowned) teeth of horses and cattle grow continuously throughout life. This assertion was disproved by V. A. K. Teriajev in 1932. (*Bull. Soc. Nat. Moscou,* sect. geol., vol. 10, no. 1, pp. 170–92.)

5. Otto Antonius, *Grundzüge einer Stammesgeschichte der Haustiere* (Jena, 1922), p. 274.

3

The Immediate Ancestors of the Domestic Horse*

Vertebrate paleontologists, from the times of Owen, Cope, and Marsh to those to the present day, have given a great deal of study to the evolution of the horse from *Hyracotherium* to *Equus*. An equal amount of attention, perhaps, has been devoted by other, more specialized, investigators to the question of the immediate ancestry of the horse and the wild forms involved in this ancestry. However, since none of the many scholarly hypotheses as to the origin of the domestic horse has as yet been accepted universally, it should be of interest and advantage to summarize here the views of some of the foremost authors on the subject.

One of the most widely quoted views is that of Dr. James Cossar Ewart, onetime Regius Professor of Natural History in the University of Edinburgh, and an expert in the fields of animal experimentation and breeding.[1] According to Ewart, the many modern breeds of horses are the descendants in varying degrees of *three* ancestral forms (wild subspecies). The first is called by him *Equus caballus celticus* and, according to him, is represented by small horses found in Iceland, Ireland (the Connemara pony), the Hebrides, and the Faroe Islands. Included also in this group is the Norwegian dun, or Norse fjord pony. This ancestral type is called by Ewart the *Plateau or Celtic variety.*

The second form is the Mongolian wild horse, *Equus caballus przewalskii*, which Ewart calls the *Steppe* variety. (For description, see Chapter 8.)

The third form is Ewart's *Forest variety*, which he defines as being represented by certain horses native to northern Europe, especially Scotland. The Gudbrandsdal horse, found mostly on the north or west coasts of Norway, is another example of this type. (For a description of the Gudbrandsdal, see p. 198.)

It should be noted that most of Ewart's descriptions of the several ancestral varieties he proposes are qualitative rather than quantitative, and that nowhere does he give *series* of measurements even of the skulls of these examples, let alone measurements and ratios of their limb bones. Rather, he confines his distinctions to the proportions of the skull and to such vestigial characters as the wartlike callosities on the lower legs known as ergots and chestnuts, respectively. And even in Ewart's mention of the latter characters, one has the impression that not many specimens were involved. Properly, in order to demonstrate the important thesis that several distinct wild forms contributed to the ancestry of today's domestic horses, a bone-by-bone comparison of *all*

---

* See also Chapter 8.

available parts of the skeleton in these forms should be made, using at least several specimens of each presumed contributing variety. Only by such means can significant distinctions and similarities be determined.

In 1908, several years after Ewart had expressed his views, another European investigator, J. U. Duerst, of the University of Bern, arrived also at the conclusion that three differing forms or types of wild horses were involved in the ancestry of the domestic horse. Duerst calls these forms respectively "steppe," "forest," and "desert" types.[2] Thus Duerst replaces Ewart's "plateau" type (Celtic pony, et al) with a "desert" or oriental type, which he names *Equus caballus pumpellii,* and which he regards as "ancestrally closely related to *Equus przewalskii* . . ." Duerst's "steppe" type is represented by a large, draft-horse form native to central Europe, which had been named previously by A. Pomel *Equus caballus robustus.* Finally, Duerst's "forest" type has as its representative another previously described type named *Equus caballus nehringi,* from which, according to Duerst, has descended the Celtic pony (Ewart's "plateau" type!).

At this point, after reviewing Ewart's and Duerst's several conflicting names for ancestral horses, Oliver P. Hay, a contemporary paleontologist of the United States National Museum, remarks, "These views illustrate the confusion of the subject; but, what is more important, they seem to justify the view that nobody knows exactly how forest horses, steppe horses, plateau horses, and desert horses differ one from another."[3]

In 1933, T. Vetulani introduced two "new" sources to substantiate his belief that the *forest tarpan* (see Chapter 8) was the probable direct ancestor of domestic horses in the east central European (Polish-Czechoslovakian) region.[4]

An interesting article on the derivation of the domestic horse, by the German zoologist Max Hilzheimer, and translated into English by Roland G. Austin, appeared in the journal *Antiquity* in 1935.[5] After discussing the various wild forms and their respective geographic habitats that other authors have regarded as possible ancestral types, Hilzheimer dismisses "cold-blooded," or heavy-built horses of draft type, from this category. He concludes, ". . . that at least the European horse, including the so-called oriental horse of western Asia and the breed of northern Africa, is to be derived from the European Tarpan in its various subdivisions."

Evidently contrary to Hilzheimer, and in line with the multiple-origin views of Ewart and Duerst, the Russian zoologist B. F. Rumjahcev is of the opinion that there were three distinct ancestral horse types in early Europe. He believes that (1) horses of what he calls the Northern Group (which includes small horses and ponies of Scandinavia, Estonia, Finland, etc.) have descended from the tarpan (*Equus caballus gmelini*); (2) horses of the Southern Group (oriental horses of light build, of southern and western Asia and North Africa) from "the wild mountain horse of Iran and the Near East," resembling Duerst's *Equus pumpellii;* and (3) horses of the Western Group ("heavy cart-horses, developed possibly in the domestic state by man") from post-glacial European horses of large, heavy build.[5] In Rumjahcev's opinion, "Przevalsky's horse has played no part in the evolution of the domestic horse."

Perhaps one of the ablest investigators of the ancestries of domesticated animals was Hellmut Otto Antonius, onetime Director of the Schönbrunn Zoological Garden, Vienna, and a former instructor in the Institute for Animal Breeding there. In a series of papers and books published between 1912–1951, Antonius discusses with authority the origin, geographic and chronologic distribution, and physical and osteometric characteristics of horses, zebras, asses, and hemionids. In 1922, under a chapter heading, "The type of *Equus ferus,*" Antonius expresses the opinion that this form (Przevalsky's horse) was the ancestor of the present-day Mongolian pony, the Szekle pony of Transylvania, and, among others, various small-statured but sturdily-built and large-headed horses of Japan, Tibet, and northern Indochina. However, he remarks also (1922, p. 291) that,

> Among the modern steppe-horses of eastern Europe and western Asia, those of Bashkiria (East Soviet Russia) seem to have predominantly the blood of *Equus ferus,* while the Kirghiz, Kalmuck, and Turkoman horses must be designated, without exception, as mixtures of the latter with the (South Russian) tarpan.[6]

Thus, Antonius expresses an opinion contrary to that of Rumjahcev (see above), who asserts that Przevalsky's horse had no part in the ancestry of the domestic horse.

Another European hippologist who, in a paper published in 1949, excludes Przevalsky's horse, as well as the earlier, "cold blood" horses of central Europe, from the ancestry of the domestic horse is Bengt Lundholm, of the University of Uppsala. Among many other listed conclusions, Lundholm states that (1) the domestic horse has a monophyletic (rather than a multiple, as Ewart and others contended) origin, and the wild progenitor is the South Russian tarpan; (2) the forest tarpan, as recognized by Vetulani, is not sufficiently distinct from the South Russian tarpan to be regarded as a separate type; (3) "There are no grounds for the assumption that the horse was domesticated in Paleolithic time"; (4) in Sweden, Denmark, and probably other parts of Europe, the horse appears to have existed continously from the last recession of glacial ice up to the time man domesticated it. Lundholm expresses also the opinion that "there is no basis for the once-held assumption that Przevalsky's horse existed in Europe during the Pleistocene."[7]

Evidently the latter "once-held assumption" is still being held, since the geochronologist F. E. Zeuner, in 1959, among many other listings of Pleistocene horses, gives dates of findings of *E. c. przewalskii* ranging from 33,000 to 110,000 years ago, in the Upper Pleistocene.[8]

In contradiction of the monophyletic origin of the domestic horse postulated by Lundholm and others is the statement by Ewart that,

> Had all domestic breeds sprung from a single wild ancestor, the individuals which ran wild would have been rapidly reabsorbed without in any way modifying the original wild stock—as tame rabbits are rapidly reabsorbed by the common wild rabbit. If, however, the escaped [from captivity] individuals had sprung from several perfectly distinct species, the result would be that, in addition to pure wild herds, one might have come across herds having a distinct infusion of tame blood, and also herds consisting of the mixed offspring of several domesticated breeds.[9]

To the present writer also it seems that the observed diversity in certain proportions of the skull and postcranial skeleton exhibited among the various breeds of the domestic horse can have no other explanation than that these breeds have descended from the cross-breeding (in nature) of at least several wild races of *Equus caballus,* as was the opinion held by Ewart, Duerst, Pocock, Ridgeway, Lydekker, Stegmann (who recognized *five* ancestral types), Hay, Antonius, Rumjahcev, and other investigators of the subject.

As to the *date* at which the horse was first tamed, there is also a wide range of opinion; some authors place it at the end of the last Ice Age (*c.* 8500 years ago?), and others no earlier than 1700 B.C., when, it is said, the animals were first used to draw chariots. J. Wilfred Jackson, in his book *Prehistoric Domestic Animals* (1934, p. 155), says,

> The occurrence of horse remains at . . . early sites, with admittedly domesticated animals, has led to discussion as to its right to be regarded as domesticated also. It is by no means clear that this animal has been tamed in Neolithic times, although it is conceivable that it may have been controlled by a nose-loop or halter of rope.[10]

On the other hand, W. Amschler gives a genealogical table of the horse and of horsemen dating back 5000 years (i.e., to c. 3100 B.C.). Amschler says that the first domestication of the horse occurred in western Siberia, and came after domestication of the dog and the reindeer. According to him, the horse came from the north and entered the Mediterranean region from the east.[11] (See also Chapter 7.)

Otto Antonius believes that *several independent centers* of the taming, or domestication, of the horse could have occurred more or less at the same time.[12]

In *Discovery* (October, 1931), Sir Flinders Petrie, the eminent Egyptologist, recorded the finding of a horse skeleton, the animal of which had been buried by Hyksos not later than 2250 B.C. This skeleton, it is said, was of a size and build similar to that of two horse skeletons unearthed from the Iron Age in Britain, dating some 2000 years later.

To sum up the foregoing discussion and add a few observations, it would appear that the various events connected with the domestication of the horse were as follows:

1. Successive migrations of horses and other Equidae from North America (central plains), over land bridges to Asia and South America, took place from perhaps as long ago as a million years up to about 9000 B.C., at which time the latest covering or inundation of the 700-mile-wide land bridge across Bering Strait took place concurrently with the recession and melting of the last glacial sheet.[13]
2. The horses and their kin in North America became totally extinct about 7800 years ago.[14]
3. One of the three possible ancestors of certain domestic breeds was the heavy, "coldblood" Pleistocene horse of western and central Europe (inclusive of its several varieties*), designated by the general term *Equus caballus robustus* Pomel. This large, forest-living horse evidently *preceded* in time the following smaller types. *E.c.robustus* is considered to have become extinct about 3000 years ago.
4. Two generally accepted pony-sized ancestors of various domestic breeds were the Mongolian wild horse (*Equus caballus przewalskii*) and the tarpan of south Russia (*Equus caballus gmelini*). The present writer, after having made an extensive study of the available published cranial and limb-bone measurements of both *E.c.przewalskii* and *E.c.gmelini,* in addition to measurements of various examples of *E.c.robustus,* believes that Przevalsky's horse is *not* an ancestor of existing "coldblood" breeds, but is more likely the *descendant* of one or more "coldblood" European horses. Przevalsky's horse, in its structural conformation, would appear to be more "warmblood" than "coldblood." (See also Chapter 8.)
5. Various specimens of fossil or sub-fossil horses from Siberia, Scandinavia, and Solutré (France) present in their structural makeup a *combination* of the

---

* For example, *E.c.mosbachensis* Reichenau, *E.c.germanicus* Nehring, *E.c.taubachensis* Freud, *E.c.abeli* Antonius, et al.

proportions typical to *E.c.przewalskii* and *E.c.gmelini,* respectively. There can be little doubt that the two latter subspecies, where exposed to each other, freely interbred.

6. In addition to the large, "coldblood" horses of Europe mentioned above, there existed in western North America during the uppermost Pleistocene a similarly formed horse, which was named by Joseph Leidy *Equus pacificus.* This horse may have been one of the many equine forms that migrated to Eurasia prior to the closing of the Bering Strait land bridge.

7. Zeuner (1959, pp. 313–318), in listing the dates of first appearance of various Equidae in Europe, gives a date of 570,000 B.P. (before present) for that of *E.c.robustus,* and 180,000 B.P. (possibly earlier) for *E.c.caballus,* the typical horse.

Notes and References

1. J. Cossar Ewart, *The Multiple Origin of Horses and Ponies, trans. Highland Soc.,* (1904) : 19 ff; republished in The Smithsonian Report for 1904, pp. 437–55).

2. J. U. Duerst, "Animal Remains from the Excavations at Anau, and the Horse of Anau in Its Relation to the Races of Domestic Horses" (Carnegie Inst. Wash. Pub. 73, 1908), vol. 2, Part 6, pp. 339–442.

3. Oliver P. Hay, "Contributions to the Knowledge of the Mammals of the Pleistocene of North America, proc. U.S. Nat. Mus., no. 2086, vol. 48 (1915) : 515–75. (A splendid osteometric treatise on fossil horses and existing species of the horse family.)

4. T. Vetulani, "Zwie weitere Quellen zur Frage des europäischen Waldtarpans" (Zeitschr. für Säugetierkunde, Band 8, 1933), pp. 281–82. (Vetulani cites two different travelers who, during the late eighteenth century, saw living wild horses in southeastern Europe.)

5. B. F. Rumjahcev, "Origin of the Domestic Horse" with a summary in English. (Akademia Nauk, Investia Seriia Biologicheskaia, No. 1, 1936), pp. 4444–48. (Like Ewart and Duerst, Rumjahcev postulates a *triparate* origin of today's domestic horses.)

6. Max Hilzheimer, "The Evolution of the Domestic Horse" *Antiquity* 9, no. 34 (June 1935) : 132–39.

7. Bengt Lundholm, *Abstammung und Domestikation des Hauspferdes.* (Zoologiska Bidrag fran Uppsala, Vol. 27, 1949), pp. 1–287. (A comprehensive survey on the origin of the domestic horse, supplemented by new, pollen-dated material on Swedish fossil and recent horses. Includes a bibliography of over 400 titles. A 9-page summary in English is given at the end of the paper.)

8. F. E. Zeuner, *The Pleistocene Period—Its Climate, Chronology, and Faunal Successions.* (London, 1959). (Chronological listing of fossil European Equidae.)

9. J. Cossar Ewart, "The Tarpan and Its Relationship with Wild and Domestic Horses," (Proc. Roy. Soc. Edinburgh, Vol. 26, 1905), pp. 7–21. (See also, by the same author, *The Wild Horse* (*Equus prjevalskii* Poliakoff), *Proc. Roy. Soc. Edinburgh,* 24 (1903) : 460–68.

10. J. W. Jackson, "Prehistoric Domestic Animals," in *Proc. 1st Int. Congress of Prehistoric and Protohistoric Sciences.* (London: Oxford Univ. Press, 1934).

11. W. Amschler, *The Oldest Pedigree Chart, Jour. Heredity* 26, (1935) : 233–38. (Horses and horsemen dating back to 5000 years ago.)

12. Otto Antonius, *Die Abstammung des Hauspferdes und Hausesels.* Naturwissenschaften, 6 Jahrgang, 1918. (Origins of the domestic horse and domestic ass.)

13. William G. Haag, "The Bering Strait Land Bridge," *Sci. Amer.,* 206, 1, January 1962; pp. 112–21. (A land width ranging from 200 miles to 1300 miles is estimated, depending upon the recession of the sea.)

14. Norman D. Newell, "Crises in the History of Life," *Sci. Amer.* 208, no. 2 (February 1963) : 81. (Newell points out that at the close of the Pliocene *new land connections* were formed between North America and the neighboring continents of Asia and South America. "The horse and camel, which had evolved in North America during Tertiary time, quickly crossed into Siberia and spread throughout Eurasia and Africa." The last such crossing must have taken place prior to about 7800 years before the present, since by the latter time, according to Newell, both the horse and the camel had become extinct in North America.)

4

Growth and Physical Structure of the Horse

The skeleton of members of the horse family (genus *Equus*), while varying in the size and proportions of its parts among these forms, is essentially of the structure and conformation shown in Fig. 11, which represents a domestic horse of light ("warmblood") build. The principal bones of the equine skeleton, including the number of each, are as follows: In the case of the limb bones, the numbers listed include both the right and left sides.

Head	Skull (including auditory ossicles, but excluding teeth) ..	34
Trunk	Vertebrae, cervical (neck)	7
	——— thoracic (back)	17–19
	——— lumbar (loin)	5–6
	——— sacral (croup)	4–6
	——— caudal (tail)	13–21
	Ribs (2 sets)	34–38
Fore limbs (both)	Scapulae (shoulder blades)	2
	Humeri (upper arm bones)	2
	Radii (forearm bones)	2
	Ulnae (elbow bones)	2
	Carpi (bones of "knees")	12
	Metacarpi (cannon bones), including splints	6
	Pisiform bones	4
	Sesamoid bones	4
	Phalanges (pastern and hoof bones)	6
Hind limbs (both)	Pelvis (haunch bone)	3
	Femora (thigh bones)	2
	Patellae (knee-caps)	2
	Tibiae (gaskin bones)	2
	Fibulae (smaller shin bones)	2
	Tarsi (bones of "hock," or heel)	12
	Metatarsi (cannon bones), including splints	6
	Sesamoid bones	4
	Phalanges (pastern and hoof bones)	6
	Total	193–210

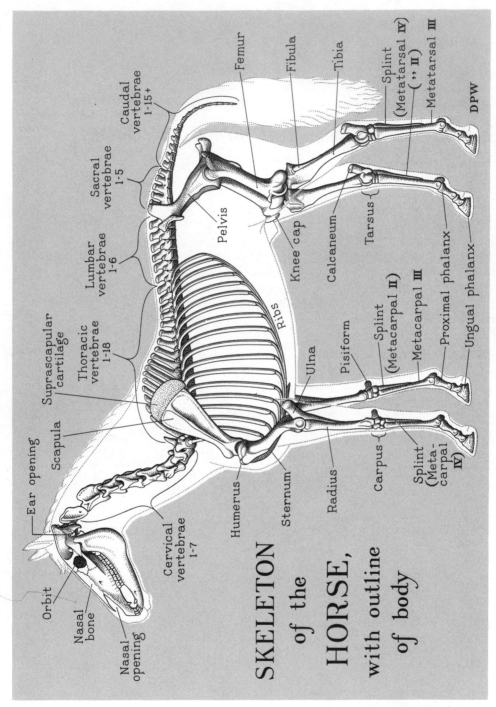

SKELETON of the HORSE, with outline of body

Orbit
Nasal bone
Nasal opening
Ear opening
Cervical vertebrae 1-7
Scapula
Suprascapular cartilage
Thoracic vertebrae 1-18
Lumbar vertebrae 1-6
Sacral vertebrae 1-5
Caudal vertebrae 1-15+
Femur
Fibula
Tibia
Splint (Metatarsal IV)
(" II)
Metatarsal III
DPW
Pelvis
Knee cap
Calcaneum
Tarsus
Proximal phalanx
Ungual phalanx
Humerus
Sternum
Ribs
Ulna
Pisiform
Radius
Carpus
Splint (Metacarpal II)
Metacarpal III
Splint (Meta- carpal IV)

Fig. 11 Drawing to exact scale of a representative "light" horse (Thoroughbred) ×1/17 natural size. (Compare with Fig. 9.)

Horses, like cattle and other members of the hoofed mammals, have no clavicles (collar-bones).

As will be observed in the above list, the numerical variations normally occur only in the vertebrae (and connected ribs). Robert Stecher,[1] in a study of the spines of 256 equine specimens, of which 190 were horses, found the following conditions. In all cases the number of cervical vertebrae was 7. While 18 is the usual number of thoracic vertebrae, in 190 horse spines eighteen had only 17 such vertebrae, and eleven had 19. However, of the eleven specimens having 19 thoracic vertebrae, nine instances occurred among 32 examples of Przevalsky's horses. In the domestic horse (including the Shetland pony), zebras, and mules, the number of lumbar vertebrae normally is 6. Frequently the number is only 5; but in all of Stecher's 256 equine specimens only one exhibited 7 lumbars, and that was a Grévy's zebra, a typically long-bodied species. In Przevalsky's horse the number is equally divided between 5 and 6. In seven examples of the Arabian horse, Stecher found six to have 6 lumbars, and only one to have 5. While the former number suggests that the Arabs may not have been purebred specimens, it is at least possible that they all *were*. On the other hand, the number of *thoracic* (rib-bearing) vertebrae in the Arab horse was found by Stecher to average only 17.43, this being the smallest number among any of the equines recorded. This shortness of the *dorsal* section of the spine in the Arab is a factor contributing to its relatively short trunk that does not appear to have been recorded, or at least emphasized, previously. In the domestic ass and the wild Asiatic hemionids the typical or dominant generic number of 6 lumbar vertebrae is reduced to 5.

The caudal (tail) vertebrae are often fused with those of the sacrum, making a variable total number, depending upon how they are counted. While variation in one part of the spine results in compensating changes in the neighboring parts, Stecher's study shows that the number of combined thoracic, lumbar, and sacral vertebrae normally averages about 28½ in domestic horses generally, 29 in Grévy's zebra, and only 28 in the Arabian horse, the donkey, the mule, and the hemionids. This is another confirmation of the general opinion that the Arabian horse has normally a shorter back than other domestic breeds. Also, the equally frequent occurrence in Przevalsky's horse of 5 and 6 lumbar vertebrae would seem to show—as does the proportions of its limb bones—that this wild ancestral horse is more "warmblood" in its makeup than "coldblood" (see Chapter 8).

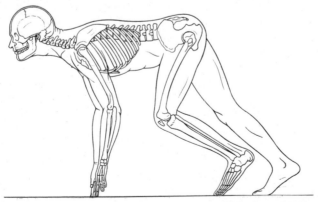

Fig. 12 Figure of a man drawn to the same scale and in a similar posture to the horse in Fig. 11, for comparison. Note that in man the scapulae (shoulder blades) lie diagonally across the back, while in the horse (and various other four-footed animals) these bones stand almost upright when viewed from the side. Man's heels are normally flat on the ground, while in the horse they are high above it, so that the animal really stands and walks on what would correspond in man to the *finger and toe nails* of the middle digits of the hands and feet. Numerous other differences will be noted by comparing Figs. 11 and 12.

While the number of cervical (neck) vertebrae in members of the horse family is normally always seven, these vertebrae, during the course of equine evolution, have become progressively longer, in conformity with the lengthening of the limbs, in order that the grazing animal may freely reach the ground with its mouth. A young foal, with its disproportionately long legs and somewhat short neck, may even have to bend at the knees in order to touch its lips to the ground (see Fig. 13). The only alternative to such an elongation of the neck in horses would have been for these animals to have developed a proboscis (trunk), as did the elephants!

Fig. 13 Notice, in the young animal, the disproportionately long legs, which oblige it to bend its knees and stretch its neck in order to bring its mouth to the ground. This precocious development of the limbs is evidently a provision of Nature to enable the young horse to run alongside its mother, and keep up with the herd, within a few hours after birth.

In their basic skeletal anatomy, horses do not differ appreciably from asses, zebras, and hemionids. Only by a measured comparison of certain details—such as the proportionate lengths and calibers of the various limb bones, the shape of the pelvis, the size and form of the hoofs, and various proportions of the skull and teeth—may the bones of true horses (*Equus caballus*) be distinguished from those of their equine relatives. In external appearance, the differences between horses and their kin are due largely to body size, coloration, and length of ears, mane, and tail. The range in size, while considerable, is not great if we limit consideration to the wild species and exclude the gigantic but man-made varieties of the draft horse. The greatest variation is in color and marking, which ranges from the fully striped zebras through the partially striped asses to the largely unicolored horse. The ears range from the relatively short narrow ones of the horse to the relatively enormous ears of the domestic ass and the broad, heavily "furred" ears of Grévy's zebra. The mane normally is short and erect in zebras, asses, hemionids, the Mongolian wild horse, and the tarpan, and long and pendant only in the domestic horse. The tail varies from the completely tufted (long-haired) tail of the domestic horse, through the intermediately haired tails of the mule and the Mongolian wild horse, to the short-tufted, or cow-like, tails of the donkey, the zebras, and the hemionids. Further comments on these physical differences are given later in connection with the descriptions of the various genera and species.

In the following list are defined some of the principal parts of the horse as illustrated in Figs. 9, 10, and 11.

Some Anatomical Terms of the Horse, and their derivation.

BRISKET: The breast or lower part of the chest in front of, between, and slightly behind the forelegs. From the Middle English *brusket,* akin to breast.

CANNON: (or cannon bone). The metacarpus or the metatarsus. So-called because of its similarity in shape to the barrel of a cannon. Since "cannon" might be construed as meaning only the unfleshed cannon bone, the term "shank" was suggested by Professor J. C. Ewart as a more inclusive name. Among horsemen, however, "cannon" is taken to mean the *whole* metacarpal or metatarsal segment. It is at the level of the slenderest part of the cannon that the "girth of cannon," commonly called "bone," measurement of a horse is taken.

CHESTNUT: One of the small round or oval horny vestigial callosities on the inner sides of the forelegs and hind legs. Named presumably from their resemblance, real or fancied, to a chestnut. Also called *castors.*

COFFIN BONE: The foot bone, or third phalanx, enclosed within the hoof. If we consider the hoof as a "coffin," or receptacle, the term is self-descriptive.

CORONET: The comparatively soft lower portion of the pastern where the skin joins the hoof. The term, meaning "small or inferior crown," has been here applied presumably because of the location and form of the upper margin of the horse's hoof.

CROUP: The place behind the saddle. Specifically, the posterior part of the back between the loins in front and the tail behind, extending sidewards the width of the pelvis. From the French *croupe,* meaning rump or buttocks.

ERGOT: A rounded, wartlike, vestigial growth, in the tufts of hair on the back of the fetlock. In the horse it averages about a half-inch in diameter. In asses and zebras it is much larger. From the French *ergot,* meaning spur.

FETLOCK: (and fetlock joint). The cushionlike projection, usually bearing a tuft of hair, on the back side of the leg above the hoof. The fetlock joint is located between the great pastern bone (first phalanx) and the metacarpus or metatarsus. Literally "foot-lock" (of hair) or "feet-lock." The fetlock joint is sometimes erroneously called "ankle."

GASKIN: That part of the hind leg between the stifle (knee) and the hock (heel). Named, presumably because of sameness of position, from the obsolete, dialectal English word *galligaskins,* meaning gaiters or leggings.

HOCK: The tarsal joint, corresponding to the ankle in man. From the Anglo-Saxon *hoh,* meaning heel.

KNEE: The joint in the foreleg between the forearm (radius) above and the metacarpal bones below, corresponding to the *wrist* in man.

PASTERN: The short, inclined part of the foot between the fetlock and the coffin joint (hoof). So-called because of the horse being tethered by this part of the foot while at *pasture.*

POLL: The summit, or most posterior part, of the head, connecting the head and the neck. From the Middle Dutch *pol,* meaning head.

STIFLE: (or stifle joint). The joint next above the hock, and near the flank, in the hind leg, corresponding to the knee in man. The word is of uncertain origin. The stifle bone is the patella, or kneecap.

WITHERS: The highest part of the ridge of the back between the shoulder blades, to which point the "shoulder height" of a four-footed animal is measured. From the Anglo-Saxon *wither,* meaning against, as in resisting the strain in pulling a load.

The general trend of bodily growth in the domestic horse from birth to maturity may be exemplified by that shown in the Arabian horse. Figure 14 depicts the average body proportions, drawn to exact scale, of a newborn male Arabian foal. This drawing is based on the principal measurements of 6 male and 5 female foals measured at the W. K. Kellogg Arabian Horse Ranch, near Pomona, California, along with a supplementary list of detailed measurements of 3 male and 2 female foals measured by the author. Table 1, following, lists the typical measurements of a newborn male Arabian as compared with those of a full-grown stallion of the same breed. All linear measurements are given in inches.

Table 1. Comparative measurements of a typical male newborn and a typical male adult Arabian horse.

Measurement	Newborn		Adult (5 yrs.)		Newborn
	Inches	% of Withers Height	Inches	% of Withers Height	Adult, %
Height, withers	38.6	100.0	59.7	100.0	64.6
" croup	39.4	102.1	59.4	99.5	66.3
" chest from ground	24.3	63.0	32.7	54.8	74.3
" elbow	26.4	68.6	35.7	59.8	74.0
" knee	15.0	38.7	18.6	31.2	80.3
" hock	19.1	49.6	23.9	40.1	80.0
Length, trunk	29.3	76.0	59.2	99.3	49.5
" head	14.2	36.9	23.3	39.1	61.0
" neck	12.8	33.2	27.5	46.1	46.7
" ear	5.8	15.1	7.2	12.0	81.4
Girth, neck	16.1	41.6	29.4	49.3	54.6
" chest	33.2	86.0	68.2	114.2	48.7
" forearm	11.9	30.9	18.1	30.4	65.7
" fore cannon	4.8	12.5	7.4	12.4	64.9
" hind cannon	5.2	13.4	7.9	13.3	65.0
Fore hoof, width	2.4	6.3	4.9	8.1	49.8
" " length	3.0	7.7	5.9	9.9	50.3
Hind hoof, width	2.4	6.3	4.6	7.8	52.1
" " length	3.2	8.2	5.8	9.7	54.6
Weight, lbs.	94	——	922	——	10.2

A study of Fig. 14, along with a comparison of the two animals in Fig. 15, will show the differences in bodily proportion of a newborn foal from an adult horse. These differences, so far as they apply to the Arabian horse, are listed numerically and percentagewise in Table 1.

The most significant difference in the newborn foal from the adult horse is the great length of the legs compared with the length and girth of the trunk. Other clearly visible differences in the young animal are the short neck, mane, and tail, and the small hoofs. In the foal the croup is higher than the withers, and the head presents a relatively shorter face and a larger cranium. The eyes, as in all young mammals, are relatively larger than in the adult. The mouth and lips, not yet used for grazing, are noticeably small.

Fig. 14 Proportions of the body in a newborn Arabian foal. Compare with the adult proportions shown in Fig. 86 and Table 1. Note the relatively long legs, short trunk and neck, high croup, small hoofs, and short, bushy tail.

As is indicated in the last column in Table 1, the legs of the newborn foal are relatively longest in their distal segments—that is, the portions below the knee and the hock, respectively. This brings up the often-heard statement that the legs of a young foal are as long as they will ever be. This statement, specifically as regards the metacarpal and metatarsal bones, is almost but not quite true. As is shown graphically in Fig. 17, the length of the metacarpus at birth is about 225 mm (8.8 in.) and at one year, when it has practically attained its full growth, about 254 (10.0 in.). Thus the metacarpus reaches virtually its full length at one year of age, after having increased about 1¼ inches since birth. A similar rapid growth takes place in the metatarsal bone of the hind limb. As is shown also in Fig. 17, the other long bones of the equine skeleton likewise grow at a rapid rate, although less rapidly than the metapodials. The femur, radius, tibia, and humerus all normally reach their full length at from 4 to 5 years of age. In individual animals the bones may lengthen to 6 or 7 years; but in most cases a horse may be considered to be "full-grown," so far as stature is concerned, at 5 years of age. Some parts of the skeleton, such as the skull and the pelvis, may continue to grow at a slow, diminishing rate throughout the lifetime of the animal. This is particularly true of the *caliber,* or thickness, of the bones, which tend to attain a size (cross-sectional area) in ratio to the weight of body they are obliged to support, which generally increases past the age at which full statural growth is reached.

Draft horses are larger at birth than are horses of the lighter breeds. Percheron foals, for example, average in weight at birth about 160 pounds, at 4 months 550 pounds, and at 2 years 1100 pounds, and at 5 years 1760 pounds.[2] Thoroughbreds have an average birth weight of about 113 pounds, and Standardbreds about 110 pounds. Male Quarter horses, according to a study made by Cunningham and Fowler, average at birth 102 pounds, and females 97 pounds; the respective weights at 5 years being 1201 and 1172 pounds.[3] Thus, roughly, a newborn foal weighs from $\frac{1}{12}$ to $\frac{1}{10}$ of its weight at 5 years, or of the weight of its parent.

Fig. 15 Skolma, an Arabian mare, and her three-day-old male foal, Shah. Photographed by the author in 1950 at the Arabian Ranch of Donald and Charles McKenna at Claremont, California.

Growth in weight of the horse and of other hoofed mammals is most rapid in the beginning and decelerates steadily until the adult age is reached. The shape of the growth curve depicting this increase is like the upper lefthand quadrant of a circle (see Fig. 16). This is in contrast to the growth curves of man, apes, and other mammals, such as the elephant, in which there is a relatively long period of infancy, a more prolonged development of the brain, and a higher age at maturity (e.g., man 20 years, anthropoid apes 10–15 years; elephant 25 years). The growth curves of

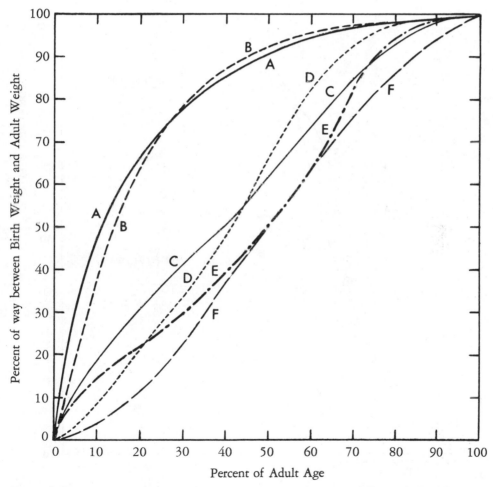

Fig. 16 Comparative growth curves for horse (A), cow (B), whale (C), elephant (D), man (E), and domestic cat (F). The curves for anthropoid apes (gorilla, chimpanzee, and orang-utan) are similar to that for man. Note how much more rapid the initial growth is in the horse and the cow.

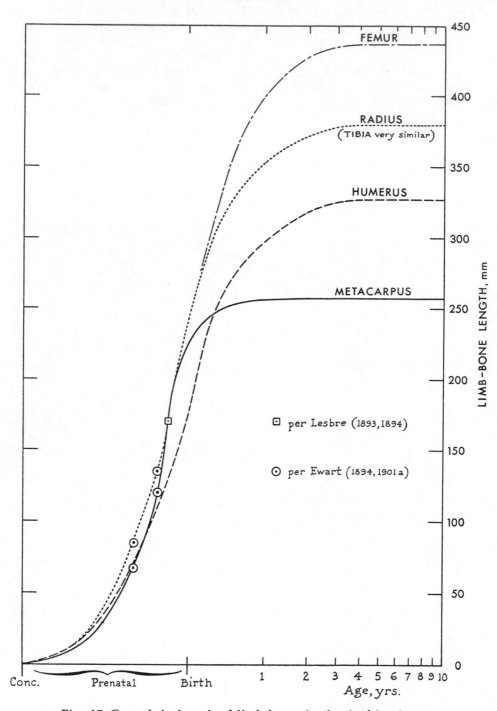

Fig. 17 Growth in length of limb bones in the Arabian horse.

these species form a sigmoid (S-shaped) curve, in which there are two stages of accelerated growth (immediately after birth and at puberty) and two stages of deceleration (just prior to puberty and as the adult stage is approached). That is to say, horses and other such animals as must depend for their survival on speed (swift and prolonged running) must grow rapidly so as to quickly attain a body size and limb length conducive to maximum speed. In contrast, in carnivores, which—even in such large forms as lions, tigers, and bears—may require no longer a period than horses in which to reach maturity, there is a less rapid growth in infancy and an ultimate greater development of the brain (along with a greater longevity relative to body size).

Further comments on the bodily size and proportioning of the adult horse are given in Chapter 18 and in connection with the respective descriptions of the various domestic breeds and wild subspecies.

Brief mention will now be made of two of the most important differential characters of the equine skeleton, namely the pelvis and the hoofs. As criteria for classification, these distinctly variable parts have been relatively neglected both by mammalogists and paleontologists, while the more commonly available elements of skull and teeth have been used as though they were the sole essentials.

Fig. 18 shows the dimensions used by the author in measuring the equine pelvis. That this part of the skeleton is a complex and confusing element is shown by the name given to the pelvis by the ancients: *os innominatum,* or "bone without a name." Each and every measurement indicated in Fig. 18 was taken by the author on over three dozen complete pelves of horses, zebras, asses, and hemionids. Exact scale drawings (in projected views) were then made of the pelves, and comparisons drawn between them for the various species and sexes considered.

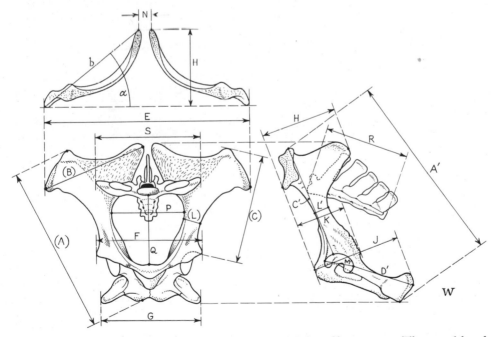

Fig. 18 Dimensions to be taken of the equine pelvis. (Shown on a Thoroughbred stallion.) Measurements shown in parentheses ( ) are *foreshortened* in the drawing due to being projected. Measurements indicated by *prime* letters (as **A'**) are direct measurements projected into the mid-sagittal plane. These measurements apply to the pelvis as viewed in *profile.*

The distinguishing features of the equine pelvis are mainly (1), the height of the two ilia compared with the bi-iliac width (index H/E); (2), the width across the ischia as compared with the width across the acetabulae (index G/F); (3), the anteroposterior *length* of the pelvic opening relative to the width across the acetabulae (index Q/F); and (4), the height of the two ilia relative to the length of the pelvic opening (index H/Q).

Sex differentiation of the pelvis can usually be determined reliably by means of either index Q/F, index H/Q, or simply measurement Q—the anteroposterior diameter of the pelvic opening. In the index Q/F in the domestic horse, mares average about *27 percent* larger than stallions. The index H/Q is consistently larger than Q/F in stallions, and consistently smaller than Q/F in mares.

The best single index for determining species or subgeneric differences in the pelvis would appear to be the height of the two ilia as compared with the bi-iliac width. In true (caballine) horses this index (H/E) is small, corresponding to a low, broad pelvis; while in asses, zebras, and hemionids the index is larger, in conformity with a pelvis that is relatively higher or steeper and less broad.*

The marked difference in this respect between the pelvis of a Shetland pony stallion and that of a male domestic ass of approximately the same general size is shown in Figs. 19 and 20.

Unfortunately, in order for an equine pelvis to provide the principal index (H/E), the two halves of the hip bone (*os coxae*) must be firmly united, not separated, so that the inclination of the two ilia is definitely established (and not brought about by restoration). Such a condition, while present in the pelves of recently deceased animals, is hardly ever encountered in those of fossil specimens, where one is lucky to obtain even one complete iliac bone (*ilieum*), let alone two joined together as in life. However, the pelves of members of the existing horse family are available intact and in sufficient numbers to establish beyond question the distinguishing characters of this part of the skeleton among the various subgenera of *Equus*.

The *hoofs* of the Equidae are likewise among the most useful criteria for distinguishing the differing subgenera within the genus *Equus*. By "hoofs" is here meant all three of the terminal foot-bones of both the fore and the hind limbs—that is, phalanges I and II as well as the foot phalanx itself, or phalanx III. These relatively small bones, in contrast to the larger and more fragile ones composing the pelvis, are solid and highly imperishable, thus providing excellent means of identification and classification, especially of fossil forms of Equidae.

Fig. 21 shows, in graphic form, how the index—phalanx III width/ phalanx I length, in the fore hoof—varies so markedly as to completely separate the range of *Equus* (*Caballus*), even the warmblood forms, from the ranges of *Quaggoides, Hippotigris,* and *Asinus,* and to separate almost completely *Equus* from *Dolichohippus*. An almost equally great range of variation can be charted by using the same index in the hind foot. It will be noted that by this foot-bone index the fossil form *Equus occidentalis* is completely separated from *E. caballus* (other limb-bone indices show the animal to

---

* The computed Standard Range (i.e., that among 1000 specimens) of index H/E among the five living subgenera of Equus for which pelves in adequate numbers have been available is as follows: Hemionus 43–52; *Asinus* 41–51; *Dolichohippus* 39–48; *Quaggoides* 37–48; *Caballus* 22–42. Doubtless, in *Hippotigris* (the mountain zebras) the index is high, as in *Asinus*. Thus, while there is considerable "overlapping" of the ranges of the index H/E among the subgenera charted, there is a clear distinction between the *typical* broad and low pelvis of the horse and the *typical* higher and narrower pelves of asses, zebras, and hemionids.

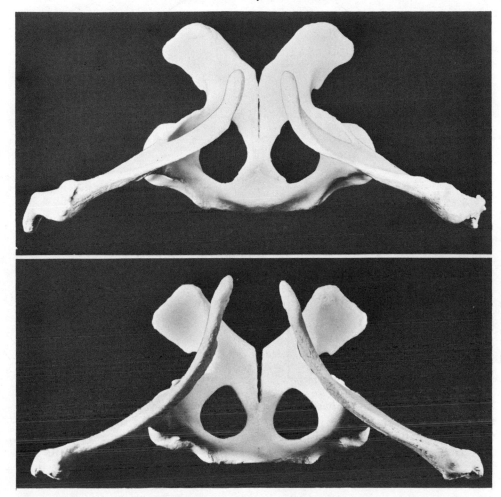

Fig. 19 Comparison, looking from before directly backwards, of the pelvis of a Shetland pony stallion (upper photograph) with that of a male domestic ass (lower photograph) reduced to approximately the same scale. These two pictures typify certain gross differences in pelvic conformation existing between (1) the true horses and (2) the asses, zebras, and hemionids. Both figures *c.* $\times$ .4 nat. size. (Compare with Fig. 20.)

have been a large, early form of *Quaggoides*); yet certain paleontologists, who studied only the teeth of *E. occidentalis,* have declared emphatically that it was "caballine" (i.e., a true horse)!

Fig. 22 shows the fore hoofs of an Arabian horse and a domestic ass for comparison, drawn to the same scale. A careful study of these two drawings will show the many differences in size and proportion existing between the broad, rounded hoofs of the horse and the small, elongate hoof of the donkey.* The three terminal foot-bones shown

* When, in order to make this cross-section, I sawed through the foot of the donkey, I was astonished at the solidity and toughness of the horny hoof. Even with a power saw, it was like cutting through ironwood! D.P.W.

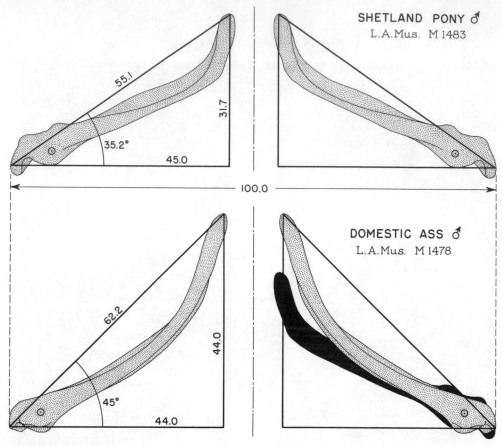

Fig. 20 Diagrammatic comparison of the two pelves shown photographically in Fig. 19, brought to the same relative bi-iliac width (100). In the lower drawing the blackened outline is that of the left ilium of the Shetland pony. The depicted differences in the inclination of the ilia accounts in the living animals for the broad and low croup of the horse and the narrow and high croup of the ass. Both figures × .4 natural size.

Fig. 21 Estimated Standard Ranges (1000 cases each) of the $\dfrac{\text{Fore Phalanx III Width}}{\text{Fore Phalanx I Length}}$ index in the six Recent subgenera of *Equus*.

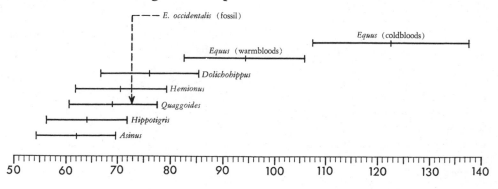

in cross-section are, counting downwards, fore phalanges I, II, and III, respectively, of which the length of phalanx I is divided into the width of phalanx III (the "coffin bone") to yield the index charted in Fig. 21. The large V-shaped structure on the hinder side of the bottom of the hoof is a horny, elastic pad called the "frog." Its function is to absorb concussion and prevent slippage. It varies in size and shape in correspondence with the general size of the hoof and the particular type of environment (e.g., hard ground, or grassy plain) peculiar to the species.

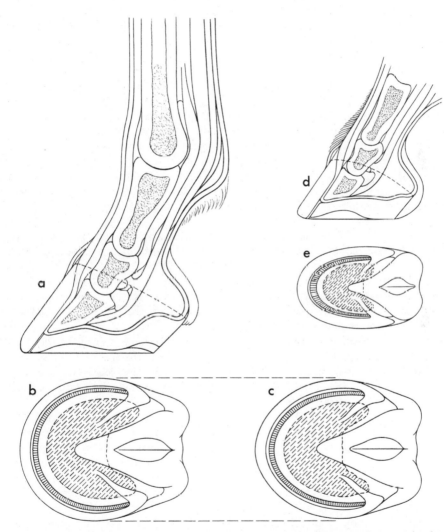

Fig. 22 Cross-sections through the hoofs of a typical domestic horse (Arab) and a domestic ass. a = Cross-section of fore hoof of Arab horse; b = Plantar view of same, showing position of coffin bone (dashed lines); c = Plantar view of hind hoof of Arab horse, showing coffin bone; d = Cross-section of fore hoof of domestic ass; e = Plantar view of same, showing coffin bone. All figures × .30 natural size.

Fig. 23, reduced to the same scale as Fig. 22, shows various additional examples of Equidae with special reference to the outer (horny) hoof as compared with the underlying (or encased) coffin bone. The known relations of these parts in existing species provide a fairly reliable basis for reconstructing the outer hoofs (which almost always undergo complete disintegration) of fossil species, as in the cases here shown of *Equus andium* and *Equus occidentalis*.

In passing from such "diagnostic" postcranial skeletal elements as the pelvis and the hoofs, it may be of interest to consider briefly those external equine characters known respectively as "chestnuts" and "ergots."

"Chestnuts" (sometimes called "castors") are the horny growths, or callosities, on the inner (medial) surfaces of a horse's legs, above the knees and below the hocks (see Figs. 9 and 10). In early-day French veterinary works these growths were termed "sallenders" (from *salandre*) or "mallenders," from the notion that they were the manifestations of disease. Even so authoritative a writer as Youatt (1880, p. 357) includes them among diseases, owing to "bad stable management," and prescribes remedies both internal and external for getting rid of them.

On each fore limb of the horse the chestnut takes the form of an oval patch of dark, warty skin, usually (in the domestic horse) about two inches long and three-quarters of an inch wide, located several inches above the knee; while on each hind limb there is a smaller patch, located several inches *below* the hock. In some breeds, as for example the Celtic pony and the Shetland pony, the hind chestnuts may be absent. In purebred domestic horses, such as Arabs and Thoroughbreds, the hind chestnuts are usually very small.

To gain an idea of how the chestnuts vary in size among different species of equidae, the reader is referred to Chapter 18, where in the conformation drawings of these species the chestnuts are shown. In the Mongolian wild horse (Fig. 242) the chestnuts are quite small—even smaller than in the Arabian horse. This suggests that in some specimens of the Mongolian wild horse the hind chestnuts may be lacking, just as they are said to be in some Arab horses.[4] In all the wild, noncaballine forms of *Equus,* the hind chestnuts *are* lacking. In the species of *Hemionus* known as the kulan or chigetai (Fig. 243), the chestnuts on the forelegs are typically large, as shown. In the domestic ass (Fig. 244) the chestnuts are somewhat smaller—about the size of those in ordinary horses. In the mountain zebra (Fig: 246) the chestnuts are relatively enormous, in marked contrast to those in the larger-bodied Grévy's zebra (Fig. 245). Chapman's zebra also (Fig. 247) has relatively large chestnuts.

The smaller growths, called ergots (meaning "spurs"), are warty structures located within the tuft of long hair on the hind surface of each fetlock. These growths are round or slightly oval in shape. They are usually about an inch in diameter in the domestic ass, somewhat smaller than this in zebras, and smallest of all in Arabian horses and Thoroughbreds. In fact, in the latter breeds they may be absent. According to Capt. Hayes, "The nearer a horse approaches the heavy draught type, the thicker is the growth of the callosities on his legs."[5]

As to the function, if any, of the ergots, Sir William Flower, an early-day British authority on the horse, believed them to be analogous to the large (middle) fatty pads or cushions on the soles of the feet in dogs. Although now rudimentary or vestigial structures, in the early ancestors of the horse the ergots were evidently functional, since in these multi-toed animals a considerable portion of the side of the foot (rather than only the tip of the middle toe) was applied to the ground.[6]

The function of the chestnuts has not been so summarily described, and differing

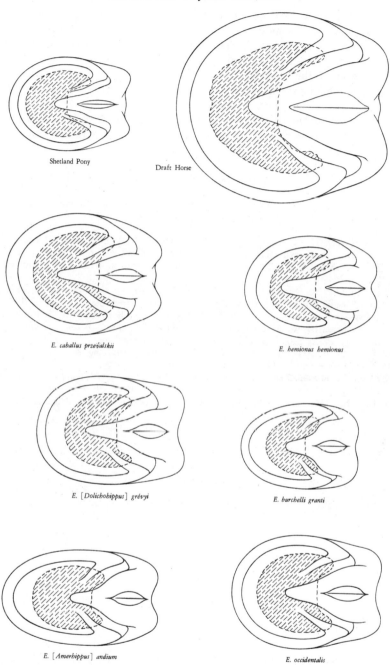

Fig. 23 Relationship of the outer fore hoof to phalanx III (coffin bone) in various forms of Equidae. The outer hoofs in the fossil species *E. andium* and *E. occidentalis* are necessarily conjectural. All figures × .30 natural size.

opinions of the purpose of these structures have been advanced by various investigators of the horse. Possibly the most plausible conclusion as to their function is that which was reached in 1912 by Richard Lydekker, who regarded the chestnuts as being glandular structures analogous to the tarsal glands of certain species of deer. In horses, the original function of the chestnuts presumably was as scent-glands (which may have served to keep a herd together when fleeing from an enemy in the blackness of night), but the function has been lost, probably from disuse. In short, Lydekker regarded the chestnuts of the Equidae as "decadent glandular structures,* the decadence being more marked in those (of both pairs of limbs) of the horse than in the single pair of the asses and zebras."[7]

Notes and References

1. Robert M. Stecher, "Anatomical Variations of the Spine in the Horse," *Jour. Mammalogy* 43, no. 2 (May 1962): 205–19. (A comparison of the spines of 9 different groups of modern Equidae.)

2. Samuel Brody, H. K. Kibler, and E. A. Trowbridge, "Resting Energy Metabolism and Pulmonary Ventilation in Growing Horses," Research Bull. 368, Univ. of Missouri Agric. Exper. Sta. (May 1943). (Tables 2a and 2b give the weights of Percheron foals at frequent stages from 3 days to 5 years.)

3. Kirby Cunningham, and Stewart H. Fowler, "A Study of Growth and Development in the Quarter Horse," Bull. No. 546, Louisiana State Univ. Agric. Exper. Sta. (November 1961).

4. This was the statement of A. Sanson (1868), an authority on the horses and ponies of North Africa (quoted by W. Ridgeway in *The Origin and Influence of the Thorobred Horse* [Cambridge: University Press, 1905], p. 13). However, some recent breeders (e.g., the late Lady Wentworth, of England) have said that the Arabian horse "always" has chestnuts on the hind legs.

5. M. H. Hayes, *Points of the Horse,* 5th ed (London: 1930).

6. William H. Flower, *The Horse—a Study in Natural History* (London: Kegan Paul & Co., 1891), p. 170.

7. Richard Lydekker, *The Horse and Its Relatives* (London: George Allen & Co., Ltd., 1912), pp. 48–52.

---

* Lydekker supports this view with the interesting observation that the chestnuts, when cut, exude a strong-smelling fluid which is attractive to other horses; and that this fluid was "formerly employed by burglars and poachers to keep dogs quiet."

5

The Equine Skull and Teeth

The distinctive feature of the skulls of horses, zebras, and other one-toed ungulates (hoofed animals) is the great elongation of the facial bones—that is, the portion of the skull in front of the socket of the eye, or orbit—as compared with the hinder part (cranium) back of the orbit. This long-faced proportioning of the skull in the horse family is an ancient character, and has evolved gradually from *Eohippus* to *Equus* concurrently with the lengthening of the limbs, the elevating of the body, and the consequent need for an increasingly longer neck and head in order for the grazing animal to reach the ground with its mouth (cropping teeth) without having to bend its legs.

A second reason for the elongation of the facial part of the skull in the *Equidae* is, according to Lydekker, "to allow space in front of the eye-sockets for the great rows of elongate, or hypsodont, grinding teeth, the marvelous dental battery of the horse. We might assume from these facts that long-headedness is correlated with long teeth, but the giant pigs (elotheres) have still longer and narrower skulls than the horse, yet all the teeth are brachyodont, or short-crowned. Again, the elephant has extremely elongate, or hypsodont, molar teeth, yet it also possesses the [relatively] shortest skull known among the Mammalia."

Again quoting Lydekker, "Another feature in the skull of the existing members of the horse family is the comparative shortness of the slit separating the front end of the nasal bones, which form the roof of the nose-chamber, from those of the upper jaw . . ." This V-shaped opening between the roof-like nasal bones and the underlying upper jaw bone is shown in Figure 6. Although designated by Lydekker as a "comparative shortness," it will be observed in these carefully exact drawings of skulls that the nasal opening extends proportionately farther back from the front end of the upper jaw in recent forms of the horse than in those of earlier genera.* This modification of structure may be correlated with the gradual change in environment from the time of the browsing, jungle-dwelling *Eohippus* to the grazing, plains-living later forms of the horse tribe, (2) the concurrent change from a humid, tropical atmosphere to a more temperate climate, and (3), because of the more cursorial nature of the later horses,

---

* With the exception, at least, of the extraordinary Pleistocene genus, *Hippidium,* of South America, shown in Figure 7, the nasal notch in which extended backward some 10 or 11 inches, almost to the eye-sockets! It has been deduced from this that the members of this genus had pronouncedly long noses, possibly forming a sort of short *trunk* comparable to that of the saiga antelope.

67

to the need of greater breathing power and larger nostrils and air-passages. However, no definitive study appears to have been made on this point.

The *growth* of the skull in equine animals proceeds at a rate that corresponds, not with the actual age, but with the *logarithm* of the age, as is shown (from the age of about two years onward) in Figure 24, which charts the basilar length of the skull in the domestic horse.

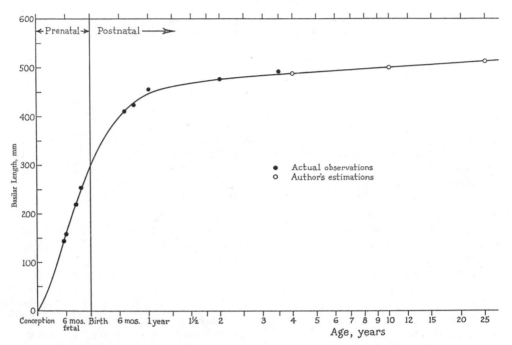

Fig. 24 Growth of the skull in basilar length in the domestic horse.

An important classifactory feature of the equine skull that appears to have been overlooked both by mammalogists and paleontologists is the extent to which the occipital crest projects rearward beyond the occipital condyles. This projection, or ratio, may be accurately determined by relating the vertex length of the skull to the basilar length. The latter two measurements, along with 22 others which have been standardized for the equine skull, are indicated in Fig. 25.* The basilar length is measurement no. 1, and the vertex length no. 2. In species where there is a pronounced backward projection of the occipital crest (or *inion*), as is shown in the Pleistocene form (*Equus occidentalis*) in Figure 6, a *nonhorselike* form—such as an ass, a zebra, or a hemionid—is indicated. Here are some vertex/basilar ratios typical for the forms named: Arab horse, 1.095; draft horses, av., 1.100; South Russian tarpan, 1.100; Mongolian wild horse, 1.106; Grévy's zebra, 1.124; *E. hemionus*, av., 1.126; Grant's zebra, 1.126; domestic ass, 1.133; mountain zebra, 1.135. It is interesting to note that this ratio in the fossil "tar-pit horse" of Rancho La Brea is 1.132, which is only one of a

---

* This drawing, like the second figure in Figure 6, is of a typical skull of the so-called "tar-pit horse" of Rancho La Brea, *Equus occidentalis* Leidy, a fossil species which has been identified by the author as being a giant form of zebra or quagga (see Chapter 15).

great many ratios of proportion that stamp the animal as having been a giant quagga, or a Burchell's zebra, rather than a true (caballine) horse.

The significance of the vertex/basilar ratio is that a large ratio indicates favorable leverage of the neck muscles on movements of the head, while a small ratio indicates relatively unfavorable leverage. The latter condition, which is characteristic of true horses, is accompanied by a compensatory development of the extensor muscles of the neck, which is evidenced in the thick, high-arched necks of stallions. Conversely, the favorable leverage present in asses, zebras, and hemionids permits a lesser development of the neck muscles as results in the relatively flat or "ewe" necks typical of these species.

Another classifactory index derived from measurements of the equine skull, and one which is a great deal more variable between species than the vertex/basilar index just mentioned, is what the author has termed the "occipital index." In this index the "overhang" of the occipital crest, as derived by subtracting the *condylo-basal* length of the skull (measurement no. 3, Fig. 25) from the vertex length (no. 2) is divided by the *width* of the occipital crest (no. 9). Thus a *wide* occipital crest, divided into a *slight* backward "overhang" of the same bone (as is typical of true horses), yields a small occipital index, whereas a *narrow* crest divided into a *pronounced* overhang yields a large occipital index. This is shown in the following typical examples of this index:

Table 2. The "Occipital Index" in various examples of the genus *Equus*.

Draft horse	27.6
Arabian horse	29.7
Shetland pony	31.6
South Russian tarpan	32.2
Mongolian wild horse	35.5
Quagga	40.3
Domestic ass	43.9
Grévy's zebra	45.6
Syrian onager	52.4
Grant's zebra	52.8
Mule	52.9
Mountain zebra	55.1
Burchell's zebra	59.3
E. hemionus (av. 3 species)	63.9

In the fossil Rancho La Brea species, *E. occidentalis,* the index is 59.5, which again contributes to the probability that this equine animal was *not* a horse. Even if a Standard Range (1000 cases) of this index is applied to the domestic horse, the index goes no higher than 37, which completely separates true horses from hemionids, and from most zebras.

Many other measurements and ratios of the equine skull could be commented upon if such items were of interest to the general reader (see also Chapter 18). However, most such ratios are so highly variable among individual animals of a given species as to be useless for distinguishing one species from another. That is, the range of variation *within a given species* is much greater than the *differences between the averages* of a measurement or a ratio in a distinct species. This shortcoming applies also to the *teeth* of horses, about which a few words may now be said.

Referring again to Fig. 25, it will be noted (measurement no. 13 in the side view

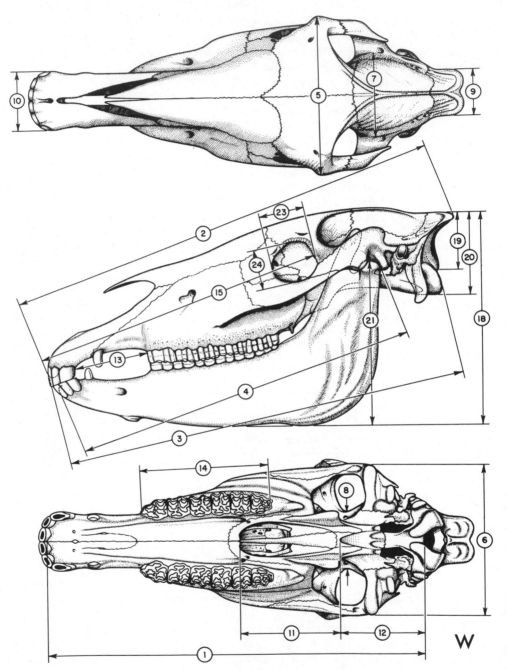

Fig. 25 Skull of a typical male specimen of the so-called "tar-pit horse" of Rancho La Brea, indicating (by the various numbers) where the standard measurements of the equine skull are to be taken. × .18 nat. size.

of the skull) that there is a considerable gap between the front (incisor) teeth, which are mainly adapted for cropping and biting, and the long row of six teeth (measurement no. 14) on each side of the face, which are appropriately called cheek-teeth, and whose function is to grind up the grass or other herbage gathered by the front teeth. The gap is called the *diastema,* and is the space in which the bit of the bridle is placed. It will be noted also that in the front end of the diastema there is shown a canine tooth in both the upper and the lower jaws. These teeth, which normally occur only in male horses, are called "tushes" (tusks). Thus the usual number of teeth in stallions is $\frac{3-1-3-3}{3-1-3-3} = 40$, while in mares, which lack the tushes, the number is 36. It has been inferred that since mares normally lack tushes, these canine teeth in stallions are used mainly, if not entirely, for fighting. Certainly they are of little or no use for gathering or masticating food.

The presence of the diastema in horses is one of the features that testify to the specialized nature of the teeth in these animals. Mammals of a more primitive type have either *all* the teeth in contact, or present only small spaces on each side of the canines when these are large. In comparing the teeth of horses with those of oxen, Lydekker remarks

A similar long gap (diastema) occurs in the lower dental series of the ox and its relatives, in which, however, they form a regular series of spatulate-crowned teeth. In the upper jaw of the ox tribe specialization has been carried to a much greater extent than in the horse, the canines and incisors having completely disappeared, and being replaced by a hard pad which takes the bite of the lower front teeth. In consequence of the retention of upper as well as lower front teeth, a horse is apparently able to graze closer than an ox.[3]

Lydekker suggests also that the function of the diastema in both the horse and the ox is to afford more room for the play of the large tongue, which performs an important part in the action of grazing. In both the horse and the ox, the grass is first gripped by the front teeth, then torn off with a tug or jerk of the head.

The incisor, or front cutting teeth, of the Equidae present a relatively complex type unique among the Mammalia. Instead of having simple conical crowns when they first erupt in an unworn state from the gums, the incisor teeth of horses and their relatives have a kind of pit, or hollow, at the surface, which is commonly called either the "cup" or the "mark" (infundibulum). This pit is lined with enamel, and extends downward more than half an inch in the center of each incisor tooth. The "mark" is black, owing to discoloration caused by food and juices. As the tooth wears down, the "mark" gradually is obliterated. It should be remembered that the teeth of a horse, unlike those of a human being, are continually being worn away with age and use as their crowns are pushed into position from their roots. When the "mark" has disappeared from wear, the dentine beneath it, which is also blackened by the aforementioned causes, wears out in its turn. The "mark" is then said to be "out," and indicates (in the lower jaw) an age of about 8 years. The "marks" in the upper incisors continue to be present until 9 years (upper central incisors), 10 years (upper intermediate incisors), and 11 years (all upper incisors, including the outer or "corner" ones). (See Figs. 26 and 27).

The forms of both the incisor and the grinding (premolar and molar) teeth of the horse may be more readily understood by reference to Figs. 28 and 29. Figure 28 represents the skull of a two-year-old colt, cut away so as to show the embedded parts of the teeth. Fig. 29 is the cut-away skull of a five-year-old horse, showing the permanent

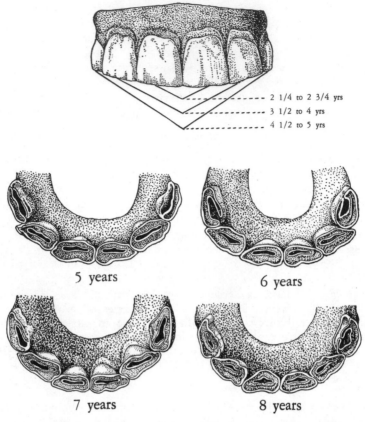

Fig. 26 In the upper figure are given the times of eruption of the *upper* incisor teeth. The lower four figures show changes in the "marks" in the *lower* incisor teeth that occur with age.

Fig. 27 Slant of the incisor teeth as an indication of age.

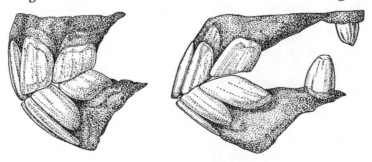

dentition in place and with the teeth just beginning to be worn. The following table, based mainly on Sisson,[4] gives the usual eruption time of the teeth in the domestic horse. The designations of the teeth correspond with those shown in Figures 28 and 29.

Table 3. Eruption time of the teeth in the domestic horse.

	Deciduous dentition (milk teeth)		Time of eruption
	1st incisor	(di 1/1)	birth to 7 days
	2nd "	(di 2/2)	4 to 6 weeks
	3rd "	(di 3/3)	6 to 10 months
	Canine	(dc)	(absorbed without eruption)
	1st premolar	(dm 2/2)	birth to 2 weeks
	2nd "	(dm 3/3)	" " " "
	3rd "	(dm 4/4)	" " " "
	Permanent dentition		
	1st incisor	(I1)	2¼–2¾ years
	2nd "	(I2)	3½–4 years
	3rd "	(I3)	4½–5 years
	Canine	(C)	4–5 years (rarely in female)
	1st premolar	(P1)	
Order of appearance	(or "wolf tooth")		5–6 months (frequently absorbed without eruption)
3	2nd premolar	(P2)	2¼–2¾ years
4	3rd "	(P3)	2½–3½ years
6	4th "	(P4)	3¾–4¼ years
1	1st molar	(M1)	10–12 months
2	2nd "	(M2)	20–26 months
5	3rd "	(M3)	3¼–4¼ years

These eruption-times are for *upper* teeth;
the lower teeth may erupt about 6 months earlier.

The cheek, or grinding, teeth of the horse normally consist of three premolars and three molars on each side of each jaw. As is seen in Figure 26, the lower teeth, although forming a row of grinding surfaces as long (from front to back) as the upper row, are considerably narrower and less square than the upper teeth. Both the upper and the lower rows of these long-crowned (hypsodont) teeth grow until 4 or 5 years of age, at which time the incisors and canines reach their full length. The cheek teeth continue to grow for a somewhat longer period, so long as their roots remain open. Concurrently with this growth in length, the teeth are "pushed" into chewing position by the steady growth of *bone* beneath them. However, the growth of the teeth does not keep pace with the shortening caused by wear, so that the teeth gradually become shorter. The exposed part of the tooth tends to keep the same height above the gums (at times higher rather than lower) with age; the decrease in length of the tooth takes place entirely in the jaw. As the tooth extrudes itself, deposits of cement take place continuously at the bottom of the teeth. New bone replaces the space under the tooth as the tooth grows into occlusal position, always remaining in contact under it.

Fig. 30 is a schematic representation of the grinding (or premolar-molar series) of teeth in the horse, showing the levels of the crowns or wearing surfaces that normally come into use at the ages indicated. A prolonged study by the writer of the dimensions and proportions of the cheek teeth in domestic horses of various known ages has

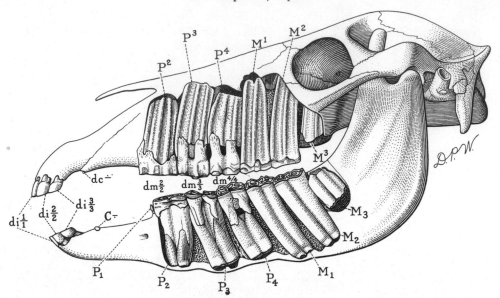

Fig. 28 Skull of a two-year-old colt, cut away so as to show the embedded parts of the teeth. The deciduous or temporary teeth are designated by lower case letters; the permanent teeth by capitals. dc = upper deciduous or milk canine; C = lower permanent canine, undeveloped; $di\frac{1}{1}$, $di\frac{2}{2}$, $di\frac{3}{3}$ = first, second and third deciduous incisors; $dm\frac{2}{2}$, $dm\frac{3}{3}$, $dm\frac{4}{4}$ = second, third and fourth deciduous molars; P_1, $P\frac{2}{2}$, $P\frac{3}{3}$, $P\frac{4}{4}$ = permanent* premolars; $M\frac{1}{1}$, $M\frac{2}{2}$, $M\frac{3}{3}$ = permanent molars. The deciduous canines are quite vestigial, and do not erupt to the stage of being functional. The usual milk-tooth formula, therefore, is: $2(i\frac{3}{3}; c\frac{0}{0}; m\frac{3}{3}) = 24$.

1	2	3	2	3	4		2	3	4
1	2	3	2	3	4	1	2	3	4

1	2	3	3	0	3
1	2	3	3	0	3

* P_1, or so-called "wolf teeth," are probably retained deciduous teeth rather than true permanent ones. Where present, they occur usually in the upper jaw and only rarely in the lower. In the adult horse these tiny premolars are on the way toward becoming vestigial. Hence the first or most anterior functional premolars in the horse are P

1	2
1	2

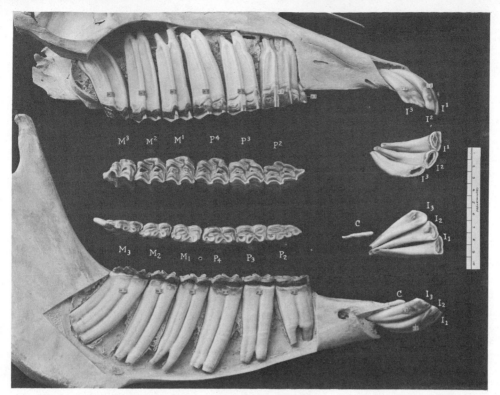

Fig. 29 Skull of a five-year-old domestic horse (New Forest pony), cut away so as to show the whole of the outer surfaces of the embedded cheek teeth. The mandible has been separated from the cranium in order to present views of the occlusal surfaces of the upper and lower tooth-rows. At the right side of the photograph, three of the six incisor teeth in each jaw are shown, top and bottom, in *situ*. In between are given views of their occlusal surfaces. Note in the upper tooth row the presence of an undeveloped P1.

shown that wear takes place, and the teeth diminish in crown length, at a rate that corresponds, not with the age of the animal *per se*, but with the *logarithm of its age.*[*] That is, under average conditions of growth and wear, the surfaces of the grinding teeth abrade as much between 5 and 10 years of age as between 10 and 20 years, and as much between 10 and 20 years as between 20 and 40 years. This logarithmic (diminishing) rate of wear is confirmed by the reduction in the fore-and-aft length of the six-tooth row that takes place as various levels of teeth come into use. The fore-and-aft dimensions of the six grinding teeth also present varying size-ratios *among each other* as successive levels move into position with age and wear. As will be observed in Fig. 30, the widest (fore-and-aft) teeth are P2 in both the upper and the lower jaw and M3 in the lower jaw. The other, intermediate teeth are (at 4 years of age) of closely similar anteroposterior diameters, although changes caused by the differing degrees of taper toward the roots of the teeth as successive grinding levels come into use alter these size-similarities.

The intricate foldings of enamel that form the "patterns" on the crowns of the

---

* It is probable that in the teeth of other types of animals also, in which there is rapid abrasion, the tooth wear takes place in ratio to the *logarithm* of the age. For example, this appears true of the molar wear in house mice, as shown by Donald R. Breakey (*Jour. Mammalogy* 44, no. 2 [May 20, 1963]: 155).

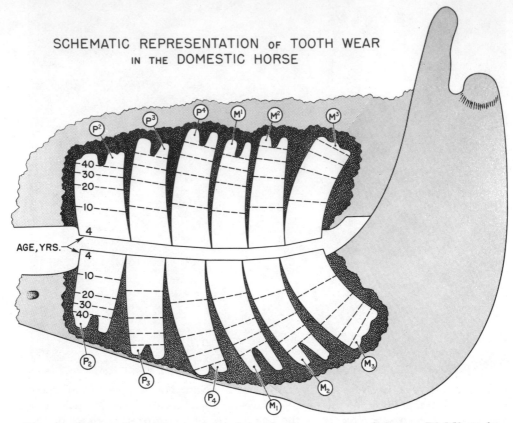

SCHEMATIC REPRESENTATION OF TOOTH WEAR IN THE DOMESTIC HORSE

Fig. 30 Schematic sections taken through the upper and lower P2-M3 series, showing the relative anteroposterior diameters and crown lengths of the cheek teeth in the domestic horse at 4 years of age. The broken lines on the teeth indicate the respective age-levels from 10 to 40 years. It is assumed that by the age of 40 the horse's teeth, under normal living conditions, will be worn down to the roots. Note that the teeth are abraded not at a uniform rate, but in ratio to the *logarithms* of the ages, the same as the diminution of the anteroposterior diameters of the teeth. $\times$ .37 nat. size.

grinding teeth of horses and their relatives have been the objects of a great amount of study by mammalogists and paleontologists during the last hundred years or more. What was being sought by these investigators in the dimensions, proportions, and enamel patterns of the cheek teeth was a means for reliably identifying given specimens of the various species and subgenera occurring within the genus *Equus*. The present writer also has endeavored to find—in the cheek teeth of numerous examples of horses, zebras, donkeys, wild asses, hemionids, and various fossil and sub-fossil equids—a means of positive identification and classification. The result has been that while *average* differences in size, proportioning, and patterning can be established or demonstrated between the various subgeneric forms of Equidae, *no reliability can be placed on the identification or classification of a given single specimen by such means.* The reason for this is that in equine teeth the degree of *individual* variability within a given species (such as *Equus caballus*) is far greater than the difference between the *mean or typical* characteristics (dimensions, proportions, or patterns) presented in the teeth of the various subgeneric types.

From a paleontologist's point of view, the teeth of any fossil animal afford the most imperishable part of its skeleton; and the hard-surfaced, prismatic, and beautifully patterned cheek teeth of fossil horses and their kind seem to promise an infallible object for exact measurement and differential classification. Unfortunately, as pointed out above, the range in *individual* variability tends to obscure or invalidate the presumed specific differences between members of the genus *Equus*. Hence, to describe a species on the evidence presented by a single tooth (which is often all that is recovered of a fossil specimen), or even an entire row of cheek teeth or a complete skull, is a risky procedure, and one that has in many cases been proved erroneous.*

Reference to Fig. 31 will show how the dental patterns of distinct equine forms can be misleading as differential criteria. Let us ignore the middle pattern, which is that of a mule (a hybrid animal and not a species) and compare the patterns of the horse (left) and the donkey (right). In the lefthand figure, the letters *pc* refer to what has been termed the *pli caballin*[5], or a portion of the enamel-folding that has been presumed to be distinctive of true (caballine) horses as contrasted with asses, zebras, and hemionids. But note the word "presumed." For it has been demonstrated that, through natural wear (or the deliberate grinding-down or sawing-through of a detached tooth), a donkey tooth may come to possess a pli-caballin, and a horse tooth to lose it.[6] In some individual horses the *pli caballin* may diminish as the teeth are worn down with age, while in other horses it may become more pronounced. Thus the tooth patterning, the same as the dimensions and proportions of the teeth, and even of the entire skull, must be used with caution and reserve (giving due consideration to the modifying influences of age and absolute size) as criteria for species identification.

Fig. 31 Molar teeth of horse, mule, and domestic ass, respectively; to show "typical" likenesses and differences in pattern. All figures natural size. (Redrawn from Osborn, *Titanotheres* 2: 820.)

The best that can be expected from the skull and teeth is that they may provide *supplementary or corroborative evidence* of the zoological position of a species as determined primarily from a study of the limb bones, pelvis, and hoof (foot) bones in the specimen. Where the postcranial skeletal elements are not available—as is commonly the case in fossil specimens—the species identification, as made from the teeth (and possibly a more or less complete skull), should be regarded at best as a tentative one. According to Antonius:

The teeth of equids depend, according to my findings, much more on the living conditions [habitats] of the animals than on their phylogenetic relations . . .[7]

Fig. 32 shows outlines of the upper grinding teeth in one example of the domestic horse, two examples of the Mongolian wild horse, two examples of the quagga (now extinct), and one example of the fossil "tar-pit horse" (actually a giant quagga or a

---

* For example, the fossil European genus *Hipparion,* which from its dentition has commonly been thought to have been ancestral to caballine horses, is clearly shown from its postcranial skeleton to have been a zebra. The same is true of the tar-pit "horse" of Rancho La Brea.

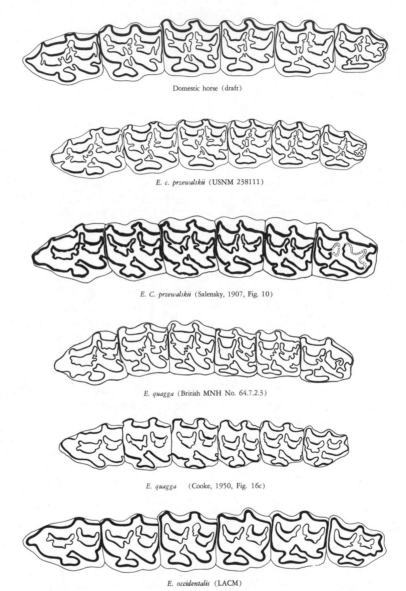

Domestic horse (draft)

E. c. przewalskii (USNM 238111)

E. C. przewalskii (Salensky, 1907, Fig. 10)

E. quagga (British MNH No. 64.7.2.3)

E. quagga (Cooke, 1950, Fig. 16c)

E. occidentalis (LACM)

Fig. 32 Upper P^2 -M^3 dental series in the domestic horse, the Mongolian wild horse, the quagga, and the fossil tar-pit quagga of Rancho La Brea. All figures $\times$ .56 natural size.

Burchell's zebra), drawn to the same scale. In the latter species a lower tooth row also is shown. When illustrations such as these are published, the lay reader may well make comparisons on the assumption that the patterns shown for each species are typical for *all the individual animals* composing that species. Such, as has been pointed out, is not the case, and the tooth-patterns of the members of the horse family, even when brought (reconstructed) to the same age, show variabilities and discrepancies resulting from the food and eating habits peculiar to each animal.

Notes and References

Chapter 5

1. Henry Fairfield Osborn, *The Age of Mammals* (New York: 1910), p. 18.
2. Richard Lydekker, *The Horse and Its Relatives* (London: 1912), p. 21.
3. *Ibid.*, p. 28.
4. S. Sisson, *The Anatomy of the Domestic Animals* (Philadelphia, 1927). (Sisson's table largely follows that of W. G. Ridewood, "The Teeth of the Horse," in *Natural Science* 6, no. 38 [April 1895]).
5. For details of the dental nomenclature in horses, see: H. F. Osborn, *Evolution of Mammalian Molar Teeth to and from the Triangular Type* (New York: The Macmillan Co., 1907); and R. A. Stirton, "Development of Characters in Horse Teeth and the Dental Nomenclature," *Jour. Mammalogy* 22, no. 4 (November 14, 1941): 434–46.
6. J. U. Duerst, "Animal Remains from the Excavations at Anau . . ." (Carnegie Inst. Wash. Pub. 73, 1908), vol. 2, Part 6, pp. 339–42. (Much useful information on the origin and relationships of the domestic horse is given in this article.)
7. Otto Antonius, *Grundzüge einer Stammesgeschichte der Haustiere* (Jena, 1922), p. 247. (Origin and history of the domestic horse and its wild relatives, by one of the greatest authorities on the subject.)

6

The Horse's Existing Perissodactyl Relatives
(Tapirs and Rhinoceroses)

Included in the same order of odd-toed animals (*Perissodactyla*) as the horses and their relatives are two existing yet less familiar groups, the tapirs (Family *Tapiridae*) and the rhinoceroses (Family *Rhinocerotidae*). As is shown in Fig. 33, the latter two families, along with the *Equidae,* are the sole surviving representatives of groups that flourished during Eocene and Oligocene times, and which had their origin in the Paleocene in an order called *Condylarthra.* According to W. B. Scott:

> The Condylarthra were a group of exceedingly primitive ungulates, which served to connect the hoofed and clawed mammals in quite an intimate manner. So few indeed were the ungulate characters which they had acquired, that it is still premature to make any positive statements regarding their geographical distribution, because unusually well-preserved specimens are required to make sure of their presence in any particular region. Concerning North America there is no room for question, and there is hardly any doubt that they existed in the Paleocene of Europe.[1]

A well-stablished representative of the condylarths was *Phenacodus,* which varied from the size of a fox to that of a small sheep. The skull was even shorter-faced than that of *Eohippus* (see Figs. 1 and 6); and although the hinder portion of the skull was relatively long, the brain was very small. The jaws were short and shallow, in accordance with the small and low-crowned teeth which they carried. The teeth showed clearly that *Phenacodus* was a plant eater, although in bodily appearance the animal resembled a small carnivore. The neck was of medium length; but the body, which had an arched back, and the tail were both relatively long. The limbs were short, and the feet had five digits each; but the middle toe of each foot was enlarged, while the two outer toes were shortened. This suggests that *Phenacodus* was already on the way to acquiring a three-toed perissodactyl foot. A second family of the *Condylarthra* was represented by the later (lower Eocene) genus *Meniscotheridae.* These animals, while no larger than *Phenacodus,* had relatively longer and lighter limbs, and their five-toed feet strongly resembled those of the modern conies, or klipdasses, of Africa and Asia Minor. Evidently by the time the genus *Meniscotheridae* appeared, the condylarths were approaching the stages in their evolution where they branched off into the numerous

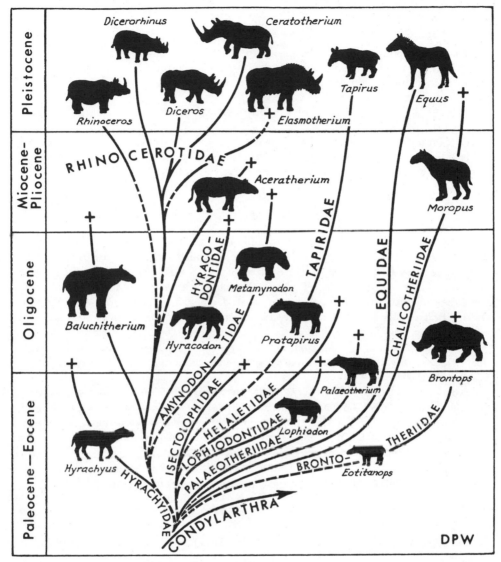

Fig. 33 Family tree of the *Perissodactyla* (horses, tapirs, rhinoceroses, and their fossil ancestors). The crosses at the tops of some stems indicate the times of extinction of those forms. Where lines are dashed, it indicates uncertain continuity.

types that led to the sole existing perissodactyl animals of today: the horses, tapirs, and rhinoceroses.

Referring again to Fig. 33, it will be noted that of the seventeen branches (suborders or families) stemming from the Paleocene *Condylarthra,* twelve branches pertain to forms that became extinct before reaching Recent time. Of these twelve forms, six became extinct in the Oligocene, four in the Miocene or Pliocene, and two in the Pleistocene. Only the horses, the tapirs, and the rhinoceroses survive today; and some of these forms, such as the Mongolian wild horse, the Asiatic species of the rhinoceros, and possibly the Malay tapir, are perilously close to extinction and can be saved only by the most stringent observance and enforcement of conservation and game laws in the countries involved.

It is now opportune to describe briefly the tapirs and rhinoceroses, calling attention in particular to those points in which—despite the widely different external appearances among these animals—the tapirs and rhinoceroses have affinities with the horse.

The Tapirs (Family *Tapiridae*).

This family is represented today by two genera (*Tapirus* and *Tapirella*) in Central and South America, and by one genus (*Acrocodia*) in southeastern Asia and Sumatra.* In the new world there are four species distributed as follows:

1. Subgenus *Tapirus Brisson*.

BRAZILIAN TAPIR (*Tapirus terrestris* Linnaeus): The common South American tapir of the lowland forests of Brazil and Paraguay and the northern part of Argentina. This species may be identified by the thick rounded crest on the neck, which is topped by a short mane of stiff hair (see Fig. 36). The chief enemy of this species, and perhaps the three other American species of tapir, apart from man, is the jaguar (see Fig. 39). Of the Brazilian tapir, besides the typical form, there are three other subspecies: *T. terrestris laurillardi* Gray, of Venezuela; *T. terrestris mexianae* Hagmann, of Mexiana Island, in the mouth of the Amazon; and *T. terrestris spegazzinii* Ameghino, of Argentina (type locality, Tucuman). All three subspecies differ only in minor respects from *T. terrestris terrestris*.

THE PINCHAQUE, or ROULIN'S TAPIR (*Tapirus roulini*). This species, the smallest of the four kinds of tapirs, occurs mainly at high levels in the Cordilleras of Columbia and Equador, 7000 to 8000 feet above sea level. The skin is uniformly covered with thick, curly hair about an inch long. There are whitish spots on the.head, and the sides of the body are bluish-hazel in color instead of brown. On the feet, just above the toes, there is a ring of bare white skin. The neck has no crest nor mane. Its numbers may today be very limited, and the species has been placed on the endangered list.

2. Subgenus *Tapirella* Palmer.

BAIRD'S TAPIR (*Tapirella bairdi*): Mexico, Honduras, Nicaragua, Costa Rica, and Panama.

DOW'S TAPIR (*Tapirella dowi*): Guatemala, Nicaragua, and Costa Rica.

The Brazilian tapir is of a nearly uniform dark brown or blackish coloration (except in young animals up to the age of about six months, which are spotted and striped in a horizontal pattern).**This species is somewhat smaller than its Malay cousin, ranging among different specimens from about 36 to 42 inches high at the shoulder,

---

* This widely separated present-day distribution is attributed to the greatly extended range that occurred in former times over a wide area of the Northern Hemisphere, and which linked together the New World and Old World species of the tapir.

** The coat-pattern of young tapirs, which is shown very clearly in Figure 36, may well represent that which was common to the remote, jungle-dwelling ancestors of the horse, such as *Eohippus*, or of the tapir, such as the Eocene genus *Systemodon*. Concerning the usual black-and-white coloration of the adult Malay tapir, Pocock remarks: "It has been stated that when lying down in a district studded with large grey boulders a Malay tapir is almost invisible; but in spite of this, it is probable that the division of the body into a dark and a light area is for the purpose of breaking up the outline of the entire animal and thus rendering it inconspicuous at a moderate distance."[3]

and weighing from 550 to 850 pounds. The hog-shaped tapirs of Central America (*T. bairdi* and *T. dowi*) are smaller than the South American species, and differ from them in having the nasal septum ossified. The coloration of these forms is brownish-black above, dirty white on the throat and chest, and somewhat rufous on the head. The gestation period in the Brazilian tapir is about 11 months (335 days).

Fig. 34 Brazilian tapir *(Tapirus terrestris)*. Note the long nose, short legs, stubby tail, and cylindrical body-form typical of tapirs in general, along with the crested, maned neck peculiar to this species. $\times$ 1/18 natural size.

3. Subgenus *Acrocodia* Goldman.

The Malay tapir is represented by a single species (*Acrocodia indica* Desmarest). Its range—before the warfare in southeastern Asia began!—was said to be the Malay Peninsula and Archipelago, southernmost Burma, and parts of Siam (Thailand), Sumatra, and possibly Borneo. But today, according to some investigators, the species is threatened with extinction. The Malay tapir is larger on the average than the American species, averaging about 44 inches high at the choulder and 3 to 4 inches higher at the rump. Its length, from tip of snout to end of tail, averages about 8 feet. The tail measures only about 3 inches. The proboscis is proportionately rather longer than in the American tapirs. The neck has no crest nor mane, but is rounded and smooth. The coloration is a striking, unique contrast of black and white. The body is dark brown or black except for a large whitish area that covers the back, rump, and sides of the belly (see Fig. 35). The tips of the ears are also whitish. The dark and light colors do not pass gradually one into the other, but are sharply demarcated, giving the animal a most peculiar appearance. A local variety of this species that is entirely black

Fig. 35 Wood engraving by the oldtime team of German animal illustrators, the three brothers Specht, showing Malay tapirs *(Acrocodia indica)* in their native haunts. Note the large whitish patch of color peculiar to this Old World species.

has been reported.[2] The newborn animals, as in the four American species, are brownish or velvety black, marked with spots and longitudinal streaks of brownish-yellow on the sides, and of white on the underside. As the change from the young to the adult coloration takes place between four and six months of age, it would appear that it concurs with the age of weaning. The period of gestation in the single offspring is usually 390–395 days—nearly two months longer than in the horse.

As to the skeletal anatomy, the most distinctive features of the skull in tapirs are the enormous size of the nasal opening, and the lack of a bony bar (postorbital process) dividing the socket of the eye from the channel on the side of the cranium (which bar is present in the skull of the horse but not of the rhinoceros). The teeth are 42 in number, or 2 less than the full typical mammalian number, the lacking teeth being the first premolar on each side of the lower jaw. The cheek teeth, which are low-crowned, are separated from the incisors by a long gap, comparable to the diastema in horses; and the tusks, or canines, are small, those of the upper jaw being inferior in size to the outermost pair of incisors. The upper cheek teeth have two transverse ridges and an outer (lateral) fore-and-aft wall, while those of the lower jaw present a pair of transverse ridges alone.

In the relatively short, sturdily developed limbs all the bones are distinct from one another, and the toe-bones (see Fig. 38, A) are encased in long, somewhat oval-shaped hoofs. On the sole the foot is furnished with a large, callous central pad, which helps support the weight of the body. Except when the soil is soft and yielding, the small outermost toe (digit V) on the fore foot hardly touches the ground. The three-toed hind foot is shown in Fig. 39. The front foot has four toes; but the weight, as in the hind foot, is borne mainly by digit III.

Both the Malay tapir and its American relatives are, so far as known, of similar habits. All species appear to be solitary (two or three together is about the extent of their sociability), nocturnal, shy, and inoffensive. Their preferred haunts are forests or savannahs with rivers or lakes nearby, into which they can take refuge when pursued. Tapirs are excellent divers and swimmers, and often take to the water to refresh themselves or to get rid of annoying insects. Like hippopotamuses, they are able to walk along the bottom of the water, instead of swim. Despite their shy, retiring habits, tapirs, if captured at a sufficiently young age, can readily be tamed, and often exhibit considerable attachment to their keeper. In the wild state, the food of tapirs is largely composed of palm leaves; but at certain seasons they subsist also on fallen fruits, swamp grasses, and water plants. In the vicinity of plantations they often do much harm to the crops of sugar-cane, melons, and other tropical products. The American species are said to be especially dreaded by the operators of cocoa-bean plantations for the amount of damage they inflict on the young plants. Like many other hoofed animals, tapirs relish salt, and they even eat salt-containing earth in order to obtain it. In captivity they are fond of sweet foodstuffs, and may become almost as omnivorous as swine.

Fig. 36 Brazilian tapir and infant young. The spotted and streaked coat-pattern seen in the young animal is believed to be similar to that which characterized adult animals of such ancestral perissodactyl forms as *Eohippus*, the "dawn horse" (cf. Fig. 2).

Fig. 37 Here is a graphic scene in the South American forest. From a convenient ambush the jaguar springs out upon a tapir, who has been enjoying herself with her young on the river bank. Frequently when a jaguar jumps on the back of a tapir the attacked animals run into a thicket. The jaguar's hold on the tapir's tough, thick hide is weak, however; and the predator is often thrown off. In this instance, the tapir can escape by diving. The jaguar will not be able to do much damage in the water.

Fossil tapir-like forms are known from the Eocene onward (see Figure 33), but many of them, as deduced from their skeletal remains, are hardly separable from the present-day species. This indicates that the modern tapir, unlike the modern horse, has retained most of its primitive characters for some 50 million years! Indeed, it is among the oldest (relatively unchanged) of living mammals.

The Rhinoceroses (Family *Rhinocerotidae*).

The name *rhinoceros* is derived from two Greek words: *rhinos,* the nose, and *keras,* horn. The German name, *Nashorn,* is completely literal, since the most outstanding outward peculiarity of the animal is the horn, or horns, growing atop its nose. The name in most other European languages is either *rhinoceros* or a derivative of it (e.g., the Spanish or Italian *rinoceronte*). However, in Japan a radical difference occurs, as there the name is reduced to *sai.*

The physical characters common to the existing species of the rhinoceros are as follows: head relatively large, with a concave forehead; muzzle prolonged; ears medium to large, prominent and erect, placed far back; eyes small (and eyesight poor); neck short and thick; body long and massive; limbs short and heavy; hips broad. The two nasal bones are fused together into a strong arch for the support of one or two horns. The "horns" are composed, not of the type of keratin that forms the hollow horns of cattle, sheep, goats, and true antelopes, but of a type that is closer to that in hair and hoofs, especially hoofs. The horn of a rhinoceros arises from the skin of the snout, and the only indication of its position on the bone of the skull underneath is an area where the bone is exceedingly roughened (see Fig. 40). In only one species is the horn usually absent, and that is in females of the Javan or lesser one-horned rhinoceros (*R. sondaicus*). The horn grows throughout life, and in the wild animal is smooth and polished, because of constant digging, rubbing, and other abrasive uses. In one zoo specimen in which the horn was torn away, it was found to regrow at the rate of about 3 inches a year.

In extinct forms of the rhinoceros the presence or absence of a horn or horns may readily be determined, since if no horns existed the nasal bone shows no roughened area for their attachment (via the skin), and the facial portion of the skull is flat or straight rather than concave. Since in many of the earlier, ancestral members of the family *Rhinocerotidae* no horns were present, some zoologists have regarded certain other features as being better means for distinguishing these animals from their relatives the tapirs. One such distinguishing feature is the cheek or grinding teeth.

In the African subgenus *Diceros* (the black rhinoceros) there are usually no front teeth; all the incisors and canines have been lost.* The other rhinoceroses have on each side of the upper jaw a large, sharp, chisel-shaped incisor, which shears against a still larger, tusk-like lower incisor, that points almost directly forward. Between the large lower tusks there is a pair of very small incisors, which evidently are of little or no use; the third lower incisors have been suppressed, as have also the canines of both jaws. The seven large cheek teeth are much less complicated in their enamel patterning than are those of horses. All seven teeth closely resemble each other, except the first premolar, which is much smaller than the rest, and is often lost early in life (see Fig. 40). The dental formula for the existing forms of the rhinoceros is normally 1

---

* Perhaps this is why the Indian rhinoceros uses its front teeth in fighting, while the black rhinoceros of Africa uses its front horn.

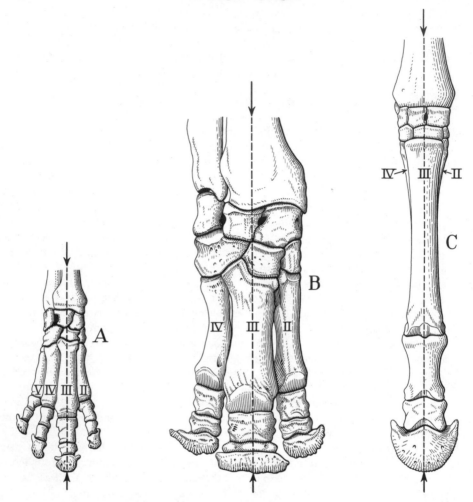

Fig. 38 Bones of the right fore feet of three existing forms of perissodactyl (odd-toed) ungulates. A, *Tapirus terrestris,* the Brazilian tapir; B, *Diceros bicornis,* the black rhinoceros; C, *Equus caballus,* the domestic horse (Standardbred). All figures × 1/5 natural size.

In all recent perissodactyls the main axis of weight-bearing, or symmetry, passes through the middle digit (phalanx III), which in consequence has become greatly enlarged, while digits II and IV have diminished. In the horse the sole remnants of these outer digits are the sliver-like "splint-bones." The foot of the tapir, with the exception of having relatively shorter metacarpal bones, represents very nearly, on a large scale, the foot of *Eohippus.*

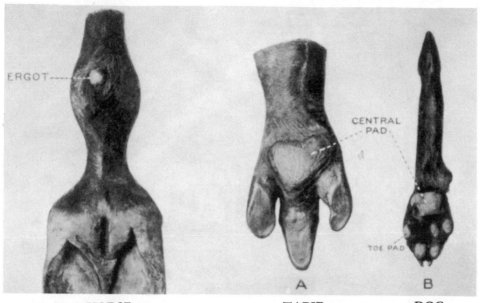

HORSE	TAPIR	DOG

Hind surface of the foot of a horse to show the ergot.

Hind feet of a tapir (A) and a dog (B) to show the pad corresponding with the ergot of a horse.

Fig. 39 Comparison of the feet of a horse, a tapir, and a dog.

(or no) upper incisors; 2 (or no) lower incisors; no canines; 4 premolars and 3 molars on each side of each jaw, making a total of 28 to 34 teeth. This is at least 10 less than in the tapir, and at least 6 less than in the horse (stallion).

The spinal column in rhinoceroses is composed normally of 7 cervical, 19-20 thoracic, 3 lumbar, 4 sacral, and about 22 caudal vertebrae. Thus the number of combined thoracic, lumbar, and sacral vertebrae in these animals normally averages about 2 less than in the horse, chiefly because of the rhinoceros's shorter lumbar section.

The feet in the rhinoceros, both fore and hind, consist of 3 toes (see Figure 38), each of which is furnished with a relatively small but broad and well-defined hoof-like nail. The gaits of this animal (walk, trot, gallop) are the same as in the horse.

The seven upper grinding teeth have a characteristic pattern, which is well adapted for crushing and chewing coarse branches, leaves, and other vegetable substances.* The pattern would appear to be a development of that seen in the ancient perissodactyl form, *Hyracotherium,* and in then-contemporary forms of hornless rhinoceroses. The cheek teeth have moderately high crowns, yet must be regarded as brachyodont, except in the grazing, broad-lipped white rhinoceros of Africa, in which the teeth may fairly be called hypsodont (high-crowned).

Rhinoceroses as a group are animals of large size, but of limited intelligence, general timid of disposition, though formidable when provoked, using their nasal horns to rip and toss their enemies. Their sight is poor, but their senses of hearing and smell compensate by being remarkably acute. With one exception (the white rhinoceros) they are browsing animals, feeding on the leaves and shoots of bushes and low-growing trees. Like many other large animals that inhabit tropical countries, they sleep

---

* In captivity, an adult rhinoceros is fed anywhere from 60 to 140 pounds of hay, oats, bread, and vegetables a day, depending upon its size.

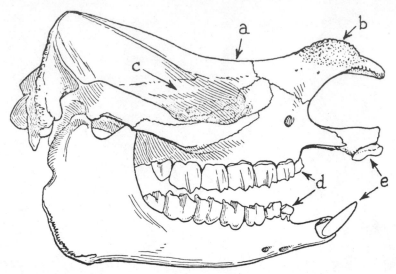

Fig. 40 Skull of Javan rhinoceros, showing features common to most species. *a*, concaveness of forehead; *b*, roughened area on nasal bone for attachment of horn; *c*, absence of bony bar behind eye-socket; *d*, reduced first premolar teeth; *e*, peculiar incisor teeth. The brain cavity is very small for the size of the skull. × 1/6 natural size.

Fig. 41 Drawing, by the author, showing a typical Great Indian rhinoceros *(Rhinoceros unicornis)*. The height, length, and weight indicated apply to an average-sized adult male. × 1/30 natural size.

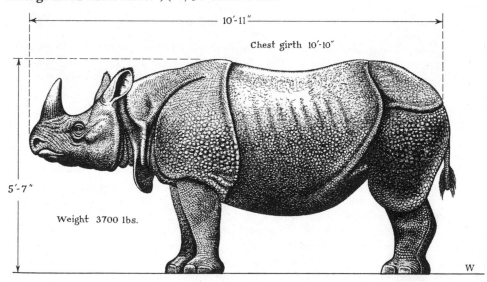

the greater part of the day, and are most active in the cool of the evening or even during the night. They are fond of bathing and of wallowing in mud (as with elephants, their skin, though thick, is nevertheless sensitive to the stings of insects). While tameable, none of the species has been domesticated. The family in earlier epochs contained many more species and was much more widely distributed than at present. At their peak of population, during the Pliocene–Pleistocene, the animals ranged over nearly all of Eurasia with the exception of Scandinavia and the high Himalayan regions. In the New World, numerous species ranged throughout what is now the United States, southward into lower Mexico. Evidently none ever reached South America. For concise descriptions of the chief fossil forms, the reader is referred to W. B. Scott.[4]

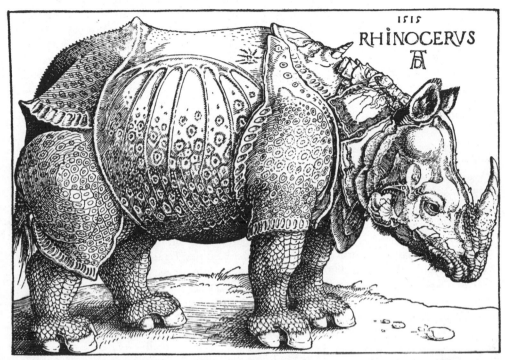

Fig. 42 Drawing (woodcut) of an Indian rhinoceros made in 1515 by Albrecht Dürer, the famous German artist. Dürer, who had only a poor sketch to work from, has made the animal appear as though it was covered with *metal* armor, and had *scales* on its lower legs. Note also the small horn above the shoulders! Gesner, in his *Historia Animalium,* published in 1551, used this illustration.

Each of the existing species of rhinoceros has its peculiarities of structure as well as habit, and these, where notable, are commented upon in the review which follows.

The family of existing rhinoceroses (*Rhinocerotidae*) is composed of one genus (*Rhinoceros*) and four subgenera. Two subgenera (*Ceratotherium* and *Diceros*) include two species each, occurring in southern and eastern Africa, and from the Sudan westward to Nigeria. Two additional subgenera (*Rhinoceros* and *Dicerorhinus*) comprise four or five species that range from India and Indochina through the Malay Peninsula to Sumatra and Borneo. Brief descriptions of these forms follow.

1. Subgenus *Rhinoceros.*

1. Great Indian rhinoceros (*Rhinoceros unicornis* Linnaeus). The name in Hindustani is *Gainda,* or *Gargudan;* in Punjabi, *Karkadan;* and in Bengali, *Gonda.* Germans call the species *Panzernashorn* ("armored rhinoceros").

This is the best-and-longest-known of the Asiatic rhinoceroses. As its specific name indicates, it has only a single horn. Fig. 37 is a drawing of a typical adult male, and shows it to be a large, heavy animal with an average shoulder height of 5 feet, 7 inches and a weight of 3700 pounds.* The hide, which is very thick, is studded with pebble-like tubercles, giving the impression of armor-like plates. Indeed, the German artist Albrecht Dürer (1471–1528) even pictured the animal thus! (Fig. 42). There are prominent folds on the neck, in front of the shoulder and behind it, and also in front of the hips and above the lower legs, fore and hind. With the exception of a fringe on the margins of the ears, and some bristly hairs on the peculiarly shaped tail-tuft (resembling that in the elephant), the coarse and massive skin is naked. The general color is uniform blackish-grey, with more or less pink on the edges of the skin-folds. The single horn in wild specimens is about the same size in both sexes, the average length when full grown being about 16 inches, with a basal circumference of about 21 inches. The record-sized horn is one that measures 24 inches in length and 24¾ inches in basal girth.[5]

As in the other forms of the rhinoceros, only one offspring at a time (every two or three years) is the rule. In the zoo at Basel a newborn male weighted 133 pounds (gestation period, 474 days), and a newborn female 147 pounds** (gestation period, 478 days).[6] However, gestation periods of from 510 days to 540 days (18 months) have been reported.

While in earlier times the range of the Indian rhinoceros extended from the North-west Frontier Province of India eastward perhaps as far as what was then French Indo-China, today it is restricted to the Assam plain, the Terailand of Nepal, and north-ern Bengal. In the early 1900s the species was close to extinction, but during more recent years, as a result of stringent conservation laws and penalties, it has slowly gained in numbers. A census taken in 1953 by the Indian biologist E. P. Gee showed a total of 350 wild specimens; while by 1966, in eight game reserves in India and Nepal, the number had increased to 740.

As to zoo specimens, those so far obtained appear in all cases to have adapted themselves well to their man-made environment, with its regular schedule of feedings and activities. Mohan, a full-grown male at the Whipsnade Zoo, London, is of a par-ticularly amiable disposition. Although his horn has for one reason or another been sawn off, he contentedly follows his keeper around his enclosure while he lets a child, or even a young lady, ride comfortably on his broad back.

As has been widely publicized, the chief cause of the decimation of the Indian rhinoceros has been the belief—which despite its lack of foundation still persists throughout most of Asia (as well as Africa)—that the horn of the animal, ground into powder, is a powerful aphrodisiac, youth restorer, and general panacea. In 1925, the value of a horn in the market at Calcutta was about half its weight in gold, and since

---

* Some of the specimens shot in earlier days, however, were much larger than this, and one big bull secured by the Maharaja of Cooch-Behar measured no less than 6 feet 4 inches in shoulder height. The weight of a giant of this height would be close to 5000 pounds, or equal to that of two very large draft horses together.

** These weights (and the listings definitely show kilograms, not pounds) are considerably greater than those reported for other newborn Indian rhinoceroses. For example, *Mohini,* a female at London's Whipsnade Zoo, in 1957 gave birth to a female that was estimated to weigh between 85 and 100 pounds. Even in the case of an African white rhinoceros the newborn animal weighed only about 100 pounds, and in one instance of the black rhinoceros the neonate weighed a mere 45 pounds.

Fig. 43 A drawing (stone lithograph) of the lesser one-horned, or "Javan," rhinoceros, by Joseph Wolf. Note, by a comparison with Fig. 41, the difference in the skin-folds from the Indian species. $\times$ 1/28 natural size.

an Indian rhino horn of average size weighs about two pounds, this meant a price of $300 to $400. Later on, this poaching was largely stopped by the passage of stringent laws, with the result that the Indian rhinoceros today has a chance, although a slim one, of holding its own.

2. Lesser one-horned rhinoceros (*Rhinoceros sondaicus* Desmarest). Called also, but inappropriately, the Javan rhinoceros. The French name is *Rhinocéros de la sonde;* the Malay name, *Badak,* and the Burmese name, *Kyan-tsheng.*

This species is closely related to the great one-horned rhinoceros, but differs from it outwardly in the mosaic patterning of its skin (which also lacks the tubercles), and by the extension of the neck fold over the back; it is also markedly smaller in body size and has a relatively shorter head and a shorter horn (see Fig. 43). The single horn in this species averages not over 8 inches, while the record-sized example is 10¾ inches long and 20 inches in basal circumference. The horn is generally lacking in the female. In shoulder height, an average-sized Javan rhinoceros stands about 4 feet 9 inches (57¼ inches) and weighs about 2200 pounds.*

According to Harper, the lesser one-horned rhinoceros is (or was, even in 1945) "one of the rarest and most famous of the large mammals now facing extinction."[7] While the animal's range formerly extended from Bengal, Assam, Burma, Siam (Thailand), and Indochina through the Malay Peninsula to Sumatra and Java, today the last few specimens survive in several remote refuges in these areas. Population estimates made in 1960 varied from 24 to 80 specimens, a sorry remnant of this once widely-ranging species. Most of the animals still existing today are in the game reserve at Udjong Kulon in western Java.

Curiously, although the Javan rhinoceros is now nearly extinct in the wild, it is represented in museum collections by a greater amount of skeletal material than any of the other Asiatic species of rhinoceros. The Dutch paleontologist, D. A. Hooijer, lists 14 skulls and 6 complete skeletons just among the specimens that he measured and studied.[8] Thus the skeletal and dental distinctions of this species are well documented.

---

* While several authors have quoted the shoulder height of a female specimen as being 5 feet, 6 inches, this is far greater than the average or typical size as determined from a series of skull and limb-bone measurements. The latter, in an average-sized Javan rhinoceros, are only about 86 percent as long as in the great Indian species, which would indicate a shoulder height in proportion.

Fig. 44 Hairy-eared subspecies of the Sumatran rhinoceros (*Dicerorhinus suma-trensis lasiotis*), in act of trotting (pacing). × 1/30 natural size.

2. Subgenus *Dicerorhinus.*

1. Sumatran rhinoceros (*Dicerorhinus sumatrensis sumatrensis* G. Fischer). Called also the Asiatic two-horned rhinoceros. The Burmese name is *Kayan* and *Kyan-shaw;* while the Malay name (the same as for the Javan rhinoceros) is *Badak.* Another native name is *teuxon.* The following description applies to the typical species. Two other sub-species (*D. sumatrensis blythi* and *D. sumatrensis lasiotis,* respectively) have been listed, but they differ from the typical form only in minor details, with the exception that both *blythi* and *lasiotis* are much more hairy.

This is the smallest and most widely distributed of the Asiatic rhinoceroses, and is the only one having normally two horns. It differs from both forms of the African two-horned rhinoceros by the presence of folds in its skin and of teeth in the front of the jaws. Only the skin-fold behind the shoulders is complete and continued across the back, and the skin is rough, granular, and more or less hairy. The general body color is brownish ash, while the underbelly and the folds of skin are of a dirty flesh coloration. The ears are small and pointed, and edged with short black hair. The upper lip, as in the browsing African black rhinoceros, is pointed and prehensile. The shoulder height of a male specimen of *lasiotis* is given as 4 feet 4 inches; length from tip of nose to root of tail, 8 feet 5 inches; length of front horn about 9 inches, and of rear horn 4 inches.* The body weight has been given as "about 2000 pounds"; however, since an average-sized Indian rhinoceros weighs 3700 pounds at a shoulder height of 67 inches, a Sumatran rhinoceros, even if as heavy-built as its giant Indian relative, would be expected to weigh only about 1650 pounds.

The Sumatran rhinoceros is a mountain-living animal, frequenting rugged hill jungles. Like all the other species, it likes to swim and to wallow in mud. Young specimens have been captured by natives and brought up as pets. In 1868, a full-grown rhino was rescued out of some quicksand and eventually sent to the London Zoo, where it lived contentedly for the following 32 years.

Like the other forms of rhinoceroses in Asia, the two-horned species has for some

---

* These measurements are far surpassed by those of the longest front horn on record, 32⅛ inches, and the longest rear horn, 14 inches. However, in each of these specimens there was no second horn; and the record for a two-horned specimen is 15 inches front and 7½ inches rear.

years been protected by law. Since it had a more extensive range to start with (nearly the entire forested area from Burma southeastward, including the Malay Peninsula, Borneo and Sumatra), it would appear to be in not quite so precarious a position numerically as the one-horned species. Nevertheless, the total population in 1966 was estimated as "not over 170." At that time, the sole captive specimen was one in the Copenhagen Zoo.

Fig. 45 Female black rhinoceros *(Diceros bicornis)* and young. Note the long and peculiarly curved anterior horn. The young calf is evidently deviating from the rules in walking alongside its mother, since it is said that in the black species the calf usually *follows* its mother, while in the white rhinoceros it *precedes* the parent, who guides it along with her horn.

3. Subgenus *Diceros.*

1. Black rhinoceros (*Diceros bicornis bicornis* Linnaeus). Called also (and more correctly) the African hook-lipped rhinoceros. For this African species, we shall not attempt to list all the native names. In Rowland Ward's *Records of Big Game* (9th ed., p. 441), 21 different names are given, varying from A to Z according to tribe or locality!

The African rhinoceroses are two-horned animals, distinguished from their Asiatic cousins by the absence or slight development of the folds of skin which form such a characteristic feature of the latter, and also by the absence of front teeth in both the upper and lower jaws. This dental deficiency shows in the jaws, the lower one being shorter in front, while the bones (premaxillae) of the upper jaw are undeveloped. Thus deprived of incisor teeth or tusks for fighting, the black rhinoceros depends upon its horns, which are longer and are mounted on sturdier nasal bones than those of the Asiatic species.

The skin, which is dark brownish-grey in color, is almost completely naked, although there are some bristly hairs on the borders of the ears and the tip of the tail. This species is distinguished from the African so-called "white" rhinoceros, not so much by being of a darker color (since actually the coloration in the two forms is almost the same) as by having a hooked rather than a square upper lip. The prehensile, somewhat pointed lip of the black rhinoceros is adapted for browsing, while the broad, flat upper lip of the white rhinoceros is clearly for grazing.

The body dimensions of an average-sized male, or bull, black rhinoceros are as follows: shoulder height, 5 feet 2¼ inches; length from tip of nose to back of rump in a straight line, 10 feet 3 inches; girth immediately back of the shoulders, 8 feet 10 inches; weight, 2565 pounds. An average-sized female, or cow, stands an even 5 feet, weighs just under 2400 pounds, and is proportionately slightly smaller than the male otherwise.* The ears in both sexes are about 9 inches in length, and the tail 24 inches. Often the ears show slits or gashes where they have been ripped and torn by the "wait-a-bit" thorns which are one of the bushes on which this species feeds. As in other species of rhinoceros, only one young is born at a time, the birth weight in the black species ranging from 45 to 75 pounds.**

The horns of the black rhinoceros have long been in demand for two reasons: (1) as a source of ground or powdered horn, of supposed medicinal potency, the horns being exported principally to Chinese dealers; (2) as sportsmen's trophies of possibly record-making dimensions. As their first use has already been mentioned in connection with the Indian rhinoceros, a few statistics on the size attained by the horns of the black rhinoceros may now be in order.

Of the two horns normally borne by this species, the anterior or front horn is usually, though not invariably, longer than the one behind it. In fact, for a long time it was believed by some that two species of the black rhinoceros existed, the distinction of which depended upon the relative lengths of the two horns. If the front horn exceeded the rear horn in length the animal was called *borele;* and if the rear horn was equal to or longer than the front one, *keitloa.* However, it is now known that horn length is a highly variable and nonspecific character, and that these once-supposed different types of rhinoceros were simply individual variations of one species.

The average length of the horns in the black rhinoceros would appear to be not over 18 inches front and about 8 inches rear. The front horn, which is relatively long and slender, is generally curved somewhat backward (although in some individuals it may point straight forward or even slightly downward), and its length is measured along the outside or front curve. The rear horn is conical or cup-shaped, and usually shows little if any curvature. The longest horn of a black rhinoceros on record is of a female specimen from Kenya Colony that was secured many years ago by K. V. Painter. The horn, which is almost uniformly slender throughout except near the base, is 53½ inches long. Roland Ward lists thirty-three front horns of 29 inches or longer, besides thirty-five others of shorter length. In only two of these 68 specimens is the rear horn longer than the front one. Curiously, in both these examples the front horn measures 29 inches, while in one the rear horn is 29½ inches long and in the other a record

---

* These rather specific dimensions result from a study and correlation made by the author of the known heights, weights, and lengths in various species of rhinoceroses as recorded by zoo-keepers and big-game hunters, among the latter principally Lieut.-Col. R. Meinertzhagen.[9]

** It is an interesting coincidence that on the very day (December 24, 1956) the first zoo-gorilla was born in the United States (Cleveland Zoo), the first black rhinoceros to be born in Europe (and the fifth born outside of Africa) made its appearance at the Frankfurt, Germany, Zoological Garden.

Fig. 46 Head of a black rhinoceros *(Diceros bicornis)* in the Bronx Zoo. The pointed "hook-lip" of this species is clearly shown as the animal stretches it out to receive food. Note also the narrow lower lip. The conch-shell-like ears, small eyes, and thick, wrinkled skin common to all rhinoceroses are likewise plainly evidenced.

Fig. 47 Foot outlines of a black rhinoceros (left) and an Arabian horse, to show relative sizes. $\times$ .30 natural size.

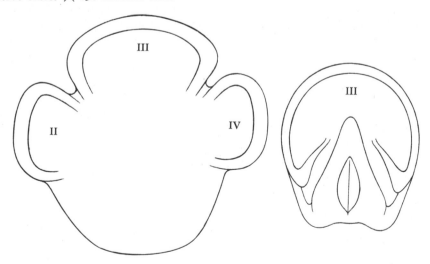

37½ inches. Several *three-horned* specimens have been reported from Kenya Colony and Rhodesia, and a *five-horned* specimen is also on record.

Much has been printed of the alleged vicious disposition of the black rhinoceros in its native haunts. However, some of the complaints may have been a matter of misinterpretation. All rhinoceroses have poor eyesight. Some of them (provided the wind is blowing *away* from them) are said to be unable to distinguish a man, standing still, from a tree stump, even a short distance away. Hence the animals must depend upon their acute senses of smell and hearing, and if the wind is wrong they are as likely to charge toward an enemy as away from it.* In captivity, it has been found that rhinoceroses, even those of the allegedly black species, are among the most tractable of all large wild animals. One of the first adult rhinos to be brought into captivity in Africa was one secured by H. R. Stanton of Nairobi. After being placed in a corral, within a month the animal showed signs of friendliness, and at the end of two months would eat out of a person's hands. By the end of the third month the rhino (a male) had lost all fear, and would whine pitifully whenever he was left alone. He changed his habits from nocturnal to diurnal, and never became tired of being patted, stroked, or rubbed. "The rhinoceros's sense of differentiation in sounds and smells is remarkable, and his ability to change his habits and instincts is probably as conclusive evidence as any of how unjustly he has been known as stupid."[10]

Lydekker gives the typical locality of the black rhinoceros as Cape Colony, where the Boer name for the animal is *zwaart rhinaster*. This species avoids wet forest country and prefers dry thorn-bush savannahs with streams nearby where it may wallow and drink. Its former range included Cape Colony, southwestern Angola, and across Cape Province to eastern Africa. Northward, avoiding the rain forests, it ranged to Somaliland and southwestern Ethiopia, and from there westward between the Sahara and the Congo and Nigerian forests to the region of Lake Chad and the French Cameroons. Of late years the black rhinoceros's once vast numbers have become greatly reduced, but the animal is still sufficiently numerous not to be added to the growing list of "endangered species." Today the black rhino is fairly abundant only in eastern Africa and some of the game reserves south of the Zambezi River. In 1960, the total number in Africa was estimated at about 12,000 animals, approximately one-half of which were in Tanzania and Kenya.

In addition to the typical form from Cape Colony, three other subspecies have been proposed. However, none of them may be sufficiently distinct to be regarded as other than a geographical variant. These asserted subspecies are *Diceros bicornis somaliensis,* a rather narrow-headed form, of Somaliland; *D. b. cucullatus,* of Abyssinia; and *D. b. holmwoodi,* of East Africa.

4. Subgenus *Ceratotherium.*

1. Southern white rhinoceros (*Ceratotherium simum simum* Burchell). Called also square-lipped or square-mouthed rhinoceros. The Boer name is *witrenoster,* and the French name *rhinocéros blanc du Sud.* Native names are *Abu garn* and *Umgirin* (Sudani), *Chuckuroo* (Bechuana), *Mohuhu* (Matabele), and *Chil* and *Mirer* (Dinka,

---

* Rhinos may be aided at times of danger by the actions of the birds (oxpeckers) which perch on their backs and feed on the ticks that infest and irritate their skins. If the rhino happens to be asleep, the shrill cries of the birds are quickly caught by his keen ears. But the rhino's only real enemy is man.

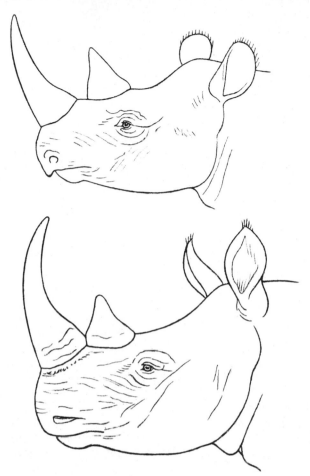

Fig. 48 Comparative sizes of the head in the two types of African rhinoceros. Top: hook-lipped or "black" rhinoceros (*Diceros bicornis*); bottom: square-lipped or "white" rhinoceros (*Ceratotherium simum*). Both figures × 1/15 natural size.

Fig. 49 Comparative sizes of a white, or square-lipped, rhinoceros (larger outline) and a black, or hook-lipped, species (darker outline). × 1/37 natural size.

Nuer, and Atwot). This rhinoceros has been known to science since 1812, at which time it could be seen in large numbers on the South African veldt. As it was "discovered" by Dr. W. B. Burchell, it was long known as Burchell's rhinoceros.

This species is the largest of the existing rhinoceroses, an average-sized adult male having a shoulder length of 5 feet 8 inches, length from tip of nose to back of rump in a straight line 12 feet, chest girth 10 feet 7 inches, length of tail 28 inches, length of ear 11 inches (see Fig. 47). An average-sized adult female stands 5 feet 3 inches. The weight of a full-grown male is about 3970 pounds, and a full-grown female 3220 pounds. Thus this species is slightly larger on the average than the great Indian rhinoceros. However, it would appear incorrect to call the white rhinoceros—as is so often done—the largest land mammal next to the elephant. For if body weight be the criterion, the white rhino is inferior to a bull hippopotamus, the average weight of which is about 5100 pounds; and if height, far inferior to the giraffe, which has an average shoulder height of 10 feet 8 inches. Even though the largest specimens of the white rhinoceros may range in shoulder height up to 6 feet 6 inches (which would indicate a weight of about 6000 pounds), there would be a corresponding increase in weight in the largest hippopotamus (c. 7700 pounds). So, about all that can be said is that in weight—the best single criterion of size—the white rhinoceros is the *third-largest* land mammal, following the elephant and the hippopotamus.

The chief external features by which the white rhinoceros is distinguished from its African relative the black rhinoceros are as follows: (1) a much greater average size: 5 feet 8 inches and about 4000 pounds, as compared with the black rhinoceros's 5 feet 2 inches and 2600 pounds; (2) a relatively longer head; (3) presence of a large, muscular hump on the back of the neck;* (4) a broad, truncated snout and straight-across lips, the lower lip having a horny edge; (5) generally larger horns, the front one having a squarish base and flattened front, from constant rubbing on the ground; (6) larger soles of the feet (to support the much greater weight). In keeping with its grazing habit, the white rhinoceros usually carries its head low, in contrast to the higher-carried head of the black rhinoceros, which is a browser. Another difference in habit is that the white rhino lives in family groups, whereas black rhinos are more solitary animals. In disposition, the white rhinoceros is normally less truculent than the black, but the latter's unpredictable outbursts may be due to its different habits; carrying its head higher than the white rhino, and depending mainly upon the "wind," it is apt to charge either toward or away from any disturbing scent, particularly that of man. An interesting point is that a mother white rhinoceros walks *behind* her calf, guiding it with her front horn, whereas in the black species the mother walks *ahead* of her calf.

As to coloration, the customary terms "black" rhinoceros and "white" rhinoceros are misnomers. Actually there is little difference in the normal coloration of the two species, since in the white rhinoceros the tone is a dark, slate grey, and in the black rhinoceros a slightly darker hue which in some specimens may have a reddish tinge to it.

It is said that the "white" coloration attributed to the larger form of the African rhinoceros probably originated from the animal having been seen after it had rolled in clayey mud, which after it dried became a light, powdery color. But the black rhinoceros—though perhaps to a lesser degree—also wallows in mud (to protect its skin

---

* Evidently this hump of muscle has power in proportion to its mass, for the hunter William Cotton Oswell (1818–1893) once, when on horseback, was tossed so violently by a white rhinoceros he had wounded that the horse turned a half-somersault in the air, coming down heavily on its back. The rhino's horn had passed completely through its body.

from insect bites), and may on occasion appear equally "white." Another explanation is that the term "white" has no connection with the rhino's color, but is a derivation of the Boer term *weid,* which refers to the *wide* (not white), square nose or lips of the animal, distinguishing it from the hook-lipped black rhinoceros.* But the terms "black" and "white," though inappropriate, are convenient to use, just as the writer is using them now!

Two geographically discontinuous races, or subspecies, of the white rhinoceros have been described, the typical form (*Ceratotherium simum simum*) being known as the Southern or Burchell's rhinoceros, while the second form (*C. simum cottoni*), which occurs over 1200 miles to the north, is referred to as the Northern or Nile-Congo race. However, the differences between the two forms are so slight that they need not be considered here. The Northern race was discovered and named as recently as 1900.

Before laws were passed prohibiting the killing of the white rhinoceros, specimens of both races were eagerly sought by sportsmen for their horns, which made fine trophies and occasionally proved to be of record dimensions. The longest front horn on record is one of a female Southern white rhinoceros in the collection of Sir William Gordon-Cumming. It measures 62¼ inches in length and 22¼ inches in basal circumference. Its length surpasses by 5¾ inches the next-longest horn, a specimen in the British Museum, which has a basal girth of 23½ inches. Possibly the Southern race has, or had, typically longer horns—front ones at least—than the Northern race, since the record-sized anterior horn in the latter race is only 45¾ inches long, although its basal circumference is 24½ inches. In Rowland Ward's 9th edition (1928) of *Records of Big Game,* there are listed 51 anterior horns measuring 20 inches or longer, along with 33 rear horns ranging from 6 inches to 21 inches. If, from these figures, an average or "typical" length of horns in trophy-sized specimens of the white rhinoceros could be established, one might say about 35 inches for the front horn and 11 inches for the rear horn. Thus, while the white rhino greatly surpasses the black rhino in the length of the front horn, the opposite is true in the case of the rear horn, where the black rhino averages (among Rowland Ward's listed specimens) about 15 inches to the white rhino's 11 inches.**

The respective habitats of the two races of the white rhinoceros, though so far apart geographically, are essentially similar in climate and surroundings. Parts of the terrain frequented by these animals are fairly arid, containing large expanses of higher-elevation brush country, where the presence of waterholes is infrequent. These surroundings are more suitable for the browsing black rhinoceros, though generally the two species live apart. But there are also vast stretches of rolling grassland, and at lower elevations

---

* And there are still other explanations. Some interesting ones occur in *Natural History Essays,* by Graham Renshaw. London: 1904, pp. 131–33.

**Possibly the factor that regulates horn size is the *volume* of material in the horn, rather than either its length or its girth. On this basis (multiplying the length of the horn by the basal circumference *squared*), it is found that the record-length 62¼-inch horn, which is very slender, has no more volume than the 56½-inch one which has a greater basal girth. Even the 45¾-inch horn, with its large basal girth of 24½ inches, by this means shows a volume equal to 90 percent of the 62¼-inch horn's volume, even though in length it is only about 73 percent as large. However, it is exceedingly unlikely that rhino horns will ever be rated on the basis of their volume, even though this would appear to be a more rational procedure than to consider only their length.

Even more coveted than sportsmen's trophies are the rhino horns secured by poachers and sold for fantastic prices to Asiatic dealers in "pharmaceutical" (aphrodisiac) products. Despite all laws and penalties, the poaching goes on, and even the rare white rhinoceros is one of the victims.

Fig. 50 Here is an excellent head-on view of the white rhinoceros *(Ceratotherium simum)*, which shows the widely separated nostrils and broad, almost straight, upper lip that separates this species from the black rhino. Note also the ever-present ticks clinging to the side of the body.

even swamps, which are much to the liking of the white rhinos. And there is a striking contrast in the vegetation between the dry and the rainy season typical of savannah regions, which causes a certain amount of back-and-forth traveling on the part of both species of rhino. In any case, an abundance of grassy plains and pasturage are an absolute necessity to the larger white rhinoceros, which is strictly a grazing animal. The cropping of the often-tough grass is facilitated by the horny edge of the lower lip, since the white rhino, like its black relative, has no incisor teeth. Also, the grassy fodder is properly masticated by the broad, flat molar teeth of the white rhinoceros, which are in marked contrast to the high-ridged and deeply-grooved smaller teeth of the black rhino.

Evidently the range of the Southern white rhinoceros was not much greater in earlier days than in more recent times. In any event, its numbers have been steadily reduced, until today the animal is extinct except in or near two reserves in Natal and possibly one or two remote spots in Southern Rhodesia. In contrast, the range of the Northern subspecies, while at first believed to be restricted to the Lado country and the immediate neighborhood of the Nile, was subsequently found to be greater. Writing in 1920, Lang says: "These white rhinoceroses are now positively known to extend from a little

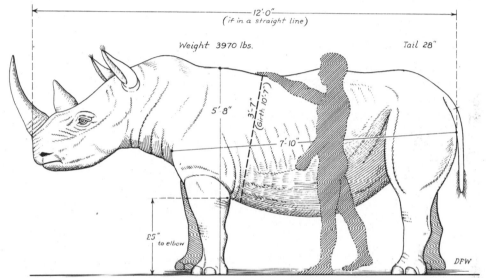

Fig. 51 Scale drawing by the author, showing an adult male white rhinoceros (*Ceratotherium simum*) of average size. The man, for comparison, is 6 feet tall. × 1/32 natural size.

north of Lake Albert to three hundred miles down the Nile to a point near Shambe. From there it stretches four hundred and fifty miles south to Rafai." (The latter being on the Bomu River at about 24 East longitude). The map in Figure 52 gives the respective former ranges of the two subspecies as determined by Lang in 1920.[12]

In a survey conducted in 1959, the following numbers of the white rhinoceros were recorded: 600 on the Umfolsi River in Zululand; 500 in the Garamba game preserve in the Belgian Congo; 300 in the rhinoceros park between the Sudan and Uganda; and 60 in the South African Hluhluwe reserve. From this it would appear that though the Northern race is in no immediate danger, the numbers of the Southern, or typical, race of the white rhinoceros have been reduced to a critical level.

In zoos in the United States, as of January 1, 1963, there were 4 male and 2 female Indian rhinoceroses; 18 male and 18 female black rhinoceroses; and 5 male and 6 female white rhinoceroses, only one pair of the latter (in the National Zoological Park) being of the Northern subspecies. As much as $14,000 has been paid by a zoo for a single white rhino of either subspecies.

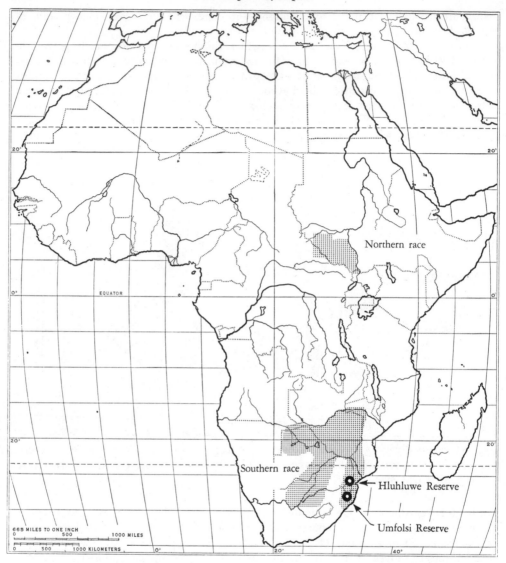

Fig. 52 Distribution of the two races of the white rhinoceros (*Ceratotherium simum*). At latest count there remained about 800 specimens of the Northern race and 660 of the Southern race, most of the latter being in the Umfolsi Game Reserve and a few in the Hluhluwe (pronounced schlu-schlu-we) Reserve.

Rhinoceros in general are an interesting family of grotesquely fashioned "living fossils." Except for developing horns on their noses, the species of today are not appreciably different from their ancestors, which roamed the grassy plains of North America ten or twenty million years ago. And despite their last stand before the high-powered rifles of the hunter and the cruel snares and pits of the poacher, they can hardly be regarded as an unsuccessful type. If man succeeds in surviving half as long, he will be doing well!

To review the foregoing commentary on tapirs and rhinoceroses, it may seem to the lay reader that there is little similarity between these exotic, primitive-appearing animals and the long-legged and man-refined horse. Superficially there may not be; but when the anatomy of the skeleton is considered it becomes evident that all three types— tapirs, rhinoceroses, and horses—are fashioned on the same basic plan and belong in the same order. Some of these similarities are as follows: (1) all the premolar teeth, except the first, have the size and pattern of the molars; (2) the bony openings in the skull, through which veins, arteries, and nerves enter and leave the head, are arranged in a way that is similar and which is different from that in artiodactyl (cloven-hoofed) mammals; (3) the femur, or thigh bone, always has a third trochanter, or bony process near the upper end; (4) the number of digits in each foot is usually "odd"— 1, 3, or 5—although in the tapirs there are 4 toes in the front foot and 3 in the hind; the important character is that in all three types of animals the main weight-bearing digit is the third. Actually the feet of the tapir and the rhinoceros are much like those of the horse, with the exception that the foot-bones are much shorter, while the "frog" on the sole of the horse's hoof is represented in the heavy, weight-bearing rhinoceros by a flexible, elastic pad. Just as in the elephant, the rhinoceros walks on tiptoe, and the hinder part of each of its feet is supported by a shock-absorbing, cushion-like pad of fibrous tissue.

Other points of similarity could be listed, but the foregoing ones should suffice to show the anatomical and zoological affinities of the three existing types of perissodactyl (odd-toed) ungulates, all of which trace back to a common ancestor in the Paleocene (see Fig. 33).

Notes and References

Chapter 6

1. William B. Scott, *A History of Land Mammals in the Western Hemisphere* (New York: Macmillan, 1913), p. 456.

2. [?] Kupper, *Proc. Zool. Soc.* (London, 1926), p. 425.

3. R. I. Pocock, in *Harmsworth Natural History.* (London: Carmelite House, 1910) 2:773.

4. W. B. Scott, *Land Mammals* pp. 326–39.

5. Rowland Ward's *Records of Big Game,* 9th ed. (London, 1928), p. 436.

6. Ernst M. Lang, "Beobachtungen am Indischen Panzernashorn," *Der Zool. Garten* (N.F.) 25 (1961) : 369–409. (Mating a pair of Indian rhinoceroses in the zoo at Basel, Switzerland.)

7. Francis Harper, *Extinct and Vanishing Mammals of the Old World.* (New York: 1945), p. 381.

8. D. A. Hooijer, *Prehistoric and Fossil Rhinoceroses from the Malay Archipelago and India.* (Leiden: Press of E. J. Brill, 1946). (A definitive study, especially of the dentitions in various species.)

9. R. Meinertzhagen, "Some Measurements and Weights of Large Mammals," *Proc. Zool. Soc. London* 108, Ser. A, Part 3 (1938) : 433–39.

10. H. R. Stanton, in *The Illustrated London News* (February 4, 1939), p. 163.

11. W. C. Oswell, *Big Game Shooting* (Badminton Library, 1894).

12. Herbert Lang, *The White Rhinoceros of the Belgian Congo, Bull. New York Zool. Soc.* 23, no. 4 (July 1920) : 67–92. (An excellent account of the life, distribution, and habits of this species, well illustrated.)

7

The Horse in History and Art

a. The horse in Europe during prehistoric and historic times.

A portion of the natural history of the modern horse and its relatives is shrouded in the past, of which today we know only a little. Part of this knowledge has been revealed in the unearthed bones of the animals, and part in the pictures of them that prehistoric man painted upon the walls of caverns or carved on fragments of ivory or antler-bone.

During the Pleistocene period wild horses were abundant over the whole of Eurasia, and they formed an important part of the food supply of contemporary man.* The remains of these horses—of which there were at least several varieties, ranging in size from ponies to large "coldbloods"—have been found in the British Isles, Scandinavia, Finland, France, Spain, Belgium, Germany, Austria, Italy, Siberia, the Near East, North Africa, and in various parts of Asia. Fig. 53 shows tracings of a number of European cave-paintings or engravings of horses of this period. Sandars, on a map of Europe, shows 167 sites of prehistoric drawings and sculptures. Of these, 96 are in France and 34 in Spain.[1]

One of the most famous caves depicting prehistoric art is that at Lascaux, in southwest France. Culturally, Lascaux cave is dated as between the upper Aurignacian and the beginnings of the Magdalenian, during the Würm, or last, glaciation of the Upper Pleistocene. This would date it as about 11,000 years ago. Painted or engraved on the walls and ceilings of Lascaux are nearly 60 figures of horses, in addition to lesser numbers of oxen, deer, wild asses, bison, ibex, bear, and large cats. Apparently the purpose of the paintings was not just to decorate the cave, but mainly to propitiate the spirits of the animals portrayed and thus insure successful hunting. Of horses, several types are shown, as described under Fig. 53.

The two main varieties of horses shown at Lascaux would appear to be the tarpan and Przevalsky's horse (see Chapter 8). However, it is not always safe to conclude

---

* One method of hunting, which was used whenever and wherever the opportunity existed, was to drive a herd of horses (or wild cattle, or even mammoths) toward the brink of a cliff, and so cause some, at least, to fall over it and be killed. This the hunters accomplished by shouting and running toward the animals while throwing spears or brandishing torches. Figure 54 shows wild horses thus being driven to their death. It was several thousand years later before the hunters switched from horsemeat to venison, using the reindeer.

Fig. 53 A few of the many prehistoric pictures of horses in French caverns.

    A. Engraving on bone (or horn) of horse, from cavern at La Madelaine, Dordogne, France.

    B. Another horse, possibly a colt, from the cavern of La Madelaine.

    C. Wall painting of a Celtic pony type in the cavern of Les Combarelles, France. The total number of designs of Equidae in Les Combarelles is 116, consisting mainly of horses but including one wild ass and two possible hemionids.

    D. Horses of the Przevalsky's type, from Les Combarelles. Note how cleverly the artist has made one mane do for two horses!

    E. Engraved pebble, dated at about 16,000 B.C., showing on one face a horse, and on the opposite face part of a horse and a woolly rhinoceros. From the rock shelter at La Colombiere, France. The pebble was originally about 4 3/4 inches long.

that all the straight or concave-faced horses are tarpans and all the convex-faced ("ram's-nosed") horses depicted are Przevalsky's horses. For it has been found that individual horses of the Przevalsky's variety may (even if from the same parents) have either straight, concave, or convex facial profiles. It has been pointed out that domestic horses do not normally exhibit such marked diversity within a given breed. Another circumstance is that the extensive migrations induced by changes in climate, together with much cross-breeding in nature, possibly hindered the development of fixed characters in the tarpans and Przevalsky's horses of Pleistocene Europe.

In another French cavern, that at Fond-de-Gaume (Dordogne), there are 15 designs of horses. In the cavern of Les Combarelles, some 750 feet underground, there are over 400 pictures of various game animals engraved or painted on the walls. Of these designs, 116 are of horses. Many of the drawings depict coats of long, wooly hair, such as develop on wild horses during cold winter months. In the Grotte de Montespan (Haute Garonne) there have been found clay figurines of horses showing the marks of spear-thrusts. This is another indication that horses were hunted for food long before they were tamed or domesticated. The age of these caves is estimated at *c.* 12,000 to 15,000 B.C. The pigments used in painting on the walls were natural minerals: ochre and haematite for the reds, yellows, and browns, and oxide of manganese for black and very dark brown, with some vegetable charcoal (Sandars, 1968, p. 49).

A famous depository for the bones of both the tarpan and Przevalsky's horse (or admixtures of the two types) was the cultural station of Solutré, near Macon (Saone-et-Loire), France. According to Ridgeway (1905, p. 84),

> On the south side of the settlement piled-up bones of horses formed a sort of protecting wall. The estimate of the number of animals represented by these relics varies from two thousand to one hundred thousand, but it is very difficult to make a just calculation, for the bones were so broken in extracting the marrow, that it was with difficulty a complete skeleton could be constructed for the museum at Lyons.

Fig. 54 Wild horses falling to their deaths at the Pleistocene "culture station" of Solutré in France. After a watercolor painting by Franz Roubal.

It is interesting to note that the proportions occurring between the various limb-bone lengths in the horse from Solutré (average of 4–10 specimens) show similarities (depending upon the particular two bones compared) to both the tarpan and Przevalsky's horse, as well as the Celtic pony and the Arabian horse. But as the majority of ratios are similar either to the tarpan or Przevalsky's horse, it strongly suggests the cross-breeding in nature of these two closely related (but differently colored) wild types. While the shoulder height of the horse from Solutré averages about 51 inches, in comparison with 50.2 inches for Przevalsky's horse and 49.4 inches in the tarpan, the figure for the Solutré horse, being derived from such a small number of specimens, may or may not be a trifle high. In any case, the three different shoulder heights are all well within the normal range of variation in any one type of the three contemporaneous equine varieties.

In the famous cavern of Lascaux, mentioned previously, as well as in the caverns of La Madelaine, Laugerie, and Les Eyzies, the bones of the horse were more numerous than those of any other animal, from which fact it may be inferred that horsemeat formed the main food of the primitive inhabitants. And the horse hides were used for various purposes, mainly for clothing. "It is clear then that during the Reindeer period the horse was found in considerable numbers in southwestern France."[2]

Fig. 55 Tracing of the head of a horse from the chariot of King Assurbanipal (669-626 B.C.) of Assyria. That the sculptor used "artistic license" in this figure is indicated by the dashed lines added by the author, which show where the outlines of the face and neck of the horse normally would come. Evidently, the Assyrian sculptors favored slender heads and thick necks on their horses, as later did the Greeks.

An important contribution by J. U. Duerst is the description of a subfossil, slender type of desert horse unearthed at Anau, Turkestan, which Duerst designates as *Equus pumpellii*. From the measurements and proportions of the limb bones of this animal (average of 2–4 specimens), it would appear that it is about 60 percent horse (*E. caballus*) and 40 percent hemionid! This raises the interesting question as to whether a horse–hemionid cross-breeding would produce fertile offspring. It appears very doubtful. *E. pumpelli* has also a number of ass-like characters, which makes one wonder on what basis Duerst identified the animal as a true (caballine) horse.

As to the first domestication of the horse, the consensus of opinion is that it took place on the treeless steppes of west-central Asia, possibly among the Scythians, in what is now the Soviet state of Kazakh. According to Ridgeway, "The fact that the

Scythians and allied tribes and their descendants down to modern times preferred and still prefer mares' milk to that of the cow naturally suggests that the Turko-Tartaric peoples had domesticated the horse before they possessed the ox, and that they tamed the former not for locomotion, but rather as a means of subsistence."[3]

The time, or date, at which the first domestication of the horse occurred is still not definitely known. "5000 years ago," as Amschler in 1935 put it, would mean about 3100 B.C. Evidently the area of domestication moved slowly in a southwesterly direction through Persia (Iran) and reached Babylonia, in the fertile lower Euphrates valley, about 2500 B.C.* There is also some evidence that the horse may have come to the west from India (where the early inhabitants were great horsemen) as well as from the steppes of central Asia although this in some accounts has been denied.[4] Interesting in this connection was the finding by the British archaeologist C. Leonard Wooley, who discovered at Ur in the Euphrates valley the remains of what may have been the Biblical Flood. Although among the remains there were the bones of various domesticated animals—cattle, sheep, and swine—there were no donkeys nor horses. Wooley dated his find as about 4000 B.C.[5] However, it has been supposed by some historians that, much later, the first cross-breeding between horse and ass took place at Ur.

Many centuries later, in the same general region, the Assyrians were great horsemen and hunters. Noteworthy were the exploits of King Ashurbanipal (668–626 B.C.),

---

* One of the oldest known representations of *any* species of the horse family is a plaque which was unearthed at Khafje, Iraq (Mesopotamia), and which is dated as about 2800 B.C. However, the plaque depicts, not horses, but a team of four onagers or Asiatic "half-asses" (see Fig. 178).

** Apart from actual dates, the *order* in which the domestication of various "useful" animals occurred is generally given as follows: first, dog and pig; next, cattle and reindeer; then sheep, goats, horse, camel, and elephant (although the latter cannot strictly be considered a *domesticated* animal).

Fig. 56 King Ashurbanipal shown on a lion hunt while on horseback (lions then inhabited Mesopotamia). Note the vertically shallow, dished facial profiles of the horses, along with their highly comparisoned trappings. The lions are shown entirely too small as compared with the man and the horses.

Fig. 57 AN ANCIENT EGYPTIAN HORSE AND RIDER
One of the earliest representations of the domestic horse extant, a painted wooden statuette dating from the XVII or XVIII Egyptian Dynasty (*c.* 1700-1500 B.C.), shortly after the horse had been introduced into that country. This historically important object is now in the Metropolitan Museum of Art.

whose prowess in lion hunting on horseback has been preserved in plaques (bas-reliefs) taken from the walls of his palace at Nineveh. The Assyrian horses were really just good-sized ponies, standing about 52 inches high at the shoulder. A peculiarity of the heads of these ponies—at least as they are represented in the bas-reliefs—is their narrowness vertically in relation to their length. The forehead immediately above the eye is shown as arching strongly above the rest of the facial upper surface—a conformation that never occurs in a straight profile view of a normal skull of any of the Equidae. This abnormal representation can therefore only be taken as an example of "artistic license" on the part of the Assyrian sculptors (see Fig. 55). To a lesser degree, such license was used later by the Greeks in their sculptural representations of horses, as well as in many a case of the human figure.

Devotees of the Arabian horse have sometimes been carried away with enthusiasm for the breed, which has extended to crediting the animals with an undocumented ancientness of ancestry. The evidence of historians in the matter, however, is that the Arabian horse was derived, through long and careful breeding, from horses of the Libyan tribes of North Africa. The testimony of two eminent Greek geographers,

Erastothenes (3rd century, B.C.) and Strabo (*c.* 63 B.C.–24 A.D.) is in agreement that the Arabs did not breed, or even possess, horses until after the beginning of the Christian era.[6] It is generally accepted that domestic horses were unknown in Egypt until the Hyksos, invading that country from somewhere to the north, introduced the animals, along with the two-wheeled war chariot (Fig. 58). This was about 1657 B.C., according to the archaeologist J. H. Breasted, but possibly as early as 2100 B.C., according to William Ridgeway.[7] The more recent historian, Robert West Howard, puts the date at 1720–1710 B.C.[8] (See also the statement by Sir Flinders Petrie on page 47.)

Fig. 58 Egyptian two-horse light war chariot. 17th century B.C.

The Greeks and Romans made many sculptured representations of horses as well as of humans. One of the best-preserved of these is a plaque recovered from Hadrian's Villa at Tivoli, dating from *c.* 117–138 A.D., showing a youth holding a horse and followed by a dog (Fig. 59). Among the Greeks horseback riding was done bareback, and often with little or no clothing worn by the rider, if the sculptures of those times are to be interpreted as factual. Of course, many a statue is of some mythological subject, such as the winged horse Pegasus, the half-horse, half-man centaur, or the team of horses drawing the sun-chariot of Apollo daily across the sky. But such representations have little connection with the natural history of the horse, except so far as they depict the general type of animal used by the Greeks.

Xenophon (*c.* 434–355 B.C.) wrote a through description of what the points of a good war-horse should be. First was a sound set of hoofs, since the Greeks never shod their horses; secondly, a set of pasterns that were neither too upright nor too sloping; thirdly, "plenty of bone in the legs, supple knee joints, strong shoulders, a broad chest (as it keeps the legs wide apart), and a high-arched neck." The head should be bony, the cheek small (for good forward visibility), the eye prominent, the nostrils wide, and the ears rather small. Finally, the back should have a good padding of muscles on each side of the spine (so as to be comfortable to sit upon), and not present a backbone "lean as a rake."[9]

Ridgeway regards the Greek horses as being predominantly of Libyan (Barb) blood, and mentions that the four-horse chariot and the ridden horse (*keles*) were only given places in the Olympic Games (the former in 664 B.C., the latter in 648 B.C.) in the same century that saw the founding of the Greek colony of Cyrene in North Africa.[10]

Evidently the Greek horses were of small stature (averaging perhaps 52 inches, or 13 hands). This is indicated in numerous statues by a comparison of the horses with the riders. It has been estimated from skeletal remains that Greek men of the Classic period averaged only 65.2 inches in height, and Greek women only about 62 inches.[11] The sitting heights for these statures would have been about 34.7 inches for the men and 33 inches for the women. Knowing that the trunk length (shoulder to rump) in "warmblood" horses is ordinarily equal to their shoulder height, or vice versa, it becomes only a matter of comparing the rider with the horse to derive the ratio of the heights of the two. The Amazon rider in Fig. 61, if 62 inches tall, is thus seen to be mounted on a Greek horse of average size. It may be added that while the bronze and marble statues of horses made by the Greeks give no indication today of the *coloration* of the horses (many of the statues were originally painted), the type of horse (Barb) which most of the statues represented was *dark bay*.

Fig. 59 Greek youth holding a horse and followed by a dog. A plaque from Hadrian's Villa at Tivoli (*c.* 117–138 A.D.), now in the British Museum. Characteristically, the head of the horse is shown relatively shallow vertically, the mane is upright, and no forelock is apparent. Additionally, the horse's body is shown too long (from shoulder to rump) for a horse of the Grecian "warmblood" type.

It would appear also that the famous horse Bucephalus, which Alexander the Great had tamed and which only he could ride, was a horse of rather small size. This is indicated in the statue in the National Museum (Naples) entitled "Alexander in Battle," attributed to the great Greek sculptor Lysippus, who was a contemporary of Alexander. Bucephalus had been bred in Thessaly by Philonicus of Pharsalus.

The point of these references to Greek and Roman horses is that the war-horses of those nations, as well as those of Libya (Barbary), Turkey, Persia, and countries farther east, were all of small size compared with riding horse of today, which by systematic breeding have been increased in shoulder height anywhere from 8 to 12 inches (2 to 3 hands) over their ancient domestic forebears.

Fig. 60 Here is a modernized interpretation of the famous Horse of Selene, which depicts perfectly the large expressive eye, small ear, tapering muzzle, and prominent nostril of the Grecian horse. The roached mane, however, was depicted less often than the full, flowing mane. Here also, as in the Assyrian horse (Figure 55), the eye is shown too close to the facial line.

The introduction of the domestic horse into other European countries continued westwardly and northerly. In due course the entire continent of Europe, along with England, Ireland, and other islands, possessed horses of one breed or another. Some of the horses, or ponies, were indigenous, while others were brought in from countries where they had already been domesticated. What with all the importations, exportations, native horses, and cross-breeding, it is no wonder that in a relatively short time many different breeds of domesticated horses existed throughout the whole of Europe. In some of the hot and humid Asiatic countries, such as India, where horses could not be raised with any great success, the animals had to be imported either from central Asia or countries farther to the west.

Wild horses existed into the Middle Ages in Spain, the Alps, and the valley of the Danube. In Switzerland in the tenth and eleventh centuries these horses were still regarded as "game animals." In the Vosges Mountains of northeast France they survived until the seventeenth century, and in Poland and Lithuania until a century later. Possibly some of these "wild" horses were actually *feral* horses or the offspring of them. "Feral horses have existed all over the world since the domestication of the horse."[12]

Fig. 61 Amazon and Greek horse. A sketch by the author, based on the bronze statuette, "Amazon," by Franz von Stuck, and on the third-century B.C. bas-relief of a horse and rider from Rhodes. In those early days, horses were often ridden bridleless.

It is not within the scope of the present volume to present a historical account of all the migrations, exportations, and importations of the domestic horse. This has already been done by a large number of historians, notably William Ridgeway (*The Origin and Influence of the Thoroughbred Horse*, 1905), from whose scholarly book numerous quotations have been made in the present chapter.* Details of the *physical characteristics* of the more important breeds of the domestic horse, as well as the other forms of existing Equidae (with which this book is particularly concerned) are given in later chapters. Below, in summarized form, are a few of the many important dates concerned with the domestic horse, specifically in the Old World.

SOME SIGNIFICANT DATES in EQUINE HISTORY in the OLD WORLD
B.C.

3100   The first domestication of the wild horse took place probably among the Scythians, on the treeless plains of west-central Asia, in what is now the Soviet republic of Kazakh.

---

* For horses in America, two excellent reference works are those by Charles S. Plumb (1906) and Robert West Howard (1965) respectively (see Bibliography).

3000   Somewhere about this date the wild Mongolian horse is said to have been tamed and used by the Chinese.

3000   The donkey appears in Sumerian art. "Long before the camel and the horse, he was at work."

3000–2500   About this time, domesticated horses were being used in the lower Euphrates valley (Mesopotamia). They had been brought there from Persia.

2800   In Mesopotamia, teams of onagers (*Equus hemionus onager*) were used to draw chariots.

2000   Horses were first tamed in the Caucasus and in the Danube Valley.

1720   Sometime about this date the Hyksos ("shepherd kings"), coming from somewhere in Asia, invaded and conquered Egypt, introducing into that country the domestic horse and the two-wheeled chariot.

1490   The earliest domestic horse skeleton from Egypt was found in the tomb of Queen Hatshepūt.

1400   The Hittites trained horses for sport and warfare.

1194–1184   In the poems of Homeric Greece, the horse was used solely for drawing chariots, and mounted cavalry was not heard of there until later times.

1000   The Chinese developed the first light cavalry, which were armed with bows and arrows.

1000   Solomon introduced into Palestine the laying of roads for chariots. He also imported from Egypt a great number of horses for his army, paying 600 shekels of silver for a chariot and its horses, and 150 shekels for a cavalry horse (a shekel being about half an ounce, and equal today to about $1.23). By this means Solomon came to possess 1400 chariots and stabling for 40,000 horses.

1000   The *riding* of horses, which had been preceded by the use of other equids (e.g., onagers) drawing chariots, was introduced into Europe from the East. (In Libya, women regularly rode horseback in the seventh century B.C., from which it has been inferred that the men learned to ride at a still earlier period.)

700   The first remains of "coldblood" domestic horses were found in Austria.

664   Four-horse chariot racing was first used in the Olympic Games. Four Olympiads later, in 648 B.C., riding bareback made its first appearance in the Games.

206 B.C.–
200 A.D.   (Han Dynasty). The ass, the mule, and the Libyan type of horse were brought into China from contacts made with the Persians and Greeks.

60   The Romans, invading the British Isles, found there a native breed (possibly the Exmoor pony) with which their heavier horses became mixed.

58–51   Possibly the first systematic breeding of the "Great War Horse" from the European wild coldblood "forest horse," or "black horse of Flanders," took place in the Flemish area.

A.D.

50–100   Breeding of the horse in Arabia began.

450   When, in this year, the Huns invaded Europe, it is said that their horses were *shod*.

622   At this time, when Mohammed led the exodus from Mecca, his Arab horses were shod with iron shoes.

619–906   (T'ang Dynasty). Polo was introduced into China, and the practice of breeding them especially for the sport was begun.

1060   Stirrups first made their appearance in Europe in the time of William the Conqueror. (Prior to that time, most warriors mounted their horses

Fig. 62 Four-horse chariot races were first used in the Greek Olympic Games in 648 B.C. They were later adopted by the Romans, who staged thrilling contests before vast audiences in open hippodromes.

	either by vaulting onto their backs, from one side or the other, or by putting one foot into a stirrup-like loop of cord attached about two feet above the lower end of their spear.)
1270	Immense numbers of war-horses were being used by the Mongols about this time. For example, the emperor Kublai-Khan was able, on at least one occasion, to amass an army consisting of 100,000 footmen and 360,000 horsemen!
1603–1625	During these years, in which the King of England was James I, Arab horses (e.g., the Markham Arab) were first introduced into that country and crossed with native light stock. It was during this time also that horse racing was legally established in England.

b. The horse in America.

The first domestic horses to be introduced into the New World from Europe were those brought by Christopher Columbus from Spain on a voyage (his second) that started on September 15, 1493, and ended on the island of Haiti in January 1494. Although a herd of twenty purebred Barbs had been sent by Queen Isabella to the embarkation point of Cadiz, by the time the grooms had arrived there they had sold the purebreds to dealers along the way and brought to Columbus only some "sorry hacks." Owing to the losses occurring during the voyage (and to the "jump and swim for it" method then used to bring livestock ashore), only six mares were landed in Haiti. Along with these horses were six donkeys, six young cattle, a hundred sheep and goats, and a hundred swine.

On his second trip to the West Indies, in 1504, Columbus brought a few horses to establish ranches in San Domingo. By the early 1500s, horse were being brought from Spain to the New World by the hundreds. These horses were of *Arab-Barb* descent, modified by local Spanish blood.

Credit for being the first to land horses on the North American *mainland* is generally given to Hernando Cortez (or Cortes), the Spanish conqueror of Mexico. On March 13, 1519, near Vera Cruz, Cortez took from his ship the famous sixteen* "first" horses. In 1527, 300 horses were first brought into the United States (Florida) by Cabeza de Vaca. However, the most general belief is that the first horses to *escape and become feral* were those (four mares and two stallions) from the respective bands of Hernando (or Fernando) de Soto and Francisco Vasquez de Coronado, in 1543. One version is that the offspring of these two mingled bands became the *first* Western horses. Another account is that Coronado, on his expedition westward in 1540, had 250 or more horsemen and perhaps 1000 extra horses (and pack mules). In western Mexico a hailstorm caused nearly all these horses to break away (and become feral?).

The following chronology lists some of the arrivals in America of various breeds of the domestic horse from 1494 to 1905. Specific information on the main breeds is given in Chapters 9, 10, and 11.

DATES OF ARRIVAL OF HORSES INTO AMERICA FROM EUROPE

1494–1663   First arrivals of domestic horses from Europe: Spain, 1494; England, 1620 and 1629; Flanders, 1660; France, 1663.

1600–1775   The Indians of the United States first became acquainted with the horse through already domesticated animals that they stole from the Spanish frontier settlements, and in a relatively short time they became expert horsemen. The first use by the Indians of horses occurred in what is now the state of New Mexico. According to Frank Gilbert Roe, by acquiring the horse

> . . . the Indian was transformed and revitalized—in war, in hunting, in social organization, and in the ability to meet the white invader on his own ground. Northward from Mexico, the horse spread through the Plains and the mountains, reaching central Saskatchewan 150 years after its dispersion had started, and bringing a new way of life to every tribe it touched. The Comanche became one of the most splendid horsemen the world has ever known, while the Cheyenne gloried in war and showed an amazing grasp of cavalry tactics. The Blackfoot were the horsemen par excellence and the Crow were the "horse traders" of the Northern Plains and mountains. The Nez Percé (who developed the Appaloosa), the Piegan, and the Flathead were noted for their wealth in horses, possessing herds which were numbered in "thousands."[14]

1665   Horse racing in the United States was introduced by Governor Nicholls of New York.

---

* More probably 17. (See *Branding of the Horses of the Conquest,* by Miguel E. Bracho, *The Western Horseman,* December 1952, p. 16.)

Fig. 63 An Indian scout and his horse. This notable monument, the work of Cyrus Dallin, stands in Penn Valley Park, Kansas City, Missouri. Both the horse and his lean, athletic rider are depicted with lifelike fidelity.

1735   In South America, the first settlers and their horses were establishing themselves where the city of Buenos Aires now stands.

1760   The Quarter Horse breed was started with the English Thoroughbred "Janus" in Virginia and North Carolina. The first examples of this breed were only 13–14 hands high, and were called Quarter Pathers, on account of their being raced over a straightaway "path" a quarter-mile long.

1760   The first purebred Arabian horse in the United States was a stallion named "Ranger"; he had been imported to New London, Connecticut. A halfbred, grey son of Ranger was presented to George Washington by General Harry Lee. This horse became known as the Lindsay Arabian. Between 1760 and 1941, 127 Arabian stallions and 151 Arabian mares were imported into America.

1771   In this year, English colonists to Virginia brought the first Thoroughbreds to America. The first of these appears to have been "Shark," imported from England. The greatest was probably "Diomed," imported in 1777, the first winner of the Derby (in 1780), England's classic race.

1787   The introduction of the domestic ass to America is said to date back to colonial times, when, soon after the Revolutionary War, the king of Spain sent as a gift to General George Washington a Spanish jack and jennet. Mule raising in the United States was commenced shortly thereafter.

1788–1822   The American trotter (or Standardbred) traces back to two main sires: the Thoroughbred "Messenger" (also known as "Imported Messenger," since he was foaled in England in 1780); and "Bellfounder" (known in the United States as "Imported Bellfounder"), who was foaled in England in 1815.

1822   The Hackney horse in America dates back to 1822, at which time the stallion "Bellfounder" was imported from Liverpool, England (see above).

1833   The foundation stock of the American Saddle Horse consisted of ten stallions, mostly Thoroughbreds, but among them two Morgans. The most distinguished of these ten sires was "Denmark," a Thoroughbred, foaled in New York about 1833.

1840   The first Percherons to be bred in America consisted of two stallions— "Diligence" and "Bonaparte"—along with several mares. The year previous, three other such horses had been brought over, but all soon died.

1842   This year saw the first two Clydesdales reach North America (Ontario, Canada). These were "Grey Clyde 78" and "Sovereign 181." The first Clydesdales to be brought into the United States, both through Canada and directly from Scotland, arrived in the 1870s.

1866   The first Belgian horses were brought to the United States in this year, at which time they were incorrectly designated as Boulonnais.

1880   The first Suffolk, or Suffolk Punch, horses (stallions) were imported from England by Powell Brothers of Pennsylvania.

Fig. 64 Napoleon on his famous war-horse, "Marengo." From the painting by Jean Louis Ernest Messonier.

1905 The largest importation of Shetland ponies to the United States occurred this year, with 201 animals being brought from England.

1920–1925 About this time, an estimated *million* "wild" horses roamed the western plains of the United States. By 1970, an estimated 17,000, distributed over nine western states, fought for survival against cattlemen, hunters, and pet-food manufacturers. However, the remaining horses have retreated to remote and rugged regions where they can be approached only with difficulty. Recently at least one refuge—that in the Pryor Mountains on the Montana–Wyoming border—has been officially established for the wild horses.

c. Some Famous Horses of Famous Generals.

Down through history, some of the finest individual horses have been those possessed by military leaders and presidents. Bucephalus, the horse of Alexander the Great, was a magnificent stallion which Alexander, as a youth, had tamed, and which would permit no other rider to get onto his back. It carried the ruler through thick and thin throughout his matchless march of conquest.*

Next to Bucephalus, perhaps the most famous military horse was Emperor Napoleon's favorite charger, "Marengo" (Fig. 64). This animal, which was named to commemorate one of Napoleon's major victories, was an almost-white Arab stallion, 57 inches (14.1 hands) in height, "with the typical black eye and wide nostril of his race." He had been acquired by Napoleon in Egypt after the Battle of Aboukir in 1799. Marengo lived to the age of 36.

"Copenhagen," which carried the Duke of Wellington to victory in the Battle of Waterloo in 1815, had borne his master for eighteen hours that day. Copenhagen was a powerful chestnut Thoroughbred, grandson of the celebrated racehorse "Eclipse." Copenhagen was foaled in 1808 and died in 1836. He had been bought by the Duke in 1813 for four hundred guineas (then about $2000).

George Washington, when made Commander-in-Chief of the American Army, in 1775, took with him to a meeting in Cambridge, Massachusetts, five fine chargers, his favorite being a spirited stallion named "Douglas." Thomas Jefferson called Washington "the best horseman of his age [time]." Another of Washington's war-horses was "Nelson," a light chestnut, 64 inches (16 hands) high, with white face and legs. Fig. 65 shows Washington on yet another charger, a white horse named "Lexington," the portrait of which was painted "from memory" by John Trumbull. The General needed a sturdy horse, since he was a big man, standing 6 feet 2 inches and weighing 215 pounds.

During the Civil War, the most celebrated horse in the Confederacy was General Robert E. Lee's "Traveller," a fine grey gelding 16 hands high, which had been foaled in West Virginia in 1857. Traveller was much admired "for his springy walk, high spirit, bold carriage, and muscular strength." That General Lee was a fancier of fine

---

* The name Bucephalus, meaning "bull-headed", was bestowed either because of the animal's wild-bull-like appearance, or because the *armor of horns* that used to be attached over the horse's forehead gave him a unicorn-like look. In a curious passage from Marco Polo's *Travels,* that author remarks: "There used to be horses in this country that were directly descended from Alexander's horse Bucephalus out of mares that had conceived from him and they were all born by him *with a horn on the forehead* [my italics. D.P.W.] The breed was entirely in the possession of one of the king's uncles, who, because he refused to let the king have any, was put to death by him. Thereupon his wife, to avenge her husband's death, destroyed the whole breed, and so it became extinct."

Fig. 65 General George Washington on his favorite white charger, "Lexington," at the battle of Monmouth (1778). From the painting by John Trumbull.

horses was indicated in his remark, "There is many a war-horse that is more entitled to immortality than the man who rides him."

General Ulysses S. Grant's favorite horse was "Cincinnati," a 16-hand, 1200-pound black charger that carried him throughout the Civil War.

Another famous black horse was "Winchester," which was ridden by General Philip H. Sheridan. The horse was of large size, standing "over 17 hands" high, and according to the General was exceedingly strong and a fast walker. With regard to walking speed, that of the average horse is about four miles per hour. "Winchester," aided perhaps by his height, could average probably about five mph, as could General Sherman's "Sam," General Meade's "Baldy," and General McClellan's "Black Dan."

d. Development and Dispersion of the Breeds of the Domestic Horse.

Figs. 66 and 67 show in diagrammatic form the development and geographic dispersion of various breeds of the domestic horse from the ancestral Light Horse ("warmblood") and Heavy Horse ("coldblood") types, respectively. These two diagrams, which are necessarily simplified, present only a sampling of the principal breeds of modern horses as used in Europe and the United States. Many additional breeds—over a hundred in all—exist today in all parts of the civilized world where horses can be utilized. Some of the breeds shown on the "warmblood" chart—for example, the Shetland pony—possess also a certain amount of "coldblood" (or draft-horse) characteristics. Similarly, many of the heavier breeds—such as the Lipizzaner and the Percheron—have some Arabian (or "warmblood") features in their makeup. The whole concept of "warmblood" and "coldblood" equine types has no basis either in physiology or geography, and should be discarded in favor of some other terms, such

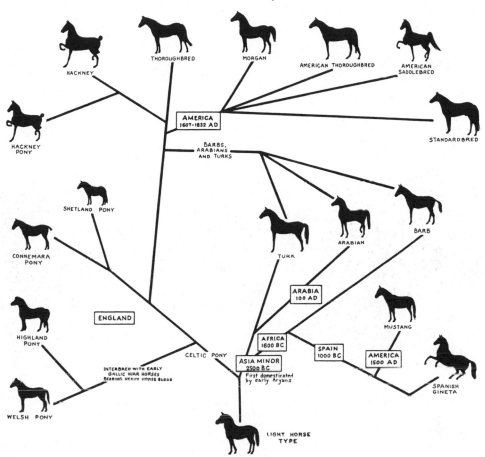

Fig. 66 Some of the principal breeds of horses derived from the Light Horse ("warmblood") type.

as Light Horses and Heavy Horses, although these designations also suggest only two distinct type and call no attention to the numerous intermediate breeds. "Oriental" and "Occidental" horses—a distinction introduced in 1875 by L. Franck in his pioneering German work on horses (*Ein Beitrag zur Rassenkunde unserer Pferde*) are geographically descriptive terms, since they place in the "Oriental" category such breeds as the Arab, Barb, Turk, and Persian; and in the "Occidental" group the large, draft-type breeds of central Europe. A more recent author, evidently desirous of separating the Arab as far as possible from the draft horse, used the respective names *Equus caballus arden* ("hot horse") and *Equus caballus frigidus* ("cold horse"), as though even the body temperatures of the two types were widely different!

Happily, the *physical* differentiation of the various breeds of the domestic horse, as well as such wild varieties as the tarpan and Przevalsky's horse, can be determined and listed simply by relating the average, or general, body *girth* of each type to its shoulder (withers) height. When this is done (as in Table 12), it is seen that the lightest-built breeds are the Thoroughbred, the Arabian, and the Standardbred, and the heaviest-built,

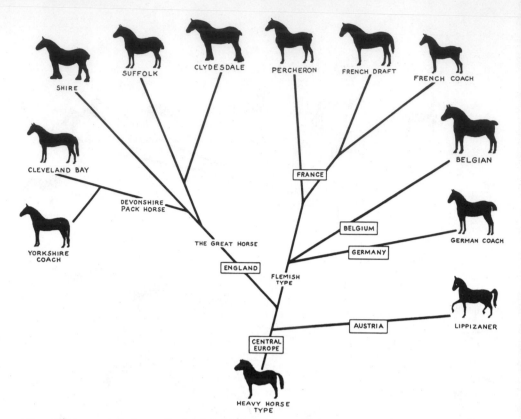

Fig. 67 Some of the principal breeds of horses derived from the Heavy Horse ("coldblood") type.

any of several breeds of the draft horse. In between these extremes are ponies and various other medium-built breeds. All may be "indexed," or classified, according to their differing body-*builds,* which removes the need for the long-used but illogically based terms "warmblood" or "coldblood." Figs. 66 and 67, with some modifications, are reproduced here with the kind permission of the Los Angeles County Museum of Natural History, by which institution the charts were originally used.

e. Horses in Art.

This is an extensive subject in itself, of which only a few examples (paintings and sculptures) can be reproduced in this chapter. Other such illustrations may be seen in the later chapters that deal with various domestic breeds. To portray a horse realistically in any art medium whatever requires an intimate knowledge of the animal's skeletal and muscular anatomy, along with familiarity of how the body and limbs properly appear when seen both in repose and in action from various angles and points of view. Many different books on the subject have appeared over the years. One of the best, however, in the writer's opinion, is *Horse Anatomy,* by Lewis S. Brown (Pelham, New York: Bridgman Publishers, Inc., 1948). In this book the author depicts the anatomy of the horse from numerous angles, often in conjunction with human figures, which help to convey the idea of relative sizes. Another fine reference work is *An Atlas of Animal Anatomy,* by W. Ellenberger, H. Baum, and H. Dittrich (New York: Dover Publications, 1949). Among the best modern *sculptures* of the horse, especially from the standpoint of muscular anatomy, are those of Anna Hyatt Huntington, two of which are reproduced here (Figs. 68 and 69).

Fig. 68 "Fighting Stallions," a powerful portrayal of the horse in action by Anna Hyatt Huntington, Brookgreen Gardens, Georgetown, South Carolina.

Fig. 69 "Female Centaur," by Anna Hyatt Huntington. In Brookgreen Gardens, Georgetown, South Carolina. (It is remarkable that the ancients who believed in centaurs apparently never wondered how the creatures would function with only one small mouth and nose to supply two sets of lungs, two hearts, a horse-sized digestive tract, etc.!)

Fig. 70 A splendid bronze statuette of an Arabian horse and rider, typifying the spirit and elegance of "the horse of the desert." (The sculptor is anonymous.)

Fig. 71 "White horse frightened by lion," by George Stubbs, 1770. (The lion which is in the left background, is almost invisible in this reproduction.)

Fig. 72 Many beautiful representations of horses occur in fanciful or mythological scenes, such as this painting by John Elliott of Diana arriving on a seashell atop the ocean waves. The four horses express the four tides—high, low, spring, and neap—controlled by the moon-goodness Diana.

Fig. 73 "Man controlling trade," a symbolic sculpture by Michael Lantz, in front of the Federal Trade Building, Washington, D.C. Here is an instance where great power is expressed by the limbs of the horse being shown disproportionately thick.

Notes and References

1. N. K. Sandars, *Prehistoric Art in Europe* (Baltimore: Pelican, 1968).

2. William Ridgeway, The Origin and Influence of the Thoroughbred Horse (Cambridge: 1905), p. 85.

3. *Ibid.*, pp. 127–28.

4. Sidney Smith, *Early History of Assyria* (New York, 1930), pp. 213–214.

5. C. Leonard Wooley, *The Royal Cemetery.* Ur excavations, Vol. 2. (London: 1934).

6. Ridgeway, *Thoroughbred Horse*, p. 201.

7. *Ibid.*, p. 232.

8. Robert West Howard, *The Horse in America* (Chicago: 1965), p. 14.

9. Ridgeway, *Thoroughbred Horse*, pp. 298–299.

10. *Ibid.*, p. 251.

11. J. Lawrence Angel, "Skeletal Change in Ancient Greece" *Amer. Jour. Phys. Anthrop.*, n.s. 4, no. 1 (March 1946): 69–97. (Height of ancient Greek men and women.)

12. Walker D. Wyman, *The Wild Horse of the West* (Lincoln: Univ. of Nebraska Press, 1966), pp. 22–23.

13. *Ibid.*, p. 30.

14. Frank Gilbert Roe, *The Indian and the Horse* (Norman: Univ. of Oklahoma Press, 1955).

8

Przevalsky's Horse, the South-Russian Tarpan, and the Ancestral "Forest Horse"

This chapter, which is an elaboration of Chapter 3, reviews in detail the three most generally accepted ancestors of the modern domestic horse. These are (1) the Mongolian wild horse, or Przevalsky's* horse; (2) the tarpan (more specifically, the South Russian tarpan); and (3) the so-called "Forest Horse," represented by a number of Pleistocene and sub-fossil varieties. A rather large literature is extant on these three forerunners of the present-day domestic horse. From this literature, supplemented by the writer's studies of the skulls and postcranial skeletons of all three types, the following particulars are derived.

a. Przevalsky's Horse (*Equus caballus przewalskii* Poliakov, 1881).

This animal, which is known also as the Mongolian wild horse, the Mongolian tarpan, and the Steppe tarpan (and by the Mongols as *Taki,* and the Kirghiz *Kertag*), is of direct importance to paleontologists as well as zoologists, since it is the only truly wild horse existing in the world today and is generally considered to be one of the ancestors of certain breeds of the domestic horse.

Przevalsky's horse—to use the term by which it is best known—was named in 1881 by the zoologist J. S. Poliakov after the Russian explorer Nikolai Mikhailovitch Przewalski (1839–1888). While crossing the central Asian steppes in 1879, Przewalski is said to have twice come across small bands of this hitherto unknown (to science) wild equine. Although Przewalski himself did not shoot or capture any of the horses, a skin was presented to him by the chief magistrate of Zaisan, who in turn had obtained it from some Kirghiz hunters. It was from this single skin that the first (?) scientific description of the animal was made by Poliakov. It should be added, however, that the "type" specimen of *E. c. przewalskii* was not a full-grown animal, but a foal of 18–20 months of age, with a vertex skull length of only 493 mm as compared with 531 mm in the average stallion.

---

* This spelling, as well as various other spellings: Prejevalsky, Prschewalski, Przhevalsky, have been adopted by certain authors on the grounds that in the Russian spelling of the explorer's name— Przevalsky, or Przewalsky—the first syllable has no English phonetic equivalent. The usual English pronunciation is puhr zhuh VAHL skee.

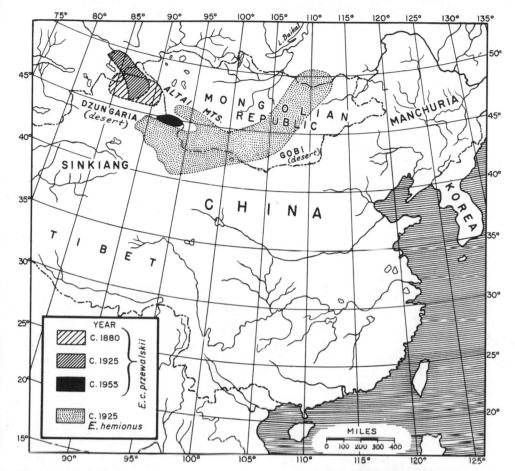

Fig. 74 Distribution of Przevalsky's horse (*E. c. przewalskii*) and the kulan or chigetai (*E. hemionus hemionus*). The three larger shaded areas are according to R. C. Andrews (1925), as shown by G. M. Allen (1940). The small black oval on 45° North indicates the last known area occupied by Przevalsky's horse in the wild state, according to A. G. Bannikov (1957).

Although Przewalski is often credited with having "discovered" the wild horse that bears his name, there is considerable confusion attending the history of the animal—so much so, that "rediscovered" would perhaps be a more accurate term for the part that Przewalski played in bringing it to public notice. As long ago as 1814, the English naturalist Col. Hamilton Smith, while in Paris, obtained from some Russian cavalry officers a first-hand, detailed description of the Mongolian wild horse, under the name of "tarpan," which corresponds essentially with the animal later to be known as Przevalsky's horse. This description was published by Col. Smith in several editions of *Jardine's Naturalist's Library,* Vol. 20, *Horses,* the first of which came out in 1841, 40 years before Poliakov published *his* description. Even earlier, the eighteenth-century German-Russian naturalist and traveler, Peter Simon Pallas (1811, Vol. 1, p. 260), gave a clear description of the wild horse, under the name *Equus ferus;* and Otto Antonius, who later wrote a great deal about this wild equine, always used the names *E. ferus* or *E. ferus przewalskii.*

Eight years after Poliakov's description of *Equus caballus przewalskii,* the brothers Grum-Grshimailo secured four specimens of this wild horse in 1889 at the oasis of Gashun, northeast of Guchen in eastern Dzungaria.[1] According to their report:

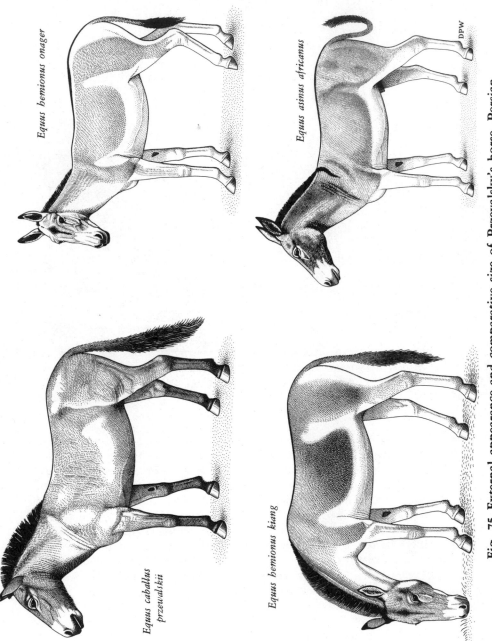

Equus hemionus onager

Equus asinus africanus

Equus caballus przewalskii

Equus hemionus kiang

Fig. 75 External appearance and comparative size of Przevalsky's horse, Persian onager, kiang, and Nubian wild ass.

Prjevalsky himself, though he crossed the desert of Dzungaria in several directions, never came across any of these wild horses, and if he wrote otherwise he was mistaking kulans he had seen in the distance for wild horses, a mistake the most experienced hunters are liable to make, for at that distance it is almost impossible to distinguish between them. We were the first Europeans who, for twenty days, made a study of these interesting animals, adding the skins of three handsome stallions to our collection.[2]

In the spring of 1900, the first living examples of the Mongolian wild horse (a stallion and two mares) to be seen in Europe were brought to the animal farm of the South Russian landowner, Friedrich von Falz-Fein, at Askania Nova. About a year later, Carl Hagenbeck, the famous animal collector of Hamburg, who had been commissioned by the Duke of Bedford, sent a large expedition to Dzungaria to obtain specimens of the wild horse for various European zoos and parks, including that of the Duke of Bedford himself, at Woburn Abbey. Hagenbeck's agents, who employed nearly two thousand Kirghiz hunters for the purpose, were unable to obtain alive any adults, but captured 32 young horses (17 colts, 15 fillies), which were fostered by domestic Mongolian mares. Until the arrival of these living specimens, Przevalsky's horse had been regarded by most English naturalists either as a hybrid between the domestic horse and the kiang, or as the offspring of escaped (feral) Mongol ponies. Some (e.g., Flower, 1891, p. 79) even considered it as "intermediate in character between the equine and the asinine group of Equidae." However, if these zoologists had had the opportunity to study the skeleton of one of the wild horses, it would have dispelled all doubt of any asinine or hemionien affinity. The large feet, rather broad hoofs (see Fig. 23), deep thorax, low and wide pelvis, small ears (in the living animal), and almost completely typical horse-like skull characterize the animal as a true equine form and one for which the specific name *caballus* has rightly been retained. Externally, the coat-color alone (especially the persistently black fetlocks and pasterns) is sufficient to separate *E. c. przewalskii* from asses or onagers, in which the legs are usually of a more or less whitish cast. Still another indication of the equine character of Przevalsky's horse is its gestation period (334–343 days), which is the same as that of domesticated horses and about a month less than that of asses and hemionids.

An average-sized Przevalsky's horse stands 1275 mm (50.2 in.) high at the withers.* While this subspecies of *E. caballus* has been correctly described as a large-headed equine, actually it represents almost exactly the *average* head-to-body proportions of the genus *Equus* in general (including the noncaballine forms). It is relatively "large-headed" only where compared with domestic horses of the taller breeds, in which the length of the legs (and as a consequence, the shoulder height) has been increased by artificial selection. Other physical characteristics of Przevalsky's horse are: a relatively long face or muzzle; eyes located far from the nostrils and near the ears; somewhat short ears; a flat crest (top surface of neck); low withers; a mane which (in the summer coat, at least) is stiff and erect, with little or no forelock; a tail the hairs of which on the upper half are short and mule-like, and on the lower half long and horselike; ergots on all four fetlocks, chestnuts usually on all four legs, somewhat long pasterns, and with the limbs moderately robust. The forehead (facial profile), which

---

* Throughout this book, to avoid duplication—with possibly attendant confusion—all dimensions refer to specimens *averaged from both sexes,* unless otherwise stated.

Fig. 76 Przevalsky's horse and foal in their short summer coats (cf. Fig. 78).

by some authors has been described as typically convex, actually may be either convex, straight, or slightly concave.

The number of lumbar vertebrae in *E. c. przewalskii* is typically either 5 or 6, the average number according to Stecher being 5.43.[3] Usually the *combined* number of lumbar and thoracic vertebrae is 24.

The coloration of Przevalsky's horse, in purebred adult specimens and in the short summer coat, has been described by Ewart (1905), Salensky (1907), and Antonius (1922). It may be summarized as follows: The general color is dun (that is, light bay, or yellow-reddish brown), becoming paler on the lower sides and flanks, and almost clear white on the throat, chest, and belly. The head, neck, and shoulders are of a strong bay or brownish coloration similar to that of the back, except that the nose, lips, and muzzle are white or light yellowish (except for the surface between the nostrils, which is grey). Around each eye there is an almost circular, whitish patch. The ears are light-brown at the base, dark-brown or black at the tips, and with the interiors white-haired. The erect (or "hogged") mane, at the middle of its extension between occiput and withers, may reach a length of six to eight inches. The color is usually dark-brown or black, although it may contain also some light-grey hairs. The mid-dorsal band is dark reddish-brown, or black, and may be as narrow as .2 inches in width; it is bordered on each side, over its full length (including the mane), by a lighter-colored strip. In some individuals a shoulder-cross is visible; and there may be faint, zebra-like stripings above the knees and hocks. The lower portions of the legs, on their front and side surfaces, are colored similarly to those of certain bay, brown, or dun domestic horses; that is, they are dark (frequently solid black), at least on the outer sides of the fetlocks, and often from the hoof all the way up to the knee or the hock. The inner and rear surfaces of the legs are usually a pinkish-grey. The tail, over its upper portion, is of the same color as the body, becoming darker downwards, and being dark-brown or black the lower two-thirds of its length.

In the winter the coat is long and wavy; the mane falls a little to one side; and the "beard" on the lower jaw and the tufts of the fetlocks may each reach a length of from three to four inches.

According to Tegetmeier (1901),[4] the 32 Przevalsky's foals brought to Europe by Hagenbeck in 1901 were obtained from three separate districts in Mongolia, and

Fig. 77 A small, early-day (June 1912) herd of Przevalsky's horses in the New York Zoological Park. The stallion on the left exhibits the peculiar hairing of the tail typical of this wild subspecies.

varied in coloration according to the locality from which each came. However, as Hamilton Smith pointed out over a century ago, true wild "tarpans" (the animals subsequently to be named *Equus caballus przewalskii*) were—even then—"not to be found unmixed except towards the borders of China."[5] According to him, the "tarpans" were at that time found in their greatest purity (1) near Lake Karakoum, south of the Sea of Aral; (2) in the Syrdaria, near Kusneh; (3) on the banks of the river Tom, in the territory of Kalkas; and (4) in the Mongolian and Gobi deserts. Those within the Russian frontiers of that time were adulterated, and distinguished by their *lack of uniformity* as compared with the pure herds farther east. Thus the divergence in coloration of the foals obtained by Hagenbeck from districts other than those in the east (nearest to China) probably resulted from their being mixed with feral horses.

With reference to more recently observed wild bands of Przevalsky's horses, Summerhays (1961)[6] says that they *interbreed freely* with the local Mongolian ponies which roam the same regions in a practically feral state.

Although Przevalsky's horse is today nearly, if not actually, extinct in the wild state, in prehistoric times its range covered the whole tract of the steppes of Europe and central Asia east of longitude 40, the latter parallel separating it eastwardly from the range of the South Russian tarpan (*E. caballus gmelini*), now extinct.[7] The last known area inhabited by Przevalsky's horse in the wild state is that indicated by the small black oval shown on the accompanying map (Fig. 74).*

Bannikov (1958) says that about 1955 the area of distribution of these wild horses was estimated to comprise about 20,000 square kilometers (about 7800 square miles). The then-surviving horses lived at altitudes ranging from 1000 to 1400 meters (about 3300 to 4600 feet), in a desert region alternated by mountains and valleys. The small bands consisted of from 5 to 11 animals (mares, colts, and fillies), each band being

---

* A 1970 report says that the few remaining wild horses in Mongolia seem to be confined to the Takhin Shar-nuru highlands in the southwest, where they are under close observation by the University of Ulan Bator[9] (under protection).

Fig. 78 A "semi-winter" hair-coat on a Przevalsky's stallion. In extreme cold, in the wild, the coat may become considerably longer and thicker, and form a veritable "beard" on the chin and jaws.

led by a stallion. The food of these wild horses comprised various plants common to deserts and semi-deserts. *"Les cereales* [grasses], *les absinthes* [woody herbs], *les oignons* [roots] *constituent vraisemblablement leur nourriture principale . . ."* They are also fond of various halophytes (plants which grow naturally in salty soil).[8] Salensky (1907) remarks that Przevalsky's horse "is said to be migratory, wandering northward in summer and returning south in fall," and that the South Russian tarpan did not do this. He also says that the Przevalsky's horses prefer the more *salty* districts of the desert, and that they are able to go for several days without water.[10]

A survey made by Volf (1958) gives the total number of Przevalsky's horses in European and American zoos, as of January 1, 1958, as 50 specimens. Of these 22 were stallions and 28 were mares. Volf felt that the number of these horses to be found in their native habitat at that time (1958) was probably *fewer* than the number in captivity.[11] Erna Mohr (1959) gives a list of 228 specimens born since 1899, 174 of which were born in captivity. She adds, however, a list of those that were still living on December 31, 1958, and which consisted only of 56 animals—23 stallions and 33 mares.[12] But evidently the species (or subspecies, to be exact) is doing well in captivity, for since 1958 there has been a gratifying increase in the number of zoo specimens. Heinz Heck (in a personal communication of the author dated June 23, 1964) said that at that time there were about 120 horses distributed all over the world. At latest report (1968) there were more than 150 wild horses in captivity, most of which had been sired at the Prague, Czechoslovakia, zoo. So evidently another important wild animal (like the American bison, grizzly bear, Tule elk, and sea otter, to name only a few) has been saved from extinction in the nick of time.

As to the modern domestic horses that have presumably descended from Przevalsky's horse, the situation may be comparable, on a shorter time-scale, to the descent of man from remote primate ancestors—*not* from any existing subhuman anthropoids. To pursue the analogy, it is at least possible that *both* the existing Przevalsky's horse and the various modern light-type domestic horses have descended from a Pleistocene common ancestor, which may or may not have been identical to the present-day Przevalsky's horse. Although the latter animal is more "warmblood" than "coldblood" in its structural conformation, there is no reason why it could not have branched off from one or more of the larger, forest-dwelling forms of the horse that have been designated, misleadingly, "coldbloods." According to the geochronologist F. E. Zeuner, the earliest known appearance in Europe of horses of the Przevalsky's type was 110,000 years ago, whereas the larger, forest-living type is recorded from as long ago as 650,000 years.[13] Accordingly, if there was an original common ancestor, it was probably the large "forest" horse which branched off from that ancestor first, after which another off-branching led to a diminution in body size and the appearance of the races known as the tarpan and Przevalsky's horse, respectively.

That the latter two subspecies interbred is indicated by the extensive geographic distribution (and overlapping of territories) during Pleistocene times of both forms, and by the assertions of early-day naturalists that several "varieties" of Przevalsky's horse were known to exist in different localities.

Therefore, in view of this overlapping distribution of Przevalsky's horse and the tarpan, and the circumstance that the "Horse of Solutré" appears to have possessed certain features of structural conformation peculiar to *each* of the foregoing subspecies, it would appear that *no clearly separated types* of these pony-sized Pleistocene horses can be designated as the ancestors of modern light-built domestic horses. Rather, the wide variety of modern breeds indicates descent from *crossbred* (in nature) ancestors.*

In the description of the South Russian tarpan, which follows, the points of its similarity to, and dissimilarity from, Przevalsky's horse are particularly emphasized.

The osteological material and osteometric data on *Equus caballus przewalskii* studied by the writer has consisted of 13 (9 male and 4 female) skeletons (two of which he measured personally); 25 skulls of both sexes (2 measured personally); and 9 additional sets of measurements of metapodial bones as given by Andreewa (1933).

---

* Numerous light breeds of present-day domestic horses are considered by various authors to have descended from wild ancestors of the Przevalsky's-horse type. Some of these authors, and the specific domestic breeds they have named as probably having sprung from the post-glacial forerunners of *E.c.przewalskii*, are as follows:

Max Nitsche (1923): Kalmuck (Mongol) horse.

S. N. Kwaschnin (1928): Lithuanian (Smudish) horse (which shows resemblances also to the tarpan and the Arab horse).

Max Hilzheimer (1935): *All* domestic breeds, both Light and Heavy; and the Celtic pony as a special type.

J. N. Dimitriadis (1937): Skyros pony; Veglia pony (also Shetland, Fell, Exmoor, and other ponies of northwestern Europe).

E. Bourdelle and—Trombe (1946): Arabian; Camargue (France). And the Celtic pony as ancestor of the Shetland.

R. S. Summerhays (1961): Mongolian pony, as well as numerous other domestic breeds from central Asia, China, Turkestan, the Himalayas, India, and the tropical and subtropical countries of Asia and Burma, along with the northern countries of Europe.

b. Tarpan; South Russian Tarpan (*Equus caballus gmelini* Antonius, 1912).

Seldom in zoological classification has an animal been the subject of such long-continued controversy as the South Russian wild horse, or tarpan. For this there are several reasons. To start with, the name tarpan was used freely by pioneer naturalists and travelers (of the eighteenth and early nineteenth centuries) in reference not only to the east-European animal of that name, but also to the Mongolian wild horse, which later on (in 1881) was given the scientific name of *Equus przewalskii*. This synonymizing—by the use of the same common name—of two distinct, geographically separated races of the wild form of *Equus caballus* has caused unending confusion.*

Fig. 79 The only known drawing from life purporting to represent the South Russian tarpan. The animal was a year-old mare, and the picture was published in Col. Hamilton Smith's book, *Horses* in *Jardine's Naturalist's Library*, 1841. The artist's name was Borisow.

Secondly, some of the earliest reputable observers of living tarpans in their natural habitat were inclined to doubt that these horses were truly wild. Pallas (1811), for example, believed that the whole population of supposedly wild horses "from the Volga

---

* And evidently *continues* to cause confusion. For example, in a recent (1965), supposedly authoritative book on horses, the scientific name of the tarpan is given as Equus *przevalskii gmelini* Antonius! This would make E. *c. przewalskii* a separate species from E. *caballus,* and E. *c. gmelini* a subspecies of *przewalskii!*

to the Ural" were the offspring of escaped domestic horses which had reverted to the wild (feral) state. He noticed in particular that those of the Volga region were usually brown, dark-brown, or silver-grey, some having white legs and other signs of inter-mixture. At an even earlier date, the traveler Forster was similarly disposed to think that "all the wild horses in Asia, from the Ukraine to Chinese Tartary," were descended from strayed domestic animals. Poliakov (1881) says:

> The information regarding the tarpan collected by Rytchkof, Gmelin, Georgi, and Pallas is of so contradictory and confusing a nature that many zoologists have de-cided that the so-called wild horses, or 'tarpans,' were not, strictly speaking, wild, but tamed horses which had resumed their wild state on recovering their liberty . . . Unfortunately, we have no reliable information on this legendary tarpan since the end of the last century, not a single traveler either in Siberia or Russia having com-municated any information concerning it during the present century.[14]

Gmelin (after whom Antonius gave the tarpan its scientific name), however, saw bands of tarpans even before Pallas and Forster had come across them; but he ex-pressed no opinion—at least, in the following account of them—as to whether they were wild or not. In 1768 he secured four specimens in the vicinity of Bobrowsk (Government of Voronesh), Russia. He describes them as mouse-colored, with short and crisp manes, legs that were black from the knee to the hoof, and "disproportion-ately thick" heads. The ears in some specimens were long, as in the ass, and hanging (?); the tail always shorter than in domestic horses, being sometimes well furnished (haired), sometimes sparsely.[15]

Salensky (1907) makes his comparison of the tarpan with Przevalsky's horse mainly on the basis of the "official" description of a tarpan that had been captured in 1866 on the Zagradoff steppes of the property of Prince Kotschubei (Chersonese Pen-insula, just north of Crimea), and which was still living in the Zoological Gardens at Moscow in 1884. This animal had a forelock, but no callosities (chestnuts) on its hind legs. Ewart, however, says that hind chestnuts *were* present.[16] The tarpan was of a dark mouse-color, the legs from hocks and knees down to the pasterns being very black, while its mane, which was 48 cm (about 19 inches) long, hung down on the left side of its neck. Ridgeway (1905), remarking on this description by Salensky, adds that: "Unfortunately no minute study was made of its tail, but, as far as can be seen from a photograph, the tail resembled that of Przevalsky's horse." After comparing the aforementioned tarpan with specimens of Przevalsky's horse, Salensky concluded that:

> . . . the tarpan is a type more specialized towards the horse than is *Equus przewalskii*. Too much stress cannot be laid on the absence of the hock callosities in the only known tarpan, for such a feature is well known among true horses. The Przevalsky horse represents a more universal form between the horses and the asses, and this leads to the assumption that more than any other kind of the genus *Equus* it comes nearest to the common stem-form of horses, asses, and half-asses.[17]

Ridgeway (1905), in contrast to Salensky, and in conformity with the opinions of Forster, Pallas, and the "many zoologists" alluded to by Poliakov, concludes that the tarpan of South Russia was a *cross* between Przevalsky's horse and feral domestic horses. He feels that such a conclusion will account for the opinion reached by the Russian paleontologist Tscherski—who had the opportunity to measure a skull of the tarpan,

Fig. 80 The tarpan, as pictured by Friedrich Specht in *Brehm's Life of Animals* (1896). Note that the artist has evidently used the *immature* tarpan illustrated by Col. Hamilton Smith (see Fig. 79) as a basis for this drawing.

and who stated that, "'the tarpan has all the marks of the group of Oriental horses, being connected on the one side with the Arabian, and on to the other with the Scottish race to which the ponies belong"[18]—since Arabian horses sometimes lack the hock callosities. As regards the coloration of the tarpan, as given both by Gmelin and Salensky, Ridgeway remarks: ". . . mouse-colour and dark mouse-colour in horses are a sure indication of an intermixture of breeds."[19] Again, he says:

As, then, the crossing of the bay Libyan blood with the dun-coloured horse of Asia and Europe has produced the same results in Spain and western Asia, we are justified in concluding that grey horses are not an original stock as has been held by some, but are the result of crossing the Libyan and Asiatic blood.[20]

Finally, in differentiating between Przevalsky's horse (the "tarpan" chiefly referred to by Col. Hamilton Smith) and the South Russian tarpan of later writers, Ridgeway says:

We may therefore conclude that whilst the tarpan of eastern Asia and the Prejvalsky horse with black legs from Zagan-norr Lake are identical, we must hold that the tarpans of eastern Europe and western Asia have probably been largely crossed with escaped domestic animals for at least two centuries, and probably much longer.[21]

One of the most widely quoted theses on the ancestry of the horse is Ewart's (1904) *The Multiple Origin of Horses and Ponies*. Ewart, who at the time was Regius Professor of Natural History at the University of Edinburgh, carried on various experiments in horse-breeding that provided the basis for the aforementioned paper. To test the assertion that Przevalsky's horse might be merely a domestic horse x kiang hybrid, Ewart produced such a hybrid by crossing a kiang stallion and a Mongolian pony

Fig. 81 Scythian horsemen training a wild horse, probably a tarpan. Part of encircling bas-relief on a silver vase found near the ancient town of Nicopo in northwestern Greece. The upper figure pictures a grazing tarpan (?) *c.* four century B.C.

mare. This hybrid foal differed from Przevalsky's horse (1) in having only the merest vestiges of chestnuts on the hind legs; (2) in not neighing like a horse; (3) in having more slender limbs and less specialized hoofs; (4) in the form of the head, lips, muzzle, and ears; (5) in having a mid-dorsal stripe over twice as wide as in the wild horse; and (6) in the absence, even at birth, of any suggestion of shoulder stripes or bars on the legs.

In a second experiment—to test the assertion that the colts brought from central Asia might have been the progeny of feral Mongolian ponies—Ewart mated a Mongol pony with a Connemara (Irish pony) stallion. The foal from this mating was in all essential characters like its Mongolian pony dam, and accordingly *not* a reproduction of Przevalsky's horse.

On the basis of these two tests, Ewart remarks (1903):

> If the Prejvalsky horse is neither a wild ass [kiang], pony mule nor a feral Mongolian pony, and if moreover it is fertile (and its fertility can hardly be questioned), I fail to see how we can escape from the conclusion that it is as deserving as, say, the Kiang to be regarded as a distinct species.[22]

It is noteworthy that Ewart, in his descriptions of his three primordial varieties of *Equus caballus* (see Chapter 3), makes no reference to the South Russian tarpan. The reason for this is that Ewart—like Ridgeway, who relied on Ewart's breeding experiments for evidence of biological relationships—believed the tarpan to be a *hybrid* animal. In fact, Ewart produced one by crossing a mouse-dun Shetland pony mare with a black Welsh pony. This crossbred equine, he says, was "as typical a tarpan as ever roamed the Russian steppes."

Geneticists, also, who have concerned themselves with the question, appear in agreement that grey (the color of the South Russian tarpan*) is *not* a basic coloration of horses, but an indication of crossing. Castle (1943), for instance, says:

> The original color of the wild horse before domestication was undoubtedly similar to that of the still surviving wild Prejvalski horse of Mongolia, a color similar to bay but lighter, with a yellowish pigment where the bay was red. This color class was recognized by Darwin as the probable ancestral type and designated by him as "dun"; not, however, to be confused with the yellow dun or buckskin of modern breeds of horses.[23]

Salisbury (1943), in a study of equine coat color, remarks that: "Gray is considered to be a basic or foundation color by some investigators. This conclusion is not upheld by this study."[24]

Salisbury lists the basic colors of horses as (1) Bay, (2) Brown, brown-black, or seal brown, (3) Black, and (4) Chestnut (see also Chapter 12).

Despite all the foregoing weight of opinion as to the South Russian tarpan's being a hybrid form rather than a true variety or subspecies of *Equus caballus,* the inclination of most zoologists during recent years has been to accept the verdict of those authors who, in contradistinction, have considered the European tarpan (*Equus caballus gmelini*) to be a distinct and genuine ancestral type. Among these authors are Nehring (1890), Salensky (1907), Duerst (1908), Antonius (1922), Hilzheimer (1935), and Lundholm (1949). At one time, most naturalists believed that all the wild horses of Eurasia were descended from a herd of Russian peasant's horses that had been turned loose for want of fodder during the siege of Azov in 1697. However, Linnaeus, while accepting that the wild horses of the Don area probably came from the aforementioned source, held that true wild horses existed in other localities, such as Bessarabia (Romania) and "Tartary."

As to the South Russian tarpan, Antonius (1922) says:

> The tarpan was first definitely described by the German-Russian scientist, S. G. Gmelin, who observed and hunted it in the Worenesch region. Later travelers, unfortunately, often confused it with feral horses, with which it undoubtedly often mingled. Thus, finally, its existence as a distinct form was questioned, even though the Russian scientist, I. Tscherski, clearly pointed out the peculiarities of its skull. So little attention was given to the animal in general that it was able to disappear from the world of living animals practically unnoticed. The Russian literature concerning the tarpan gives it little recognition,** since it concludes that the little European wild horses to which osteological attention was given [by Tscherski] were no longer a truly wild form. I believe that I was the first to repeatedly point out that, despite its probable admixture of blood from domestic horses, the tarpan, as above mentioned, was a genuine type of wild horse, and, as such, of greatest importance in connection with the origin of the domestic horse.[25]

---

* It is to be noted, however, that European zoologists, in referring to the tarpan as "mouse grey" (Ewart, quoted above, says "mouse-*dun*"), do not mean the type of grey common to certain domestic horses which grow whiter with age. Antonius, too (1922) uses the term "mouse-dun" rather than ` mouse-grey."

** In view of the recent definitive monographs on the tarpan contributed by the Russian zoologist, Viera Gromova, this statement by Antonius is no longer true.

The chief question connected with the acceptance or rejection of the Russian tarpan as a true variety of wild horse would appear to be its alleged partial derivation from domestic breeds. A parallel to this situation is found in Prof. Ewart's statement that the "eel-backed dun" horse of Norway was not a true breed, since it could be produced by crossing two distinct Scottish breeds. To this assertion, Lydekker (1912) replied:

> . . . if this view is admitted, the typical rock-pigeon is not a true breed, let alone a species, because, it was pointed out by Darwin in his *Animals and Plants Under Domestication* (1868, Vol. 1, p. 64), several distinct breeds of pigeons will, when crossed, revert to that type. And as what holds good for pigeons will likewise obtain in the case of horses, it follows that the production of duns by crossing affords decisive evidence of the antiquity of the type, being, in fact, a case of reversion to the ancestral form.[26]

Again, Ridgeway, despite his conclusion that the South Russian tarpan was a hybrid animal rather than a true wild horse, felt that, in the parallel case of the alleged Przevalsky-Mongol crosses:

> . . . there was a primitive variety of horse which had these characteristics [absence of forelock, upright mane, peculiarly-haired tail] so strongly marked that they cannot be easily blurred by crossing with horses of the ordinary domestic type.[27]

Thus we have two prominent hippologists agreeing in effect with Antonius that the offspring of wild horses crossed with feral ones could still be valid representatives of an ancestral wild race.

Fig. 82 A herd of "back bred" tarpans *(E. caballus gmelini)* in the Hellabrunn Zoo, Munich.

The present writer is of the opinion that the South Russian tarpan did, indeed, represent a true race of wild horse, despite the admitted probability that many of the tarpan stallions enticed domestic mares into their herds, thus producing an admixture of blood but in no way eradicating the basic physical character of the type.

The final surviving wild specimen of the tarpan—an aged mare which at the last had been domiciled with domestic horses—died in the village of Askania Nova (located just north of Crimea, in the Ukraine) about the beginning of the year 1880. A full account of this animal, as related by the South Russian landowner and zoologist, F. Falz-Fein, is given by Antonius.[28] Evidently the scientific value of this specimen was not realized at the time, as its skeleton was not preserved.

While the known osteological remains of the tarpan are by some authors (*e.g.*, Ridgeway, 1905, p. 42; Salensky, 1907, p. 62; Lydekker, 1912, p. 81) stated to be two skeletons, actually there would appear to be only one skeleton and two skulls. The sole publicized combined skull and skeleton is in the collection of the Zoological Institute of the Academy of Sciences, Moscow (ZIN catalogue no. 521). This skeleton, which was presented to the Zoological Institute in 1862 by I. N. Schatiloff, is of an eight-year-old gelded male, and had been measured and described by Tscherski (1892), Salensky (1907), and Gromova (1959). The most complete set of measurements, both of the skull and the postcranial skeleton, is that given by Gromova.[29] This skeleton is sometimes referred to as the "Crimean" specimen, evidently in reference to the locality from which the living animal came. It is without doubt the most precious (Recent) equine osteological specimen in existence, being the sole authentic evidence of the structural conformation of the members of its race.

The second tarpan skull, which it would seem was formerly in the collection of the St. Petersburg (Leningrad) Natural History Museum, is now evidently (along with specimen no. 521) in the ZIN at Moscow, although no catalogue number is given for it. This skull is of a half-blooded stallion, about 20 years old, which may have been the tarpan that was captured in 1866 on the Kherson steppe and which assertedly was still living in the Zoological Garden in Moscow in 1884.

While, as previously mentioned, in earlier days there was much confusing of the South Russian tarpan (*E. c. gmelini*) with the wild horse of Mongolia (*E. c. przewalskii*), both the skeletal structure and the external appearance of the tarpan proves it to have been a distinctly different wild variety of *Equus caballus* from Przevalsky's horse. Some of the main external differences between these two wild subspecies are given in Table 4.

As to the original range of the tarpan, Antonius suggests that during late Pleistocene time this mouse-dun wild horse may have been "spottily" distributed within the more extensive range of *E. c. przewalskii*, "probably as the remnants of a larger, old-European horse population." He points out that a parallel instance is seen in the case of the mountain zebra (*Equus zebra*), which lived until recently "island-like" within the more extensive range of the Burchell's zebra group of South Africa, without ever mixing with the latter because of the living-grounds of the two species being distinctly separated.* He (Antonius) remarks (1938): "The home of the mouse-dun tarpan

---

* It should be noted, however, that the mountain zebra and the Burchell's zebra group are two distinct subgenera, whereas the South Russian tarpan and Przevalsky's horse are only *subspecies* or varieties of the same animal. That the latter two forms interbred freely when exposed to each other can hardly be doubted. Indeed, this may account for the differences in coloration ascribed to the "tarpan" by various early observers of the animals in the wild.

extended eastward over the river Don and probably to the right bank of the Volga."[30] Hilzheimer, as mentioned previously, put the probable eastern limit of the tarpan's range (during historic times, presumably) as the 40th degree of longitude—roughly, the longitude of Archangel on the north and Rostov, southward, on the eastern shore of the Sea of Azov. Antonius's estimate would extend it five degrees farther to the east, to the longitude of the present city of Volgograd (Stalingrad). Just how far the tarpan spread westwards is not exactly known, although Aurignacian, Solutrean, and Magdalenian paintings and carvings showing this type of wild horse have been found in various caverns in France and Spain. Indeed, it is said that the fierce, wild horses that the Roman legionnaires encountered in Spain were tarpans.

Much interest has been aroused during recent years from the widespread publicity given to the "back-breeding" experiments of two German zoo directors, Lutz and Heinz Heck. One of the extinct animals "re-created" by them was the urus, or aurochs, the primeval ancestor of domestic cattle; the other was the tarpan. While, as mentioned previously, Prof. Ewart of Edinburgh produced (about 1904) a "back-bred" tarpan by crossing a mouse-dun Shetland pony mare with a black Welsh pony, Heinz Heck (then Director of the Hellabrunn Zoo, in Munich), aided by his brother Lutz (former Director of the Berlin Zoological Park), used Celtic ponies, "koniks" (small horses) from Poland and Galacia, and other ponies and small horses from Scandinavia, Iceland, Gotland, and the easterly border states of Europe. Mares of these breeds were mated with a Przevalsky's stallion. In due course, by successive cross-breedings, Heck eliminated the large head, thick bones (?), and reddish coloration of the Przevalsky's horse and got the more slender build and mouse-dun coat-color of the tarpan. His conclusion was that many of the traits of a primitive or ancestral species are dominant, so that when the more primitive-looking descendants of such a species are cross-bred, the characteristics of the ancestral animals are quickly reproduced.[31]

An interesting revelation is that the foals of the back-bred tarpans are not colored like their parents. Rather, they are born with a peculiar blond-brownish coat-color, and without any stripings on the legs. After a few months, the darker coloration of the adult horses is gradually acquired. Another development is that the hoofs of the tarpans, in contrast to those of domestic horses, which have to be shod, have been found to be almost unbelievably tough and durable. One of the back-bred stallions, which was made to pull a cart all the way from Munich to a breeding-farm in the Ukraine, a distance of over 900 miles, arrived, though unshod, with its hoofs in perfect condition.

The first of the Heck brothers' back-bred tarpans was born on May 22, 1933. Shortly thereafter there was a herd of over a dozen of the little horses; and as of the year 1953, no fewer than 58 back-bred tarpans had been produced at the Hellabrunn Zoo (see Fig. 82). The first of these "wild" horses were derived by mating female crosses between Icelandic ponies and Gotlandic ponies with a Przevalsky's stallion. Foals from these parents exhibited all the characters of the true South Russian tarpan (including its skull formation) as the latter had been described by traveler-zoologists who observed this wild horse in its natural state. Further details of the methods employed in back-breeding the tarpan are given by Lutz Heck in a 1954 publication.[32]

Interestingly, the shoulder (withers) height of an average-sized tarpan, 1254 mm or 49.4 inches, is approximately halfway between the height of a typical pony from Gotland, 1222 mm or 48.1 inches, and a typical Przevalsky's horse, 1275 mm or 50.2 inches.

To summarize, the chief external differences between Przevalsky's horse and the South Russian tarpan are given in the following table.

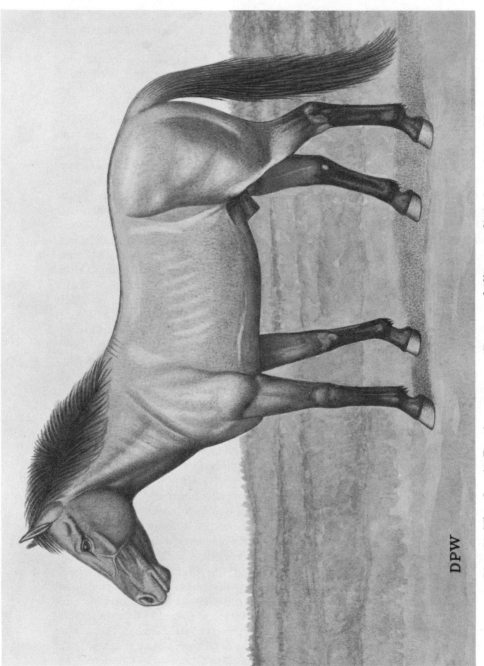

DPW

Fig. 83 The South Russian tarpan (*Equus caballus gmelini* Antonius). Now extinct as a wild form, but generally considered to have been one of the main ancestors of the domestic horse, particularly in the lighter breeds. The horse has a "mouse dun" color and is more slender than Przevalsky's horse (Fig. 84). × .07 natural size.

DPW

Fig. 84 Mongolian wild horse (*Equus caballus przswalskii* Poliakov). The second principal ancestor of the domestic horse (also, like the tarpan, of the lighter breeds). Saved in the nick of time from extinction, this wild subspecies of *Equus caballus* is now on the increase in many zoos. Numerous points of difference exist between Przevalsky's horse and the tarpan, as partially indicated in Fig. 83 and this illustration. × .07 natural size.

Table 4. External differences between the South Russian tarpan
and Przevalsky's horse.

South Russian tarpan (*Equus caballus gmelini*)	Character	Przevalsky's horse (*Equus caballus przewalskii*)
Body, mouse grey or mouse dun; legs, black up nearly to chest	Coat color	Body, reddish dun or russet; legs, black up to fetlocks and sometimes to above knees and hocks
1254 mm (49.4 inches)	Av. Withers height	1275 mm (50.2 inches)
Shorter and more refined; usually with a straight or a concave facial profile	Head	Long and heavy, usually with a convex or a straight facial profile
Relatively short and broad; vertically deep	Face and Muzzle	Long and not broad; less deep vertically than in the tarpan
Semi-erect, curly, very thick and brush-like (usually no forelock)	Mane (in summer)	Stiff and upright; little or no forelock
From 10 mm to over 40 mm wide (about .4 in. to 1.6 in.)	Dorsal stripe	Only about 5 mm wide (.2 in.)
Chestnuts small and short; ergots small or lacking (?)	Leg callosities	Chestnuts large and long; ergots on all four legs
Tail usually several inches above ground, and "differently-haired" from that of Przevalsky's horse	Tail length	Usually reaches ground

In addition to the above external distinctions, the two varieties of the wild horse also exhibit differences in the skull and teeth. However, as these metrical differences would be understandable only to a trained zoologist or paleontologist, they are omitted here. (To those interested, these and numerous other osteometric statistics are available in the writer's technical paper on *Pleistocene and Recent Equidae* on file in the Department of Vertebrate Paleontology at the Los Angeles County Museum of Natural History.)

To recapitulate, the three chief ancestral types of caballine horses which flourished in Europe during Pleistocene and post-glacial times were, according to most authors: (1) the tarpan, or an earlier form closely akin to it; (2) Przevalsky's horse, or other types closely resembling it; and (3) the Forest Horse, as defined by Ewart and as indicated in Pomel's *E. c. robustus,* Nehring's *E. c. germanicus,* and various other heavy-built "coldblood" horses such as *E. sussenborensis* Wüst, *E. moshachensis* von Reichenau, and *E. abeli* Antonius. In addition, there is the important smaller horse from Solutré, France, which is often identified with *E. c. przewalskii* but which more likely could be the result of cross-breeding (in nature) between *E. c. gmelini* and *E. c. przewalskii.*

c. "Forest Horse" (*Equus robustus* Pomel, 1853).

The origin of the great majority of modern breeds of the domestic horse, especially the ponies and smaller horses, can with considerable confidence be attributed to the pony-sized wild horses of Pleistocene times that roamed in countless thousands over practically the entire continent of Eurasia from the Atlantic to the Pacific. Of these wild, ancestral horses of small size, two distinct subspecies or varieties have been identified. One is the South Russian tarpan (*E. c. gmelini*), and the other the Mongolian wild horse or Przevalsky's horse (*E. c. przewalskii*). Both forms have just been described.

However, in order to account for the larger breeds of domestic horses, especially the heavy draft types, it becomes necessary to assume one of two possibilities: (1) that certain groups of smaller horses split off from the main population and gradually evolved into larger animals; or (2) that today's draft-horse breeds developed directly from one or more heavy-built horses of the European Pleistocene, and attained their final size partially through selective breeding by man. Several items of evidence point to the latter alternative as being the more probable explanation.

For one thing, the remains of horses of the heavy, "coldblood" type (*e.g., Equus robustus*) are recorded from as long ago as the beginning of the Pleistocene period, approximately a million years B.P. (Before Present).* In contrast, Przevalsky's horse— or an earlier form of it—is not recorded until 110,000 B.P.

Secondly, large hoofs in the horse, in the natural state, usually although not always indicate a forest or meadow habitat, and small hoofs a steppe or desert habitat. The exceptions to the rule were certain large horses that presumably lived on the steppes, and certain small horses that presumably lived in forests. A theory applied to the forest-dwelling "coldblood" horses of the Pleistocene is that their confining habitat lessened the possibility of escape by speedy, prolonged running, and was compensated by the development in these horses of greater size, strength, and fighting ability.

Despite all this, there were successive warm (interglacial) periods during which most of Europe was forested, and when the majority of *both* large and small horses had forest habitats. Heinz Heck (1936) remarks that although the recession of the last ice-sheet in Europe left large steppe areas upon which the steppe horses flourished, the subsequent climatic changes brought forests over these areas.** The steppes were thus gradually reduced to island spots, and the steppe horses [*E. c. przewalskii*] caused to migrate into Asia.[34]

While most present-day zoologists are agreed that the domestic horse in its numerous and diverse breeds had to have both "coldblood" and "warmblood" ancestors, much confusion still exists as to which ancestral types contributed the "coldblood" and which the "warmblood." It has been convenient for many to assume that the "refined" South Russian tarpan was the progenitor of most "warmblood" domestic horses, and that the "coarse" Przevalsky's horse was one of the ancestors of "coldblood" breeds.

---

* Zeuner, however, assigns to the Pleistocene an age of only 600,000 (rather than 1,000,000) years; but he still places the "coldblood" horses earlier than the "warmbloods."[33]

**This forestation of practically all parts of Europe would make unnecessary the recognition of a local "forest" variety of the South Russian tarpan, as proposed by T. Vetulani,[35] unless at one time the "wood-tarpan" existed in forests in Poland and Czechoslovakia while tarpans elsewhere lived on the steppes. Also, living under forest conditions would account for the significantly large hoofs of both the Celtic pony and the horse of Solutré (France).

But a careful study of the dimensions and proportions of the limb bones in the various forms of Pleistocene horses does not uphold such an assumption.

The principal limb-bone proportions useful in distinguishing "coldblood" and "warmblood" horses from each other are, in the "coldblood" group, a relatively *long* scapula and humerus (to make possible the great vertical depth of chest), a *long* calcaneum (heel, or "hock," bone), and a relatively short radius, metacarpus (front cannon-bone), and metatarsus (hind cannon-bone). In other words, "coldblood" horses have vertically deeper chests and shorter legs than "warmblood" horses of the same shoulder height. In addition, in "coldbloods," the metapodials (metacarpus and metatarsus) are very *thick,* especially in relation to their length, and the second and third (hoof) phalanges are *long.* Also, the hoofs, relative to their face length, are usually *broad,* sometimes exceedingly so. Nevertheless, some varieties of otherwise "coldblood" Pleistocene horse developed narrower hoofs than usual, perhaps by living on prairies or steppes rather than in softer-ground forests.

While, as mentioned above, Przevalsky's horse is sometimes (in contrast to the South Russian tarpan) regarded as a "coldblood" ancestral type, actually, in its limb-bone ratios, it is almost wholly "warmblood." Only in two out of twenty such ratios is *E. c. przewalskii* significantly closer to the draft ("coldblood") type than to the typical "warmblood" horse. In -fact, in twelve of the limb-bone ratios, the average warmblood horse stands *between E. c. przewalskii* and the draft horse. Put in another way, Przevalsky's horse is even further away from the "coldblood" type than are such domestic North-European pony breeds as the Fjord, the Celtic, and the Shetland, all of which appear to have a minor amount of "coldblood" characters in their structural makeup. For that matter, *E. c. przewalskii* itself may have descended from a larger-sized ancestor in which the percentage of "coldblood" was higher than it is in the existing Mongolian wild horse.

Various paleontologists, especially in England and continental Europe, have come to regard as one of the Pleistocene ancestors of the domestic horse the species known as *Equus stenonis* (Steno's horse). Of this species at least two distinct forms have been described (e.g., *E. stenonis typicus* and *E. stenonis major*). *E. stenonis typicus,* which stood in life about 1340 mm (52.8 in.) high at the shoulder, occurred mainly in the Lower Pleistocene, while *E. stenonis major,* a fully horse-sized animal, stood about 1607 mm (63.3 in.) and survived, so far as is known, only until the beginning of the Pleistocene (see the "family tree" in the Appendix). But the proportions of the limb bones in both these forms show them to have been *zebras,* not caballine horses. *E. stenonis typicus,* in particular, is so akin in its skeletal proportions to the existing Grévy's zebra (*Equus grévyi*) as to possibly have been ancestral to the latter. A study of the writer's chart, *Phylogeny of the Genus Equus,* in Chapter 18, should help clarify these relationships. In any event, *E. stenonis* can be left out of consideration as a possible ancestor of the domestic horse, which stems from early forms of *E. caballus.*

Of the heavy-built "coldblood" forms of *caballus,* probably the best-documented are *E. c. mosbachensis, E. c. abeli,* and *E. c. germanicus.* Since *abeli,* which came later than *mosbachensis,* presumably died out sometime during the Late Pleistocene, the most logical of these three "coldblood" types to have continued into post-glacial times and so possibly to have given rise to the modern draft horse is Nehring's *E. c. germanicus.*

The latter wild horse is, or was, a typically caballine "coldblood" type, with relatively thick bones and broad hoofs. As deduced from the skeletal measurements of 1–10 specimens, *Equus caballus germanicus* had on the average a living shoulder (withers) height of 1503 mm (59.2 in.), and weighed presumably about 544 kg (1200 lbs.).

Its body build, while not so thickset as that of a domestic draft horse, was fully equivalent to that of a present-day Quarter Horse, which it evidently closely resembled both in height and weight. What its coloration was is, of course, unknown; but geneticists favor the view that animals living in moist forests tend to have *black or red* hair-coats.*

In any event, provided some of the population of *E. c. germanicus* survived into post-glacial times, this early variety of *caballus* could well have been ancestral to some, at least, of the present-day draft breeds. This, to the present writer, appears the most logical explanation of the derivation of the domestic draft horse, and concurs with the belief held by Ewart (1904), Ridgeway (1905), Duerst (1908), Pocock (1910), Lydekker (1912), Hay (1915), Antonius (1922), Stegmann (1931), Rumjahcev (1936), and doubtless other investigators, that a large "forest horse," or some variety akin to it, must have entered into the genetic constitution of modern "coldblood" horses.

Fig. 85 Restoration of extinct "coldblood" horse, *Equus caballus abeli,* after Otto Antonius, 1913. (While the artist has succeeded in giving this horse the appearance of large size, there seems no reason for the "ram's-nose" facial profile, drooping eye, and receding lower lip depicted.)

But the over-expressive terms "warmblood" and "coldblood" should be abandoned; if not now, then by the adoption and gradual familiarizing of some more appropriate terms, such as "light" horses and "heavy" horses, or "Oriental" horses and "Occidental" horses.

Finally, it should be borne in mind that fossil, or even sub-fossil, remains of members of the horse family are of comparatively rare occurrence, and that for every such

---

* This coloration probably has to do in part with the balance between sunlight and vitamin D. When the habitat of individual animals is changed from the open into the forest, their coats tend to darken. Some earlier zoologists (*e.g.,* Bonavia, 1896) have regarded dappling as the ancestral coat-pattern of horses; but a more recent geneticist, W. E. Castle, considers dappling to be a "sport," or mutation, *not* an ancestral color pattern. "That it occurs in various breeds of horses is no evidence that it was present in a common ancestor. White markings are even more widespread than dappling, yet they are clearly recent and mutational in origin."[36]

species or subspecies unearthed and described there may have been ten, twenty, or even more forms that once existed but which were not preserved (or found). Hence, it is probable that some, possibly many, Pleistocene forms of *E. caballus* other than the three described in the present chapter have contributed to the ancestry of the domestic horse.

Students and scholars alike who have investigated the problem agree that both the evolution and the immediate derivation of the domestic horse—well-explored though these subjects have been—are still only partially elucidated. The present writer, who has tackled the problem from many angles, principally that of osteometry, can only hope that in this book he has succeeded in some small measure in clarifying various controversial or heretofore unsolved points of the subject.

Further comments on the derivation of certain breeds of the horse from Pleistocene ancestral types are given in Chapters 9, 10, and 11, following.

Notes and References

1. C. G. Wrangle, *Die Rassen des Pferdes* (Stuttgart: 1908) 1:217–18.

2. E. D. Morgan, "Expedition of the Brothers Grijimailo to the Shan Oases and Lob-nor," *Proc. Roy. Geog. Soc.*, n.s., 13, no. 4 (1891): 208–26.

3. Robert M. Stecher, *Anatomical Variations of the Spine in the Horse, Jour. Mammalogy*, 43, no. 2 (May 1962): 205–19.

4. W. B. Tegetmeier, in *Field* (London), August 31, 1901, p. 391. (Quoted by William Ridgeway, The Origin and Influence of the Thoroughbred Horse [Cambridge, University Press, 1905], pp. 26–28).

5. Col. Hamilton Smith, "Horses," *Jardine's Naturalist's Library* 20. (London: 1866). (Quoted by Ridgeway, 1905, pp. 31–32).

6. R. S. Summerhays, *The Observer's Book of Horses and Ponies* (London: Frederick Warne and Co., Ltd., 1961), p. 238.

7. Max Hilzheimer, "The Evolution of the Domestic Horse," *Antiquity* 9, no. 34, (June 1935): 135–36.

8. A. G. Bannikov, "Distribution géographique et biologique du cheval sauvage et du chameau de Mongolie," *Mammalia* (Paris) 22 (1958): 152–60.

9. Philip, Duke of Edinburgh, and James Fisher, *Wildlife Crisis* (New York: Cowles, 1970), p. 94.

10. W. Salensky, *Prjevalsky's Horse*, trans. Capt. M. H. Hayes and O. C. Bradley. (London: 1907).

11. J. Volf, "Pour le sauvetage des Chaveux de Przewalski," *Mammalia* (Paris) 22 (1958): 498–600.

12. Erna Mohr, *Das Urwildpferd* (Wittenberg: 1959).

13. F. E. Zeuner, *The Pleistocene Period—Its Climate, Chronology and Faunal Successions* (London: 1959), pp. 313–28.

14. M. Poliakov, "Supposed New Species of Horse," *Annals and Magazine of Natural History* (London), ser. 5, vol. 8 (1881), pp. 16–26. (One of the first accounts of Przevalsky's horse.)

15. J. F. Gmelin, *Reise durch Russland*, 1770. (Quoted by Ridgeway, p. 41.)

16. J. Cossar Ewart, *The Multiple Origin of Horses and Ponies,"* trans. Highland Soc., (1904), pp. 19 ff; republished in *The Smithsonian Report for 1904*, pp. 437–455).

17. Salensky *Prjevalsky's Horse.*

18. J. D. Tscherski, *Wissenschaftliche resultate. . . ,* 1892. Mem. de l' Acad. imp. des Sci. de St. Petersbourg, ser. 7, vol. 40, 511 pp. (Pleistocene and recent wild and domestic Equidae.)

19. Ridgeway *Thoroughbred Horse*, p. 43.

20. *Ibid.*, p. 261.

21. *Ibid.*, p. 43.

22. J. Cossar Ewart, *Multiple Origin*, pp. 467–468.

23. W. E. Castle, *Color Inheritance of Horses, Western Horseman,* January–February 1943, p. 8.

24. G. W. Salisbury, *The Inheritance of Equine Coat Color, Horse Lover,* February–March 1943, p. 17.

25. Otto Antonius, *Grundzüge einer Stammesgeschichte der Haustiere.* (Jena: 1922), p. 257.

26. Richard Lydekker, *The Horse and Its Relatives.* (London: George Allen & Co., 1912), p. 104.

27. Ridgeway, *Thoroughbred Horse,* p. 41.

28. Otto Antonius, *Grundzüge einer Stammesgeschichte der Haustiere.* (Jena, 1922), pp. 258–59.

29. Vera Gromova, "On the Skeleton of the Tarpan and of Other Present-Day Wild Horses, Part 1," *Bull. Moscow Zool. Soc.* 64 (1959): 99–124. (In Russian.)

30. Otto Antonius, *On the Geographical Distribution, in Former Times and Today, of the Recent Equidae, Proc. Zool. Soc. London* ser. B, 107 (1937): 558.

31. Heinz Heck, *Die Rückzüchtung Ausgestorbener Tiere, Bull. Hellabrunn Zoo,* Munich (n.d.). ("Back-breeding" of the South Russian tarpan. Also personal communications of 2–7–49 and 11–12–49.)

32. Lutz Heck, *Animals—My Adventure.* (London, 1954), pp. 156–58.

33. F. E. Zeuner, *The Pleistocene Period* . . . (London: 1959), p. 313–28.

34. Heinz Heck, *Die letzten und die ersten Urpferde* ("The Last and the First Primitive Horses"). *Das Tier und wir* (monthly bulletin of the Hellabrunn, Munich, Zoo) June 1936.

35. T. Vetulani, *Zwei weitere Quellen zur Frage des europäischen Waldtarpans.* (Zeitschrift für Säugetierkunde, Band 8, 1933), pp. 281–82.

36. W. E. Castle, (Personal communication, 1–29–46).

9

Some Representative Breeds of Light
and Medium-Heavy Domestic Horses

NOTE: In the present discussion, which is principally from the standpoint of zoology rather than of horse breeding or horsemanship, no attempt is made to describe the many breeds, or cross-breeds, of the horse that depart from a given type only by reason of the *uses* to which they are put, and not because of a difference in *size and body proportions*. The Hunter, for example, shows no physical differences sufficient to distinguish him from a Thoroughbred. The same is true of various so-called breeds of show horses, whose main distinguishing feature is their gaits. Other horses, such as the Palomino, which are cross-bred mainly to reproduce a certain coloration, likewise cannot be differentiated as physical (especially osteometric) types. Accordingly, in the following review the emphasis is on distinct breeds (i.e., purebred types), in which the *physical differences* are as manifest as the activities for which the horses are used. In later pages lists are presented in which a great number of horse breeds the world over are tabulated according to *nativity* and *geographical distribution*.

a. The Arab Horse.

The origin of the Arabian horse is unknown. The name also is somewhat misleading, since systematic breeding of the animal in Arabia did not occur until the 6th century A.D. Long before that, Oriental horses of the Arab type were being used in Palestine, Syria, Mesopotamia, and other countries of southwestern Asia. About 1700 B.C., horses of the light, chariot-drawing type were introduced into Egypt by the invading Hyksos, a Ural-Altai race of horsemen.

Most authorities are of the opinion that there were no *wild* horses originally in Arabia or Egypt, and that the tamed animals later introduced there had to be helped by man in order to survive in the barren, almost waterless deserts. The prevailing assumption is that the Arabian horse of today is largely the result of systematic breeding by man, and that its prehistoric ancestor was probably a tarpan-like wild horse of central Asia, not necessarily *E. c. przewalskii,* but perhaps an animal of similar size having a smaller skull with a "dished" facial profile. Whether the Barb (Barbary) horse of North Africa was derived from the Arab, or vice versa, is a question that has yet to be answered.

Fig. 86 depicts a typical desert-bred Arab stallion, with the various length, breadth, and girth measurements expressed in inches. Table 29 in Chapter 18 expresses the same measurements as *percentages* of the shoulder (withers) height. From the latter

152

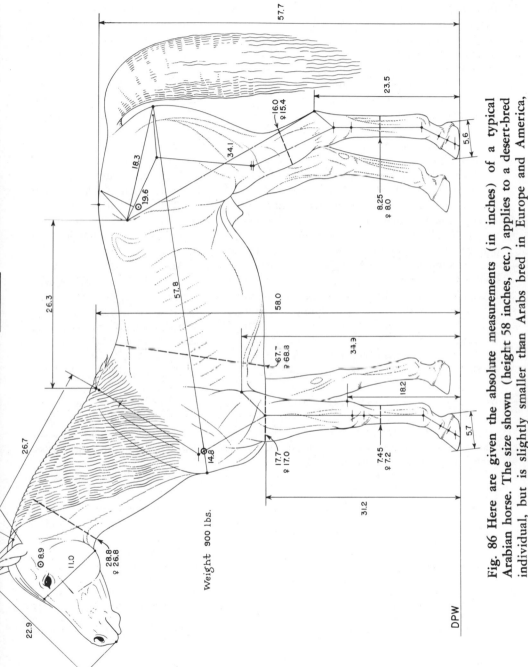

Fig. 86 Here are given the absolute measurements (in inches) of a typical Arabian horse. The size shown (height 58 inches, etc.) applies to a desert-bred individual, but is slightly smaller than Arabs bred in Europe and America, which average 59.3 inches in withers height and about 922 pounds in weight. Wherever two measurements are given for the same part, the lower measurement applies to mares.

table the typical *proportions* of the Arab horse may be calculated for individual animals of any given shoulder height. In Fig. 86 the width or breadth measurements are indicated by a *dot with a circle,* and the girth measurements by *dashed lines.* For example, in Fig. 86 the typical width across the shoulders (for an Arab 58 inches high) is 14.8 inches, and the width across the hips (croup) 19.6 inches. Note that wherever the measurement for a mare differs significantly from that for a stallion (at the *same* shoulder height), both measurements are given, the mare's measurements being indicated by the female sign ♀. For example, the girth of both the fore cannon and the hind cannon (the former being referred to by horsemen as "bone" measurement) is .25, or a quarter-inch, greater on the average in stallions than in mares. On the other hand, the girth of chest is often greater in mares than in stallions.

Fig. 86 was drawn by the writer from the average external measurements of 79 Arab stallions and 121 mares, checked against the skeletal measurements of 6 Arab stallions and 2 Arab mares, and the skull measurements of 24 specimens of both sexes. These average measurements were then compared with the *proportions* shown in numerous profile photographs of both stallions and mares. The result, it is hoped, is a strictly accurate, true-to-life profile drawing of the dimensions and outlines of the body in an "ideal" Arab horse. The same procedure has been followed in drawing other domestic breeds and existing wild forms of Equidae as described in later pages.

The shoulder (withers) height of typical desert-bred Arabian horses is, as is shown in Fig. 86, 58 inches (14½ hands).* However, in Europe and the United States, where better feed for horses is available, the average shoulder height and other measurements are somewhat greater. In Europe, 51 purebred Arab stallions measured by Christo Madroff had an average height of 1516.1 mm (59.7 inches), and 87 mares a height of 1497.4 mm (59.0 inches).[1] These Arabs were measured at breeding stations in Yugoslavia, Rumania, Bulgaria, Hungary, and Czechoslovakia. Similar heights prevail in the United States. Madroff measured also 46 halfbred Arab stallions (Arab x Thoroughbred), the average height of which was 1524.6 mm (60.0 inches), and 74 halfbred Arab mares, of the average height of 1505.9 mm (59.3 inches). The fact that the halfbred (Anglo-Arab) horses, both stallions and mares, were only about .3 inch taller than the purebred Arabs, yet at least *3 inches* less in height than the parent Thoroughbreds, would seem to indicate, in the transmission of height at least, immense prepotency on the part of the Arab sires and dams.

It will be noted that in both the Arab and the halfbred Arab horses measured by Madroff the shoulder height is about 18 mm (.7 inch) greater in stallions than mares. Such a difference, more or less, is typical of *all* breeds of domestic horses, and is due to a greater development of the scapulae and the scapular (*i.e.,* 4th, 5th, and 6th thoracic) spinal processes in the stallions.**

---

* The writer does not share the view of those horsemen who hold that the height of a horse should always be measured and expressed in "hands" (a "hand" = 4 inches). Such a measure is as archaic as a cubit, or as the length of one's middle finger. Why measure a horse's height at 60 inches, then divide by four and call it 15 hands? In Europe, and all other places where the metric system is standard, a horse's height (and other measurements) is expressed either in centimeters or millimeters; and averages may be stated even in *tenths* of a millimeter. There is nothing complicated about such measurements; on the contrary they are simple and exact. But until the United States adopts the metric system, let us at least use *inches* (and fractions thereof, preferably *decimal* fractions) as the means of expressing the measurements of horses and their kin.

** The withers and the croup in the Arab are relatively high above the lowest point of the back, in this respect conforming with domestic horses generally and differing from wild Equidae—even Przevalsky's horse—in which the spines of the withers are markedly shorter, although usually the croup is quite high.

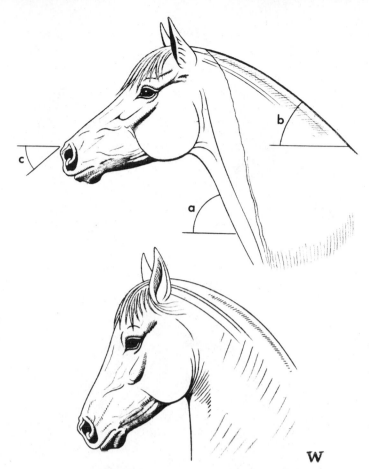

Fig. 87 Head of Arabian horse in normal attitude (above), and in "Classic" or "swan's neck" attitude (below). For explanation of angles *a*, *b*, and *c*, see text.

The individual *variability* in size among animals of a given kind may be fairly gauged by using what is called the *Standard Range,* which refers to a population of 1000 individuals.[2] In equine animals of all kinds the Standard Range in shoulder height is plus or minus about 7 percent. This, in Arab stallions, would mean a range of from about 56 inches to 64 inches, and in Arab mares from about 55 inches to 63 inches. The tallest well-known Arabian stallion was perhaps Nureddin, who stood just under 64 inches high. Khaled, whose skeleton is in the American Museum of Natural History, stood 63.5 inches, as did Rijm, one of the Crabbet stallions.

In weight, Madroff's 51 purebred Arabian stallions averaged about 409 kg (901 pounds), and his 87 Arab mares about 432 kg (952 pounds). At the Kellogg (Pomona Remount Station), in California, 25 stallions chosen at random averaged 59.3 inches in height and 922 pounds in weight; 25 mares, at the same ranch, averaged 59 inches and 922 pounds, respectively. The weight range in the 25 stallions was from 775 to 1080 pounds, and in the 25 mares from 850 to 1140 pounds. Some of the mares, however, may have been in foal.[3] Khaled, mentioned above, who stood 63.5 inches, weighed 1160 pounds. Mesoud, another purebred stallion, at ten years of age stood 58 inches and weighed 920 pounds. The writer's standard for stallions is 59.7 inches and 922 pounds, and for mares 59 inches and the same weight (922 pounds). The mean weight of the 25 Kellogg stallions was 915 pounds. The Standard Range in weight (in either sex) is from 720 pounds to 1180 pounds.

W

Fig. 88 Heads of an adult Arabian horse (top) and a newborn foal brought to the same head-length for comparison. Note in the foal the relatively large eye and ear, the small muzzle, the bulging forehead, the undeveloped mane, and the long, fuzzy hair over the neck and jowls. A newborn foal has only 16 teeth as compared with the normal 40 of its dam and 44 of its sire. See also Fig. 14.

Fig. 87 depicts the head of a typical Arabian stallion in two postures: (1) the normal, looking-straight-ahead stance, and (2) the "swan's-neck" pose occasionally assumed, and which is often to be seen in Greek sculptures (*e.g.,* Fig. 61). The main reason these two sketches are presented is because certain writers, or artists, on the Arab horse, in purporting to show the "ideal" conformation of the head and neck, have presented drawings in which the degree of neck flexion is almost as extreme as that shown in the lower drawing of Fig. 87. Actually, in the normal head and neck position, the typical angle *a* is 65 degrees (not 90!), angle *b* 33–34 degrees, and angle *c* about

Fig. 89 The "Horse of the desert," pictured in its native surroundings. This drawing of an Arabian stallion was made in 1877 by the German illustrator W. Camphausen, and was reproduced in many editions of *Brehm's Life of Animals.*

48 degrees. In Thoroughbred horses these angles are typically 56–57 degrees, 29 degrees, and 51–52 degrees, respectively, showing that normally the Arab holds its head a little higher, and with the muzzle a little farther away from the neck, than the Thoroughbred.

Fig. 88 shows the heads of an adult Arabian horse and a newborn foal, reduced to the same head length in order to compare the *proportions*. In the newborn animal these differences occur: (1) the eyes are relatively larger and placed farther forward, making the face relatively shorter and the braincase longer; (2) the forehead is more bulging; (3) the ears are much larger; (4) the mouth and lips are smaller (because the foal is nursing rather than grazing); (5) the nostrils are smaller; (6) the mane and tail are short and scanty; often, however, in the foal there is long, fuzzy hair over the body and head, especially on the jaws and neck; (7) a newborn foal has only 16 teeth as compared with the normal 40 of its dam and 44 of its sire (see Fig. 28). It is commonly believed that there is little growth in the length of the cannon-bones after birth, but actually these leg bones normally grow more than an inch between birth and the age of 1½ or 2 years (see also Table 1 and Fig. 14).

In the usual descriptions of the physical characteristics of the Arabian horse, these "distinctions" are stated:

(1) The head is small, with a "dished" face, tapering muzzle, and small ears.
(2) The eyes are large and lustrous, and are placed more forwardly in the head than in other horses.
(3) The neck is long and graceful.
(4) The shoulders are oblique.
(5) The back is short, due to there being only 5 lumbar vertebrae, rather than the usual 6.
(6) The pelvis is placed more nearly horizontal than in other horses, and the tail consequently is "set on high."

Because of these, and certain other lesser asserted differences, some hippologists have claimed the Arab horse to be a distinct subspecies of *Equus caballus*. Some even say a distinct *species* of *Equus*. Let us examine more closely these claimed distinctions, dealing with them under the following headings:

HEAD

The head of the Arabian horse is somewhat short, being only 39.1 percent of the withers height rather than the 40 or 41 percent typical of light-built horses generally. However, if the head length be compared with the *trunk length* (rather than the withers height), the ratio in the Arab becomes 39.4 and in the "typical" (average of all breeds) horse 39.9. Some of the *appearance* of small head size in the Arab may result from the relatively small muzzle, the vertical depth of the muzzle just behind the lower lip being only slightly more than *half* the greatest depth from forehead to jowl. In contrast, the muzzle depth in the heavy-headed Przevalsky's horse is 63 or 64 percent of the jowl depth.

The facial profile of the Arab is typically concave or undulating, and the forehead is relatively broad. In some individuals the facial outline may be straight, but never *convex*.

The ears, in relation to head length, are of average, not "small" size. Contrary to the statement by Lady Wentworth that the ears of mares are larger than those of stallions, the writer has found no difference, the ear length in each sex being on the average .3086 times the head length.

The asserted large eyes of the Arab may be large mainly *relative* to its small head and to the fact that the size of the eye in *any* animal varies very much less than the size of the head or body. There appears to be no measurable difference between the eye of an Arab horse and that, say, of a Thoroughbred or a Lipizzaner. This means that while the eye of the Arab is *relatively* larger than that of the other two breeds, it is so only to the extent that the heads of the Thoroughbred and the Lipizzaner are larger than the head of the Arab.

The asserted "low" or forward placement of the eye in the Arab is not borne out by measurements of skulls, in which the "facial length" is accurately obtained with a calipers. The facial length in a horse's skull is the distance from the base of the central incisors (*i.e.,* the median alveolar point) to the most lateral point of the rear edge of the orbit (eye socket), the measurement being taken *diagonally.* This is measurement No. 15 in Fig. 22; only there it is shown *projected* to the median plane. In Arabian horses the facial length (unprojected) averages 383 mm. The basilar length of the skull (measurement No. 1 in Fig. 22, and to which various other measurements are commonly related) in the same breed averages 493.7 mm. The facial length, multiplied by 100 and divided by the basilar length, yields what is called the facio-cephalic index. In the Arabian horse this index is, accordingly, 383 x 100/ 493.7, or 77.6. In the Thoroughbred it averages 76.4, in the Celtic pony 77.2, in draft horses generally (and also the Icelandic pony) 77.8, in the South Russian tarpan (only two skulls in existence) 77.6 and 78.7, in the Shetland pony 78.2 and in Przevalsky's horse 79.0. In 23 different domestic breeds the index averages 77.76. Thus it is seen that the relative length of the face—and distance of the eye from the nose relative to the length of the head— in the Arabian horse is almost exactly the same as that of domestic horses in general. One never hears of the eye in the Thoroughbred being placed "low" in the head, yet it is a fraction "lower" than in the Arab. Here, then, is another purely imaginary (or illusional) difference in the Arabian horse. It can only be added that a *short* face and long braincase in the horse is an *infantile* character (*cf.* Fig. 88).*

---

* The belief that the Arab horse has a short face would seem to trace back to Major R. D. Upton, who in 1879 remarked: "The centre of the eye more nearly divides the length of the head into equal parts than is observable in other horses . . ." (Quoted by Ridgeway, 1905, p. 172).

Fig. 90 "Arab and Horse," by Adolph Schreyer (1828–1899). Schreyer, a German, was the most famous painter of Arabian horses. He produced some 200 canvases, all of which sold for high prices. His horses impart the correct impression of small size and elegant conformation, and the men on them show how Bedouins of the nineteenth century looked.

Fig. 91 The Darley Arabian (1700–1733), one of the three foundation sires of the Thoroughbred horse. From the painting by George Ford Morris based on his study of the early paintings by Sartorious and Wooten done during the horse's lifetime.

The "dished" face (more correctly, undulating or sinuous facial profile) attributed to the Arab, while a distinctive character, is not unique, being present occasionally in other Oriental breeds such as the Barb, the Turk, and the Persian. It appears also, of course, in Anglo-Arabs and other cross-breeds derived from the Arab. And while there is no direct connection in the fact, a sinuous or undulating facial profile may be seen in certain specimens of Burchell's zebras.

NECK

The neck is not "long," as is often claimed, but rather is of *average* length in relation to withers height (namely, 46 percent). However, the Arab horse's neck gives the impression of being long by reason of its slenderness at the throat. Also a greater neck length on the *under side* results from the small head. The high-arched crest of the purebred Arab, especially in stallions, contributes a spirited effect. The neck vertebrae of Thoroughbred horses are appreciably longer than those of Arabs, even in relation to the Thoroughbred's greater general size.

TRUNK

The "short back" claimed for the Arab is a more or less typical feature of the breed, depending upon the number of thoracic (rib-bearing) and lumbar vertebrae in the individual animal. If an Arab has only 17 thoracic and 5 lumbar vertebrae, it is certainly entitled to be called short-backed. But there are other individual Arabs, purebreds included, which exhibit the full complement of 18 and 6 vertebrae, respectively. As if to compensate for the tendency toward a short back, the croup (from point of buttock to anterior point of hip bone) in the Arab is relatively long. In fact, in relation to back length, the croup in the Arab is longer than in any other domestic breed or wild subspecies of *Equus,* averaging no less than 72.5 percent. For comparison, this ratio in the Thoroughbred is 68.7 percent, in the draft horse 67.3 percent, and in Przevalsky's horse 66.8 percent. It reaches its lowest proportion in Grévy's zebra, with only 62.2 percent, indicating in this type of equine a very long back and short croup. In the typical Arab the pelvis is inclined less than in other breeds, and the sacrum accordingly elevated so that the tail is carried high. It should be added, however, that the inclination of the pelvis (fore-and-aft angle) within a given domestic breed or wild species is an *individually highly variable character.* When this feature is studied in relation to all the subgeneric forms of *Equus,* about all that can be safely stated is that the angle is from 5 to 7 degrees greater in draft horses than in equines of light body-build.

Fig. 92 Chestnut stallion SAHM, owned by Dr. and Mrs. R. W. Cosby, Los Angeles. A fine example of a well-bred Arab.

LIMBS

The long, slender, yet strongly-muscled limbs of the Arab horse, together with its somewhat short back, are well adapted for weight-carrying, a fair degree of speed, and endurance under the trying conditions of the desert. Especially long in ratio to various other bones of the skeleton are the cannon-bones (metacarpus and metatarsus). The latter bones, together with a long forearm (radius) and long pasterns, give the Arab a total length in the forelimb, compared with the withers height, of 59.8 percent, while in the Thoroughbred the relative length is 60.1 percent, a negligible difference. In both the Arab and the Thoroughbred the height of the croup is slightly *less* than that of the withers, the croup in each breed averaging .3 inch lower.

In some accounts of the conformation of the horse, the Arab included, it is stated that the pastern should incline at an angle of 45 degrees with the ground. Only when the horse is in motion does such a low inclination at times occur. Standing at rest, the typical angle that the pasterns make with the ground in light-built horses is 63 degrees in the forelimb and 65 degrees in the hind limb. In draft horses, where greater weight has to be supported, these angles are 66 degrees and 68 degrees, respectively. The relative size and shape of the hoofs in the Arab is shown in Fig. 22.

In some accounts it is stated that the Arab's "short back" may be due in part to sloping shoulders (scapulae). Indeed, in one drawing purporting to show the "ideal type" Arabian, the scapula is shown inclined at an impossible 30 degrees (!) from the horizontal. The normal, characteristic inclination of the scapula in the Arab, the same as in other light-built or "warmblood" horses, is from 57 to 59 degrees (see Fig. 86). In draft horses the scapula becomes more upright, having an average inclination of 62 degrees; but never, in normally-structured horses, does this angle go below 50 degrees.[5] See Fig. 134.

TAIL

Writers who wish to point out all possible distinctions of the Arab horse invariably add that this breed has only 16 caudal (tail) vertebrae in comparison with the 18 of other horses. But this character, like the inclination of the pelvis, is highly variable individually. As will be seen by consulting the list of bones in Chapter 4, the number of tail vertebrae is shown to vary from 13 to 21; and even this range may not represent the extreme variation, since the number of horses showing the 13–21 range is not stated. So here, as in the case of some other anatomical characteristics, about all that can be said is that the Arab horse shows a typical, though not an invariable, difference from other breeds.

As to some of the other physical characteristics of the Arabian horse, the mane is only moderately developed, fairly long, but not thick or profuse; the mane has a long forelock; the tail is long and flowing. The chestnuts on the forelegs are usually small, while those on the hind legs are either very small or absent altogether. The ergots (on the backs of the fetlocks) are likewise very small, sometimes hardly distinguishable.

The predominant colors of the Arab are bay, grey, chestnut, and brown, in that order. Roans, piebalds, skewbalds, duns, and yellows are not found in purebred Arabs, although the latter two colors occur occasionally in Barbs. Pure white or black are rare. White marks—stars, strips, blazes, and snip noses—on the head are common, as

Fig. 93 Stallion RIFAGE and mare, showing the characteristics of a fine Arab head.

are one or more white feet or stockings. Solid white, while much prized by some horsemen, is rare, although some years ago a snow-white newborn foal ("a unique sport") was reported. The skin-color of the Arabian horse is normally blue-black. According to Ridgeway, it is "so marked a feature [of Al-Khamseh horses] that it has furnished the generic name for the breed [Kohl]."[4]*

To sum up, the question of whether or not the Arab horse should be regarded as a distinct subspecies of *Equus caballus* would seem to hinge on whether its true distinctions have resulted from natural evolution or are, rather, the result of centuries of breeding by man for specific physical traits and qualities. If the latter, the Arab—in contrast to Przevalsky's horse (*E. c. przewalskii*) and the South Russian tarpan (*E. c. gmelini*)—can hardly be designated as more than a distinct *breed* of the domestic horse.

It is generally accepted by hippologists that the Arabian horse has existed as a pure (*i.e.,* inbred and "uncontaminated") breed since the time of Mohammed, c. 630 A.D. Although the comparatively recent introduction of mechanized transportation into the Near East has changed the entire status of horse-breeding there, it may be of interest to quote here a passage from Youatt, who in his book, *The Horse* (London, 1880, pp. 25–26) tells about the breeding of the Arabian horse by the Bedouins of that period:

It is an error into which almost every writer on the history of the horse has fallen, that the Arabian is bred in the arid deserts, and owes the power of endurance which

---

* Kohl, or Kuhl, is the Arabian word for antimony, a substance used by Arab women to blacken their eyebrows and eyelashes.

he possesses in his adult state to the hardships which he endured while he was a colt. The real fact is, that the Arabs select for their breeding-places some of those delightful spots, known only in countries like these, where, though all may be dry and barren around, there is pasture unrivalled for its succulence and its nutritious or aromatic properties. The powers of the young animal are afterwards developed, as they alone could be, by the mingled influence of plentiful and healthy food, and sufficient, but not, except in one day of trial, cruel exercise . . .

The parentage and birth of the foal are carefully recorded by competent witnesses, whose certificate includes the marks of the colt, and the names of the sire and dam. The colt is never allowed to fall on the ground at the period of birth, but is caught in the arms of those who stand by, and washed and caressed as though it was an infant. The mare and her foal inhabit the same tent with the Bedouin and his children. The neck of the mare is often the pillow of the rider, and more frequently, of the children who are rolling about upon her and the foal. No accident ever occurs, and the animal acquires that friendship and love for man which occasional ill-treatment will not cause her for a moment to forget.

At the end of a month the foal is weaned, and is fed on camel's milk for one hundred days. At the expiration of that period, a little wheat is allowed; and by degrees that quantity is increased, the milk continuing to be the principal food. This mode of feeding continues another hundred days, when the foal is permitted to graze in the neighbourhood of the tent. Barley is also given; and to this some camel's milk is added in the evening, if the Arab can afford it. By these means the Arab horse becomes as decidedly characterised for his docility and good temper, as for his speed and courage. The kindness with which he is treated from the time of his being foaled, gives him an affection for his master, a wish to please, a pride in exerting every energy in obedience to his commands, and, consequently, an apparent sagacity which is seldom found in other breeds.

The following eulogy, which is re-quoted from *Brehm's Life of Animals,* 1896 edition, p. 410, is typical of the sentiments of nineteenth-century Arab horsemen:

Do not tell me that this animal is my Horse; say that he is my son. It runs more quickly than the wind of a storm, more swiftly than the glance that sweeps the plain. It is pure as gold. Its eye is clear and so keen that it sees a hair in the dark. It overtakes the gazelle in its course. To the Eagle it says: I hurry on like you! When it hears the shouts of girls, it neighs with joy, and the whistling of bullets rejoices its heart. From the hands of women it begs for alms; the enemy it beats in the face with its hoofs. When it can run to its heart's desire, it weeps tears. It recks not whether the sky be clear or the blasts of the desert obscure the light of the sun with dust; for it is a noble steed and despises the rage of the storm. There is no other in this world that could vie with it. Swift as a Swallow, it courses on; so light is its weight that it could dance on the breast of your beloved and not annoy her. Its pace is so gentle that you could drink a cup of coffee on its back, when its speed is highest, and not spill a drop. It understands all like a son of Adam, and all it lacks is speech.

It may be added that the Arab horsemen of those days never used a bit or bridle, and substituted for those controls a plain silken cord tied around the horse's head. (Perhaps this was at an earlier period than that pictured by Adolph Schreyer in Fig. 90, where the horse is shown not only equipped with a bridle but with *blinders!*). It is further said that a horse-owner could summon his untethered mount out of a line of hundreds simply by whistling to it. The horse and its rider were perfectly coordinated and symbiotic.[6]

Today this picture has practically vanished, and most Arabian horses are being bred and used by Europeans and Americans either as saddle horses, cow ponies, or for cross-breeding. The inherent beauty of the Arab is not being lessened; on the contrary, by better-controlled feeding and grooming, and less harsh living conditions, the breed is being improved.

Further mention of the Arabian horse is made in the following pages in connection with those breeds, particularly in America, to which he has contributed his qualities. (See especially the comparison of the Thoroughbred with the Arabian.)

---

b. The Thoroughbred.

The origin of the Thoroughbred, in contrast to the nebulous beginning of the Arabian horse, is at least partially established. The Thoroughbred as we know it today dates back to approximately the year 1700. To be sure, there was horse-racing in England long before that date, but it was not the organized affair that it later became. The earlier races were usually matches between two horses, and it was only occasionally that more than three or four horses competed in the same race. The contests were usually decided in heats of various lengths, with two or more heats being run to determine the winter. Jockey weights were much higher than at present; in 1739, by royal edict, no races could be run at Newmarket with a rider weighing less than 12 stone, or 168 pounds. Usually horses were required to be completely mature before they raced, although four-year-olds were sometimes allowed to compete. There were no grandstands of the modern type; and except for a few farmers who might be on foot, the races were watched from horseback or from carriages. No admission was charged; and since there was no income from this source, the prizes were usually the result of private stakes. There were no racetracks as at present, and the races took place over empty fields with stakes marking the courses. "A rope from stake to stake was the ancestor of the rails which surround modern tracks."[7]

To digress for a moment, it is said that the change from heavy, armor-bearing horses to lighter and more active ones in warfare was brought about by the introduction of gunpowder and firearms, which altered the course of military tactics and led indirectly to the breeding of horses for speed and racing.

During the seventeenth and even the sixteenth centuries, many horses were brought from other countries into England, mainly for the purpose of racing, but also to cross-breed with the native British horses, which included ponies of the Celtic, New Forest, Highland, and other medium-sized breeds, but which for the most part were probably Cleveland Bays. The imported horses, according to Thomas Blundeville, writing in 1580, were not only Barbs and Turks, but also Spanish, Neapolitans, and Sardinians. Evidently all these imported horses were stallions, since the original owners, especially those in North Africa and the Near East, were reluctant to part with their mares.

On the authority of William Ridgeway and other eminent hippologists, it has come to be generally (although not universally) accepted that the English Thoroughbred owes nothing to the native horses of Britain, but is "purely foreign in origin."[8] He came into being during the time of King Charles II, who reigned from 1660 to 1685, with the importation of an Oriental stallion known as the Byerly Turk. This horse was foaled about 1679, and was still being used as a sire as late as 1698. He had been owned by a

Fig. 94 An interpretation by George Ford Morris of the "Godolphin Arabian," 1724–1753, one of the three original foundation sires of the Thoroughbred line. The cat in the picture was a constant companion of the horse, and after the horse died, pined away and shortly followed him.

Captain Byerly, who had used him as a charger in Ireland during King William's wars (1689, *et seq*). Little else is known of him. The second of the three acknowledged foundation sires of the Thoroughbred* was the Darley Arabian, a bay stallion (see Fig. 91). He was bought in Aleppo, Syria, and arrived in England in 1700, at the age of four. The third sire was the so-called Godolphin Arabian, which by most authorities is regarded as having been a Barb. (He had been owned by the Earl of Godolphin, hence the name.) He was a brown bay, "about 15 hands high," and had been foaled about 1724.

Every Thoroughbred in the world today traces in male line back to one of these three foundation sires; but the present-day descendants are substantially improved animals, standing fully a hand higher than their original forebears and possessing greater speed and at least equal endurance.

One more important sire should be mentioned, since he appears to have been responsible for the color of virtually all the *grey* Thoroughbreds now living. This was an imported grey stallion called Alcock's Arabian. According to Estes and Palmer, "It should be familiar to the student that a grey horse must have at least one grey parent, and if the greys are followed through a pedigree, they will, with the scantiest of exceptions, go to the Alcock Arabian, though some of them will also trace, also in an unbroken sequence of greys, to the Brownlow Turk."[9]

In equine genealogy, "male line" means from son to sire to grandsire, etc. In modern pedigrees, however, male lines are traced only to three descendants of the three original

* By "Thoroughbred" is meant a stallion or a mare bred especially for racing under the saddle, and whose pedigree is registered in the Stud-Book kept by the official agents of the Jockey Club, in London. American Thoroughbreds are similarly registered in the Jockey Club, New York City.

Fig. 95 "Eclipse," the most famous of early-day racehorses, as portrayed from life by the English painter, George Stubbs, about 1770.

foundation sires, as follows: The Godolphin Arabian is the grandsire of Matchem (1748); the Byerly Turk is the great-great-grandsire of Herod (1758); and the Darley Arabian is the great-great-grandsire of Eclipse (1764). No other branches of the original male lines exist, and the pedigrees of present-day Thoroughbreds can be traced only to Herod, Matchem, or Eclipse, in male line.

To comment on the vast number of prominent Thoroughbred horses which have descended from Herod, Matchem, and Eclipse is beyond the scope of the present volume,* the aim of which is to treat of the horse from the zoological rather than the historical standpoint. Comprehensive historical accounts are given by Ridgeway (1905), Plumb (1906), in the *Cyclopedia of American Agriculture* (1908), and *The Encyclopedia Britannica* (11th edition, 1911). A more recent review is presented in *The History and Romance of the Horse,* by David Alexander (1963). Perhaps the best coverage as a sport is in *The Encyclopedia of Sports,* by Frank G. Menke (4th Ed., 1969). We shall, therefore, confine our comments at this point to the most famous of the three foundation sires of the modern Thoroughbred.

"Eclipse," reputedly the fastest of the early English racehorses, was so named from having been foaled on the day of a solar eclipse, April 1, 1764. Eclipse has been variously described by various writers, but most seem to agree that he was low in the withers and high in the croup. However, a list of relative measurements of him (based on head length), which were taken by M. St. Bel and were quoted by William Youatt (1880, p. 72), makes these two body heights the same. Again, the height of the withers in Eclipse has been variously stated as 61, 62, and 63 inches (the latter figure being given by Ewart). To the contrary, the measurements of the limb bones in a skeleton in the British Museum, said to be of Eclipse, indicate a living withers height of only 59 or 60 inches, and a croup height considerably lower. And there are other skeletons also pur-

---

* For example, over a period of, say, 200 years, with the average time between generations being 12 years,[10] the theoretical number of horses would be 2 doubled 17 times, or 131,072; and even if only one horse in ten was noteworthy, there would still be some 13,000 names to contend with!

portedly of this racehorse, so that it would appear practically impossible to learn what the living animal's body dimensions really were. The well-known painting of Eclipse by George Stubbs, which was made about 1770, shows the withers and the croup of the horse to be equal in height, the body to be rather long (1.04 times the height), the quarters very long, the head disproportionately small, and the neck exceedingly long and slender (Fig. 95). In portraying the latter parts, Stubbs was probably influenced by the fashion of horse-painters of his day, which was to make the head and neck too small (slender) and the quarters too large. The painting shows also the conspicuous white stocking on Eclipse's right hind leg, which made it easy to identify the horse who was so far ahead of his competitors that the saying arose: "Eclipse first, the rest nowhere!"

Eclipse, who had been bred by the Duke of Cumberland, was at first considered so ordinary that he was not put into a race until he was five years old. He later became the sole property of a Colonel O'Kelly, who had recognized the horse's potential. During Eclipse's short racing career of seventeen months, he was never closely threatened, let alone beaten, and he earned for O'Kelly more than $125,000. The horse was afterwards put at stud, and produced the extraordinary number of 334 winners, which in turn netted their owners more than $800,000, not counting awards of plates and cups. Herod, however, outdid Eclipse in the latter respect, producing no fewer that 497 winners, who gained for their owners upwards of $1,000,000. Matchem, the first of the "Second Trinity," went to stud in 1763 and sired 354 winners whose total earnings were about $750,000.

As to the racing ability of Eclipse, he is said to have had a stride of 25 feet, and to have run a 4-mile race in 6 minutes, 2 seconds (!). When it is considered that over eighty years later (that is, in 1855) the famous American Thoroughbred "Lexington" established an official record by covering the same distance in 7 minutes, 19¾ seconds, or at about only 82 percent of the speed attributed to Eclipse, it is evident that either the timing of Eclipse's race, or the distance measured, must have been sadly inaccurate!

We may now conveniently leave the uncertain fields of the past, and consider the known physical characteristics of the modern Thoroughbred, which in this respect as well as in performing ability is doubtless the best documented of all breeds of the horse.

Fig. 96 gives the measurements (in inches) of a typical Thoroughbred stallion, while Table 29 in Chapter 18 expresses these measurements as percentages of the shoulder (withers) height. A comparison, by means of the latter table, of the body proportions (relative to the withers height) of the Thoroughbred and the Arab, shows the following similarities and differences in these two breeds:

(1) The trunk length is relatively longer in the Thoroughbred.
(2) The head length in the Thoroughbred is even smaller, relatively, than in the so-called small-headed Arab.
(3) The width of forehead and length of ear in the Thoroughbred are each slightly smaller relative to withers height, but about the *same proportion relative to head length* as in the Arab.
(4) The neck length in the Thoroughbred is notably longer than in the Arab (49 percent of the withers height as compared with 46 percent, respectively).
(5) The relative girth of chest in the Thoroughbred is smaller, though only slightly, than in the Arab, while the relative girths of the neck and limbs are essentially the same in both breeds.

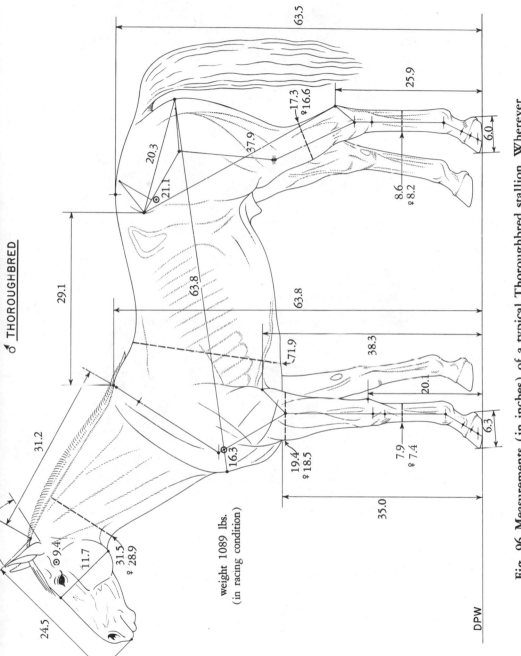

♂ THOROUGHBRED

63.5

25.9

17.3
♀16.6

37.9

20.3

21.1

6.0

8.6
♀8.2

29.1

63.8

63.8

71.9

38.3

31.2

16.3

19.4
♀18.5

20.

7.9
♀7.4

6.3

weight 1089 lbs.
(in racing condition)

9.4

11.7

31.5
♀28.9

35.0

24.5

DPW

Fig. 96 Measurements (in inches) of a typical Thoroughbred stallion. Wherever two measurements are given for the same part, the lower measurement applies to mares.

Fig. 97 Two early-day racehorses, as drawn by H. Fieg and engraved by Carl Gottlob Specht. At the top is Hanover, a chestnut American Thoroughbred stallion, foaled in 1884. In 48 races, Hanover was first 32 times, second 13 times, and third 3 times. His total winnings were $118,872. Hanover's skeleton, which was measured for the author by Dr. Dewey G. Steele, is in the museum of the Agricultural Experiment Station of the University of Kentucky.

Below is Doncaster, a chestnut Thoroughbred stallion foaled in 1870. The drawing of Doncaster is more realistic than that of Hanover, since the latter shows the disproportionately small head and thin neck typical of the early-day paintings of English racehorses.

(6) The length of the back in the Thoroughbred is slightly greater, and the length of the croup slightly smaller, relatively, than in the Arab.

(7) The relative length of the limbs in the Thoroughbred and the Arab are practically identical, as in the width of shoulders.

In body-build, the average-sized Thoroughbred stallion is slightly more slender at a height of 63.8 inches and a weight of 1089 pounds than is the average Arabian stallion at 59.7 inches and 922 pounds. This, however, is only where the Thoroughbred is weighed in racing condition. Off the racetrack, the typical Thoroughbred may weigh anywhere from, say, 1110 to 1190 pounds, at which stage he will equal or surpass the body-build (girth relative to length) of the typical Arab.

The Standard Range (1000 cases) in height of Thoroughbreds is from about 60 inches to 68 inches, although in rare instances the height may be 69 inches or so. Man o' War, one of the greatest racehorses, was 65.6 inches high at the withers and in racing condition weighed 1150 pounds. Seabiscuit (Fig. 98), another great performer, stood only 62 inches high and weighed 1040 pounds. Whirlaway (Fig. 99), at four years was 63 inches and 1070 pounds, with a chest girth of 72 inches. At the age of nine, at stud and no longer racing, he had increased to 64 inches and 1185 pounds, with a girth of 73 inches.

Assuming the foregoing range in height, and a uniform body-build, the Standard Range in weight in the Thoroughbred (in racing condition) is from about 900 pounds to 1300 pounds.

The coat-color in the Thoroughbred may be either bay, brown, chestnut, or black. Less frequently the color is grey. Irregular and conspicuous white markings are common.

A great number of imaginary virtues continue to be attributed to the Thoroughbred, just as to the Arabian horse. Both are splendid animals, in some respects the most highly developed of all equine forms, but this does not warrant the effusive encomiums applied to them by sentimental writers. Such qualitative descriptions as "large," "small," "moderately large," "well-sprung," "sloping," "springy," etc. are meaningless unless accompanied by *quantitative* measurements in the form of exact heights, lengths, widths, girths, and angles. While all the latter measurements are seldom taken in the United States, in Europe they have been recorded for nearly all the principal breeds present there, with the result that the external bodily conformation of any particular breed is a matter of definite knowledge rather than subjective opinion. Of the Thoroughbred horse, for example, Alfred Plischke (1927) records no fewer than 65 linear measurements and 9 angular measurements, for horses aged 1, 2, 3, 4, and 5 years, respectively. J. Stratul (1922) gives 16 linear measurements and 6 angular measurements of 102 Thoroughbred stallions and mares. Gutsche (1914) gives 64 linear measurements and 8 angular measurements of Trakehner horses (a fine East-German breed, slightly larger than the Thoroughbred). Christo Madroff gives 14 to 16 body measurements and the weights of 79 Lipizzan stallions and 128 mares (1935), 323 Large Nonius and Small Nonius (1936), 89 Gidran (Anglo-Arab) stallions and 113 mares (1936), and 138 purebred and 120 halfbred Arabians (1937). The foregoing references represent only a small fraction of the papers published in Europe (chiefly in the German periodical *Zeitschrift für Züchtung*), dealing with the body and limb measurements of horses of numerous breeds, including ponies and the heavy draft types. (See list of authors on European breeds, Appendix).

So, in view of this extensive and exacting literature, there is little excuse for those who describe horses by such terms as "good quarters," "roomy barrel," "oblique

Fig. 98 Seabiscuit, after having been retired from the track, posing beside the life-sized statue of him modeled by Tex Wheeler and unveiled at Santa Anita Park, California, in 1941. Seabiscuit died at the age of 14 years, on May 18, 1947. He was a grandson of the famous stallion Man o' War (1917–47).

shoulders," etc. The latter specification, in particular, is invariably presented, on the premise that the more sloping the scapulae, the freer-moving the limbs. However, a study made in 1933 by Dr. von Müller on 237 horses of various European breeds, including Thoroughbreds, trotters, and Rheinish-Belgian draft horses, showed that the performing ability of a horse cannot be judged from its skeletal build and body proportions. In fact, in a group of East Prussian horses judged to have a "free stride," the inclination of the shoulder was slightly *greater* on the average than in another group judged to have a "short stride." Another of Dr. von Müller's findings was that *endurance* in a horse, while probably aided by a large chest and capacious lungs, is more dependent upon efficient *functioning* of the organs than upon their *size* (as inferred from external measurements).[11]

It is stated by some writers that the most carefully developed breed of horse, and the culmination of its type, is the Arab. It is generally agreed that the Arab horse has been maintained in pure form (that is, uninfluenced by the introduction of foreign blood) for a longer period of time than any other breed.* However, the breeding of the Arabian horse has not been stimulated by *economic* reasons to anywhere near the extent that has occurred during the last 200 or 300 years in racehorses, particularly the

---

* This is evidently another of the points in the Arab upon which undue emphasis has been placed.

Dewey G. Steele (1944) in a genetic analysis of various horse breeds, says "The current use of lengthy pedigrees lacks genetic significance. For all practical purposes individuals beyond the third generation may be ignored."

Thoroughbred. And where possible financial gain is a factor, there will one find man's greatest interest and application! For this reason, despite all the romance and sentiment surrounding the horse of Arabia, it must be evident that the culmination of the equine animal, so far as its chief quality—speed—is concerned, is represented by the modern Thoroughbred horse, and only to a slightly lesser degree by the American trotter (Standardbred), with which we shall now deal.

Fig. 99 Whirlaway, one of the greatest money-winners of his day, was the fifth horse in racing history to win all three "big" stakes—the Derby, the Preakness, and the Belmont. Whirlaway, foaled in 1938, was by Blenheim II out of Dustwhirl. His "Triple Crown" was won in 1941.

c. THE STANDARDBRED, or HARNESS HORSE.

Harness racing, while looked upon by some as a comparatively recent sport, actually traces back to the dawn of history, when men, often of royal blood, raced one another in light, two-wheeled chariots drawn either by Oriental horses or by onagers. Such use of the horse preceded that of racing under the saddle (or even bareback) by hundreds of years. The latter probably did not take place until systematic breeding had produced horses large enough to be ridden, which would have been about 800 B.C., when the Greeks started to ride their small but sturdy all-purpose steeds.

Fig. 100 One of the finest photographs of a racehorse ever taken. It depicts the early American champion, George Wilkes (1856–1882), who from 1868 to 1872 held the world's one-mile trotting record of 2:22. George Wilkes was a handsome brown stallion, 60 inches in height, who upon his retirement from the track sired a numerous progeny of celebrated trotters and pacers.

Modern harness racing dates officially from the year 1806, when the first records started to be kept. The Standardbred horse is a breed derived mainly from the Thoroughbred, but tracing also to the Norfolk (English) trotter, the Narragansett pacer, and to other light breeds, including the Arab. Horsemen who are partial to the Thoroughbred give chief credit to Imported Messenger (1780–1808); while others favor Imported Bellfounder (1815–1843), the first noteworthy Norfolk trotter stallion ever imported from England.

Messenger, a grey stallion 63 inches high, was a descendant of the Darley Arabian. As a three-and-four-year-old, he won several races under the saddle on tracks near London. In 1788 he was sold to a Thomas Benger of Philadelphia. As Pennsylvania law then forbade horse racing, Messenger was driven to New York and sold to a brother of John Jacob Astor. The horse, however, while a trotting sire, had no immediate notable descendants. He gained his chief fame through his son Mambrino, a Thoroughbred, who in turn sired Abdallah I, a trotter of real prepotency. Abdallah sired the famous Goldsmith Maid, Hambletonian 10, and other top-ranking trotters of the 1870s and 1880s.

Bellfounder, known also in the United States as Imported Bellfounder, was foaled in 1815, and was brought from Norfolk, England, in 1822. He was a bright bay, 60 inches high, with black "points" (mane, tail, and lower legs), and was a natural trotter of great speed and power, being capable of 17 miles in an hour. He, like Messenger, went into stud service in New York State, where he sired numerous fast trotters and pacers. Bellfounder died on Long Island in 1843.

Hambletonian 10*, sired in 1849 by Abdallah I out of the Charles Kent Mare, proved the founder of the most famous American family of trotters (see Fig. 104). In 1851, Hambletonian 10 began service in stud, which, with the exception of one year (1868), he continued until 1872. During those 21 years of service he sired 1287 foals, among them such famous sons and daughters as Alexander's Abdallah, Electioneer, George Wilkes (see Fig. 100), Aberdeen, Volunteer, Happy Medium, Harold, Strathmore, Dictator, Dexter, Nettie (who trotted a mile in 2:18), Orange Girl 2:20, Gazelle 2:21, Jay Gould 2:21½, and Bella 2:22. Hambletonian 10 was considered the greatest progenitor in American trotting history. (There is an often-reproduced painting of Hambletonian, but it shows such a ridiculously long-bodied and swaybacked animal that the present writer refrains from showing it here!)

Other important families of trotting horses were the Mambrino family, dating from 1844, the Clay family (from 1816), the Pilot family (from 1828), and the Hal family, from Kentucky (or Tennessee?), somewhere about the same time. It is interesting to note that Charles Plumb, in his book, *Types and Breeds of Farm Animals* (1906, p. 39), names the stallion Justin Morgan, foaled in 1789, as the founder of a family of trotters as well as of the Morgan horse breed. Certainly, at 56 inches and 800 pounds, Justin Morgan was of very similar body-build to the typical (larger) trotter or pacer.

The physical characteristics of the Standardbred (light harness trotter and pacer) may be deduced from the following body measurements of six champion trotters and eleven "roadsters." That the latter type was virtually identical with recent trotters is shown by a comparison of the figures in the last two columns.

Table 5. Comparative measurements (in inches) of six champion trotting stallions and the average measurements of eleven Roadsters (10 males, one mare).

Measurement	Directum 4 2:05¼	Cresccus 2:02¼	The Harvester 2:01	Lee Axworthy 1:58¼	Spencer Scott 1:57¼	Grey-hound 1:55¼	Average, 6 Trotters	Average 11 Roadsters (1893)
Height at withers	60.5	64.1	66.0	60.0	63.2	65.3	63.19	62.72
Height at croup	59.0	63.9	64.6	60.0	63.0	63.6	62.35	62.48
Length of body	61.8	63.1	64.0	59.5	63.5	61.2	62.19	63.91
Length of head	27.0	27.0	25.0	22.5	25.0	23.5	25.00	24.86
Length of neck	29.0	30.0	32.0	29.0	30.0	31.0	30.17	34.64 (29.50)
Girth of chest	71.0	70.7	74.0	67.8	71.8	70.5	70.96	70.09
Height of elbow	36.5	36.0	37.0	34.0	37.0	(37.5)	36.34	37.50
Girth of forearm	18.5	21.5	21.0	17.0	20.0	17.8	19.29	20.05
Girth of fore cannon	7.7	8.0	9.0	7.5	7.8	7.5	7.92	7.95
Girth of hind cannon	8.0	9.0	9.5	8.3	8.5	8.1	8.56	8.84
Height of hock	21.5	25.5	24.5	23.3	23.5	23.5	23.62	24.64
Point of hip to hock	37.0	40.5	40.0	37.0	37.5	37.4	38.23	38.50*
Width of shoulders	18.0	16.0	18.0	14.0	14.6	(16.5)	16.19	17.11
Width of hips (croup)	23.0	20.8	22.7	18.5	23.5	18.0	21.08	21.91
Weight, lbs. (est).	1039	1122	1253	936	1120	1100	1092	1118

* This length, when projected to the median plane as in Fig. 101, becomes 37.8 inches.

* The number 10 refers to the horse's number in the Trotting Register.

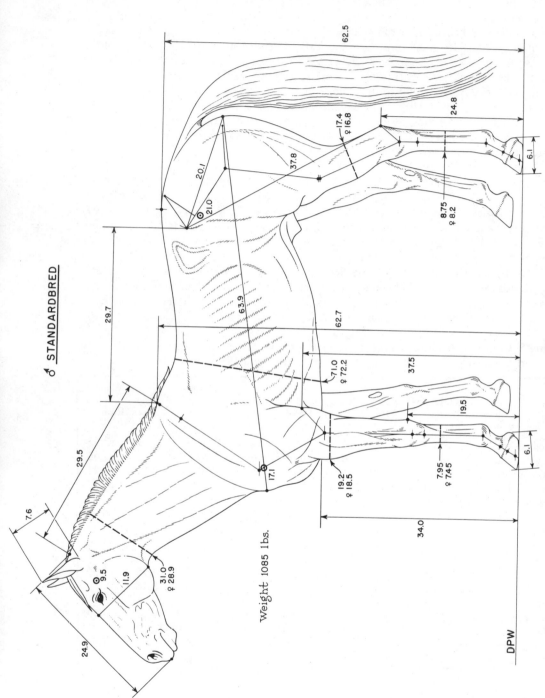

♂ STANDARDBRED

weight 1085 lbs.

Fig. 101 Measurements (in inches) of a typical Standardbred stallion. Wherever two measurements are given for the same part, the lower measurement applies to mares.

In Table 5, measurements of the first five listed trotters are taken from *The Harness Horse for* December 10, 1941, p. 112. Those of Greyhound are from the same periodical for December 14, 1938, p. 127. The average measurements of the eleven "roadsters" are from *The External Conformation of the Horse,* by E. A. A. Grange, 1894 (of horses exhibited in 1893 at the Columbian Exposition, Chicago, and the Michigan State Fair). Allowances must be made for possible faulty measuring (or recording) in the case of such measures as length of body (whether horizontal or slantwise), length of neck, width of shoulders, height of hock, and other parts where the individual recordings show too high a range. For example, the neck length as recorded by Grange is manifestly too large, and suggests that the horses were measured with their heads somewhat lowered and the neck thereby extended. Hence the corrected average neck length listed (under the 34.64 by Grange) as 29.50 inches in the last column of Table 5. The length 29.50 is based on the average length of the neck *vertebrae* in the Standardbred as compared with that in the Arab horse and the Thoroughbred, respectively.

The weights of all the horses listed, with the exception of Grange's "roadsters" in the last column, are estimated from the formula:

$$\text{weight, lbs.} = \frac{\text{chest}^2 + \text{forearm}^2 + \text{fore cannon}^2 + \text{hind cannon}^2}{32.07} \times \text{withers height}$$

This formula, for a Standardbred horse of the measurements shown in Fig. 101, gives a weight of 1085 pounds. Grange's average of 1118 pounds for his eleven roadsters is unduly high by reason of his inclusion of an oversized stallion that stood 68 inches high and weighed 1388 pounds. With this horse deleted from the list, the average weight becomes 1091 pounds.

The Standard Range (1000 cases) of withers height for Standardbred horses is from 59 to 67 inches, and for weight from 900 to 1300 pounds—the latter being the same as for Thoroughbreds.

In earlier days, before automobiles had monopolized transportation, the Standardbred was used to draw light carriages as well as to be raced on the track. It was also used as a saddle horse. Today its use is almost exclusively for professional harness racing. As the financial rewards for winning became even greater, all possible means for increasing the speed of the horses were applied. Although the size of the Standardbred horse has increased on the average very little during the last century, improvements were constantly made in the design of the racing vehicles, or sulkies, in which weight was reduced to a minimum (from 75–100 pounds to about 35 pounds in wood, and finally to 28 pounds in tubular aluminum), the wheels changed from four to two, and light, wire-spoked wheels with pneumatic tires made standard equipment. All these mechanical aids, plus greater competition resulting from a larger number of racing horses, gradually lowered the trotting time for the mile from 2:48½ (in 1810) to 1:58½ (in 1903), a reduction of no less than 50 seconds, or about 30 percent. But in Thoroughbred racing the reduction in the time during the same period would appear to be even greater, from about 2:27 in 1810 to 1:37.4 in 1903, a reduction of 49.6 seconds, or 33.8 percent. However, further lowering of the mile record during the last 60 or 70 years both by Thoroughbreds and by harness horses has taken place at a markedly slower rate, indicating that a potential maximum speed in both types of racehorse is being neared. A further discussion of racing speeds is made in Chapter 11.

Compared with its chief constituent, the Thoroughbred (see Figs. 96 and 101, and Table 13), the Standardbred is seen to be about the same in weight, about an

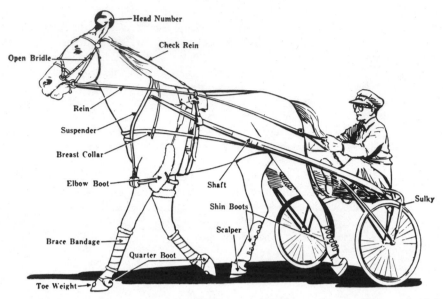

Fig. 102 (Above). Harness and rigging for a trotter: a *diagonally gaited horse* that moves with a high-stepping, straight-ahead gait, with left front and right hind legs moving forward in unison, and vice versa.

Fig. 103 (Below). Harness and rigging for a pacer: a *laterally gaited horse* that moves with a swaying motion, swinging the right front and right hind legs forward at the same time, etc. Details of the *shoeing* of the two types of horses varies in accordance with the gaits.

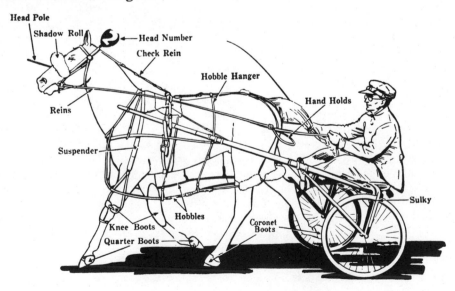

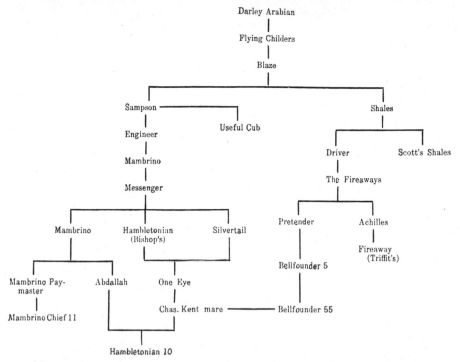

Darley Arabian
|
Flying Childers
|
Blaze

Sampson — Useful Cub

Shales

Engineer

Driver — Scott's Shales

Mambrino

The Fireaways

Messenger

Mambrino   Hambletonian   Silvertail
            (Bishop's)

Pretender   Achilles

Mambrino Pay-   Abdallah   One Eye
master

Bellfounder 5   Fireaway
                 (Triffit's)

Mambrino Chief 11

Chas. Kent mare — Bellfounder 55

Hambletonian 10

Fig. 104 Descent of Hambletonian 10 from the Darley Arabian, *et al.* Hambletonian 10 was the founder of the famous Hambletonian family of American trotters and pacers.

inch less in height, longer-bodied relative to height, shorter-necked, slightly larger in head size and relative shoulder width, and practically identical in the lengths and girths of the limbs and the girths of the neck and body relative to withers height. It is often stated that the head of the Standardbred is less "refined" than that of the Thoroughbred; but this is another of those subjective generalizations that is certainly contradicted by many an individual trotter or pacer. In coloration, the Standardbred is essentially the same as the Thoroughbred; that is, generally bay, brown, chestnut, or black. Grey, roan, and dun, however, are occasionally to be seen.

Whether a Standardbred foal becomes a trotter or a pacer is determined by its training. The gait is regulated by the manner in which the legs are hobbled and induced to work. It has been found also that lightweight shoes encourage a horse to pace, as does also even the shifting of the bit.

Before leaving the subject of light harness horses, a few words may be said about the Orloff trotter, a Russian breed of racehorse, which is slightly smaller but otherwise very similar to the American Standardbred.

d. The Orloff, or Russian Trotter.

This popular Russian horse takes its name from Count Alexius Grigorievich Orloff (1737–1808), who evolved the breed, beginning in 1780, by crossing Thoroughbred, Arab, Dutch, Danish, and Mecklenburg horses. The first sire was an Arabian stallion named Smetanka, which Orloff—as an emissary of Catherine II of Russia to Constantinople—obtained from the Sultan of Turkey in 1780. Smetanka was described as . . . an animal of superior breeding and unusual size and strength." This Arab horse was bred to a Danish mare, and produced a male foal which was named Polkan 1. In turn, the latter horse, bred to a Danish mare named Hartsdraver, sired a male foal named Bars 1, which was regarded as the first representative of the true Orloff breed of trotters.

Trotting has long been a popular sport in Russia, and the Orloff breed was developed primarily for that purpose. It is used also as a carriage horse, and in its earlier form was also a saddle horse. Today there are two types of the Orloff: one a heavy type, which is generally black; and the other a more slender variety, usually grey, possessing certain Arab features. It is the latter type that is used for racing. However, the fastest listed time for the mile by an Orloff trotter is 2:06, which was accomplished in the United States as long ago as 1892, and which is a long way behind the present American trotting record of 1:54.8. Even in proportion to its smaller size the Orloff should go faster than it does, which indicates that it is subject to considerable improvement in speed.

In the *Cyclopedia of American Agriculture,* 1908, Vol. 3, p. 474, C. S. Plumb states that in the Orloff "A well-accepted height is sixteen hands, with a weight of 1100 to 1300 pounds." Evidently Plumb is referring to the larger, more draft-like type of Orloff. In contrast, the average sizes of 261 stallions and 192 mares of the Orloff trotter, as recorded by S. Afanasieff in 1930,[12] are as follows (the measurements being converted from millimeters to inches):

Table 6. Measurements (in inches) of Orloff trotters.

	Stallions	Mares
Height at withers	62.1	61.8
Height at croup	61.4	61.5
Length of head	23.1	23.2
Width of shoulders	16.1	15.7
Width of croup	20.3	21.2
Length of croup	21.1	21.3
Girth of chest	68.1	68.9
Height of elbow	37.9	37.6
Height of hock	23.6	23.3
Girth of cannon (fore)	7.64	7.48
Weight, pounds	958	958

Fig. 106 Billy Direct, 1:55, holder from 1938 to 1969 of the world record for pacing a mile, with his driver, V. Fleming. In a comparison of the records at various distances, the pace is seen generally to be faster than the trot, though only to a very slight degree. The reason for this is said to be that in pacing the feet of the horse are brought down more in a line, causing less lateral movement of the limbs and body.

From the table it will be seen that the Orloff trotter, as compared with the American Standardbred, is (1) about an inch less in withers height, (2) relatively smaller in head length, (3) relatively about the same in shoulder width and croup width, (4) relatively smaller in chest girth, (5) relatively smaller in cannon girth, and (6) possibly longer limbed; all in all, a slightly smaller and somewhat slenderer model of the American Standardbred horse, with relatively longer legs.

The color of the Orloff is most often grey, white, or black, although chestnut and bay occur.

While the Orloff is not so fast a trotter as the American Standardbred over short distances, it is said that on long stretches of several miles or more he is the faster, stronger, and more enduring animal.

Crosses have been made between the Orloff and the American trotter; but today the purebred Orloff is the preferred breed in Russia, and it is not seen to any great extent outside that country. It is said that in pre-Revolutionary Russia there were no fewer than 3000 stud farms devoted to the breeding of the Orloff trotters; but it is not possible to say how many of these breeding establishments still exist.

Fig. 105 The "mechanism" of a harness horse on the track is shown to good advantage in this action photograph of Watson Hanover, 2:02 3/4, of the famous family of trotting horses of the Hanover, Pa., Shoe Farms. Details of interest are the "knee boots" on the front legs and the "strikes" on the hind hoofs. These are for protecting the legs and hoofs from injury in case, during the fast action, one limb should strike another. Shown, too, is the position of the driver in his racing-sulky, close-up behind the horse. Harness racing, always popular, has during recent years enjoyed ever-increasing patronage in America. The driver here is Harry Pownall.

Fig. 107 (Above). Greyhound, at the age of 13 years, with "Doc" Flannery driving. This greatest of all trotters, in 1938, at the age of 6 years, set a record for the mile of 1:55 1/4, which stood for 28 years. Exceptionally tall for a trotter, Greyhound was 65 1/4 inches in withers height.

Fig. 108 (Below). On September 27, 1940, Greyhound trotted a mile under saddle, carrying Mrs. James B. Johnson, in 2:01 3/4, a record which still stands. Greyhound is shown being paced by his regular driver and trainer, Sep Palin, who is driving Dad's Choice, a Thoroughbred.

e. The Morgan Horse.

This breed may be regarded as a smaller model of the Standardbred, perhaps even a replica of what the Standardbred was in the early days of its development. The Morgan horse evolved virtually from a single progenitor, a prepotent bay stallion with black points named Justin Morgan. This name was given the horse later to commemorate his second owner, a man who had acquired him as a two-year-old in partial payment of a debt. The horse, Justin Morgan, was foaled in 1789* in West Springfield, Massachusetts. His owner, Morgan, broke the colt to harness, took him to Vermont, and rented him to a neighbor named Robert Evans, who soon discovered to his surprise that the horse, small as he was, could out-pull, out-run, and out-work any of the other horses of the area.

When Morgan, the man, died, his horse, which had by then attained his full size of 56 inches and 800 pounds—really only that of a large pony—was sold to pay creditors. Because of the horse's remarkable stamina and speed, neighboring farmers brought their mares to him. The foals were predominantly like their sire, and like him possessed more all-around ability and usefulness than the offspring of other horses. Thus was the Morgan breed started. Justin, the founding sire, died from an injury at the age of 32, in 1821.

One of the greatest of Justin's sons was Sherman, foaled in 1808. From Sherman came Black Hawk (foaled in 1833—note the time between generations), who became a celebrated sire of American trotters. One of Black Hawk's innumerable offspring was Ethan Allen, foaled in 1849, who in 1853 made a world's trotting record (mile) of 2:25½—the first time 2:30 was beaten—and was the winner of 33 out of 55 races.

While eventually the Hambletonian became the most famous family of American trotters, fanciers of the Morgan breed point out that Justin Morgan antedated the horse Hambletonian by 60 years, and that George Wilkes, who headed the greatest Hambletonian line, had for his dam Dolly Spanker, an accredited Morgan mare. It is believed also that Morgan blood entered into the constitutions of such record-making trotters as Uhlan, Lee Axworthy, The Harvester, and Hamburg Belle. The Morgan is one of the oldest of American breeds, and is regarded by those who sponsor it as an ideal all-around light horse. In the west its main use is as a stock horse; in the central states, as an all-purpose breed; and in the east chiefly as a saddle horse.

While the ancestry of Justin Morgan is unknown, it is generally accepted that his all-around excellence and great prepotency could have come only from Thoroughbred or Arab (possibly Barb) forebears.

If Justin Morgan represented his immediate offspring in the matter of size, then during the last 150 years the breed has increased in height from 56 to about 61 inches, and in weight from 800 to about 1000 pounds. Thus the *build* of the breed has remained about the same. Figures obtained by the writer in 1948 from W. M. Dawson of the Bureau of Animal Industry (Washington, D.C.) showed eight three-year-old Morgan stallions to average 59.86 inches in height. Their weights were not given. Ten three-year-old Morgan mares averaged 59.72 inches in height and 930 pounds in weight. Since normally a horse gains about 1½ percent in height from three to five years of

---

* The name Justin Morgan was given to the horse after his owner of the same name had died. During the period that Morgan had owned the horse, he was known as "Figure." While some researchers give the year of the horse's birth as 1793, that given here (1789) is the year accepted by the Morgan Horse Club.

Fig. 109 Statue presented in 1921 by the Morgan Horse Club to the U.S. Department of Agriculture, in memory of Justin Morgan, the founder of the Morgan breed, who died in 1821. The sculptor of the statue was F. G. R. Roth of Englewood, New Jersey.

Fig. 110 Justin Morgan, as interpreted by the eminent American painter of horses, George Ford Morris.

age, this would indicate an average height at five years of 60.8 inches for stallions and 60.2 inches for mares. The corresponding average weight would be about 1010 pounds in each sex. The Standard Range in height would be from 57 to 65 inches, and in weight from 820 to 1240 pounds. Thus the Morgan horse averages an inch or so taller than the Arab, and close to a hundred pounds heavier. While no illustrations from life of Justin Morgan appear available, Figs. 109 and 110 are representations of him as interpreted by a capable sculptor and a well-known painter of horses, respectively.

And although it may be without significance here, the name "Morgan" is ancient Welsh, in which language it meant "sea dweller."

Fig. 111 Ethan Allen, the first trotter to cover a mile under 2:30. He did 2:25 1/2 in 1853. He was regarded as a perfect representative of the Morgan breed.

f. The Quarter Horse.

In this sturdy breed we encounter one of the heaviest-built of the so-called Light (or "warmblood") horses—a breed whose body-build places it about halfway between the Thoroughbred and the heaviest-built of draft horses. To draw a human analogy, the Quarter Horse is comparable to a strongly-built sprinter standing between a slender distance runner and a powerfully-muscled shot-putter or weightlifter. Each type of horse, or human athlete, is developed in conformity with the tasks that his muscles are called upon to perform.

The Quarter Horse was originally (in the seventeenth century) called the American Quarter Running Horse, and it is the earliest distinct type developed in the United States. It originated in Virginia in 1611 with the importation of 17 native English stallions and mares. These English horses were not Thoroughbreds, since at that early date not even the foundation sires of the latter breed had been brought into England. The 17 horses (one author refers to them as having been Irish hobbies and Scotch Galloways) imported into the American Colonies were crossed with horses of Spanish-Barb (Andalusia) origin, and from these crossings came a new type of horse that was unsurpassed for quickness, agility, and running speed over short distances. By 1656, horse racing was popular in Virginia, and by 1665 the American Quarter Running Horse was recognized throughout the Colonies as a superior type of short-distance racer. In addition to being used for racing, which took place on weekends and holidays, the horse was found also to be a good general animal for working around the farm and rounding up cattle. His speed, energy, and versatility made him a perfect cow horse. As the saying went, "He can turn on a dime, and toss you back nine cent's change." So, in due course, the Quarter Horse came to be recognized as an ideal breed for ranch work, rodeo performing, and short-distance racing.

Fig. 112 Conformation photo of a one-time world's champion Quarter horse, Paul A. P-19794. Owned by R. Q. Sutherland of the R. S. Bar Ranch, Kansas City, Missouri.

The Quarter Horse played a part in the development of the American Thorough-bred, which breed was established some 160 years later after the Quarter Horse had become a recognized breed. Some, however, say that the Quarter Horse, while a distinct *type* since the seventeenth century, became recognized as a *breed* only upon the founding of the American Quarter Horse Association, which occurred on March 15, 1940, at Fort Worth, Texas. Credence is given the latter statement by the fact that neither Ridgeway (1905), Plumb (1906), the *Cyclopedia of American Agriculture* (1908), nor various other comprehensive sources in the early 1900s even mention the Quarter Horse.

Concerning the Quarter Horse's prime point of excellence, namely his speed in covering a quarter-mile (440 yards), it should be noted that his superiority in this respect is due mainly to his speed in *starting,* and that once under way, the fastest Quarter Horse is no faster than the fastest Thoroughbred racehorse. Hence the respective records of Big Racket, a Thoroughbred mare who covered a quarter-mile in 20⅘ seconds, and Woven Web, a Quarter Horse mare who did the same distance in 22 seconds flat, are about equal in merit, since Quarter Horse races are from a *standing start* and Thoroughbred races from a *running start* (the start being from 20 to 60 feet, and usually averaging about 45 feet). (See Chapter 11 item f).

The Quarter Horse has been described qualitatively thus: "small alert ears, short head, big jaws, well-developed neck, deep sloping shoulder, great heart girth, short back and full loin, low flank, heavily-muscled thighs and forearms, short cannons and moderate (?) pasterns, heavily-muscled quarters and hind legs."[13] But most of these specifications, especially those having to do with girth in relation to height, can be deduced from the general sturdy build (weight/height cubed) of Quarter horses as indicated in the following list.

Table 7. Heights and weights of some well-known Quarter Horses.

Stallions —	Height, in.	Weight, lbs.	Body Build
Colonel Clyde	59.75	1050	0.966
Black Wolf	58.5	1050	1.018
Peppy	61	1200	1.026
Steeldust's Cowboy	56	925	1.042
Buckskin Joe	57.75	1065	1.073
Joe Reed II	61.25	1280	1.081
Bert	59	1150	1.086
Leo	58	1100	1.094
Hard Twist	58	1100	1.094
Dee Dee	59	1165	1.101
Silver King	60	1240	1.114
Little Joe, Jr.	58	1150	1.144
Harmon Baker Star	59.5	1250	1.152
Joe Hancock's Steeldust	59	1260	1.191
Oklahoma Star	58	1200	1.194
Hobo	58	1245	1.238
Dan Waggoner	58	1300	1.293
Average (17)	58.75	1160	1.110
Mares			
Salty	58	1000	0.995
Gray Annie	57	1000	1.048
Lady Coolidge	57	1100	1.152
Jane Hunt	57	1175	1.231
Average (4)	57.25	1069	1.104

If, to the above 17 stallions, Cunningham and Fowler's[14] series of thirteen 5-year-olds is added, the 30 stallions average 59.3 inches in height and 1178 pounds in weight. The same two author's sixty 5-year-old mares average 58.5 inches and 1172 pounds, respectively. The body-build of the two sexes combined is about 1.110,* which as before mentioned above indicates a build about midway between the Thoroughbred (0.831) and the heaviest-built of draft horses (e.g., Percheron champions, with 1.403; see Table 12). The body-build, as expressed in the average of 1.110 for Quarter Horses, indicates that in this breed the various girth measurements and widths are, on the average, *11 percent larger than those of horses of medium body-build at the same withers height.*

The Standard Range in height in the Quarter Horse is from 55 to 63 inches, and in weight from 940 to 1440 pounds. As will be seen from Table 7, however, the usual range in height is from 57 to 61 inches and in weight from 1000 to about 1300 pounds. Some average measurements of 13 five-year-old Quarter Horse stallions and 60 five-year old mares, as taken by Cunningham and Fowler (1961), are given in Table 8, following.

Table 8. Average measurements (in inches) of Quarter Horse stallions and mares at 5 years of age.

	Stallions	Mares
Height at withers	60.0	58.5
Length of body	61.9	61.8
Length of head (not total)	23.2	23.3
Length of neck	29.2	28.3
Girth of chest	73.0	72.3
Height of elbow	35.8	34.8
Height of hock	23.3	22.5
Girth of cannon (fore)	7.9	7.4
Weight, lbs.	1201	1172

Considerably more measurements were recorded by Cunningham and Fowler than are quoted in the foregoing table, but since the measurements they chose and the techniques they used are not directly comparable with those adopted here, the other measurements are not included in Table 8. Also in their study, Cunningham and Fowler present measurements of Quarter Horses at birth, 3 months, 6 months, 12 months, 18 months, and 2, 3, and 4 years, in addition to the adult age of 5 years. The *rate* of growth in these horses appears to be about the same as that in other breeds.

The most common colors in the Quarter Horse are chestnut, sorrel, bay, and dun; but also may be palomino, black, brown, roan, or copper-colored.

Fig. 113 shows the main lines of descent of many noteworthy Quarter Horses. Note that Bob Wade, for many years the holder of the quarter-mile running record (21¼ seconds), was sired by Roan Dick by Black Nick by Stewart's Telegraph. The latter horse is said to have been "straight Morgan."

---

* The body-build as used herein is derived from the author's formula:

$$\text{Build} = \text{weight, lbs.}/\text{height, in.}^3 \times 194.1$$

The latter multiplier yields a figure of approximately 1.000 for the average of *all* breeds of the domestic horse (see also Table 12).

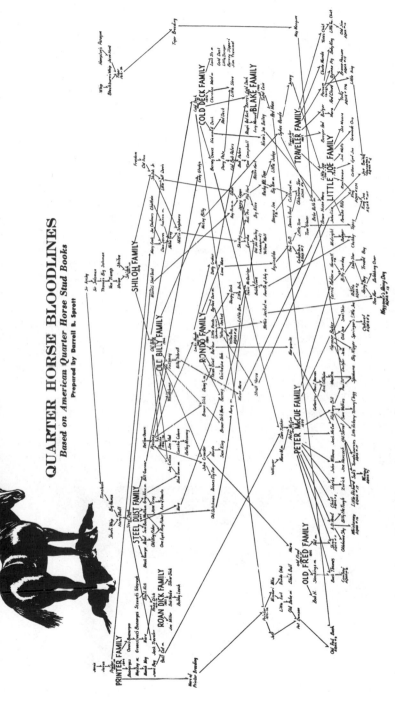

Fig. 113 This chart is reproduced here in order to show how complicated the pedigree of a horse may be! Note that there are 12 main families represented, to one or more of which all existing Quarter horses trace their descent. The chart was designed by Darrel B. Sprott (who does not claim it to be complete) and appeared in *The Cattleman* (Fort Worth, Texas) 33, no. 4 (September 1946); 129.

Writing in 1961, Cunningham and Fowler remark: "Probably no breed of animal has gained such widespread popularity in so short a period of time as the American Quarter Horse. In the short period of twenty years, the Quarter Horse, as a breed, has developed to the point where, today, its registry is growing more than three times as fast as any other horse breed registry in the world." At the end of 1970, 704,159 had been registered, 16,510 of which were in 42 foreign countries.

g. The Criollo Horse.

The Criollo may be regarded, both in physique and utility, as the South American counterpart of the Quarter horse or cow-pony. Accordingly, since we have noted that the Quarter horse is one of the heaviest-built Light horses, it follows that the Criollo horse may be looked upon likewise. While the Criollo is somewhat smaller both in height and girth than the Quarter Horse, its body *proportions* are remarkably similar to those of the latter breed, giving it in consequence about the same body *build*. The ratio of chest girth to withers height, for example, is practically identical in the two breeds. With such similarity in body conformation, the inference to be drawn is that the Criollo, in general, must possess about the same abilities and potentialities as the Quarter horse. While the Criollo is not so renowned for its speed as the Quarter horse, it nevertheless stands in high favor among the *gauchos,* who use the animal in every possible way as an indispensable companion and worker.

Concerning Argentine horses in general, Dr. Emilio Solanet, an authority on the Criollo, points out that in 1942 there were 6,756,534 horses registered in that country, and that in 1930 a census had showed no fewer than 9,858,111 animals.[15] So probably even today, the Republic of Argentina has more horses in ratio to its human population (*c.* 22,000,000 in 1964) than any other horse-producing country—at least one horse to every three persons! And among the total horse population in Argentina, where some twenty breeds or types are represented, the Criollo is the only native breed.

According to Roberto C. Dowdall (1945), the Criollo traces its origin to the Celtic and Solutréan ponies of ancient Spain, and to horses introduced into Spain by the Mussulmans and Goths, respectively. Dowdall considers that any Arab influence

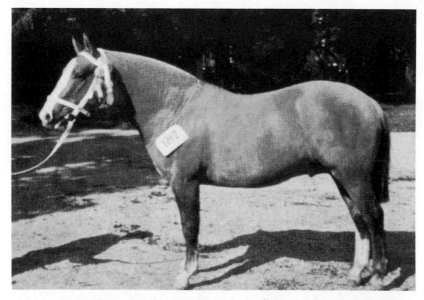

Fig. 114 Typical Criollo conformation and marking is shown here by champion stallion "Coriaci," winner at the Exposition of Palermo in 1945.

in the ancestry of the Criollo is negligible.[16] At least, one rarely sees a "dished" facial profile in the Criollo, whose tendency in this respect is toward either a straight or a slightly *convex* profile.

The typical coloration of the Criollo is dun (grey, yellow, or reddish*), with a chestnut mane, a dark, narrow mid-dorsal stripe, and frequently a white blaze. White feet or stockings, especially on the hind legs, also are common.

Some body measurements of 79 Criollo stallions and 16 mares recorded at the Exposition of Palermo in 1946 are as follows.[17]

Table 9. Measurements (converted from meters to inches) in 95 purebred Criollo stallions and mares. Both averages and ranges are given.

	Stallions		Mares	
Height at withers	56.85	(55.1–59.8)	56.26	(55.1–57.7)
Girth of chest	68.90	(63.8–74.0)	69.41	(66.9–72.4)
Girth of cannon (fore)	7.56	(6.9–8.1)	7.16	(6.9–7.5)

Fig. 115 Head of a Criollo horse, showing characteristic facial profile.

The body weight indicated by the height and girth measurements of the Criollo horse is, on the average, about 1014 pounds in stallions and 1040 pounds in mares. These figures give the Criollo an average body build of 1.102—a build practically identical to that in the Quarter Horse. The Standard Range of the Criollo in height is from 53 to 61 inches, and in weight from about 820 to 1280 pounds.

The physical powers of the Criollo are on a par with its robust build. One of the most famous of all long-distance horseback rides was that made by Aime Tschiffely, who, during the years 1925 to 1928, using two native Argentine horses named "Mancha" and "Gato," rode 13,350 miles from Buenos Aires to New York, over mountains (the highest being 19,250 feet!) and deserts, jungles and city streets, through every conceivable kind of weather. Tschiffely and both his horses, nevertheless, com-

---

* A buckskin hue called *gateado* is said to be the preferred color.

Fig. 116 A Criollo cow-pony is tough as his *gaucho* rider.

pleted the trip in good condition.[18] On each day's ride they had averaged 26½ miles.

A popular polo pony in South America is the Anglo-Argentine, produced by crossing Criollos and Thoroughbreds.

h. The Lipizzan Horse.

The Lipizzan* (German: Lipizzaner) may be described summarily as a beautiful, "white" horse of Austrian origin, specially trained or "schooled" to perform spectacular leaps and other exhibition maneuvers in response to subtle cues from its rider.

There are several theories about the origin of the Lipizzan. In one account the breed is said to have descended from three Andalusian (Spanish-Barb) stallions and 24 mares imported from the court of Spain and crossed with horses from Denmark, Polesina, Lombardy, Naples, and native Karst (Yugoslav) stock.[19] A second attribution of the breed is, ". . . a cross between the Kladruber and a small Italian horse of northern Italy—especially near Trieste and in Gorizia—with a later admixture of Arab blood."[20] William Ridgeway, in his scholarly discussion of horses of all breeds, says the Lipizzan is "chiefly of Eastern origin," crossed with English half-bred horses.[21] The consensus of opinion would seem to be that the Lipizzan is a descendant of the no-longer-bred Bohemian Kladruber horse, which in turn was developed in late Renaissance times "by crossing Spanish and Eastern stallions with the heavy native horse of the Alps."[22]

The first stud farm for breeding Lipizzan horses was founded in Lipizza (or Lippiza) in 1580 (some accounts say 1563) by the Archduke Charles. The horses were bred especially for "high school" equitation and for drawing state coaches. Today their use is mainly as performers in the Spanish Riding School at Vienna. About 25 Lipizzans are born each year at the school's study farm in Piber. Only those foals that show special aptitude and temperament are chosen for training at the school in Vienna. The

---

* Also spelled Lippizan from the town of Lippiza, near Trieste, a Yugoslav seaport between Italy and Yugoslavia.

training begins when the horses are about 4 years old, prior to which time all the horses know of discipline is a halter. The first training is limited to about 45 minutes a day so that the horse never leaves the lesson either tired or disappointed. Gradually, the Lipizzan learns the convenional walk, trot, and gallop, then a series of increasingly difficult maneuvers: the *passade* (high-stepping walk), the *piaffe* (stationary trot), the circling *pirouette,* and finally the *levade* (bending back and raising the forelegs), the *courbette* (jumping on the hind legs), the *croupade* (leaving the ground with the legs bent under), and the *capriole* (rising into the air with the hind legs outthrust and the mane and tail flying). The Lipizzans seem instinctively to know all parade maneuvers, which may trace back to the days when their ancestors carried knights and had to dance and dodge in combat.

Fig. 117 **Head of a Lipizzan stallion, by the author.**

While some overenthusiastic writers have described the coloration of the Lipizzan horse as "snow-white," more accurately it is whitish grey, often flecked with tiny black spots (see Fig. 118). The foals are born black, and gradually turn lighter with age. The mane and tail are flowing and luxuriant. The hoofs are dark. Some authors attempt to stress the element of Arab blood in the Lipizzan, but this is not evident in a comparison of measurable physical characteristics in the two breeds.

Christo Madroff,[23] who secured measurements of 138 purebred Arabian horses and 207 Lipizzans respectively, presents average figures for each breed from which the following ratios have been derived (the two sexes being here combined).

	Arabs	Lipizzans
Head length x 100 / Withers height	38.9	42.5
Head width x 100 / Head length	38.4	37.0
Croup height x 100 / Withers height	98.5	99.5
Tail height x 100 / Croup height	96.0	94.8
Trunk length x 100 / Withers height	98.2	100.8

While some of these differences may seem trivial, in a group as markedly homogeneous as that of the horse they may be significant. The ratios show that the Lipizzan horse, compared with the Arab, has (1) a longer, narrower head, (2) a higher croup, (3) a lower-placed tail, and (4) a longer trunk. In addition, one rarely sees a "dished" facial profile in the Lipizzan; on the contrary, owing to its descent from the "ram's-nosed" Kladruber breed, the facial outline has a tendency to be *convex*.

Fig. 118 Pluto XX, a Lipizzan "high school" performing horse of the Spanish Riding School in Vienna. Foaled in 1935, height 61 inches. (There are six main lines, or families, of the Lipizzan breed; Pluto, Neapolitan, Conversano, Maestoso, Favory, and Siglavy, respectively. The breed is kept pure by restricting registration to these six families.)

Fig. 119 A Lipizzan at the Spanish Riding School in Vienna, performing the spectacular *capriole*. A long controlling rein leads from the horse to the dismounted rider.

Some other measurements of Lipizzan horses as given by Madroff (and here converted from millimeters to inches) are listed in the following table.

Table 10. Average measurements of 79 Lipizzan stallions and 128 mares.

	Stallions	Mares
Height at withers	60.08	59.16
Height at croup	59.73	58.96
Length of head	25.42	25.20
Width of head	9.47	9.27
Length of trunk (horiz.)*	60.31	59.94
Width of shoulders	16.04	15.67
Length of croup	20.48	20.04
Width of croup	18.94	19.58
Girth of cannon (fore)	8.04	7.65
Weight, lbs.	1102	1015

* The length of a horse's trunk when taken *slantwise* (as by the writer) from front of shoulder to point of buttock, is, on the average, 1.0134 x the length taken horizontally (as by Madroff). Measured slantwise, Madroff's stallions would have a trunk length of about 61.1 inches, and his mares, 60.7 inches.

The Standard Range in height of Lipizzan horses is from 56 to 64 inches, and in weight from about 840 to 1280 pounds.

A number of Lipizzans were imported by the United States Army in 1946, and since then have been bred in this country to help preserve the breed.

---

i. The Pony Group.

While, as mentioned in Chapter 2, the word "pony" is a rather loose term, it is always applied to horses of 13 hands (52 inches) or less in height, and often to those of 13½ hands (54 inches) and even 14 hands (56 inches). However, when it comes to the polo "pony," which may be anywhere up to 16 hands (64 inches) high, depending upon which *breed* the particular animal represents, it is obvious that the term "pony" is simply a convenient designation rather than a size-classification. Also, the term "cow-pony" is frequently applied to horses used for rounding up cattle, irrespective of such horses' size.

More strictly, the term pony applies to the various recognized breeds of small horses in Europe and the British Isles, none of which, on the average, stands higher than 56 inches.

An ancient, ancestral type of pony is the Celtic, whose essential likeness is pictured in a number of paintings and engravings on the walls of prehistoric caverns in France and Spain (see Fig. 53-c). In turn, the Celtic pony is considered by some authorities to be descended from the European (i.e., South Russian) tarpan. More specifically, it may have come from the prehistoric horse of Solutré (France).

Just as in the case of full-sized horses, much speculation surrounds the question of the origin of the various pony breeds. Even national rivalry is involved; and wherever it can be convincingly argued, modern horses (or ponies) of a particular country will be attributed to an ancestor of the same region. Nevertheless, some agreement occurs where the evidence is sufficient to cause it. Various authorities concur in the opinion that the Celtic pony (or its remote ancestor) gave rise to most of the present-day British breeds of ponies, such as the Irish Connemara, the Welsh mountain pony, the Scottish Highland pony, and the Exmoor, Dartmoor, Fell, Dales, and New Forest breeds, respectively, of English feral ponies. Dr. L. Stejneger[24] (1907) says that the Fjord pony of Norway is mainly of Celtic pony origin (along possibly with some genetic influence from the larger "forest" horse [*Equus caballus robustus*] of central Europe?), and that both these ponies and the South Russian tarpan belong to the same stock.

In size and coloration, the various British and European breeds of ponies on which the writer has found descriptive data are as follows.

Table 11. Shoulder height and typical coloration in various breeds of ponies.

Breed	Locality	Height, in.	Predominating or preferred colors
Shetland	Shetland Islands	39–40	Black, bay, brown chestnut
Exmoor	England	48	Bay, brown, dun (black points)
Dartmoor	England	48	Dark bay, black, brown
Viking	Gotland	48	Black, bay, sorrel, dun
Icelandic	Iceland	51	Grey, dun
New Forest	England	53	(various)
Viatka	Baltic States	54	Bay, grey, roan, mouse-dun
Konik	Poland, Galicia	54	Mouse-grey with dark dorsal stripe
Connemara	Ireland	54	Grey, black, bay, brown, yellow-dun
Welsh mountain	Wales	54	Bay, brown, grey; any color except piebald or skewbald
Fell	England	55	Black, dark brown, dark bay
Dales	England	55	Black, bay, brown, grey
Haflinger	Tyrol	55	Black, dark bay (whitish mane)
Highland (3 types)	Scotland	52–55–58	Black, brown, foxy-brown (silver mane and tail)
Fjord	Norway	56	Cream-dun (dark lower legs and dorsal stripe)
Zemaitukas	Lithuania	56	Dun (light tail and mane)

From the foregoing table it will be seen that ponies in general average about 52 inches in height. While this would be small for a horse, it is probably about two inches greater than the typical height of the horse's prehistoric tarpan-like ancestors. That is to say, ponies of today, especially those that exist in a semi-wild or feral state, are fair representations, so far as size is concerned, of the ancient, wild progenitors of domestic horses generally. Doubtless that is why Heinz Heck, in re-creating the ancestral European tarpan by a process of "back-breeding," selected for his purpose *ponies* rather than horses. He chose in particular ponies of presumed ancient lineage, such as the Scandinavian, Icelandic, Viking (Gotland) and Polish "konik" breeds, respectively. mating mares of these breeds with a Przevalsky stallion (see Chapter 8).

From various data on the measurements of the skeleton in the ancestral Celtic pony, it can be estimated that the average height in life of this breed, or possibly subspecies, is 51.6 inches, and the average bodyweight about 720 pounds. These figures correspond very closely with those of the present-day Icelandic pony. Fortunately, we are able to show a photograph of a Celtic pony, a stallion which lived many years ago in the New York Zoological Park (Fig. 120).

Fig. 120 Celtic pony, an ancient type ancestral to the Shetland, Icelandic, Connemara, Norwegian, and other pony breeds.

Another interesting photograph is Fig. 121, which depicts a Fjord pony in its native western Norway surroundings. Although the photograph was published originally by Richard Lydekker in 1912, it shows that the Fjord breed then was essentially identical to that of the present day.

The great Swedish naturalist Carolus Linnaeus in classifying the domestic horse gave it in 1758 the Latin name *Equus caballus*. However, in doing this he did not designate any particular breed as the *type,* or typical form, of the subspecies. Lydekker therefore proposes the Norwegian Fjord horse, or pony, as the typical representative of Scandinavian horses in particular and of the domestic horse in general.[25] In view of this important circumstance, a few additional particulars about the Fjord pony may be appropriate.

As is listed in Table 11, the Fjord pony has a shoulder (withers) height of 56 inches on the average, is of a cream-dun coloration generally, and has a dark mid-dorsal stripe. This stripe runs from the base of the tail along the back, and through the mane to the forelock. The dark markings on the legs, according to Lydekker, occur on the front surfaces of the limbs and on the fetlocks. Photographs, however, show most ponies of this breed with the pasterns as well as the fetlocks black. The mane, in show specimens at least, is clipped so as to form an arched crest 4 or 5 inches high. Zebra-like markings on the legs sometimes occur. While cream-dun is the typical coat-coloration, bay and brown are also occasionally seen.

The general body-build of the *fjord-hest,* as the pony is called in Norway, is quite sturdy; some specimens resembling miniature draft horses. The weight, however, seems nowhere to be listed. For an average-sized individual 56 inches high a fair estimate would be about 1000 pounds. A larger breed of horse, called the Gudbrandsdal or *doele-hest* ("valley horse"), is found not only in eastern Norway but also in Sweden and Poland. It is markedly different in appearance from the Fjord pony, being black or dark brown in coloration and with its long dark mane left hanging. Both the Fjord and the Gudbrandsdal breeds are used as all-purpose farm horses, mostly for drawing carts rather than for riding.

A small horse, resembling the Fjord pony in Fig. 121, appears on the one-krone coin of Norway.

Referring again to the list of ponies in Table 11, the Connemara appears to be one of the few British breeds for which a series of skull measurements is available. Dr. Robert F. Scharff, in a paper published in 1909,[26] lists the basilar skull length (see Fig. 22) of three stallions and two mares, the average length of which is 457.2 mm (18 inches). This indicates a living head length of about 546 mm (21.5 inches), or almost exactly 40 percent of the average living shoulder height of 54 inches. Such a relatively short head suggests possible derivation from the Arabian horse, as does also the *width* of the head in relation to its length (39.4 percent as compared with 38.4 percent in the Arab). Thus, these skull or head proportions tend to support the opinion of Professor J. C. Ewart that the resemblance of Connemara ponies to "Eastern" horses must be due to an introduction of Arab blood.[27] Dr. Scharff mentions that the Connemara ponies were a recognized breed as early as the year 1296. This negates the opinion held by certain other writers that the breed owes its origin to horses saved from the wreck of the Spanish Armada on the rocky coasts of Scotland and Ireland in 1588.

As to the *coloration* of ponies generally, in most of the British breeds almost any color is permitted, provided it is not piebald (black-and-white) or skewbald (brown-and-white). Since the latter splotchings indicate crossing, evidently they are prohibited in order to preserve purity of breed. It will be noted in Table 11 that white is not listed. However, in some ponies designated as grey the hairs may be almost white; also, one or more white feet may occur in otherwise dark animals. But the predominating or preferred coloration in most breeds is solid black, bay, or brown. A dark mid-dorsal stripe is typically present in the Polish *konik* (a general term, meaning "little horse"), which is one of several characters in this breed and in the Fjord pony indicating descent from the mouse-dun European tarpan, which also had a dark mid-dorsal stripe.

One of the best-documented pony breeds, so far as body measurements are concerned, is the Shetland. The native home of this popular little horse is the rocky, wind-swept islands that lie about 200 miles north of Scotland (of which they constitute a county). The Shetland is the smallest, and probably also the oldest and purest of British breeds, having existed in its present habitat since prehistoric times.

In the United States, during recent years, breeders decided to make the original Shetland pony type lighter and flashier by crossing it with the Hackney pony. Today, in consequence, many of such so-called Shetlands have so much Hackney blood that they are no longer the gentle animals formerly suitable for small children. But the lighter build and varied colors of the American "Shetlands" make them popular and eye-catching in horse shows.

The following measurements and other statistics refer to Shetland ponies of the purebred type still to be found in the British Isles and various European countries.

Table 12. Average measurements (in inches) of purebred Shetland ponies.
(to be compared with the *percentage* measurements in Fig. 241).

	Stallions	Mares
Height at withers	39.84	39.37
Height at croup	40.04	39.74
Length of trunk (slantwise)	43.23	43.23
Length of head	17.65	17.41
Width of forehead	6.85	6.76
Length of ear (on outside)	5.30	5.23
Length of neck	18.37	18.37
Girth of neck (at throat)	22.99	21.42
Girth of chest	49.08	49.29
Width of shoulders	12.47	11.81
Height of chest from ground	20.20	19.96
Height of elbow	23.38	23.15
Height of knee	11.99	11.85
Girth of forearm	12.63	12.13
Length of back	20.16	20.85
Length of croup (projected)	12.63	11.94
Width of croup	14.14	14.37
Length from hip to hock (projected)	24.74	24.62
Girth of gaskin	11.51	11.18
Girth of cannon (fore)	5.30	5.08
Girth of cannon (hind)	5.86	5.59
Height of hock	15.78	15.60
Length of fore hoof (sole)	4.50	4.17
Length of hind hoof (sole)	4.54	4.25
Weight, lbs.	354	354

Fig. 121 Fjord or Western Norwegian pony (after Lydekker, 1912).

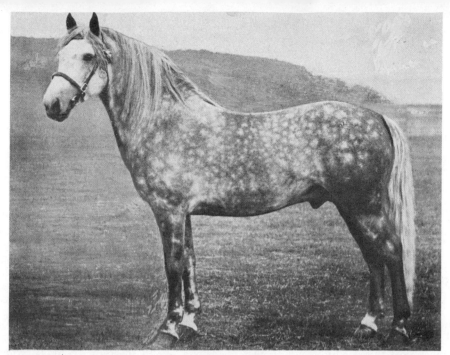

Fig. 122 Highland pony stallion. An example of one of the smaller types of this breed, from the Hebrides or western islands.

The Shetland pony (in Scotland called "Sheltie") is commonly referred to as a "miniature draft horse." So far as its working capacity is concerned, that is one of the things that it is. However, in its physical makeup there are a number of features in which, quite apart from absolute size, the Shetland is either similar to or different from its gigantic relatives. Similarities to the draft horses are its (1) large head, (2) somewhat short neck, (3) long back and trunk, (4) long hip-to-hock distance, (5) low-from-the-ground chest, (6) thick neck, and (7) large chest. In relative forehead width and ear length the Shetland is somewhat larger than the draft horse; however, a *relatively* larger brain, head, eyes, ears, etc. are typical for the smaller representatives of a given type of mammal, including man. In various other features the Shetland is intermediate between the draft type and the typical light-built horse. These features are (see Table 29): relative croup height, elbow height (which is comparable to foreleg length), hock height, shoulder width (closer to draft), croup width, and in the girths of the forearm, gaskin, and cannons, although in the three latter girths it is relatively closer to light-built horses than to the draft type.

The greatest divergence of the Shetland from the draft horse is in the proportioning of its *feet* (cannon-bones, pasterns, and hoofs), which from a geometric standpoint could be said to represent those of a draft horse if this giant equine were reduced to one-fourth or one-fifth of its normal weight. In other words, a quadruped's feet are generally of a size proportionate to the *body weight* of the animal (see Table 36 in the Appendix). Hence the relatively small feet of ponies generally compared with the huge, weight-bearing feet of heavy draft horses.

In view of the Shetland's being bred in some quarters especially for small size, there is a great variation within this breed between the largest and the smallest specimens. The typical shoulder (withers) height may be said to be from 38 to 42 inches. A purebred Shetland, to be registered, must not exceed the latter height. Unfortunately, in the United States there appears to be a large percentage of crossbred

Fig. 123 Head of a typical purebred Shetland pony stallion. A study by the author.

ponies of heights up to 46 inches (and with an unduly high proportion of piebald and skewbald individuals) which are nevertheless referred to as genuine Shetlands. So much does this condition prevail that to many a person the term "pony" is synonymous with Shetland pony. While parti-colors may indeed occur in purebred Shetlands, the basic color is *black,* with variations of bay, brown, sorrel, and dappled grey. In Germany, about one Shetland out of every seven is *white.*

The typical measurements of adult Shetlands given in Table 12 have been derived principally from the data of Dr. J. E. Flade (1959),[28] who gives figures on two groups of Shetlands in Germany: one group of 148 ponies under 120 cm (47¼ inches) high, and another group of 70 ponies under 107.5 cm (42.3 inches) high. The animals in both groups were four years old or older. These measurements by Dr. Flade of living ponies were supplemented here and checked against measurements of 7 skulls and 3 to 5 postcranial skeletons recorded by other investigators.

G. Ullmann (1939)[29] gives the average birthweight of the Shetland as 14.5 kg (32 pounds) for males and 14 kg (31 pounds) for females. The average withers

Fig. 124 A purebred Shetland pony stallion in his rough winter coat. A first-prize winner.

height at birth in both sexes is 625 mm or 24.6 inches, and the average chest girth 540 mm or 21¼ inches. The fore cannon measures a tiny 3.6 inches.

Data are available on a few newborn Shetlands that were even smaller than the foregoing figures. For example, Mr. and Mrs. T. P. Parker, owners of the Royal Crescent Shetland Pony Farm at Arlington, Texas, at one time had a foal named "Tiny Bit" which stood only 18 inches high and weighed only 10 pounds (!) at birth. This foal's dam was only 32 inches high. The smallest adult Shetland of which the writer has record was one that measured only 26 inches in height and weighed about 100 pounds (see, however, Chapter 17). To draw a human analogy, this would be equivalent to a full-grown man who stood only 3 feet 9 inches and weighed 44 pounds—about the size of a normal six-year-old child.

In artificially-inseminated crosses between Shetland ponies and Shire (English draft) horses, the foals of Shire mares were found to weigh about the same as purebred Shire foals. That is, the physique of the mother appeared largely to control the size of the offspring. On the other hand, the foals born to Shetland mares were only about one-third the size of the Shire-mothered foals. Here again was shown the influence of the female parent. The Shetland-mothered foals grew slower than purebred Shire foals, but nevertheless much faster than purebred Shetland foals.

The derivation of the Shetland from the Celtic pony of earlier times is indicated in one respect by the usual absence in both types of the chestnuts on the hind legs. In individual ponies in which these chestnuts are present they are very small. Dr. J. C. Ewart had a Shetland mare in which the right hind chestnut measured only .40 x .16 of an inch, while the left was only .20 inch in diameter. The front ergots (fetlock callosities) were absent, and the hind ones were very small.

While in former years Shetland ponies were widely used in the British Isles as miniature draft horses, today their use in all countries is almost exclusively that of a saddle horse. Nonetheless, this breed of pony, despite its small size, has long been recognized as a remarkably strong weight-carrier.

j. Variation in body-build according to breed.

Before describing the draft horse in detail, it may be well to present in summarized form a list of the typical heights, weights, and body-builds of well-known breeds of horses of all types. This is done in Table 13. In the righthand column, labeled "Reference," the source of the height and weight is given. Some of the sources listed are identified more fully in the lists of references to various chapters given on later pages. However, this should be unnecessary in Table 13, since the heights and weights for most breeds are common knowledge and appear in numerous readily-available books and articles on horses.

As will be seen, there are few substantial differences in body-build between one breed and the next. Rather, domestic horses, like human athletes, present an almost continuous gradation of body-builds, from the slender running type at one end to the massive, weight-moving type at the other. Between these extremes is a long series of intermediate body-builds, each corresponding to the particular muscular and skeletal development required or induced by the form of physical activity engaged in.

The most slender breeds are the light, running horses of predominantly Arabian blood, nos. 1-7 inclusive. The light harness horses closely follow. The Thoroughbred is the lightest-built horse only when he is in "trained-down" racing condition. After a short period at pasture he would weigh anywhere from 40 to 100 pounds more, which would bring his body-build rating up to .830 or even .850. But he would still be typically a light-built horse.

The basis for the body-build ratings here adopted is girth or diameter (width or thickness) in relation to length. This ratio may be derived by relating the body weight to the shoulder (withers) height *cubed*. The formula employed here is:

$$\text{Body-build} = \frac{\text{Weight, lbs.}}{\text{Height, in.}^3} \times 194.1$$

The latter multiplier was derived experimentally by using the figure 1.000 to express the *average* body-build of domestic horses generally. In Table 13, several obviously "overweight" examples among draft horses (nos. 36, 38, and 40) were excluded in averaging the remaining 37 breeds. Had these three repetitious heavyweights been included, the average body-build would be raised from 0.994 to 1.017. Further references to draft horses are made in Chapter 10. As will be noted, no specific breed corresponds in height and weight with the average of all breeds. The closest in this respect would appear to be the Finnish horse (no. 25).

Fig. 125 Half-wild (feral) Hungarian horses during a storm. From an engraving by M. Plinzner.

Table 13. Typical height, weight, and body-build in various breeds of the domestic horse. Sexes are combined. ( ) = estimated measurement

Order of Build	Breed	Height at withers		Body weight		Body build	Reference
		cm.	in.	kg.	lbs.		
1.	Orloff trotter	157.2	61.9	434	958	0.784	S. Afanassieff (1930)
2.	Thoroughbred	161.0	63.4	484	1066	0.812	(various)
3.	Barb (North African)	144.8	57.0	(363)	(800)	(0.838)	(various)
4.	Persian (Arab)	144.8	57.0	(363)	(800)	(0.838)	(various)
5.	Turk (Kurdistan)	144.8	57.0	(363)	(800)	(0.838)	W. Ridgeway (1905) p. 160
6.	Gidran (Anglo-Hungarian)	157.0	61.8	471	1039	0.855	C. Madroff (1936)
7.	Arabian	150.8	59.4	418	922	0.856	C. Madroff (1937)
8.	Morgan	154.2	60.7	458	1010	0.876	W. M. Dawson (1948)
9.	Standardbred	158.9	62.6	507	1118	0.886	E. A. A. Grange (1894)
10.	Hackney horse	160.0	63.0	522	1150	0.893	(various)
11.	Halfbred Arabian	151.6	59.7	445	981	0.897	C. Madroff (1937)
12.	Hackney pony	134.6	53.0	317	700	0.912	(various)
13.	East Prussian (Trakehner)	161.3	63.5	548	1208	0.915	von Nathusius (1891)
14.	Small Nonius (Anglo-Norman)	158.5	62.4	523	1153	0.920	C. Madroff (1936)
15.	"Coach" (light)	162.3	63.9	578	1274	0.948	E. A. A. Grange (1894)
16.	Hanoverian (German)	162.7	64.0	586	1292	0.956	von Nathusius (1891)
17.	Holstein (German)	163.5	64.4	597	1317	0.957	von Nathusius (1891)
18.	Large Nonius (Anglo-Norman)	165.4	65.1	620	1366	0.961	C. Madroff (1936)
19.	Lipizzaner (Austrian)	151.5	59.6	480	1036	0.969	C. Madroff (1935)
20.	Mezohegyes (mares only)	161.2	63.5	583	1286	0.976	K. Gregory (1931)
21.	Cleveland Bay	165.1	65.0	635	1400	0.989	N. C. Nye (1968)
22.	German Coach	161.1	65.0	635	1400	0.989	C. S. Plumb (1906), p. 84
23.	Danish-North Schleswig	162.1	63.8	602	1327	0.991	von Nathusius (1891)
24.	Oldenburg (German)	163.9	64.5	635	1399	1.011	von Nathusius (1891)
25.	Finnish	153.2	60.3	520	1146	1.015	V. Svanberg (1928)
26.	French Coach	162.6	64.0	633	1396	1.033	C. S. Plumb (1906), p. 77
27.	Icelandic pony	129.5	51.0	327	720	1.054	Gov't. Horse Breeding Ad.
28.	"All-purpose"	161.3	63.5	632	1393	1.056	E. A. A. Grange (1894)
29.	Criollo (Argentine)	143.7	56.6	(466)	(1027)	(1.102)	*Raza Criolla*, May 1947
30.	Quarter Horse	149.6	58.9	533	1175	1.110	Cunningham & Fowler (1961)
31.	Shetland pony	101.8	40.1	175	385	1.164	J. E. Flade (1959)
32.	Clydesdale (in 1891)	163.5	64.4	739	1630	1.185	von Nathusius (1891)
33.	East Friesian (Dutch)	161.6	63.6	719	1586	1.197	von Nathusius (1891)
34.	Belgian	161.9	63.7	728	1605	1.203	von Nathusius (1891)
35.	Percheron (typical)	162.3	63.9	736	1623	1.207	(various)
36.	Clydesdale ("standard")	165.1	65.0	794	1750	1.237	Am. Cyclop. Agric. (1908), p. 455
37.	Suffolk	162.6	64.0	771	1700	1.259	M. E. Ensminger (1969), p. 247
38.	Percheron ("standard")	163.9	64.5	794	1750	1.266	C. S. Plumb (1906), p. 102
39.	Shire	167.6	66.0	930	1862	1.281	(various)
40.	Percheron ("champions")	166.9	65.7	930	2051	1.403	1941 International Comp.
	Average, 37 breeds	155.2	61.11	530	1168	0.994	

The familiar terms "warmblood" and "coldblood" are used almost universally by horsemen to indicate relationships to (or derivations from) horses of light build or heavy build, respectively. Yet these terms, which suggest a difference in the *temperature* of the blood, are wholly without basis. There is no more difference in this respect between a Siberian horse and an Indian (or other Oriental) horse than there is between a Siberian tiger and a Bengal tiger. The only difference is in the thickness of the animal's furry covering.

As Table 13 suggests, the classification of horses of differing physiques should be quantitative (i.e., *numerical*) rather than qualitative ("light," "heavy," etc.). Why not use *a scale of body-build* as the basis for classifying the various breeds?

A further indication of the misleading nature of the terms "warmblood" and "coldblood" is illustrated by the Quarter Horse. Here is a breed which stands, in point of body-build, three-quarters of the way between the lightest-built and the heaviest-built horses. From this, should it be inferred that the Quarter Horse is one part "warmblood" and three parts "coldblood"? So far as is known, the amount of "coldblood" in the Quarter Horse—if there be any at all—is negligible. Its somewhat heavy body-build was *bred,* or developed, by the particular *uses* to which the breed was put.

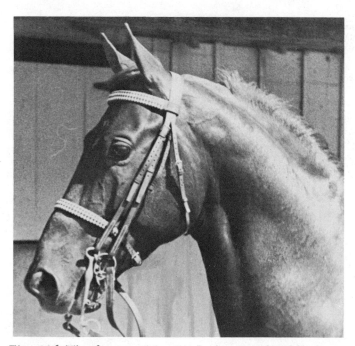

Fig. 126 **The fine, sensitive head of a gaited saddle horse.**

Next to the Quarter Horse (no. 30 in Table 13), and of slightly heavier build, is the Shetland pony. The proportions existing between various bones of the skeleton in the Shetland indicate that this sturdy little animal is about 60 percent light horse and 40 percent draft horse. This again shows the futility of attempting to classify a horse by its breed affinities. In the latter case the Shetland should have a body-build of about .95 or .96, rather than the 1.10 or higher that it actually exhibits. Even some of the heaviest draft breeds, such as the Percheron, may possess a certain amount of Arab

Fig. 127 **Wing Commander (63 in., 1100 lbs.), a one-time World's Grand Champion Five-gaited Saddle Horse. Earl Teator up. It would be difficult to show more spirited picture of a gaited horse in action.**

blood, yet if this fact were not known would anyone deduce from the Percheron's physique that it had an Arabian ancestor? The point of all this is that *measurable classification* of a horse breed by means of its body-build provides a uniform, scientific method, whereas attempted classification by means of the terms "warmblood" and "coldblood" is on a par with astrology or tea-leaf reading.

At this stage too it would seem appropriate to present a table of horse breeds listed according to nation or geographical locality. This is done in Table 14. While in this table a reasonable effort has been made to include all important breeds, doubtless there are many minor breeds, types, or varieties of horses in remote localities which have escaped the writer's research. Nevertheless, it is hoped that this "geographical" list may prove a revelation to readers who had previously thought that practically *all* horses were those found in the United States and Europe! Most of the information in Table 14 is based on a list published by Dr. G. Rau, Dr. Valentin Stang, and others in the German encyclopedia *Tierheilkunde und Tierzucht* (Berlin and Vienna: Urban and Schwarzenberg), 1936, Vol. 8, pp. 19–75. Perhaps the best recent survey is *Horses of the World,* by Daphne Machin Goodall (New York: The Macmillan Co., 1965), in which are listed many types or local varieties as well as generally recognized breeds. Another source of information on over a hundred different breeds of horses is the excellent little volume, *The Observer's Book of Horses and Ponies,* by R. S. Summerhays (London: Frederick Warne & Co., Ltd, 1961). A fourth source is the German book, *Welches Pferd Ist Das?,* by Jasper Nissen (1961).

Table 14. Breeds of races of the domestic horse, listed geographically.

EUROPE

AUSTRIA: Furioso; Gidran; Haflinger (small draft); Lipizzan; Nonius; Noric draft or Pinzgauer; Murinsulaner; Przedswit (semi-draft); Veglia Island pony.

BELGIUM: Belgian draft horses, light and heavy; Ardennais draft; Brabant draft; Gelderland; Flemish.

BULGARIA: Bulgarian farm horse; crosses between Bulgarian horse and Anglo-Arab, Nonius, and Thoroughbred.

CZECHOSLOVAKIA: Light horses in Bohemia: Oldenburg, English half-breds (Furioso, Nonius, and Przedswit), Hannover, East Friesian, Holstein, and Kladrub; in Moravia: Oldenburg, English half-breds (Furioso, Nonius, and Przedswit), Arab half-breds (Shagya, Gidran), Norfolk, American trotter. In Silesia: Arab half-bred and Lipizzan; in Slovakia: English and Arab half-bred and purebred, large Nonius, Lipizzan. In the Carpathians: Huzulen, Lipizzan, and small Arabian. Draft breeds: Belgian, Noric, and Netoliter.

DENMARK: Frederiksborg horse; Jutland draft; Knabstrupper; Lowenberg horse; imported Russian, Icelandic, and other small horses.

ESTONIA: Unveredeltes farm horse; Torgelscher strain; Smudish horse; crosses between farm horse and Ardennais draft; Klepper.

FINLAND: Finnish draft; Finnish horse; crosses between Finnish horse and Norfolk trotter and Gudbrandsdal (Norwegian valley) horse; Klepper.

FRANCE: Anglo-Arab; Anglo-Norman; Arab; Ardennais draft; Picardy; Brabant; Augeron draft or pack horse; Auvergne draft; Belgian; Boulogne draft (both small and large types); Breton draft; (various strains, such as the Norfolk-Breton); Camargue horse; Charolais horse; Comté (or Comtois)* horse; Poitou horse; Corsican pony; Schlettstadt pony (Alsace); Flemish draft; Gascogne moor horse; Limousin horse; Maconnais horse; Nivernais draft; Percheron (both small and large strains); Nivernais (Percheron x "native"); Demi-sang trotter; Noram trotter; Trait du Nord; Poitevine draft.

GERMANY: *Draft breeds:* Noric (Pinzgauer or Upland draft); Oberlander (a lighter form of the Noric breed, from the Austrian Alps); Rhenish-German draft; South German draft; Schleswig draft; Jutland draft. *Lighter breeds:* Hannover; Holstein; East Friesian; East Prussian or Trakehner; Brandenburg; Oldenburg; Freiberger; Württemberg; Pfalz-Zweibrucker; Schlettstadt pony; Westfale; Dülmener pony (feral); Beberbecker. Black Forest draft; Mecklenburg draft.

GOTLAND: Viking or Skogsruss pony.

GREAT BRITAIN AND THE REPUBLIC OF IRELAND: Cleveland Bay; Clydesdale; English Thoroughbred; Hackney horse; Hackney pony; Hunter; Shire; Suffolk; Yorkshire Coach; Irish draft; Connemara (Irish) pony; Dartmoor pony; Exmoor pony; New Forest pony; Fell pony; Dales pony; Shetland pony; Welsh pony; Welsh mountain pony; Polo pony; Scottish Highland pony or Garron (3 types).

GREECE: Greek horse (plains and mountain types); Peneia pony; Pindos pony; Skyros pony; imported horses from Yugoslavia and Hungary.

HOLLAND: Friesian draft; Hackney; Gelderland horse; Groningen; Holland horse; Belgian; Military horse; English Thoroughbred; Drenthe horse; Dutch draft.

HUNGARY AND YUGOSLAVIA: Babolna horse (Arabian purebred and halfbred); Haflinger; Kisberer horse (English halfbred); Gidran; Lipizzan; Mezöhegyes English halfbred (Furioso North-Star); Nonius (large and small types); Tolnatamas horse.

ICELAND: Icelandic pony.

ITALY: Avelignese Italian light horses crossed with Anglo-Arab, Throughbred, Hackney, and Belgian; Norfolk-Breton draft; Haflinger (small draft of the Tyrol); Karster horse; Maremmana (Salerno) horse.

LATVIA: Danish draft; Friesian draft; East Prussian horse.

LITHUANIA: Zemaitukas pony; Pange horse.

NORWAY: Döle trotter; Gudbrandsdal horse; Fjord pony; Northlands pony.

POLAND: Anglo-Arab; "Konik"; Mierzyn; Ardennais draft; Huzulen horse; Masure horse; Beberbeck; also cross-breeds between Arabs, Thoroughbreds, Hannover, Oldenburg, and East Prussian horses; Sok'olsk.

PORTUGAL: Portuguese horse; Portugal horse (Altér and Lusitano breeds); Minho pony.

RUMANIA: Bulgarian or South-Bessarabian horse; German-Bessarabian horse; Huzulen horse; Rumanian farm horse (4 strains); Dobrutscha horse; mountain horse; Moldavian horse; Transylvanian horse ("Seven cities" and Jalomitz strains); also numerous imported breeds.

RUSSIA: (including Asiatic Russia): Amur (Siberian) horse; Viatka pony (two types); Strelets horse; Bachmatten horse; Baschkiren horse; Bitjug (Woronesch) draft; Buratish horse; Jomuden horse; Kabardin (Caucasus) horse; Don (Cossack) horse; Akhal-Tekin (Central Asian desert); Lokai horse (Central Asia); Kazakh (nomad) horse; Orloff trotter; Baluchistan horse; Kalmuck horse; Karabagh horse; Karabair (Uzbekistan); Kirghiz horse; Kokand or Bucharest horse; Kurdish horse; North Russian forest horse; Iomud (north Turkmenia); Dagestan horse; Azerbiajan (Caucasus); Megrel (Caucasus); Shav (Caucasus); East Siberian horse; "Schwarzerdegebiet" horse; Siberian forest horse; Adayev (south Kazakh steppes); Transbaikal (far east, endures 40 degrees below zero); South Russian and Ukrainian steppe horses; Turkoman horse (5 breeds); Central Kazakistan horse; Altai horse; Assinsho-Tschiliker horse; Najman horse; West Siberian horse; and various draft and semi-draft breeds; Toric horse; Lithuanian; Latvian; Kustanair; M'eh's trotter; Vladimir draft.

SERBIA AND CROATIA (Yugoslavia): Bosnian konik; English Thoroughbred and halfbred; Karster horse; Lipizzan; Nonius (large and small strains); Noric draft; Posavina horse; Hungarian horse; also a number of imported breeds.

SPAIN: Andalusian horse; Tarbenian horse; for military use: Arabian, Thoroughbred, and Breton horses. MAJORCA: Majorca pony. POTTOKAK, or pony of the Pyrenees; Sorraia (Garranos); CARTHUSIAN.

SWEDEN: Ardennais draft; Gotland pony; Hannover horse; North Swedish horse; Norwegian horses (Gudbrandsdal and Fjord); East Prussian horse; Gotland (Skogsruss) pony; North Swedish ("coldblood") trotter.

SWITZERLAND: Ardennais draft; Burgdorfer heavy draft; Freiberg horse; Einsiedler; Erlenbuch horse; Laumont horse; Willisburg horse; Irish and Hungarian military horses, plus a number of imported breeds, including the Nivernais (French) draft, Percheron, Holstein, and Shire.

AMERICA

UNITED STATES: four developed breeds: Morgan, Saddlebred, Quarter Horse, and Standardbred. Some would add to these the Mustang, the Chincoteague (Maryland) pony, the Appaloosa, the American Cream Horse, the Colorado Ranger, and the Tennessee Walking Horse. Also numerous imported breeds.

CANADA: French-Canadian cob; Walpole Island pony; also various imported breeds.

MEXICO: Mustang; Galiceño pony; various imported breeds, including Thoroughbreds for racing in Mexico City.

SOUTH AMERICA: Criollo; Mestizo (half-bred); Anglo-Argentine cross-breds; Chilian pony; Peruvian Paso; Morochuco, curly-coated pony; Bagual (feral) horse. Numerous imported breeds, including: Arab, Anglo-Normand, Polo pony, Thoroughbred, Percheron, Clydesdale, Shire, Suffolk, Boulonnais, Hunter, Hackney, Standardbred, Belgian, Norman, Norfolk, Shetland pony, Yorkshire, Ardennais, Orloff trotter, Welsh pony, Breton, Oldenburg, Holstein, and others. Brazil has the Crioulo, Campolino, and Mangalarga breeds.

PUERTO RICO: Paso Fino horse.

AFRICA

ABYSSINIA: Dongala horse; Galla horse (Arab x Barb cross).

ALGERIA: Arabian; Barb; Dongala horse.

CAMEROONS: Fullah horse; Lakka pony.

CENTRAL AFRICA: Togo pony.

CONGO (Zaire): (no domestic horses, because of the tsetse fly).

MADAGASCAR: Madagascar horse; horses from Abyssinia, Algeria, Arabia, and Tarbes (Spain).

MOROCCO: Arabian; Barb; Dongala horse; Libyan Leopard horse; imported Breton, Percheron, and Boulonnaise draft horses.

NILE REGION (upper): Dar-Fur horse; Dongala horse; Kordofan horse.

SENEGAL and GAMBIA: Bagazan or Kinabuta horse; Dongala horse; Arab-Barb crossbreeds.

SOMALILAND: Galla horse; Somali horse.

SOUTH AFRICA: African horse; Cape horse; Basuto pony.

SOUTHWEST AFRICA: Native S.W. African horse; imported East Prussian, Gidran, English Thoroughbred, and other British breeds.

SUDAN: Sudanese horse.

TOGOLAND: (West Africa): Descendants of Barb horses; Togo pony.

TRIPOLITANIA (Libya): Arabian; Barb; cross-breeds from the foregoing.

TUNISIA: Arabian; Barb; Beradin horse; "Bou Chareb"; English Thoroughbred; mountain pony.

ASIA and Pacific Islands (see also RUSSIA)

AFGHANISTAN: Afghan horse; Kabul horse; Kandahar horse.

ARABIA: Arabian horse, with 16 sub-breeds.

CHINA: Manchurian horse; Mongolian horse (various breeds); Chinese Pony.

INDIA: Burma horse; Baluchistan horse; Butea pony; Cozakee horse; Kathiawar horse; Marwari horse; Manipur horse (Assam). Various imported British breeds.

INDOCHINA: Cambodian, Burmese, South-Annam, Tonking and other native horses; various imported breeds.

INDONESIA: Bone horse; Bugine horse; Toorky horse; Macassar horse; Tattoo horse; Mandar horse. *Java:* Java horse; Preanger horse (crossbred from native mares and imported Oriental horses); *Smaller Sunda Islands:* Flores horse; Sandelholz horse; Savol horse; Soembawa-Bima horse; Timor horse. *Sumatra:* Batak pony; Bovenland horse; Sulu horse.

IRAN: Hyksos-Persian horse; Circassian horse; Persian horse; Iranian horse; Persian mountain pony; Darashoori (Shiragi); Turkoman; Tchenarani.

IRAQ: Karabac horse.

JAPAN: Crossbred Anglo-Arabian, Anglo-Norman, Thoroughbred, Gidran, Nonius, and Percheron, plus various native breeds.

PHILIPPINES: Sulu horse (from Sumatra); Philippine pony (various types).

SYRIA: Anaze horse.

TURKEY: Anatolian horse; Arabian; Capadoz horse; Mesopotamian horse; Kurdish horse; Rumelish horse; Tschukur-Owa horse; Usunjaila horse; Turkish pony; Karacabey horse.

AUSTRALIA

Cross-bred Arabian, Indian, and Persian horses; English Thoroughbred; Timor pony; "Waler" (an Anglo-Indian horse bred in New South Wales and exported to India for cavalry service).

As mentioned previously, Table 14 is undoubtedly incomplete. Also, since many of the breeds named were taken from the list compiled by Drs. Rau and Stang in 1936, changes have meanwhile been made in the names of various horse breeds, as well as in the military uses to which horses were put, while perhaps some former breeds no longer exist. It would certainly help matters if some world-traveler (who was also a horseman, or horsewoman) could check on the horse and pony breeds, indigenous and imported, existing today in all the countries where horses are used!

Fig. 128 A stallion of the "leopard-spotted" horse, which lived in Holland in 1743. Spotted horses have been known since the days of the Cro-Magnons, who painted them on the walls of their caves. In England such horses used to be called Chubarries or Blagdons; in France, Tigres; in Denmark, Knabstruppers; in Argentina, Pintados; and by the Nez Percé Indians of Washington, Oregon, and Idaho, Appaloosas.

Fig. 129 Cleveland Bay horse. After an engraving by Carl Gottlob Specht from a drawing by H. Fieg, c. 1875. (The three German brothers—August, Friedrich and Carl Gottlob Specht—were the foremost animal illustrators of that period.)

As to the number of breeds present in the principal horse-using nations at the present time, the USSR clearly heads the list with possibly about 50 different breeds; second is the United Kingdom and the Republic of Ireland, with some 20 breeds; third, Germany, with at least 18 breeds; and fourth, France, with perhaps 16 breeds. The United States has only 4 or 5 recognized breeds, as do a number of other nations. All together, it would appear that there are today at least 180 different breeds of the domestic horse extant.

The four leading horse-breeding nations are (1) the USSR, with 9,400,000 horses in 1962; (2) Brazil, with 8,374,000 horses in 1962; (3) China, with 7,411,000 horses in 1956; and the United States, with 6,675,000 horses in 1968.[30] Then follow, in diminishing order, Mexico, Argentina, Poland, France, India, and Turkey, with horse populations ranging from over 4 million down to perhaps 1½ million. To what extent the number of horses has diminished in foreign countries due to the introduction of mechanized farming equipment is a question. However, in the United States a peak population was reached during World War I, at which time there were approximately 27,000,000 horses and mules in use. This number steadily declined to about 14,000,000 in 1940, and to a "low" of about 3,000,000 in 1949. Since the latter year there has been a gratifying rise in the equine population of the United States, mostly through the increasing use of saddle horses, to an estimated 8,250,000 animals in 1971.

Tables 13, 14, 15, and 16 are appended as convenient reference lists for the general reader. Zoologically there is no point in listing and describing all the races, breeds, or crossbreeds of the domestic horse that have been produced artificially by man. The interest of the zoologist or paleontologist is confined, so far as the domestic horse is concerned, to (1) those wild species or subspecies which have contributed to its origin or descent; (2) the changes in physical structure that have resulted from domestication; and (3) the geographical dispersion and distribution of the horse from the time of its origin in Pleistocene or late Pliocene times to the present day. Table 16 is added also for the reason that many foreign breeds of horses and ponies, some of exceptional interest, are not mentioned in the usual American and British books on horses. This table, though not complete, should serve also to indicate the enormous number of breeds of horses and ponies in use in the world today.

Fig. 130 "German coach horse" was the name given to horses formerly bred in the United States from imported sires of the German types known as Oldenburg, Hanoverian, and East Friesland, respectively. These German coach horses are the heaviest of the so-called light breeds, ranging in weight from 1300 to 1500 pounds. They were developed originally for use as artillery horses. At present they are used in Europe as general-purpose farm and heavy harness horses, but the cross-breeding of them in America has been discontinued.

Table 15. Characteristics of some leading breeds of light horses in the United States.

Breed	Place of origin	Primary uses	Average height, in.	Average weight lbs.	Predominating or preferred coloration
American Saddle Horse	United States: Fayette, Ky.	3- and 5-gaited saddle horses; fine harness horses; pleasure horses	62	1100	bay, brown, grey, chestnut, or black
Appaloosa	United States: by the Nez Perce Indians of Oregon, Washington, and Idaho	stock horses (cow ponies); pleasure horses; parade horses	60	950	usually white over loins and hips, with dark round or oval spots thereon
Arabian[1]	unknown	saddle horses; stock horses	59.4	922	bay, grey, or chestnut, often with white markings on face and legs
Cleveland Bay	England: Cleveland district of Yorkshire	general utility; to crossbreed heavy hunters	65	1400	always solid bay, with black points
Hackney	England: eastern and northeastern counties of Suffolk, York, and Norfolk	heavy harness or carriage horse to crossbreed hunters and jumpers	63	1150	chestnut, bay, or brown; sometimes roan or black; often with white markings
Morgan[2]	United States: West Springfield, Massachusetts	saddle horses; stock horses	60.7	1010	bay, brown, black, or chestnut; white markings rare
Palomino	United States: from horses of Spanish origin	stock horses; parade horses; pleasure horses; saddle horses; fine harness	61	1030	golden, with white, silver, or ivory mane and tail; often white markings on face and feet
Quarter Horse	United States: Virginia	stock horses; racehorses	58.9	1175	chestnut, sorrel, bay or dun; but may also be palomino, black, brown, roan, or copper-colored
Shetland Pony[3]	Shetland Islands (Scotland)	children's mounts; harness show use (American types)	39.8	354	purebred: basically black; American types: all colors, including piebald and skewbald
Standardbred[4]	United States: Colonial States	harness racing: trotting or pacing; harness horses in shows	62.6	1118	bay, brown, chestnut, or black; sometimes grey, roan, or dun
Tennessee Walking Horse	United States: Tennessee (Middle Basin)	plantation walking horses; pleasure horses	62	1100	sorrel, chestnut, black, roan, white, bay, brown, grey, and golden, often with white markings on feet
Thoroughbred[5]	England	racing; riding; stock horses; polo ponies; hunters	63.4	1066	bay, brown, chestnut, or black; sometimes grey
Welsh pony	Wales (mountains)	children's mounts; harness show use	54	730	bay, brown, grey; any color except piebald or skewbald

For a detailed account, see (1) pp. 152-165; (2) pp. 183-185; (3) pp. 199-203; (4) pp. 173-179; (5) pp. 165-173.

Table 16. Brief descriptions of some lesser-known breeds of light horses and ponies in the United States and elsewhere, arranged in alphabetical order.

ACCHETTA: See Sardinian pony.

AMERICAN ALBINO: A breed developed at the White Horse Ranch, Naper, Nebraska. Snow-white hair, pink skin, preferably dark eyes. Height ranges from 32 to 68 inches, thus including both ponies and horses.

AMERICAN BUCKSKIN: Named after its typical coloration. Has a dark, mid-dorsal stripe and sometimes zebra-like stripes on the legs and across the shoulders. Used as a stock horse, for pleasure, or for show purposes.

AMERICAN CREAM: A medium-heavy, cream-colored horse with white mane and tail. The breed is said to have descended from a mare of unknown ancestry in central Iowa in the early 1900s. Like the so-called Albino Horse, the American Cream has pink skin and dark (in this case, amber) eyes. It is used mainly for draft purposes and as a show horse.

AMERICAN GOTLAND PONY: Called also Viking pony. Bred in the United States from ponies imported from the Baltic island of Gotland. Height, 45–51 inches. Color: black, grey, sorrel, or dun. Used for children's mounts and as a pony-sized trotter (racing).

AMERICAN PAINT, or PINTO: A horse of Spanish derivation, colored either piebald or skewbald. Used as a stock horse, riding or racing, and for show purposes (see also Pinto).

AMERICAN SADDLE HORSE (see Table 15).

ANDALUSIAN: An ancient Spanish breed of saddle or harness horse, derived from Barb (Moorish) stock. Said to be the ancestor of such breeds as the Lipizzan, Hanoverian and Trakehner (Germany), Criollo (Argentina), American Quarter Horse, and others. Bred in Spain in the regions of Cordoba, Seville, and Cadiz, and along the Guadalquivir River. Characterized by a convex facial profile ("ram's nose"), sturdy build, and flowing mane and tail. Color: usually black. Height, 58–64 inches. In earlier times there were two types, the light Jennet and the heavier Villanos (the latter bred mainly in Castile).

ANGLO-ARAB: Called also Halfbred Arabian. A light breed of riding horse, used for racing, hunting, etc. Developed in France by crossing Arabs and Thoroughbreds. As shown in Table 12, this cross-breed is only slightly taller and heavier than the purebred Arab, thus indicating the prepotency of the latter breed.

ANGLO-ARGENTINE: A South American cross between the native Criollo cow-pony and the Thoroughbred. Popular as a polo pony.

ANGLO-NORMAN: Any of several breeds or types developed in France by crossing Norman horses with English Thoroughbreds. A cavalry type, no longer bred, was typical of this crossing. A present-day draft type has an admixture of Percheron and Boulonnais (French draft) blood; while an Anglo-Norman trotter, which was evolved between 1834 and 1860, was a cross between Norman horses and Norfolk (English) trotters.

APPALOOSA: See Table 15. A pony-sized breed of the Appaloosa also is recognized.

ARABIAN: See Table 15 and p.152.

ARDENNES (French: ARDENNAIS): A French or Belgian draft breed of two types: one a small (58–61 inch) mountain type, the other a taller, heavier draft type. The breed traces back to the beginning of the Christian era.

BALEARIC: Known also as Majorca pony. An ancient breed found on the island of Majorca. A peculiarity of the Majorca pony is that in galloping it carries its head (lower jaw) in close contact with its neck (rather than stretched out forward as in Algerian and Andalusian horses). For this and other reasons it is believed by some that these ponies may be descendants of the Greek horse of Classic times, which was usually portrayed with its head and neck in the flexed attitude described.

BARB (or BERBER): The typical light riding horse of North Africa, which region was formerly known as the Barbary States. Possibly an admixture of Arab and Moroccan or Algerian blood. About the same size as the Arab, but with a less refined head and a lower-set tail. Color: usually dark bay, brown, chestnut, black, or grey. Several strains of the breed exist in various parts of Africa.

BASUTO PONY: Formerly known also as the Cape horse. A breed developed from the introduction of English horses into South Africa. It was much used during the Boer War, but it is now on the decline as a "pure" breed.

BATAK (or DELI) PONY: A small, Arab-derived pony bred in the Batak hills of Sumatra. The color is generally brown, although skewbald specimens occur. Height: 44–50 inches.

BEBERBECK (German: BEBERBECKER): So-named from its origin in the Beberbeck region of Germany. Derived from English Thoroughbreds crossed with Arabs and with previously bred native (Beberbeck) horses. Now bred also in Poland.

BEETEWK, or BITJUG (or WORENESCH HORSE): A medium-heavy, active, Russian draft breed. Originated in the time of Peter the Great (1672–1725) with the importation of Dutch stallions, which were crossed with native Russian mares. Later, some Orloff trotter blood was added. These powerful horses are among the most favored breeds on Russian farms.

BELGIAN: See Chapter 10.

BHUTIA: See Spiti pony.

BLACK FOREST (German: SCHWARZWÄLDER) DRAFT: A German breed of medium-heavy build, in size about halfway between the Austrian breeds of the Haflinger and the Pinzgauer. Height: 58–62 inches. Color: usually sorrel, with light mane and tail.

BOSNIAN MOUNTAIN HORSE: A strong, hardy and enduring Yugoslavian breed, of pony-size. (52–56 inches). There is some Arabian blood in its makeup.

BOULONNAIS: A strong, fast-moving French draft horse, bred for centuries near Boulogne and adjacent Belgian districts. It resembles the Percheron both in size and coloration. Bred also in Picardy, Artois, Haute Normandy, and in parts of Flanders.

BRABANÇON (or BRABANT): A tall and heavy draft breed used in France, Belgium, and Holland. Bred also in the Gorki province of Russia. Essentially of the same type as the Rheinish-Dutch draft horse.

BRANDENBURG: A German horse of medium-heavy build, resembling generally the Hanoverian.

BRETON: A strong, massive French farm horse of three different types, ranging from light to heavy draft. Height: 59–64 inches. Colors: usually grey or bay.

BURMESE (SHAN) PONY: Bred mainly by the hill-tribes of the Burmese Shan States. Similar to, and possibly a relation of, the Mongolian pony. Characterized by great strength for its size, and a rugged constitution.

CAMARGUE HORSE: An ancient, small horse which originated in southeastern France on the Rhone River delta called Isle of Camargue. Once extensively used throughout France as a small cart horse. Color: usually white or chestnut. Average height: about 54 inches. Regarded by some as descended from the prehistoric horse of Solutré.

CHICKASAW HORSE: A breed of horses developed in the early eighteenth century in South Carolina and Georgia. Named after the Chickasaw Indians—the first Indians with whom the English colonists came in contact. The Chickasaw breed descended from the horses introduced by the Spaniards into Florida, similar to the way in which the Mustang descended from the escaped horses of the Spanish explorers of the western United States. Evidently the Chickasaw was only of pony size, since it is said that few of them were over 13½ hands (54 inches) in height. They were used both for riding and for draft.

CHINCOTEAGUE PONY: A feral breed originating in Colonial days and named after an island of that name lying off the coast of northern Virginia. Presently, the ponies live on a larger island, farther offshore than Chincoteague, named Assateague. The ponies are believed to be of Spanish origin. The original height was about 56 inches and the color was either bay, brown, black, or chestnut. During recent years the Chincoteague stock has been "diluted" by the infusion of Pinto, Shetland, and Welsh pony blood; and this has reduced the height to 48–54 inches. The resulting offspring, when tamed, are said to be gentle animals suitable for children's riding.

CLEVELAND BAY (see Table 15).

CLYDESDALE (see Chapter 10).

COACH HORSE: Before the era of the automobile, several breeds of the so-called Coach horse were developed for drawing vehicles of various types. In an average of five stallions, two geldings, and one mare, listed as "Coach" horses and exhibited at the Columbian Exposition at Chicago in 1893, the height was 63 7/8 inches (62–66) and weight 1274 pounds (1175–1375). See Table 12. Accordingly, these horses were very similar in size to the present-day German breed known as Hanoverian. Presumably the Coach horses at the Columbian Exposition included importations of both the French Coach and the German Coach breeds.

COB: A name applied to various types (not breeds) of riding horses of sturdy build, generally described as being short-legged and of large girth. The Welsh Cob, however, is a definite breed, of two types, used for riding and for draft, respectively.

COLLIER: Sometimes called a Pitter. A small draft type used in West Wales in the coal mines. Has short legs with feathered fetlocks, a wide croup, and great strength and endurance. All colors, but mainly grey or bay. Height: 55–61 inches.

COLORADO RANGER: A spotted breed established in 1938 in Denver, Colorado. The "leopard spotting" consists of small spots of any color on a white, cream, or grey background. In one type the body is dark and the hips or croup white, as in the Appaloosa. The breed is said to have originated in 1894, when two stallions—one a grey Arabian and the other a leopard-spotted Barb—were presented to General U. S. Grant by the Sultan of Turkey. These horses were sent to Beatrice, Nebraska, for stud service. Another leopard-spotted Barb constituted the third foundation sire of the American breed. The Colorado Ranger should not be confused with the Appaloosa, even though some individuals may exhibit similar coloration. The Appaloosa originated in central Asia, and the Colorado Ranger from the leopard-spotted horse of Morocco.

CONESTOGA HORSE: Said to have been the first native American breed of draft horse. It appeared in Pennsylvania sometime between 1700 and 1730. It was used largely for drawing the Conestoga freight wagon, a vehicle which was designed during the same years. While the origin of the Conestoga horse is unknown, it is believed to have been bred from horses of draft type that were imported into New York. Long before 1900, the Conestoga breed had been absorbed and disappeared.

COMTÉ (or COMTOIS): A medium-sized French horse believed to have descended from the old original Ardennes draft breed.

CONNEMARA PONY: Sometimes called Hobbie. The native pony or small horse of Connemara, West Galway, Ireland. An ancient breed, dating back into the thirteenth century or earlier. Used for riding, jumping, and in harness. 51–57 inches. (See also p. 199).

DALES PONY: One of the nine recognized breeds of ponies in the British Isles today. Its native locality is the east valley side of the Pennine Mountain Range in northern England. It is a general-utility small farm horse. Height: 52–58 inches. Colors: black, bay, brown, or grey.

DANISH HORSE: See Frederickberg horse; Jutland horse; Knabstrupper; and Lowenberg horse.

DARTMOOR PONY: A half-wild breed of pony, living on the rugged plains of Dartmoor in the extreme southwest of England. Essentially a riding pony. Height: 45–51 inches. Colors: dark bay, black, or brown; but any color permitted except piebald or skewbald. In some quarters cross-breeding with Shetlands has served to obliterate the purebred Dartmoor pony.

DON HORSE (called also COSSACK HORSE): One of the many breeds or types of small riding horses or ponies ranging over the steppes of Russia and Siberia. The Don (river) horse is probably a cross of Thoroughbred, Arab, and Orloff trotter on native Cossack stock. Colors: usually golden chestnut, or bay. Height: 56–60 inches. A number of types of the Don horse are recognized.

DÜLMENER: A medium-sized, half-wild horse of the North Rhine, Westphalian region of Germany. It is said to have been bred there for over 600 years. It is a mixture of the Welsh mountain pony, Polish konik, Baschkiren (Russian) pony, and Arab. Regarded as the last living race of feral horses in Germany. Height: 52–56 inches.

DUTCH DRAFT: See Friesian draft.

EAST PRUSSIAN HORSE: See Trakehner.

EXMOOR PONY: An English breed, believed to be an indigenous animal descended from the wild horse of Britain of prehistoric times. Like the Dartmoor pony, the Exmoor lives on the high, bleak, sparsely inhabited moors of southwest England, especially in the county of Somerset. Living under inhospitable conditions of climate and limited food supply, the surviving Exmoor ponies have developed great hardiness and stamina. Height: 45–51 inches. Colors: bay, brown, or dun, with black points; no white markings.

FELL PONY: The home of this pony is on the western side of the Pennine Mountain (or hill) Range in northern England, across the ridge from the Dales pony on the eastern side. About the turn of the century these two ponies were considered to be a single breed. The colors of the two are about the same, as are their sizes, although some say that during recent years the Fell pony has become slightly taller and heavier than the Dales pony, the increase in size resulting from the introduction of draft-horse blood. Like the Dales pony, the Fell is, or was, primarily a small, all-purpose horse.

FINNISH HORSE: A breed in Finland described as "a medium-sized work-horse." Height: 57–64 inches. Weight: 1000–1300 pounds. Color: mainly chestnut. The present breed began about the year 1550 from imported Swedish horses, which in turn had come largely from the Friesian (Holland) draft breed. It is said that 200 years ago the Finnish horse was only 52 to 56 inches in height, and that the great increase in size since that time has come from better feeding and living conditions, plus cross-breeding with larger horses.

FJORD (Norwegian) PONY: (described on pp. 198–199).

FLEMISH HORSE: This Belgian breed is considered to stem directly from the "Great Horse," or "black horse of Flanders," which in Medieval times was developed to carry knights clad in heavy armor into battle. The Flemish horse is believed to be closely related to the Friesian (Holland) draft horse. Belgium has always been one of the chief users of heavy horses, and it is said that probably nine out of ten horses there are, or were, of the draft type.

FRENCH DRAFT: See Chapter 10.

FRIESIAN HORSE: A breed of heavy draft horses indigenous to Holland, raised mainly in the province of Friesland. The color is always black, although a small star is sometimes present. In this breed the mane and tail are never trimmed or docked. Another, heavier breed of the same country is called the Dutch draft. Its colors are bay, chestnut, or grey, with black rarely being seen. A third breed is the East Friesian, a tall horse of 68 inches or over.

FURIOSO-NORTH STAR (known also as the MEZÖHEGYES HORSE): A fine Hungarian riding horse, bred from English Thoroughbred stallions crossed with native mares from Hungary, Austria, and South Germany. The Mezöhegyes ranges in height from 60 to 68 inches, and averages in weight about 1290 pounds, thus being practically identical in size with the Hanoverian horse of Germany.

GALICEÑO: A riding pony from Mexico, standing 48–54 inches and weighing 625–700 pounds. Colors: mostly solid; either bay, black, chestnut, buckskin, grey, brown, or palomino. The breed originated in Galicia, a province in northwestern Spain. While ponies of this lineage were brought to America by the conquistadores, it was not until 1958 that they became a recognized breed in the United States.

GARRON: See Highland pony.

GELDERLAND: The name of this breed comes from the Dutch province of Gelderland. The breed originated from the crossing of English Thoroughbreds, Norfolk trotters, Holsteins

(Germany), and Anglo-Normans. The Gelderland is used as a riding horse, a farm horse, or a show horse. Height: 60–66 inches.

GIDRAN: A Hungarian breed developed by crossing native mares with English Thoroughbred and Anglo-Arabian stallions. The breed stems from the chestnut Arabian stallion "Siglavi-Gidran," foaled in 1810. The Gidran is closely associated with the Furioso-North Star or Mezöhegyes horse, and with another Hungarian breed called the Nonius. The Gidran is a handsome saddle horse, standing on the average 61.8 inches and weighing 1039 pounds (see Table 12). Its color is usually chestnut or brown, sometimes accompanied by a light-colored mane and tail.

GOTLAND PONY (called also SKOGRUSS, and VIKING PONY): A small, ancient breed, native to the island of Gotland in the Baltic Sea off the mainland of Sweden. Believed to be directly descended from forest-dwelling ponies that inhabited north-central Europe 10,000 years ago. Height: 45–51 inches. Colors: black, bay, sorrel, or dun. In winter the haircoat grows to about 3 inches long. These ponies are now being bred also in the United States and Alberta, Canada, as well as in Gotland and Sweden.

GRONINGEN: A Dutch farm horse of light draft build. Height: 60–66 inches. Is used also as a carriage horse or heavyweight riding horse.

GUDBRANDSDAL: Known as the Norwegian eastern "valley horse," as distinguished from the Fjord pony of the western coastal region. Whereas the Fjord pony stands only about 56 inches and is of a cream-dun coloration, the Gudbrandsdal is taller, heavier, and dark-colored, with a long, dark mane and tail (the mane not being trimmed short and upright as in the Fjord pony). Both breeds are of ancient origin, probably from the Celtic type that was ancestral to the pony-sized horses of northwestern Europe.

HACK: A British term used in reference to a refined *riding* horse. To be differentiated from Hackney, which refers to a *harness* horse originally known as the Norfolk trotter.

HACKNEY HORSE: (see also Table 14): A popular breed of light carriage horse used both in the British Isles and the United States as a high-stepping, show-ring horse. The breed is said to have originated in Norfolk, England, about 1729, from two stallions—an Arabian and a Yorkshire—bred to Norfolk county mares. The original breed, no longer in existence, was known as the Norfolk Roadster. The height, weight, and body proportions generally of the Hackney horse are essentially the same as those of the Standardbred (see Table 5). The word "hackney" is said to have come from "nag," a nondescript horse, and from the Norman (French) *hacquenée,* which combined the Latin *Equus* and the Anglo-Saxon *knegan* (neigh). See also Chapter 1.

HACKNEY PONY: Essentially a pony-sized derivation of the Hackney horse, having similar gaits, and like the larger horse used today almost exclusively in the show-ring. Height: usually 50–54 inches. Colors: mostly bay, brown, or black, often with white markings on the head and feet.

HAFLINGER: A breed of small but sturdily built horses from the Austrian Tyrol. Used as an all-purpose pony in rugged, mountain country. Height: 53–57 inches. In the 1930s, Arab blood was introduced into the original Haflinger, and since then a new type of the breed, "less peasant and more aristocrat," has been developed. The color is no longer dark bay or black, but more of a palomino—a "golden roan," as one observer put it. The long, flowing mane and tail are of the color of "bleached straw." The high intelligence of the Haflinger, along with its unchanged placid disposition, makes it an ideal circus horse. The breed is popular in Holland, and has more recently been introduced into England and other countries. It is there used both as a draft animal and a riding pony.

HANOVERIAN (German: HANNOVERANER): A well-known German breed evolved largely from English Thoroughbred stock. The inclusion, however, of "native" blood has resulted in a heavier type of horse of about the same height as the Thoroughbred (see Table 12), although the Hanoverian of today may be somewhat larger than at the turn of the century. The Hanoverian is popular in Germany as a hunter and jumper. Colors: bay, brown, chestnut, or black; sometimes grey or white; often with white markings on the head and feet.

HIGHLAND PONY (called also GARRON): Three types, or sizes, of Scottish Highland ponies exist today. The smallest ponies are from the island of Barra and other islands (the Outer Hebrides) lying off the western coast; they stand from 50 to 54 inches. The second type is a riding pony of 53–57 inches; and the largest and strongest ponies are those of the Central Highlands, called "Mainland," standing 56–60 inches. Obviously the latter are small *horses*. Colors: dun, grey, black, or brown; sometimes bay or chestnut. Mane and tail are usually silver. A dark mid-dorsal stripe is often, though not invariably, present. These Highland ponies are believed to have had an infusion of Arab blood.

HOLSTEIN (German: HOLSTEINER): A medium-heavy German breed, suitable either for riding, driving, or as a hunter. The original breed was believed to be of Andalusian origin. From about 1825 on, in a "reorientation" of breeding, there was an introduction of the Yorkshire Coach horse along with some half-bred stallions. This reorientation was said to have improved the breed. As is listed in Table 12, the Holstein horse averages 64.4 inches and 1317 pounds, being slightly larger but of almost identical build to the German Hanoverian breed. Color: usually brown, often with white feet.

HUNGARIAN SHAGYA: A primitive, hardy breed of small horses, believed to have descended from the cross-breeding (in nature) of the South Russian tarpan and Przevalsky's horse. Later on, numerous Turkish invasions of Hungary introduced into the native horses Arab, Persian, and Turkish blood. The foundation sire of the present-day breed was an Arab stallion named "Shagya," from which the breed is named.

HUNTER: This type, not breed, of horse is classified according to the weight of the rider. British standards define a *lightweight* Hunter as one which is expected to carry a rider weighing under 182 pounds; a *middleweight* Hunter, from 182 to 205 pounds; and a *heavyweight* Hunter, over 205 pounds. The height of a Hunter is usually from 63 to 66 inches. The weight generally ranges from about 1100 pounds for lightweight Hunters to 1300 pounds for heavyweights. Hunters are derived mainly from Thoroughbreds, often crossed either with American Saddle, Standardbred, Hackney, or Cleveland Bay horses, depending upon which weight-class of Hunter is desired. Sometimes even draft blood is used if a particularly heavy Hunter is wanted.

HUZULEN: A mountain pony native to Rumania, but used also in Poland and perhaps other European countries. Height: 53–57 inches. Colors: black, dark brown, or dark bay, sometimes with white markings on the head and feet. Like many another pony breed, the Huzulen has Arab blood in its makeup.

ICELANDIC PONY: Believed to have lived on the island of Iceland since Norsemen arrived in the year 874 to settle there. The horses, or ponies, brought to Iceland by the Norsemen were probably Norwegian (Fjord?) and Irish (Connemara), which in turn had descended from the aboriginal Celtic-type pony of northwestern Europe. Height: 48–54 inches. Whereas the original colors were mainly grey or dun, now it is said they are sorrel and chestnut, along with white, palomino, and black, and only an occasional dun. Iceland today has some 35,000 native ponies, about half of which roam free throughout the year. The breed was introduced into Canada in 1959 and the United States shortly thereafter.

IRISH HORSE: See Connemara.

JUTLAND HORSE: A Danish draft breed which originated on the peninsula of Jutland, where it is still in common use. Height: 62–66 inches. Colors: usually chestnut, but also brown, bay, roan, black, or grey. While primarily a farm horse, the Jutland has during recent years been used also in Danish cities and towns for draft purposes. The Schleswig draft horse of northwest Germany is considered identical to the Jutland breed. In the Middle Ages the Schleswig was used to carry heavy armored knights, and later as an artillery horse and a heavy draft horse.

KABARDA (or KABARDIN): One of a number of medium-sized horse-breeds found in the Caucasus mountain regions of the U.S.S.R. Other Russian breeds of the same size (60–64 inches), but varying in coloration, have similar and sometimes confusing names: Karabair,

Karabakh (or Karabagh), Kazakh, etc. Altogether, Russia has today perhaps fifty breeds or types of horses. Most of these horse breeds are listed in Table 13, but space forbids a more extended reference to them. One of the most famous breeds, the Orloff trotter, is described on p. 179.

KATHIAWAR: An ancient breed of horses native to the Kathiawar district of Pakistan. According to Ridgeway, these horses, or ponies, are a cross between the Arab and the dun-colored pony of Mongolia. This crossing has in some specimens resulted in a reversion to the ancestral type, this being indicated by dark stripings on the legs, sometimes traces of shoulder stripes, and always by a narrow, dark mid-dorsal stripe. The ground color is usually dun, or slate-colored, although chestnut and brown occur. Height: 56–60 inches. The slender build of the Kathiawar horse is comparable to that of a small-sized Thoroughbred.

KENTUCKY SADDLE HORSE: Same as American Saddle Horse; see Table 15.

KLADRUBY (German: KLADRUBER): A discontinued breed of large Spanish horses, once maintained at the imperial stud at Kladrub in Bohemia, developed from horses of Spanish and Italian stock brought into Austria in late Renaissance times. The chief characteristics of the Kladruby horses were their great height (68–72 inches), coloration (either black or white), Roman noses, arched necks, heavy crests, and the upright position of their necks when drawing the royal carriages. Their trotting gait was extravagant, and limited them to a speed of 2–3 mph. From the Kladruby has been derived the present-day Lipizzan horse of Austria.

KLEPPER: A breed of ponies or small horses native to the U.S.S.R.'s Baltic provinces of Estonia, Livonia, and some of the islands of that region. They exhibit the characteristic primitive coloration of dun with black points (mane, tail, and lower legs), along with a dark mid-dorsal stripe (often termed eel-striping). In common with other pony breeds of northern regions, the Klepper is able to remain strong and enduring while subsisting on a meager food supply. Height: 52–60 inches.

KNABSTRUP (German: KNABSTRUPPER): Called also the Danish spotted horse. A type of the Frederiksberg coach or utility horse. Color: grey or white with "leopard" spotting. The foundation sire of the Knabstrup breed was a Frederiksberg stallion of palomino color bred in 1812 to a famous spotted mare named "Flaebehhoppen," which had been left behind in Denmark by Spanish officers during the Napoleonic Wars.

KONIK (native: KONIJK): A general term, meaning "little horse," applied in particular to ponies of primitive type native to Poland and Galicia. Height: 52–56 inches. Color: mouse-grey (or mouse-dun), with a dark mid-dorsal stripe; sometimes showing transverse zebra-stripings on the legs. Some of the ponies turn white during winter, with only their face, mane, tail, and fetlocks retaining the normal grey color. The ancestry of the Konik is believed to trace back to the South Russian tarpan.

LIBERTY HORSE: Not a breed, but any of various types of horses, usually all of the same color, used in the circus to perform singly or in groups while unridden and undriven and controlled only by a ringmaster on foot.

LIMOUSIN: A half-bred heavyweight hunter originated in Limousin, France, trained especially to gallop and jump while carrying a heavy rider. Height, up to 68 inches. The breed is today practically discontinued.

LIPIZZAN: See p. 192.

LUNDY PONY: A mixed breed of ponies native to Lundy Island, off the coast of Devonshire, England. Presumably the breed has died out, since it is not included among the nine pony breeds recognized in the British Isles today.

MANIPUR PONY: An ancient breed named after the state of Manipur in Assam, India. Bred as long ago as the seventh century, primarily for use as polo ponies, Manipur being one of the original homes of the sport. Height: 44–52 inches. Weight: 500–700 pounds. The Manipur, like various other pony breeds of Asia, is believed to have descended from a crossing of Arab horses and Mongolian ponies.

MAREMMANA: A breed of Italian all-purpose horses produced in the Maremmana district of Tuscany, cross-bred from Oriental and native stock. Height: 61–64 inches. Colors: generally bay or brown; sometimes black; less often chestnut or grey.

MASURE: A Polish riding horse derived from the Trakehner (*q.v.*). Color: brown. Height: 63–66 inches.

MECKLENBURG (German: MECKLENBURGER): A German breed which has passed through several stages. Although originally developed for drawing carriages and as a light-heavy draft type of cavalry horse, later on there were repeated infusions of English Thoroughbred blood, which resulted in a lighter, more active type of riding horse.

MISSOURI FOX-TROTTING HORSE: A recently evolved American breed, or type, of gaited horse. The "fox-trot" is an interrupted or divided gait wherein the horse walks with his front feet and trots with his hind feet—a gait similar to the running walk. Besides as a show-ring horse, this breed is used as a pleasure horse, a stock horse, or for trail riding.

MONGOLIAN PONY: One of the most ancient types of the domestic horse, found in both a wild (feral) and a domesticated state over the whole of Mongolia. As a result of the severe climate and meager food supply of their desert surroundings, these small horses are exceedingly hardy and enduring. They differ from the truly wild Mongolian horse (*Equus caballus przewalskii*) in being 2 to 3 inches taller (*i.e.,* 50–55 inches), having hanging manes with forelocks, tails that are long-haired even at the roots, and a somewhat lighter body-build. Along with these differences is their coloration, which is either grey, chestnut, bay, or sorrel, with dun (the typical color of the wild horse) being comparatively rare. The semi-wild Mongolian ponies interbred freely with Przevalsky's horse before the latter was reduced in its native haunts almost to extinction. Too, the Mongolian pony, or its ancestors, by having mixed with Arabian horses, are said to have produced the Turkoman horse of Turkestan, along with numerous pony breeds native to India, Burma, and the countries and islands of southeastern Asia in general.

MORGAN: For description, see p. 183.

MUSTANG (or BRONCO): The so-called "wild" horse of the plains of the western United States. The name comes from the Spanish mesteño, a group of stockraisers (see Chapter 1). The first Mustangs were horses (mostly Andalusian) that had escaped either from the Spanish conquistadores or from the corrals of later-established ranchers in the southwest and had become feral. J. Frank Dobie, in his book *The Mustangs* (1952), devotes 376 pages to telling just about everything about Mustangs except their size. Other sources indicate that the animals, if not cross-bred, ranged in height from about 52 to 58 inches, and in weight from 600 to 850 pounds, thus being about the size of the Highland ponies of Scotland. In coloration, according to Dobie, the Mustangs were "bay and sorrel, brown and grullo [dark grey], roan, dun, and grey, with here and there black, white, and paint" (Dobie, pp. 111–12). In short, they exhibited about every color that a horse could exhibit. As is stated in Chapter 7, in 1970 about 17,000 Mustangs, distributed over nine Western states, were left of the estimated *million* that had roamed the country about fifty years earlier.

NARRAGANSETT PACER: A breed of horses developed early in the 1700s on Point Judith and neighboring stud farms in Rhode Island. Although pacers, they were generally ridden under the saddle, and were said to neither tire themselves nor their riders. Sometime about the mid-1800s the breed came to an end. It was believed to have originated from a stallion imported from Spain.

NEW FOREST PONY: One of the nine presently recognized breeds of ponies in the British Isles. The New Forest is today a stretch of sparsely wooded grassland in Hampshire, comprising about 60,000 acres (or 94 square miles). In it an estimated 1500 ponies run free throughout the year, along with grazing cattle. Like other British semi-wild breeds, these ponies have inherited hardiness and endurance from having had to live on a poor food supply, especially during the winter, when they have had to dig out the sparse grasses from under the snow. Height: 49–57 inches. Colors: any, except piebald or skewbald, although bays and browns predominate. The origin of the breed is obscure, but it is thought to have descended either from the Exmoor pony (q.v.) or from a common ancestor of the two breeds. New Forest ponies are today being used in Sweden, Denmark, Holland, and other European countries as children's mounts and as show-ponies. Since the late 1950s they have also been imported into the United States.

NONIUS: Two breeds of this fine saddle horse exist: the Large Nonius and the Small Nonius. The parent breed was evolved in France in 1814 from Anglo-Norman stock. Today the Nonius—usually both the Large and the Small breeds—is used in Austria, Bulgaria, Hungary, Yugoslavia and Czechoslovakia. The coloration in both breeds in solid brown, without markings. In size (see Table 13), the Large Nonius averages 65.1 inches and 1366 pounds; the Small Nonius 62.4 inches and 1153 pounds. Thus the Large Nonius is somewhat the heavier in build of the two forms. Also in the Large Nonius the back is relatively longer and the tail placed lower than in the Small form. In both breeds the chest girth in stallions averages larger than in mares, thus showing a reversal of the proportions typical of Arabs, Thoroughbreds, Standardbreds, and most other light horse breeds. Despite this, the bodyweight in mares of the Large Nonius averages 12 pounds more than in stallions, and in the Small Nonius 18 pounds more (C. Madroff, 1936)

NORIC: See PINZGAUER.

NORWEGIAN HORSE: See FJORD PONY and GUDBRANDSDAL HORSE.

OLDENBURG (German: OLDENBURGER): A German horse of medium-heavy build, standing on the average 64.5 inches and weighing 1399 pounds (see Table 13). In build it is thus about halfway between a Thoroughbred and an average-sized draft horse. It is said that the introduction of English Thoroughbred blood during recent years did not improve the breed.

ORLOFF TROTTER: For description, see p. 179.

PALOMINO: For many years, Palominos were regarded simply as a color type rather than a breed. Today, however, horses of Palomino coloration, which also meet certain other breed requirements, may be registered in either of two American associations for the purpose. The Spanish word *palomilla*, from which *palomino* is said to be derived, means, among other things, "a cream-colored horse with white mane and tail." Palomino horses have been known at least since the days of the Spanish conquistadores. Today the stipulation for color is "golden, with mane and tail of white, silver, or ivory." Although Palomino coloration may occur in horses or ponies of any size, the usual height of the animals used for riding and parade purposes is 58–64 inches, and the weight from 1000 to 1200 pounds. This combination of height and weight represents the body-build of a sturdy saddle horse.

PASO FINO: A Latin-American riding horse, dating from the sixteenth and seventeenth centuries, native to Puerto Rico, Cuba, Peru, and Colombia. Its gait is one which may be described as a broken pace. The Paso Fino is used as a pleasure horse, a parade horse, and for endurance rides. Color: any, although solid colors are preferred.

PERCHERON: See Chapter 10.

PERSIAN: One of the three principal Oriental races of the domestic horse, the others being the Arab and the Turk. The original Persian breed has been variously described as both larger and smaller than the Arab, and as being either ancestral to the latter or descended from it. Perhaps all that can be said with certainty is that the Persian was a small horse of southwestern Asia, developed for the same purposes as the Arabian horse and closely resembling the Arab both in size, coloration, and running ability. Today in Iran (Persia) there are so many different breeds—some indigenous but others mostly introduced, especially from the U.S.S.R.—that a single, distinct "Persian" horse can no longer be identified.

PERUVIAN PASO: A riding horse bred in Peru since the early 1500s, but not imported in numbers into the United States until 1960.

PFALZ-ZWEIBRUCK: An elegant German breed of large-sized riding horses evolved in 1755 by the crossing of Arab, Persian, and Norman stock. Height: 63–67 inches. Color: usually sorrel, often with white markings on the head and feet.

PICARDY: See Chapter 10.

PINTO: (called also Painted Horse, or "paint"): Any horse or pony which exhibits the black-and-white or brown-and-white coloration known otherwise as piebald or skewbald, respectively. In Britain especially, the latter terms are the only ones used to designate such blotch-colored horses. Feral horses or ponies often display a "pinto" coloration, and horses of such coloring were common among the mustangs, Indian ponies, and the once-great herds that overran the South American pampas. Various *patterns* of coloration in Pinto horses and ponies are recognized by certain breed associations; but the Pinto horse is not a breed but a *color type*.

PINZGAUER: See Chapter 10.

POLO PONY: Any horses or ponies of any breed used in playing polo. From a height in this type (not breed) of 48–52 inches in the sixteenth century to 60–64 inches in 1940, it may be seen that progressively larger mounts have been used to improve the game; so much so that the designation "pony" no longer strictly applies. However, the name will doubtless continue to be used even if the horses eventually reach 17 or 18 hands!

POMERANIAN (German: POMMER): A riding horse developed in Germany and Pomerania (now part of Poland), combining the attributes of the Hanoverian and the Mecklenburg breeds.

PONY OF THE AMERICAS: A western-type breed originated as late as 1954, in Mason City, Iowa. It is a cross-breed of Arabian and Quarter Horse in miniature, with Appaloosa coloring. Height: 46–54 inches. Weight: 450–750 pounds. Used mainly as a riding pony for children and teen-agers.

QUARTER HORSE: For description, see Table 15 and p. 185 .

RHENISH-DUTCH DRAFT: See Chapter 10.

ROTTAL: A medium-heavy horse, strong and of fine appearance, bred in Bavaria and Rottal, derived from the Oldenburg breed (*q.v.*).

RUSSIAN SADDLE: As is mentioned above in connection with the Kabarda horse, Russia today has perhaps fifty breeds or types of horses. Most of these are used for riding, some for general utility, and some for draft, both light and heavy. A breed named the Russian Saddle horse, or Orloff-Rostopchin horse, was developed by crossing the Orloff trotter with the Rostopchin Saddle horse, the latter being an Anglo-Arab breed. Summerhays states (1961, p. 192) that efforts were being made in Russia to evolve a breed comprised of 3/4 Russian Saddle Horse, 1/8 Arab, and 1/16 English Thoroughbred. Presumably the other 1/16 was contributed by several existing Russian breeds.

SARDINIAN PONY, or ACCHETTA: A native pony of Sardinia, believed to have been derived from Barb stock. Height: 55–59 inches. Like many another pony breed, the Sardinian is characterized by an exceptional longevity, some individuals still being active at the age of 30–35 years.

SCHLESWIG: See Jutland horse.

SHETLAND PONY: See Tables 11, 12, and 15, and p. 199 .

SHIRE: See Chapter 10.

SKOGRUSS: See Gotland pony.

SKYROS PONY: A small breed of Greek pony indigenous to the island of Skyros of the Sporades group. Height: 38–46 inches. J. N. Dimitriadis (1937) gives the body measurements of three mares of this breed, along with the skull measurements of three mares and three stallions. He regards the Skyros as being similar to the ponies of northwestern Europe generally, and also to the Veglia pony.

SOUTH GERMAN DRAFT: A heavy draft horse bred in Baden-Württemberg and at the stud farm at Marbach. Similar in build to the Austrian Pinzgauer. Height: 63–67 inches.

SPANISH (see also ANDALUSIAN): A breed dating from the time of the invasion of Spain by the Saracens in 711 A.D. The Arab and Barb horses brought in by the invaders were crossed with indigenous Spanish horses. From this came a new breed which was called the Gineta (Jennet). This horse was characterized by a Roman nose (convex facial profile), a "mule-like" croup, and extravagant (high) leg action. The horses of Andalusia (*q.v.*) in particular were the ones most valued.

SPITI PONY: A breed of mountain ponies native to Kashmir and Nepal, in northwestern India. It is believed to have descended from the wild horse of Mongolia. Height: 46–50 inches. Another pony breed, also from Nepal, as well as parts of the Punjab, is the Bhutia. It is similar to the Spiti with the exception of being larger: 51–55 inches. In both breeds the usual coloration is grey or iron-grey. These ponies are used as sure-footed pack animals over the high and dangerous trails in the Himalayas.

STANDARDBRED: See Tables 5, 13, and 15, and p.

STRELETS: A Russian riding horse, predominantly of Oriental type, produced by crossing Ukrainian mares with Anglo-Arab, Turkish, Persian, and pure Arabian stallions. The Strelets horse (so-named from the stud farm of that name) is of about the same size as the Gidran (q.v.).

SUFFOLK, OR SUFFOLK PUNCH: See Chapter 10.

SWEDISH HORSE: This general term includes a number of breeds, both native and imported, used primarily for agricultural work. The great majority of horses in Sweden are either of heavy draft (65 percent of the horse population) or light draft (31 percent). Only 4 percent, or perhaps 20,000 horses, are of light, riding breeds.

TARBENIAN: A French breed of riding horse from the region of Tarbes, at the foot of the Pyrenees. Mostly of Anglo-Arab derivation. Height: 57–63 inches. Colors: usually dark brown or chestnut, seldom grey.

TENNESSEE WALKING HORSE: Called also PLANTATION WALKING HORSE: See Table 15.

THOROUGHBRED: (see Tables 13 and 15, and p. 165).

TIMOR PONY: A sturdy breed of pony used in Australia and New Zealand both for riding (particularly, stock work) and in harness. The Timor comes in virtually all colors, including an Appaloosa type having a dark ground color with light spots and a light mane and tail. Although small in size, the Timor pony is capable of carrying a heavy rider for hours on end without tiring.

TRAKEHNER, or EAST PRUSSIAN HORSE: A fine riding horse, generally considered to be the most perfected breed in Germany. The Trakehner Stud was founded in 1732 by Frederick William I of Prussia. By 1786, systematic breeding on a large scale was carried on in East Prussia. In its physical makeup the Trakehner is practically identical with the English or American Thoroughbred. Height: 60–68 inches. Weight: 1000–1400 pounds. Colors: mostly sorrel, brown, or black.

TURK: One of the three principal foundation breeds or races of Oriental horses. Today, of these three breeds only the Arab horse still exists in pure form. Today's so-called Persian and Turkish horses are all of mixed blood. The asserted "Turk" horses which contributed to the foundation stock of the English Thoroughbred were no longer in evidence after the year 1700. R. S. Summerhays (1961, p. 228) says that the most typically indigenous horses in Turkey are the Kurdistan ponies bred near Sivas. However, these ponies are a cross between the "native" (?) mares and Arabian stallions, which has resulted in a breed almost the size of the Arab (namely, 56–58 inches) and mostly of bay or grey coloration. Evidently the early Turkish horse was quite similar to the contemporary Barb horse of North Africa.

VEGLIA: The native pony of the island of Veglia (Austria) in the Adriatic sea. Height: 46–52 inches. Albert Ogrizek (1923), who gives the body measurements of seven stallions and one mare of this breed, considers the Veglia pony to be similar to the Icelandic pony, and that it is probably descended from the South Russian tarpan.

VIATKA: A Russian breed derived from the Baltic pony known as the Klepper (*q.v.*), crossed with the Finnish horse. Height: 52–56 inches. Colors: bay, grey, roan, or mouse-dun. In the wintertime these ponies develop a heavy coat of woolly hair, along with a thick layer of subcutaneous fat, as a protection against the intense cold. Two slightly smaller strains, known as Obvinkas and Kazankas, respectively, each average about 52 inches in height.

VIRGINIA SADDLE HORSE: Same as AMERICAN SADDLE HORSE.

WELSH COB: A long-established breed derived from the Welsh Mountain Pony. In turn, the Welsh Cob has contributed to the development of at least three other British breeds: the Hackney horse, the Hackney pony, and the Fell pony. The Welsh Cob is generally similar to the Welsh Mountain Pony except for being on the average about two inches taller (i.e., 54–58 inches). It can be of any color except piebald or skewbald.

WELSH MOUNTAIN PONY: A feral or semi-wild pony indigenous to the mountains and moorlands of Wales. Height: 52–56 inches. Colors: any, except piebald or skewbald, although the colors most preferred are bay, brown, or grey. Although the Welsh Mountain Pony was formerly much used in coal mining, with the mechanization of the latter industry it has been converted mainly into a riding pony for children and teenagers.

WESTFALE: A strong, fine, German riding horse of the Hanoverian type, but less purebred.

WORONESCH HORSE: (see BEETEWK).

WÜRTTEMBERG: A medium-heavy German riding horse of Anglo-Norman type without Arab admixture. Named after the province in which it is mainly bred.

YORKSHIRE COACH: A British breed of heavy harness horse that was popular 150–200 years ago, but which has since virtually died out. The Yorkshire Coach was produced mainly by crossing English Thoroughbreds with Cleveland Bay horses. Another derivation was by crossing Arab and Barb stallions with Yorkshire draft mares. These crossings resulted in a horse of refined appearance, up to 66 inches in height, suitable for drawing the elegant coaches of fashionable Londoners.

ZEELAND HORSE: See FRIESIAN HORSE.

ZEMAITUKAS: An ancient breed of large ponies or small horses of Lithuania, typically dun in color with light mane and tail and a dark mid-dorsal stripe. Mouse-grey and bay colors also occur. Physically the Zemaitukas is a well-documented breed, as lists of body measurements are given by Urusoff (1899), Moraczewski (1912), Mockus (1925), Zébenka (1933), K. Alminas (1937), and others. The average height is 56.6 inches for stallions and 55 inches for mares; the average weight, 893 pounds for stallions and 872 pounds for mares. Average birth weights are 84 pounds for male foals and 82 pounds for females.

A review of the foregoing breeds of the domestic horse indicates that the great majority of them have been produced through cross-breeding, and that the principal progenitors of these cross-breeds have been stallions of the Arabian horse, the Barb, and the English Thoroughbred, mated with "native" mares either of "coldblood" (draft) or pony origin. Actually, of the known wild races or subspecies of *Equus caballus,* only four appear to have had a part in the ancestry of the domestic horse. These are the Mongolian wild horse (*E. c. przewalskii*), the South Russian tarpan (*E. c. gmelini*), the so-called "forest horse" (*E. c. robustus,* or a derivative thereof), and the Celtic pony (*E. c. celticus*), which latter may have represented a western extension of the wild horse of Mongolia. Too, there were doubtless cross-breeds in nature between any or all of the numerous types of wild horses or ponies that ranged over almost the whole of the vast continent of Eurasia.

Fig. 131 "Paladere," a former International Champion French Coach stallion. The main source of this breed, which is no longer imported into the United States, was Normandy, where the horses, derived from Thoroughbred and trotter stock, were produced largely for military purposes.

Notes and References

1. Christo Madroff, *Araberpferd und seine Zucht in den Donauländern.* (Zeitschrift für Zuchtung, Band 39, Reihe B, 1937), pp. 43–66.

2. George G. Simpson, "Range as a Zoological Character," *Amer. Jour. Sci.* 239 (November 1941): 785–804.

3. Major Charles B. Team, in charge of Pomona Remount Station. Personal communication of 5-18-49.

4. William Ridgeway, *The origin and influence of the Thoroughbred horse.* (Cambridge: University Press, 1905), p. 466.

5. C. Kronacher, and A. Ogrizek. *"Exterieur und Leistungfahigkeit des Pferdes . . . ," Zeitschrift für Zuchtung* 23 (1932): 183–228. (Diagram showing measurements of articular angles in the horse, and listings of the angles in various European breeds.) Kruger, Wilhelm. "Uber Wachstumsmessungen an den Skelettgrundlagen . . . ," *Zeitschrift für Tierzüchtung und Zuchtungsbiologie* 43 (1939): 145. Same as above, only measured from different articular points, and confined to Trakehner and Mecklenburg horses.)

6. George H. Conn, *The Arab and his horse, The Cattleman,* September 1946, p. 180.

7. J. A. Estes, and Joe H. Palmer. *"An Introduction to the Thoroughbred Horse," The Blood-Horse* (August 1943), p. 1.

8. Ridgeway, *Thoroughbred Horse,* p. 381.

9. Estes, and Palmer, "Introduction," p. 4.

10. Dewey G. Steele, "A Genetic Analysis of Recent Thoroughbreds, Standardbreds, and American Saddle Horses," Kentucky Agric. Exper. Station Bull. 462 (May 1944), p. 21.

Fig. 132 Two European tarpan stallions about to fight for the possession of a herd. From a watercolor painting by F. Jung.

11. von Müller, "Die Bedeutung des Schulter (und Brustmasse) für die Buerteilung des Pferdes," *Zeitschrift für Veterinark.* 45 (1933) : 175–85, 204–23, 255–64, 321–50.

12. S. Afanassieff, *"Die Untersuchung des Exterieurs . . . beim Traber,"* *Zeitschrift für Züchtung* 18 (1930) : 171–209.

13. Helen Michaelis, Personal communication, 1948.

14. Kirby Cunningham, and Stewart H. Fowler, "A Study of Growth and Development in the Quarter Horse," Louisiana State Univ. Agric. Exper. Sta. Bull. No. 546 (November 1961).

15. Dr. Emilio Solanet, *El Caballo Criollo* (Buenos Aires: Editiones Agro, 1943), p. 46.

16. Roberto C. Dowdall, *"Conformacion de la Raza Criollo,"* *Anales de la Sociedad Rural Argentina,* no. 8 (1945), p. 607.

17. *Raza Criolla* (Buenos Aires) 23, no. 27 (May 1947): 37–38.

18. Fred Harvey, "Tschiffely's Horses," *The Western Horseman* 24, no. 9 (September 1959) : 26.

19. Lida F. Bloodgood and Piero Santini. *The Horseman's Dictionary.* (New York: E. P. Dutton & Co., 1964).

20. R. S. Summerhays, *The Observer's Book of Horses and Ponies* (London: Frederick Warne & Co., Ltd., 1961), p. 150.

21. Ridgeway, *Thoroughbred Horse,* p. 346.

22. Kladruby Horses—a Historic Breed Represented at Olympia, *Ill. London News,* December 28, 1929, p. 1152.

23. Christo Madroff, "Das Lippizanerpferd und seine Zucht in Europa," *Zeitschrift für Züchtung* 33, Reihe B): 169–84.

24. L. Stejneger, "Den celtiske pony, tarpanen og fjordhesten," *Naturen,* vol. 28., reprinted in *Smithsonian Misc. Proc.* 48 (1907): 469 ff.

25. Richard Lydekker, *The Horse and Its Relatives* (London: George Allen & Co., 1912), p. 104.

26. R. F. Scharff, *On the Irish Horse and Its Early History, Proc. Irish Acad.,* no. 6, (1909), pp. 81–86.

27. J. Cossar Ewart, *The Ponies of Connemara. Jour. Dept. Agric. Ireland,* 1900.

28. Dr. Johannes Erich Flade, *Shetlandponys* (Der Neue Brehm Bucherei, 1959).

29. G. Ullmann, Entwicklung und Wachstum bei Shetlandponys," *Tierarztliche Rondschau,* 45, no. 16:312.

30. M. E. Esminger, *Horses and Horsemanship* (Danville, Illinois: The Interstate Printers, 1969), p. 34.

10

The Draft Horse and Its Derivation

It is now opportune to devote a chapter to the draft horse, not because he is different physiologically from smaller horses, but because he represents a *race* of the domestic horse developed specifically for the purpose of exerting immense strength at slow speeds. The draft horse in its various breeds represents the maximum divergence from the light, fast, and graceful breeds of running horses of Oriental origin.

It is generally considered that the various modern breeds of the draft* horse stem principally from the "black horse of Flanders," a large, heavy type developed during Medieval times for the purpose of carrying knights clad in heavy armor. In some cases the knight and his armor (including that of the horse) together weighed as much as 450 pounds; and to carry such a load through the course of a battle required a horse of great strength and stamina. Speed and maneuverability in both horse and rider were probably conspicuous by their absence. Indeed, in some battles where the opposing forces used light, fast, unencumbered horses, the victory went to them because of the greater mobility of both horse and rider.

The ancient ancestor of the Medieval "Great Horse," as it was called, was presumably one of the large and fairly heavy-built horses of the Pleistocene; most probably, in the writer's opinion, the central European "forest horse" named *Equus caballus germanicus* Nehring (see Chapter 8). It should be emphasized, however, that there is no evidence among the skeletal remains of Pleistocene horses that there ever existed in Europe a race, or subspecies, of *E. caballus* that possessed the size and heaviness of build presented by the domestic draft horse.

Most present-day breeds of the draft horse, while differing in minor respects, such as coloration, amount of hair on fetlocks, etc., are so markedly similar in height, weight, and conformation of the body and limbs generally that a single draft "type" can be defined on the basis of the average or typical measurements of the Percheron. These measurements, as determined for both sexes, are listed in Table 17.

---

* Also spelled draught, and said to derive from the Anglo-Saxon word *dragon*, meaning "to draw or haul."

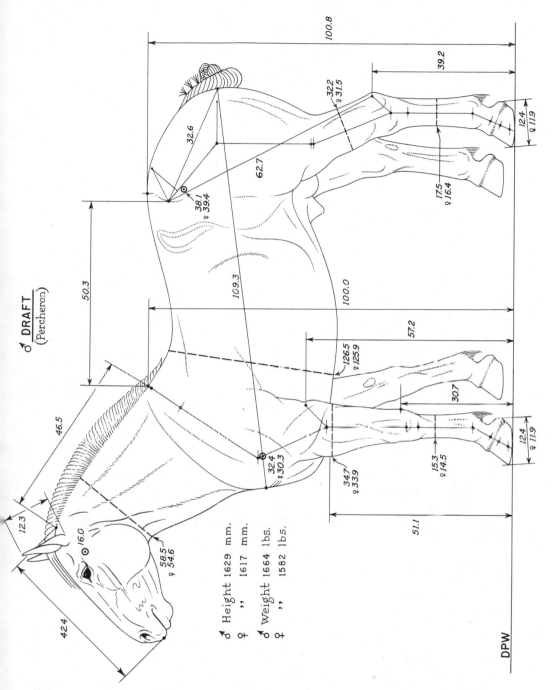

Fig. 133 Body outline of a typical draft stallion (Percheron, Belgian, or Nor[d]ic), showing proportions relative to shoulder height. Actually, this drawing represents a stallion of "championship" caliber (weight about 1850 pounds), rather than one possessing the girth measurements indicated here for the typical weight of 1664 pounds.

Table 17. Measurements (in inches) of the typical draft horse.
(to be compared with the *percentage* measurements in Fig. 133 and Table 30).

	Stallions	Mares
Height at withers	64.13	63.66
Height at croup	64.64	64.09
Length of trunk (slantwise)	70.09	70.09
Length of head	27.19	27.03
Width of forehead	10.26	10.19
Length of ear (on outside)	7.89	7.84
Length of neck	29.82	29.64
Girth of neck (at throat)	37.52	34.76
Girth of chest	81.12	80.14
Width of shoulders	20.78	19.29
Height of chest from ground	32.77	32.53
Height of elbow	36.68	36.41
Height of knee (top of pisiform)	19.69	19.54
Girth of forearm	22.25	21.58
Length of back	32.26	33.40
Length of croup (projected)	20.91	19.86
Width of croup	24.43	25.08
Length from hip to hock (proj.)	40.21	39.84
Girth of gaskin	20.65	20.05
Girth of cannon (fore)	9.81	9.23
Girth of cannon (hind)	11.22	10.44
Height of hock	25.14	24.95
Length of fore hoof (sole)	7.95	7.58
Length of hind hoof (sole)	7.95	7.58
Weight, pounds	1664	1582
Body build	1.225	1.190

The three best-documented "coldblood" Pleistocene horses are perhaps *Equus caballus mosbachensis* Reichenau, *E. c. abeli* Antonius, and *E. c. germanicus* Nehring. Restorations by the writer of the living body dimensions of these fossil horses indicate that the Mosbach (Germany) horse stood about 64.8 inches high, weighed about 1370 pounds, and had a body build (see Table 13) of 0.975; Abel's horse, 65 inches, 1425 pounds, and a build of 1.007; and "the horse of Germany," 59.2 inches, 1200 pounds, and a build of 1.124. Thus the heaviest-built of these wild forms, *E. c. germanicus,* had a physique almost identical with that of the present-day Quarter Horse. Accordingly, even *germanicus* was considerably below the heavy build (1.200 and over) of the modern draft horse. While *mosbachensis* and *abeli* equalled the draft horse in height, their limb bones were relatively longer and less heavy, and their hoofs considerably smaller, indicating a semi-cursorial (running) type of horse. However, one theory has it that the "forest horse" was big enough and strong enough to be a formidable fighter, and was thereby less dependent upon saving himself by flight.

In any case it is evident that a fair amount of the size of the domestic draft horse has been developed, or bred, over the centuries by man. In this connection it may be noted that Sir Walter Gilbey, an authority on the Shire horse—the largest of English draft breeds—considered this horse to have been derived "probably from the chariot-horses of the Britons of Caesar's time," and by the time of King John (1199–1216) to have become the recognized English war-horse.[1] If the Shire (64.5 inches, 1700 pounds, av.) could have been developed by man from native British horses that probably stood no higher than 56 inches and weighed perhaps 750–800 pounds, and if the sturdy Quarter Horse during a period of only 300 years could have been similarly developed from relatively light-built English and Andalusian stock, there seems no reason why the draft horse (or "Great Horse" of the Middle Ages) could not have been as readily derived from any of the heavy-built wild horses still existing in the forests of Europe during historic times.

The body measurements listed in Table 17 are those typical of an average-sized specimen of either the Percheron, Belgian, Pinzgauer (Austrian) or Rheinish-Dutch draft breeds. Other breeds may vary slightly from this general physical type, but the degree of such variation is usually slight.

In the typical draft horse (Fig. 133) most of the body proportions may be said to be in extreme contrast to those of the light-built, racing type of horse typified by the Arabian. About the only features in the draft horse that are similar to those in the Arab are the relatively small ears, the somewhat short neck, the prominent development of the withers, and the fairly long croup. Interestingly, in contrast to its shortness of legs otherwise, the relative height of the "knee" (pisiform bone) in the draft horse is almost equal to that in the Arab, owing to the large size (in length, as well as in caliber) of the three phalanges or terminal foot-bones in the draft horse. In marked contrast to the Arabian horse are the long back and trunk of the draft type, the long head, thick neck, great length from hip to hock, low-from-the-ground chest, low elbow and hock heights, and exceedingly broad shoulders and croup along with great girth of chest, the latter being due more to width or lateral expansion than to vertical (withers to sternum) depth. Greater still, in the draft horse, are the relative calibers or girths of the limbs, which increase downwardly from the forearms (which average 14 percent thicker, relative to withers height, than in the Arab), to the cannons (25 percent thicker relative to height) and finally the hoofs, which average 29 percent longer and over 31 percent broader, relative to withers height, in the draft horse than in the Arab. In connection with the draft type it should be considered that many of the large ratios shown in Fig. 133 *are* large only because the various parts have been related to withers height rather than to trunk length. If compared with the latter dimension the "long" head of the draft horse is seen to be actually somewhat short, while the relative lengths of the neck and limbs become shorter still.

Another difference in the draft horse as compared with light-built horses is the more upright positioning of the limb bones, owing to the need for supporting a heavier weight. Typical angles (in relation to the horizontal) of the various inclined limb bones are as follows.

Table 18. Typical inclinations of the limb bones in Light and Heavy horses.
(compare with Fig. 134)

		Light horses	Draft breeds
a.	Scapula (shoulder)	58	62
b.	Humerus (upper arm)	60	62
c.	Pastern (fore)	63	66
e.	Pelvis (ilium)	25	40
f.	Femur (thigh)	87	90
g.	Tibia (gaskin)	69	72
h.	Pastern (hind)	65	68

It should be noted that the limb-bone inclinations as recorded by various investigators vary slightly in accordance with the points chosen for measuring them. The

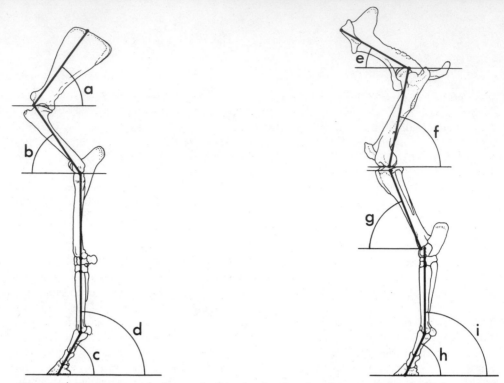

Fig. 134 Diagrams of the articular angles in the fore and hind limbs, as applicable to members of the genus *Equus*. (See also Table 18.)

points adopted by the present writer are those shown in Fig. 134. The steeper inclination of the iliac bone of the pelvis in the draft horse accounts for its more sloping croup and lower-placed tail, as compared with that in light-built horses generally and in the Arabian horse in particular. Fig. 134 illustrates the foregoing limb-angles. The angles labeled *d* and *i* may each be taken as 90 degrees in all breeds of horses and in the wild forms of the genus *Equus*.

A short digression at this point may be useful. In the Percheron, the Belgian, and doubtless other breeds of draft horses, there have often been specimens entered in championship competitions that have been fattened up (i.e., overfed) until they *looked* very fit and impressive, but were really "overweight" for the size of their skeletal structure, just as men and women can thus be overweight.* The best means of determining what the optimum, or "ideal," weight of any particular horse should be is to derive the weight from the *girth of the cannon, squared, multiplied by the withers height* and then by a factor which varies according to the *breed* of horse in question. For this purpose it is convenient to use the fore, or front, cannon, since it is the one most generally used to obtain the so-called "bone" measurement.

An example will show how this weight-estimation is to be made. In Arabian stallions the optimum bodyweight (in pounds) is equal to the fore cannon girth (in inches) squared, multiplied by the height at the shoulder (withers) in inches, times the factor 0.2851. For Arabian mares the latter multiplier is 0.3080. The larger multiplier for mares is owing to the fact that, typically, mares have larger body girths relative to

---

* Some years ago, in various horse-breeding periodicals, a discussion went on during which a number of prominent breeders expressed their belief that the most efficient weight of a farm (draft) horse was between 1200 and 1400 pounds. Of course, it would take a long time to bring the heavier draft breeds down to such weights; but that many individually overweight draft horses of today could be reduced an appreciable amount with marked benefit is certain.

their comparatively slender cannon girths. Thus an Arabian stallion with a fore cannon girth of 7.4 inches and a height of 60 inches would have an optimum bodyweight of 7.4^2 x 60 x 0.2851, or 938 pounds. Allowing, say, 3 percent for individual variation in body density and proportions, would make the estimated optimum bodyweight 938 pounds with a range from 911 to 966 pounds. This is a far cry from cases, particularly among draft horses, in which the actual bodyweight may be *several hundred pounds* over the optimum weight.

For some representative breeds of horses, both light and heavy, popular in the United States, the following ratios apply.

Table 19. Factors for estimating the optimum bodyweights of horses from the girth measurement of their fore (front) cannons.

Breed	Sex	Height, in.	Weight, lbs.	Cannon, in.	Factor
Arabian	stallions	59.7	922	7.36	0.2851
Arabian	mares	59.0	922	7.13	0.3080
Thoroughbred	stallions	63.8	1089	7.91	0.2740*
Thoroughbred	mares	63.0	1043	7.37	0.3049*
Standardbred	stallions	62.7	1085	7.96	0.2722*
Standardbred	mares	62.0	1055	7.38	0.3124*
Quarter Horse	stallions	60.0	1201	7.92	0.3191
Quarter Horse	mares	58.5	1172	7.43	0.3629
Shetland pony	stallions	39.8	354	5.29	0.3172
Shetland pony	mares	39.4	354	5.08	0.3479
Draft (typical)	stallions	64.1	1664	9.81	0.2696
Draft (typical)	mares	63.8	1582	9.23	0.2917

* In racing condition; otherwise about 0.29 to 0.31 for stallions, and about 0.32 to 0.34 for mares.

If the factors in the above table were all the same, say about 0.3000, it would mean that all domestic horses, regardless of breed, would possess the same amount of muscle for a given caliber of bone. But since the factors vary from breed to breed, it indicates that in some breeds (e.g., those having large factors, such as the Quarter Horse and the Shetland pony) the muscles are large in relation to the bones, while in other breeds (e.g., the Arab, Thoroughbred, Standardbred, and Draft horse) the muscles are smaller in relation to the bones. That the Thoroughbred should have slightly larger muscles relative to the thickness of his bones than does the draft horse is an unexpected revelation, until it is realized that in heavy graviportal (weight-bearing) animals the bones tend to become *disproportionately* thicker in relation to the amount of weight they have to support (see *Baluchitherium,* in Appendix). Hence the big hoofs and relatively thick leg bones in the draft horse.

We may now consider separately some of the leading breeds of draft horses with respect to their geographic locus, coat-coloration, and other departures, if any, from the generalized draft type.

Fig. 135 The early-day (c. 1870) Percheron stallion "Victor." An engraving by C. G. Specht from a drawing by H. Fieg.

a. The Percheron.

The origin of the Percheron draft horse is unknown; but the breed is considered to be an ancient one, possibly descended from the "black horse of Flanders." The breed is native to the district of La Perche, an area of 53 by 66 miles in southeastern Normandy (northwestern France). The La Perche horse is generally considered to have been crossed with Arab and Barb blood during the Saracen (Moorish) invasion of France in 732 A.D. In 1755 the native stock was crossed again, this time with Danish horses, the breed of which is not stated. Still later, English and Belgian horses added their blood to the Percheron. In 1820, two grey Arab stallions, evidently of high prepotency, influenced the breed. It was evidently these Arabians which to a large extent induced the grey or dappled coloration now prevalent in the Percheron. It was not, however, until the 1870s that the Percheron became generally recognized as a distinct breed.

Typical* body dimensions of this breed are given in Table 17. It should, in view of these actual measurements (along with the comparison with the Arabian horse already made) be unnecessary to add any of the usual (and often ridiculous) "qualitative" descriptions such as "ample bone," "good feet," "wide chest," "well-flexed hocks," etc. Suffice it to say that the Percheron, in common with other well-bred draft horses,

---

* "Typical" is used here in the sense of *average* or possibly *optimum*. Much heavier horses, especially in the "championship" class have been recorded; but most such animals are "overweight" in relation to their skeletal size. Moreover, the excess weight is not often accompanied by proportionate pulling power (see Chapter 11).

Fig. 136 "Don Juan," of the Crocker Ranch. A close-up study of a typical Percheron head.

is the Hercules of the equine tribe, and accordingly the antithesis of the light, fast, mostly Oriental breeds, which it can greatly surpass in its own specialty—the drawing of heavy loads.

In coloration the Percheron is predominantly (i.e., in about 9 out of 10 cases) grey or black, although bay, brown, chestnut, and roan are occasionally seen; the latter colors are accompanied by black points.

Today the Percheron is the most popular of the various draft breeds in the United States. In 1966 the population was 250,298. The breed is equally popular in France, its home, the British Isles, Canada, and various countries of Europe and South America.

Fig. 137 "Calypso," chosen by one hundred judges as the ideal type of Percheron stallion. Calypso's 67 inches and 1900 pounds would be proportionate to 64.13 inches and 1667 pounds (see Table 17), thus being in exact ratio to the typical body-build of a draft horse.

Fig. 139 A prize-winning eight-horse hitch of Percherons exhibited by the W. K. Kellogg Institute of Animal Husbandry at Pomona, California.

b. The Belgian.

The modern Belgian draft horse is generally considered to have descended from the "Great Horse" of Medieval times, which in turn probably sprang from the "black horse of Flanders." It is believed that the original, primitive "forest horse" of northern Europe had no admixture whatever of Oriental or South European blood. Some authorities consider the body-build of the Belgian to more nearly resemble that of the Flemish horse than does the build of any other breed.

The shoulder (withers) height of Belgian stallions as measured by three different hippologists (von Nathusius, 1905; Leyder, 1905; and Boicoianu, 1932[2]) was 1618 mm, 1650 mm, and 1644 mm, respectively. The average of these three series is 1637 mm, or 64.46 inches. For Belgian mares the corresponding figures are 1620 mm, 1635 mm, and 1643 mm—an average of 1633 mm or 64.28 inches. If these heights are compared with those in Table 17, it will be seen that the Belgian stallion averages only about a third of an inch taller than draft stallions generally. Mares of the Belgian breed, however, are very nearly the same height as stallions, which makes their height about 5/8 of an inch taller than that of draft mares in general. But these are trivial differences; and when the measurements and proportions of all parts of the body and limbs are considered it becomes evident that the general body-build of the Belgian horse is essentially the same as that of the average draft type. However, individual Belgian horses, both stallions and mares, sometimes attain a greater height and weight than is seen in other draft breeds, with the possible exception of the Shire. This is indicated by the fact that the heaviest (if not the tallest) horse on record was a Belgian stallion

Fig. 138 "Nerva," a champion Percheron mare of exceptional size: 67½ inches and 2285 pounds.

Fig. 140 A fine example of a blond-maned Belgian stallion.

(see Chapter 17). Dinsmore and Hervey (1944) correctly point out that the head of the Belgian is not so broad as that of the Percheron.[3] However, for a given head length the difference in forehead width is only 1/4 inch; and whether this slightly narrower head in the Belgian constitutes a fault or a disadvantage is a question.

In coloration, the typical Belgian is preferably a dusty chestnut, with a flaxen mane and tail and a white blaze (see Fig. 140), although bay, roan, brown, grey, and black are also to be seen.

Next to the Percheron, the Belgian is the most numerous breed of draft horse in the United States. By 1966 the total number of registrations was 69,641. The Belgian, like the Percheron, is popular also in many parts of Europe and South America.

c. The Clydesdale.

The Clydesdale originated in the vicinity of the river Clyde, in the county of Lanark in southern Scotland. It is practically the only draft breed found or favored in that country. The modern Clydesdale is said to have come into being about the year 1715, when a black Flemish stallion, evidently of great prepotency, was brought from England into Lochlyoch (Clydesdale) and bred to native mares of that region. From these matings came a superior strain of draft horses for that period. The Clydesdale breed met with special favor during the late 1700s and early 1800s. During that period there were a number of importations of heavy horses of Flemish extraction, from England, Belgium, and Holland, which accordingly influenced the Scottish breed (as well as the English Shire and Suffolk breeds). Shire horses also were crossed with Clydesdales, so that in the mid-1800s the latter horses were definitely a mixed breed. During more recent years, however, the Clydesdale has been maintained as a pure breed.

Fig. 141 "Strathore Guard 29109," a Grand Champion Clydesdale stallion. Owned by Nelson Wagg of Claremont, Ontario, Canada.

In height and weight the Clydesdale is slightly smaller than the typical draft type dimensioned in Table 17. Clydesdale stallions average about 63.5 inches and 1615 pounds, and mares about 63.3 inches and 1555 pounds. These figures refer to Scottish-bred horses. As to Clydesdales—as well as other draft breeds—in the United States, the tendency is to breed larger animals—if the heights and weights given in various popular books on horses may be relied upon. It would appear, however, that most such published heights and weights are either estimations or mere unsubstantiated quotations, since rarely if ever is the source of the measurings stated. In the case of championship-class animals one should of course expect larger specimens, but such individuals cannot be considered as *typical* representatives of their particular breed. Accordingly, the average measurements of numerous animals[4] provide a more reliable basis of comparison than do the larger measurements of a few—sometimes only one—selected specimens.

In coloration, the ancestral color of black predominates, although it is often modified into a very dark brown or a brown-bay. A chestnut color is said to indicate Shire blood. White markings on one or more of the feet or hocks are common, as is a white star or a blaze on the forehead. A distinguishing feature of the Clydesdale is the long, fine hair (called "feather") on the cannons, fetlocks and pasterns, both front and hind. While Scottish farmers claim that the hair protects the skin of the leg, and is indicative of superior "bone," the average buyer finds the long hair a nuisance where mud, dirt, and dampness must be contended with.

The number of Clydesdale horses in use in the United States is decidedly less than that of Percherons or Belgians. Up to 1965 the total number of registrations was 25,698.

Fig. 142 "Gallant Prince," five times a Grand Champion Shire stallion. Owned by Fred H. Bixby of Rancho Los Alamitos, Long Beach, California.

d. The Shire.

The Shire is said to be the largest of all the heavy draft breeds, although it is possible that the average size has been overstated.* Von Nathusius gives the average height of 48 stallions as 1636 mm (64.4 inches) and the average weight às 772 kg (1702 pounds).[4] Percherons and Belgians, as well as Shires, attain heights of over 68 inches and weights of over 2000 pounds, but such dimensions pertain to exceptionally large individuals, not average or typical specimens. And as pointed out elsewhere, while oversized horses may make impressive exhibition specimens, they are not necessarily superior animals in point of physical efficiency and stamina. Rather, they may represent a departure from the average almost to the stage of gigantism, just as is presented in some human athletes who weigh over 300 pounds. (Specific figures on the relative pulling powers of horses of various sizes are given in Chapter 11).

Like a number of other breeds of the draft horse, the Shire is believed to have come from the "Great Horse" of the Middle Ages, and so, originally, from the primitive "forest horse" of northern Europe. Its name comes from its surroundings, which were the *Shire* counties in east-central England, particularly Lincolnshire and Cambridgeshire. Like the Clydesdale, the Shire breed has been modified at various times by crossing it with draft horses from the Low Countries of continental Europe.

---

* Perhaps as a matter of national pride, for in one publication on British breeds of live stock it says that a Shire stallion should stand "at least" 17 hands high and weigh "not less" than 20 hundredweight (2240 pounds)!

While in the past the Shire has been criticized for its excessively thick "bone," super-abundance of "feathering" (i.e., hair on lower legs), shelly-textured hoofs, sluggish disposition, and other alleged faults, these objections have during recent years been largely overcome by careful breeding.

For hundreds of years the Shire was known as the "Old English Black Horse," that color having been distinctive of the breed. Today the Shire is more usually bay or brown, although black is often seen. More rarely the coloring may be grey, chestnut, or roan. White markings on the legs and face are typical.

The number of Shire horses registered in the United States up to 1965 was 22,030, this being slightly less than the number of Clydesdales and less than a *tenth* the number of Percherons.

e. The Suffolk.

This English breed is also commonly called Suffolk Punch, the latter half of the name referring to the horse's "punched-up" conformation, or thickset body on short legs. It would seem also that "punch" may have come from *puncheon,* a wine or beer cask, in allusion to the Suffolk's thick, rotund body.

The name Suffolk comes from that county in England where the breed is known to have existed as far back as 1586. For this reason the Suffolk has become known as the oldest draft breed. However, the Suffolk horse as it stands today traces its pedigree to a stallion of unknown sire, foaled in 1768 and known as the "Crisp horse" (after the name of its owner). The Crisp horse was a bright chestnut in color, stood 62 inches high, and proved of exceptional prepotency. According to Charles Plumb (1906), "In the development of the Suffolk since his [Crisp's] time, four attempts have been made to introduce foreign blood and thus improve the stock. In no case, however, has this blood held its own, but has been completely absorbed and the breeding lost."[5]

Unlike the other British breeds of draft horses—and possibly all the continental European heavy breeds as well—the Suffolk does not trace its ancestry to the "black horse of Flanders"; ". . . no sluggish Flemish blood flows in the Suffolk's veins."[6] The chestnut color typical of the Suffolk breed is said by some authors to have come from its enforced crossing with horses introduced into England by the Vikings about a thousand years ago. On the other hand, William Ridgeway (1905) says, "The large head, thick body and sorrel colour all point to the animal (Suffolk horse) having been chiefly developed from old European horses of the Solutré type."[7] So here again is an instance where the origin of a breed is not definitely known.

As to Ridgeway's reference to the Suffolk horse's head being large, there is no evidence that it is proportionately larger than that of draft horses in general. If anything it is a trifle *small,* especially in relation to the long trunk in this breed. Photographs of well-bred specimens of the Suffolk horse show clearly and invariably that its legs are shorter relative to the length of the trunk than in other draft breeds. Hence its shoulder (withers) height is somewhat less. Suffolk stallions average about 63.5 inches and mares about 63 inches. The weight of stallions averages about 1650 pounds, and of mares about 1600 pounds.

The color of the Suffolk is always chestnut, varying from light to dark. Often the mane and tail are flaxen or cream-colored. Such white markings as occur are generally unobtrusive. The relatively short legs are particularly free from long hair or "feather," and the caliber of the bones is small in comparison with the heavily muscled body and limbs.

Fig. 143 Imported "Beau Boy," a many-times champion Suffolk stallion. Owned by L. B. Wescott, Clinton, N.J.

Considering the good qualities of the Suffolk—great strength and stamina, a docile disposition, spirited action, etc.—it is rather surprising that the total number of this breed in the United States today is only a few thousands.

f. The Rhenish-Dutch Draft.

This heavy draft horse comes from the Rhine Provinces of Germany, where during the Middle Ages great armor-bearing "war-horses" were developed. Presumably, therefore, the Rhenish-Dutch, like many another draft breed, has descended from the "black horse of Flanders."

The only measurements seen by the writer of this breed are those recorded by A. Hering (1925).[8] The chief measurements (as converted from millimeters) given by Hering for stallions are: height 64.17 inches, trunk length 67.2 inches, chest girth 84.2 inches, front cannon 10.3 inches. For mares the corresponding figures are 63.07, 67.6, 79.0, and 9.02 inches, respectively. The bodyweights commensurate with these linear measurements would be about 1700 pounds for stallions and 1500 pounds for mares. This weight difference between stallions and mares is much greater than that generally present in draft breeds.

The usual colors in the Rhenish-Dutch horse are sorrel, sorrel-roan, sorrel-brown, or sometimes brown-roan. The mane and tail are usually flaxen-colored.

Early in the 1900s German breeders established a Rhenish-Dutch Stud Book. In it the most successful founders of bloodlines are "Albion d'Hor," "Lothar III," and "Indien de Biévène."

g. The Pinzgauer, or Norische Draft.

This breed, which is also called the Noric, is native to the Austrian Tyrol. It is believed to have descended from the early Friesian (Holland) draft horse, and so, by extension, from the "black horse of Flanders." It was bred first in the Pinzgau district of Styria (southeastern Austria). Later on, its breeding was extended to the highlands of Austria.

The Pinzgauer is a typical draft breed, powerfully built and well adapted for the drawing of heavy loads.

Measurements of Pinzgauer horses at 1 year, 2 years, 3 years, and adult are given by Adolf Weiss-Tessbach (1923).[9] According to his figures (converted from millimeters into inches) the principal measurements of Pinzgauer stallions are: height 64.88 inches, trunk length 67.16 inches, chest girth 77.95 inches, front cannon girth, 9.84 inches. For mares the corresponding average measurements are: 64.17 inches, 67.48 inches, 76.97 inches, and 9.25 inches, respectively. Estimated weights (by the writer) are: stallions 1650 pounds, mares 1540 pounds.

A peculiarity of the Pinzgauer or Norische horse is its Appaloosa-like coloration. The ground color is generally roan, with a lighter area over the hips and croup on which there are dark spots or splotches. The fetlocks and lower legs are free from long hair.

A somewhat smaller type of the Norische breed is the Oberlander or Highland Austrian horse. Its principal breeding area is in Upper Bavaria, at an average elevation of 5000 feet.

h. The French Draft.

The name "French Draft" (French: *"Cheval de Gros Trait"*) is applied broadly to all draft breeds of French origins and does not refer to any specific breed from that country. It includes such breeds as the Percheron, Boulonnais, Nivernais, Breton, Brabant, Augeron, Auvergne, Ardennais, and Picardy.

The Boulonnais is native to northern France in the vicinity of Boulogne and in adjoining districts in Belgium. It was bred in that region as early as the eleventh century, and was later crossed with Arab and Barb stallions brought from the Middle East by the French Crusaders. The Boulonnais is said to be a trifle larger, on the average, than the Percheron, which breed it resembles rather closely in type, coloration, and general draft ability. As in the Percheron, the infusion of Oriental blood is said to have given the Boulonnais a certain refinement in spite of its massive bodily size.

The Nivernais is another heavy draft breed similar generally to the Percheron, from which it is derived, but usually black in color. Its home is in central France, in the Department of Nièvre, but its numbers even there are small.

The Ardennais has been described as a small type of the Belgian (see Table 16).

The Picardy has been variously termed a variety of the Belgian breed or of the Boulonnais. It is a large draft horse, generally bay in color, and is bred both in northern France and in Belgium.

With the exceptions of the Percheron, the Boulonnais, and the Nivernais, no French breeds have been imported in appreciable numbers into the United States.

To sum up, the draft horse has been developed or bred by man evidently from one or more smaller wild horses of post-glacial northwestern Europe which had the potentiality of becoming larger. During the Middle Ages, horses of more than ordinary size were needed for the purpose of warfare. They were developed to carry knights clad in heavy armor. Later, the breed or breeds so developed were converted into vehicle-drawing animals; the size of the horse was adapted to the heaviness of the load drawn. Ultimately a maximum normal height and weight were attained, at which stage the best-bred of such huge horses were used for competitive exhibition purposes. Today—in the United States, at any rate—draft horses are being replaced more and more by mechanized farming and hauling equipment. The only definite statement that can be made regarding the future of these animals is that it is uncertain.

Notes and References

1. Sir Walter Gilbey, *The Great Horse, or Shire Horse* (London, 1899).

2. Constantin Boicoianu, "Studien über das belgische Pferd," *Zeitschrift für Züchtung,* 23 (1932) : 25–54.

3. Wayne Dinsmore, and John Harvey. *Our Equine Friends,* 2d edition (Book No. 277, Horse and Mule Ass'n. of America, 1944), p. 21.

4. See in this connection especially: Simon von Nathusius, *Messungen an Hengsten, Stuten und Gebrauchspferden,* Berlin, 1905. Nathusius's tables of measurements are also quoted in a number of German textbooks on animal breeding.

5. Charles S. Plumb, *Types and Breeds of Farm Animals* (Boston: Ginn & Co., 1906), p. 140. (Plumb's book would appear to be the basis for most of the heights and weights of domestic horses quoted in various popular books on the subject, including articles in encyclopedias.)

6. *The chestnut breed of draft horses,* a descriptive booklet issued by the American Suffolk Horse Association, Lynden, Washington.

7. William Ridgeway, *The Origin and Influence of the Thoroughbred Horse* (Cambridge: University Press, 1905), p. 370.

8. A. Hering, "Ein Beitrag zur Kenntnis der Jugendentwicklung des rheinish-deutschen Kaltbludpferdes," *Arbeiten der Deutsch Gesellschaft für Zuchtungskunde,* no. 27 (1925).

9. Adolf Weiss-Tessbach, *"Studien über das Pferd des Pinzgaues," Arbeiten der Lehr. für Tierzucht an der Hochschule für Bodenkultur in Wien,* vol. 2 (1923) : 157–215.

11

Life History, Physiology, Intelligence, and Physical Powers of the Horse

a. Life History of the Horse.

Although some of the information that follows has been given already in Chapters 4 and 5, it may be appropriate to include it here among various associated items.

In the domestic horse and its wild relatives (horses, zebras, asses, hemionids) normally only one foal is born at a birth. Twins are rare (occurring once in several thousand births) and are undesirable, as often both offspring are inferior. Gestation in light breeds of the domestic horse averages 337 days, or about 2 days over 11 months. The time is from 1½ to 4½ days shorter, on the average, for female foals than for males. There are, however, wide individual differences in the gestation period, Tessier reporting a range of 287–419 days, or about 9½ to nearly 14 months, among 582 mares. Draft horses average about 332 days, or 5 days less than light-built horses,[1] while pure-bred Shetland ponies average 333 days. Foals born in the spring average 13 or 14 days longer than those born in the fall.[2]

The foal is born fully covered with fine, short, wooly hair, which differs in color from that which develops later. The foals of grey horses are almost black, while those of chestnuts or bays are lighter in color than the parents. The newborn foal can see and very shortly stand, and within 4 or 5 hours can follow its mother about. It is weaned at about 5 or 6 months (after which, to the age of one year, it is called a "weanling"), and at that time grows its first adult coat. Young mares, or "fillies," can breed in their second year, although 3 years is a better age for this. Mares may breed until an advanced age: 14 to 16 years is common; while 25 years and a most extraordinary age of 32 years have been recorded.* Mares are in season, or "heat," for about 3 days to a week, beginning early in the spring or on the ninth to eleventh day after foaling, and again at 21-day intervals (with a range of 10–37 days) during the summer. The date of pairing is dependent upon the time the breeder desires the foal to be born. In temperate climates, such as the United States and the British Isles, the best time for breeding is from April to June, so that the foal will be born in the spring warmth, and when grass for the mare

---

* More recently, a Suffolk draft mare is said to have given birth to a healthy foal at the age of 39 years!

is at its best. Many horses live throughout the year in climates where either the heat or the cold are extreme. Some even have to dig through snow for their food. While such horses are able to endure heat and cold, they suffer if the weather is windy or wet, and during such periods, at least, should be provided with shelter.

As to the potential maximum longevity of the horse, under optimum living conditions, it would appear to be about 44 years.[3] A captive zebra has been known to reach 38 years, an Arab horse 40 years, a mule 43 years, a donkey 47 years, and a Shetland pony 48 years. Considerably higher ages have been claimed for various common horses, but without adequate substantiation. It would serve no useful purpose to review these claimed cases here. Alex Comfort, a biologist who has made an extensive study of animal longevity, has provided authentic survival curves for 419 British Thoroughbred mares. The average age at death of these horses was 22 years, and the maximum age attained by any one of them was 31 years.[4] On this basis it can be estimated statistically that only one horse in 500,000,000 should be expected to reach 40 years.* Hence such claimed ages as 52 years, 54 years, and in one instance 62 (!) years, would correspond to such exceedingly unlikely human ages as 136, 140, and 160 years, respectively. The present writer's estimate of 44 years as the maximum age for a horse (though not a pony or a donkey) corresponds to a maximum human age of 117 years, which may well have been attained, although the highest documented age is of a man in Canada, one Pierre Joubert, who reached 113 years and 124 days. As regards equine longevity, it may be questioned whether racehorses live as long as other breeds, even draft horses.

The daily life of a horse depends mainly upon the purpose for which it is used. Horses, unlike cattle and sheep, do not usually sleep steadily throughout the night. They are restless, and frequently get up from their sleep to feed. Some horses sleep while in a standing position, but this is considered a bad habit, as the animal might fall and injure itself. According to a German investigator, I. Norr, who made a study of the sleep of horses, the following details were learned. During a period of 10 hours in the stall, the average length of time spent by a horse in sleeping is 4½ to 5 hours, and while awake but in a lying position, 2½ hours. During a full day (in the stall and outdoors), the average time spent in sleeping is 7 hours, and in a lying position 2¾ hours. The average number of *times* that a horse sleeps during 10 hours in the stall is 5, and the number of times that he lies down, 4. During a full day, the horse sleeps 9 times and lies down 4 or 5 times. In either a hard-working or an idle horse, the average duration *of any one period* of its sleep is 2 hours and 9 minutes (ranging from 45 minutes to 4 hours and 45 minutes); and the average length of time of any one period of *lying* is 1 hour (45 minutes to 1¼ hours). To sum up, a horse rarely sleeps for more than 2 hours or so at a time, nor lies down for more than an hour at a time.[5]

A horse when at work should be fed three times a day, as owing to its relatively small stomach** it needs frequent small feedings and waterings rather than large amounts at one time. It should be watered before feeding and after working. If watered *after* feeding, it may suffer an attack of colic. When not working, a horse should have water always within reach. If not treated inconsiderately, a horse is rarely if ever vicious.

---

* In a larger series, of 2742 racehorses, the oldest animal reached 34 years. Assuming a normal distribution, this would predict an age of 40 years in one horse out of 10,000,000.

** A horse's stomach has a capacity of only 8 to 16 quarts, as compared with the 200-quart capacity of a cow, a ruminant which has a four-compartmented stomach.

Fig. 144 Domestic horses that escape from captivity and roam free soon revert to the feral, or wild, state. Here is a small herd of such horses in the sagebrush desert of southeastern Oregon. Their convex facial profiles and uniform colorations show the effects of generations of inbreeding, while the horse second from the left seems almost to have an erect mane.

Horses are naturally high-strung animals, ready for instant flight from danger. They have an instinctive reaction to sudden movements of unfamiliar objects, especially if above their heads. Possibly this is an inherited fear of being pounced upon by a tree-dwelling carnivore. In fighting, especially against another stallion, a horse uses his powerful front teeth as well as the hoofs of all four feet. When he kicks, he lays back his ears and looks back, showing the whites of his eyes. When in a state of fear, he will sweat and shiver. But a horse trained for battle may show extreme courage, determination, and even apparent initiative. The favorite horses of Alexander the Great and of Julius Caesar, to cite only two such instances, were so habituated to their masters that they would tolerate no other riders on their backs. According to T. H. White, "When their master is dead or dying, horses shed tears—for they say that only the horse can weep for man and feel the emotion of sorrow."[6]

The food of the horse is herbivorous or gramnivorous. When in a pasture, he will select the shorter and tenderer grasses. When fed in a stable—as he must be if working —he may be given hay and seeds of almost any kind: oats, beans, peas, lentils, barley, maize, or bran. Wheat is regarded as unwholesome. Apples and sugar are relished. A 1000-pound horse at medium work requires each day about 23 pounds of feed (oats, corn, or hay, or their equivalent in pasturage).[7] Variations in body size and activity may substantially alter the average feed ration. For example, the "fuel" requirement of an 1100-pound horse walking at 3 miles per hour is 273 calories; at 3½ miles per hour, 310 calories; and when trotting at 5¼ miles per hour, 445 calories.* Horses

* As an interesting sidelight, it may be noted that the average horse consumes about 9 quarts of oats a day. In comparison, the Thoroughbred Assault, while preparing for a race (1946), consumed 11 quarts; and an English Thoroughbred named Windsor Lad, no less than 13½ quarts—a "record" appetite for a racehorse, it was claimed.

are raised for a more varied and useful life than other farm animals, and should not be given the same feeds. Indeed, it has been said that from a scientific point of view "horses are the most poorly nourished of all domestic animals . . ."[8]

When resting on the ground, a horse sometimes lies flat, on one side and cheek, but more often it lies on the bent legs of one side, with its head and neck upright and inclined to the other side. To lie down, a horse gathers its legs together under it, then kneels and sinks down. To rise, it straightens and gets up on its forelegs first. This is in contrast to a cow, which rises on its *hind* legs first.

Horses are usually very silent, but will "neigh" when excited or alarmed. If in great pain, they will shriek. A soft, low "whinny" is used to call the foal or to attract attention.

A horse does not normally enjoy swimming, but when compelled by man will perform well in the water and, in the case of trained circus or carnival horses, even dive from a high tower into a tank. Horses, furthermore, are subject to seasickness—so much so that many a Thoroughbred, after a rough sea voyage, has been unfit to race for as long as six months. To avoid this possibility, travel by air was initiated in the 1940s, and the first such cargo ever to cross the Atlantic was six racehorses flown from Limerick, Ireland, to Los Angeles, California.

b. Physiology of the Horse.

The following items of information, which have been gleaned from many sources, are presented for whatever comparative value they may have, rather than as a treatise on equine physiology, which belongs properly in the province of veterinary medicine.

The average body (rectal) temperature of the horse is 100.5 degrees F., with a normal range of from 99 to 100.8 degrees. In a day-old colt it was found to be 102¾ degrees. In the domestic ass the average is about 101 degrees, and in the mule, 102 degrees. Among farm animals, horses are the nearest to man's average of 98.6 degrees. Cattle average 101.5, sheep 102.3, swine 102.6, and goats 103.8 degrees.

The pulse rate and the breathing rate vary inversely according to the size of the animal. In the horse the normal range in the pulse is from 32 to 44 beats per minute, and in the respiratory rate from 8 to 16 breaths per minute, the latter increasing rapidly with exercise. For comparison, man averages 72 heartbeats per minute, an elephant only 30 beats, and a shrew 1000 beats. In fact, someone has figured out that the typical number of heartbeats per minute in mammals is equal to the bodyweight in pounds raised to the minus 0.27 power (i.e., heartbeats = bodyweight, lbs. $^{-0.27}$).

The lung capacity in a 1000-pound horse is about 2500 cubic inches; and each ordinary inhalation accounts for about 250 cubic inches. These figures are nearly ten times those of the average man, weighing about 155 pounds. The weight of the lungs in a horse weighing 1320 pounds was found to be 11.9 pounds.[9] In proportion to bodyweight, this is over 40 percent greater than in cattle, in which the demand for endurance and great breathing power is much less.

In keeping with the need in the horse for prolonged running ability and exceptional cardiovascular efficiency, the weight of the heart in relation to bodyweight is over *twice* as great as in cattle. Brody and Kibler give the weight of the heart in a 1320-pound horse as 9.4 pounds (or about 1/14 of the bodyweight) while in a 1540-pound steer it was only 5.1 pounds (1/30 of the bodyweight).

Among various other animals which were tested, the horse has been found to be the champion sweater. During a 24-hour period while at rest, an average-sized horse lost 6.4 pounds of perspiration; in trotting, this was increased to 14 pounds. Donkeys and mules sweat less profusely than do horses.

The digestive tract in a horse is anatomically and physiologically quite different from that in a cow or other ruminating animal. The stomach consists of a single compartment, whereas in ruminants there are four compartments. In the horse the small intestine is somewhat smaller than in the cow, while the large intestine has a capacity twice as great. In a horse 61 inches in height, the total length of the intestines was over 98 feet, or nearly 20 times the shoulder height of the animal. In a donkey the ratio was over 15 times the height, and in a zebra only about 11 times the height.[10] Thus the domestic horse has relatively a very long digestive tract. This is mainly on account of the great length of the *small* intestine. In relation to trunk length, the alimentary canal in the horse is about *twice* as long as that in man.

The muscular and skeletal development of the horse is a subject of special interest, since it is directly correlated with the ability of the animal to perform in its particular field (e.g., running or load-pulling). The following particulars on muscular and skeletal anatomy in the horse have been taken from various earlier studies, mostly by German zoologists, who laboriously derived the information through careful dissections and measurings.

In a horse of the German Trakehner or cavalry breed, weighing 456 kg (1005 pounds), the separate weights of various parts and organs were as follows: bones of each forelimb (fresh, not dried), about 12 2/3 pounds; each hind limb, 16.3 pounds; trunk, 56.4 pounds; skull (including lower jaw), 18 1/3 pounds; total, 132 2/3 pounds, or 13.2 percent of the living bodyweight. In the same (freshly dissected) condition, the bones of an average man constitute about 15 percent of his bodyweight, and of a well-trained athlete about 13 3/4 percent. After the bones, either of a horse or a man, have become thoroughly dry, they weigh only about 57 or 58 percent as much as when fresh. Hence in the above 1000-pound horse, the *dry* bones would weigh about 76½ pounds, or 7.6 percent of the bodyweight. That a general correspondence between skeleton weight and bodyweight exists among mammals of various sizes and types is indicated by the fact that in the domestic cat the relative fresh weight of the bones is about 13.6 percent of the bodyweight; in dogs (well nourished but not fat) 14–15 percent; in beef cattle 14.7 percent; and in small bats 14.6 percent. In animals which normally carry a great deal of fat the ratio is correspondingly lower. Thus in guinea pigs it averages only 8.8 percent, in mice 8.4 percent, in rabbits 8.1–9.2 percent, and in fat swine only 6.3–6.7 percent. Surprisingly, in the elephant, whose ponderous bulk consists mainly of bone and muscle rather than fat, the weight of the skeleton rises to over 18 percent of the living bodyweight.

The relative weights of the muscles of the horse and other animals show a similar correlation with that of the entire body. In both the horse and in man the muscles comprise, on the average, about 48 percent of the bodyweight. In domestic sheep the ratio is about 40 percent; in albino mice, 45.4 percent; and in the elephant about 51.5 percent. The amount of blood in a 1000-pound horse is about 66 pounds, or approximately 1/15 of the bodyweight.

While many of the muscles of the horse are analogous in position and action to those in man, we need concern ourselves here only with those involved in the chief activities of the horse: walking, running, and jumping. All the joints of the limb of the horse are essentially "hinge joints" that act only in one plane (fore-and-aft). Hence the muscles acting on these joints are mostly either simple "flexors" (which bend the distal segments backward on the segment above) or "extensors" (which return the segments to the straight position). The structure of the joints prevents the segments being bent forwards much beyond a straight alignment with the segment above. Also, the limbs cannot be swung very far to the sides. Because of this, some of the extensor muscles (e.g., those which extend the feet) are located on the front surface of the limb, and some of the flexor muscles on the rear or hinder surface; and the muscles are grouped so as to provide maximum power in a fore-and-aft direction.

Muscles are like rubber bands; and when they move a bone to which they are attached, they do so always by *pulling,* never by pushing. Thus, either in man or in the horse, the action of any particular muscle, or combination of muscles, may be deduced from the points on the bones to which the muscle is attached. From this principle it follows that a horse's limbs are drawn forward by muscles on the fronts of them, and are pushed backward by muscles on the rear surfaces of the limbs. Accordingly, the muscles involved in the principal actions of the horse—walking, running, and jumping—are mainly muscles of the limbs, in particular those on the backs of the upper segments of the limbs, which supply the power to propel the body forward or upward.

While horsemen constantly point out the need in a horse for great power in the extensor muscles of its hind limbs, actually there is an equal need for such power in the corresponding muscles of the *forelimbs.* This may be observed in the action of a horse which is exerting its maximum power in drawing a heavy load (see Fig. 162). In such an effort the triceps and forearm extensor muscles of the front legs are as heavily taxed as are the rear-thigh and buttocks muscles of the hind legs. The same need for proportionately strong *forelimb* muscles exists in all four-legged cursorial mammals, including the horse, in such habitual actions as running and jumping. In most such animals a larger portion of the bodyweight has to be borne by the forelegs than by the hind ones. This probably accounts for the girth of the forearms in the horse being greater than that of the gaskins, and for the triceps muscles of the upper arms being comparable in power with the large extensor muscles of the hip joints.

Fig. 145 shows some of the principal muscles of the horse, while Table 20 lists the names of these muscles and gives their actions.

The specific gravity of a horse's body averages about 1.026. This is practically identical to the same ratio in the cat, dog, deer, and other four-footed mammals in which the measurement has been taken. In man the SG is generally given as 1.040, which higher figure may be due to his relatively heavier limbs and smaller chest and abdominal cavities.

The surface area (in square feet) of a horse is equal, on the average, to the cube root of the bodyweight in pounds squared, times .5233. Thus in a 1000-pound horse the area would be about 52.33 square feet; and in a 2000-pound horse, about 83.08 square feet.

In the above-cited 1000-pound Trakehner horse the head weighed about 39½ pounds, the hide (without hoofs) 33 1/3 pounds, the four hoofs 6½ pounds, the heart 7.2 pounds, and the brain 25.36 ounces or a little over 1½ pounds. This brings us to the subject of brain weight and intelligence in the horse as compared with certain other animals.

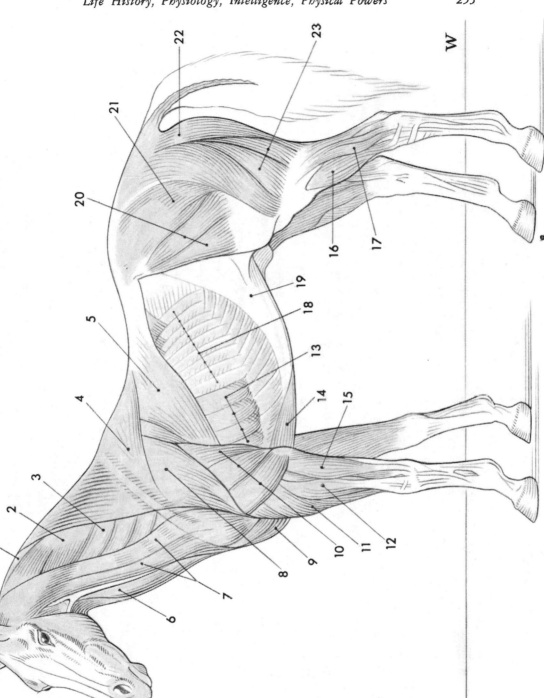

Fig. 145 Some of the principal muscles of the horse (outer or superficial layer). For names and actions of the muscles numbered, see Table 20.

Table 20. Some of the principal muscles of the horse (see Fig. 145).
(outer or superficial layer)

No.	Name	Meaning of Latin Name	Action
1	Rhomboideus	"Rhomb-shaped muscle"	Draws shoulder upward and forward.
2	Splenius	"Splenid muscle"	With 1, 3, and 4, raises neck and head; acting alone, inclines head to one side.
3	Serratus cervicus	"Saw-toothed neck muscle"	Supports neck between shoulder-blades; acting on one side only, shifts weight to leg on that side.
4	Trapezius	"Table-shaped muscle"	Raises shoulder and carries it forward or backward, depending upon which of its fibers contract.
5	Latissimus dorsi	"Broadest of the back muscle"	Draws the upper arm upwards and backwards; flexes the shoulder joint; if foreleg is fixed, moves body forward.
6	Sterno-mandibularis	(derived from attachments of muscle)	Both right and left muscles together pull head down to neck; one muscle only pulls head toward that side.
7	Sterno-cephalicus	(derived from attachments of muscle)	Both right and left muscles together pull head down to neck; one muscle only pulls head toward that side.
8	Deltoiceus	"Triangular or delta-shaped muscle"	Abducts and raises the upper arm (foreleg).
9	Pectoralis major	"Greater breast muscle"	Draws the upper arm forward and inward.
10	Triceps brachii	"Three-headed extensor of the forearm"	Extends forearm; flexes upper arm on scapula.
11	Extensor carpi radialis	"Extensor of the wrist ('knee') on the radial side"	Extends the wrist ("knee").
12	Extensor digitorum communis	"Common extensor of the digits (pasterns)"	Extends the phalanges (pasterns) of the forelegs.
13	Serratus thoracis	"Saw-toothed side-chest muscle"	Elevates the ribs in inspiration (inhalation).
14	Pectoralis minor	"Lesser breast muscle"	Depresses the point of the shoulder.
15	Extensor carpi ulnaris	"Extensor of the wrist ('knee') on the ulinar side"	Extends the wrist ("knee").
16	Extensor digitorum longus	"Long extensor of the digits (hind pasterns)"	Extends the phalanges (pasterns) of the hind leg.
17	Extensor digitorum pedis lateralis	"Extensor of the side toes"	Extends the hind foot.
18	Intercostalis	"Between-the-ribs muscle"	Raises and lowers the ribs in breathing.
19	Obliquus abdominis externus	"External oblique muscle of the abdomen"	Bends the trunk sideways; arches the back.
20	Tensor fascia lata	"Tightener of the broad fascia"	Tightens the fascia, flexes hip joint, extends stifle joint.
21	Gluteus maximum	"Largest buttock muscle"	Extends, abducts, and rotates thigh (hind leg) outward.
22	Semitendinosus	"Half-tendinous muscle"	Acts with other back-leg muscles to extend hip and hock joints and flex leg (gaskin).
23	Biceps femoris	"Two-headed flexor of	Flexes and rotates the leg (gaskin) outwards in

c. Intelligence of the Horse.

Opinion on this point would appear to be sharply divided between horse-lovers, who assert positively that their favorite mounts can really think, and zoologists, including veterinarians, who point out that the horse lacks that portion of the brain—the pro-encephalon—which makes thinking possible. That many kinds of lower animals can be *trained* to perform certain actions, and to respond apparently with intelligence when placed in certain situations, is a matter of common observation. Animal psychologists, however, say that the true measure of intelligence is *the capacity to learn* (or to solve new problems by drawing on past experience), and that some adjustments, such as reflexes and instincts, occur naturally without learning and without involving the brain.

As means for establishing the degree of intelligence of animals (i.e., nonhuman ones), two resources are available. One is called the anecdotal approach, the other the objective (experimental) method. By "anecdotal" is meant *accounts* of occurrences assertedly seen either first-hand or transmitted by presumably reputable reporters. By the "experimental method" is meant tests made under laboratory conditions by trained observers using uniform, measurable techniques. While the latter approach has its shortcomings—such, for example, as not duplicating the natural environment of an animal—it has the virtue of being objective and not dependent upon what an observer *supposes* or declares that he saw. The anecdotal approach is also to be regarded with caution and reservation because of its often seeming credibility, especially when championed by a clever orator or novelist.

As an example of how even experienced observers can be deceived by the *apparent* intelligence of an animal, there is the case of "Hans, the educated horse." Hans was one of three such horses which were owned by a Herr von Osten, of Berlin. In 1901 von Osten announced to the press that his horse, Hans, could solve difficult mathematical problems and could understand and reply to spoken or written questions. The problems were written on a large blackboard, and the horse gave the answer by tapping on the ground with his forehoofs, indicating units with the right foot and tens with the left. When verbal answers were required, Hans would spell out his reply by tapping a certain number for each letter of the alphabet, the latter being arranged before him on a large chart. Investigators who had marvelled at the horse's apparent ability discovered that this ability was dependent upon von Osten's presence. Whenever the master was absent the animal would act like any ordinary horse and would be quite unable to solve the simplest problems or spell even a single short word. The horse had learned to respond to very slight, involuntary cues given by von Osten, and would start tapping under certain conditions and stop when his master changed position slightly or relaxed when the right number of taps had been given. Von Osten had sincerely believed that Hans performed independently of cues, and was very crestfallen when he learned that this was not the case.

Additional instances of such "thinking" horses could be presented. There was, for example, the highly publicized "Lady Wonder—Mind-Reading Horse," of Richmond, Virginia, who in the early 1950s fooled even trained psychologists. It took a professional magician to point out that all of Lady Wonder's tricks could be remote-controlled by a person in another room who was tuned into the questions asked the horse, and that the desired answers could be given irrespective of what the animal did. Evidently "clairvoyance," with a horse as the "medium" could explain the whole affair.

Where laboratory intelligence tests were given, as at Columbia University by Prof. C. J. Warden in 1950, it was found that the ranking of various chosen animals was usually about as follows: (1) chimpanzee, (2) orangutan, (3) gorilla, (4) monkey, (5) dog, (6) cat, (7) raccoon, (8) elephant, (9) pig, (10) horse. But there have been many criticisms of these ratings by "outdoor" observers not in sympathy with laboratory methods of testing intelligence. Particularly have horsemen objected to the pig being placed before the horse. However, most observers agree that both the donkey and the mule have more "horse-sense" than the horse, although this may result from the former two animals having more stable emotional makeups than the horse, rather than a higher degree of intelligence.

Again, many types of wild animals (types seldom listed in the usual "intelligence" tests) are decidedly more brainy and quick-witted than domestic animals of comparable species. Otters, for example, have given abundant evidence of being smarter and more adaptable (within their physical limitations) than any dog. Foxes are proverbially cunning in outwitting their canine pursuers, and much of this reputation is based on observed facts. Wild rabbits have far-better-developed brains than domestic ones. And the same natural superiority may exist in the brains of wild horses.

The comparative anatomist Daniel P. Quiring has prepared lists showing how many different types of animals compare in what he calls the "cephalization coefficient." This may be taken as the ratio of brain development to body size (weight). On this basis, if we let man's ratio be represented by 1.00, the ratios of certain lower animals become as follows: anthropoid apes .35, elephant .29, baboon .23, polar bear .18, caribou .16, arctic fox .15, horse .14, lower monkeys .13, dogs (generally) .12, lion .11, weasel .10, domestic cats (average) .09, cattle .09; rats, mice, and other rodents (average) .04, and shrews .02.[11] While this method of appraisal should satisfy horse-lovers (since the pig ranks only about .11), it will probably be met with indignation by owners of white mice, rabbits, and golden hamsters!

It should be noted that in Quiring's method high values are found for most aquatic animals. Seals and walruses, for instance, have an average rating of .22, and cetaceans (whales) no less than .61! As Quiring says, "If brain size were correlated directly with intelligence, the cetaceans (whales) should be the most intelligent of all animals excepting man . . ." Nevertheless, his method gives in many cases a more dependable index of the probable intelligence of animals than do some of the laboratory tests which express the animal's reactions only.

That probable intelligence may be inferred from certain anatomical measurements is shown by the following list of ratios, in which the weight of the brain is divided by the weight of the spinal cord.[12]

Weight of Brain / Weight of Spinal Cord		
	Ratio	Relatively
Man	33.00	1.000
Dog	5.14	0.156
Cat	3.75	0.114
Donkey	2.40	0.073
Pig	2.30	0.070
Horse	2.27	0.069
Ox	2.18	0.066

While Sisson's *The Anatomy of the Domestic Animals* (Philadelphia, 1927) gives ratios of 2.98 for the pig, 2.63 for the horse, and 2.04 for the ox, it maintains the respective standings of the three animals.

A "Relative Intelligence" ratio discovered by the writer is the following.

Table 21. Intelligence in relation to Adult Age / Gestation Length.

Species	(A) Adult Age, yrs.	(B) Gestation, yrs.	(A)/(B) Adult Age Gestation	Relative Intelligence*
Man	21	0.746 (272 days)	28.2	1.00
Gorilla	12.5	0.712 (260 days)	17.5	0.39
Chimpanzee (& Orang)	11	0.630 (230 days)	17.5	0.39
Elephant (Asiatic)	25 ?	1.750 (640 days)	14.3	0.26
Whale (Blue)	9.5 ?	0.850 (310 days)	11.2	0.15
Lion (African)	3	0.296 (108 days)	10.1	0.13
Dog (av.)	1.5	0.178 (65 days)	8.4	0.09
Cat	1	0.160 (58 days)	6.3	0.05
Horse	5	0.923 (337 days)	5.4	0.037
Pig	1.7	0.315 (115 days)	5.4	0.037
Cow	4	0.767 (280 days)	5.2	0.034
Donkey	5	1.027 (375 days)	4.9	0.030
Sheep	1.5	0.414 (151 days)	3.6	0.013
Mouse (house)	0.25	0.069 (20 days)	3.6	0.013

* In order to be more directly comparable with the study of Quiring, this factor is derived by taking the *square root* of A/B for the species in question divided by A/B in man.

Table 21 is presented to show that evidently the longer it takes for an animal to reach maturity, as compared with the length of the gestation, the greater its intelligence. In other words, if the brain is hurried in its postnatal development, the degree of its functioning power is lessened, and vice versa. Hence the superior intelligence of man, the anthropoid apes, and the elephant, all of which have a long period of postnatal growth as compared with the length of gestation. In Table 21, as in the sequences determined by Dr. Quiring, next to man come the anthropoid apes and then the elephant. Quiring, however, ranks the horse above the dog and the cat, while in Table 21 (and rightly, it would appear), this sequence is reversed. Other lists omit marine mammals, such as the whale, the dolphin, and the porpoise, which species are now known to be among the most intelligent of all nonhuman animals. And for once, Table 21 places the horse on a par with the pig and above his lowly cousin the domestic ass.* One suspects, however, that over-sentimental animal fanciers, in evaluating intelligence, are apt to be unduly influenced by what they regard as beauty of appearance,** and so to assign inferior places to such inelegant creatures as the donkey and the pig. Perhaps if the latter two animals were not so homely their places in the scale of animal intelligence would be more generally acknowledged!

One should bear in mind that in so-called intelligence tests what is being recorded is the animal's *manifestations* of intelligence, not necessarily the intelligence itself. Hoofed mammals, such as the horse and the cow, cannot be expected to exhibit the manual dexterity of apes, with their hands and fingers, or of the elephant, with its universally useful proboscis. Hence the basic brain development of hoofed animals,

---

* Major Lamb, in his book *Horse Facts* (1947), p. 47, points out that a high degree of reasoning power, as opposed to memory, is not desirable in a horse, as it makes the animal impatient of control by man. Lamb says that "useful" intelligence depends on a high degree of instinct, not "reason," and that the action of instinct is *impeded* by a large brain.[13]

** In this connection see especially the rhapsodical praise given by an Arab to his horse (p. 164).

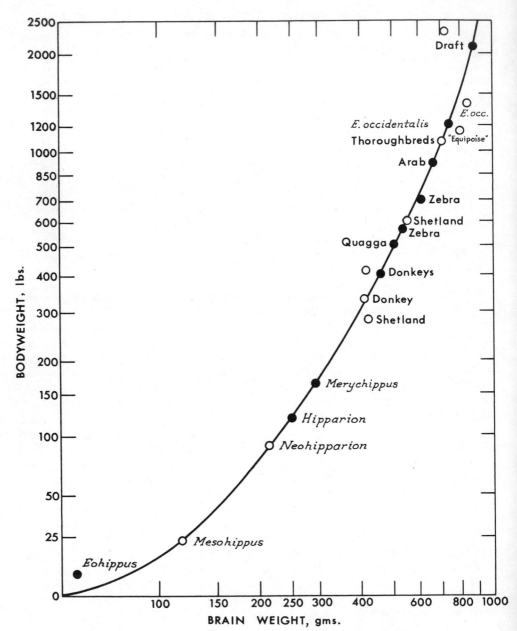

Fig. 146 Brain weight vs. body weight in the Equidae.

for example, may not be so inferior as their physical limitations indicate. In any case, man should accept and admire each lower animal species for its individual, particular abilities, and not degrade it for lacking powers that are contrary to its structural and physiological makeup.

Fig. 146 shows the evolutionary increase in the size of the equine body and brain that has taken place during the 55,000,000 years separating *Eohippus* and *Equus*. The typical trend of brain weight in relation to bodyweight is seen to follow a definite curve, irrespective of genus, species, or breed. From *Neohipparion* to *Equus* the correlation formula is: Brain Weight, grams $= 607$ (log Bodyweight $+ 100$) $- 1179$. For a 1000-pound horse this gives an average brain weight of 673 grams (or about 24 ounces), and for a 2000-pound horse 838 grams (or about 30 ounces). One of the largest brains in a Thoroughbred was that of Equipoise, who at a bodyweight of about 1150 pounds (in racing condition about 1090 pounds) had a brain weight of 800 grams. This was nearly 100 grams more than that of an average-sized brain in a horse of Equipoise's weight. The heaviest brain weight charted in Fig. 146 is that of a draft horse weighing about 2100 pounds who had a brain weight of 900 grams or nearly 2 pounds.

d. Gaits of the Horse.

This subject has been so thoroughly expounded in numerous previous treatises* on horsemanship that it will be dealt with lightly herein, where the emphasis is on zoology rather than equitation.

Gaits are classified according to the sequence of limb movements, number of feet upon the ground at successive instants, and similar points. The gaits most commonly referred to are the walk, the trot, the pace, and the gallop. From these basic gaits have been developed numerous artificial ones, such as the canter, the amble, the stepping pace, the fox trot, the running walk, and the rack. In addition there are such movements as the transverse or side step, in which the animal simply steps alternately to one side and the other without moving forward or backward. Such movements are purely for show or exhibition use, and have no connection with the natural modes of locomotion peculiar to the horse in its native habitats.

The WALK is a natural, slow, flatfooted, four-beat gait; the latter meaning that each footfall is separate and evenly spaced. At all speeds of the walk there is always at least one foot on the ground. The walk is said to be the most nearly ideal form of locomotion, since in it any deviation from the horizontal is minimal, and support and propulsion are both uniform and continuous. In walking, the sequence of steps is (1) left fore, (2) right hind, (3) right fore, (4) left hind, etc. A horse's speed in the walk is ordinarily 4–4½ mph, 5 mph being considered fairly rapid. In walking, cattle expend less energy than humans, and horses less than cattle.

The TROT is a natural, rapid, two-beat, diagonal gait. The sequence of steps is

---

* See especially the series of gaits described and beautifully illustrated in *Horse Anatomy*, by Lewis S. Brown (N.Y.: Bridgman, 1948). A thorough, technical analysis of the various gaits of four-footed animals, particularly the horse, is given in *Speed in Animals*, by A. Brazier Howell (Univ. of Chicago Press, 1944, pp. 217–47). A third, more recent, treatise is *Animal Locomotion*, by James Gray (N.Y.: W. W. Norton, 1968). Finally, for those desiring a treatment of the subject from the standpoint of *evolution*, there is the highly technical paper, *Notes on the Principles of Quadrupedal Locomotion and on the Mechanism of the Limbs in Hoofed Animals*, by William K. Gregory (Annals N.Y. Acad. Sciences 22 (October 18, 1912): 267–94.

(1) left fore and right hind, and (2) right fore and left hind, etc. There is an instant when all four feet are off the ground and the animal seemingly floats through the air. There is also a walking or slow-tempo trot, with a step-sequence of (1) both fore and both hind, (2) left fore and right hind, (3) both fore and both hind, and (4) right fore and left hind, etc. Speed in the trot is ordinarily 8–9 mph, but may rise to over 30 mph in the case of champion trotters drawing light sulkies. The trot is the least tiring of the paces to a horse, for going long distances at a fair rate of speed, but it is fatiguing to the rider, who generally would prefer a canter or a walk.

The PACE is a specialized, two-beat, lateral gait in which the fore and the hind feet *on the same side* work together, the step-sequence being (1) left fore and left hind, (2) right fore and right hind, etc. The possibility of speed in the pace is practically identical with that in the trot, but the pace is more tiring even though there is a lesser side-to-side (i.e., rocking) movement. By training, and the use of leg-controlling straps or hobbles, a young trotter may be converted into a pacer, or vice versa.

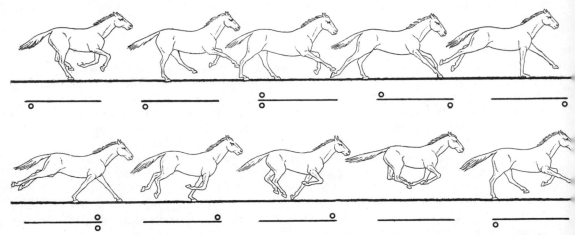

Fig. 147 Ten phases of the action of a horse in full transverse gallop. Under each phase is the corresponding footfall formula. As is shown in phase 9, at one stage of the gallop a horse has all four feet off the ground.

The GALLOP is a natural, fast, four-beat gait wherein the feet strike the ground separately, the sequence being (1) left hind or right hind, (2) right hind or left hind, (3) left fore or right fore, and (4) right fore or left fore, etc. The double-bound (i.e., *two* "off the ground" periods during a stride) of the cheetah—which action requires a *much more flexible backbone* than does a gallop—gives the feline a potential speed about 50 percent greater than that of a racehorse, which has all four of its feet off the ground only once during a stride.* Fig. 147 shows the successive placements of a horse's feet in the gallop. Ordinary speed in a gallop is about 16 mph, but in championship class racehorses it may reach 40 mph or over.

The CANTER** is a slow, restrained, three-beat gait, or "collected gallop." The

---

* A "stride" is the full series of movements of all legs until they regain the position from which they started. As a measure of distance, it is the length from any footprint to the next footprint of the same leg.

** The word CANTER is said to have come from the pace used by the Canterbury pilgrims.

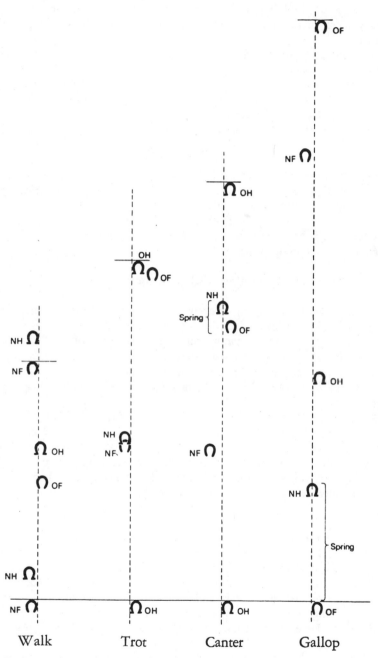

Fig. 148 Foot tracks of a horse in various gaits. From the bottom to the top foot in each line (gait) is a single stride. NH= near or left hind; NF= near or left fore; OH= off, or right, hind; OF= off, or right, fore.

sequence of steps is (1) left hind, (2) right hind and left fore, and (3) right fore, etc. Ordinary speed in the canter is about 12 mph, and the average length of a stride is about 12 feet.

Fig. 148 depicts the foot tracks of a horse at various of the above-described gaits.

The AMBLE is a slow, easy, pacing movement. Although it is an unnatural gait for the horse, some foals do it before learning to trot. Standardbred racehorses often amble after being footsore from too much fast trotting. According to Major A. J. R. Lamb, natives of Iceland breed amblers, and Dutch farmers in South Africa "make a considerable use of amblers."[13] The amble is the natural gait of the camel and the elephant.

The RACK, which was formerly (but is now only rarely) called "single-foot," is a fast, artificial, four-beat gait in which each foot meets the ground separately at equal intervals. The rack is said to be the most popular gait in the American show-ring, being fast, flashy, and eye-catching.

Other gaits, such as the stepping pace, the fox trot, the running walk, etc., are exclusively show-ring steps, and in this connection are described in detail in treatises on the techniques of horsemanship.

e. Running Ability in the Horse.

Years ago, the writer made an extensive investigation of the running abilities of cursorial mammals of various kinds, in an endeavor to ascertain if possible what physical (anatomical) factors determine running speed. One of the outcomes of this research was a formula relating speed to size, weight, and build. It may be said, in a very general way (which applies to the *average or typical* characteristics of a *species*, but not nectssarily to *individual* animals), that the relative running or sprinting speed of mammals possessing a given type of skeletal conformation is correlated with the size and build of those animals. Horses are one type of such animals; deer, antelopes, and gazelles are another type; cats, a third type; dogs, a fourth type; man, a fifth type; and so on.

If we have the speed formula for a racehorse we can apply it to a draft horse, a donkey, a zebra, or even another type of perissodactyl (odd-toed) hoofed animal, the rhinoceros, provided we know the height, weight, and other essential body measurements (particularly the length of the limbs) of the animals for which we wish to estimate the speed.

In determining the running power of a wild animal, the investigators usually drive an automobile behind or alongside the fleeing creature and clock it over a variable distance by the speed of the car. The information thus obtained is customarily recorded as the maximum sprinting speed of the animal. The distance over which the animal has been urged to its utmost speed is in most cases in the neighborhood of a quarter-mile, and the timing is not commenced until the animal presumably is going at near its top speed. In some cases certain species of game animals have been run to a standstill by being pursued by automobile for mile after mile. However, such instances have served more to demonstrate the *endurance* of the fleeing animal than its utmost sprinting *speed*.

The domestic horse has become the classic basis for comparison with the known or presumed maximum speeds of various swift-footed animals in the wild. But it should be recognized in making such comparisons that the horse, like the wild animal, should be timed only after it has had an ample running start (and not from a standing

Fig. 149 "Equine freedom," a study in arrested motion. Ghaniha, a four-year-old purebred Arabian stallion, bred and raised at the San Simeon Stables, Hearst's Ranch, San Simeon, California. Ghaniha is in phase 1 of the gallop as illustrated in Fig. 147. Note, however, that Ghaniha's feet are in the position of a *lateral* rather than a *transverse* gallop.

start), and that due allowance should be made for the slowing-down effect of the weight of the jockey and his trappings on the horse. It has been argued, and admittedly with some force, that a skilled jockey can urge a racehorse on to its maximum speed; but it is still probable that the same animal, freed of all encumbering weight and running for its life, would attain even greater speed. A third consideration is that all sprinting races should be run and timed over a straight, not a curved, course. This, however, is standard practice when the distance is limited to a quarter-mile.

Presumably it has become an axiom that no individual horse can excel both at short and middle distances, such, for example, as 220 yards and one mile. This is certainly true of human runners, and hardly ever is there a champion in the 100-yard sprint who shows up equally well at any distance beyond 220 yards. Actually there is a different training technique, and different record holders, in races at 1/8 mile, 1/4 mile, 1/2 mile, and a full mile, respectively. So, to apply the same considerations to racehorses, it would appear unreasonable to expect a Thoroughbred trained to run at distances from 1/2 mile to 1 1/4 miles to run equally well at so short a distance as a quarter-mile or less. Nevertheless, occasional match races between selected Thoroughbreds (i.e., those having sprinting ability) and Quarter Horses have indicated that, with specialized training in quick starting, the Thoroughbred might well run the shorter distances in as fast times as the Quarter Horse. However, about all that such an achievement would demonstrate would be that the Thoroughbred had increased its starting speed. With both a champion Quarter Horse and a champion Thoroughbred in full stride, at any distance between 50 yards and 500 yards, it would indeed be a

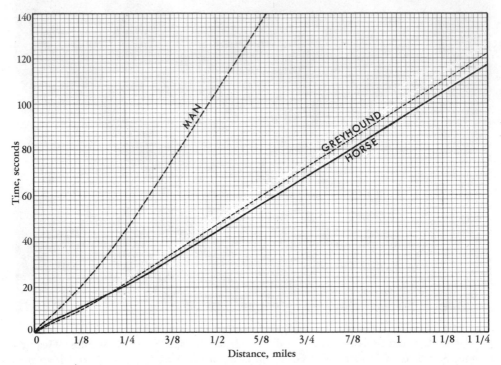

Fig. 150 Running time, in relation to distance, for man, greyhound, and race-horse, respectively. For further explanation see text. (Cf. Fig. 151.)

question as to which horse was the faster. But just how fast can the fastest horse run when fully "under way"?

To answer the latter question is the purpose of the two accompanying graphs (Figs. 150 and 151, respectively). For comparison are given also the speed curves of man and greyhound. The respective curves for man, greyhound, and horse have been derived from the best official records available for each, for the various distances indicated. For the horse, the most dependable records, for distances up to and including a quarter-mile, are those of the Quarter Horse. From 3/8 mile upward, Thoroughbred records fall into line with those of the Quarter Horse, provided the amount of the running start is in each case known and the corresponding time added to the Thorough-bred time as recorded. (Quarter Horse races are from a *standing* start, and Thorough-bred races from a *running* start of 20–60 feet, averaging 45 feet.* With a 45-foot start, 0.9 second should be *added* to Thoroughbred records to make them directly comparable with Quarter Horse records (i.e., those of 1/4 mile or less), and vice versa).

In graphing the running records for various distances, it is seen that certain records are better than others when judged by the general trend of all the records from 100 yards to 440 yards (see Fig. 143). For man, the present official amateur records for 100 yards (9.1 seconds), 220 yards (with turn, 20.0 seconds), and 440 yards (44.7

---

* However, to complicate matters, this distance may vary among different tracks and for longer races. At Santa Anita (Calif.), for example, the distance allowed for a running start in a *mile* race is about 50 *yards*.

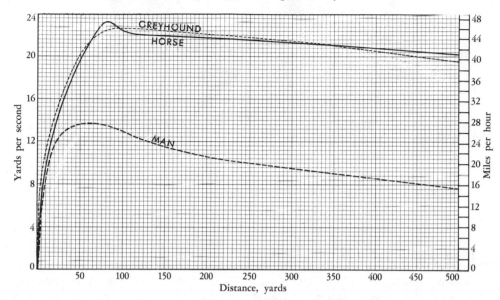

Fig. 151 Speeds, at given distances, as derived from the curves plotted in Fig. 150. It is seen that the horse attains its maximum speed at about 80 yards (23.22 yards per second or 47.5 miles per hour), the greyhound between 90 and 120 yards (22.73 yards per second, or 46.49 miles per hour), and the man between 60 and 75 yards (13.636 yards per second, or 27.893 miles per hour). The horse, which takes off less rapidly than the dog, but which on the average travels 6.5 percent faster, overtakes and passes the dog at somewhere between 340 and 350 yards and from there on maintains the lead.

seconds), respectively, are approximately equal in merit.* For greyhound, the relatively best marks are for 100 yards (5.4 seconds) and 345 yards (17.1 seconds). For Quarter Horse, the relatively best marks are for 100 yards (6.1 seconds) and 440 yards (22.0 seconds). When the best time made from a *running* start (by a Thoroughbred) is considered, the latter time (i.e., for 440 yards) becomes about 20.8 seconds.

Every so often one will read where, over a short distance, some human sprinter outran a racehorse. Such a statement is true only where the horse has been handicapped in some way. Most Standardbred horses, for example, are of necessity slow starters,** and it is possible for a first-class human sprinter to beat such a horse at any distance up to about 50 yards. But in a race with a horse ridden under the saddle, especially a fast-starting Quarter Horse, no man has a chance. In one race of this kind, the horse was up and away before the man was even out of his crouching start, and the man was one of the greatest sprinters of all time.

---

* More precisely, it would appear that 20 seconds flat in the 220 yards (with turn) is equivalent to 9.06 seconds for 100 yeards and 44.52 seconds for 440 yards. Hence the record for 220 yards is slightly more meritorious than those for the two other distances.

** Yet some such horses are evidently able to make a quick start despite having to draw a sulky. One horseman says that he had a pacing mare that could "stand flat-footed and catch the fastest boy in the community inside of 35 yards."

Fig. 152 "They're off!" The start of a race between a human sprinter, a **Quarter Horse**, and a greyhound. For details, see text.

A greyhound is a very fast animal for its size, and because of its smallness is able to make a faster start than even the quickest-starting Quarter Horse. It leaves its starting gate literally like a "bolt from the blue," and is overtaken by a horse only after some 350 to 400 yards of galloping. Theoretically, the fastest racehorse enters its full stride at about 50 yards, which it covers in 3.84 seconds. The same distance is covered by the fastest human sprinter in about 5 seconds flat, and by the fastest greyhound in about 3.1 seconds. Faster even than the greyhound, however, is the cheetah, or hunting leopard, which is said to have been timed at 44 yards in 2 seconds flat! This would be equal to 50 yards in about 2.2 seconds, an example of almost unbelievable accelerative power in a four-footed running machine.

A detailed analysis of the accompanying graphs, on a larger scale, has been made by the writer, and from this analysis it has been possible to determine the precise distances, theoretically, between which the fastest man, the fastest greyhound, and the fastest Quarter Horse reach their respective maximum speeds. Man's utmost sprinting speed (to date, at any rate), as is shown in Fig. 151, is about 13.64 yards per second or 27.9 mph. This speed was attained by sprinter Bob Hayes in St. Louis on June 21, 1963, in a 100-yard race in which he was clocked at 25-yard intervals. In that race, Hayes covered the distance between 50 and 75 yards in 1.9 seconds, or at the rate of 26.9 mph, and in all probability covered the distance between 60 and 75 yards in 1.1 seconds, which would have equalled the aforementioned 27.9 mph. This is a more accurate method of determining a sprinter's true *maximum* speed (even if it can be maintained for only 10 or 15 yards) than by taking his time over 100 yards from a standing (or crouching) start and figuring the average speed, which in Hayes's case would have been 22.22 mph.

On the same graph (Fig. 151), the greyhound's maximum speed is indicated as 22.73 yards per second or 46.49 mph. This speed is based on an estimated time for 75 yards of 4.3 seconds and for 100 yards of 5.4 seconds. The maximum speed. is maintained roughly between 90 and 120 yards, after which there is a gradual deceleration which almost parallels that in man.

The Quarter Horse, curiously, reaches a peak of 23.22 yards per second or 47.5 mph* at about 80 yards, after which the speed rapidly decreases to 22.3 yards per

---

* Minus a 116-pound rider, this brief spurt should increase to 50 mph!

Fig. 153 Miss Princess (Woven Web) setting a Quarter Horse world record of 22 seconds flat for 440 yards (= 40.91 mph). On the left is Lightfoot and in the background Stella Moore, whose time, according to this photograph, would have been 22.1. The race took place at Del Rio, Texas, on April 30, 1948.

second (or 45.6 mph) at 100 yards, and to an even 22 yards per second (45 mph) at 130–140 yards. From the latter distance onward the deceleration in speed takes place very gradually, indicating a slower onset of fatigue than occurs in the greyhound or in man. The best records for the Arabian horse would come between the curves for the greyhound and the Quarter Horse, being on the average about .925 as fast as those of the latter horse.

The Quarter Horse's fastest quarter-mile is, theoretically, between 50 yards and 490 yards. This distance, with the standard load of 116 pounds, the horse covers in 20.58 seconds, a speed of 21.38 yards per second or 43.73 mph. Riderless, the speed should increase to 46.00 mph, and it is *this* speed (over the customary quarter-mile, with an ample running start) which should be used in comparing a racehorse's maximum sprinting speed with that of other animals timed in their natural surroundings by observers following in automobiles. Of course, if there are obstacles in the natural running course, or if the animal runs in zig-zag fashion rather than in a straight line, the slowing-up effect of these or other factors should be taken into account in arriving at a fair estimate of the pursued animal's speed.

Table 22, following, lists the world records in Thoroughbred racing up to August 16, 1970, at which date the present record for 6½ furlongs (13/16 mile) was established by the horse Turbulator. In addition to the actual records, the table lists "predicted" times for the various distances as computed from a formula that correlates their general trend from ¼ mile to 4 miles. Actually, the speed from ¼ mile to 1 mile decelerates at a slightly slower rate than at distances over a mile, and from about 5/8 mile onward reduces more rapidly so as to meet the tempo of the longer distances. From 1 mile onward (to 4 miles, at any rate) the correlation between time and distance can be expressed by the logarithmic formula: log Time, sec. = 1.119 log Distance, miles + 1.9618.*

This formula yields the times listed in Table 22 under the heading Time, sec., Formula, and shows that some of the listed records are highly meritorious as they stand, while others are subject to considerable improvement. As would be expected, most of the better records are those at 1/4-mile intervals, while many of the other listed marks, at 1/16 and 1/8 mile intervals, are credited to horses of lesser ability. Above 1 1/4 miles, 1/16-mile distances have been omitted from the table on account of their uniform inferiority.

In this connection, the attention of the reader is called to a remarkable earlier study of the subject, entitled *An Approximate Law of Fatigue in the Speeds of Racing Animals,* by A. E. Kennelly. In this paper Kennelly presents curves and formulas equating the running records of trotting horses, pacing horses, Thoroughbreds, and of men walking, running, rowing, skating, bicycling, and swimming. In all cases the type of correlation formulas used by Kennelly produce a more or less straight-line "curve" when plotted on a double logarithmic grid.

Kennelly found that in all the aforementioned events the same principle applied, namely that "The time varies approximately as the ninth power of the eighth root of the distance." In the case of running (i.e., Thoroughbred) horses, Kennelly's formula is: log Time, seconds = 9/8 log Distance, meters — 1.6274. This may be converted to read: log Time, seconds = 1.125 log Distance, miles + 1.9801. For comparison, the present writer's formula, as noted above, is: log Time, seconds = 1.119 log Distance, miles + 1.9618. The need of a larger additive in Kennelly's formula is occasioned by the horse-racing records in 1906 having been lower than the records of today.

A criticism that may be made of Kennelly's equation is that he extends it downward clear to 1/4 mile, allowing no diminution in speed over the shorter "getting under way" distances. As a result, his formula predicts times of only 20.08 seconds for 1/4 mile, 31.69 seconds for 3/8 mile, 37.68 seconds for 7/16 mile, and 43.79 seconds for 1/2 mile. Only at 9/16 mile does his predicted time (50.01 seconds) approximate today's record for the distance. Beyond 9/16 mile the times predicted become progressively larger (or slower) and accordingly less conformable with the records listed in Table 22.

Nevertheless, Kennelly's pioneering work constitutes a most informative and useful reference study. For example, one of his recommendations that finds support today is that record-breaking performances are most likely to occur where the athlete maintains a *uniform* speed throughout a race. Again, Kennelly suggests that those who would establish new records should select an event or distance in which the present record is below the predicted level of possibility. This procedure is indicated also by a perusal of Table 22. Remarkably, Kennelly's curve for human runners predicted a time in the mile of 3:58 way back in 1906, when the existing record was 4:12 3/4.

With reference again to Table 22, it may be seen that the relatively best existing records are, in order of merit, those at 2 1/4, 2, 4, 2 1/2, 1 3/4, and 3/8 miles, respectively. But it should be noted that some of the listed marks are by many horsemen regarded with suspicion. At 1/4 mile, for instance, the Thoroughbred mare **Big Racket** is credited with the world record time of 20.8 seconds. Yet in 22 other races

---

* A consequence of this formula is that above one mile (but not for shorter distances) each doubling of the distance increases the running time by 2.1719.

run by this horse, the time averaged 22.7 seconds, ranging from 22.2 to 23.6, all with a running start. In the case of the claimed 20.8 seconds, the start would have had to be at least 50 yards, and may have been considerably more. And when the running start for a short-distance race amounts in itself to anywhere from 100 to 200 yards, as sometimes actually occurs on minor racetracks, little significance can be attached to "records" made under such conditions.

Table 22. World records in Thoroughbred racing.

Distance, miles	Time	Name of Horse	Age, Yrs.	Weight carried	Date	Track	Speed, mph, Actual	Time, sec., Formula
'4	0:20.8	Big Racket	4	111	Feb. 5, 1945	Hipodromo, Mex. City	43.27	20.58
16	0:26.6	Pichirilo	2	117	Mar. 25, 1954	Hipodromo, Mex. City	42.29	26.36
8	0:32.0	King Rhymer	2	118	Feb. 27, 1947	Arcadia, Calif.	42.19	32.15
16	0:39	Joe Blair	5	115	Feb. 5, 1916	Juarez, Mexico	40.38	37.95
2	0:44.8	Tamran's Jet	2	118	Mar. 22, 1968	Sunland, New Mexico	40.18	43.76
16	0:49.8	The Pimpernal	2	118	May 17, 1951	Belmont Park, N.Y.	40.66	49.58
8	0:55.4	Zip Pocket	3	122	Apr. 22, 1967	Phoenix, Arizona	40.61	55.42
16	1:01.6	Zip Pocket	3	129	Nov. 19, 1967	Phoenix, Arizona	40.18	61.28
4	1:07.4	Zip Pocket	2	120	Dec. 4, 1966	Phoenix, Arizona	40.06	67.18
16	1:14	Turbulator	5		Aug. 16, 1970	Renton, Washington	39.53	73.15
8	1:20	El Drag	4	115	May 25, 1955	Inglewood, Calif.	39.37	79.19
16	1:31.2	Restigouche			May 22, 1908	Belmont Park, N.Y.	37.01	85.32
	1:32.2	Dr. Fager	4	134	Aug. 24, 1968	Arlington, Illinois	39.04	91.59
16	1:39	Swaps	4	130	June 23, 1956	Inglewood, Calif.	38.64	98.02
3	1:46.4	Bug Brush	4	113	Feb. 14, 1959	Arcadia, Calif.	38.06	104.50
16	1:52.6	Fleet Bird	4	123	Oct. 24, 1953	Albany, Calif.	38.10	111.01
1	1:58.2	Noor	5	127	June 24, 1950	Albany, Calif.	38.07	117.55
	2:12.4	Cool Prince	5	114	July 3, 1965	Stanton, Delaware	37.39	130.78
2	2:26	Meneleck	6	116	July 1, 1961	Haydock, England	36.98	144.15
	2:38.2	Swaps	4	130	July 25, 1956	Inglewood, Calif.	36.98	157.66
	2:50.8	Swartz Pete	6		Jan. 1, 1966	Auckland, New Zealand	36.88	171.29
	3:13.8	Pharawell	5	119	Apr. 8, 1947	Hallandale, Florida	34.83	185.04
	3:15	Polazel	3	142	July 8, 1924	Salisbury, England	36.92	198.91
	3:37.6	Dakota	4	116	May 27, 1927	Lingfield, England	37.22	226.93
2	4:14.6	Miss Grillo	6	118	Nov. 12, 1948	Baltimore, Md.	35.35	255.33
	4:48.8	Shot Put	4	126	Aug. 14, 1940	Homewood, Illinois	34.28	284.01
	5:15	Farragut	5	113	Mar. 9, 1941	Agua Caliente, Mex.	34.29	313.02
	7:10.8	Sotemia	5	119	Oct. 7, 1912	Louisville, Ky.	33.43	432.02

Note: All the times listed from 1/4 mile to 9/16 mile were made on *straight* courses.

In 1926, Take My Tip is said to have run 3000 meters (1.864 miles) in Paris in 3:10.4. This equals 35.25 mph.

The average age of the horses is 4 years (2-6 yrs.) and the average weight carried, 120 pounds (111-142 pounds).

* This mark is inferior to the American record of 1:29 made by Aurecolt (3 yrs., 122 lbs.) on Nov. 12, 1957 (= 37.92 mph).

As Table 22 indicates, there are a number of existing running records in which the time could be substantially improved. This applies especially to the distances of 1 7/8, 15/16, 2 3/4, 1 3/4, 3, 1 1/8, 1 1/2, and 1 3/16 miles, respectively, in that order. At 1 7/8 miles the time could seemingly be reduced from 3:13.8 to about 3:05, and at 1 3/16 miles from 1:52.6 to 1:51, with the other distances just listed having proportionately intermediate reductions.

Relatively the best of all the records listed would appear to be that at 2 1/4 miles attributed to Dakota, at Lingfield, England, with a time of 3:37.6, which is over 9 seconds under the time predicted by the formula. However, it should be noted that many of the racetracks in England are measured along the *middle* of the track and not, as they should be, a few feet from the inner rails. If this is true of the track at Lingfield, it would account for the remarkable time credited to Dakota, since the 2 1/4 miles as measured might be anywhere from 1/16 to 1/4 mile shorter than if measured a few feet out from the inner rails. A similar situation may have prevailed in connection with the 2-mile time of 3:15 credited to Polazel.*

The significance of all this is that new world records should be attempted for *every* distance listed in Table 22 in which the formula time is better than the actual or credited time; likewise for all distances in which the listed records were made on tracks not properly measured.

Fig. 154 Here, in a high-speed photograph, is shown the muscular anatomy of a champion racehorse in action. Seabiscuit, who was foaled in 1933, at the Ridgewood Ranch, Willits, California, was retired from the track seven years later by his owner, Charles S. Howard, after having won (during 89 races) the then-record amount of $437,730. During his retirement to stud he sired numerous worthy descendants. His rider here is G. Woolf.

---

* This is suggestive in view of a time of 3:19.2 being made by the great Thoroughbred Kelso over forty years later, and carrying only 124 pounds to Polazel's 142.

A factor which appears to have been ignored in the rating of Thoroughbred racing records is the *date* of the horse's performance. Since horse-racing records in general have improved by a certain average amount over the years, world records should be expected to improve by somewhat the same amount. The writer has expounded this proposition at length in connection with human athletic records,[15] and there appears no reason why the same principle should not be applied in the rating of records made by racehorses.

Fig. 156 shows how trotting records have improved during the last 100 years. A similar degree of improvement has taken place in pacing records and in running (i.e., Thoroughbred racing) records. Although Fig. 156 shows only the leading performances over the years, it is evident that a corresponding degree of improvement prevailed among the *entire population* of racehorses from which the best records were drawn. And just as the curve connecting the best records proceeds at a level above the *average* performances, so a 100-percent "reference" curve, to which the record performances may be related, can be postulated. The dotted line in Fig. 149 indicates such a 100-percent reference level.*

Fig. 155 This remarkable "triple dead-heat"—a handicapper's dream—occurred in the Carter Handicap, at the Aqueduct Race Track, Jamaica, N.Y., June 10, 1944. It was the first time in the history of stake racing in New York State that three horses fought it out down the stretch and hit the finish wire at precisely the same instant. The horses were (No. 6) Brownie; (No. 1) Bossuet; and (No. 3) Wait-a-Bit. The distance was seven furlongs and the time 1 min. 23 2/5 seconds.

---

* The writer is presenting this method of evaluation not as a final conclusion, but rather as an experimental working basis from which horse-racing records may be rated more fairly than by their magnitude alone. Constructive criticisms from interested readers will be welcomed.

The *average* time taken by a contemporary Thoroughbred to cover a mile may be assumed as 2 minutes flat, or 120 seconds. The best time to date, as listed in Table 22, is 1:32.2, or 92.2 seconds. If a rating of 50 percent (or 500 points) be allotted to the former time (120 seconds), and a rating of 100 percent (or 1000 points) to the time of 92.2 seconds, intermediate timings may be rated proportionately by standard statistical procedures. In 1968 (the year in which the record of 92.2 seconds was set) there were in the United States about 23,000 Thoroughbreds in action. From this it follows that one horse in 23,000 covered the mile in 92.2, and that the *expected* time for one horse in 10,000 would be 93.5 seconds; one in 1000, 98 seconds; and one in 2, 120 seconds. For readers interested in statistical measurements, it may be added that the Standard Deviation in the records of Thoroughbreds running the mile is 6.80 seconds, and the Coefficient of Variation, 5.67 percent. In human mile runners the latter measure is 7.73, which indicates that men are nearly 40 percent more variable in ability in a mile race than are horses.

After the aforementioned factors have been taken into account for *contemporary* running records, it remains only to consider the *date* (year) of performance in order to bring all records to the same time-basis for rating.

Table 23, following, lists the respective time-factors that correspond with the trend of the records as charted in Fig. 156. These factors apply not only to trotting records, but also to records made in pacing and in running (galloping). To find the factor for any intermediate year, simply interpolate the figures listed for 10-year intervals.

Table 23. Reduction factors for rating horse-racing records.

Year	Factor
1970	.9930
1960	.9893
1950	.9856
1940	.9818
1930	.9780
1920	.9742
1910	.9703
1900	.9664
1890	.9625
1880	.9586
1870	.9546

The trend of the time-factors listed in the above table implies that a factor of 1.0000, or the presumed limit of performance, will be reached about 1990, at which time the mile record will be reduced to 1:31.5, or 91.5 seconds. Coincidentally, as long ago as 1903, Francis E. Nipher presented a paper to the St. Louis meeting of the American Association for the Advancement of Science in which he concluded that the final limit to the running mile would be 91.5 seconds. Prof. Nipher, however, did not predict the year in which this limit was to be reached (see Kennelly's reprinted paper, p. 453).

The writer's "formula" for rating the mile running records of Thoroughbreds is as follows: Rating, in percent = 208.14 — (1.182 predicted time, seconds)

The predicted time is derived by multiplying the actual time of the horse over a mile, in seconds, by the factor in Table 23 for the year in which the horse made the record. For example, Man o' War ran a mile in 1:35.8 (95.8 seconds) in 1920. What is his rating? 208.14 — (1.182 × 95.8 × .9742) = 97.83 percent. This may be expressed as 978 points, since the last digit is inconsequential.

By the same procedure, the point-ratings of various Thoroughbreds are found to be as follows:

Dr. Fager	(1:32.2 in 1968)	1000
Salvator	(1:35.5 in 1890)	995
Citation	(1:33.6 in 1950)	992
Roamer	(1:34.8 in 1918)	991
Equipoise	(1:34.4 in 1932)	989
Coaltown	(1:34.0 in 1949)	987

It need not be emphasized that these ratings give a fairer evaluation of running ability than do the records themselves, which ignore the date of performance. Salvator's 1:35.5, for instance, stood as the world record for 28 years, and was surpassed in merit only after 78 *years.*

However, a racehorse's potential cannot always be gauged by his ability at a single distance (such as the mile). Some horses have done their best at distances varying from 3/4 mile to 4 miles. For example, Man o' War's 1920 world record of 1 3/8 miles in 2:14.2 was equivalent (on the basis of the estimated times in Table 22) to one mile in 1:34.0. This yields a rating of 999 points instead of 978.

Clearly, Man o' War was a "super-horse." Among other Thoroughbreds who in other years were considered to be in this category were Sysonby (1904), Exterminator (1918), Equipoise (1932), and Citation (1948). Also to be considered among the greatest Thoroughbreds are the winners of the Triple Crown (Kentucky Derby, 1 1/4 miles; Preakness Stakes, 1 3/16 miles; and Belmont Stakes, 1 1/2 miles, respectively). To date there have been only eight such winners: Sir Barton (1919), Gallant Fox (1930), Omaha (1935), War Admiral (1937), Whirlaway (1941), Count Fleet (1943), Assault (1946), and Citation (1948).*

In a nation-wide poll conducted in 1950, Man o' War was voted the greatest racehorse of the first half of the twentieth century. After Man o' War, in order, came Citation, Whirlaway, Seabiscuit, and Exterminator. By many, though, Citation was considered to have been superior to "Big Red." But when the element of *time* (date of performance) is taken into consideration, it is revealed that Man o' War's best running times were superior to Citation's (made 28–30 years later) at 3/4 mile, 1 3/16 miles, 1 1/4 miles, and 1 3/8 miles, and inferior only at 1 mile and 1 1/8 miles.

Man o' War was rather large for a Thoroughbred, standing 65 5/8 inches and weighing in racing condition about 1150 pounds. He had the longest stride—27 feet—of any top-ranking racehorse. Accordingly, when "Big Red" galloped 1 3/8 miles in 2:14.2, he took about 269 strides, averaging almost exactly 2 strides per second.

For comparison, Seabiscuit was 62 inches and 1040 pounds, and had a stride that averaged 20 feet 11 3/4 inches. War Admiral was 62 1/2 inches and 960 pounds, and had a stride of 21 feet 1 3/4 inches. Both the latter strides were considerably shorter than the average for Thoroughbreds, which is about 23 feet. Gallant Fox stood 65 inches and weighed 1125 pounds, which was almost as large as Man o' War. Bull Lea was even larger: 66 inches and about 1250 pounds. Equipoise presented the typical Thoroughbred dimensions of 63 3/4 inches and 1090 pounds. One of the

---

* The above was written before Secretariat became, in 1973, the ninth horse to win the Triple Crown.

smallest top Thoroughbreds was Assault, who stood only about 60 1/2 inches, and who probably had to average well over 2 1/2 strides per second to negotiate a mile in 1:35. Among the tallest Thoroughbreds have been Civil Code (69 1/2 inches), Roseben (71 inches), and the present-day record-holder for height, Limbo, with 73 inches. Possibly the heaviest Thoroughbred ever to compete was Burgomaster, a champion two-year-old in 1905, who weighed 1300 pounds.

When a racehorse is in full gallop, with his neck normally extended, his overall length (including his tail) is about 11 feet. So, if a horse is said to have won by three lengths, it means by about 33 feet or 11 yards.

A comparison and rating of *all* the leading contenders for the title of "greatest racehorse" could be made, converting the various distances run by each horse to their equivalent timing for one mile, and then applying the factor of *date* of performance. Such a comparison and rating would doubtless be revealing, but it is beyond the scope of the present brief review of the subject.

Some miscellaneous data on Thoroughbreds.

In 69 Kentucky derbies, 68 of the races were won by colts or geldings. In 22 races, a filly won only once.

The first Thoroughbred imported into the United States was Bulle Rock, a stallion brought from England in 1730.

The number of horses that are allowed to run in a race depends mostly on the width of the track. On the larger tracks 14 or 15 horses may run at one time, five feet of width being allowed for each horse. However, in the Grand National Steeplechase at London in 1929, 66 horses competed.

The oldest Thoroughbred to win a race is generally considered to have been John Burwell. In 1925, at the age of 19, he competed 19 times, won once, was second twice, and earned $570.

The all-time leading money-winning Thoroughbred (through 1967) was Kelso, with earnings of $1,977,896. He was also voted Horse of the Year a record five times, during 1960, 1961, 1962, 1963, and 1964.

In 1967, the approximate number of people attending horse races in the United States was 68 million (of which nearly 39 million were to Thoroughbred races, 27 million to harness races, and over 2 million to Quarter Horse races). For comparison, the numbers attending other sporting events were as follows: automobile racing 40 million, football 36 million, and baseball nearly 35 million. During the same year there were about 140 major recognized racetracks in the United States.

As of 1968, there were about 23,000 Thoroughbred horses listed in the Jockey Club's registry (New York), and 10,232 harness horses in the United States Trotting Association (Columbus, Ohio). The entire racehorse population in this country was then about 125,000. The total number of horses (all breeds), donkeys, and mules during 1968 was about 6,675,000. As of 1971, the total equine population was estimated to have *increased* to 8,250,000.

f. Trotting Ability in the Horse.

Both trotting and pacing, in contrast to galloping, are for some horses acquired rather than natural gaits. Harness horses (i.e., trotters and pacers) move at lesser speeds than runners (gallopers), not because of having to draw a vehicle (sulky), but because of the gaits themselves being slower. That the drawing of a sulky does not hinder the speed of a trotter or a pacer is shown by the fact that whenever one of these harness horses has been put to running a mile under saddle his time has been anywhere from 6 to 9 seconds *slower* than if he had been pulling the vehicle.

In general, the fastest trotters are about 76–80 percent as fast as the fastest Thoroughbreds; and the fastest pacers are about 77–81 percent as fast. That is, the gait of pacing is consistently about one percent faster than that of trotting.

The list of different racing events recognized by harness-horse associations is extensive. There are (1) mile records for stallions, mares, and geldings, respectively; (2) mile records for yearlings, 2-year-olds, 3-year-olds, 4-year-olds, and 5-year-olds, respectively; (3) without record at beginning of year; (4) respective mile times by double-gaited (i.e., trotting and pacing) performers; (5) distances other than a mile; (6) mile by lady driver; (7) to wagon (now discontinued); (8) team to pole; (9) tandem team; (10) three-abreast team; (11) four-in-hand; (12) with running mate; and (13) under saddle (now discontinued). In addition, there are records made in heat racing and in the fastest heats, and all the aforementioned styles of racing performed on a half-mile rather than a mile track. Finally, all the foregoing categories are recognized for pacing as well as trotting horses. For our purpose here, it should suffice to list simply the best times recorded for various distances over a mile (curved) track. These records for trotters appear in Table 24, and for pacers in Table 25.

Table 24. World trotting records.

Distance, miles	Time	Name of Horse	Sex	Age, yrs.	Driver	Date	Speed, Actual	mph, Formula	Time, sec., Formula
1/4	0:27	Uhlan	g	9	Chas. Tanner	Oct. 6, 1913	33.33	33.33	27.00
1/2	0:56¼	Uhlan	g	7	C. K. G. Billings	1911	32.00	32.34	55.66
5/8	1:14½	Crawford	g	5	T. W. Murphy	1925	30.30	32.11	70.05
3/4	1:28¼	Peter Manning	g	6	T. W. Murphy	1922	30.59	31.91	84.60
7/8	1:46¼	Truax	h	4	R. D. McMahon	1925	29.65	31.66	99.46
	1:54.8	Nevele Pride	h		Stanley Dancer	Aug. 31, 1969	31.36	31.36	114.80
1/16	2:05.6	Senator Frost				Oct. 17, 1959	30.45	31.10	123.00
1/8	2:17¼	Cupid's Albingen	g	8	W. R. Cox	1925	29.51	30.86	131.27
3/16	2:22.8	Scotch Victor				Nov. 6, 1954	29.94	30.63	139.59
1/4	2:30.6	Pronto Don				Nov. 24, 1951	29.88	30.41	147.97
1/2	3:02½	Greyhound	g	5	S. F. Palin	Sept. 14, 1937	29.49	29.66	182.06
	4:06	Greyhound	g	7	S. F. Palin	Sept. 19, 1939	29.27	28.51	252.51
	6:49½	Lee Stout	g	9	F. D. Gilbert	Oct. 7, 1939	26.37	27.00	400.02
	10:12	Senator L.	h	6	J. Castro	Nov. 2, 1894	25.17	25.93	555.32
	12:08½	Imogene Constantine	m	10	J. Gauvin	1919	24.71	25.15	715.70
	26:15	Pascal	g		L. H. Burke	Nov. 2, 1893	22.86	22.86	1575.00
	58:21	Black Rod	g	6	Rupert Parker	Mar. 25, 1942	20.57	20.80	3461.55
	1:47:59	General Taylor	h	10	J. M. Daniels	Feb. 21, 1857	16.67	19.68	5488.83
	3:55:40½	Ariel	m		C. Simmons	May 5, 1846	12.73	18.34	9811.40
	8:55:53	Conqueror	g	11	George Spicer	Nov. 12, 1853	11.20	16.68	21,577.90

Table 25. World pacing records.

Distance, miles	Time	Name of Horse	Sex	Age, yrs.	Driver	Date	Speed, Actual	mph, Formula	Time, sec Formula
1/4	0:26¾	Directum I.	h	9	T. W. Murphy	Sept. 14, 1916	33.65	33.65	26.75
1/2	0.55¾	Directum I.	h	9	T. W. Murphy	Sept. 14, 1916	32.29	32.67	55.09
5/8	1:12½	Phil O'Neill	g	7	W. T. Crozier	1925	31.03	32.44	69.35
3/4	1:26¼	Prince Alert	h				Sept. 23, 1903	31.30	32.24	83.72
7/8	1:45½	Star Ruth	g	7	S. F. Palin	1925	29.86	31.99	98.41
1	1:53.6	Bret Hanover	h				Oct. 7, 1966	31.69	31.69	113.60
1 1/16	2:03.2	Adios Vic	h				Oct. 23, 1965	30.55	31.43	121.72
1 1/8	2:15¼	Calumet Dubuque	g	4	H. H. Thomas	1934	29.94	31.19	129.90
1 1/4	2:33½	Phil O'Neill	g	7	W. T. Crozier	1925	29.32	30.73	146.44
1 1/2	3:05.4	Right Time				1961	29.13	29.97	180.21
2	4:17	Dan Patch	h	7	M. E. McHenry	Nov. 30, 1903	28.02	28.89	250.00
3	7:31½	Elastic Pointer	h	15	A. J. Wood	1909	23.92	27.23	396.59
4	10:10	Joe Jefferson	h	12		Nov. 13, 1891	23.61	26.17	550.17
5	11:54	Angus Peter	h			Sept. 10, 1933	25.21	25.38	709.25

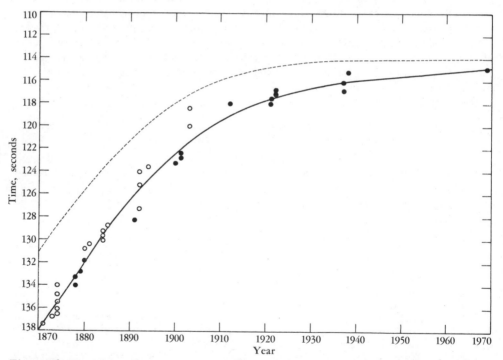

Fig. 156 World trotting records over the years. The first recognized mark, one of 2:17, was set by the celebrated Goldsmith Maid in 1871. The present record of 1:54.8 was made by Nevele Pride in 1969. The best intervening records were those made by Goldsmith Maid in 1874 (2:14), Nancy Hanks in 1892 (2:04), Lou Dillon in 1903 (1:58½), and Greyhound in 1938 (1:55¼). The open circles denote mares and the solid circles geldings and stallions. The dotted line represents the 100-percent rating level proposed by the writer (see text).

As Table 24 shows, trotting records are consistently about 20 percent slower than running (Thoroughbred) records, and even more so during the early stages of a race. This is owing to the extra time—perhaps a second or so—required to get the sulky under way. For while the Thoroughbreds and harness horses both are timed from a moving start, the runners are able to get into their stride faster than are the horses that draw vehicles. Once under way, however, the speed of the harness horse is remarkably uniform, diminishing between 1/2 mile and 2 miles only from about 32 to 29 mph.

The average length of the stride in a trotter is about 21 feet, as compared with a Thoroughbred's galloping stride of 23 feet. Hence a champion trotter, in covering a mile in 115 seconds, takes about 250 strides at the rate of 2.174 strides per second; while a galloping horse, doing a mile in 93 seconds, takes 230 strides at the rate of 2.473 strides per second. Thus the galloping horse attains a greater speed both by his longer stride and by the greater rapidity of his leg movements. This would seem to confirm the idea that the gallop is the *natural* gait for enabling cursorial animals, such as the horse, to attain their greatest speed.

Table 24 lists the world trotting records as of August 31, 1969, when Nevele Pride set the present one-mile record of 1:54.8. As in the case of running records (Table 23), it is seen that many of the timings could be bettered. This is true especially of the records at 5/8, 3/4, 7/8, and 1 1/8 miles, and at the longer distances of 30, 50, and 100 miles. The latter, each made over a hundred years ago, are indeed subject to spectacular improvement, provided a trotter can be found today which is capable of negotiating the distances.

Clearly the best records listed in Table 24 are those at 1/4, 1/2, 1, 1 1/2, 2, 5, 10, and 20 miles, respectively; and the best of all these marks is Greyhound's remarkable 2-mile record of 4:06, which is 6 1/2 seconds faster than the time predicted by the formula. The latter, for trotters, is: log Time, seconds = 1.137 log Distance, miles + 2.0600. This formula, as in the case of Thoroughbred records, applies only for distances of a mile or over. It is equivalent to saying that each doubling of the distance (above a mile) increases the trotting time by 2.1992.

The same procedure for rating the performances of trotting and pacing horses may be applied as in the previously described instance of running horses. The only changes needed are to modify the figures in the formulas so as to fit them to the lesser speeds of the harness horses. The formula for trotters then becomes:

Rating, in percent = 267.57 — (1.470 predicted time, seconds)

This equation, applied to the outstanding trotting records plotted on Fig. 156, gives the following ratings:

Greyhound	(1:55 1/4 in 1938)	1014
Nevele Pride	(1:54.8 in 1969)	1000
Lou Dillon	(1:58 1/2 in 1903)	990
Nancy Hanks	(2:04 in 1892)	920

Goldsmith Maid, alas, with her best record of 2:14 set in 1874, gets a rating of only 792 points. Why?, because 2:14 is only 42 percent of the way between the *average* trotting performance of 2:28 and the best performance of about 1:55. That Goldsmith Maid was, in some respects, a most remarkable horse is generally acknowledged. But so far as speed goes, she simply was not in the same class with more recent champions such as Lou Dillon (1903), Uhlan (1912), Peter Manning (1922), and Greyhound (1938). For one thing, the sulkies used in the Maid's day were large-wheeled, heavier vehicles than is the case today. This, along with other varying factors, actually makes it unfair to compare such early-day trotting performances with those of recent years.

Although considerable difficulty attends the selecting of the greatest Thoroughbred, less confusion exists in the case of the greatest trotting horse. Clearly, it was Greyhound. As is seen in the list of ratings above, at one mile Greyhound's time of 1:55 1/4, performed in 1938, is 14 points (or 1.4 percent) better than Nevele Pride's 1:54.8 made 31 years later. Moreover, Greyhound's 2-mile world record of 4:06, performed in 1939, is equal in merit to one mile in only 1:51.8 (as per the formula timings in Table 24). The latter time, if only it had been performed, would gain a rating of no less than 1060 points! Similarly, Greyhound's record of 3:02 1/2 for 1 1/2 miles, if converted to the proportionate time for one mile, gains a rating of 1017 points. Another fine record made by this super-trotter was his mile under saddle of 2:01 3/4 at the age of 8 years, in 1940 (see Fig. 108).

Greyhound, like Man o' War, was of above-average size for his class, standing 65 1/4 inches and weighing about 1100 pounds. His detailed body measurements are listed in Table 5. Also, like Man o' War, Greyhound had a long stride—23 feet—as compared with 21 feet for trotters generally. Titan Hanover, another great trotter, had a stride of 22 feet.

Some miscellaneous data on trotters

Uhlan trotted 1/8 mile under saddle in 13 1/2 seconds (1914).

A 1/4 mile in 0:27 was run by Lou Dillon (1903) as well as by Uhlan (1913).

When Greyhound made the 2-mile world record of 4:06 (1939), he ran both the first and the second miles in the same time—2:03. Between the ages of 2 and 8 years (1934–1940), Greyhound ran 82 races, finishing first 71 times. In his later years he was virtually unbeatable.

Messenger, the founding father of today's Standardbred in America, arrived in Philadelphia in 1788. Messenger was a grey Thoroughbred stallion, standing 63 inches, who had distinguished himself on racetracks in England.

The first mile to be trotted in less than 3 minutes (probably under saddle) was registered by a gelding named Yankee, in 1806, at a trotting track in Harlem, N.Y. By 1839, when sulkies had come into use, the time had been reduced to 2:32, by Dutchman; and in 1845 to 2:29 1/2 by Lady Suffolk, at Hoboken, N.J.

The most remarkable trotting horse is generally considered to have been Goldsmith Maid (1857–1885), who was a farm horse until the age of 6. At 8 years she became a champion, and remained so until her retirement at age 20. The Maid trotted in 426 heats and won more than 350 of them. In 123 separate races, she finished first 97 times. She repeated her best time of 2:14 (made in 1874) in 1876, when she was 19. On only two occasions did she win more than $5000, yet her lifetime earnings reached $364,200.

The peak year for harness racing is said to have been 1892, when 17,000 horses raced in some 2000 meets.

The average age at which both trotters and pacers have made world records is about 7 1/2 years. (In Thoroughbreds, the average is only 4 years.)

The fastest times for a double-gaited harness horse are those set by Steamin' Demon, who paced a mile in 1:58.8 and trotted a mile in 1:59.2. For a mare, the best double-gaited times were made by Calumet Evelyn, who paced in 1:59 1/4 and trotted in 1:59 1/2.

The leading money-winning trotter (through 1969) was Roquepine, a French mare, who during the years 1963–1969 had total earnings of $956,161.

g. Pacing Ability in the Horse.

Pacing, as has been mentioned, is about one percent faster than trotting. The consistency with which this ratio is present at all distances from 1/4 mile to 5 miles is truly remarkable. Although no records beyond 5 miles appear to have been made by pacers, probably the 101:100 ratio would hold for longer distances also.

In Table 25 it is seen that the poorest records are those listed for 3 and 4 miles, while, in contrast, the record at 5 miles is highly meritorious, being only 4 3/4 seconds slower than the theoretical best time predicted for that distance. Most of the other marks, with the exception of those at 1/4 mile and 1 mile, could each be lowered by anywhere from 0.66 second (at 1/2 mile) to 7 seconds or over (at 7/8, 1 1/4, and 2 miles, respectively). The best *contemporary* record in the table is perhaps that at one mile, by Bret Hanover, of 1:53.6. But as explained previously, for fair rating the *date* of performance also must be taken into account. The following formula does this for pacers:

Rating, in percent $= 264.76 - (1.462$ predicted time, seconds) *

This formula, applied to the outstanding pacing records over the years, gives the following ratings:

Dan Patch	(1:56 in 1904)	1006
Bret Hanover	(1:53.6 in 1966)	1001
Billy Direct	(1:55 in 1938)	998
Adios Butler	(1:54.6 in 1960)	990

It is evident that just as Greyhound was the greatest trotter, so Dan Patch (1896–1916) was the greatest pacer. This is acknowledged by a great many racing authorities, quite apart from his rating as determined by the above formula.

Dan Patch is credited also with a time of 1:55 1/4 (1905), but this was made with the aid of a Thoroughbred pacemaker who galloped in front and was equipped with a windshield. Perhaps Dan Patch's superiority was best shown by his consistency on the track: he covered a mile in 2:00 or under on no fewer than 30 different occasions. This in itself constituted a record which, so far as the writer knows, still stands. Dan paced 2 miles in 4:17 (1903), which was equivalent to a mile in 1:56.8, and which has a rating of 996 points. Dan Patch was retired from the track in 1909, at the age of 13. Strangely, in 1916, both he and his owner, M. W. Savage, of Minneapolis, died from heart ailments, the horse on July 11 and Savage the next day.

---

* The formula applying to the *contemporary* predictions of pacing time in Table 25 is:

log Time, seconds $= 1.138$ log Distance, miles $+ 2.0554$

This equation implies that each doubling of the distance (above a mile) increases the pacing time by 2.2007.

h. Racing Records by Arabians and Ponies.

The only running records known to the writer for Arabian horses in the United States are one of 1:50 for the mile and another of 0:53 for the half-mile, each with 135 pounds up, made in 1928. In his book, *Newmarket and Arabia,* written in 1873, Major Roger D. Upton says that the fastest mile run by an Arab horse in races in India was 1:50, and that the half-mile was run on the average in 0:54. But possibly Major Upton had not heard about the following. William Youatt, in his book *The Horse* (1880, p. 31), tells about a 2-mile race held in Calcutta in 1828, between an English Thoroughbred named Recruit and an Arab named Pyramus, "the best Arabian in Bengal." Recruit, who carried 152 pounds, won in 3:57, which was equivalent to a single mile in about 1:49. But it is added that at the mile mark Pyramus, who carried only 115 pounds, was "neck and neck" with Recruit. From this it would indicate that even as early as 1828 there was an Arabian horse who could cover a mile in at least 1:50 and possibly 1:49. Today, however, on the basis of the Arabian horse's size and build, the mile record for this breed should be about 1:39, and the half-mile about 0:47.

In harness racing by ponies, extensive records are kept by the United States Trotting Pony Association. As in the case of full-sized harness horses, the latter association recognizes numerous categories of age, sex, and gait (trotting or pacing), and in addition, various champions listed according to shoulder height. The best trotting record from among all these classes, as of the year 1963, would appear to be that of the pony stallion (breed not stated) King D., who covered a half-mile in 1:31.4 at Frankfort, Indiana, on April 4, 1963. King D. was 47 3/4 inches tall; the race was on a half-mile track; and the driver was D. Lemler. This pony record was at the rate of 19.69 mph, or only .615 as fast as the half-mile record made by the Standardbred Uhlan. The speed is considerably below what should be expected from a pony 47 3/4 inches tall. Possibly the races are made from a standing start.

Another organization, known as the Miniature Horse Racing Association, states that a pony has been known to gallop a quarter-mile in 26 seconds, with 80 pounds up (presumably with a running start). This is very fast time, and suggests that the "pony" must have been about 50 inches in height.

Back in 1831, a Shetland pony mare, "barely 44 inches high," *trotted* a mile in 3:44. Whether in harness, under saddle, or riderless, is not stated.

i. Miscellaneous Records of Running Speed and Endurance.

Note: The following instances have been collected from all available sources. They are not listed in any particular order, and are included here to show that many interesting and some extraordinary performances have been made other than on racetracks under standardized conditions. The first six items listed have been taken from T. S. Andrew's pocketbook of sports records, 1917 edition.

1. 10 miles in 18:17, by Mme. Maranette, changing horses. Lansing, Mich., June 2, 1883.
2. 50 miles in 1:50:03 1/2, by Carl Pugh, using ten horses. San Bernardino, Calif., July 7, 1883.
3. 100 miles in 4:19:40, by George Osbaldison, using 16 horses. Newmarket, England, Nov. 5, 1831. Osbaldison also rode 200 miles in 8:42:00, using 28 horses. Each horse was ridden a distance of 4 miles. Thus there were 50 mountings and dis-

mountings. The actual running time was 7:19:00—an average rate of 27.33 mph. For this feat, Osbaldison collected 1000 guineas (then about $5000) from a colonel who had wagered that no rider could cover 200 miles in less than 10 hours.

4. 200 miles in 8:00:00 and 300 miles in 14:09:00, by Neil H. Mowry, using 30 horses, changed at will. San Francisco, Calif., August 2, 1868.

5. 559 miles, 754 yards. Won by the Thoroughbred Pinafore, against other horses and men in a 6-day race. San Francisco, Calif., October 15–20, 1879.

6. 1071 1/2 miles in 6 days of 12 hours each (= 72 hours), by C. M. Anderson, changing horses at will. San Francisco, Calif., April 15–20, 1884.

7. In a race of 47 miles, staged in 1825 between two Cossack and two English horses, one of the latter, named Sharper, won in 2:48:00, after having covered the first half of the distance in only 1:14:00. Thus the 47 miles was run at the rate of 16.79 mph, and the first 23 1/2 miles at 19:05 mph. The latter, in particular, was excellent time under the circumstances.

8. In the United States Mounted Service Cup Endurance Test, the horse and rider must cover 300 miles in five days, at 60 miles a day. In 1919 this event was won by Ramla, an Arab mare, in 51 hours and 26 minutes, carrying 200 pounds. In 1920 it was won by an Arab gelding, Champion Crabbet, in 52 hours and 33 minutes, carrying 245 pounds. In 1921, Champion Crabbet again won, carrying 245 pounds, in 49 hours and 4 minutes. In 1923, it was won by an Anglo-Arab named Gouya, in the record time of 45 hours, carrying 225 pounds. Interestingly, in the latter two winners the time is seen in each case to have equalled one/fifth the weight of the rider.

9. (This, and the following three instances of the speed and stamina of early-day English racehorses, are taken from Youatt, 1880, pp. 69–70.) In October 1741, in Ireland, a Mr. Wilde, using ten horses, rode 127 miles in 6 hours and 21 minutes. Allowing for the changings and a moment's rest, he rode for 6 hours at the rate of 20 mph.

10. In 1745, an Englishman named Thornhill exceeded this, for he rode 213 miles in 11 hours and 34 minutes, changing horses (the number of which is not stated). Here was a speed of about 18 mph, continued for no less than 11 hours "on the turnpike-road and uneven ground."

11. In 1762, a Mr. Shaftoe, with ten horses, five of them being ridden twice, rode 50 1/4 miles in 1 hour and 49 minutes, at the rate of 26 mph. He also rode 2900 miles in 29 days, using 14 horses. On one day he was compelled to ride 160 miles (!), "on account of the tiring of his first horse."

12. In 1786, a racehorse named Quibbler ran 23 miles "round the flat at Newmarket," in 57 minutes and 10 seconds (= 24.14 mph).
   (Could any racehorse of today run for an hour at this rate? In other words, has the *speed* of the modern racehorse been increased at the expense of *stamina?*)

13. Youatt (1880, pp. 68–69) says that the celebrated English racehorse Flying Childers galloped over the round course at Newmarket (about 3.8 miles) in 6:40, and over the Beacon course (about 4.2 miles) in 7:30. The 3.8 miles would thus have been at the rate of 34.23 mph, and the 4.2 miles at the rate of 33.63 mph. On the basis of the figures listed in Table 22, the world record time for 3.8 miles today would be 6:48; and for 4.2 miles, 7:36 2/3. Note the remarkable and almost consistent superiority of Flying Childers' alleged timings over the latter ones. Could a racehorse really have been that fast in the early eighteenth century, or were the racetracks in England improperly measured?

14. Back in the sixteenth century, the Abbé Nicquet, who was a courier of the King of France, rode horseback from Paris to Rome, a distance of 1050 miles, over poor roads, in 6 days and 4 hours, an average of 170 miles a day! How many horses were used during the ride was not stated.

15. A Cossack named D. Pieszkow covered nearly 6000 miles during six months while riding a small Russian steppe horse.
16. Several remarkable rides were made by early-day *gauchos* in South America. In 1767, for instance, a man named Merlo carried an important message from Buenos Aires to Lima—a distance of at least 3000 miles—in 40 days, averaging 75 miles a day through all sorts of conditions. Even with an occasional fresh mount, enormous distances had to be covered.
17. Another such ride was when, in 1810, a Major Corvalan rode from Buenos Aires to a town named Mendoza, located in the foothills of the Andes, in 5 days, averaging 133 miles a day. Still another Argentinian rider, a Lieutenant Samaniego, in 1818 rode from Buenos Aires to Santiago, Chile, a distance of 240 miles, in only 27 hours.
18. In 1967, G. Steecher rode a single horse for 100 miles in 11 hours and 4 minutes, in Victoria, Australia. This, however, is surpassed by the record of Conqueror (see Table 24), who back in 1853 *trotted* 100 miles in just under 9 hours, at Union Course, Long Island.
19. In September 1848, for a wager, a French-Canadian named "Little Aubry" (François Xavier Aubry) rode the 800 miles between Santa Fe, New Mexico and Independence, Missouri, in 5 days and 16 hours. The actual time on the road was 4 days and 12 hours. Thus the 800 miles was covered at the average rate of 7.41 mph. Part of the ride was made at the rate of 250 miles in 24 hours (= 10.42 mph); and over one stretch of 200 miles—*using a single horse* ("my yellow mare")—the distance was covered in 26 hours (= 7.69 mph). On this extraordinary ride, "Little Aubry" killed 6 horses and broke down 6 others. J. Frank Dobie (*The Mustangs*, p. 279) regarded this ride by Aubry as "supreme in the whole riding tradition of the West."
20. Buffalo Bill, as a Pony Expressman, exceeded Aubry's record as to distance covered within a given period of time, namely 322 miles in 24 hours and 40 minutes (= 13.05 mph). "On that ride, however, he had a score of station men to help him along, and used 21 horses in relays. A fresh horse freshens the rider. No two horses have the same gait. Jaded cowboys on jaded ponies sometimes swap with each other to the relief of both man and mount." (Dobie, p. 285).
21. The most prolonged example of riding—although no effort was made to establish a time record—was when, in 1924, an Argentinian, Aime F. Tschiffely, rode two Criollo horses from Buenos Aires to Washington, D. C. For details of this ride, see p.191 .

From the above listings it would appear that the greatest distance covered *by a single horse* in one stretch was the 200 miles (in 26 hours) accomplished by the buckskin mare in "Little Aubry's" ride of 800 miles. This run, while *faster* than a man could do it, was over a trivial distance compared with what some of the greatest human endurance runners have accomplished.

For example, in 1836, the famous Norwegian courier, Mensen Ernst, ran from Calcutta to Constantinople—a grueling course of some 5625 miles—in 59 days. If a deduction be made of eight hours' sleep per night, the time Ernst spent in running becomes 39 1/3 days; and each day he would have had to average 95.34 miles in 16 hours, or practically 6 miles per hour.

In New York City, on February 27, 1882, an English 6-day runner named Hazael traveled 600 miles and "one lap" (185 feet?) on an indoor race track in 144 *consecutive* hours, at the average speed of 4 1/6 miles per hour.

As another example of prolonged endurance, Wally Hayward, a 45-year-old runner from South Africa, during a period of 24 hours jogged 637 laps around a 1/4-mile track—a distance of 159 miles 562 yards, averaging about 6 2/3 miles per hour.

In a 6-day race in London in 1924, between an English marathon runner named George Hall and a racehorse named Black Jack, the horse was withdrawn from the race on the fifth day, with Hall 15 miles ahead and still going strong.

---

j. Jumping Ability in the Horse.

In connection with the physical power manifested in jumping—whether the jump be made by a man or by a four-footed animal such as the horse—the essential consideration is not the height (or width) of the object cleared, but rather how high or how far the jumper's *center of gravity* (CG) has been displaced by his effort. Horses, with heavy heads on long necks, have a center of gravity nearer the shoulder than the hip. This distribution of the animal's bodyweight confers certain advantages both in running and jumping. Since in running most of the forward thrust comes from the hind limbs, the forward-placed center of gravity keeps the animal from rearing as its speed accelerates. And in jumping, especially for height, the horse's long body and hind legs enable it to clear any height up to nearly four feet without raising its CG (that is, without lifting its weight) at all.*

Fig. 157 shows the position of a horse's CG in a lateral view. Bilaterally, the CG may be assumed to come midway between the right and left sides of the body. Fig. 157 is based on a diagram showing the position of the CG in the horse as determined by Goubaux and Barrier (1892).

Fig. 158 illustrates the approximate position of a horse and rider at the beginning of a high or hurdle jump. (For reasons of space in the drawing, the horse is shown only about *half* the distance away from the hurdle as he should be). The height of the top bar on the hurdle as shown is 5 feet (60 inches); and the height of the 16-hand horse's CG, 58.5 inches (measurement A in Fig. 158). That is, in the reared-up position from which the horse starts his jump, his CG has been raised about 15 1/4 inches from the position (see Fig. 157) it occupies when the animal is standing at rest. In order for the horse's flexed forelegs to clear the bar in the hurdle, the underside of his body must pass at least 4 inches above the bar (see stage 3 in Fig. 159). And since the horse's CG is about 8 inches above the lower surface of his body, it (the CG) must accordingly pass about *12 inches above the bar.* Hence in making a jump of 60 inches, as is depicted in Figs. 158 and 159, a 16-hand horse has to raise his CG only about 13 1/2 inches.

Note, in the horse's preliminary position (Fig. 158), that his hind legs are bent at the hocks and stifle-joints just enough to supply maximum power when they are explosively straightened as in Fig. 159, stage 2. In the preliminary position, the CG, as would be supposed, comes vertically above the two hind feet. This position, however, is a transitory one, and as the horse straightens its legs in the takeoff, its CG is immediately moved forward and upward in the direction that its body is being propelled (Fig. 159, stage 2).

---

* When a horse stands quietly at rest, the animal can readily lift one of its hind legs off the ground, removing all weight from it. However, in order to lift a *foreleg,* the horse must first *shift its weight rearward* until the CG lies behind the intersection of the diagonals of its feet.

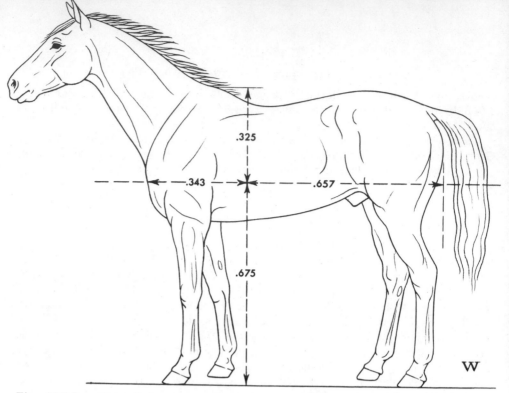

.325

.343 .657

.675

W

Fig. 157 Location of the center of gravity in a typical light horse. In a horse 16 hands (64 inches) in height the CG would be about 43¼ inches above the ground and 22¼ inches backward from the point of the shoulder.

The distance B from the hurdle (Fig. 158) is ordinarily about 1 1/2 times the distance horizontally from the upright on the hurdle, so that the angle of the takeoff (i.e., the direction in which the long axis of the horse's body is moving) is somewhere about 30–35 degrees. However, the angle varies, according to the height to be jumped, the speed of the approach, and the particular "technique" in which the horse making the jump has been trained.

While a jump may be made from the trot, it can be made more freely and to a greater height from the canter or gallop. But experts in the matter advise that a horse should not be made to go *too fast* at either a high jump or a broad jump, or the animal will be unable to raise his forequarters high enough to clear the maximum distance. The greater the speed in approaching the jump, the smaller the angle of the takeoff.

In *landing* after a jump, the horse's two forelegs are kept straightened out, and close together until near the ground, when one foot comes down closely followed by the other. After clearing the hurdle and landing, the horse moves on usually at a canter. (A detailed analysis of all the stages in a horse's jump, which are unnecessary to repeat here, are given in various treatises on riding, one of which is the excellent little book, *Horse Facts,* by Major A. J. R. Lamb,[16] and another, *Fundamentals of Riding,* by Gregor de Romaszkan[17]).

It has been stated that a jump of 3 feet would appear a very good one for any animal.[18] By this is meant, not the height of the obstacle jumped over, but *the height that the animal raises its center of gravity.* For a 16-hand horse to raise his CG 3 feet would be equivalent to his making a jump over a bar 6 feet 10 1/2 inches high.* This,

* Fitzsimons (1920, p. 185) says that a mountain zebra (q.v., Chapter 16), which was confined in a small stone krall having walls exactly six feet in height, cleared the wall in a standing leap "without touching the top." This was equivalent to a 16-hand horse clearing a height of at least 7 feet 3 inches.

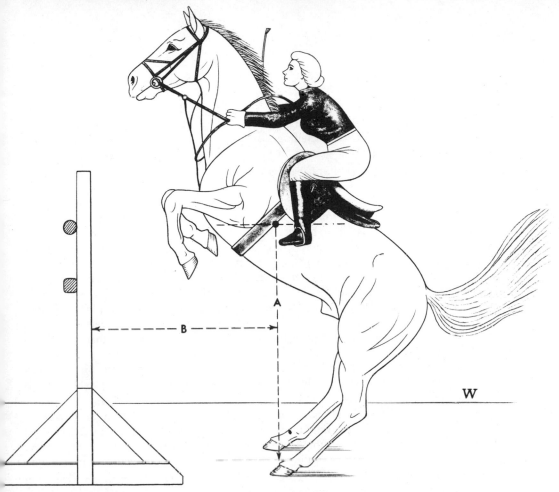

Fig. 158 A jumper about to go over a five-foot hurdle. For details of the mechanics of a jump, see text.

while an excellent jump, is considerably under the height that has been attained in high jumping by horses of championship class in the event. The first official record of this kind of which the writer is aware was made by the American horse Biskra and equalled by the French horse Mount Joie III, at Voages, France, August 18, 1912. The height jumped was 7 feet 8 1/2 inches. Sometime prior to 1923 a horse named Confidence, at Ottawa, Canada, raised the record to 8 feet 0 1/2 inches. Unofficially, he is said to have done 8 feet 2 inches. Another unofficial record was that made by Heatherbloom between 1901 and 1903, of 8 feet 3 inches. Officially, the first record to follow that of Biskra and Mount Joie III was made by Greatheart (see Fig. 160) on June 9, 1923, at Chicago, with a leap of 8 feet 0 13/16 inches (note the accuracy!). The present record, which stands at 8 feet 3 1/2 inches, was made in November 1925 by King's Own, a jumper owned by Fred Wettach. On February 5, 1949, a horse named Huaso cleared 8 feet 1.6 inches.

It will be observed in the photograph of Greatheart that the horse appears rather large and may have been well over the 16 hands in height assumed for the comparisons made heretofore. In that case the horse's center of gravity would have been higher from the ground and his CG consequently raised a lesser distance than in the case of a horse standing 16 hands high. This may well have been the case with the record-holder, King's Own, also. If it be assumed that King's Own stood 66 inches high, his

CG at the instant of takeoff would have been about 60 1/2 inches above the ground. Accordingly, in making his jump of 8 feet 3 1/2 inches, he would have raised his CG no less than 51 inches. If it be further assumed (since the figure appears unavailable) that the weight of King's Own, including that of his rider, was 1350 pounds, the horse's effort in raising his CG 51 inches would be: $\sqrt{1350} \times 51$, or 1874 inch-pounds.*

Sometimes a horse's high jump has been compared with that of a human athlete's, but such a comparison ignores the many differences in the respective jumping *techniques* used by the man and the horse. The man makes his high jump by approaching the bar at an angle (i.e., partly from one side), taking off on *one* foot, then rolling his body sidewise over the bar in a manner that requires the least possible raising of his CG in order to clear the bar. In contrast, the horse approaches the obstacle directly from in front, takes off on *both* feet together, then goes over the bar with its forelegs followed by its hind legs. The latter action is comparable to a tumbler doing a forward dive, rather than to a track and field athlete performing a high jump. Nevertheless— despite the highly technical gymnastics required in the latter event—world champions (i.e., those who attain a height of 7 feet 6 inches) are required to raise their CG about 48 inches, which even with the bouncing take off is an extraordinary height to attain.[19]

If, then, we credit the best human jumper with an ability to raise his CG to a height of 48 inches, and assume his bodyweight as 175 pounds, the product of his effort becomes: $\sqrt{175} \times 48$, or 635 inch-pounds. The horse King's Own, in similarly raising a total load of 1350 pounds, as related above, and thereby gaining a score of 1874 inch-pounds, is seen to be (in jumping) 1874/635, or about three times as strong as a human champion jumper. From the cross-section of the horse's muscles generally (assuming the animal, without a rider, to weigh 1200 pounds), its strength in relation to the man's would be expected to be: $(\sqrt[3]{1200/175})^2$, or 3.6. Hence it would appear that the man is more *efficient* in making a high jump than is a horse; and that for the horse to be equally efficient he should be able to jump nearly a foot higher, that is, over 9 feet. That this comparison is not being unfair to the horse is indicated by the fact that some champion tumblers (who take off on *both* feet together, with a bound at the end of a row of flip-flaps) are able to raise their center of gravity possibly as high as 60 inches.

It should be unnecessary to present an illustration of a horse making a *broad* jump, since the action is almost self-explanatory. The animal simply gallops or canters up to the obstacle to be jumped, then takes off just as in the high jump but with a lesser raising of its CG and a greater speed and propulsion of its body *forward*.

However, in judging the jumping ability of any four-footed animal, allowance should be made for the difference in *physique and posture* of such an animal from that of a human athlete. When a horse leaps across, say, a 10-foot ditch, it does not perform a standing broad jump in the manner of a human jumper. In the case of the latter, the man takes off from his toes and alights on his heels, so that actually he covers the width of the ditch *plus* the length of his foot (including the shoe). In a four-footed animal, the take off is made from the *hind* feet and the landing made on the *front* feet, so that the distance covered by the body in a horizontal jump is actually

---

* In calculating the effort involved wherever a weight is propelled *off the ground*, as in throwing a ball, putting the shot, or jumping (i.e., moving one's own weight), the *square root* of the weight of the object propelled, rather than the weight *per se*, must be used.

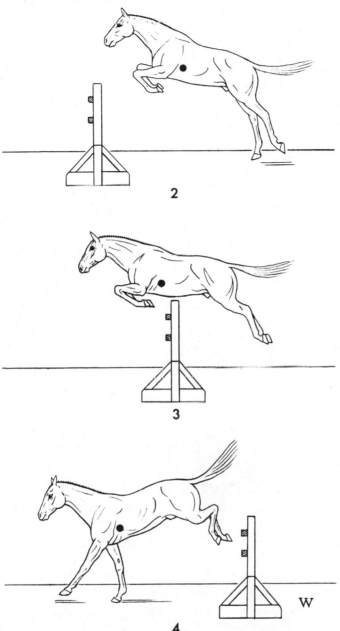

Fig. 159 Successive stages of a high jump. Note how little a horse has to raise its center of gravity (black dot) in order to clear a four-foot hurdle. For details see text.

the width of the jump *minus* the length from the hind feet to the forefeet of the animal when it is stretched out. As this minus-length in a horse of average size is no less than 8 feet, it means that in jumping a 10-foot ditch the horse moves its CG horizontally only about 2 feet. And this 8-foot deduction is to be made in the asserted length of every broad jump made by a horse.

Several broad jumps of 30 feet or over (as measured) by horses are on record. But evidently no such jumping—so far as *distance* is concerned—has taken place within recent years. At Liverpool, England, in 1839, a horse named Lottery, in winning the first Grand National Steeplechase,* is said to have made a jump of 36 feet while carrying a 138-pound rider. Another horse, Chandler, in 1847, in Warwickshire, England, surpassed the foregoing jump by assertedly clearing 39 feet. Three horses—Master Crump, Roustabout, and Overall—each jumped 36 feet. A United States Army mount, Nigra, jumped 35 feet, and another such mount, Touraine, 33 feet. A gunhorse of the English battery at Arras, France, in 1918 jumped a ditch 32 feet wide. Accepting Chandler's jump of 39 feet as the best horizontal leap accomplished so far by a horse (presumably mounted), and from it deducting 8 feet for the distance between the hoofs of the horse's outstretched fore and hind limbs, leaves a net jump, or forward repositioning of the horse's CG, of 31 feet. For comparison, the best broad jump (repositioning of the CG) made by a human athlete, after deducting an arbitrary 2

---

* Incidentally, the largest steeplechase jump in the world is one in the Liverpool Grand National Steeplechase, at Aintree. It is 5 feet 2 inches high, 3 feet 9 inches wide (thorn hedge), with a ditch on the take-off side 6 feet 2 inches wide and 2 feet 6 inches deep. Possibly it was this jump where the horse Lottery made his record broad jump.

Fig. 160 Greatheart setting a world record of 8 feet 13/16 inches in the high jump. South Shore Country Club Horse Show, Chicago, June 9, 1923.

Fig. 161 The Arabian stallion Mustafir, photographed from an unusual angle. For the author's comparison of Mustafir's rearing position with the takeoff position in a high jump, see text.

feet for the forward lean of the body at the start of the jump and the backward lean
at the finish, is about 27 feet. Assuming the human jumper's weight as 160 pounds,
his foot-poundage score thus becomes $\sqrt{160} \times 27$, or 342; while that of the horse
becomes, say, $\sqrt{1350} \times 31$, or 1139. This gives the horse a score of 1139/342, or
3.33, in comparison with the man (and with the expected ratio of 3.84), and indicates
a somewhat higher degree of efficiency on the horse's part than in the high jump,
possibly on account of the greater horizontal speed and momentum, along with the
lessened need for raising its center of gravity. But in order to equal human efficiency
in the running broad jump, the horse would have to increase his jump (as measured)
from 39 to 43.7 feet.

Fig. 161, taken from an unusual angle, shows a horse rearing in a position that
would immediately follow that in Fig. 158. That is, the horse's legs are more nearly
straightened as it approaches the take off position shown in Fig. 159, stage 2. Note the
display of the muscles of the back, as well as those of the powerful hind legs. The
horse is Mustafir, of the Palmer Arabian Stud Farm, Portland, Oregon.

k. Pulling (Draft) Ability in the Horse.

Here we shift our attention from light racing and jumping horses to others of
great bulk and massive build, whose physical powers are expressed in their ability to
draw heavy loads at slow speeds. For the draft horse, too, has its moments of glory!

In the time-honored county fair event of horse-pulling, the draft horse has today
regained much of his former popularity. Horse-pulling offers an exciting and enter-
taining exhibition of animal strength directed by man. There are active horse-pulling
associations in Kentucky, Wisconsin, Michigan, New York, and New England, plus
many smaller associations. For the month of August 1971 alone, no fewer than 81
sanctioned horse-pulling competitions were listed for the six New England states as
well as New York, Pennsylvania, Ohio, and West Virginia. And this did not represent
all the contests, as there were many others staged by minor associations.

These horse-drawing contests are popular events in rural communities, where
crowds gather to cheer the giant draft horses on to victory and to make wagers on
their favorite animals. In simple, early-day contests, the teams would merely draw a
loaded stoneboat over a specified distance. But, as would be expected, the "technique"
of the event has become more elaborate with increased competition, and for at least
the last fifty years a special dynamometer has been used to accurately record the amount
of weight pulled. This method involves the use of weights (suspended on each truck)
which are raised by the horses' pulling power until a certain degree of force (that which
the team is striving to overcome) is registered. At that point the brakes on the truck
are automatically released. The truck itself is a specially built vehicle with four dual
pneumatic-tired wheels, chains over the tires, and all wheels locked. A contest consists
of a team of horses (usually closely matched in weight) which strives to move the
truck for the required distance of 27 1/2 feet while the dynamometer continues to
register the hauling force attempted. Why the odd distance of 27 1/2 feet was
agreed upon, the writer does not know, for even in metric measure the distance does
not come out even, being equal to 8.4 meters.*Contests are held both for teams weighing
under 3000 pounds, and for teams weighing over 3000.

The following table, which is based on the best data available, shows the relationship
of pulling power to bodyweight in *individual* horses. For *team* comparisons, the body-

---

* Since writing this, I have learned that the distance of 27.5 feet was adopted because of its relation
to a *horsepower:* $27.5 = 1/20 \times \frac{\text{lbs. x ft.}}{550 \text{ x sec.}}$ D.P.W.

weights and the amounts pulled should each be *doubled*. Horses entered in team contests seldom if ever weigh less than 1200 pounds each. However, the following formula, upon which Table 26 is based, applies also to smaller horses and ponies down to a bodyweight of 400 pounds. The formula is: Dynamometer load, pounds = 1977 log Bodyweight pounds — 4500. The equivalent *weight that can be started* on a "granite block pavement," or other smooth, hard road, is 13 1/3 times the tractive dynamometer pull; and the *rolling load that can be pulled* on a similar surface is 66 2/3 times the dynamometer pull or 5 times the starting load.

Table 26. Pulling power in relation to bodyweight in draft horses.

Bodyweight of horse, lbs. (BW)	Dynamometer pull, lbs. (DP)	$\dfrac{DP}{BW}$	Equivalent weight, lbs., *started* on a granite block pavement	Equivalent *rolling load* on a granite block pavement
1200	1587	1.322	21,160	105,798
1300	1656	1.274	22,079	110,397
1400	1720	1.229	22,933	114,665
1500	1780	1.187	23,733	118,665
1600	1835	1.147	24,467	122,335
1700	1887	1.110	25,160	125,800
1800	1936	1.076	25,813	129,067
1900	1982	1.043	26,427	132,133
2000	2026	1.013	27,013	135,067
2100	2068	0.985	27,573	137,867
2200	2108	0.958	28,107	140,533
2300	2146	0.933	28,613	143,067
2400	2182	0.909	29,093	145,467
2500	2218	0.887	29,573	147,867

Since 1926, when a pair of geldings named Cap and King, weighing together 3700 pounds, made a dynamometer pull of 3475 pounds, the best records in this test at all bodyweights have advanced nearly 10 percent, or roughly 8 to 10 pounds a year. In 1943, a pair of grade Belgian geldings named Dan and Rowdy, weighing together 2990 pounds, set a then-record for "lightweight" horses by pulling the same amount (3475 pounds) as had been pulled 17 years earlier by the team of Cap and King, weighing 3700 pounds. Today (1972), as may be derived from Table 26 by interpolation, a team weighing 2990 pounds should be expected to pull 3554 pounds.

Also in 1943, a then "heavyweight" record was set by two grade Belgian geldings named Rock and Tom, weighing together 4650 pounds, which pulled 4100 pounds. Today (per Table 26), a team weighing 4650 pounds should be expected to pull 4310 pounds. Both the 1943 lightweight and heavyweight pulling records were made at Hillsdale, Michigan, which for many years has been a leading center for dynamometer pulling contests.

Fig. 162 shows Rock, together with another big Belgian, Tom, setting an earlier (1935) record pull of 3900 pounds. This record, which was widely publicized at the time, is shown in Fig. 163 in what would have been an equivalent "rolling load" of 260,000 pounds.

But there are also other contests of horse-pulling in which no dynamometer is used. In these simplified events the team of horses pulls, or drags, a wooden sled which is loaded, usually by means of a heavy block of stone, to an agreed-upon starting poundage.

After some of the competing teams have succeeded in pulling this amount of weight the required distance (and often within a prescribed period of time), the weight is increased by piling more rocks onto the sled. The best performance of this kind known to the writer is where two draft horses, named Buster and Sam, owned by Richard Wallingford of West Forks, Maine, dragged a sled loaded to 12,400 pounds a distance of 4 feet 7 inches "in one continuous draw."

Fig. 162 Rock and Tom, a team of grade Belgians each weighing over a ton, pulling a tractive dynamometer load of 3900 pounds for a world record in 1935, Hillsdale County Fair, Michigan.

Oxen, on account of their cloven hoofs, are in some respects able to gain more traction than are horses, and accordingly to draw very respectable loads. The best record of oxen-pulling relative to size is possibly that of a German team at Munich in 1893, which pulled a wagon weighing with its load 4000 kilos (8818.5 pounds) a distance of about 2 1/2 miles in 41 minutes, 36 seconds, at the rate of 3.6 mph. The pair of oxen weighed together 3300 pounds.

For direct comparison with the latter performance there is one which was made by a Russian draft stallion named Pepper, of the heavy breed raised in the Vladimir and Ivanovo regions. Pepper singly pulled a wagonload weighing 4000 kilos (8818.5 pounds) a distance of 6.2 miles in the time of one hour, 39 minutes, 49 seconds, at the rate of about 4 mph. If we apply to these two instances the familiar "horsepower" formula, and multiply together the factors of weight, distance, and time, and divide by the weight of the two oxen and by the one horse, respectively (assigning to the horse a weight of 1600 pounds), it is found that the horse's performance outdoes that of the oxen's in the ratio of nearly 6 to 1!

To refer again to Table 26, it is seen that the smaller the horse, the stronger it is in relation to its own weight, and vice versa. This is in contrast to the strength of human athletes, which reaches a peak of efficiency at 130–140 pounds, and diminishes at

Fig. 163 If converted to an equivalent "rolling load" of 260,000 pounds, Rock and Tom's dynamometer pull of 3900 pounds (See Fig. 162) could be represented by five railroad boxcars plus a caboose, as here shown. But the wheels would have to be smooth-turning, metal-tired ones, not chain-covered rubber tires like those on the dynamometer, as the artist has depicted them.

bodyweights both lighter and heavier than those of that median zone. However, when the most efficient pulling strength of a horse is based on *muscular cross-section* (or weight per inch of height), it is found that the greatest efficiency comes at a body-weight of about 24 pounds per inch of height. This, in a draft horse standing the average height of about 64 inches, would indicate an optimum weight of about 1540 pounds. This, in turn, shows the folly of breeding oversized draft horses, unless wholly for show purposes, since such huge animals cost a great deal more to feed and otherwise maintain than their limited usefulness justifies.

1. The Circus Horse.

Before leaving this chapter, perhaps a few words should be said about the horses that perform in the circus; because some such horses represent the results of training carried to the highest possible levels. Circus horses are used for three main purposes: (1) bareback riding, (2) "high school" or dressage exhibitions, and (3) as "Liberty horses," which perform their routines without a rider. In addition to these equestrian demonstrations, some smaller circuses and carnivals feature wild west or rodeo riding, along with such specialties as calf roping, dressage routines, trick riding, bareback bronco busting, etc., all of which involve horses either trained or untrained.

Quite apart from their own performances, circus horses have in numerous instances been associated with outstanding acts presented by human athletes and acrobats. In fact, many old-time circus families have been identified with acts in which horses, used in one way or another, have been indispensable co-workers.

When, for example, a cantering Percheron* is taught to allow human performers to leap onto his back, the animal learns exactly what to expect at a given moment, and to conform with it. Especially exacting on the horse's part as well as the man's is where a *somersault* is turned from the back of one horse to that of another. In one such act, which had taken years to perfect, some disgruntled person poisoned the perfectly trained horse that the family had relied on, and the act had to be discontinued until another horse could be schooled to take its place.

Again, some big, round-the-ring horses have been taught to *support* as many riders as can find room on their backs. Often the last to attempt such a tandem ride is a clown, who finds no more room on the horse's croup and ends up by hanging onto the animal's tail and being dragged around the ring! In order to support 700 pounds or more on its back, a horse has to be unusually robust as well as long-trained.

Many an equestrian act has featured a "supporting" feat, in which the bottom man (or, sometimes, woman) stands with one foot on the back of one horse and one on another, while the two animals canter around the ring side by side. In this straddling position the bottom (standing) rider supports another person on his (or her) shoulders. However, it is doubtful if there was ever another such act in which the bottom man, or supporter, stood *between* two horses with each of his feet in a stirrup, while supporting *three* partners on his shoulders as he directed the animals around the ring.** So extraordinary was this equestrian feat that we have attempted to give an illustration of it (Fig. 166). The "supporter" was Laurent, son of the famous circus founder Antonio Franco. The three persons supported consisted sometimes of three men, and sometimes Laurent's wife, her sister, and one man (as shown in Fig. 166).

An act that was once popular but which is rarely seen anymore, is where a horse "dives" from an elevated platform into a large tank of water about 30 feet below. In some such acts there is a rider, usually a pretty girl, who splashes into the water along with the horse. Years ago, when a performance of this kind was being given in London, some critics were of the opinion that the horses were being dealt with cruelly

---

* The reason why horses chosen for bareback riding are generally grey or dappled is because the light-colored backs of such horses do not show spots from the rosin used on the rider's slippers.

** A standard circus ring measures 41 feet in its inside diameter. So accustomed do performers and their horses become to this size of ring that if they have to perform in one of a different size they have to practice awhile especially for it.

Fig. 164 A circus horse being reared completely upright by its pretty rider. Some of the best-trained of all equine animals are the "high school" horses seen in the larger circuses of Europe and the United States.

in order to make them dive. A thorough investigation by the S.P.C.A. followed, whereupon it was learned that the horses dived of their own free wills and apparently *enjoyed*
the experience!

Fig. 165 "Bronco-busting" at a Western rodeo. The *Bronco* of the present day
may be regarded as having descended mainly or wholly from horses which were
lost by American cross-country pioneers, rather than from the original *Mustang*
or feral (semi-wild) horse of the earlier Spanish explorers. The latter (mustang)
type of horse, strictly speaking, became extinct about 1880, except for a few
individuals which were captured, broken to use, and bred by Indians.

Fig. 166 A mighty feat combining humans and horses. Shown here is Laurent Franco as he presented his act, *Les Forces d'Hercule,* in Paris about 1800. Laurent would support *three* members of his troupe as shown, with a foot in each of the stirrups, while his pair of matched Percherons cantered around the ring. Usually, in addition, a girl stood on each of the horse's backs.

Notes and References

1. Adolf Staffe, "Untersuchungen über die Trachtigkeitsdauer bei Lippizanern," *Mittelungen der landwirtschaftlichen Lehrkanzeln der Hochschule für Bodenkultur in Wien,* vol. 3 (1918): 547–595.

2. C. E. Howell, and W. C. Rollins, "Environmental Sources of Variation in the Gestation Length of the Horse," *Animal Science* 10, no. 4 (November 1951): 790.

3. David P. Willoughby, "Animal Ages," *Natural History* 78, no. 10 (December 1969): 56–59.

4. Alex Comfort, *The Process of Ageing.* (New York: New American Library, 1964), p. 26.

5. I. Norr, "Der Schlaf des Pferdes" *Zeitschrift für Veterinarkunde* 49, no. 6 (1937): 193–232.

6. T. E. White, *The Book of Beasts.* (New York: G. P. Putnam's Sons, 1954), p. 86.

7. J. O. Williams, *Care and Management of Farm Work Horses,* U.S. Dept. Agric. Farmer's Bulletin No. 1419 (1940), p. 7.

8. M. E. Esminger, *Horses and Horsemanship.* (Danville, Ill.: The Interstate Printers, 1969). (This book has the most up-to-date, comprehensive coverage of the feeding of horses—125 of its 907 pages—yet seen by the present writer.)

9. Samuel Brody, and H. H. Kibler, Relation between Organ Weight and Body Weight in Growing and Mature Animals, Univ. of Missouri Agric. Res. Bull. 328 (1941), p. 16.

10. E. Bourdelle, "Quelques characters anatomiques du zebra de Hartmann," *Bull. Mus. Nat. Hist.,* 2d ser., vols. 7–8 (1935–36): 473–77.

11. Daniel P. Quiring, "A Comparison of Certain Gland, Organ, and Body Weights in Some African Ungulates and the African Elephant," *Growth* 2, no. 4 (1938): 335–46.

12. Capt. M. H. Hayes, *Points of the Horse.* (London: 1930), p. 38.

13. Major A. J. R. Lamb, *Horse Facts* (London, 1947), p. 27.

14. A. E. Kennelly, *An approximate law of fatigue in the speeds of racing animals. Proc. Amer. Acad. Arts and Sci.* 42 (1906): 275–331. (Reprinted in the volume *Classical studies on physical activity,* edit. by Roscoe C. Brown, Jr. and Gerald S. Kenyon. (Englewood Cliffs, N.J.: 1968).

15. David P. Willoughby, *The Super-Athletes* (South Brunswick (N.J.) and New York: A. S. Barnes and Co., 1970), pp. 585–593.

16. Lamb, *Horse Facts,* pp. 36–41.

17. Gregor de Romaszkan, *Fundamentals of Riding* (New York: 1964), pp. 91–104.

18. R. A. R. and B. J. K. Tricker. *The Science of Movement* (New York: 1967), p. 122.

19. Willoughby, *The Super-Athletes,* p. 475.

20. Robert C. Procter, et al. "Efficiency of Work in Horses of Different Ages and Body Weights," Res. Bull 209, Univ. of Missouri Agric. Exper. Sta. (May 9, 1934), p. 18.

12

Coat Coloration in the Domestic Horse

Many different coat colors are to be seen among the numerous breeds of the domestic horse. Some of these colors are termed *basic* and others *color patterns*. While authorities differ on minor points, the following list, which is abstracted from a study made by Fred Gremmel (1939),[1] would appear to be one of the most systematic classifications made so far.

Classification of coat colors in horses.

Basic Colors

I. BLACK: body color in true black (disregarding weathering).
    A. Black—true black without light areas.
    B. Seal brown—black with light areas, to include muzzle, under eyes, flanks, and inside of upper legs, termed "light points."
II. BAY (reddish-brown): shades from tan to brown, with black "points" (mane and tail and often lower legs).
    A. Mahogany bay—the brown shades of bay, often called brown.
    B. Blood bay—the red shades of bay.
    C. Sandy bay—the light shades of bay.
III. CHESTNUT (red-yellow brown): shades from yellow-gold to dark brown; mane and tail not black but approximately the color of the body.
    A. Liver chestnut—the dark shades, some appearing dark brown with an auburn hue.
    B. Sorrel—the reddish shades of chestnut. Sometimes in the lighter shades the mane and tail are of the color described as "crushed strawberry."
IV. YSABELLA: a color group having flaxen (straw-blond) or silver manes and tails.
    A. Red ysabella—red sorrel-like; flaxen mane and tail.

Color Patterns

I. GREY: causes gradual displacement of colored hair by white hair as age advances.
    A. Iron or steel grey—usually a high percentage of colored hair, indicating a young animal.
    B. Dappled grey—having the colored hair in such distribution as to give a dappled effect.
    C. White—almost devoid of colored hair.

II. At certain ages grey, black roan, and grey roan are practically indistinguishable, but true genetic differences exist. Grey is foaled solid color; any roan is foaled roan; and grey roan whitens with age the same as does grey. Roan, a more or less uniform mixture of colored and white hairs, occurs in a number of combinations.

    A. Black roan—black and white hair mixed, usually called "blue."

    B. Blue roan—usually described as black and white hairs mixed, but almost invariably having some red hairs.

    C. Bay or red roan—roaned bay.

    D. Chestnut or strawberry roan—roaned chestnut.

    E. Paint roan—roaning imposed on the colored areas of paint.

    F. Dun roan—roan in combination with the dun factor.

    G. Grey roan—roan in combination with the grey factor.

III. DUN: always with dorsal stripe; often zebra stripes on legs and transverse stripes over withers and shoulders; coat appears diluted.

    A. Mouse dun—dun imposed on black, seal brown, dark mahogany bay, or dark liver chestnut, giving a smoky effect.

    B. Buckskin dun—dun imposed on blood or sandy bay.

    C. Claybank dun—dun imposed on sorrel.

IV. PAINT or PIED: irregular colored and white areas.

    A. Piebald—white and black.

    B. Skewbald—white and any color other than black.

In addition to the foregoing basic colors and patterns of the hair-coat itself, there are minor markings of the head and feet and colors of the long hair of the mane and tail. On the forehead or face there may be a "spot," a "star," a "blaze," or any of the other markings illustrated in Fig. 167. On the feet there may be any of the markings shown in Fig. 168. The mane and the tail may each be different in coloration from the body, and similar to or different from each other.

Another investigator of equine coat color, Dr. G. W. Salisbury of Cornell University, makes the following definitions of the basic colors.[2]

1. BAY: A bay horse or pony is one having a black mane and tail, black feet and legs often as high as the knees and hocks, and a body color that may range from light reddish-brown to dark cherry-red. [The most prized Arabian horses are those of a blood-bay color.]

2. BROWN, BROWN-BLACK, or SEAL BROWN: Brown is often confused with bay, and sometimes, if the brown is very dark, with black. The brown body color is accompanied by black "points" (mane, tail, feet, and legs). However, the muzzle, the region about the eyes, the flanks, and the inner sides of the upper legs may be a lighter shade of brown.

3. BLACK: A uniform color found most commonly in the Percheron draft and Shetland pony breeds. If bleached from sunlight, the black color may present a reddish tinge to the hair which approaches bay or brown.

4. CHESTNUT: Any one of the three chestnut shades defined by Gremmel (see above). Much confusion exists in the defining of these colors. Some breeders call them all chestnut, while others classify all except the liver chestnuts as sorrels. The mane and tail of this color group are the same color as the body, or lighter, sometimes nearly pure white. The pasterns and legs are generally lighter in shade than the body.

Further to the above definitions, the following details should be noted.

a. GREY: According to Salisbury,[2] grey is not a basic color. Grey horses or ponies are black at birth. The white hairs appear when the foal's hair is shed, and the animal becomes progressively whiter with age. It would appear that grey is produced by a dominant gene epistatic to the basic colors. Dapple grey color generally comes between the second and fifth years. Young grey horses are often looked upon as "blue roans." When small specks of black hairs occur the grey is called "flea-bitten." When a young grey horse has a great deal of black in his coat he is termed "iron grey"; or if the black makes a pattern, "dappled grey."[3]

b. WHITE: Most horses referred to as "white" are really grey. According to Prof. W. E. Castle, a true albino mutation in horses is unknown. "The most nearly complete degree of albinism known among horses is probably that found in the albino horses of Butte, Nebraska [the American Albino, see Table 16], which have an all-white coat including the eye lashes, but with pigmented eyes described as blue or brown. Some colts, however, may have a coat of very pale yellow color which later becomes white." "There is also a type of albino horse which has a cream-colored coat, even when adult, with pink skin and blue 'china' eyes. It is known as 'cremello,' both the type of animal and its descriptive term being importations from Mexico . . ."[4] White *markings,* such as those which commonly occur on a horse's face or feet, or not to be regarded as atavistic ("throwbacks"), but rather as mutations of contemporaneous origin (Castle).

c. DUN: This is a coat color in which yellow hair predominates. If it is light and mixed with white, it is called "cream." Horses of such a color never have black points. If the coat is pure golden, the color is called "palomino." Such horses always have *white* points. If the coat is yellow mixed with red (sorrel), the horse is a "clay-bank" and has reddish points. Dun mixed with blood bay or sandy bay is a "buckskin," and always has black points. Dun mixed with brown or black is called "grullo" (grew-yo), a dark grey. Grullo horses, however, are not classified as true duns, even though they have a dark mid-dorsal stripe and sometimes zebra-like stripings on the legs and withers, because of the dominance of brown or black over yellow-dun. It should be noted that the color of the ancestral wild horse, designated by Darwin as "dun," was a color similar to bay but lighter, with a yellowish pigment where the bay has red. This color should not be confused with the yellow-dun or "buckskin" of modern domestic horses.

d. BAY: Denhardt likens "bay" to the color of a well-baked loaf of bread. Pocock (1909) says, "Bays with black points are rufus-brown horses, with mane, tail, and lower half of the legs black."[5] Bay horses may be distinguished from Sorrels because of the latter having a red (or occasionally flaxen or blond), rather than black, mane, and tail.

e. PINTO: This is a Spanish term referring to horses or ponies of "calico" coloration. A "pinto" horse may be either *piebald* (black and white) or *skewbald* (white and any color other than black). Terms synonymous with pinto are "painted" or "paint." All refer to horses having large, irregularly shaped patches or spots. Smaller-sized spots, as in the Appaloosa, do not constitute pinto coloration.

Many theories have been advanced as to the probable coloration of primitive or ancestral horses. In order to give the reader an idea of the agreements and disagreements of these theories, the following quotations—all from authorities of high standing—are appended.

Charles Darwin (1859). Darwin believed that the first horses were dun in color and marked more or less with dark stripes, and that this coat-pattern later passed into spots and dapplings.[6]

Emmanuel Bonavia (1896). "In my opinion, the Zebra stripes, like those of the Tiger and other feline animals, owe their genesis to spots or rosettes or dapplings,

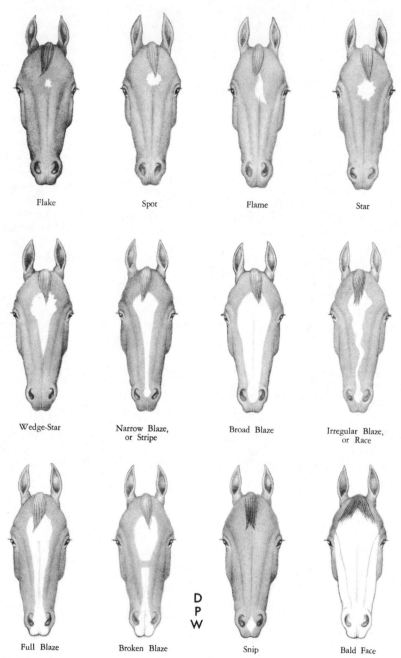

Fig. 167 Sketches by the author, showing some common head markings in the domestic horse.

which had become disposed in transverse rows. . . . Subsequently the rows of spots coalesced into beady bands, and ultimately became the sharp-edged bands we see in Zebras."[7] (i.e., in Bonavia's opinion stripes came *after* rosettes or dapplings.)

Harry Johnston (1903). "The true horse, *Equus caballus,* which succeeded it [the wild horse], in its early forms probably bore dark stripes on the limbs and perhaps on the shoulder, and dapplings on the body."[8] Johnston's theory of the original markings of the horse group were not zebra-like (dark) stripes, but *white or pale spots and stripes on a dark ground-color.*

Reginald Innes Pocock (1909). "Thus there appear to me to be very good reasons for thinking that Johnston's view of the coloration of the Equidae is correct, namely, that they are descended from dark-colored animals patterned with white spots, running into longitudinal lines originally, and at a late stage in evolution becoming arranged in transverse bars over the neck and body."[9] Pocock, like Bonavia (see above), believed that a pattern of dappling *preceded* that of zebra-like (vertical, or transverse) stripings.

Fred Gremmel (pers. comm., 2–27–46). "Persistent cropping up of a pattern [e.g., dappling] to me does not at all indicate it to be more primitive."

W. E. Castle (pers. comm., 1–29–46). "I consider dappling as a 'sport,' i.e., a genetic mutation, *not* an ancestral color pattern. That it occurs in various breeds of horses is no evidence that it was present in a common ancestor.[*] White markings are even more widespread than dappling, yet they are clearly recent and mutational in origin." Further, Prof. Castle remarks: "It would be unjustified speculation to go farther back than the Przevalsky horse in search of an ancestral pattern for domestic horses. That horse *has* an ancestral pattern, which is present in the domestic bay type, and especially the dun. . . . This ancestral pattern involves, as effects of a single dominant gene probably, the following details: (a) spinal stripe, (b) dark "points" (legs, mane, tail, ears), (c) lighter general body color (yellow in dun, red in bay), (d) occasional faint zebra stripes on legs and across withers."

A. G. Searle (1968) gives an analytical review of the coat colors of horses, donkeys, zebras, tapirs, and rhinoceroses.

In connection with white markings on the legs and feet of domestic horses, the following table, after C. Grevé (1887),[**] shows the frequencies of various markings observed in 2000 work-horses having white markings on one or more of their feet. No grey horses were recorded, as these naturally are frequently possessed of white foot markings. The colors of the horses observed were black, brown, chestnut, and Ysabella.

---

[*] This view was held also by William Ridgeway (1905). Pocock, however, (1909, p. 410) offers a contrary explanation, namely, that dapple-grey *could* very well be a primitive coat-pattern.

[**] In the *Zoologische Garten,* 28:338–39.

Table 27. Distribution of white markings on the feet of 2000 domestic horses.

		Number in 2000	Percent	Approx. one in:
1.	LEFT hindfoot white	512	25.6	4
2.	BOTH hindfeet white	408	20.4	5
3.	RIGHT hindfoot white	320	16.0	6
4.	NONE of the feet white	256	12.8	8
5.	ALL of the feet white	236	11.8	8
6.	LEFT forefoot and BOTH hindfeet white	60	3.0	33
7.	RIGHT forefoot and BOTH hindfeet white	48	2.4	42
8.	LEFT forefoot and RIGHT hindfoot white	28	1.4	71
9.	RIGHT forefoot and LEFT hindfoot white	28	1.4	71
10.	LEFT forefoot white	24	1.2	83
11.	RIGHT forefoot white	20	1.0	100
12.	LEFT forefoot and LEFT hindfoot white	20	1.0	100
13.	BOTH forefeet and LEFT hindfoot white	16	0.8	125
14.	BOTH forefeet and RIGHT hindfoot white	12	0.6	167
15.	RIGHT forefoot and RIGHT hindfoot white	8	0.4	250
16.	BOTH forefeet white	4	0.2	500
		2000	100.0	

It is interesting to note, from this table, how the *right* feet are white only 80 percent as frequently as the *left,* whether they be fore or hind; and that consequently, when two right feet are white they occur only 40 percent as frequently as two left feet, etc. It would be interesting to know, further, whether the above distribution is applicable to brown and black horses of the *lighter* breeds, such as Arabians, Thoroughbreds, et al. Finally, someone should make a similar study today, to determine whether or not the distribution of white markings among horses is the same now as it was when Grevé made his examinations in 1887.

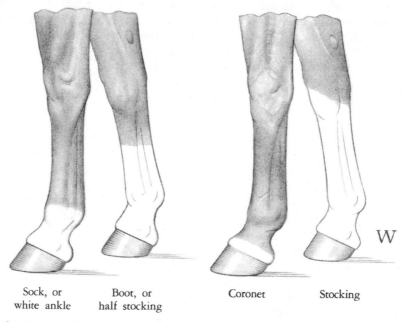

| Sock, or | Boot, or | Coronet | Stocking |
| white ankle | half stocking | | |

Fig. 168 Four of the many light markings common to both the fore and the hind limbs of domestic horses. The marking may range from a spot on the coronet to full whitening of the legs below the knees and the hocks.

An animal's physiology, as well as its coat color, is influenced by its natural habitat. In this connection a number of "rules" have been advanced by zoologists to account for such things as coat coloration, heat conservation, etc. Three of these so-called rules are as follows:

GLOGER'S RULE: that animals living in moist forests tend to have black or red haircoats. This probably has to do in part with the balance between sunlight and Vitamin D. Animals and birds obtain Vitamin D by licking fur and preening feathers. Vitamin D is produced in body oils by ultraviolet irradiation, which, in dim light, may be more efficient with black or red coats than with buff or grey ones. The latter colors afford camouflage that is not needed in the dim light of the forest. When individual animals are taken from the open into the forest, their coats tend to darken.

BERGMANN'S RULE: that animals living in colder regions are larger than those of the same type inhabiting warmer regions. This is because of the need of all warm-blooded animals to maintain a constant internal temperature. The larger the animal, all else being equal, the greater its volume in ratio to surface area, and the lesser the loss of heat through the skin. Conversely, in hot, dry climates, survival depends on the body's ability to lose heat by radiation, convection, and evaporation, and the smaller the body the greater its efficiency to these ends.

ALLEN'S RULE: desert-living animals tend to have long ears (for heat loss) and long limbs (for traveling swiftly between far-separated oases or feeding-places). Conversely, in cold regions, the ears tend to be much shorter (even in rabbits), to prevent their freezing and to *conserve* heat.

Notes and References

1. Fred Gremmel, "Coat Colors in Horses," *Jour. Heredity* 30 (1939): 437–45.
2. G. W. Salisbury, "The Inheritance of Equine Coat Color," *Jour. Heredity* 32 (1941): 235–40. (Reprinted in *The Horse Lover*, February-March 1943, pp. 15–17.)
3. Bob Denhardt, "What Color Is He?" *The Western Horseman*, January–February 1948, p. 19.
4. W. E. Castle, "The Genetics of Coat Color in Horses," *Jour. Heredity* 31 (1940): 127–28. (Reprinted in *The Western Horseman*, January–February 1943), p. 8.
5. R. I. Pocock, "On the Colours of Horses, Zebras, and Tapirs," *Ann. & Mag. Nat. Hist.*, ser. 8, vol. 4 (1909): 404–15.
6. Charles Darwin, *The Origin of Species* . . . (London, 1859).
7. Emmanuel Bonavia, *Studies in the Evolution of Animals* (London, 1896), p. 87.
8. Harry Johnston, *British Mammals.* (London, 1903), pp. 275–76.
9. R. I. Pocock, *On Colours of Horses*, p. 415.
10. A. G. Searle, Comparative Genetics of Coat Colour in Mammals (New York: 1968), pp. 200–207.

13

The Domestic Ass and Its Wild Ancestors

3. SUBGENUS *ASINUS* (J. E. GRAY, 1825)

a. *Equus* (*Asinus*) *asinus asinus* (domestic ass; donkey; jack; burro).

When Linnaeus, in 1758, classified the common domestic ass, giving it the Latin name *asinus*,* he designated it simply as a member of the genus *Equus,* and did not assign it to a subgeneric group, as did the British systematist J. E. Gray in 1825. Again, Linnaeus based his *Equus asinus* on the domesticated ass of continental Europe, since the animal was not in general use in Sweden, the climate there being too cold for it. Accordingly, no particular breed or strain of the domestic ass, either in Europe or elsewhere, can be taken as the type of the species as classified by Linnaeus.

While the familiar grey-coated animal, commonly known as the donkey, is found almost throughout the habitable world, it occurs in greatest abundance in climates that suit it best, such as southern Europe, North Africa, the Near East, India, Mexico, the West Indies, South America, and other hot (and preferably arid) countries. The animal was known in England prior to 1000 A.D., but later died out and was not reintroduced until sometime in the 1500s.

As to size, the average shoulder height of the common donkey may be assumed as being just under 40 inches (for body proportions, see Fig. 244). However, great variations occur from this average in the case of certain small or large local breeds, such as the dwarf donkeys of Sicily, India, and Ceylon, which may be as little as 24 inches high at the shoulder (see Fig. 169), and the large Majorca (Spanish island) ass, which averages no less than 62 inches. This size-range between dwarf and giant breeds of the domestic ass is even greater, proportionately, than that which exists between small (e.g., Shetland) ponies and the largest draft horses.

Various European donkey breeds of large size, the stallions of which are known as jacks and the mares as jennets, include the Maltese jack (average height 56 inches) the

---

* The Latin name was really *asininus,* from which was derived the French *asinus,* the Anglo-Saxon *assa,* and the German *esel.* The Latin name was preceded by the Greek *asnos* or *osnos,* which had come from the Hebrew *athôn.* The name donkey came much later, possibly in the 18th century, and is believed to have resulted from a combining of the words *dun,* the animal's coat-color, and *kin,* meaning small. (It should be noted, though, that the donkey's color is *grey,* not dun.) The name was formerly pronounced dunk-e, to rhyme with monkey, before becoming the present dong'ki.

Fig. 169 Sicilian donkey (*E. asinus asinus*), one of the smallest breeds of the domestic ass.

long-haired Poitou jack (57 inches), the Catalonian jack (60 inches), the Andalusian jack (60 inches), and the aforementioned Majorca jack (62 inches). These breeds—from Malta, France, northeast Spain, and southern Spain, respectively—have been imported in large numbers to the United States. From them, and a few lesser-known European strains, has been developed the American jack, a strongly constructed animal, black with light points and white muzzle, standing 62–63 inches in height, weighing 1150–1200 pounds, and which is used principally for breeding with draft mares in the production of draft mules. The American jack is one of the few distinct breeds of domestic animals to have originated in the United States.* The range in size of the American jacks is extensive. Plumb (1906, p. 159) gives the variation in height of only 100 individuals as from 56 to 66 inches, averaging 61 inches. The average height of jennets is given as 58 inches.

As to the domestication of the ass in the Old World, it is known to have occurred considerably earlier than that of the horse. On this point the historian Peake remarks:

> The ass was used at a very early date, both in Egypt and in Mesopotamia, but it is impossible to say at present to which region to ascribe the priority. Towards the close of the predynastic period in Egypt, just before 3400 B.C., the Libyan tribes,

---

* The American jack stock is said to have had its origin in the importations from Spain and Malta of General George Washington, Henry Clay, and two breeders in Kentucky named Young and Everett. However, a breeder named Theodorick Bland, Jr. in 1776 advertised his jacks for public service. As this was 12 years prior to Washington's advertisement, it shows that jacks and mules were well known in the Colonies prior to 1776. "They were descendants of asses brought into Florida by the Spaniards, which had increased there and in the nearby Colonies—Georgia, the Carolinas, and Virginia."

who dwelt in the desert to the west of the Nile Delta, possessed large herds of asses, and this indicates that this animal had been known to and possessed by them for a long time. At Ur, in Mesopotamia, asses were used by those kings and queens who were buried in the famous death-pits, accompanied by their slain retainers, and these must be relegated to quite as early a date, and are probably much earlier. All our evidence goes to show that asses had been tamed, and were used as beasts of burden, both in Egypt and Mesopotamia, between 4000 and 3000 B.C., and may have been domesticated at a considerably earlier date."[1]

In contrast to the diversity of opinion still prevalent regarding the origin of the domestic horse, present-day zoologists are in general agreement that the immediate ancestor of the domestic ass, or donkey, is one of the existing (or recently extinct) forms of the wild ass of North Africa. The external appearance of the domestic animal, as compared with its wild progenitor, with the exception of certain differences in coloration, is almost identical, and a comparison of the proportions of the skull and the postcranial skeleton confirms this similarity. While at one time it was commonly believed that the so-called Syrian wild ass, or hemippus, entered into the ancestry of the domestic donkey, an analysis of the skeletal proportions in the two types demonstrates so many dissimilarities as to rule out any hemionien ancestry completely.

Taking the average-sized domestic donkey as a typical representative of the subgenus *Asinus,* some of the major differences between this equine and a horse are as follows: (1) in the ass, there are no chestnuts on the hind legs; (2) the number of lumbar vertebrae in the ass is usually 5, rarely 6, whereas in the horse it is usually 6, although in the Arab and some other Oriental breeds it averages 5 or 5½; (3) the ears of the ass are disproportionately long compared with those of the horse, and in the domestic subspecies are usually marked at the base, as well as at the tip, with a large black or dark-brown patch; (4) the mane of the ass is short, stiff, upright, and usually without a forelock, while in the horse it is long and hanging and with a forelock, although in true wild horses it is either erect or semi-erect; (5) the hoofs of the ass are small and narrow, while those of the horse are large and round (see Fig. 19); (6) the tail of the ass is cow-like, having long hairs only at its end, whereas in the domestic horse the tail is flowing and long-haired from root to end; (7) the croup of the ass, seen from behind, is sloping and angular; that of the horse is flatter and more rounded (see Figs. 19 and 20); (8) the male ass ("Jack") has two rudimentary teats; (9) the period of gestation in the ass averages 370 days or at least twelve months, whereas in the horse it is only about 337 days or just over eleven months; (10) the ass, in comparison with the horse, more frequently produces twin offspring; (11) the coloration of the ass (here, specifically the domestic form), which may be black or any shade of grey to creamy white, is never brown, bay, chestnut, red or blue roan, or any of the other reddish or brownish colors so common to horses; again, the ass commonly has a narrow, vertical shoulder-stripe (as well as a dark, narrow dorsal stripe), which is never present in the horse; (12) neither does the ass ordinarily have any of the white markings common to horses, such as (on the forehead) a spot, star, or blaze, or (on the feet and legs) socks, boots, stockings, or white points; however, piebald or pinto donkeys and burros occur, in which the black and white blotches are spread irregularly over the entire head, neck, body, and legs; (13) the longevity of the donkey is, on the average, probably greater than that of the horse, although ages of 50 years have assertedly been attained by both species (but see p. 248); (14) the call of the donkey is a bray, whereas that of the horse is a neigh; (15) among the

Fig. 170 Two jacks on a street in Naples. Note the *rope* halters and the unshod hoofs.

Fig. 171 "Old and young." A Study of donkey heads by Benno Adam.

wild asses of Nubia and Somaliland the mares and their young form separate herds, led by a mare; the males joining them only at the breeding periods. This is in contrast to the social setup prevailing among wild horses, in which the entire herd is controlled and led by a master stallion; finally (16), the ass is sure-footed, while the horse is not.

The material used by the writer in determining the osteometry of the domestic ass has consisted of 30 adult skulls (2 measured by the writer) and from 12 to 15 complete or partial postcranial skeletons (2 measured by the writer).

NOTE: The mule, which is not a species, is dealt with in Chapter 16, along with other equine hybrids.

b. Nubian wild ass (*Equus asinus africanus* Fitzinger, 1857).
Arabic name: *Himar el wadi* ("ass of the desert").

This wild forbear of at least some of the domestic asses of North Africa differs from the latter in its somewhat larger size (although it is very much smaller than the domestic asses or jacks used for breeding mules), and to a certain extent in its coloration. In its cranial and post-cranial skeletal proportioning it is very near indeed to the ordinary donkey.

The shoulder height of the Nubian wild ass would appear to range between the wide limits of 38 and 47 inches. A very large male specimen that lived in the New York Zoological Park from 1925 to 1949, and whose skeleton was later measured by the writer, must have stood in life about 46½ inches. A photograph of this animal is shown in Fig. 172 (see also Fig. 75).

In this wild race of *asinus,* as in the domestic donkey, the ears are very long, the hoofs small and narrow, the tail-tuft of moderate length (the terminal hairs being mixed black and grey), and the dark mane short and upright and without a forelock. The general coat-color is greyish-fawn, with a narrow, dark dorsal stripe running the full length of the spine, well onto the tail. The muzzle, a circular patch around each eye, the under surface of the lower jaw, the inside of the ear, the underparts of the body, and the inner sides and much of the lower portions of the legs are whitish. On the inner side of the lower part of each foreleg is a chestnut patch.

Pocock (1909) says:

These . . . (Nubian) asses differ from ordinary domestic asses in the sharp contrast between the white of the legs and the greyish-fawn of the head, neck, and body. They also . . . differ at all events from the majority of English domestic asses . . . in having scarcely any black or brown on the ear, except at the tip and on the margin.[3]

Pocock feels that the true ancestral form of the wild ass must have been a race possessing the markings both of the ears and of the legs commonly seen in domestic donkeys—namely, a large black or dark-brown patch at the base of the rear of the ear, and with legs the same (greyish) color as the body and indistinctly barred with black. *E. africanus* is without the latter striping of the legs, although, as in the domestic ass, it has a short but distinct shoulder-stripe running vertically for a distance of 5 to

Fig. 172 Nubian wild ass (*E. asinus africanus*). A male specimen that lived in the New York Zoological Park for 24 years.

6 inches over each scapula and across the withers. The wild form has also a dark patch on each side of the front fetlock.

While the Nubian wild ass has frequently been referred to in zoological treatises also as the Abyssinian wild ass, according to Lydekker (1922) the range of the species:

> . . . formerly extended as far as the fifth cataract of the Nile, and eastwards to the River Atbara and the Danakil district, but not including Abyssinia.[4]

Year by year the range of this species has become even more restricted.* Brocklehurst (1931) says that the wild ass (meaning *E. africanus*):

> . . . is found in the Sudan in the neighborhood of the Atbara River in the provinces of Berber and Kassala; it is also found in the Red Sea Province south of Suakin.[5]

---

* In a personal communication from I. Kadny, Director of the Zoological Gardens at Giza, Egypt, dated June 28, 1944, the writer was informed that it was the practice of the Bedouins in the Nubian Desert, when their domesticated she-asses approached the mating time, to tie them up and leave them in the desert to be mated by the males of the wild asses, which at that time still existed in small herds in the area.

It is believed that the small herds, supposedly of *E. africanus,* reported in 1960 near Tibesti-Enni in Chad, and in 1965 not far from Giarabub in Libya, may, like other such groups west of the Nile, have been domestic asses running wild rather than survivors of the true *E. africanus.*[6] In this connection it may be noted that the wild asses of Nubia and Somaliland form herds of females accompanied by their young and led by a female; the males join them only at the reproductive periods.*

The available, or published, material on skulls and skeletons of the Nubian wild ass is exceedingly limited. For the writer's study there was only one complete male skeleton available (American Museum of Natural History Cat. No. 135017), the skull of which was not measured. However, the close similarity of the skeletal proportions of the domestic ass, the Somali wild ass, and the published data on the Nubian wild ass indicate that all the other subspecies of this animal from North Africa, whether living or recently extinct, were probably of a very similar structural pattern—a pattern that has remained about the same, despite the effects of artificial breeding, for at least 4000 years.

c. Somali wild ass (*Equus asinus somaliensis* Noack, 1884).

Native names: *Gumburi; Dameir dibbaded.*

This race of wild ass is distinguished from the Nubian subspecies by its generally larger size, somewhat heavier build, and partially different coloration. The shoulder height of *somaliensis* is said to range from 47 to 49 inches. A male specimen, the skeleton of which was measured by the writer, had an estimated living shoulder height of 47.3 inches. Heights up to 56 inches have been given by various authors, but such dimensions may have been made from carcasses in the field, and over the curves of the body and forelegs. Pocock (1909, p. 528), in discussing such exaggerated measurements, points out that the actual height of a fine stallion then living in the London

Fig. 173 Somali wild ass (*E. asinus somaliensis*). A mounted group collected and prepared by Carl E. Akeley in 1896. Its larger size, along with the absence of a shoulder stripe and the presence of distinct stripings on the legs, distinguishes this subspecies from the Nubian Wild Ass. (Cf. Fig. 172.)

Zoo was not over 48 inches. The height at the croup, as in all other forms of *Asinus,* is greater than at the withers, the superiority being from 3 to 4 percent or approximately 1 to 2 inches. The head or skull is proportionately large, the length of the head in the living animal being about 47½ percent of the shoulder height. A point of distinction in the Somali race is that the facial length of the skull, in ratio to the cranial length, is notably greater than in the domestic ass or donkey.

In coloration, the Somali wild ass differs from *africanus* by the somewhat lighter ground color of the coat, the partial or complete absence of shoulder stripes, the slightly developed and discontinuous dorsal stripe, and the distinct dark striping of the legs (mainly on the front and outer side surfaces), which on the hind pair extends above the hocks, and on the forelegs up to within several inches of the level of the chest (see Fig. 173).

The center of the geographical range of *Asinus somaliensis* would appear to have been the Berbera district of British Somaliland (now Somaliland Protectorate), near the south coast of the Gulf of Aden, and about 500 miles south and 800 miles east of the typical locality of *Asinus africanus* (Atbara, in the Nubian Desert). About the turn of the century it extended northward along the coast of Eritrea nearly to Massawa, and from there southward into the wasteland of Danakil, in Ethiopia. The main population in 1965 is said to have consisted of only 200–350 animals located in the Sardo area of Ethiopia; and it is believed that other herds may have survived at Lake Hertale in Ethiopia, Buri in Eritrea, and Wadi Nogal in north Somalia.[7]

A comparison of the relative lengths of the limb bones in the domestic ass with those in *E. a. africanus* and *E. a. somaliensis* gives these results: the Nubian wild ass resembles the domestic donkey most in general size (being 7 or 8 percent taller), but in only 5 out of 20 limb-bone length indices. The Somali ass is larger (20 percent taller than the donkey), but is somewhat closer to the donkey in most of its skeletal proportions.

The skeletal material of *E. asinus somaliensis* used in the writer's study has consisted of 6 skulls (4 male, 2 female), and one complete male skeleton (Chicago Nat. Hist. Mus. No. 18851), the limb bones of which were measured by Dr. Paul O. McGrew and the pelvis by the writer. A few other skeletal measurements have been published by the Soviet zoologist Viera Gromova (1955) and by H. G. Stehlin and P. Graziosi (1935).

---

d. Ethiopian wild ass (*Equus asinus taeniopus* Heuglin, 1861).

While this alleged race of the African wild ass was described before either *africanus* or *somaliensis,* there has always been a lack of exactitude regarding its geographical habitat, and even an insufficiency of information as to the animal's physical appearance. About the only definite statement concerning the latter is that *taeniopus* possessed both the shoulder and dorsal striping of *africanus,* and the leg striping of *somaliensis.* Since apparently the race no longer exists, and since (to the writer's knowledge, at least) there is not a single complete adult postcranial skeleton of *taeniopus* in any museum in the United States, there is no way of determining whether the physical makeup of this species was nearer to *africanus,* to *somaliensis,* or to the average domestic ass.

It is rather remarkable that while much effort has been expended by various authors to substantiate *taeniopus* as a distinct race—possibly the chief one concerned in the ancestry of the domestic ass—no one has suggested the possibility that the small number of specimens so far attributed to *taeniopus* may all have been merely the hybrid offspring of *africanus* and *somaliensis*. The geographically intermediate position of *taeniopus* would increase the likelihood that such cross-breeding has occasionally taken place. Again, the coat-patterns occurring in the offspring of zebra–horse and zebra–donkey crosses indicates that—if a crossing of *africanus* and *somaliensis* could be made—the offspring could very well inherit the shoulder and dorsal stripings of the former along with the leg striping of the latter.

The sum of the foregoing discussion is that the domestic ass is definitely descended from one or more of the present-day or recently extinct races of the wild ass of North Africa. As to which race, Pocock (1909)[8] and Antonius (1918)[9] give good reasons for presuming that it was one which combined both the shoulder striping of *a. africanus* and the leg striping of *a. somaliensis,* but which had in addition (Pocock) a form of ear marking not characteristic of any of the existing wild races but usually present in domestic donkeys.

Notes and References

1. H. J. Peake, *Early Steps in Human Progress* (Philadelphia, 1933), pp. 98–99.

2. *Jacks, Jennets and Mules* (Book No. 286, Horse & Mule Asso. of America, Inc. 1945), p. 6.

3. R. I. Pocock, "On the Agriotype of Domestic Asses," *Annals & Mag. Nat. Hist.*, London, ser. 8, vol. 4 1909:523.

4. Richard Lydekker, *Guide to the Specimens of the Horse Family . . . in the British Museum* (Natural History). (London, 1922), p. 41.

5. H. C. Brocklehurst, *Game Animals of the Sudan . . .* (London, 1931), p. 15.

6. Philip, Duke of Edinburgh, and James Fisher, *Wildlife crisis* (New York: Cowles, 1970), p. 242.

7. *Ibid.,* p. 242.

8. R. I. Pocock, *op. cit.*

9. Otto Antonius, *Die Abstammung des Hauspferdes und Hausesels.* (Naturwiss., 6 Jahrg., 1918).

14

The "Half-Asses" (Hemionids) of
Mongolia, India, and the Near East

2. SUBGENUS *HEMIONUS* (P. PALLAS, 1775).

a. Kulan; Kulon; Chigetai; Dziggetai (*Equus hemionus hemionus* Lydekker, 1904).

While this fleet-footed equid is often referred to as the Mongolian wild ass, the name is warranted only to the extent that it differentiates the animal from true horses. Actually, the kulan, and other members of the subgenus *Hemionus,* are neither wild donkeys nor horses, but animals having certain characteristics of each, along with distinctive features of their own, both in coloration and in skeletal conformation.

Structurally, the most notable characteristic in the hemionids is the great elongation of the metapodials (metacarpal and metatarsal bones). In this respect the animals differ markedly from all other members of the genus *Equus*—both Recent and Pleistocene—and suggest derivation from some earlier long-limbed genus, possibly *Astrohippus* or *Neohipparion* (see Fig. 5). It is rather remarkable that most otherwise-thorough describers of one or more species of the *Hemionus* group (e.g., Pallas, Radde, Carruthers, Matschie, Blanford, Jerdon, Pocock, Lydekker, Schwarz) make no reference whatever to the disproportionate length of the lower limb bones in these equids. Antonius alone appears to be the exception to this oversight, since he correctly observes:

> The skeleton of the half-ass is distinguished from the skeletons of all other equids by its relatively short humeri and femora and extremely long and slender metapodials, which express themselves in the living animal by slender joints and long limbs.[1]

On the other hand, Antonius would appear to be in error where, in the same account, he says that the pelvis in hemionids is entirely different from that in the ass. In five pelves of *Hemionus* measured by the writer, the iliac bones, at least, are all of the same steep, high and narrow shape typical of the pelves of *Asinus* generally, and are in conspicuous contrast to the low and broad croups of *Equus caballus*.

The *kulan,* as it is known to the Kirghiz; or *chigetai,* to the Mongols; is the typical hemionid of the desert areas of central Asia. Although it is probably the most numerous

Fig. 174 Kulan or chigetai (*Equus hemionus hemionus*), at one time the most populous subspecies of the subgenus *Hemionus*. The animal here shown is galloping at a speed of 40 mph!

species of its kind, it, like its more localized relatives, is becoming scarcer year by year (see map, Fig. 74). At one time the range of the kulan

> . . . apparently covered the greater part of Outer Mongolia (except the present Tannu-Tuva), small areas in Siberia and Manchuria, and the northern part of Chinese Turkestan (chiefly north of the Tian Shan).[2]

In the central Gobi, in 1922–1925, R. C. Andrews found considerable numbers of the kulan (or chigetai) in the vicinity of Orok Nor and Zagan Nor. The total range of these animals at that time was, so far as could be determined, as indicated herein on the map shown in Fig. 74. Andrews remarks:

> During the first two years of our work in the Gobi, we never saw wild asses in herds of more than fifteen or twenty, but we did not arrive in their country until after the breeding-season. In 1925 the herds numbered thousands. Evidently they collect at favorable localities just before the young are born. . . . The young are dropped about the beginning of July, and the asses seek a flat plain, undoubtedly for protection from wolves.[3]

In 1934, Sven Hedin found tracks of kulans in the Ghashun Gobi. This location would seem to have constituted the southwestern limit of the then-known range of these animals.[4]

Describing the terrain inhabited by the kulan, Carruthers (1915) says:

> The wild ass, or kulon, is unlikely to be seen unless a special attempt is made. . . . The kulon is a rare animal, excessively wild, and lives in very difficult country. Featureless plains, bitterly cold in winter, waterless and sunbaked in summer, are its habitat. The kulon ranges . . . through Dzungaria to the edge of the Gobi. We have seen them at the lowest elevation in the heart of the continent, and at 7,000 to 8,000 feet above the sea, in localities not very far distant from each other.[5]

Fig. 175 Kulans in their native habitat, the steppe-like plains of the Gobi Desert.

It would appear that the vast herds of the kulan seen by Andrews and others as recently as 1925 have now been almost entirely exterminated, for at latest report (c. 1968) the estimated number of the animals still surviving was only about 750.

In a report by Andrews (1933),[6] the following information is given about the kulan as it then existed. Although, when pursued, these animals often seek the shelter of the "bad lands," with their ravines and gullies (see Fig. 176), they seem to prefer more open plains where they can see and avoid their lupine enemies. The large herds break up just before the young are born (usually in July and August). It is the females that form the stable element in the herds; during the breeding season the stallions take possession of three or four females with their foals and protect them against the advances of other males. Kulans associate habitually with the desert-living gazelle, *G. subgutturosa hillieriana.* Andrews found that when pursued by a car the kulans could run at a speed of 40 mph for a mile or so, and would then slow down to about

Fig. 176 Hunting the kulan (*Equus hemionus hemionus*) in the Altai Mountains (Mongolia). From a drawing (*c.* 1875) by August Specht.

35 mph. A stallion pursued on the open plain was run down only after 29 miles, during 16 miles of which he averaged 30 mph. Thus the top speed of these animals is greater than that of a record-making Thoroughbred horse. The advantage of the kulan's long legs is therefore evident, since it enables it to outrun the desert wolves, whose top speed is 36 mph.

In appearance the kulan is a handsome, asslike animal, adapted for swift running and colored in conformity with its sandy, desert habitat (see Figs. 174 and 175). The

coloration varies noticeably with the season, however, being in winter greyish and
with the hair thick and long (about an inch); in summer the hair is shorter, and the
color changes to a bright rufous chestnut or reddish sandy, with a more or less marked
tinge of greyish fawn on the neck. According to Lydekker (1922), ". . . the muzzle,
the inside of the ear, the throat, underparts, the inner side of the legs, and a streak on
the buttocks are white or buffish white"; and

> . . . A relatively narrow dark dorsal strip reaching the tail-tuft, and (in most cases,
> at any rate) not bordered with white, is present; but there is no shoulder stripe,
> or dark barrings on the limbs, although there is a dark ring immediately above the
> hoofs.[7]

The forelock is very short, the mane short (about 4 inches) and erect, the tail
black above and with its terminal half provided with a tuft of long black hairs. The
ears, in comparison with those of *E. asinus,* are relatively somewhat smaller; and in
contrast to those of the kiang, have no dark patch at the base; the middle of the rear
surface is largely white. The hoofs are relatively large and broad (see Fig. 23).
According to Hedin (1899),[8] the nostrils are very much larger than a horse's, in
adaptation to a rarefied atmosphere. The shoulder height of the kulan averages about
48.4 inches. As in the subgenus *Asinus,* all hemionids are appreciably taller at the
croup than at the withers. However, the difference is not so great as a hand (4 inches),
as stated by some writers, but is rather from about 1½ to 2 inches. For the body
proportions of this animal, see Fig. 243.

The Mongolian name, *tchikhetei* or *chigetai* (German spelling: *dziggetai*) is said to
mean "long-eared." Perhaps this is to distinguish these wild equids from the relatively
short-eared domestic horses and ponies used by the Mongolian tribesmen. Some of the
earlier accounts (e.g., Smith, 1841)[9] bear out this description by reporting that the
ears of the chigetai are about ten inches long. If this statement is true—and photographs
of various specimens of the living animal would seem to confirm it—the kulan has
ears more akin to those of the long-eared asinines than to the short-eared caballines.

Other points of distinction in the kulan (chigetai) and other members of the
subgenus *Hemionus* are: (1) the coat-color, which is yellowish, reddish, or a dilution
thereof, without any of the ashy or bluish grey characteristic of the true (i.e., North
African) asses; (2) the voice, which has been described as a shrieking bray, although
nearer to the neigh of the horse than to the noisy bray of the ass. The alternating deep
notes so characteristic of the bray of the ass are in hemionids entirely absent; (3) the
presence of a dorsal stripe, but almost always the *absence* of shoulder stripes or dark
markings on the limbs (with the exception of the chocolate-brown ring just above the
hoofs).

Conformity with the *Asinus* group is indicated (1) in the hemionids' preference
for dry and desert-like habitats, and (with the exception of the kiang) to their aversion
to water; (2) in their period of gestation, which is approximately twelve months, the
same as that of the ass; (3) the absence of chestnuts on the hind legs, and the large
size and smooth surface of those on the forelegs.

According to Motohashi (1930), the hoofs of the chigetai are very hard, black, and
almost like a half cone; roundish above, and very deeply hollowed on the soles. This
author also found that the facial length of the skull in the chigetai was relatively
longer (and, accordingly, the cranial length relatively shorter) than that in any of
five other equine species, including *E. c. przewalskii.*[10] This result has been found also
by the present writer.

Antonius (1922) remarks: "During the Quaternary epoch, kulans were distributed all the way into Western Europe, along with other fauna typical of the mid-Asiatic steppes . . . their bones are frequently found intermingled with those of other animals of the Ice Age . . . often the remains have been confused with those of other equids, although their slender conformation is readily distinguishable."[11]

The osteometric material on the kulan used by the writer has consisted of 3 adult male skeletons and 3 adult female skeletons (one of each sex measured by the writer); 33 adult skulls; one 3–4 week-old male skull, and one 3-week-old female skull.

---

b. Kiang (*Equus hemionus kiang* Moorcroft, 1842).

Closely similar to the kulan in size, conformation, and coloration is the Tibetan subspecies known as the kiang (ki-ang', as in *kit* and *rang*). The range of this animal, which extends through certain lofty valleys of the Himalayas, lies at least 800 miles to the southwest of that of the desert-living kulan. While the two races are manifestly of the same species, each has evolved certain distinctive characters since the time of its geographical separation from the other and in keeping with its respective habitat. According to Lydekker (1912):

The kiang was first brought to scientific notice by Moorcroft, one of the early explorers of Kashmir and Ladak, whose travels, which contain an excellent account of the habits of the animal, were published in London in 1841. In Ladak the kiang is to be met with a few marches to the eastward of the city of Leh, and abounds in the great Chang-Chenmo plain and the arid country around the wonderful Pangong Lake, the home of the chiru or Tibetan antelope, and formerly, the yak. Thence it extends northwards to the Kuen-Lun and eastwards into Tibet, where the limits of its range are still unknown. Scant as seems to be the nutriment in these barren countries, which in summer are scorched at midday by a burning sun, but become bitterly cold at night, it suffices to keep these animals, as well as hares and marmots, in prime condition.[12]

Pocock (1910) adds:

North of the Himalaya the kiang ranges at least from Lhasa to Ladak, at elevations up to about 16,000 feet above sea-level. They live in the plains in small troops. The feeding herd is guarded by a sentinel, which watches the surrounding country at a distance of 100 or 200 yards from the rest, and when danger threatens gives a signal of alarm, whereupon the whole herd makes off at a brisk trot or canter, stopping now and again and wheeling round, as if in curiosity, to inspect the pursuer. They are never found far from water, and are strong and fearless swimmers, boldly crossing broad and swift-flowing rivers. In this respect they are unlike African asses, which are notorious for their dislike of fording streams.[13]

In appearance, the kiang is generally regarded as the most handsome of the hemionids, as well as being the largest. In shoulder height the animal is slightly taller than the kulan, averaging 49.2 inches. The height as taken by naturalists in the field is, as in the cases of other wild equids, anywhere from one to several inches more

Fig. 177 Kiang (*E. hemionus kiang*), a Tibetan hemionid almost identical to the kulan of the Gobi Desert.

than this, because of being measured over the curves of the recumbent (stretched-out) animal.

The kiang is a more richly colored equid than the kulan, perhaps in conformity with its less desert-like habitat. The general color of the coat (in summer, when it is short) is pale chestnut or reddish. In the winter coat, which is long and shaggy, the color becomes darker and browner. The muzzle, the back of the jaw, the lower part of the neck, the belly and legs, and the backs of the thighs up to or slightly above the root of the tail, are creamy white, producing a sharp contrast to the darker coloring of the upper body. The black stripe along the spine is narrow and extends backward clear to the tail-tuft, as in the kulan. The ears, which are somewhat short and horselike, are distinguished from those of the kulan by having a dark patch at their base as well as at their tip, the basal patch being lacking in the kulan. Another distinguishing feature of the kiang is that the legs are white throughout (see Figs. 75 and 177). In the kulan, these members are *light sandy-fawn* right down to the hoofs.

The form of the hoofs of the kiang (width as compared with length, of the sole) is intermediate between that of the horse and the ass. The frog extends far back, as in the ass and the mule, and touches the ground. The hoofs, which are slightly smaller than those of the kulan, are deeply hollowed, probably for adaptation to rocky ground.

In the proportions of its limb bones, the kiang is generally very similar to the kulan. It differs mainly in having a somewhat longer humerus than the kulan. This feature may possibly be correlated with a deeper chest in the kiang, which would be expected in an animal living in a high and rarefied atmosphere. However, there is no correspondingly longer scapula in the kiang, so perhaps the humerus length in this animal (as compared with that in the kulan) is simply a random or nonsignificant development.

The data recorded and studied by the writer on the cranial dimensions and proportions in the kiang indicate, as do the limb bones, that this animal is essentially the same as the kulan, being merely a geographical subspecies or variety. The skull of the kiang is, in general, slightly larger than that of the kulan, but this is simply a concomitant of the kiang's slightly larger bodily size. In 21 out of 26 cranial indices, there is no statistically significant difference between the two animals, and what discrepancies exist may be due to the small number of specimens measured, rather than to actual biological divergence. However, there may be a real difference in the relative width of the forehead, since the cephalic index (skull width × 100 divided by skull length) in the kiang averages 45.0 and in the kulan only 44.0, indicating a narrower forehead in the latter animal. A feature noted by the present writer, but not commented on by other authors, is the marked development of the *anterior nasal spine* in adult skulls of the kiang; this is possibly a concomitant of the animal's adaptation for a high altitude.

To sum up, the kiang (*Equus hemionus kiang*) is almost identical in its skeletal size and proportioning to the kulan or chigetai (*Equus hemionus hemionus*). Both races are representative examples of the subgenus *Hemionus,* having relatively short humeri and femora and exceedingly long (and therefore relatively *slender*) metapodials. Fossil forms exhibiting this conformation are, accordingly, readily identifiable and classifiable.

The osteometric material on the kiang used by the writer has consisted of 3 adult male skeletons, 2 adult female skeletons, and one two-year-old male skeleton (4 of the 6 skeletons having been measured by the writer); 7 adult skulls, and 3 sub-adult skulls (3 of these 10 skulls having been measured by the writer).

---

c. Persian onager (*Equus hemionus onager* Boddaert, 1784).

This is a somewhat smaller hemionid than the kulan or the kiang; an average-sized specimen stands just over 46 inches high at the shoulder. The so-called Persian onager formerly ranged over the south Russian steppes, northwest Afghanistan, and north Persia. It is now extinct in Afghanistan, and much reduced in Russia, where it is presently confined to the 290-square-mile Badkhyz Reserve, which was established especially for it in 1941, and where at latest report it has become stabilized at about 700 head. In Iran, small isolated populations, numbering a few hundred, may survive near Gum and Meshed.[14] In 1963, a census taken by the American Association of Zoological Parks and Aquariums showed that there were then 17 Persian onagers (7 males and 10 females) in zoos in the United States, with the largest troop at the Catskill Game Farm in New York, where there were 4 males and 6 females. The AAZPA's list also showed 3 specimens (1 male and 2 females) as then being in the West Berlin (Germany) zoo.*

The onager was well known to the ancients, who commonly referred to it in words meaning the "wild ass." One of the oldest known representatives of this animal—or, indeed, of any kind of equine—is a scene on a stone plaque unearthed at Khafaje, Iraq, which is dated as of about 2800 B.C. The scene depicts four harnessed onagers

---

* A pair of onagers was acquired by the Topeka (Kansas) Zoological Park in 1970. In that year, according to the International Zoo Yearbook, only 32 zoos in the world possessed onagers.

driven by a man on foot and pulling an empty chariot (Fig. 178). The animals shown drawing a Greek chariot in Fig. 179 also, with their exceedingly long and slender limbs, suggest onagers, although their tails, which seem to be braided, are too fully-haired to be of other than horses. A third illustration—a mural painting from Thebes, reproduced by Antonius, 1922, Fig. 36—shows that the ancient Egyptians also used the onager to pull their light war chariots. So, while the members of the *Hemionus* group in general are of an exceedingly wild and wary nature, it is evident that the onager, at any rate, can be tamed (though probably not domesticated).

Fig. 178 Plaque from Khfaje, Iraq, showing a team of onagers in ancient Mesopotamia drawing an empty chariot. The plaque is dated as of *c.* 2800 B.C.

The following description by Hablizl (here slightly abridged) of the Persian onager was made from a living male specimen that he observed away back in 1783.[15]

The top and sides of the head are half-reddish, the under side (throat) and the muzzle white; the outer surface of the ears is reddish-yellow at the base and the tip, and white in the middle area between; the sides of the neck, body, and fore part of the croup are reddish-yellow (isabelline); the mane is light brown, and is composed of hairs 3 to 4 inches long; a light-brown dorsal stripe, up to 2½ to 3 inches wide, and bordered on each side by a narrow strip of white, extends from the mane to the beginning of the tail (sometimes clear to the tuft); on the shoulders a narrow dark stripe crosses the dorsal stripe at right angles; the lower neck, lower shoulder, breast, belly, buttocks, flanks, and legs are white; the tail is like a cow's, ending in a long tuft of light-brown and white hairs.

Fig. 179 Greek coin of *c.* 480 B.C., showing a team of horses (or onagers?) drawing a light racing chariot.

Fig. 180 Persian onager (*E. hemionus onager*), the "wild ass" of the Bible. It is now nearly, if not actually, extinct in the wild state.

From the foregoing description, it would appear that the coloration of the Persian onager is, with the exception of the transverse shoulder stripes, very similar to that of the kiang, although somewhat lighter. However, other accounts indicate that the shoulder stripes are more often absent than present; and where present, are usually in male individuals. Goodwin (1940) describes the summer coat as either avellaneous (orange-brown) or light pinkish-cinnamon, with a faint shoulder stripe; and the winter coat as sayal (dull orange) brown, without a shoulder stripe.[16] Lydekker (1912) remarks:

In winter, when it grows much longer and rougher, the coat becomes more or less decidedly grey, and in one race is distinctly mouse-grey, with sharply-defined white areas.[17]

Despite the foregoing descriptions of coat color given by Hablizl and Goodwin, respectively, other observers of the onager (specifically, the Persian variety) ascribe to it a much lighter coloration. Pocock, for example, says that the typical onager

> . . . is very white, and in fact might be described as a white animal with a yellowish blotch on the side, another on the neck, and some yellow on the head.[18]

Certainly the two onagers shown by Bolton (1900, p. 55), from which the writer's drawing in Fig. 75 was made, likewise indicate generally *light* coloration (despite the summer coats). Indeed, the white "asses" mentioned in the Bible (Judges, v. 10) may well have been, instead, onagers especially selected for their coloration and then tamed for riding. Possibly, therefore, two or more color varieties of the onager exist in the Persian area, or did exist, ranging in the darker portions of their pelage (in various individuals) from chestnut to light fawn or silvery grey. Fig. 180 depicts a zoo specimen in which the coloration appears to be definitely defined between the dark and light areas.

Brehm (1896) gives the following general description:

> The Onager is perceptibly smaller than the Dziggetai, although it is taller and possessed of finer limbs than the common Ass. The head is proportionately longer and larger than the Koulan's; the fleshy lips are thickly covered with stiff, bristly hair to their very margins; the ears are tolerably long, though shorter than those of the Ass. The prevailing color is a beautiful white with a silvery lustre, merging into a pale sorrel tint on the upper part of the head, the sides of the neck and body and the hips. On the side of the withers a white stripe of a hand's breadth runs down; a second stripe runs along the backbone and down the back of the hind legs; in its centre is a smaller brown stripe. The hair is softer and silkier than that of the Horse. The winter hair may be compared with Camel's wool, while the summer hair is exceedingly smooth and delicate. The mane stands erect and consists of soft, wooly hair about four inches long; the tuft on the tail measures from seven to twelve inches.[19]

The onager is similar to the kulan and differs from the kiang in lacking the dark patch at the base of the ear. Its coat pattern is somewhat different from both that of the kulan and the kiang in that the white of the rear thighs and buttocks is *continuous* with the narrow white strips running down each side of the dark dorsal stripe.

Of the Persian onager, the writer has measured only a single skull and skeleton. This was of an aged female specimen in the Academy of Natural Sciences of Philadelphia (Cat. No. 12576). This specimen, while falling in general within the typical *Hemionus* range in skeletal proportioning, is characterized by exceedingly small *feet* (including the calcanea), long scapulae and tibiae, and a somewhat large *skull* (the latter thus conforming with Brehm's description). The reconstructed shoulder height (46 inches) of this specimen also corresponds closely with the average for the Persian race.

According to some of the ancient Greek historians, it would appear that a local race of the onager existed as far westward as Anatolia (the western peninsula of Turkey in Asia). However, this animal has long since been exterminated, and there is no way of determining whether it was a form of the Persian onager or of the smaller race from Syria known as the hemippus. East of the Persian onager's most easterly occurrence, other geographical forms occur, or did occur formerly, one of which is the following.

d. Indian onager; Ghorkhar (*Equus hemionus khur* Lesson, 1827).

This animal is perhaps more closely related to the kulan and the kiang than to the more westerly-dwelling Persian onager. That, at least, is what the proportions of the limb bones indicate, although in shoulder height the animal is practically identical to the Persian subspecies. The coloration of the ghorkhar is so similar in general to that of the Persian onager that a description of it would be repetitious (see Blanford, 1891: *The Fauna of British India*). Blanford gives the field measurements of an adult female ghorkhar shot by him on the Punjab-Sind frontier in 1882 as: shoulder height, 46 inches; body length, nose to root of tail (over curves), 83 inches; tail length, including tuft, 26 inches; ear length, from crown, 9 inches. Incidentally, the Hindustani name, *ghorkhar* (or *ghoor-khur*), like the Near-East name *onager* (derived from the Greek *onagrus*), may be translated as "wild mule"—a designation quite appropriate for the entire *Hemionus* group.

Fig. 181 Indian onager, or ghorkhar. (From a photograph taken in India.)

As to the former range and status of the Indian onager. Jerdon (1874) gives the following details:

The *ghorkhur* is found sparingly in Cutch, Guzrat, Jeysalmeer and Bikaneer, not being found further south, it is said, than Deesa, or east of 75° east longitude. It

also occurs in Sindh, and more abundantly west of the Indus river, in Beluchistan
. . . . It appears that the Bikaneer herd consists at most of about 150 individuals. . . .
The foaling season is in June, July, and August, when the Beluchis ride down and
catch numbers of foals, finding a ready sale in the cantonments for them, as they
are taken down on speculation to Hindustan. They also shoot great numbers of
grown-up ones for food, the ground in places in the desert being very favourable
for stalking.

It is said also that among the ghorkhars the groups of females, accompanied by
their young, live apart from the males for about three months after giving birth.

Between 1946 and 1956, the total population of Indian onagers was estimated at
3000 to 5000, including several herds each consisting of more than 200 animals.
Within a few years thereafter, more than three-quarters of the population had died
off, presumably from disease. During the Indo-Pakistan war the population was again
halved, and an aerial census made in 1969 by the Indian conservationist E. P. Gee
placed the total number at about 400 head. Most of these animals were then living in
the area known as the Little Rann of Kutch. Those in the Rann have to compete for
the sparse grazing with large numbers of domestic livestock—cattle, sheep, goats, and
donkeys. Besides the main population in the Little Rann, there were (in 1969) some
20–30 head in the Great Rann of Kutch.

Several other forms of the kulan, or the onager, have by various authors been
proposed as distinct subspecies, or races. However, of them the writer has no skeletal
measurements and so is unable to evaluate their systematic positions from an osteometric
standpoint. In 1929 the systematist Ernest Schwarz[20] used as a subgeneric classifactory
term for this group the name *Asinus* rather than *Hemionus,* a procedure which—in
view of the pronounced skeletal and external differences between the two groups of
equines—is incomprehensible to the present writer. More recently, two other taxonomists, C. P. Groves and V. Mazak,[21] have followed Schwarz's procedure, placing both
Asinus and *Hemionus* in the same subgenus! Clearly, both Schwarz and the two later
authors could have made no osteometric study of the limb bones of these two distinctly
different forms of equids and arrived at such a conclusion as to their identity.

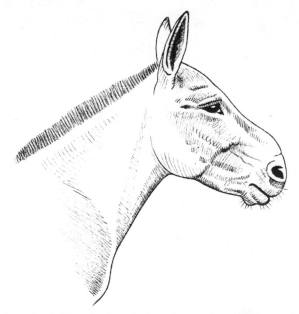

Fig. 182 Head of a ghorkhar. A sketch by the author after a photograph by E.
Schneider, Berlin, 1929. Note the bulging nasal region, a characteristic of
hemionids in general.

It is probable that in earlier times—even as recently as 200 years ago—the various local races of the *Hemionus* group ranged, more or less continuously, all the way from southern Russia (in Europe) eastward to the eastern border of the Gobi desert and possibly even into Manchuria, southward into Syria, Mesopotamia (Iraq), and Persia (Iran), and from there eastward through Afghanistan and Baluchistan into northern India and Tibet. Indeed, during the upper Pleistocene, these animals, as evidenced by their fossilized remains, ranged westward into Central and Western Europe. The scattered and greatly decimated races existing today are therefore merely the remnants of what, in former times, was a vast geographical distribution of this distinct desert-and-steppe-dwelling division of the genus *Equus*. The most westerly-ranging of the recent hemionids is the form now about to be described.

e. Syrian onager; Hemippus (*Equus hemippus* Geoffroy, 1855). Arabic name: *akhdar* ("wild ass").

This diminutive member of the *Hemionus* group had, it would appear, a sufficient number of distinctive characteristics to warrant its being considered a separate species from the kulan, the kiang, and the onager. While it was probably the most frequently mentioned "wild ass" of the Bible, it is now totally extinct.

The first distinction of the hemippus ("half-horse") was its small size; an average-sized adult stood only about 40.2 inches high at the shoulder, or about the height of an average-sized Shetland pony. The hemippus, however, was somewhat slenderer in build than the caballine Shetland. Secondly, there are marked differences in the skeletal proportioning of the hemippus. One of these distinctions is *very small* hoofs; another is the great length of the hind first phalanx as compared with the fore first phalanx, the proportioning in this respect being similar to that in the horse. The skull of the hemippus, while somewhat small even in relation to the general skeletal dimensions, nevertheless is essentially hemionid-like. Externally, however, the head was more like that of a fine Oriental horse than of an ass (Hilzheimer, 1941).

Antonius remarks:

> The skull of the hemippus has the same basilar length as that of a Shetland pony . . . and is similar to the latter also otherwise in more than one respect, above all in the very strikingly *concave* profile, the large orbits, and the proportionately very large and decidedly vaulted cranium . . . Of . . . exterior characteristics there remain to be mentioned the very short, nimble ears, the splendid large and fiery eyes, and the very disproportionately wide nostrils.[22]

Again referring to Antonius for a description of the coloration of the hemippus, we read:

> The general color of the male is avellaneous (orange-brown), becoming a sort of mouse gray with age; the color is lightest on the head, darkest on the haunches, a light area in front of hips; buttocks, belly, and inner side of legs dirty grayish white; outer side of legs, lower side of neck, and outer surface of ears "tilleul buff"; tips of ears originally dark brown, later almost white; mane rather long, "natal brown"; vertebral stripe, of the same color, extending from the mane to the tail tuft, and bordered by a lighter area; surface above the nostrils grayish white; nostrils very large and nasal region swollen.[23]

Fig. 183 The recently-extinct Syrian "wild ass," or hemippus (*Equus hemippus*), as shown in a plaque dating from King Assurbanipal of Assyria.

As to the one-time geographical distribution of the hemippus, Tristram (1884) says:

> This . . . rather smaller than the true Onager, and confined to Syria, Mesopotamia and North Arabia, very rarely enters the north of Palestine from the Syrian desert, but is still common in Mesopotamia. It does not extend into India, but in summer herds of this animal frequently visit the Armenian mountains. It is the Wild Ass of Scripture and of the Ninevite sculptures.[24]

According to Carruthers (1935):

> It is almost certain that they (Syrian wild asses) have now been exterminated in their last refuge, north of the Euphrates, the Jabal Sinjar, none having been seen since 1927. Whether or not there are a few left in South Arabia, or in the Oman hinterland, seems doubtful.[25]

Antonius (1928, pp. 19–20), records a male hemippus that had been obtained in 1911 from the "desert north of Aleppo," Syria, and was still living in the Schönbrunn Zoo in Vienna in 1928; he also mentions three preserved specimens that had lived in the same zoo during the latter part of the nineteenth century.

According to Harper (1945):

No modern zoologist seems to have met with this subspecies in the field, and wild-killed animals are evidently among the rarest of all museum specimens.[26]

Of illustrations of the hemippus, there are (1) the photographs of a zoo specimen shown by Antonius in his paper dealing with the species (1928),[27] and (2) the photographs of the bas-reliefs in the British Museum showing King Assurbanipal of Assyria (669–626 B.C.) hunting and lassoing these animals (Fig. 183). Various hippologists, including Ridgeway (1905) and Antonius (1922) have interpreted the equine animals in these bas-reliefs as being onagers, but there can be little doubt that they actually represent the hemippus. The small size of the equids as compared with the men, their moderate croup height as compared with shoulder height, their thick and horselike necks, small ears, straight (or even slightly *concave*) facial profiles, and prominent eyes and nostrils all testify that they are hemippi, not typical onagers. This conclusion was reached also by Hilzheimer (1941).[28]

That the Persian onager and the hemippus coexisted in the Syria-Mesopotamia region in earlier times is practically a certainty. Why the hemippus was killed off first may have been due to its smaller numbers; and it is sadly evident that drastic conservation laws will have to be enforced to preserve the relatively few remaining Persian onagers.

The osteometric material on the hemippus studied by the writer has consisted of the following: One adult male skull and skeleton (Phila. Mus. Nat. Hist. 1637) measured by the writer (see Fig. 178); one adult female skull and skeleton (per Antonius, 1913);[29] partial measurements of two female skulls and skeletons (per George, 1869);[30] and some comparative limb-bone ratios by Bourdelle (1933).[31]

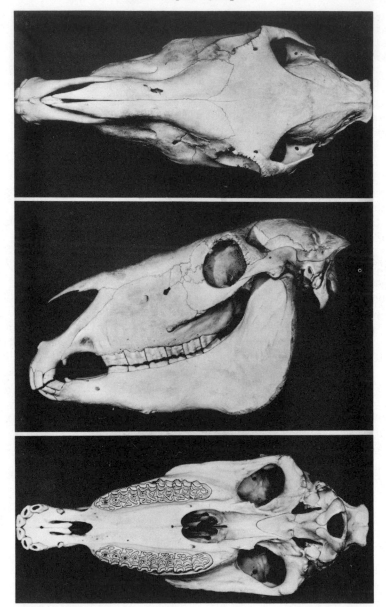

Fig. 184 Superior, lateral, and inferior views, respectively, of the skull of a male hemippus (PMNH no. 1637), of 8 to 9 years of age. All figures approximately x 1/5 natural size. (For greater clarity, the tooth patterns and some of the sutures have been inked in.)

Notes and References

1. Otto Antonius, *Grundzüge einer Stammesgeschichte der Haustiere.* (Jena, 1922), p. 251.

2. Francis Harper, *Extinct and Vanishing Mammals of the Old World* (New York: 1945), p. 354.

3. Roy Chapman Andrews, "Living Animals of the Gobi Desert," *Natural History* 24, no. 2 (1924) : 150–59. See also 26:132–45, 299–302; and 33:3–16.

4. Sven Hedin, *The Wandering Lake* (New York, 1940), pp. 195, 197, 200.

5. D. Carruthers, *The gun at home and abroad. The big game of Asia and North America* (London, 1915), p. 154.

6. Roy Chapman Andrews, "The Mongolian Wild Ass," *Natural History* 33, no. 1 (1933) : 7.

7. Richard Lydekker, *Guide to the Specimens of the Horse Family . . . in the British Museum* (Natural History), (London, 1922), pp. 29–30.

8. Sven Hedin, *Through Asia.* (New York & London, 1899) 2:1005.

9. Col. H. Smith, *Jardine's Naturalist's Library. Vol. 20, Horses.* (London, 1866), p. 309.

10. H. Motohashi, *Craniometrical Studies on Skulls of Wild Asses from West Mongolia.* (Tokyo: Mem. Tottori Agric. College, 1930) : 1–62.

11. Antonius, *Grundzüge,* pp. 249–250.

12. Richard Lydekker, *The Horse and Its Relatives* (London, 1912), pp. 179–180.

13. R. I. Pocock, in *Harmsworth Natural History,* 3 vols. (London, 1910) 2:793.

14. Philip, Duke of Edinburgh, and James Fisher. *Wildlife crisis.* (New York: Cowles, 1970), p. 242.

15. C. Hablizl, *Bemerkungen in der persischen Landschaft Gilan und auf den Gilanischen Gebirgen.* (Neue Nord. Betytrage, Vol. 4, 1783), pp. 89–92.

16. G. G. Goodwin, *Mammals Collected by the Legendre 1938 Iran Expedition.* (Amer. Mus. Novit., 1082, 1940), p. 17.

17. Richard Lydekker, *The Horse and Its Relatives,* p. 182.

18. R. I. Pocock, In: William Ridgeway's *The Origin and Influence of the Thoroughbred Horse.* (Cambridge: University Press, 1905), p. 46.

19. A. E. Brehm, *Brehm's Life of Animals.* (Chicago: A. N. Marquis and Co., 1896), p. 415.

20. Ernst Schwartz, *Ein sudpersischer Wildesel im Berliner Zoologischen Garten.* (Zool. Garten, N.F., Vol. 2, Nos. 4–6, 1929), pp. 89–94.

21. C. P. Groves, and V. Mazak. *On Some Tavonomic Problems of Asiatic Wild Asses, Etc.* (Zeitschrift für Säugetierkunde, Vol. 32, No. 6, 1957), pp. 321–355.

22. Otto Antonius, In: Max Hilzheimer, *Animal Remains from Tell Asmar.* (Orient. Inst. Univ. Chicago, Studies in Ancient Oriental Civilization, No. 20, 1941), p. 6.

23. Otto Antonius, *Beobachtungen an Einhufern in Schonbrunn. I. Der Syrische Halbesel.* (Zool. Garten, N.F., Vol. 1, 1928), pp. 21–22.

24. H. B. Tristram, *The Fauna and Flora of Palestine.* (London: 1884), p. 3.

25. D. Carruthers, *Arabian Adventure to the Great Nafud in Quest of the Oryx.* (London: 1935), p. 149.

26. Francis Harper, *Extinct and Vanishing Mammals of the Old World.* (New York: Amer. Committee for Internat. Wildlife Protection, N.Y. Zool. Park, 1945), p. 370.

27. Otto Antonius, *Grundzüge,* 1928, pp. 19–25.

28. Max Hilzheimer, *Animal Remains from Tell Asmar,* (see No. 22 above).

29. Otto Antonius, *Equus Abeli, nov. spec.,* etc. (Beitrag. Paleont. Geol. Oster.-Ungarn, u. d. Orients, Vol. 26, 1913). (A comprehensive general treatise on cranial and limb-bone measurements in the Equidae).

30. H. George, *Etudes Zoologiques sur les Hémiones,* etc. (Annales des Sciences Naturelles, Zoologie et Paleontologie, Ser. 5, Vol. 12, 1869), pp. 1–48.

31. E. Bourdelle, Notes ostéologiques et ostéometriques: No. 6, *E. hemippus.* (Bull. Mus. Hist. Nat. Paris, Ser. 2, Vol. 5, 1933), pp. 435–442.

15
Zebras and the Quagga

Preliminary Note:

The common interpretation of a zebra is that it is a striped horse, or a striped donkey. But it would probably be more accurate to regard horses and donkeys as zebras in which the stripes have been partially or completely lost. For during the 60,000,000-year evolution of the horse tribe from the tiny *Eohippus* ("Dawn-horse") to the modern genus *Equus,* spots and stripes came *before* the more uniform colorations that we see in horses and donkeys today.

For a long time, zebras have been exclusively African animals. Yet there is a strong possibility that these striped or semi-striped equines originated in the forests and plains of North America, in what is now the United States. One of the results of a 13-year study of modern and Pleistocene (Ice Age) horses made by the writer* is that the so-called fossil "horses" of the tar-pits of Rancho La Brea, in Los Angeles, were in all probability giant zebras, or giant quaggas, rather than horses. Again, there is good evidence that the present-day species known as Grévy's zebra may have evolved from the Pliocene form *Plesippus* (see Fig. 241), which roamed the plains of the western United States several million years ago. And as the emigration from America to Asia could have taken place at numerous times when the Bering Strait was a land bridge, zebras could have evolved in America yet ended up in Africa.

When the term "zebra" is mentioned to the average person, about all that he or she can picture is a striped animal like a horse or a donkey, and which may be seen in a zoo. No conception is had of the different *kinds* of zebras, although it is generally known that these equine animals live only in Africa. Even some "popular" writers on natural history lump all the different species of zebras together, as though they are scarcely worthy of individual description. Yet there are a great deal more structural (i.e., skeletal) differences between some forms of zebras than there are, for example, between a lion and a tiger—two animals which no popular writer would dare to classify as being identical.

---

* "The genus *Equus,* a Paleo-zoological survey of the Recent and Pleistocene Equidae, with especial references to *Equus occidentalis* of the Rancho La Brea tar-pits," by David P. Willoughby. (The manuscript of this extensive technical paper is on file at the Los Angeles County Museum of Natural History. Included in the paper is an annotated bibliography of over 700 references).

Fig. 185 Grant's (Bohm's) zebras on the East African veldt. After a sketch by Walter J. Wilwerding.

At the present time, only three distinct species (actually *subgenera*) of zebras exist, out of the dozens of forms that must have ranged over Europe, Africa, Asia, and North America during the time that Cro-Magnon man lived in Europe.* The three extant forms are Grévy's zebra, the mountain zebra, and several varieties of Burchell's zebra, the original species of which became extinct about 1910. Another recently exterminated species was the quagga, of South Africa, the last living specimen of which died in 1883 (see Fig. 186). We shall now deal with these three forms of zebras in the order just named. Fig. 187 shows the present, or recent, geographical distribution of the existing zebras and the recently extinct quagga.

II. EQUIDAE WITH STRIPED COATS.

4. Subgenus *Dolichohippus* (E. Heller, 1912).

a. Grévy's zebra (*Equus grévyi* Oustalet, 1882).

Native names: in Swahili, *kangani;* in Samburru, *kanga*; in Somali, *faro.*

Although this large, finely striped member of the zebra tribe was well known to the ancient Romans, who used the animal in the arena and called it "Hippotigris" (tiger-horse), it was not made known to modern Europeans generally until 1882, when its distinctive characters were described by the French zoologist Edward Oustalet.[1] During that same year, a live specimen was sent by King Menelik of Shoa (now central Ethiopia) as a gift to the then-President of France, Jules Grévy, after whom the species of zebra was named by the zoologist Alphonse Milne-Edwards. The type specimen sent by King Menelik was housed in the menagerie of the Jardin des Plantes, in Paris, but unfortunately died after a short period in captivity. Its skin was mounted and placed on exhibition in the gallery of the Natural History Museum, in the Jardin des Plantes.

---

* A correlation of the indices found in twenty different comparisons of limb-bone lengths, *among 16 forms of Equidae,* shows that the *typical* representative of the living genus *Equus* was not a horse, an ass, nor a hemionid, but rather a *zebra.*

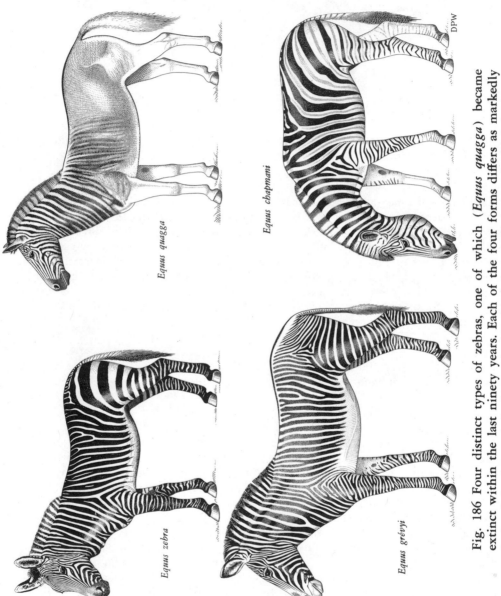

Equus quagga

Equus chapmani

Equus zebra

Equus grévyi

DPW

Fig. 186 Four distinct types of zebras, one of which (*Equus quagga*) became extinct within the last ninety years. Each of the four forms differs as markedly in its skeletal proportioning as in its coat pattern, the latter of which is shown here for comparison.

At first, Grévy's zebra was by some naturalists assumed to be merely a northern variety of the Cape mountain zebra (*Equus zebra*); however, a comparison of several skins of the two forms, while in some respects similar, showed beyond question that they belonged to specifically different animals.

Whereas most other zebras—that is, the members of the subgenus *Hippotigris,* along with those of the Burchell's group—stand less than 50 inches in shoulder height, *Dolichohippus* is more than 4 inches higher, an average specimen of the species standing 54.1 inches.* Along with this outstandingly larger size, the narrow and numerous stripings on the head, body and quarters, the very large and broad ears, the short and thick neck, and the peculiarly long and narrow head identify *E. grévyi* as a form distinctly different from all other existing zebras. Indeed, Heller (1912) felt that the Ethiopian zebra deserved full *generic* rank.[2]

The following general description of the physical features of Grévy's zebra is taken from Pocock (1910):

> The stripes on the head, body and legs, which are fully marked to the hoofs, are narrow, numerous, and close-set. On the middle of the neck they are commonly broader. On the body they run vertically from the spinal area as far back as the quarters, but do not pass on to the belly. . . . The spinal stripe is broad and separated from the upper ends of the body stripes from the beginning of the lumbar region by a pale area which widens considerably on the croup, the croup itself being marked with very narrow stripes inclining obliquely downwards and backwards, and passing into the narrow longitudinal stripes on the thighs. The muzzle is mostly ashy grey. The neck is deep and short, and the head correspondingly long and heavy, so that the mouth may reach the ground for grazing. . . . The ears are long and flexible, but their most remarkable characteristic is their great width, a feature in which they are quite unlike the ears of all known members of the horse tribe. The callosities are exceedingly small, and the hoofs, though small, are oval, with the 'frog' broad behind. In the typical race from the highlands of Shoa, the coloration is markedly black and white; but in Somaliland there occurs a different race, known as *E. grevyi berberensis,* in which the dark stripes are chocolate-brown, and the intervening light stripes ochre, the entire tint of the animal being much more uniform.[3]

It will be noted in the above quotation that Pocock recognizes the Grévy's zebras from Somaliland as constituting a different race from those found in Ethiopia. However, although there was a lot of discussion on this point, most mammalogists today recognize only the typical (Ethiopian) species. Renshaw (1904) suggests that the brownish (rather than black) stripes of certain specimens of this zebra may be due to their being *immature* individuals.[4]

The following descriptive notes on *E. grévyi* are given by Roosevelt and Heller (1914):[5]

> Stands out in shape of skull and proportions of head and body further from the other zebras and asses than does the horse, which is commonly regarded as the most highly specialized member.

---

* While some overenthusiastic writers have attributed to Grévy's zebra the size "of a horse", a more accurate description would be "a good-sized pony", such as a Connemara, a Welsh mountain pony, or a konik.

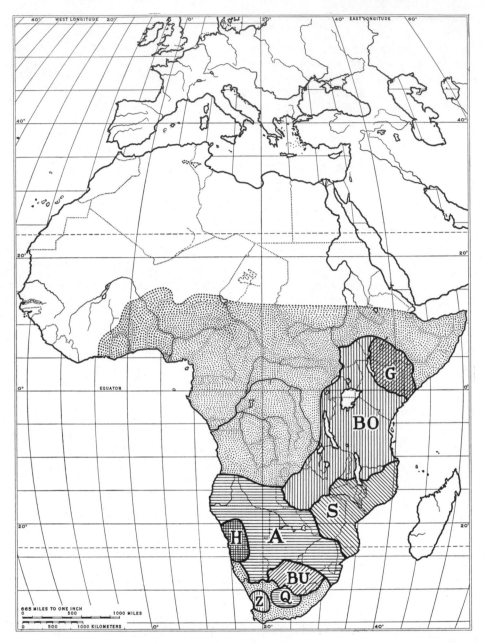

Fig. 187 Approximate distribution of the zebras, based on the most reliable sources. G = *Equus grévyi;* BO = *E. burchelli böhmi;* S = *E. burchelli selousi;* A = *E. burchelli antiquorum;* BU = last recorded range of *E. burchelli burchelli;* Q = last recorded range of *E. quagga* sp.; Z = *E. zebra zebra* (now extinct in the wild state); H = *E. zebra hartmannae.* Note the extension of the range of *E. b. böhmi* over that of *E. grévyi.* The large, dotted area indicates the presumed former range of zebras collectively, after their emigration from Eurasia during the Middle (?) Pleistocene. *E. quagga* became totally extinct in 1883, and *E. burchelli burchelli* about 1910.

ZECORA QVADRUPES PULCHERRIMA
Lusitanis Burro do Matto Priscis
Oi Græyp Θ: Asinus sylvestris.

Fig. 188 Grévy's zebra. This curious old engraving is reproduced from the book, "A History of Ethiopia," by the German historian, Job Ludolphus, 1681. It is perhaps the first modern illustration to depict the large, finely striped Abyssinian zebra which was later (1882) named after the then-President of France, Jules Grévy. It is most interesting to compare the artist's conception with life-photographs of Grévy's zebras. Observe, from the caption above the engraving, that in Ludolphus's day the zebra was called (in Abyssinia) "zecora."

The most distinctive feature of the skull is the great width of the occipital crests and their production backwards beyond the occipital condyles. (The great length of the head is due largely to the lengthening of the rostrum and the diastemae, and is accompanied by a long nasal cavity.)

Cheek teeth relatively better developed (and relatively larger) than in the Burchelline zebras.

The assumption that *E. grévyi* is the least specialized of the living Equidae (on the ground that its coloration represents that of the ancestral stock) is not borne out by the extremely long-headed nature of this zebra and the somewhat higher specialization of its dental apparatus. In the latter two features (long head and elongated teeth with complex folds) the Grévy zebra is slightly more advanced than any of the other living horse-like ungulates.*

E. grévyi is an inhabitant of the low desert or semiarid country (Rift Valley), very different in character from the cool, moist Abyssinian highlands of the capital (where it has been assumed to occur—as on the plains of Shoa).

Met with on the bare, grassy plains, and more rarely in the thorn-bush scrub, in small herds of from six to 30 or 40 individuals. Sometimes a herd of several hundred individuals assembles from the smaller parties and troops. They mix freely with

---

* However, Paul McGrew (1944) says: "The dental characters of *Dolichohippus* are like those of *Hippotigris* and the two are probably more closely related than any other two living horse genera."[6]

Fig. 189 A Grévy's zebra in the San Diego Zoo. This species is characterized, among other features, by its fine and numerous stripes, long and narrow head, and broad, thickly-haired ears. Its call is very like an ass's or a mule's bray—not a "bark" as in other zebras.

the oryx herds and the smaller species of zebra—but they never breed with the latter. *E. grévyi* herds usually contain one master stallion, and the stallions fight viciously with one another.*

The gaits of the big zebra are a slashing trot and a gallop, whereas the small zebra canters.

Its very long ears, thrown forward in curious interest, enable it to be recognized at a distance.

Tail-tuft small and confined to extreme tip of tail.

Color pattern in general resembles that of *E. zebra* more than *E. burchelli.*

Body stripings consist of 20–22 vertical dark stripes 1 to 1½ inches wide, with light innerspaces ¾ inches wide. Neck stripes number 9 or 10, the widest of which measure 2½ to 3 inches.†

---

* Contradicting this statement is that by E. Bourdelle, in his *Natural History of Mammals* (1964, p. 246), in which he says: "Grévy's zebras form only small herds in which the stallions play no permanent or dominant part, and it is the same with the mountain zebra."

---

† Numerous photographs indicate that the probable range of the neck stripes is from 10 to 16, and of the body stripes from 18 to 26 (D.P.W.).

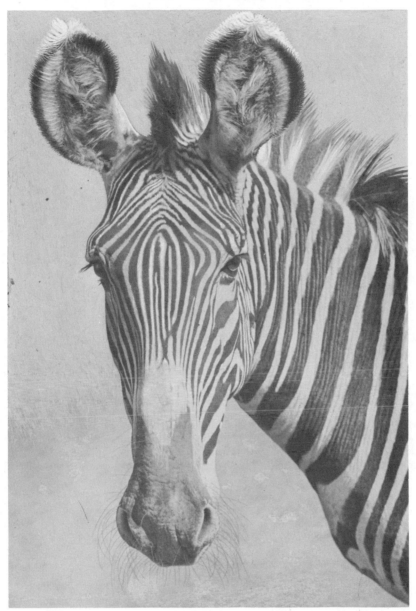

Fig. 190 A close-up, head-on view of the zebra in Fig. 189. Here are shown to advantage the long, narrow head and muzzle and the broad, internally "furry" ears peculiar to this species. Faintly visible also about the muzzle are the sensory (tactile) hairs, which in the Grévy's zebra are coarser and of greater length than in most other members of the horse family.

Fig. 191 Rear view of a Grévy's zebra, showing the striping pattern of the croup and hind legs peculiar to this large, Abyssinian species.

Heller (1912) says:

The alarm or call note of the Abyssinian zebra is a series of deep grunts interrupted by a whistle-like squeal. At a long distance only the grunts are audible, and they are scarcely distinguishable from the grunting noise made by the lion. The sharp barking kwa-ha of the Burchell zebra or the bray of the ass are strikingly different sounds.[7]

Heller, in his differentiation of *E. grévyi* from all other living Equidae, states that the two distinct subgenera, *Asinus* and *Hippotigris,* ". . . show no skull characters which will separate them." Actually a number of indices, or ratios, can be made from cranial measurements which will clearly separate the skulls of the smaller zebras from those of either domestic or wild asses of the same general size. Two such indices are measurements 23/5 and 5/18 (see Fig. 25). In the former index: measurement 23/measurement 5 the average in three ass skulls was found by the writer to be 26.6, and in five zebra skulls 31.4. This is a difference of 18 percent, which in any comparison made within such a homogeneous group as the living Equidae is highly significant.

The geographical range of *E. grévyi* is given by Roosevelt and Heller as from the Northern Guaso Nyiro drainage and the north bank of the Tana River northward to Lake Zwai in Abyssinia (Ethiopia), westward to the eastern shore of Lake Rudolf and the Omo River, and east to the limits of Abyssinia, but not known to occur actually within British Somaliland. It may be added that much of this same territory is shared by one or two local races of the Burchell zebra group. As to Roosevelt and

Fig. 192 Grévy's zebra (*Equus grévyi*), the largest of the existing wild Equidae. Note, even in this female specimen, the unusually thick, as well as short, neck.

Heller's statement that *E. grévyi* "is not known" to occur within British Somaliland, it would indicate, if a fact, that even as early as 1912 the alleged Somali race of this species, as recognized by Pocock, Ridgeway, and Lydekker, was extinct. Sorrell (1952)[8] says that Grévy's zebra does not "appear" to exist in southern Ethiopia (see map, Fig. 187).

The skeleton of *E. grévyi* differs from that of the smaller zebras in its relatively very long and narrow skull, short cervical vertebrae, and very long scapulae. From *Asinus* it is removed even further by its scapula/radius ratio of 105.5 as compared to 91.6, its scapula/humerus ratio of 121.5 as compared to 109.7, and its scapula/tibia ratio of 100.4 as compared to 86.8 in *Asinus*. Actually, in many. of the proportions of its limb bones, Grévy's zebra is more horselike than the members either of the subgenera *Hippotigris, Asinus,* or *Hemionus,* or of the group classified as Burchelline zebras. However, like all the latter forms, *E. grévyi* has the relatively high and narrow conformation of the pelvis (iliac bones) that distinguishes it completely from the low and broad pelvic (croup) conformation typical of *E. caballus*.

The osteometric data on Grévy's zebra used by the writer has consisted of 4 adult skeletons (2 male, 2 female), all measured by the writer, and 25 adult skulls (12 male, 13 female), one of which was measured by the writer.

Fig. 193 This lifelike habitat group is in the Simson African Hall of the California Academy of Sciences, San Francisco. It depicts a herd of Grévy's zebras on the grassy plains of northeastern Kenya. In the background are shown the orchard-like groves of flat-topped thorn trees, interspersed with patches of thorny scrub and volcanic rock, typical of the surroundings of these zebras.

Fig. 194 Here is a reproduction of one of the earliest known representations of the mountain zebra. It is a copy of an engraving made by George Edwards in 1751 for his work, *Natural History and the Gleanings of Nature*. The engraving is a fairly accurate representation of this species (cf. Figs. 186 and 195), with the exception of the strangely disproportionate head and muzzle and the cow-like tail.

5. Subgenus *Hippotigris* (H. Smith, 1841).

a. Mountain zebra; Cape mountain zebra (*Equus zebra zebra* Linnaeus, 1758).

Preliminary Note: This species is the *type* of the subgenus *Hippotigris,* as fixed by Sclater in 1900.[9] However, as will be seen from the description below, *E. zebra* is an animal so markedly different from the zebras of the Burchell's group as to warrant its being considered *subgenerically* distinct from the latter. Or, to state the matter in its proper order, there is ample zoological evidence for believing that the group of Burchelline zebras, including the quagga, should be placed in a subgenus of its own. Accordingly, a new subgenus, *Quaggoides,* is herein proposed to accommodate the zebras of the Burchell's group, and to separate them from the asiniform zebras to which the name *Hippotigris* was originally applied. Details of the proposed new subgenus *Quaggoides* are given on p. 352.

The mountain zebra,* Cape mountain zebra, or *wildepaard* ("wild horse") of the Boers has had a long and interesting history in its native habitat (Cape Colony), and was the first of the zebras to become known to modern Europeans. However, during recent years it has become extinct in the wild state. In 1937, only 47 individuals remained; but owing largely to the development of the Mountain Zebra National

---

* In zoological parlance, wherever the term "zebra" is used without further qualification, it should be taken to mean the true, or mountain, zebra rather than any one of the Burchell's zebras.

Park in South Africa, the population had by 1965 been brought up to 75 strictly protected animals.[10] A few other individuals exist in various zoos throughout the world.

Pocock (1910)[11] and Lydekker (1912)[12] elaborate on the distinguishing features of *E. zebra zebra,* and from their descriptions the following notes are drawn:

From the other zebras, this species is distinguishable at a glance by its more ass-like appearance—especially the relatively great length of the narrow ears—and by the full development of a "gridiron" pattern of transverse stripes on the croup (see Figs. 197 and 198). With the exception of the belly, on which the barrel stripes are either very faint or totally absent, the mountain zebra is covered with numerous stripes over the head, neck, body, and the legs down to the hoofs (Fig. 186). The ground color of the body is either white or pale ochre. The blackish stripes are mostly narrow and close together, except on the thighs, where they are very broad and are separated by white spaces of similar width. All the transverse body stripes stop short of the middle line of the belly, leaving a white space on each side of the longitudinal ventral stripe. The mid-dorsal stripe is very narrow and straight, and is connected throughout its length with the transverse stripes of the body, most of which run vertically up to it, except the two uppermost of the stripes on the thighs, which are much broader than the rest and which are bent obliquely downwards and forwards onto the flanks. The uppermost of the latter, called the croup-stripe, passes on each side of the root of the tail, forming a triangular space, within which are nine or ten transverse stripes which form the "gridiron" and which become progressively shorter towards the tail (Fig. 198). Although some of the northern races of Burchell's zebras show traces of a "gridiron," it is never so strongly developed as in *E. zebra.*

Fig. 195 Cape mountain zebra (*E. zebra zebra*), a species now on the verge of extinction and no longer found in the wild state.

Fig. 196 Hartmann's zebra (*E. zebra hartmannae*), a larger subspecies of the Cape mountain zebra.

The muzzle of the mountain zebra is of a bay or tan color, darkening to black towards the mouth. Smith (1866) differentiates the sexes in stripe-color, stating that while in the male the stripes are black, in the female they are "of a less intense, or rather brownish colour."[13]

Of all the species of living zebras, the Cape mountain zebra is the smallest, averaging less than 46 inches in shoulder height. As noted previously, the ears are long and donkey-like. On the rear surface they have a white tip, and below this a black area to about the mid-level of the ear.* The head is relatively somewhat longer than in *E. burchelli*. The throat is unique among existing Equidae in possessing a dewlap. The hoofs, which are blackish in color, are small and narrow, although the hinder portion of the sole, or "frog," is remarkably broad and unconstricted. The tail is sparsely haired at the top and tufted (with dark-brown hairs) at the end, similar to a donkey's. The chestnuts (which are present on the forelegs only) are larger than in any other existing species of equid. Sclater (1900)[14] gives the size as about 3 inches by 2 inches. Another distinctive feature is that the hairs on the mid-dorsal stripe, from the withers to the croup, grow in a *forward* instead of backward direction. Again, in contradistinction to Burchell's zebras and the quagga, the mountain zebra has only two mammae or teats (inguinal), instead of four. Finally, this species is relatively quiet, vocally.

In its natural habitat, the Cape mountain zebra lives—or formerly did live—in troops usually of from three or four to ten individuals, one of which acts as a sentinel (giving the alarm with a shrill neigh). These zebras feed during the early morning, in the evening, and at night; during the heat of the day they rest beneath overhanging crags. They venture down into the valleys at night to drink, but are always back in their highland haunts before dawn. Their powers of endurance, speed and surefootedness in their rocky homes are simply astounding, and denote long residence in mountainous habitats.[15]

---

* Sclater (1900) says: ". . . ears long and rather narrow, posteriorly the basal two-thirds striped, the terminal third black, and the extreme point white."[14]

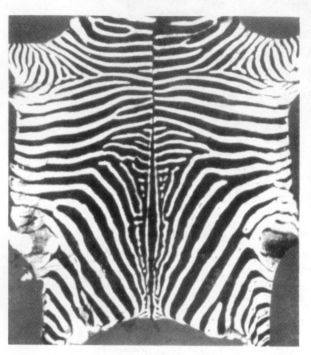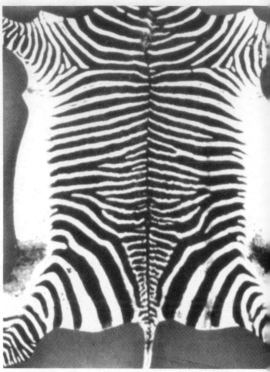

Fig. 197 Coat patterns of Burchell's zebra (left) and mountain zebra (right). Note in the latter the "gridiron" pattern on the croup, a distinctive feature of this species. After A. Griffini, 1913.

Concerning the phylogeny of *Equus zebra,* it would certainly appear that this species is distantly related to *E. grévyi,* or, in any event, that the two types have descended from a fairly recent common ancestor. On this subject, Tegetmeier (1895) says:

If I might be bold enough to express an opinion, I would say that *Equus grévyi* and *Equus zebra* are the same animal modified by a long residence, possibly for many thousands of years, in different localities. . . . There are to be seen in both animals the same transverse bands on the legs, the same general disposition of the stripes on the body, and on the neck. There are even in the *E. grévyi* the rudiments of the gridiron marks on the hind quarters of the *E. zebra,* and almost the only difference is the larger number and the smaller width of the stripes in *E. grévyi.*[16]

To this can be added the fact that in both *E. grévyi* and *E. zebra* the vertical body stripes at their lower ends stop short of the middle line of the belly, leaving a white space between the stripes of the two sides. In *E. grévyi* this space is broken by the fore-and-aft ventral stripe, while in *E. zebra* it is nearly or completely unmarked. In contrast, the body stripes of all the races of the Burchelline zebras continue downward and *join* at the middle of the belly. In the quagga, as in the mountain zebra, the body stripes do *not* so join; the mid-space of the belly is pale ochre or white.

In the early 1900s, a supposed subspecies of the mountain zebra was named by Prof. Ewart "Ward's zebra," after Rowland Ward, the London taxidermist, in whose establishment the skin was said to have been discovered. The interesting fact about this specimen is that the living animal had been shot in South Somaliland—a location

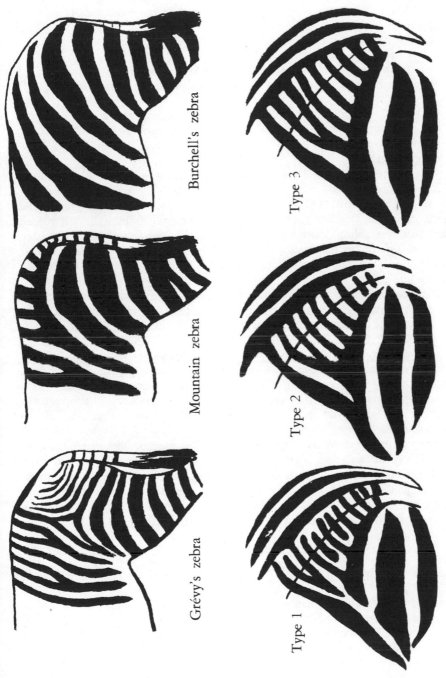

Burchell's zebra

Mountain zebra

Grévy's zebra

Type 3

Type 2

Type 1

Fig. 198 Patterns of croup-striping. (Above) in the three subgeneric forms of zebras. (Below) three types of the "gridiron" pattern in the mountain zebra. After A. Rzasnicki, 1931.

over 2000 miles northeast from the nearest habitat of the mountain zebra of the Cape. Unfortunately, only this single individual was recorded, so that there is no way of determining whether a local race of *E. zebra* once existed in the mountainous areas of northeast Africa.

Ridgeway (1909) offers the opinion that

. . . it was in the northern part of British East Africa that the differentiation of the three species [subgenera], not only in colour, but also in osteology, had begun.[17]

Antonius (1935) partially concurs with Ridgeway, in expressing the judgment that the "quagga-group" (Burchell's zebras) is of East African origin and is a comparatively recent invader of South Africa, ". . . the original South African striped horse being the mountain zebra."[18]

In any case, there appears to be agreement among most students of the subject that (1) *E. grévyi* represents—in its coat pattern, at least—the most primitive type of existing striped equid; that (2) *E. zebra* could have evolved from *E. grévyi*; and that (3) the group of Burchell's zebras could have evolved from a heavily-striped common ancestor resembling, more or less, *E. zebra. E. quagga,* as is shown later, represents in its limited striping the extreme differentiation from *E. grévyi* and *E. zebra,* although in certain other respects it is nearer to these fully striped forms than are the Burchelline zebras.

With reference to skeletal material, while there may be a fair amount on *E. zebra* scattered through museums in various European countries and in South Africa, the number of postcranial elements actually measured and reported in the literature is exceedingly limited.

Equus zebra zebra (and, in the main, *Equus zebra hartmannae* also) is distinguished skeletally from the Burchelline group of zebras by: (1) a relatively long radius; (2) a relatively long femur; (3) a fairly long tibia; (4) a relatively short metacarpus; (5) a relatively short metatarsus; and (6) very small hoofs. The species has also, relative to its bodily size, a larger and more asslike skull, ears, and head than any of the Burchelline zebras.

The osteometric material on the Cape mountain zebra used by the writer has consisted of 3 adult male skeletons; one adult female skeleton; one 1½-year-old male skeleton; one newborn male (?) skeleton, complete except for phalanges; the metapodials, carpals, and calcaneum only of a 4-year-old male; the metapodials only of a newborn (sex not stated); and 25 adult skulls. Of this material, 3 complete skeletons, and the bones of the 4-year-old male, were measured by the writer.

---

b. Hartmann's zebra; Hartmann's mountain zebra (*Equus zebra hartmannae* Matschie, 1898).

This animal, while manifestly closely related to the Cape mountain zebra, differs from the typical species in its distinctly larger size and more widely spaced stripes (Fig. 196). Whereas the mountain zebra from the Cape stands about 45.7 inches at the shoulder, Hartmann's zebra averages about 49.3 inches. This 8 percent superiority in height indicates a superiority in weight (assuming the two races to be of similar body *build*) of about 25 percent—a substantial difference. The limited amount of osteometric data on Hartmann's zebra in the writer's possession suggests that in the

smallness of its hoofs it departs further from the Burchell's zebras than does even
E. zebra sp.

The geographic locus of Hartmann's zebra is the dry upland of the western and
northwestern parts of South West Africa and northward about 50 miles across the
Cunene River into southwestern Angola (map, Fig. 187). According to Bigalke (1958),
this zebra

> . . . within its rather restricted range . . . is numerous.* Questionnaires revealed
> that it is widespread only in the districts of Outjo (48% of all farms), Karabib
> (45%), Windhoek (21%), Luderritz (21%), and Maltahohe (39%). It is
> also reported to be common in the Native Reserves in the Omaruru district and
> is found in the eastern part of Game Reserve III. No records were received from
> Tsumeb, Grootfontein and Gobabis, and in the remaining districts it is rare. It
> is therefore in the mountain ranges bordering the Namib, from the vicinity of the
> Orange River northward to Angola, that this species is most at home. Shortridge
> describes a similar range.[19]

The towns of Maltahohe, Windhoek, and Outjo, mentioned above, all lie from
150 to 200 miles inland from the west coast of South West Africa (now Namibia),
which is bordered immediately by the Namib Desert. It is evident that in these districts
the zebra's original range has been taken over by farmers, and that in these large
areas the wild equines still roam. Blaine (1922)[20] states that the spoor of *E. z. hartmannae*
may sometimes be seen on the wet sand of the beach at low tide, and that these zebras
are often to be observed grazing on the flat plateaus within a mile of the ocean. The
distance inland from the coast that *E. z. hartmannae* ranges (according to the distribution map presented by Shortridge, 1934)[21] is from about 74 miles to an extreme of
150 miles (see Fig. 187).

In its coat coloration and striping, Hartmann's zebra, while similar generally to the
typical or Cape mountain zebra, differs from it in that the respective areas occupied
by the dark stripes and the light ground are transposed—that is, the animal is *lighter-
colored* in general than *E. zebra zebra* on account of the light interspaces in its coat
pattern being wider, generally, than the dark stripes. As in *E. z. zebra*, the hairs on the
mid-dorsal stripe of *E. z. hartmannae*, from the withers to the croup, grow in a *forward*
direction instead of backward. There is also present in *hartmannae* the prominent
dewlap which, among existing Equidae, is a unique character of the species *E. zebra*.
Again, as in the typical form of the latter species, the chestnuts on the forelegs in
hartmannae are *large*. To sum up, about the only respect in which *E. z. hartmannae*
differs significantly from *E. z. zebra* is its larger bodily size—not one in a thousand
specimens of the Cape species is likely to attain the shoulder height of an average-
sized Hartmann's zebra.

During the season of light rains, according to Blaine (1922),[22] herds of the local
race of bontequagga (*E. burchelli antiquorum*), commonly known as Chapman's zebra,
migrate from the interior to the coast for the fine new grass, and are often to be seen
on the same plain with small troops of Hartmann's zebra, but never associating with
them. (This is a parallel to the situation in Abyssinia and northern Kenya, where

---

* In 1969, the wild population in southwest Africa was estimated at about 7000 head. As of 1963,
there were 21 specimens in zoos in the United States, 17 of these being in the Game Farm at
Catskill, N.Y., where two were born in captivity.

individuals, or small parties, of Grévy's zebra share the living space with herds of the smaller but more numerous *E. burchelli böhmi*. D.P.W.). Sometimes a herd of Hartmann's zebra may consist of as many as 20 head, although the average number is from 6 to 12. Old stallions often wander about by themselves.

The osteometric material on *E. zebra hartmannae* studied by the writer has consisted of 8 adult male skulls, 9 adult female skulls, one adult male skeleton, 2 adult female skeletons, one adult female skeleton (metapodials and phalanges only), and a one-day-old hybrid skeleton of *E. z. zebra* and *E. z. hartmannae*.

6. Subgenus *Quaggoides,* subgen. nov. (D. P. Willoughby, 1966).*

a. Burchell's zebra; bontequagga (*Equus burchelli burchelli* Gray, 1825).
NATIVE NAMES: Amaxosa, *Iqwara*; Zulu and Swazi, *Idube*; Basuto, *Makwa*; Matabele and Bechuana, *Peetsee* (or *Pitsi*); Hottentot, *Dauw* (or *Daow*).

Much confusion has been, and continues to be, attached to the group, or species, of zebra of which this is, or was (since it is now extinct): the form originally named after the explorer William J. Burchell. The popular names of the several geographic or color races of this species likewise are taken after the names of African explorers or travelers: e.g., "Böhm's zebra," "Grant's zebra," "Selous's zebra," "Chapman's zebra." Neither these names nor the corresponding scientific designations of the same zebrine races refer (with a single exception) to the geographic *ranges* of the animals nor to their coloration (striping), with the result that the names—whether popular or scientific—provide no help whatever in identifying the various races of this zebra. Table 28 lists the numerous names which were proposed at various times for supposed new forms of the two (only) species of Burchelline or quagga-like zebras (namely, *Equus burchelli* and *Equus quagga*).

Another complicating factor is the unfortunate use, in some quarters, of the term "bontequagga" as an embracive title for the various members of the Burchell's zebra group. This term, which, translated from the Boer Dutch, means "painted (or variegated) quagga," implies a close relationship of the Burchelline zebras with the true (extinct) Cape quagga—an animal which was more likely a distinct species of semi-striped equid than merely an extreme color-variant of the "bontequagga." Some authors have gone even further in causing confusion, by designating *all* the Burchell's zebras as "quaggas."

---

* The subgenotypic species of this proposed new classification of quagga-like zebras is the now-extinct true quagga itself: *Equus {Quaggoides} quagga quagga* Gmelin, 1788. By the inclusion within this subgenus of the fossil species *Equus occidentalis* Leidy, 1865, the geologic range extends from the latest Pleistocene of California to the Recent of South Africa.

The osteometric differences which separate the living species of the subgenus *Hippotigris* (within which subgenus the quagga-like zebras were previously included) from those of *Quaggoides* are given in detail in the writer's 1966 paper. The external (body) proportions of the two types, as represented by *Equus zebra zebra* and *Equus {Quaggoides} burchelli* chapmani (=-böhmi), respectively, are given in Figs. 246 and 247 and in Table 29.

Fig. 199 Two true Burchell's zebras (*E. burchelli burchelli*) formerly in the London Zoo. Note the virtual absence of markings on the legs.

Table 28. Synonymy of terms proposed or used for zebras of the Burchell's species and the quagga. (Names followed by an asterisk are the original and valid subspecies names.)

Proposed name of species or subspecies	Author	Year	Proper name of species or subspecies
annectens	W. Rothschild	1906	burchelli selousi
antiquorum	Hamilton Smith	1841	burchelli antiquorum*
böhmi	P. Matschie	1892	burchelli böhmi*
borensis	E. Lönnberg	1921	burchelli böhmi
burchelli	J. E. Gray	1825	burchelli burchelli*
campestris	Hamilton Smith	1841	burchelli burchelli
chapmani	E. L. Layard	1865	burchelli antiquorum
crawshayi	W. E. de Winton	1896	burchelli böhmi
cuninghamei	E. Heller	1914	burchelli böhmi
danielli	R. I. Pocock	1904	quagga quagga
festivus	Wagner	1834	burchelli burchelli
foai	Trouessart-Prazak	1899	burchelli selousi
goldfinchi	W. Ridgeway	1911	burchelli böhmi
granti	W. E. de Winton	1896	burchelli böhmi
greyi	R. Lydekker	1902	quagga quagga
isabellinus	Hamilton Smith	1841	quagga quagga
jallae	L. Camerano	1902	burchelli böhmi
kaokensis	L. Zukowsky	1924	burchelli antiquorum
kaufmanni	P. Matschie	1912	burchelli antiquorum
lorenzi	R. Lydekker	1902	quagga quagga
mariae	J. P. Prazak	1898	burchelli böhmi
markhami	Tichomirow	1878	burchelli antiquorum
montanus	F. Cuvier	1826	burchelli burchelli
muansae	P. Matschie	1906	burchelli böhmi
paucistriatus	M. Hilzheimer	1910	burchelli burchelli
pococki	L. Brasil–G. Pennetier	1909	burchelli antiquorum
quagga	J. Gmelin	1788	quagga quagga
selousi	R. I. Pocock	1897	burchelli selousi*
tigrinus	H. Johnston	1897	burchelli böhmi
transvaalensis	J. C. Ewart	1897	burchelli antiquorum
trouessarti	L. Camerano	1908	quagga quagga
typicus	F. C. Selous	1899	burchelli burchelli
wahlbergi	R. I. Pocock	1897	burchelli antiquorum
zambeziensis	J. P. Prazak	1898	burchelli böhmi
zebroides	R. Lesson	1827	burchelli burchelli

For a long time, in the classification of the zebras referable generally to the Burchell's group, it would happen that an alleged new subspecies or race (sometimes a "distinct species") was proposed solely on the basis of some variation in color-pattern, or striping —a feature now known to be exceedingly variable individually. A decided clarification of the synonymy concerning the species was made by Cabrera (1936),[23] who accomplished in a convincing manner the reduction of some thirty previously proposed forms (see Table 28) to four geographic and/or color races.

Since there appears to be no significant skeletal or cranial variation among the various members of Equus burchelli (with the exception of size alone), it has been found expedient to adopt here the classification proposed by Cabrera. This grouping, which recognizes one species, 4 valid subspecies, and about 30 described forms, is as follows:

1. *Legs never wholly striped; shadow stripes generally numerous.*
   a. *Equus burchelli burchelli* (Burchell's zebra). The typical form, now extinct. Legs without stripes below elbow and below stifle, with the exception of a few traces on hocks occasionally. Belly usually unstriped, except for ventral longitudinal stripe. Comprises only the original species (Figs. 199 and 200).
   b. *Equus burchelli antiquorum* (Damaraland zebra). Legs more or less striped below elbow and below stifle, but never completely so. Includes 8 named forms, as listed in Table 27. (See Fig. 201).
2. *Legs wholly striped to the hoofs; shadow stripes very few and frequently absent.*
   a. *Equus burchelli selousi* (Selous's zebra). Stripes and interspaces on neck and body narrow and numerous; neck stripes 10 to 13 in number, vertical stripes 4 to 8. Includes Foa's zebra and "Annect" zebra (Fig. 203).
   b. *Equus burchelli böhmi* (Böhm's zebra). Stripes and interspaces on neck and body wider and less numerous than in Selous's zebra; neck stripes 7 to 10, vertical stripes 3 or 4. Includes 11 named forms, as listed in Table 27. (See Fig. 202).

Thus it will be seen that in the Burchell's zebra group there were, in addition to the 4 valid species described by Cabrera, at least 25 other described forms. All the latter supposed distinct races of zebras were, as previously mentioned, proposed on the basis of *individual variations in coat-pattern,* and not, as would have constituted a valid basis, on (1) measurable differences in the proportioning of the skeleton, or (2) consistent pronounced differences in the number and placement of the coat stripes.

It may be mentioned that, long prior to Cabrera's classification, Matschie (1894)[24] had subdivided *Equus burchelli* into four geographical or color races, these being: *E. b. burchelli, E. b. antiquorum, E. b. chapmani,* and *E. b. böhmi.* Thus, Cabrera's classification differs from Matschie's only in the substitution of *E. b. selousi* for *E. b. chapmani.* Sclater, in 1900,[25] increased the number of valid subspecies from the four recognized by Matschie to seven, eliminating *E. b. böhmi* and adding the four races of *E. b. transvaalensis, E. b. wahlbergi, E. b. selousi,* and *E. b. crawshayi.* In this classification, Sclater originated the form of description (relative to the extent of the striping) adopted by Cabrera and repeated, with certain additions, above.

Cabrera gives the present or recent geographic distribution, along with the respective type localities, of the four subspecies of *Equus burchelli* as follows: (The newer names of certain of the localities are added in parentheses).

Equus burchelli burchelli. Formerly Southern Bechuanaland (Botswana) and Orange River Colony (now extinct). Type locality: Little Klibbolikhoni Fontein.

Equus burchelli antiquorum. From Benguela (in Angola) and Damaraland (north-central Namibia), across Bechaunaland (Botswana), to Transvaal (in north-eastern South Africa) and Zululand (in east-central South Africa).

Equus burchelli selousi. Lower Zambesi basin, from Victoria Falls; Southern Rhodesia; Mozambique; northward to southern Nyasaland (Zambia). Type locality: Manyami River, Mashonaland.

Equus burchelli böhmi. Southern Sudan, east of Bahr el Gebel; south Ethiopia; extreme southwest Somaliland (Somalia), west of the Juba; Kenya Colony; Uganda; Tanganyika (Tanzania); northern Nyasaland (Zambia); northern Rhodesia, to the upper Zambesi. Type locality: Pangani River.

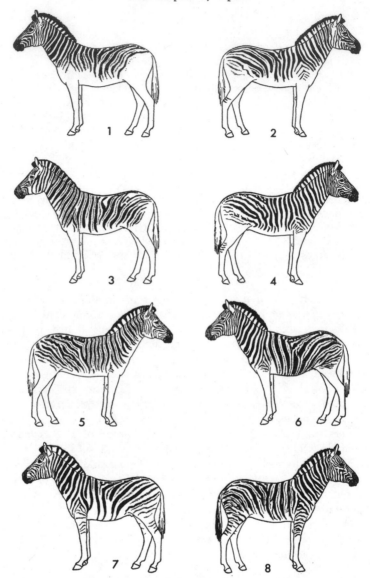

Fig. 200 Examples of Burchell's zebra. 1. *Equus burchellii burchellii.* ♂, Mainz Museum. (Type of *paucistriatus*). 2. *Equus burchellii burchellii.* ♀, Jardin des Plantes, Paris, 1826. Adapted from F. Cuvier's plate. 3. *Equus burchellii burchellii.* Type, from Little Klibbolikhoni Fontein. Adapted from Gray's original plate. 4. *Equus burchellii burchellii.* ♂, Knowsley Park, about 1845. Adapted from a drawing by **B. Waterhouse Hawkins.** 5. *Equus burchellii burchellii.* ♀, **Knowsley** Park, about 1845. Adapted from a drawing by **B. Waterhouse Hawkins.** 6. *Equus burchellii burchellii.* ♂, Dresden Zoological Garden. Adapted from H. Lang's photograph. 7. *Equus burchellii antiquorum.* ♂, from Rietfontein West. Munich **Museum.** Adapted from E. Schwarz's photograph. 8. *Equus burchellii antiquorum.* Type, from Angola. Adapted from Hamilton Smith's original figure. (After A. Cabrera, 1936).

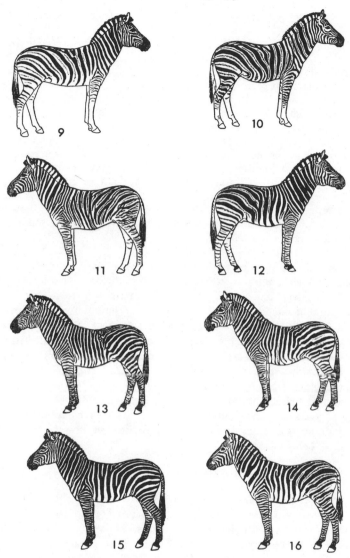

Fig. 201 Examples of the Damaraland zebra. 9. *Equus burchellii antiquorum.*
♀, from eastern Transvaal. Adapted from Stevenson-Hamilton's photograph. 10.
Equus burchellii antiquorum. ♀, from west of Lake Ngami. Madrid Zoological
Park, 1902. 11. *Equus burchellii antiquorum.* From Zululand. Adapted from a
photograph published by Pocock under the name *E. quagga wahlbergi.* 12. *Equus
burchellii antiquorum.* ♂, from eastern Transvaal. Adapted from Stevenson-
Hamilton's photograph. 13. *Equus burchellii selousii.* From Angoniland. Paris
Museum. Type of *foai.* 14. *Equus burchellii selousii.* ♀, from the Tendo of
Nyspindire. Rouen Museum. Adapted from a photograph published by Brasil
and Pennetier under the name *E. b. zambeziensis.* 15. *Equus burchellii selousii*
From Fort Jameson. Tring Museum. Type of *annectens.* 16. *Equus burchellii
böhmi.* ♀, from east of Lake Naivasha. Bâle Museum. Adapted from a photograph
published by Roux. (After A. Cabrera, 1936).

To the information on geographic distribution, Cabrera adds these comments:

Geographic distribution combined with individual variation within the same range indicate that racial difference in the Burchell zebra has little to do either with altitude or with the fact that the animals inhabit grassy plains, park countries or deserts. Differentiation seems rather to depend on latitude, and in some cases rivers appear to act as barriers of distribution. Assuming that striping is an archaic feature in horses, the most primitive form should be that found in the lower Zambesi basin. Northward the stripes appear to be less numerous and both these and the interspaces become wider as though in compensation. The same fact is observed to the south-ward, but the character here is accompanied by a gradual obliteration of the stripes on the limbs and an increase of the shadow stripes. A great river, the Orange, is, or rather was, the southern limit of the species. Another river, the upper Zambesi, divides the range of *antiquorum* from that of *böhmi,* and the lower Loangwa appears to separate this last from the range of *selousi.* East of this river, however, it seems that *böhmi* is found in the north, while the zebra living in the south belongs to the Mashonaland race.[26] (i.e., *selousi.*)

To sum up, the problem of *individual variation* in coat pattern in the Burchell's zebras has long been a hindrance to their proper zoological classification. Yet as early as 1876, T. E. Buckley, in discussing Burchell's zebras, remarked that "out of five of these animals shot in one herd there were individuals showing variation of color and marking from the yellow and chocolate stripes to the pure black and white, the stripes in some cases ceasing above the hock and in others being continued distinctly down to the hoof."[27] Besides this actual range in variation, there is a complicating factor: under differing degrees of lighting—as at midday and at dusk, respectively—the coat patterns of zebras may appear either light or dark; and numerous observers in the field, under one or the other of these conditions, have accordingly recorded their descriptions. Now that zebras are generally known among sportsmen as well as zoologists to be subject to this great individual diversity in outward appearance, we hear no more of some "new species of zebra" being discovered.

The history of the typical Burchell's zebra, like that of the mountain zebra and the quagga, is a history of extermination at the hands of colonists. The quagga became extinct in 1883, the true Burchell's zebra sometime around 1910*; and the Cape mountain zebra is today represented probably by fewer than 100 individuals, all in a captive state. While, even as late as 1850, Burchell's zebra was present on the South African veldt in immense herds, only a quarter of a century later it was almost gone. Buckley, in 1876, wrote:

Some few years ago the three species of this genus were in little repute for their skins as compared with the wildebeest and blessbok; but of late years it has been discovered that they are in great use for, I believe, connecting-bands for machinery; at any rate, their value increased so much that they have been shot down, until

---

* Antonius (1938, p. 563) says that the last surviving true Burchell's zebra was a stallion that died in the Schönbrunn (Vienna) Zoo in 1908. However, Harper (1945, p. 340) states that the London Zoo had a specimen which was "received apparently in 1909," and which lived presumably for some time after that.

you may go for a week through the 'High Veldt' and not see one, although there will be thousands of other animals.[28]

In appearance, *Equus burchelli burchelli* was a handsome animal. Nott (1886) describes its external aspect thus:

The ground color of the short and glossy coat is of a sienna brown, and the stripes with which it is banded are not quite so dark in hue as those of the zebra (*E. zebra*, D.P.W.), nor are they so numerous. Instead of covering the entire body and limbs, as a rule they are only seen on the head, neck, and upper part of the body and legs, the ventral surface and lower portion of the limbs being pure white.[29]

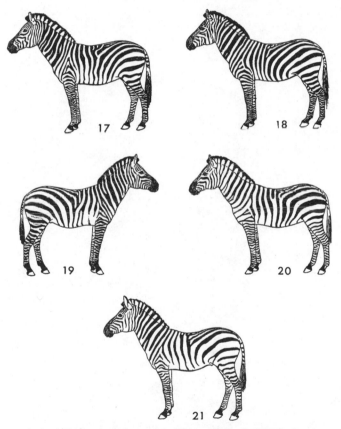

Fig. 202 Examples of Böhm's zebra. 17. *Equus burchellii böhmi*. From Marotse-land. Type of *zambeziensis*. 18. *Equus burchellii böhmi*. From the Kiliman-jaro district. Hagenbeck's Tierpark, Stellingen, 1905. 19. *Equus burchellii böhmi*. ♂, from southern Ethiopia. London Zoological Gardens, 1901. The same specimen as figured by Sclater in left side view. 20. *Equus burchellii böhmi*. From Masailand. Adapted from a photograph by C. G. Schillings. 21. *Equus burchellii böhmi*. ♂, from east of Lake Naivasha. Bâle Museum. Adapted from a photograph published by Roux with the name *E. b. mariae*. (After A. Cabrera, 1936).

Of the vertical stripes in the true (extinct) Burchell's zebra, there were about 10 on the neck, one on the shoulder, 4 on the body, and 3 or 4 on the flanks, the latter curving obliquely backwards and crossing the croup and upper thigh. The shadow stripes on the hindquarters were strongly marked, and were narrower than the main stripes. The light interspaces containing the shadow stripes became progressively broader as they ranged backwards from the body onto the thighs. The legs, from the lower level of the body downwards, were usually white and unstriped; and the vertical body-stripes usually stopped several inches above the ventral longitudinal stripe, leaving the belly mostly white. Fig. 200, especially the first five examples, gives a good idea of how the originally described Burchell's zebra must have appeared.

As to the body size (shoulder height) of the true Burchell's zebra, while stated respectively by various authors as being 48 inches, 52 inches, and even as much as 56 inches, the limb-bone lengths of several specimens indicate an average height of 48.8 inches (about 1240 mm). This, and an average vertex skull length of about 535 mm, denote a size practically identical to that of the existing Chapman's zebra (*E. burchelli antiquorum*), Figs. 201, 205, and 206.

Fig. 203 Selous's zebra (*E. burchelli selousii*). A mounted specimen in the Chicago Natural History Museum. This southeast African species was named in 1897 after the famous hunter of African big game, Frederick Courtenay Selous (1851–1917). Note that in museum specimens the mane lacks its lifelike erectness.

Concerning the details of coloration of the typical Burchell's zebra, Cabrera (1936, p. 94) gives the opinion:

. . . I regard as typical *burchelli* all the members of the species having all legs white from the elbow and the stifle joint, except for the occasional presence of a few short markings across the hocks, and with the thighs free of complete and well-defined dark stripes behind the stifle stripe.

In their points of differentiation from the Cape mountain zebra, *Equus* [*Hippotigris*] *zebra zebra,* with which subgeneric group they were heretofore included, the four races of the Burchell's zebra collectively present the differences listed in the following table.

Table 29. External differences between the Cape mountain zebra and Burchell's zebra.

Cape mountain zebra (*Equus zebra*), typical species	Character	Burchell's zebra (*Equus burchelli* and subspecies)
1160 mm (45.7 inches)	Shoulder (withers) height (average of each form)	1165 to 1240 mm (45.9 to 48.8 inches)
10 to 14 neck stripes; 8 to 11 vertical body stripes; "gridiron" striping on croup; no shadow stripes; body stripes do not join on belly	Coat pattern	7 to 13 neck stripes; 3 to 8 vertical body stripes; no "gridiron"; often shadow stripes; body stripes usually join on belly
Very narrow, with hair reversed from croup forwards to withers	Dorsal stripe	Much broader, especially over croup (see Fig. 198)
About 250 mm (9.8 inches)	Ear length	190 to 210 mm (7.5 to 8.3 inches)
Shorter and less dense, with no forelock	Mane	Longer and thicker, sometimes with the suggestion of a forelock
Present	Dewlap	Absent
Less bushy and more ass-like	Tail	More bushy and horselike
Very large and broad (about 3 x 2 inches)	Chestnuts (on forelegs)	Much smaller (about 2 x 1 inches)
Small and narrow; deeply hollowed	Hoofs	Broader; less concave on soles

Much speculation has been raised as to whether the differentiation in coat-pattern in the various geographic races of *E. burchelli* has any phylogenetic significance; or conversely, whether the variation in habitat has produced significant changes in structure

Fig. 204 Here is a striking wildlife photograph taken in Kruger National Park, showing zebras (Chapman's variety) and blue wildebeeste drinking. Zebras are "thirsty" animals, and are seldom found farther than five miles from water. They drink preferably at least twice every twenty-four hours. The time of drinking may be anywhere from early morning until late evening, or even at night, depending on the season and the weather. Usually, however, the night is spent in feeding, the hottest time of the day in resting, and the visits to drinking places are made in the very early morning and at sunset. Zebras are noisy animals when assembled near a pool or stream; and their barking cry, "qua-ha, qua-ha-ha," is one of the commonest sounds on the veldt.

and appearance. In general, the more southerly the race, the less dense the dark striping, especially on the legs, and the greater the tendency to shadow-striping. That is, the most densely striped forms are to be found chiefly among the races of *E. b. böhmi* and *E. b. selousi,* next among *E. b. antiquorum,* and the least striped forms among *E. b. wahlbergi* and the now-extinct *E. burchelli burchelli.* However, that this regional, or latitudinal, change in coloration—so far as leg-striping is concerned—may have no genetic implication is seen in the fact, pointed out by Lydekker (1912, p. 197), that in the giraffe a completely opposite condition prevails. In this animal, it is as the species ranges northward, rather than southward, that the legs become progressively more white and unstriped. Of course, it is possible also that these conditions of coloration, in the zebras and the giraffes, respectively, have no relationship whatever.

b. Böhm's zebra; Kilimanjaro zebra (*Equus burchelli böhmi* Matschie, 1892).
Native names: Swahili, *punda milia* ("striped *donkey*");
Duruma, *forru.*

Within this widespread northern race of Burchell's zebra are included the varieties *granti, crawshayi, tigrinus, zambeziensis, mariae, jallae, borensis, muansae, goldfinchi,* and *cuninghamei,* respectively. As Cabrera (1936) points out, these ten described forms may properly be regarded as synonyms of *Equus burchelli böhmi.* It is interesting to note that Sclater (1901), who describes seven varieties of Burchell's zebra, does not include *E. b. böhmi* among them, but considers the latter as a synonym of *E. b. chapmani.*

Böhm's zebra, in its typical form (if the expression may be used) ranges, according to Roosevelt and Heller (1914):

. . . from the lowlands of the coast drainage from 3000 feet to sea-level, north in British East Africa [Kenya] as far as the south bank of the Tana River, and inland to the limits of the desert nyika zone; limits of range in German East Africa [Tanzania] unknown.[29] [See map, Fig. 187].

Fig. 205 Chapman's Zebra. This photograph shows to advantage the difference in striping which distinguishes the subspecies known as Damaraland zebra (of which Chapman's zebra is one form) from those known respectively as Böhm's (Grant's) and Selous's zebras. In the latter subspecies the legs are striped clear down to the hoofs, while in the Damaraland zebras the striping below the knees and hocks is broken and incomplete and there are shadow-stripes on the flanks and hind legs.

Fig. 206 Chapman's or Damaraland zebra (*E. burchelli antiquorum*). A female specimen in the San Diego Zoo, showing strong shadow-striping.

The type locality of this zebra is Pangani, on the east coast of Tanzania near the Kenya border.

Grant's zebra (*E. burchelli böhmi,* var. *granti*) was described originally by De Winton in 1896. In contradistinction to Böhm's zebra, it is essentially an *upland* type, its habitat, according to Roosevelt and Heller (1914, p. 687) being:

> The highlands of British East Africa [Kenya] westward through Uganda to the Edward Nyanze and northward on the east side of the Nile as far as the Mongolla district and the headwaters of the Sobat River northwest of Lake Rudolf, east to the eastern edge of the highland plateau down to an altitude of 3000 feet in British East Africa [Kenya], and north as far as the south bank of the Tana River; southern limits of range in German East Africa [Tanzania] unknown.

Thus, from the foregoing descriptions, while the horizontal ranges of the typical Böhm's zebra and of Grant's zebra in some places concur, the vertical ranges are different. This altitudinal divergence possibly has produced minor differences in the cranial and hoof conformations of the two types, although the skeletal material studied by the writer has not been sufficiently extensive to demonstrate this.

As has long been known, there are places in the semiarid and desert country of northern Kenya and southern Abyssinia where the range of *E. burchelli böhmi* (var. *granti*) overlaps that of the large Abyssinian zebra *E. grévyi*. Wherever this occurs, the two species share the living space compatibly, mingling together but not normally interbreeding, although a single possible instance of a *burchelli* x *grévyi* hybrid is on record. In contrast to this mutual interspecies tolerance, it is said that wherever, in South Africa, groups of *E. burchelli* and *E. zebra* have come together, the two species have kept strictly apart.[30] That Böhm's zebra is in no danger of extinction is evident from the 1962 wildlife census of the Serengeti Plain (northern Tanzania), which enumerated some 150,000 zebras in that area alone.[31]

With respect to available skeletal material, *E. burchelli böhmi* is probably the best represented of any of the existing zebras. In the collection of the United States National Museum alone there are (or were in 1943) no fewer than 52 skulls of this subspecies, most of which were gathered by the Roosevelt-Heller African Expedition of 1912. These skulls, which range in vertex length from 495 to 561 mm,* include among the smaller specimens many examples of *granti,* the average skull length of which is 501 mm. The average living shoulder height in granti is 1165 mm (45.9 inches), as compared with 1236 mm (48.7 inches) in the lowland (typical) form of *böhmi.*

Allen (1909)[32] gives certain measurements, both external and cranial, of seven specimens of *E. burchelli granti* that were collected by the Tjader Expedition of 1906 and which are now in the collection of the American Museum of Natural History.

St. Leger (1932)[33] gives some measurements of Heller's type specimen of *E. burchelli cuninghamei,* an immature individual, in comparison with six specimens of typical *böhmi.* Her conclusion, like that of Cabrera's, is that *cuninghamei* is a synonym of *böhmi.*

The writer's series of cranial data, collated from the literature, comprises 5 detailed sets of measurements of *E. b. burchelli,* 5 of *selousi,* 20 of *antiquorum,* and 41 of *böhmi* (including 2 *cuninghamei* and 3 *crawshayi*). It was possible for the authors of these measurements to accurately classify the various crania as to the subspecies represented, because, in most cases the skins also were preserved and the geographic localities recorded.

The average *male* vertex skull lengths of these forms are, respectively: *cuninghamei,* 500 mm; *granti,* 504 mm; *crawshayi,* 528 mm; *selousi,* 530.5 mm; *böhmi* (typical form), 533 mm; *antiquorum,* 537 mm; and *burchelli* (typical form), 537 mm. In addition, the writer has recorded 8 sets of limb-bone measurements (7 *granti* and one *chapmani*).

---

* While the shoulder height and other body measurements of quadrupedal mammals, including members of the horse family, are commonly (for the benefit of those who read only English) expressed in inches as well as metric units, measurements of the *skeleton* (i.e., the skull and the bones of the body and limbs) are *always* taken, recorded, and published either in centimeters or millimeters. The latter units are the most convenient for publication, since (except in the case of very small specimens, where tenths or even hundredths of a millimeter may be used) they avoid the use of decimal points. It is for this reason that all *skeletal* measurements expressed herein are in *metric* units. Why record a measurement as 19.72 inches when 501 mm says the same thing?

Fig. 207 This view, in "grazing" posture of the same specimen as in Fig. 206, reveals a number of interesting anatomical points. It shows the "chestnut" (rather small, in this individual) on the inner side of the front leg; the absence of one on the hind leg; the "broadening" of the stripes on the neck as that part is stretched; the disposition of the stripes on the underside of the jaw; the straightness of the top of the spine when the neck is stretched downward; and the location of one of the two nipples (the dark spot on the belly, just to the left of the last or rearmost body stripe).

c. Selous's zebra (*Equus burchelli selousi* Pocock, 1897).

In this east-central race, as in the more northern *E. b. böhmi,* the legs are fully striped to the hoofs and shadow stripes are either faint or absent altogether. In contrast to *böhmi,* the neck and body stripes and interspaces are narrow and numerous, the neck stripes ranging from 10 to 13 (*böhmi,* 7 to 10), and the body stripes from 4 to 8 (*böhmi,* 3 or 4). See Fig. 203.

The distribution of Selous's zebra is stated by Roberts (1951) to be:

Mashonaland and possibly eastward into Portuguese South-East Africa (Mozambique) south of the Zambesi River. The forms to the north of the Zambesi River are different in having no shadow-stripes, and the black bands as broad or even broader than the intervening white bands; the nearest of these is *E. b. annectens* of Fort Jameson, north-east Rhodesia, which is regarded by some authors as synonymous with *E. b. böhmi.*[34] [See map, Fig. 187].

As to the skeletal material on this subspecies, the writer has collated the skull measurements of 3 adult males (one measured personally) and 3 adult females, but no measurements whatever of the postcranial skeleton. The skull length of *selousi* indicates that this zebra stands, on the average, probably about 1230 mm (48.4 inches) high at the shoulder, or very nearly the same height as *E. b. böhmi* typ.

d. Damaraland Zebra; Chapman's zebra; Congo dauw; Angola dauw (*Equus burchelli antiquorum* Smith, 1841).

Cabrera (see Table 27) considers this subspecies of *burchelli* to embrace the seven additional forms *chapmani, kaokensis, kaufmanni, markhami, pococki, transvaalensis,*

Fig. 208 Here is a head-on view of a Chapman's zebra, showing the numerous thin stripings on the forehead and face. The dark borders and the light tips of the ears also are evident.

Fig. 209 A view from an unusual angle of another Chapman's zebra, showing
the broad stripes and light interspaces on the hindquarters. Note how the spinal
stripe is continued on the tail.

and *wahlbergi,* respectively. While the species name *antiquorum* (Smith, 1841)
precedes that of *chapmani* (Layard, 1865), the animals corresponding with the description of *antiquorum* are now so generally called Chapman's zebras that the prior designation has become more or less forgotten, except among taxonomists. Although some of
the earlier authors (e.g., Matschie, 1894; Sclater, 1900) differentiate between *antiquorum*
and *chapmani,* the distinctions they make are confined to minor variations in coat-
pattern. Later investigators, such as St. Leger (1932) and Cabrera (1936), give ample
reasons for considering the two forms as merely geographical or individual variations
of the same subspecies.

Thus interpreted, *E. b. antiquorum* has a wide range, extending from the coasts of
Angola and Southwest Africa on the west to the Zambesi and Limpopo Rivers on the
east, and from central Angola on the north to the southern borders of Southwest Africa,
Bechuanaland, the Transvaal, and Zululand on the south—a total area of nearly 1,000,000

Fig. 210 Out on the veldt, while feeding, zebras keep more or less in a crescent formation, and nearly always with their heads pointing upwind. In approaching or leaving a drinking place, however, they string out in Indian file, meanwhile keeping a careful lookout for their chief enemy, the lion. A troop is usually under the leadership of a master stallion.

Fig. 211 Despite the general similarity of the coat-patterns of the zebras in this picture, close comparison will reveal that no two individuals are striped exactly alike. The same is true of the other countless thousands of these animals that roam the South African plains. The zebra, indeed, furnishes an interesting example of the rule in Nature that each individual is different, in one way or another, from all others of its kind.

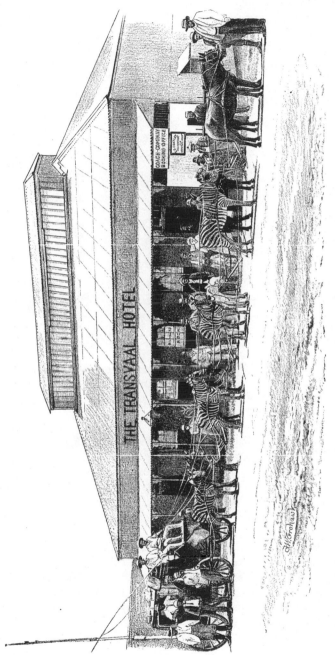

Fig. 212 *Burchell's zebras broken to harness:* This drawing is from a photograph taken in 1892 of a combination team of zebras, donkeys, and mules used to draw a coach in Petersburg, Transvaal. The experiment was made to determine the practicability of using the zebra (which is immune to the tsetse-fly and to climatic diseases that affect the horse) as a transport or draft animal in Africa. Since, however, no large-scale attempts at domestication were subsequently made, it can only be concluded that this species of zebra, despite its certain advantages, proved unsatisfactory as a substitute for the horse.

square miles (see map, Fig. 187). This makes it the most widely distributed wild form of any of the living Equidae.

Shortridge (1934) gives some field measurements of 6 adult male and 5 adult female specimens of *E. b. antiquorum,* the averages of which are: head and body length (in a straight line) 2300 mm (90.5 inches); hind foot 570 mm (22.5 inches); tail 506 mm (19.9 inches); and ear 168 mm (6.6 inches), the latter measurement having been taken presumably to the internal notch rather than the external base of the ear, which latter would make it about 40 mm longer. These body measurements indicate a form about 6.4 percent larger than *E. b. granti* and of approximately the same size as the recently extinct *E. burchelli burchelli.*

The skeletal material on *E. b. antiquorum* studied by the writer has consisted of 10 adult male skulls, 12 adult female skulls, 1 sub-adult male skull (measured personally), and 6 sets of limb bones (3 male, 3 female).

---

e. Quagga; Cape quagga (*Equus quagga* Gmelin, 1788).
Native names: Hottentot, *khoua khoua;* Xhosa, *iqwaha, idube;*
So. Suthu, *quoha.*

This recently-extinct semi-striped zebroid was in some respects the most interesting of the post-Pleistocene Equidae. Part of the reason for this, no doubt, was that the animal—which formerly roamed the grassy plains of South Africa in countless thousands—became totally exterminated in the wild state within less than forty years. Harris (1840), for example, in describing the clatter of the hoofs of a herd of quagga, says:

> I could compare it to nothing but to the din of a tremendous charge of cavalry, or the rushing of a mighty tempest. I could not estimate the accumulated number at less than fifteen thousand, a great extent of country being actually chequered black and white with their congregated masses . . .[35]

Yet as early as 1860 the quagga was extinct in Cape Colony, and by 1878 throughout the entire dominion of South Africa. The cause of this wholesale extermination was principally the shooting of the animal by the Boer farmers for its hide, which was made into shoes, meal sacks, leather belting, and every other possible commodity. The meat was used as food for the Hottentot and other native servants of the Boers. In captivity, the last living quagga—an aged mare—died in the zoological garden at Amsterdam in 1883.

While many mammalogists have regarded the quagga as merely a partially-striped zebra of the Burchell's group, others have maintained that it is a distinct species, differing not only in coloration but in cranial, dental, and skeletal makeup from the aforementioned type of zebra. The results of the writer's study contribute to the latter conclusion— namely, that *Equus quagga* was a semi-striped equid of distinctive external and skeletal characters, and not simply an extreme color-modification of *Equus burchelli.*

Previous authors, while in some cases going to great lengths to show minor cranial differences between the quagga and Burchell's zebra, have all neglected to point out a major difference: the respective body sizes of the two animals. Whereas the extinct Burchell's zebra stood on the average about 1240 mm (48.8 inches) in shoulder height, the typical quagga—which occupied much of the same territory as *E. burchelli burchelli*

Fig. 213 Edwards's quagga, from a stone lithograph made in 1751 and reproduced in color in Edwards's *Gleanings of Natural History* (1758).

Fig. 214 Daniell's quagga, from Daniell's *African Scenery* (1804–1808), No. 15.

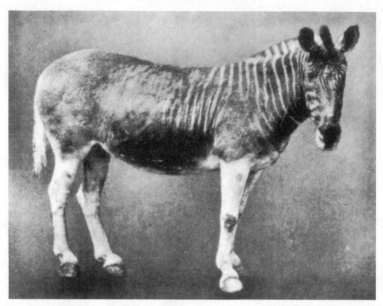

Fig. 215 A rare picture of the female quagga in the London Zoo (1851–1872). This quagga was possibly the only one ever to have been photographed during life.

Fig. 216 Another photograph, taken by F. York in 1872, of the same quagga shown above.

—averaged only 1165 mm (45.9 inches) in the same dimension. The only existing Burchelline forms of such relatively small size are Grant's zebra (1165 mm) and Cuninghame's zebra (1155 mm). However, these two forms exhibit a maximum differentiation in coat-color from the sparsely striped quagga, as well as in certain skeletal differences characteristic also of the larger Burchell's zebras.

Externally, the quagga was a handsomely-colored, zebra-like animal, the stripes of which, as a rule, covered only the head, neck, shoulders, and fore part of the trunk. The hind half of the body and the legs (both fore and hind) were in most individuals free of stripings. The usual ground color of the striped parts was yellowish-red or chestnut. Downwardly this color gradually faded, becoming pale fawn or white on the belly, legs, and tail. Along the middle of the back was the dark stripe (in this species quite broad) common to so many of the Equidae. The mane was dark brown with fawn bands, although in stuffed specimens the latter color faded to white and the mane lost its upright, "trimmed" appearance. Renshaw (1904) in this connection remarks:

> Careful examination of several museum specimens has . . . convinced me that the mane of the female quagga was longer than that of the male.[36]

The tail of the quagga is described by early travelers (who saw the animal in the flesh) as being long (reaching the hocks), white, wavy, and much more horselike than that of the Burchelline zebras.

The name quagga comes from the Hottentot words *khoua khoua* (or Quahkah), and refers to the animal's barking cry. Evidently the cry, or neigh, was identical with that of Burchell's zebra. By the Boers it was pronounced *kway-hay'* (*not* kwagger, or kwog'-ah), the last syllable being much prolonged.

In its geographic distribution the true quagga never had a very wide range. During its period of greatest abundance historically, it was to be found from the central plains of Cape Hope to and over much of the veldt of the Orange Free State, its northern limit being probably the Vaal River, its western limit a line running from the mouth of the Vaal River toward Swellendam, its southern limit the shoreline of Cape Colony, and its eastern limit the Kei River. This is only a small fraction of the extent of the present range of *E. burchelli antiquorum* (see map, Fig. 187).

The first mention of the quagga in modern times appears to have been that made by G. Tachard in 1685. He called the animal "wilde esel" (wild ass), but described it in such fanciful terms that his account is useless for zoological purposes. Probably the first reputable description of the quagga was that made by George Edwards (1758), who showed a colored plate of a quagga mare, which he erroneously supposed to be the female of the mountain zebra (*Equus zebra*).[37] Edwards's curious illustration is reproduced here in Fig. 213. A few years later, the first authentic, detailed account of the quagga was published by a Dr. Allamand from notes received from Col. Gordon of South Africa. This account was reprinted by the French naturalist Buffon in 1782. Toward the year 1800, a Dr. Sparrman corrected Edwards's idea that the quagga was the female of the mountain zebra. He went on to say further, in his book of travels, that the quagga was highly valued by the colonists because it would protect their sheep from the attacks of wild dogs and hyenas. On this point, Renshaw (1904) comments:

> *If the old stories are true,* the quagga showed a high degree of courage in facing animals (Cape hunting dogs, D.P.W.) able to conquer the lion. Bay horses, however, are noted usually for their spirit, and this tint entered largely into the coloration of the quagga![38]

Fig. 217 The stuffed skin of the male quagga (*Equus quagga greyi*) that had lived in the London Zoo (Regent's Park) from 1858 to 1864. This skin, and the skull and skeleton, are in the British Museum. Many such an early example of taxidermy gave a poor idea of how the animal looked in life.

In its natural environment, the veldt, the quagga seemed to prefer the company of black wildebeests (white-tailed gnus), ostriches, and sometimes hartebeests and sassabies. In this respect it differed from the Burchell's zebras, which associated habitually with the brindled gnu or common wildebeest. Moreover, it is said that the quaggas did not mingle with the herds of Burchell's zebras, but remained in separate groups.

Two of the most interesting specimens of living quaggas were the male and the female which once lived contemporaneously in the Regent's Park Zoo in London. As there has been much confusion attending the identities of these two quaggas—which were among the last living representatives of their race—the writer should like here to clear up some of the errors involving dates, animals, and final disposition of skins and skeletons. In 1858, Sir George Grey presented to the Zoological Society of London a male quagga. This animal lived in Regent's Park until June, 1864, when, "by breaking down some boarding," it injured itself so severely that it had to be killed. The skull and skeleton of this quagga are in the British Museum (No. 64.7.2.3.), as is also the prepared skin. Evidently this animal was quite young when Sir George presented it to the zoo, as from its teeth as examined in the preserved skull it was probably not over eight years of age at the time of its death.

Fig. 218 *Quagga Foal:* This photograph, although of a poorly prepared specimen, depicts probably the only mounted quagga foal in existence. This specimen, which came from Beaufort West, Cape of Good Hope, about 1860, has long been on display in the South African Museum, Cape Town. Note the thick, soft hair-coat and the restricting of the body stripes to the head, neck, and shoulders. G. C. Shortridge, who has personally examined this supposed quagga foal, says there is no special history concerning it, and believes that it may be rather a hybrid between a quagga or mountain zebra and a horse, owing to the absence of a mid-dorsal line, which is present in the foals of zebras, and usually indicated even in donkey foals. This unique specimen was taken from the Museum to the grounds outside and photographed especially for the writer.

The second Regent's Park quagga here under discussion, a female, was purchased by the Zoological Society on March 15, 1851 and died on July 7, 1872. It was noteworthy on account of having been photographed in life, two different pictures having been taken in the summer of 1872 by Mr. Frederick York. These two invaluable photographs are herein reproduced (Figs. 215 and 216). Another photograph—the sole other one of a living quagga—was taken of this London Zoo female specimen in 1870 by a Mr. Frank Haes.* After death, the skin of the animal, being said to be in "bad" condition, was lost track of. The skeleton, however, *was* preserved; although no one, evidently, knew where it was until it was "rediscovered" by the present writer in March, 1952. The story about this long-lost quagga skeleton is as follows.

After the animal died, in 1872, the body was sold to a taxidermist named Edward Gerrard, of London. Gerrard evidently disposed of the skin, but prepared the skeleton for mounting. In a letter dated April 14, 1873, sent to the American paleontologist, O.

---

* This photograph is reproduced by Antonius (1931, p. 99, and 1951, p. 135).

C. Marsh, Gerrard offered the quagga skeleton for £10-0-0. This offer was promptly accepted by Marsh, who presented the skeleton to the Peabody Museum of Natural History of Yale University (specimen No. 1623). This skeleton (including the skull) was measured in 1952 by the writer, through the courtesy of Dr. Joseph T. Gregory, Curator of the Peabody Museum. Since the skeleton was of an *aged female* quagga, which was known to have been purchased by Prof. Marsh from Edward Gerrard (who bought it in 1872 from the Zoological Society of London), it answers at long last the 80-year-old mystery of the missing female quagga photographed by York. It has been stated by many different authors that the latter photographs represent the last living quagga. This, however, is an error. Perhaps what was meant was the last quagga to have been *photographed*. The last living quagga was another female, that lived in the zoological garden at Amsterdam from May 9, 1867 to August 12, 1883. The skull and the prepared skin of this quagga are in the Amsterdam Museum. One other quagga, too, survived the London female; this was the female in the Berlin Zoo, which lived

Fig. 219 Mounted skins of various individual quaggas indicate that in coloration this species, as in Burchell's zebra, was widely variable. Some individuals were strongly striped only on the neck, while in others, as in the above specimen, distinct striping extended as far back as the hip. The above individual, a four-year-old stallion, was obtained by the Senckenberg Museum of Frankfurt in 1831, through exchange with the Leyden (Holland) Museum. It is one of the best-mounted specimens in existence and shows, probably very closely, how this interesting animal appeared in life.

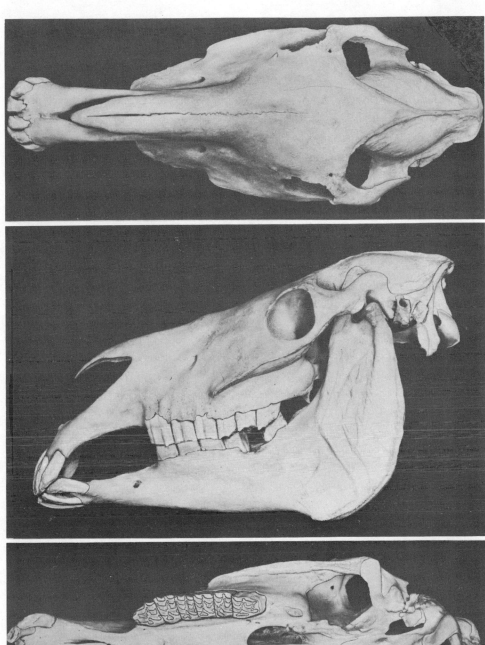

Fig. 220 Superior, lateral, and inferior views, respectively, of the skull of an aged female quagga which had lived in the London Zoo from 1851 to 1872. In all probability, the skeletal remains of this quagga, which were "lost" to science since 1873, were those "discovered" by the author in 1952 in the Peabody Museum of Natural History, Yale University (no. 1623). The cheek-tooth patterns have been gone over with India ink, for greater clarity. All figures approximately x .24

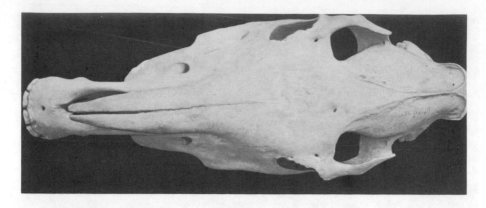

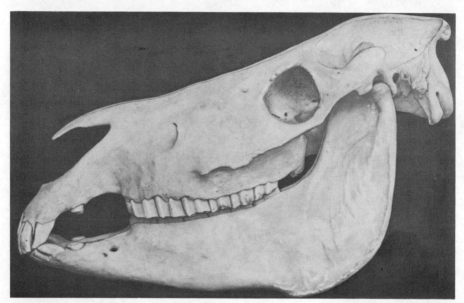

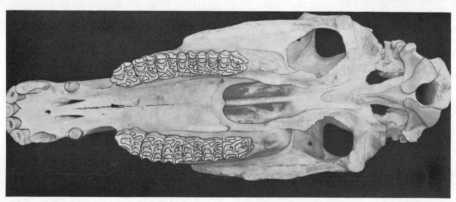

Fig. 221 Superior, lateral, and inferior views, respectively, of the skull of an adult male quagga (*E. quagga* greyi) which died in the London Zoo in 1864. The living animal was presented to the London Zoological Society by Sir George Grey in 1858. The stuffed skin and the postcranial skeleton, as well as the skull, are in the British Museum (Natural History). These three photographs of the skull were made especially for the author, who here acknowledges his gratitude. All figures approx. x .25

until 1875. Photographs of the skulls of the two London quaggas are reproduced here in Figs. 220 and 221.

Of the remains of the quagga in existence, the number of specimens and their respective locations appear to be fairly well established. Renshaw (1904)[39] lists 25 specimens, consisting variously of skulls, skeletons, and mounted skins. These specimens are located principally in museums in England and central Europe. Ridgeway (1909)[40] figures and describes 12 of the 25 quagga examples cited by Renshaw, and introduces two more. Rzasnicki (1949)[41] lists most of the specimens named by Renshaw and Ridgeway, respectively, and to these adds six other skins. To all the foregoing quagga specimens may be added these:

1. Stuttgart, Germany, Museum of Natural History. The skull and certain leg and foot bones of a four-year-old male quagga. Figured by Hilzheimer (1912).[42]
2. Leiden. Dutch State Museum of Natural History. The skull and foot bones of an immature quagga, about 1½ years old. Hilzheimer (1912).
3. Transvaal Museum, Pretoria, South Africa. The skull of a female, about ten years old. Lundholm (1951).[43]
4. Bloemfontein Museum, South Africa. The skin of an adult quagga. Fitzsimons (1920).[44]
5. Peabody Museum, Yale University (Cat. No. 1623). The complete skull and skeleton, in all probability of the aged female quagga that died in the London Zoo in 1872. Measured by the writer in 1952. For skull, see Fig. 220.

The identification of the latter specimen is of particular significance, since by certain authorities on the quagga (notably Hilzheimer, 1912) the living specimen to which the skeleton belonged was considered as the *type* of *Equus quagga* sp. By Hilzheimer, four other subspecies of the quagga were recognized, namely:

2. *E. quagga lorenzi* (Vienna Museum);
3. *E. quagga greyi* (British Museum);
4. *E. quagga danielli* (see Fig. 214);
5. *E. quagga trouessarti* (Turin Museum).

To the five presumed subspecies of the quagga just cited may be added another: *E. quagga isabellinus,* as proposed by Hamilton Smith in 1841 (see Table 27). However, other investigators, including the present writer, believe that there was only *one* species of the Cape quagga, the supposed various races being merely examples of a highly variable coat-pattern, comparable to those in the Burchelline zebras *E. burchelli böhmi* and *E. burchelli antiquorum,* for instance.

Harper (1945)[45] gives a list of 19 examples of quagga remains taken from the lists of Ridgeway (1909) and Hilzheimer (1912). Also, on pp. 334–337, he gives one of the best general descriptions of this animal.

A review of the foregoing lists gives a grand total of 22 skins (4 male, 10 female, and 8 of unspecified sex); 10 more or less complete postcranial skeletons (4 male, 3 female, and 3 of unspecified sex); 4 partial skeletons; 13 skulls (including those accompanied by postcranial skeletons) of 6 males, 6 females, and one immature specimen; 2 skins of foals (one mounted); one skin of a fetus; and one mounted head and neck. How many of these specimens may have been destroyed in World War II (with the exception of two skulls in the Royal College of Surgeons' Museum, London,* which

---

* These two quagga skulls, along with hundreds of other osteological specimens, were destroyed in the May, 1941 bombing of London.

have already been deducted), the writer does not know.

As mentioned previously, much discussion has waged among interested zoologists as to whether the Cape quagga should be regarded as a distinct species of wild equine or merely a partially-striped local variety or subspecies of Burchell's zebra. Perhaps the most prominent defender of the latter point of view was Reginald Innes Pocock, who expressed his opinion to that effect in 1902. Pocock's conclusions were shared by many other eminent naturalists of his day, including J. Cossar Ewart, William Ridgeway, and the famous English big-game hunter, Frederick Courtenay Selous.

On the other hand, Graham Renshaw as early as 1904 pointed out that the true or Cape quagga differed from Burchell's zebra not only in coat-pattern, but also in certain aspects of its cranial and postcranial structure. Renshaw's judgment in this respect has been strengthened by the independent studies of Hilzheimer (1912),[42] Schwarz (1912),[46] Cabrera (1936),[23] Cooke (1943),[47] and Lundholm (1951).[43] The writer has found a number of significant skeletal differences between the quagga and even the most closely allied of the races included in the Burchell's zebra group. Some of these differences are as follows: in the skull, (1) the occiput is less projecting posteriorly than in *burchelli;* (2) the cranial length of the skull as compared with the palatal length is markedly shorter; (3) the dental index is greater; (4) the ratio of palate-to-vomer length to upper dental series length in *burchelli* averages 73.8, whereas in *quagga* it is only 65.5; (5) the diastema length relative to the upper dental series length also is shorter in the quagga. (For the locations of the foregoing cranial measurements, see Fig. 25).

The principal differences in the long bones of *E. quagga* as compared with those of *E. burchelli* are, in the former: a very short humerus, a somewhat long femur, and long phalanges (large hoofs). Additional differences are indicated in the tables of skeletal dimensions and proportions (Tables 31 and 32).

While—as may be said also of other closely related members of the genus *Equus*—no *pronounced* differences between *E. quagga* and *E. burchelli* sp. exist in the postcranial skeleton, a careful consideration of the differences that *do* exist, along with those that occur in the cranium and the dentition (as well as the known *external* differences already mentioned), indicate that *E. quagga* was more likely a true, distinct species of semi-striped zebroid than, conversely, an extreme color-variant of *E. burchelli.* That, at least, will be the conclusion of the writer, unless and until further information to the contrary may appear.

Even during recent years there have been occasional reports of living quaggas being rediscovered in some of the less-travelled parts of South Africa. (See, for example, *A quagga chase in South-west Africa,* by Bernard Carp, *African Wild Life,* Johannesburg, vol. 6, no. 2 (June 1952): pp. 101–05). In most of such cases to date, the presumed "quaggas" have turned out to be zebras of the subspecies known as Hartmann's, which, as previously described, is a large form of the mountain zebra and which lives in precipitous surroundings that were rarely if ever visited by the veldt-dwelling Cape quagga. The latter animal is definitely gone forever; and, unlike the tarpan, or wild horse of Europe, or the aurochs, or wild ox—both species of which have assertedly been re-created by "back-breeding"—the quagga cannot be so re-created, since it has left no living descendants. A special interest attaches to the cranial and skeletal proportions of the quagga, which in some respects suggests affinity with various of the Pleistocene Equidae, both in North America and in Europe.

Let us conclude this sad chronicle of extermination with these lines from the South

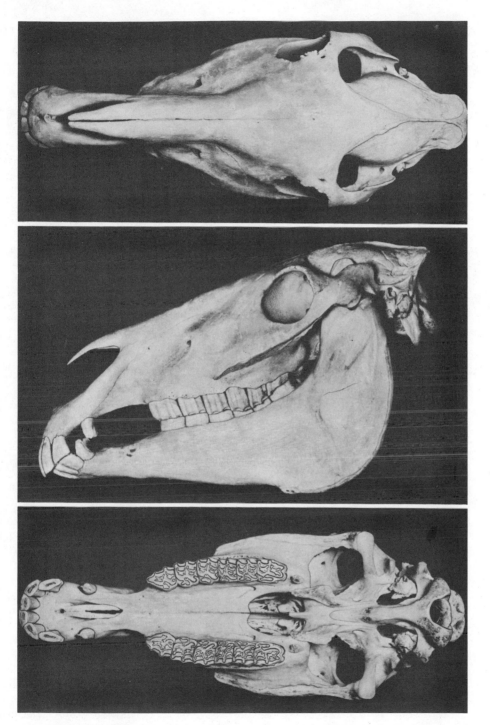

Fig. 222 Superior, lateral, and inferior views, respectively, of the skulls of a male quagga, of about 9 years of age, which was presented to the Academy of Natural Sciences, Philadelphia, by E. D. Cope. The skull is no. 6317.

African poet, Thomas Pringle, who saw the quagga in its days of abundance and who wrote:

> Afar in the desert I love to ride,
> With the silent bushboy alone by my side;
> O'er the brown Karroo, where the bleating cry
> Of the springbok's fawn sounds plaintively,
> And the timorous quagga's shrill whistling neigh,
> Is heard by the fountain at twilight grey,
> Where the zebra wantonly tosses his mane,
> With wild hoof scouring the desolate plain.

The osteometric material on the quagga used by the writer has consisted of 8 postcranial skeletons and 12 skulls (some of which went with the skeletons). It is fortunate indeed that the measurements of some of these specimens appeared in published form before the specimens themselves were bombed out of existence.

Fig. 223 A mountain zebra stallion that had been broken to the saddle. Mrs. M. H. Hayes up.

Before concluding our review of living and/or recently extinct zebras, it may be of interest to mention some of the attempts that have been made to break these wild and seemingly untameable equine animals to harness.

It will be noted that one of our illustrations (Fig. 212) shows a team of zebras drawing a stagecoach in South Africa. But it will be noted also that the team is being *led* by a pair of mules, and that each of the four zebras is teamed with a donkey. It would appear safe to conclude from this that an eight- or ten-horse team made up of zebras alone would be difficult to control, or at least be so much of a bother as to render such a team impracticable. Later experiments along this line showed indeed that while zebras are immune to the tsetse-fly and to African "horse sickness," they do not possess the stamina of the horse, the mule, or the donkey, so far as being used as beasts of burden is concerned. In any case, just as the first experiments in so using zebras were getting under way, the auto came into increasing use, with the result that *all* transportation in the localities to which the zebra is native gradually turned from horses, oxen, and camels to power-driven vehicles.

Nevertheless, zebras *can* be tamed, if not domesticated, and can even be broken to the saddle. In this connection it has been found that the ass-like mountain zebra is much wilder and more intractable to handle than the more horselike Burchell's zebra. Yet nearly 200 years ago, in Philip Astley's Circus, there were mountain zebras tame enough to be let loose in the ring. On the other hand, Captain M. H. Hayes, the well-known authority on hippology, was unable upon inquiry to find a single instance, in Cape Colony, where a mountain zebra had been *ridden*. Whereupon he was justifiably proud of having been able, within the short space of two days, to break in an old stallion to the stage where his wife could ride on his back (see Fig. 223).

Speaking of the taming of horses, zebras, et al, a few words should perhaps be said about a man who evidently was the greatest of all horse-tamers. This was John Solomon Rarey, a young Ohio farmer who claimed that he could take any horse, no matter how wild or savage, and within three hours at the most make him gentle as a lamb. In 1858 Rarey visited England, where word of his unprecedented successes with broncos and other "untamable" horses had preceded him. At a command performance for Queen Victoria, Rarey within less than an hour subdued and gentled three vicious and unbroken stallions that had been condemned to die. In each case he had entered the horse's stall and locked himself in it until he had gained the animal's confidence and gentled its behavior. While Rarey did not reveal his training methods, he claimed that kindness, firmness and patience were the essentials, and that anything else was brutal, inhumane, and ineffective. Before returning to the United States, Rarey visited France, Sweden, Germany, Egypt, and Russia, and in each country received the highest bestowable honors for his demonstrations. Ill-health caused this supremely capable animal trainer to die at the age of 38, but his teachings lived on.

f. Western quagga (*Equus* [*Quaggoides*] *occidentalis* Leidy, 1865).

During the early 1900s, large quantities of fossilized bones were exhumed from the tar-pits of Rancho La Brea, in the western section of Los Angeles. Prominent among these remains were bones of the dire wolf (*Canis dirus*), the saber-toothed cat (*Smilodon californicus*), and the western Pleistocene "horse" (*Equus occidentalis*), which, as will be shown, was in all probability a giant form of Burchell's zebra or of the quagga.

The exhumed bones, after being thoroughly freed of asphalt, were segregated as to species, and as to what particular part of the skeleton they represented, and were then filed more or less systematically in two places—the Los Angeles County Museum of Natural History, and the Paleontological Museum of the University of California at Berkeley.

The skulls and limb bones of *Equus occidentalis* in the latter collection were measured by the writer's mentor, Dr. Chester Stock, while he was a student at the University during the years *c*. 1909–1920. Dr. Stock, in turn, was a student of the paleontologist Dr. John C. Merriam, who had much to do with the early exploration of the tar-pits at Rancho La Brea. The bones of *E. occidentalis* in the Los Angeles County Museum, which in general were more numerous than those at Berkeley,* were measured by the writer during the years 1940–1953 at the California Institute of Technology in Pasadena, where Dr. Stock was Professor of Paleontology (and, concurrently, Director of Science at the Los Angeles County Museum). At the same time the writer was measuring the skulls and postcranial bones of *E. occidentalis,* he was measuring also these elements in various species of existing Equidae, the skeletons of which were loaned for the purpose by natural history museums throughout the United States.

The subgeneric identity of *E. occidentalis* with members of the existing Burchell's zebras and with the recently extinct quagga is clearly depicted in Fig. 224, which shows that *E. occidentalis* in its skeletal conformation corresponds with remarkable closeness to the other Burchelline zebras and the quagga in all 20 limb-bone indices. The horizontal line (zero-zero) on the chart shows the proportionate averages of these indices in the domestic horse, *E. caballus caballus.* The probability of this correspondence —of *E. occidentalis* with the Burchelline group—being due to chance is infinitesimally small.

Equus occidentalis, of the tar-pits of Rancho La Brea, is thus shown to have been a large form of *E. [Quaggoides] burchelli* or *E. [Quaggoides] quagga.* From the lengths of its limb bones, it can be computed that *occidentalis* stood on the average about 1461 mm (57.5 inches) high at the shoulder; and since the animal was rather heavily built, it probably weighed on the average about 1150 pounds. Details of the measurements of its skull, dentition, and postcranial skeleton are given in the Appendix. Fig. 248 shows the body outline, with measurements.

Several Carbon-14 datings obtained by the writer indicate that the Western quagga flourished on the grassy plains of what was to become Southern California some 13,000 to 16,000 years ago, or shortly (relatively speaking) before the final recession of the Pleistocene ice-sheet. A very slightly smaller subspecies was recovered from the asphalt deposits of McKittrick, California (about 120 miles northwest of Los Angeles), but the bones indicate virtual identity with the La Brea form. Just how widely *E. occidentalis* ranged is not known. For some remarks on the possible derivation and phylogenetic affinities of this species, see the Appendix.

Notes and References

1. Edward Oustalet, *Equus grévyi.* (*La Nature,* Paris, Vol. 19, No. 2, 1882), p. 12.

2. Edmund Heller, *New Genera and Races of African Ungulates.* (Smithsonian Misc. Coll., Vol. 60, No. 8, 1912), pp. 1–16.

3. R. I. Pocock, In: *Harmsworth Natural History.* (London: Carmelite House, 1910, Vol. 2), p. 791.

4. G. Renshaw, *Natural History Essays.* (London: Sherratt & Hughes, 1904), p. 162.

---

* The Rancho La Brea material studied by the writer has consisted of 26 adult skulls, numerous cheek teeth, and hundreds of separate limb bones, the latter being equivalent to 28 complete skeletons. Of the McKittrick remains (see above) several skulls and 10 sets of limb bones were measured. This skeletal material, in the aggregate, was probably the most extensive ever brought together for the study of a single, fossil species of *Equus.* As all existing mounted skeletons of *E. occidentalis* are composite specimens, made up from unrecorded numbers of individuals, no *type* specimen—outside of Leidy's single upper third premolar tooth from Tuolumne, California —is extant. The latter tooth is in the collection of the Museum of Comparative Zoology of Harvard University.

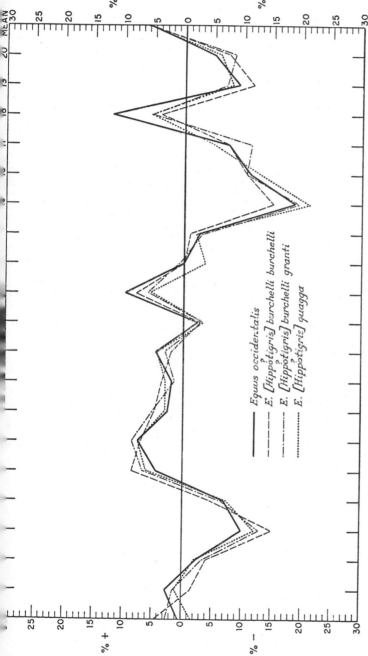

Fig. 224 It would be difficult to present a more conclusive demonstration than this of the *subgeneric identity* of *Equus occidentalis* Leidy with members of the existing and/or recently extinct *quagga-burchelli* group of striped Equidae. However, to differentiate the *Asinus*-type zebras from the *quagga-burchelli* type, if the subgeneric name *Hippotigris* be used for the former, the name *Quaggoides* should be applied to the latter. In that event, all the above forms (those charted on the graph) should have the subgeneric name *Quaggoides* rather than *Hippotigris*. The proper designation of the so-called tar-pit "horse" of Rancho La Brea should then be *Equus [Quaggoides] occidentalis*.

The final or mean Index Number (No. 21) is always on the *plus* side, due to all negative deviations having been recorded as positive before averaging.

5. Theodore Roosevelt and Edmund Heller, *Life Histories of African Game Animals.* (New York, 1914, Vol. 2), pp. 698–700.

6. Paul O. McGrew, *An Early Pleistocene (Blancan) Fauna from Nebraska.* (Pub. 546, Geol. Ser., Field Mus. Nat. Hist., Vol. 9, No. 2, 1944), pp. 33–36. Footnote, p. 63.

7. Edmund Heller, *New Genera and Races of African Ungulates,* p. 3.

8. D. S. Sorrell, *Wild life in Southern Ethiopia.* (*Oryx,* Vol. 1, No. 6, August 1952), p. 285.

9. P. L. Sclater, *The Fauna of South Africa* (2 vols.) (London: 1900, Vol. 1), p. 294.

10. Prince Philip, Duke of Edinburgh, and James Fisher. *Wildlife Crisis.* (New York: Cowles, 1970), p. 242.

11. R. I. Pocock, *Harmsworth Natural History,* p. 790.

12. Richard Lydekker, *The Horse and Its Relatives.* (London: George Allen & Co., 1912), pp. 211–212.

13. Col. Hamilton Smith, *Horses. Jardine's Naturalist's Library,* Vol. 20. (London: 1866), p. 325.

14. P. L. Sclater.

15. F. W. Fitzsimons, *The Natural History of South Africa* (4 vols). (London: 1920, Vol. 3), pp. 183–184.

16. W. B. Tegetmeier and C. L. Sutherland, *Horses, Asses, Zebras, Mules, and Mule Breeding.* (London: Horace Cox, 1995), p. 49.

17. William Ridgeway, *Contributions to the Study of the Equidae.* i: *The Differentiation of the Three Species of Zebras.* (Proc. Zool. Soc. London, 1909), p. 557.

18. Otto Antonius, *Zur Geograph. Verbreitung des Burchell-Zebras und des echten Quaggas.* (Zool. Garten, N.F., 8, 1935).

19. —— Bigalke, (The range of Hartmann's mountain zebra). (Mammalia, Paris, Vol. 22, 1958), p. 487.

20. G. Blaine, *Notes on the Zebras and Some Antelopes of Angola.* (Proc. Zool. Soc. London, 1922), pp. 330–333.

21. G. C. Shortridge, *The Mammals of South West Africa* (2 vols). (London: Vol. 1, 1934), p. 390. (See also: *Hartmann's Mountain Zebra.* Jour. Soc. Preservation Fauna Empire, N.S., Part 22, 1934), pp. 13–15.

22. G. Blaine, *Notes on the Zebras and Some Antelopes of Angola.*

23. Angel Cabrera, *Subspecific and Individual Variation in the Burchell Zebras.* (Jour. Mammalogy, Vol. 17, No. 2, May 14, 1936), pp. 89–112. (Perhaps the best single review of this species.)

24. Paul Matschie, *Die Afrikanische Wildpferden, als Vertreter zoographischer Subregionen.* (Zool. Garten, Vol. 35, 1894), p. 33.

25. P. L. Sclater, *Horses.*

26. Angel Cabrera, *Subspecific and Individual Variation in the Burchell Zebras,* pp. 108–109.

27. T. E. Buckley, *On the Past and Present Geographical Distribution of the Large Mammals of South Africa.* (Proc. Zool. Soc. London, 1876), p. 277.

28. *Ibid.*

29. Theodore Roosevelt and Edmund Heller, p. 693.

30. Allen Keast, *Interrelationships of Two Zebra Species in an Overlap Zone.* (Jour. Mammalogy, Vol. 46, No. 1, February 1965), pp. 53–66.

31. D. R. M. Stewart and L. M. Talbot, *Census of Wildlife on the Serengeti, Mara and Locka Plains.* East Afr. Agric. & Farm. Jou.r, Vol. 28, 1962), pp. 58–60.

32. J. A. Allen, *Mammals from British East Africa, Collected by the Tjader Expedition of 1906.* (Bull. Amer. Mus. Nat. Hist., Vol. 26, 1909), p. 160.

33. Jane St. Leger, *On Equus Quagga of Southwestern and Eastern Africa.* (Ann. Mag. Nat. Hist., London, Ser. 10, Vol. 10, 1932), p. 589.

34. A. Roberts, *The Mammals of South Africa.* (Johannesburg: 1951), p. 29.

35. W. C. Harris, *Portraits of the Game and Wild Animals of Southern Africa.* (London: 1840).

36. G. Renshaw, *Natural History Essays,* p. 176.

37. G. Edwards, *Gleanings of Natural History.* (London: 1758), p. 29.

38. G. Renshaw, *Natural History Essays,* p. 176.

39. *Ibid.,* pp. 182–194.

40. William Ridgeway, *Contributions to the Study of the Equidae.* ii: *On Hitherto Unrecorded Specimens of Equus Quagga.* (Proc. Zool. Soc. London, 1909), pp. 563–588.

41. A. Rzasnicki, *Complete List of Skeletons and Skins of Equus Quagga Quagga,* etc. (In Polish.) (Annals Musei Zoologici Polonici, Vol. 14, No. 5, 1949), pp. 69–73. (See also his paper on zebras and quaggas in the same journal, Vol. 14, No. 16, 1951), pp. 203–251.

42. Max Hilzheimer, *Die in Deutschland aufbewahrten Reste des Quaggas.* (Abh. Senckenberg Naturforsch. Gesellsch., Vol. 31, No. 2, 1912), pp. 83–105.

43. Bengt Lundholm, *A Skull of the True Quagga (Equus quagga) in the Collection of the Transvaal Museum.* (So. Afr. Jour. Sci., June 1951), pp. 307–312.

44. F. W. Fitzsimons, *The Natural History of South Africa.* (London: 1920, vol. 4), p. 179.

45. Francis Harper, *Extinct and Vanishing Mammals of the Old World.* (New York: 1945), pp. 337–339.

46. Ernst Schwarz, *Beitrage zur Kenntnis der Zebras.* (Arch. Naturg., Berlin, Vol. 78, Part A, No. 7, 1912), pp. 34–57.

47. H. B. S. Cooke, *Cranial and Dental Characters on the Recent South African Equidae.* (South African Jour. Sci., Vol. 40, 1943), pp. 254–257.

16
The Mule and Other Equine Hybrids

a. The domestic mule.

"Without pride of ancestry or hope of posterity." This characterization of the mule was first made in the 1890s by Ignatius Donnelly, when he likened the Democratic Party to that much-maligned creature. Since then the phrase has been repeated in practically every article dealing with the mule, and almost always with the approval of the author. In a recent survey of the animal, however, Theodore Savory[1] points out that the phrase is both unfair and inaccurate. The care with which the mule-breeder chooses both parent-animals affords the offspring a merited pride of ancestry; and while male mules are, it is true, sterile, females can and do occasionally produce foals and so have a "hope of posterity." Actually, up until the general replacement of work animals by machines, few hybrid animals have been economically more valuable or biologically more interesting than the mule.

The origin of the mule, so far as the practice of breeding it is concerned, dates back at least 3000 years, and probably much earlier. Mules were used in the Bible lands earlier than 1000 B.C., and in those times replaced the donkey as the royal beast. As the Israelites were prohibited from breeding their own mules (Leviticus 19:19), they imported them from Armenia and other Near-East sources. About the same time, mules were bred in Greece, where they were widely used as draft animals and in farming. Homer, in *The Iliad*, mentions that these hybrid animals originally came from Henetia, in the Black Sea region of Asia Minor. Mules were even used in chariot racing in the Olympic Games, beginning about 500 B.C., and continuing through at least a dozen Olympiads.

The Greek word for mule was *hemionus*, meaning "half-ass"; and from this term has come the scientific designation of the equine animals described here in Chapter 14. The Greeks called a female donkey *muchlos*, from which came the Latin *mulus*, the Old French *mul*, and the English mule. In addition to the term *hemionus*, the Greeks gave another name, *oreos* or *oureos* ("the mountain animal"), to such mules as were used to carry loads of wood from the mountains to the plains.

Although most mules are bred by crossing a male donkey, or jack, and a female horse, the converse can also be done, in which case the offspring (a cross between a *female* donkey, or jennet, and a male horse, or stallion) is called a hinny. The latter word comes from the Latin *hinnus*, which in turn was derived from the Greek *hinnos*, or *ginos*. The term "mule," however, has come to be used also for various other hybrids, for example a "mule-canary."[2]

Fig. 225 The mule, as represented in a 2400-year-old Grecian vase, found in 1930 at Agrigentum (now Girgenti) Sicily. The rare plaster vase, which was made sometime between 510–500 B.C., is in the collection of the Italian National Museum, at Palermo.

Later history contains many references to the mule. Marco Polo, in his famed *Travels,* praised the Turkoman mules he saw in central Asia. In the 1700s, mule-breeding was an extensive industry in Italy, Spain, and France. In the latter country alone, in the province of Poitou, some 50,000 mules were bred yearly. Two types of Poitou mules, the light and the heavy, were produced, but the heavy type was in greater favor, since they were more economical as draft animals. Male mules are called in French *le mulet,* and females, *la mule.* The hinny is there known as *le bardot.*

In England the mule was not bred to any appreciable extent until the late 1700s. In the United States there were mules at the Spanish settlements in Florida and New Mexico before 1625, and it was not long before the Indians of those areas learned the

Fig. 226 Attendants leading a mule, laden with nets, on one of the hunts made by Ashurbanipal, King of Assyria. Note the disproportions of the head and neck of the animal, the same as those of the Assyrian horse shown in Fig. 55.

procedure of mule-breeding. However, it was not until after the Revolution that the breeding of mules was conducted on a large scale in the Colonies. In 1786 General George Washington received as a gift from the King of Spain a jack and a jennet, of the Andalusian breed, and later a Maltese jack from the Marquis de Lafayette. On Tuesday, March 11, 1788, the two jacks were advertised by Washington for public service, although one, the large Andalusian, had sired a number of jacks, jennets, and mules the previous season.

A large number of jacks and jennets were subsequently imported from Spain and France, these being mainly of the breeds known as Andalusian, Maltese, Catalonian, Majorcan, and Poitou, respectively. The first important and valuable importation was that made by Henry Clay in 1827. The census tables of 1850–1860 showed that the number of mules produced had "increased in a greater ratio than those of any other kind of farm stock," and that during that decade the total number of mules had more than doubled.[3] The mule population in the United States increased until 1925 (ten years after horses had begun to decline), when it reached a peak of 5,918,000 animals. The number of mules decreased proportionately less than that of horses because of their continued extensive use in the Southern states, where labor was cheaper and more available and the farms smaller in size.[4]

During World War II, mules became known as "Jungle jeeps" because of their usefulness in transporting weapons and supplies on the island battlegrounds of the Pacific. Such trained Army mules are calm under fire and bombing. The only thing that frightens a mule in the jungle is an elephant, and the elephant is likewise terrified of the mule. In their encounters, both animals run away at top speed, filling the air with their braying and trumpeting.

It has come to be generally accepted that the mule resembles its male (donkey) parent in all its extremities; that is, in ears, legs, feet, and tail. In a comparison of the proportions of some of the limb bones of the skeleton, as made by the writer, it was found that (1) the scapula of the mule was practically identical to that of the horse; (2) the humerus only slightly less so; (3) the radius, phalanges, and tibia about midway between horse and ass; (4) the metacarpus, near horse; (5) the femur even shorter, relatively, than in the ass (which has a relatively shorter femur than the horse); (6) the metatarsus somewhat nearer to ass than to horse. While in many respects the mule resembles the ass more than the horse (e.g., in its cowlike tail, narrow hoofs, long ears, whitish muzzle, white ring around the eye; and in its disposition, surefootedness, bray, dislike of water, etc.), yet in a mule bred for draft use—its principal purpose—it is said, "The nearer the mule approaches the ideal desired in a draft *horse,* the more valuable he is from a market standpoint."[5]

In some respects the mule differs both from the horse and the ass. In body temperature, for example, the horse normally ranges from 99.5 to 100.4 degrees F., the ass from 99.5 to 101.3 degrees, and the mule from 100 to 102.2 degrees.

In point of size, in the mules bred in the United States there is great variation, ranging from small 48-inch-high mining mules, pack mules of 60 inches and cotton mules of 61-63 inches, to large draft mules standing 70 inches at the shoulder. In weight, the corresponding range is from 600 to 1600 pounds. The mean values of these figures are: height 58 inches, weight 965 pounds. In the conformation of its hindquarters the mule is often ass-like, having an angular, steeply sloping croup (seen from behind), too sloping hips (seen from the side), too narrow thighs, and sickle-shaped hind legs—all regarded as undesirable traits. Mule dealers therefore seek out such animals as have not inherited these defects of conformation.

The coloration of the mule is a uniform dark brown, sorrel, steel-grey, or black, without light markings on the face or feet, and without the white belly of the paternal parent, although some mules are completely "white" (i.e., light grey).

In its blood relationships, the mule appears to be somewhat less closely related to the horse than is the hinny, the mule being about 53 percent of the way from the donkey to the horse, and the hinny about 67 percent of the way.[6] Although far less frequently bred than mules, hinnies are long-lived animals, generally of marked stamina. A reason why hinnies are usually smaller than mules is because of the smallness of the dam, from which parent its size is inherited. The hinny has been bred more in Ireland than elsewhere, and owners of a first-class hinny are always well pleased with the animal.

Mules are bred for three principal purposes: pack work, draft work, and riding. As pack animals they probably reach their greatest efficiency. Mules for this purpose, standing usually from 52 to 58 inches high and weighing from 700 to 1000 pounds, can carry a total weight of 300–350 pounds and with it march 20 to 25 miles in a day. Draft mules are larger—64 to 70 inches and 1200 to 1600 pounds—and are (or have been) used principally for heavy teaming in the warmer states, although the largest animals often find their way to lumber camps. Market classes and sizes of work mules also include those listed as farm, suger, cotton, and mining.[7] Mules used for riding can be of whatever size is desired. The respective sizes of the mules used for these varied classes of work is determined by the sizes of the parent animals used

Fig. 227 **Mules drawing a cart in Seville. After a painting by Alex Wagner.**

for breeding them. Four Percheron dams, weighing from 1300 to 1900 pounds, gave birth to two female foals weighing 114 and 117 pounds, respectively, and to two male foals weighing 106 and 108 pounds. The weight of the jack (sire) is not given.[8]

Mules in general, as compared with horses, are credited with having greater strength in proportion to their size; more endurance; more activity and sure-footedness; a need for less food; better eyesight and hearing; a lesser susceptibility to disease; a greater tolerance of both heat and cold; and a greater instinct of self-preservation. "In

Fig. 228 A fine example of a Poitou mule; the mare "Brunette," height 65 inches.

short, he is possessed of more of the essentials of an ideal beast of burden than is any other animal."[9]

Much controversy has from time to time taken place regarding the possiblity of a female mule becoming pregnant. Since the earliest days of animal breeding it has been known that male mules are invariably infertile, and that couplings of mule and mule are fruitless. This is a genetic consequence of the incompatibility of the chromosomes. However, a female mule sometimes, once in some 200,000 cases, becomes pregnant from a stallion. During the eleven years from 1932 to 1943, there were five recorded mule foals (*Time,* Nov. 15, 1943, p. 88). In 1952 there was another, in Darwin, Australia, where stockmen regarded the occurrence with amazement. To date, there must have been at least a dozen such births. But among female hinnies, fertility is even rarer, possibly because there have been fewer hinnies to work with. And one reason for the lack of hinnies is because jennets are poor breeders, averaging only a 40 percent pregnancy, whereas horses average from 60 to 80 percent.

In the Bible there are numerous references to mules, early ones being in second Samuel (3: 29) and first Chronicles (12:40); but some of these references may have been to *onagers,* whom the ancients regarded as wild mules, rather than to horse–donkey hybrids.

NOTE: For an account of "miniature mules," see Chapter 17.

b. Other hybrid Equidae.

For the last 200 years, at least, attempts have been made to breed zebras with horses and donkeys. A considerable amount of such breeding was carried on, first

(in 1896) by Professor James Cossar Ewart and his staff, of the University of Edinburgh, and later by the Bureau of Animal Industry in Washington, D.C. More recently,
in the 1940s, a farmer named Raymond Hook, in Kenya, captured a young male
Grévy's zebra and raised it to adulthood along with his herd of domestic horses. When
the zebra had reached the age of six years, his matings with mares began to bear fruit,
in the form of very handsome hybrid offspring. Hook also bred hybrids between
donkeys and Burchell's zebras, in which case he found that where the sire was a
zebra the offspring had more stripes than where the sire was a donkey. It was found
also that where a Grévy's zebra stallion was mated with a mare, the hybrid foal grew
to a slightly larger size than the mare, whereas when a donkey stallion was mated

Fig. 229 Mountain zebra mare and her foal sired by a Somali wild ass. For
comments on markings, see text.

with a horse the resulting mule never attained the size of the mare. Armand Denis's
magazine, *Animals,* 1, no. 7 (1962 ?, n.d.), presents a number of photographs of
zebra x horse and zebra x donkey hybrids in full color, and the animals certainly appear
exotic and beautiful. A black-and-white photo of one of Raymond Hook's zebrules
appears in *The Book of the Horse* (Hamlyn, 1970, p. 9), where it is erroneously
referred to as a "Grévy zebra."

   Long before the aforementioned breedings, the first zebra hybrid on record would
appear to have been bred about 1776, by a Lord Clive, who mated a jackass and a
female mountain zebra. The first *series* of breedings was carried on in 1806, in Paris,
using zebras and donkeys. Later there came crosses between zebra mares and horses,
and, later still, hybrids between male zebras and ordinary mares. The famous animal-
dealer, Carl Hagenbeck, crossed a Shetland pony stallion with a mountain zebra mare.
The offspring was striped around the chest, on the belly to halfway up the sides, and

on the legs; the striping on the rear legs extended clear up to the croup. There was, however, little or no distinct striping on the rear half of the back and on the flanks. Fig. 229 shows another instance in which the dam was a mountain zebra, but the sire a Somali wild ass. As will be seen, the resulting foal has only a shoulder stripe on the body, while its legs are fairly well striped from the body down to the fetlocks. The foal's long ears appear to follow the color-pattern of its dam.

The Bureau of Animal Industry, in its hybrid-breedings, used principally a Grévy's zebra stallion. Attempts to mate this zebra with various mares were unsuccessful, and it was only after being with a female donkey, or jennet, almost daily for eight months that the zebra finally mated. After that, several matings with jennets occurred. Fig. 230 shows one of the Grévy's zebra x jennet hybrids. Otto Antonius, in his definitive monograph, *Die Tigerpferde,* pictures a number of equine hybrids, among them a beautiful foal from an Arab stallion and a Chapman's zebra mare.

Occasionally one reads in the newspapers where a "zebdonk," or a "zebronkey" has been born in some zoo. By such terms is meant a hybrid between a donkey stallion, or jack, and a zebra mare. But a better name for such an animal is zébret. In 1951, Professor Antonius (referred to above) proposed the following names for various horse-zebra-donkey hybrids:

Male zebra and female horse = zébrule
Male donkey and female zebra = zébret
Male zebra and female donkey = zébryde

It is interesting to note that while the usual gestation period of the horse is 337 days (see Chapter 11), and of the donkey 370 days, that of Grévy's zebra is about

Fig. 230 Hybrid zebra-donkey, or zébryde. This interestingly marked female is a cross between a Grévy's zebra stallion and a female donkey, or jennet.

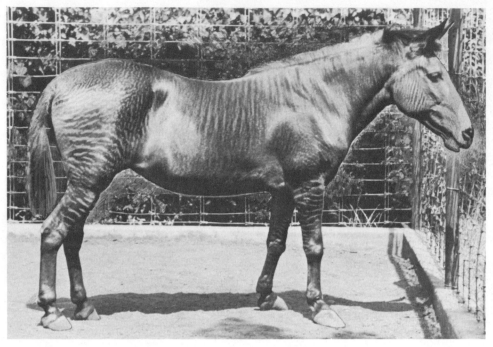

Fig. 231 Hybrid zebra-horse, or zébrule. This mare, Juno, was 31 years of age when this photograph was taken at the Washington, D.C., Zoo in 1943. She was the offspring of a Grévy's zebra stallion, "Jerry," and a Morgan mare, "Baby Gates." The zebra stripes appear as though filtered through a screen.

390 days, and of hybrids between Grévy's zebra and jennets about 378 days. Some investigators have suggested that a possible reason for the infertility of mules in general is the differing lengths of the gestation period in the species mated.

Through the courtesy of the Bureau of Animal Industry, the writer is able to show here a photograph of a second (a zebra x mare) hybrid. This interesting animal —a female named "Juno"—was a cross between the Grévy's stallion ("Jerry") mentioned above, and a Morgan mare ("Baby Gates"). "Juno" was born in 1912, and at the time the accompanying photograph was taken was 31 years of age. The diffused zebra stripings on "Juno" may represent a type, or types, of coloration that occurred in evolutionarily earlier species of the horse family. It should be borne in mind that in all primitive coat-patterns the ground coloration is the *darker,* not lighter, of the hues represented; and that a zebra's stripes are not black on white, but *white on black.* As regards the pattern of markings commonly seen in zebra x horse hybrids, Pocock (1911)[10] says: "The above-stated facts suggest that, with the possible exception of the ear-patch in horses, the shoulder and spinal stripes as well as the stripes on the legs have been lost *comparatively recently by the species that are without them.*" (The italics are mine, D.P.W.)

Whether it will ever be practicable to use zebra hybrids in Africa as pack animals has yet to be determined. Raymond Hook, mentioned above, attempted such use with some success, as the hybrids were much like mules and more tractable than zebras. However, if they were not watched closely, they were inclined to run away, and had in each case to be coupled with a trained horse. And although the zebroids are more sure-footed even than mules, it has not as yet been established whether they have the strength and stamina to be used as regular pack animals. Also, their full potential is not reached until they are about six years old.

Notes and References

1. Theodore H. Savory, *The Mule. (Sci. Amer.,* Vol. 223, No. 6, December 1970), pp. 102–109.

2. Richard Lydekker, *The Horse and Its Relatives.* (London: 1912), p. 226.

3. W. B. Tegetmeier and C. L. Sutherland, *Horses, Asses, Zebras, Mules, and Mule Breeding.* (London: 1895), p. 115.

4. M. E. Ensminger, Horses and Horsemanship. (Danville, Ill.: 1969), p. 24.

5. J. O. Williams and S. R. Speelman, *Mule Production.* (U.S. Dept. Agric. Farmer's Bull. No. 134, 1938), p. 14.

6. Alan Boyden, *The Blood Relationships of Animals. (Sci. Amer.,* July 1951), pp. 59–63.

7. Williams and Speelman, *op. cit.,* pp. 17–25.

8. H. H. Kibler and Samuel Brody, *Field Studies on . . . Mules.* (Res. Bull. 394, Univ. Missouri Coll. Agric., September 1945), p. 6.

9. *Jacks, Jennets, and Mules in the United States.* (Pub. No. 1, Standard Jack & Jennet Registry of America, Kansas City, Missouri). No date.

10. R. I. Pocock, (Remarks upon two hybrid zebra-wild ass foals). (Proc. Zool. Soc. London, 1911), pp. 988–994.

17

Anomalies of Size and Development in the Domestic Horse

a. Giants of the equine species.

In the year 1342 the emperor of China received as a gift from the Pope a German "war horse" (knight's charger) that was "11½ feet long and 6 feet 8 inches high." The Chinese people who saw the gigantic animal could scarcely believe their eyes. This historical incident shows that even during the Middle Ages some horses reached gigantic proportions. During more recent times a few even larger individuals have been exhibited in Europe and the United States.

One of the first of these publicly exhibited equines was "General Washington," who stood 6 feet 9 inches high and weighed 2800 pounds. He appeared, appropriately enough, in the days of the Revolution, and was owned by a Mr. Carter, who had raised the animal somewhere in the New England states.

Next, chronologically (so far as the writer's records go) was a horse named "Dr. Le Gear." The name was taken after the horse's owner, who was a manufacturer of health products for farm animals. The horse, a seal-brown, dappled Percheron, was foaled in 1902. At maturity he stood 7 feet tall, weighed 2995 pounds, and wore a 33-inch collar and a size 10 shoe. It was said also that the horse measured "16 feet from nose to tail." In that case the measuring must have been done over the curves of the head, neck and body, and down to the ends of the hairs of the tail. A 31-inch "arm" was also claimed, by which was probably meant girth of *forearm*. "Dr. Le Gear," the horse, died in 1919, in St. Louis. While in some accounts the horse was claimed as the tallest on record, there have since been claims to a similar height on behalf of at least two other giant horses, as follows.

About 1906, a horse named "Hiram," of Danbury, Connecticut, was said to be 7 feet tall and to weigh 3065 pounds. This animal was shown in a Ripley's "Believe It or Not" cartoon of January 21, 1936. "Hiram" was a light-grey gelding, possibly a Belgian.

Another horse of claimed 7-foot height was "Pat," a Suffolk stallion foaled about 1925 and exhibited by R. J. Conners of Phelps, New York, during the years 1934–1940, in which latter year the animal died. The statement that this horse measured "9 feet" (8 feet 9 inches?) to the top of its head in a normal standing position would seem to confirm its gigantic shoulder (withers) height. The weight of "Pat" was given as 2810 pounds.

Fig. 232 Giant and dwarf farm animals. From an old German engraving by H. Leutemann.

Two other horses of 2800 pounds and 6 feet 8 inches each were "Goliath," owned by Robert E. Jones of Pleasantville, New Jersey, and "Laddie," a Clydesdale foaled in 1963 and currently being exhibited by its owner, Bill Rieske, of Salt Lake City, Utah. "Laddie" wears a 36-inch collar; and each of his shoes, which measure 9½ inches wide by 10½ inches long, weighs 4½ pounds.

"Texas," a Belgian from Richardson, Texas, is said to stand 6 feet 8 inches and to weigh 3000 pounds. If so, he may be the largest horse in the world today.

Fig. 233 shows "Lubber," another 6 foot 8 inch giant, with a weight of 3120 pounds, and requiring a 36-inch collar. "Lubber" was foaled on April 29, 1929. His sire was a 1700-pound Percheron, and his dam a 1500-pound Belgian and Clydesdale cross. Lubber was owned by A. E. Ponton and Sons, of Winsor, Nebraska.

Fig. 234 shows "Brooklyn Supreme," probably the heaviest horse on record, even though his height of 6 feet 6 inches was considerably below the tallest. But this shorter height, along with his 3200 pounds, gave him the largest girths, including a collar size of 40 inches (!)* and a record-sized chest girth of 102 inches (erroneously recorded

* Size of collar refers to *one-half* the inside circumference of the collar as measured where it rests at the base of the neck against the shoulders.

in some accounts as 10 feet 2 inches). Each of his enormous shoes weighed 7½ pounds. "Brooklyn Supreme" was a red-roan Belgian stallion, who before becoming oversized had been Grand Champion of his breed in many state fairs. He was a great-grandson of the famous Farceur 7332. "Brooklyn Supreme" was foaled on June 6, 1930, on the farm of Earle Brown in Minneapolis. He died sometime in 1950. He was too large for breeding. He was owned by C. G. Good of Ogden, Iowa, who exhibited the giant horse throughout the United States during the late 1930s and early 1940s.[1]

All eight of the horses just listed were either stallions or geldings. The largest mare which appears to have been authenticated was "Boughbrood Lady Grey" of England (breed unstated), who in 1937 stood 6 feet 5 inches and weighed 2352 pounds. A weight of no less than 3100 pounds has been attributed to a Shire mare named "Nebraska Queen," but no height or other details were given.

It is interesting to note that the *average* shoulder height of draft horses in general is about 64 inches—the same as the standing height of the average young American woman. Yet 7-foot giantesses, rare as they are, are not so rare as 7-foot horses. There are two reasons for this. First, horses are only 60 to 70 percent as variable in height as humans; and secondly, there are a great many more humans than horses, which

Fig. 233 "Lubber," a huge yet well-proportioned draft horse standing 6 feet 8 inches and weighing 3120 pounds. His owner, shown holding him, is A. E. Ponton of Winsor, Nebraska. This photograph shows Lubber as a 5-year-old, in 1934.

Fig. 234 "Brooklyn Supreme" (1928–1948), probably the heaviest if not the tallest domestic horse on record. He is being held by his owner, C. G. Good, of Ogden, Iowa.

circumstance in itself extends the range of human variability. Accordingly, it would appear that a horse measuring 7 feet in shoulder height would be equivalent, so far as rarity goes, to a human giant about 8½ feet tall, or to a human giantess of perhaps 7 feet 10 inches.

The foregoing instances of giant horses have necessarily been confined to draft breeds, since those are the types in which the largest bodily (and skeletal) dimensions prevail. In horses of light build, the greatest height recorded would appear to be that of the Thoroughbred gelding, Limbo, who stood 73 inches high at the shoulder. And in weight, a racehorse has seldom exceeded 1400 pounds, or about half that of a record-sized draft horse.

In a number of books on the subject,* it is stated that no wild or prehistoric horse has ever attained the size of a modern draft horse. Yet how is one to know how big horses may once have been, when the world was experiencing a peak period of vegetation and a consequent maximum growth of many animal forms? Elephants (proboscidians), for example, were in Pleistocene times larger than they are today; so also were the giant bison and some species of deer (e.g., the Irish elk). So why not some species of horses? There is at least one item of evidence that makes the latter a possibility.

In the paleontological collection of the American Museum of Natural History (specimen No. 8616, Cope coll.), there is a very large upper second molar tooth which was found in southwest Texas. In its fore-and-aft length (across the crown) the tooth measures 41.5 mm or 1.63 inches, and in transverse width 36 mm or 1.41 inches. The tooth was considered by the paleontologist J. W. Gidley to represent a new species of fossil horse, which he named *Equus giganteus*.

If the tooth-row in *giganteus* were in proportion to this M^2 tooth, it would be about 275 mm (nearly 11 inches) long!; the vertex length of the skull would be at least 800 mm (31½ inches)!; and the living shoulder height of the animal would be about 2250 mm or about 7 feet 4½ inches! Yet all that Dr. Gidley says of the tooth is that it is "very large." It is, in fact, the largest equine tooth listed in any paleontological collection in the world. And who can say that this accidentally-found tooth represents the largest of its kind, or that still-larger owners of such giant teeth may not at one time have roamed the plains or ranged through the heavily-wooded forests of Pleistocene Texas?

---

b. Miniature ponies, donkeys, and mules.

During recent years, a number of breed organizations have specialized in the production of ponies, donkeys, and mules, respectively, of the smallest obtainable sizes. Foremost in the breeding of miniature ponies would appear to be Julio Cesar Falabella, of Buenos Aires, Argentina. So popular have Falabella's little horses become that they are now exported to various parts of the world, despite the fact that they are not inexpensive (as of 1965: $1500 for a gelding, $2000 for a mare, and $3000 for a stallion). At the present time there is at least one branch association in the United States that sponsors the Falabella ponies. The animals range ordinarily from 26 to 32 inches in height. While the breed was founded on Shetland stock, the ponies now come colorwise in bays, browns, blacks, greys, pintos, and even Appaloosas.

A "midget" pony is one under 32 inches in height. Mr. Smith McCoy, of Roderfield, West Virginia, has (or had, in 1965) a herd of 40 midget ponies, among which was a stallion of 28½ inches and a mare, "Sugar-dumpling," of only 20 inches and 30 pounds, making it probably the smallest adult horse in the world. "Sugar-dumpling" died sometime in 1965. Other small ponies exhibited by McCoy were: "Cactus," 26 inches and 95 pounds; "Traveler," 24 inches and 60 pounds; and "Tom Thumb," 23

---

* For example, *The Ages of Life,* by Lorus J. Milne and Margery Milne (New York, 1968), wherein (pp. 105–106) the authors say: "No wild horse ever achieved the dimensions bred into a Percheron, for no earthly conditions made so big a size worthwhile until man provided them for his own benefit."

Fig. 235 Equine extremes. Here is how the giant Belgian, "Brooklyn Supreme," and the 5-hand pony, "Sugar Dumpling," would have sized up if placed together. The unprecedented neck development of "Brooklyn Supreme" made it necessary for the rider to sit farther back than would otherwise have been the case. The rider, incidentally, is not a midget, but stands 5 feet, 4 inches.

inches and 45 pounds. The almost incredibly small size of the mare "Sugar-dumpling" is depicted in Fig. 235, along with a horse of the other size-extreme.

Sometimes there will be a report of a normal-sized horse giving birth to an unusually small foal. This is especially likely to happen in the case of twin foals. In 1954 a Thoroughbred mare on Woodland Farm, near Red Bank, New Jersey, had twins, one of which was normal-sized (but shortly died) while the other, which was named "Big Bertha," was only about 20 inches tall and weighed less than 15 pounds. Remarkably, the little foal survived. A month later she stood 31½ inches and weighed 55 pounds, thus having become nearly as large as an average-sized twin foal at birth.

Another tiny foal was "Cricket," a 15-pound offspring of a Shetland mare named "Tiny" (36 inches, 210 pounds) on the farm of Homer Houser, Dayton, Ohio. However, this foal was less remarkable than "Big Bertha" in that she came from a small-sized dam.

Before leaving the subject of small horses, mention should perhaps be made about the midget horses alleged to run wild in a remote offshoot of the Grand Canyon. The most charitable thing that can be said in this connection is that the whole story was

Fig. 236 "Arabella Matilda, 827," a month-old miniature donkey jennet, waiting for her bottle. Danby Farm, Millard, Nebraska.

a hoax, drummed up in the late 1930s by a man who must have been hard up for publicity. Yet he managed to take in a surprising number of people, including editors who were gullible enough to publish his fabricated story. Details of the alleged "dwarf horses of the Grand Canyon" are given in an article by the writer which appeared in *The Western Horseman* for September–October 1945, pp. 10–11, 38–40.

The smallest donkeys are bred chiefly on the Mediterranean islands of Sicily and Sardinia. The little animals are of a friendly nature, quick to learn, and make gentle pets for small children. They may be either ridden or driven, just played with, or kept as novel pets. Known as Miniature Donkeys, the animals range in color from mouse-grey through reddish-brown to almost black. All, however, have the cross-stripe on the shoulders, along with a dark mid-dorsal stripe, which are typical markings of donkeys in general.

The Miniature Donkey Registry of the United States, with its home office in Omaha, Nebraska, accepts for registry no donkeys taller than 38 inches. Most individuals are under 34 inches, with an average height of about 31 inches and average weight of

Fig. 237 A six-mule hitch of miniature mules bred by August Busch, Jr. Note the uniformity in size and coloration of the animals.

about 150 pounds. One very small foal measured only 15½ inches high at birth and weighed 16 pounds. Breeders of Mediterranean donkeys point out that these animals should not be confused with Mexican burros, which are of a less tractable nature and not suitable as children's pets.

Miniature mules did not come into prominence until 1950, when the first individuals were bred by August A. Busch, Jr., of St. Louis, Missouri. The mules are produced by breeding Sicilian donkeys (jacks) to Shetland pony mares. They range usually between 29 and 31 inches in height, and 200 to 250 pounds in weight. To date, it would appear that Mr. Busch is the only breeder who has been successful in obtaining this small a miniature mule.

---

c. Other oddities of equine development.

Many years ago, there was a fad, which seems to have died out, of raising horses with extraordinarily long and profuse manes and tails. Fig. 238 shows one of these horses, "Oregon Wonder," whose mane was between 9 and 10 feet in length, and

Fig. 238 "Oregon Wonder," a horse with a 10-foot mane and tail.

whose tail was equally long. In *Nature,* for January 9, 1892, there is an account of a Percheron whose mane was 13 feet long and whose tail was almost 10 feet, "probably the greatest example of excessive mane development on record." But evidently not, since in 1942 a Mr. George Zillgitt of Inglewood, California, had a horse named Maud which was credited with an 18-foot mane.

Fig. 239 shows a horse, or pony (probably in China), whose hoofs were allowed to grow too long, and could not then be trimmed without cutting into blood vessels and causing the animal to bleed to death. A pitiful instance of animal neglect.

Speaking of hoofs, there are places in the lowlands of Holland and Germany where the ground is so marshy that the hoofs of the horses have to be encased in wooden shoes (like those of the peasants) in order to prevent them from sinking into the ground. It is said that when horses accustomed to hard ground are transferred to a marshy region, their hoofs grow at more than the usual rate in order to provide the needed extra support.

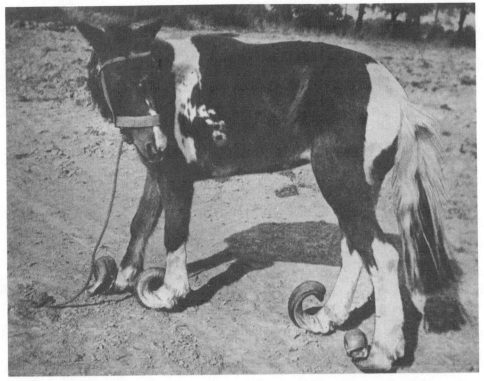

Fig. 239 Deformed hoofs give this horse a "rocking chair" appearance. Such hoofs cannot be removed because of blood vessels running through the horny substance, which if cut would cause the horse to bleed to death.

Note and Reference

1. (Personal communication from C. G. Good, dated December 7, 1942).

Appendix

a. Equine measurements and conformation diagrams.

Under this heading the writer shall attempt what may be an impossibility, namely, to hold the interest of the general reader while at the same time presenting pertinent statistics (of concern to technicians) on the bodily and skeletal measurements of various existing members of the horse family. While many a reader may be averse to tables of figures, there is nothing that will take the place of such numerical information if an exact dimensional description is desired. And in the great majority of books on horses published heretofore, such essential information has been conspicuous by its absence. A reason for this, no doubt, is that it is a long-drawn-out and laborious process to measure all the bones of numerous skeletons, to say nothing of visiting many museums and having them forward the skeletons for study and measurement. The information in the following tables, limited as it is, is more extensive than any published previously. That which is presented here has been abstracted from more comprehensive listings, which include the measurements of many Pleistocene forms of Equidae. For simplicity's sake the measurements are given in whole numbers (i.e., without using decimal points), except in the case of ratios or indices, where it is customary to carry the accuracy to at least one decimal place. And, of course, as in all zoological studies, the measurements listed here (specifically in Table 30) are in *metric* units (millimeters).

Fig. 240 indicates the principal external measurements of the horse, along with the positions of the head, neck, and limbs in which the measurements are to be taken. While similar diagrams have been employed by earlier students of the subject, in them the only species referred to has been the domestic horse (usually one of a "warmblood" breed). Here, by means that will be duly explained, the measurements and proportions of the equine physique have been determined not only for *Equus caballus,* but for domestic and wild asses, hemionids, and the principal species or subspecies of zebras. Indeed, once the measurements of the main bones of the skeleton are known, the external or fleshy measurements and contours of any extinct or fossil species of *Equus* may be determined with considerable accuracy, on the basis of the known relationships of muscle to bone in the various living species.

Fig. 240 is based on a diagram originated by E. A. A. Grange (1894), which was subsequently adopted by various German authors on the subject. Grange applied his system of measurements to several breeds of horses that were exhibited in 1893 at the Columbian Exposition (Chicago) and at the Michigan State Fair of that year. These horses consisted of 11 "Roadsters" (harness horses practically identical to the present-day Standardbred; see Table 5), 8 Coach (light carriage) horses, 6 "General purpose" (light draft) horses, and 25 heavy draft horses. The only departures from Grange's measurements made here (Figs. 133 and 241–248 inclusive) are that the slantwise length of the croup (R^p) and the length from hock to hip (T^p) are converted from actual (observed) measurements to *projected* ones. This has been necessary in order to show in two-dimensional drawings measurements which, as taken on the animal, *do not run parallel with the fore-and-aft mid-plane of the body*. That is, the projected measurements, as shown on the drawings, are always slightly smaller than were the actual lengths as measured on the horses. Absolute dimensions, in inches (rather than proportions), of the Arab, Thoroughbred, and Standardbred horses are given in Figs. 86, 96, and 101, respectively.

The measurements shown in Fig. 240 (which are illustrated on a horse of Standard-bred proportions) are as follows:

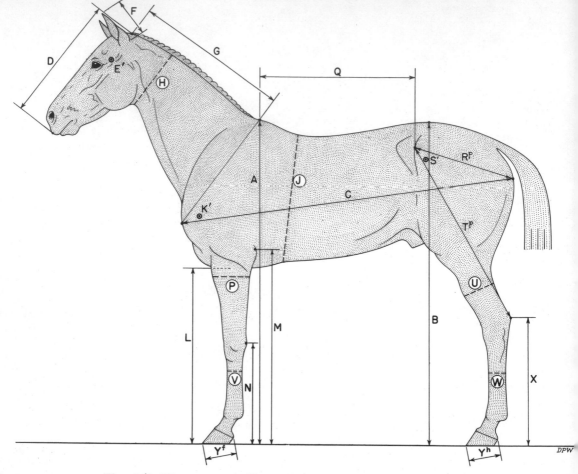

Fig. 240 Diagram to indicate the external measurements of the horse.

A: Height of withers
B: Height of croup
C: Length of trunk, slantwise, from shoulder to buttock
D: Length of head (total)
E': Width of forehead, maximum
F: Length of ear (externally)
G: Length of neck, from poll to point of withers
H: Girth of neck, minimum, at throatlatch
J: Girth of chest, maximum, behind withers
K': Width of shoulders, maximum, across heads of humeri
L: Height of chest from ground
M: Height of elbow (top of olecranon)
N: Height of knee (top of pisiform)
P: Girth of forearm, maximum
Q: Length of back, from point of withers to a line connecting the most anterior
    points of the two ilia
R^p: Projected slantwise length of croup, from point of hip to point of buttock
S': Width of croup, maximum, across heads of femora
T^p: Projected length from point of hip to point of hock
U: Girth of gaskin, maximum
V: Girth of fore cannon, minimum
W: Girth of hind cannon, minimum
X: Height of hock (top of calcaneum)
Y^f: Length of fore hoof (sole)
Y^h: Length of hind hoof (sole)

Table 30. Typical proportions of the body in various examples of Equidae.
Shoulder (withers) height = 100.0
As illustrated in Figs. 80, 95, 126

Note: Wherever two rows of figures are listed for a given measurement (ratio), the top row indicates male and the bottom row female.

Subgenus	*Equus (caballus)*						*Hemionus*	*Asinus*		*Dolichohippus*	*Hippotigris*		*Quaggoides*			
Measurement*	Arabian	Thoroughbred	Standardbred	Shetland	Draft	Przevalsky's horse	Kulan or Chigetai	Domestic ass	Somali wild ass	Grévy's zebra	Mountain zebra	Hartmann's zebra	Chapman's (Damara) zebra	Grant's (Böhm's) zebra	Quagga (extinct)	*Equus occidentalis* (fossil)
A. Height of withers	100.0	100.0	100.0	100.0	100.0	100.0	100.0	100.0	100.0	100.0	100.0	100.0	100.0	100.0	100.0	100.0
B. Height of croup	99.5	99.6	99.7	100.5	100.8	102.3	103.7	103.3	104.9	101.8	102.6	103.3	102.8	103.9	103.8	102.9
C. Length of trunk	99.3	100.0	101.9	108.5	109.3	107.0	103.0	108.1	105.8	108.1	110.6	109.6	109.1	110.6	111.2	110.3
D. Length of head	39.1	38.4	39.7	44.3	42.4	47.2	45.4	47.5	46.8	47.9	48.4	47.1	46.9	46.7	47.7	45.8
E′. Width of forehead	15.0	14.7	15.2	17.2	16.0	15.2	17.6	19.7	19.4	15.7	18.2	16.5	16.7	15.9	16.9	16.2
F. Length of ear	12.0	11.8	12.1	13.3	12.3	14.1	20.0	23.7	23.4	21.0	21.8	18.2	16.8	16.7	14.3	14.7
G. Length of neck	46.1	49.0	47.0	46.1	46.5	46.0	48.9	47.5	49.3	42.8	46.6	46.2	46.7	46.9	48.0	50.3
H. Girth of neck	49.3	49.4	49.4	57.7	58.5	59.7	57.1	60.9	61.4	67.1	64.3	60.5	59.1	58.4	59.0	60.5
	47.0	45.9	46.1	54.4	54.6	55.6	53.4	57.0	57.5	62.6	60.0	56.5	55.4	54.8	55.3	56.6
J. Girth of chest	114.2	112.7	113.2	123.2	126.5	118.5	111.3	115.1	116.0	117.7	117.0	121.1	117.8	116.3	117.0	120.7
	117.3	114.2	115.2	125.2	125.9	119.0	111.6	115.1	116.0	116.9	117.0	122.0	118.6	117.1	117.8	123.5
K′. Width of shoulders	25.5	25.5	27.3	31.3	32.4	27.6	27.2	27.7	27.9	28.3	28.3	29.3	28.8	28.1	28.7	29.7
	25.3	25.1	26.9	30.0	30.3	27.2	26.9	27.4	27.6	28.1	28.2	29.2	28.5	27.8	28.4	29.6
L. Height of chest from ground	54.8	54.9	54.2	50.7	51.1	52.6	55.5	54.0	53.1	52.9	53.2	51.2	53.5	54.2	53.9	53.3
M. Height of elbow	59.8	60.1	59.8	58.8	57.2	59.6	62.8	62.1	60.3	60.0	61.3	60.8	60.6	59.9	61.0	60.5
N. Height of knee	31.2	31.5	31.1	30.1	30.7	32.3	34.0	32.2	31.4	31.9	31.7	31.7	32.4	32.1	32.9	32.5
P. Girth of forearm	30.4	30.4	30.6	31.7	34.7	31.7	30.0	30.3	30.6	32.7	33.7	34.1	33.9	33.5	33.7	35.0
	29.7	29.4	29.5	30.8	33.9	30.8	29.0	30.0	30.3	32.4	33.4	33.8	33.8	33.4	33.6	34.7
Q. Length of back	45.1	45.7	47.4	50.6	50.3	49.1	49.1	54.0	51.5	51.6	53.4	52.9	51.6	52.3	51.9	52.2
R^p. Length of croup	32.7	31.8	32.1	31.7	32.6	32.8	30.8	31.3	32.0	32.1	32.9	32.6	33.9	34.4	33.2	34.3
S′. Width of croup	33.2	33.1	33.4	35.5	38.1	33.9	32.9	29.5	29.8	32.7	33.5	33.2	34.7	35.0	33.8	35.0
	34.3	34.1	34.5	36.5	39.4	35.0	33.1	29.6	30.0	33.3	33.8	33.5	37.5	35.5	34.1	36.7
T^p. Length, hip to hock	58.4	59.4	60.3	62.1	62.7	61.8	57.3	60.4	61.4	59.2	61.8	62.8	62.8	64.9	63.5	61.9
U. Girth of gaskin	26.7	27.5	27.7	28.9	32.2	28.3	27.4	27.4	27.7	29.5	32.3	32.6	32.5	32.9	33.0	33.6
	27.1	26.6	26.8	28.4	31.5	27.6	26.6	27.0	27.3	29.5	31.5	32.0	31.9	32.2	32.3	31.9
V. Girth of fore cannon	12.4	12.4	12.7	13.3	15.3	13.8	12.8	12.8	13.7	13.6	13.2	13.8	14.6	14.8	14.9	14.7
	12.1	11.7	11.9	12.9	14.5	13.1	12.4	12.4	13.4	13.3	12.7	13.1	14.3	14.4	14.5	14.0
W. Girth of hind cannon	13.3	13.5	13.9	14.7	17.5	15.2	14.1	13.9	14.9	15.6	15.3	16.0	16.7	16.9	17.0	17.1
	13.0	13.0	13.1	14.2	16.4	14.4	13.4	13.5	14.6	15.2	14.7	15.2	16.3	16.4	16.5	16.1
X. Height of hock	40.1	39.9	39.6	39.6	39.2	41.2	43.1	40.4	41.0	40.5	39.6	39.3	41.1	40.0	41.3	41.9
Y^f. Length of fore hoof	9.9	9.9	9.7	11.3	12.4	11.5	10.2	11.6	11.0	9.1	9.9	9.9	9.6	9.0	9.3	9.8
	9.1	9.2	9.0	10.6	11.9	10.6	9.6	11.2	10.6	8.6	9.5	9.5	9.1	8.6	8.9	9.1
Y^h. Length of hind hoof	9.7	9.4	9.7	11.4	12.4	11.3	10.5	11.8	11.2	9.1	10.0	10.0	9.2	9.0	9.3	9.8
	8.9	8.8	9.0	10.8	11.9	10.4	9.9	11.4	10.8	8.6	9.6	9.6	8.7	8.6	8.9	9.1
Avg. height of withers, in.	59.7	63.8	62.7	39.8	64.1	50.5	48.6	39.6	47.6	54.4	45.9	49.6	49.1	46.1	46.1	57.9
	59.0	63.0	62.0	39.4	63.7	49.9	48.2	39.4	47.2	53.9	45.4	49.1	48.5	45.7	45.7	57.2
Avg. bodyweight, lbs.	922	1089	1085	354	1664	688	483	320	550	830	533	715	647	553	560	1144
	922	1043	1055	354	1582	661	457	302	530	830	512	685	633	533	540	1144

* For location and definition of measurements, see Fig. 240 and accompanying text.

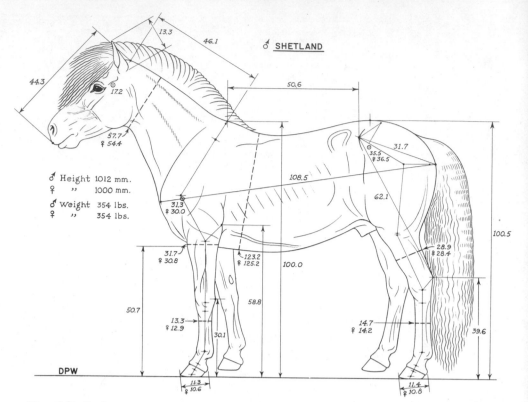

Fig. 241 Body outline of a typical Shetland pony stallion. For definition of measurements, see accompanying text. x .07

In Table 29, a number of equine species for which drawings were *not* made are listed as to their body proportions. This table enables comparisons in *proportion* to be made between any of the 16 breeds or wild forms considered. The figures should also serve to confirm or repudiate the proportions popularly attributed to certain breeds of the domestic horse, as for example the "long" neck and "short" back of the Arabian, the "long" legs of the Thoroughbred, and the "draft-horse build" of the Shetland pony. Actually, the Arabian *does* have, on the average, the shortest back (only 45.1 percent of the shoulder height), but its neck length also is *short*, rather than long, in comparison with the other forms listed, among which the Thoroughbred has the longest neck of any domestic breed. As to long legs, if the relative height of the elbow be taken as the criterion, the Thoroughbred's leg length is surpassed by eight of the fifteen other forms; and this superiority is even more pronounced if the lower leg length only (i.e., the height of the knee) is compared, whereupon it is seen that the longest-legged equine is the kulan (*E. hemionus hemionus*). This relative long-leggedness occurs also in the other hemionid forms: kiang, ghorkhar, Persian onager, and hemippus, respectively.

As to the Shetland pony being a miniature draft horse, it can be seen that in some of its proportions (e.g., trunk length, back length, and girths of neck and chest) it *is* similar to the draft type; but that in other respects (e.g., size of head and ears, girths of limbs, and size of hoofs) it is far removed from the proportions of the larger animal.

The relatively largest (longest) heads are those of the zebras, the asses, and Przevalsky's horse, although this relative large-headedness in most cases is a consequence of the animal itself being relatively small, along with the almost universal fact that small animals have relatively larger heads (and brains) than do larger forms of the

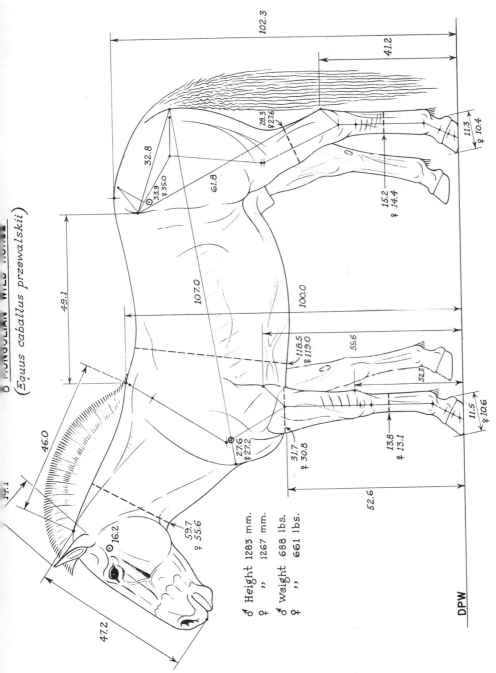

Fig. 242 Body outline of a typical stallion of Przevalsky's horse, E. *caballus przewalskii*. For definition of measurements, see accompanying text. x .07

♂ MONGOLIAN WILD HORSE
(*Equus caballus przewalskii*)

♂ Height 1283 mm.
♀ ,, 1267 mm.
♂ weight 688 lbs.
♀ ,, 661 lbs.

102.3
41.2
28.3
♀27.6
32.8
33.9
♀ 35.0
61.8
11.3
♀ 10.4
15.2
♀ 14.4
49.1
107.0
100.0
118.5
♀119.0
55.6
32.3
46.0
27.6
♀27.2
31.7
♀ 30.8
13.8
♀ 13.1
11.5
♀ 10.6
52.6
17.1
59.7
♀ 55.6
16.2
47.2
DPW

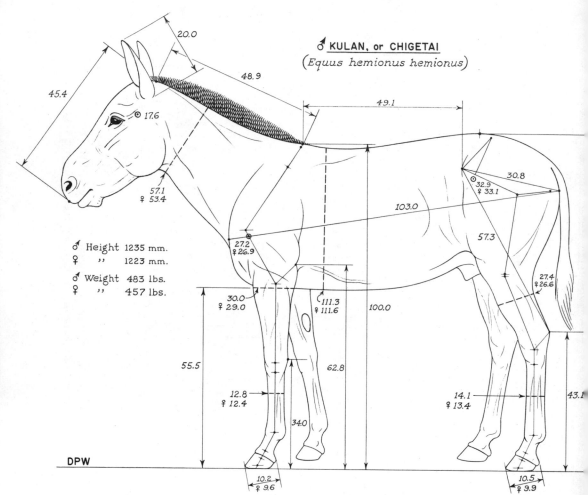

20.0

♂ **KULAN, or CHIGETAI**
(*Equus hemionus hemionus*)

48.9

49.1

45.4

⊙ 17.6

103.0

⊙ 32.9
♀ 33.1

30.8

57.1
♀ 53.4

57.3

♂ Height 1235 mm.
♀ ,, 1223 mm.
♂ Weight 483 lbs.
♀ ,, 457 lbs.

27.2
♀ 26.9

27.4
♀ 26.6

30.0
♀ 29.0

111.3
♀ 111.6

100.0

55.5

62.8

14.1
♀ 13.4

43.1

12.8
♀ 12.4

34.0

DPW

10.2
♀ 9.6

10.5
♀ 9.9

Fig. 243 Body outline of a typical stallion of the Kulan or chigetai, *E. hemionus hemionus*. For definition of measurements, see accompanying text. x .07

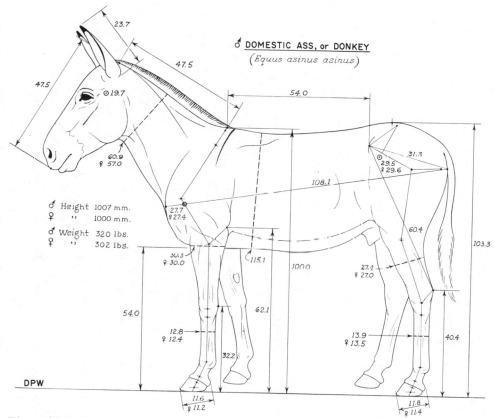

Fig. 244 Body outline of a typical stallion of the domestic ass, *E. asinus asinus.*
For definition of measurements, see accompanying text. x .07

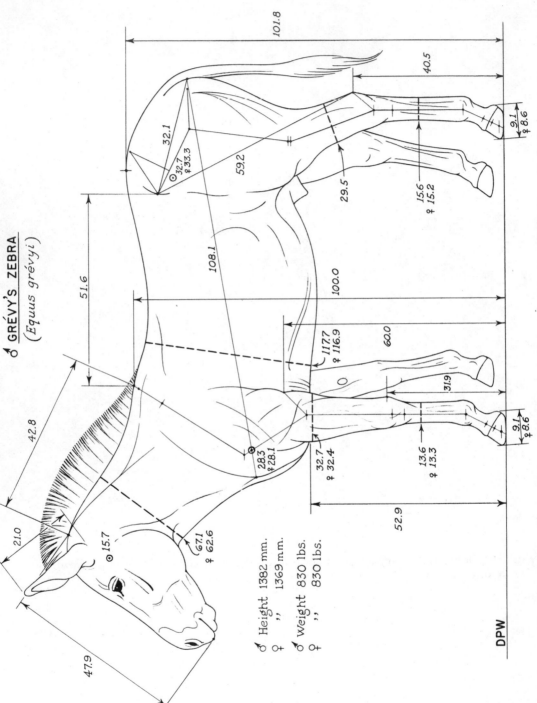

♂ GRÉVY'S ZEBRA
(*Equus grévyi*)

♂ Height 1382 mm.
♀   ,,   1369 mm.
♂ weight 830 lbs.
♀   ,,   830 lbs.

DPW

Fig. 245 Body outline of a typical stallion of Grévy's zebra, *E. grévyi*. For

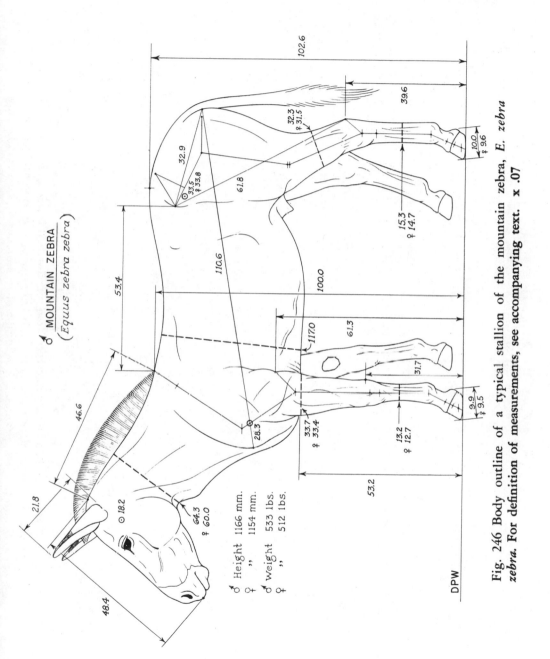

MOUNTAIN ZEBRA
(*Equus zebra zebra*)

♂ Height 1166 mm.
♀ ,, 1154 mm.
♂ weight 533 lbs.
♀ ,, 512 lbs.

DPW

Fig. 246 Body outline of a typical stallion of the mountain zebra, *E. zebra zebra*. For definition of measurements, see accompanying text. x .07

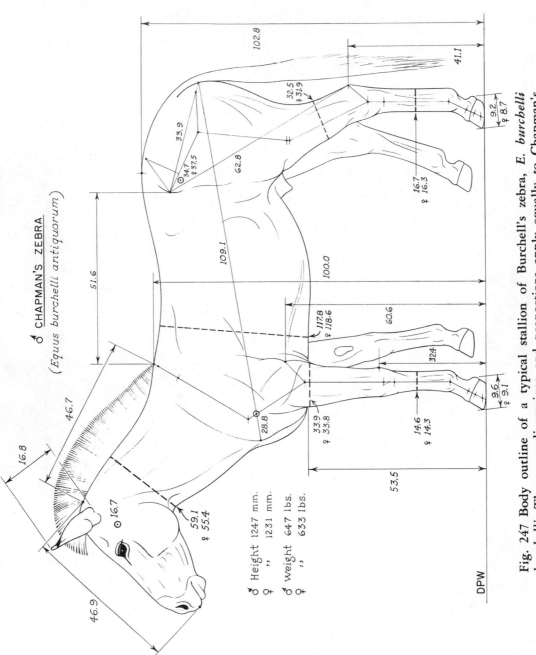

CHAPMAN'S ZEBRA
(*Equus burchelli antiquorum*)

♂ Height 1247 mm.
♀ ,,   1231 mm.
♂ weight 647 lbs.
♀ ,,   633 lbs.

DPW

Fig. 247 Body outline of a typical stallion of Burchell's zebra, *E. burchelli burchelli*. The same dimensions and proportions apply equally to Chapman's zebra, *E. burchelli antiquorum*. For definition of measurements, see accompanying

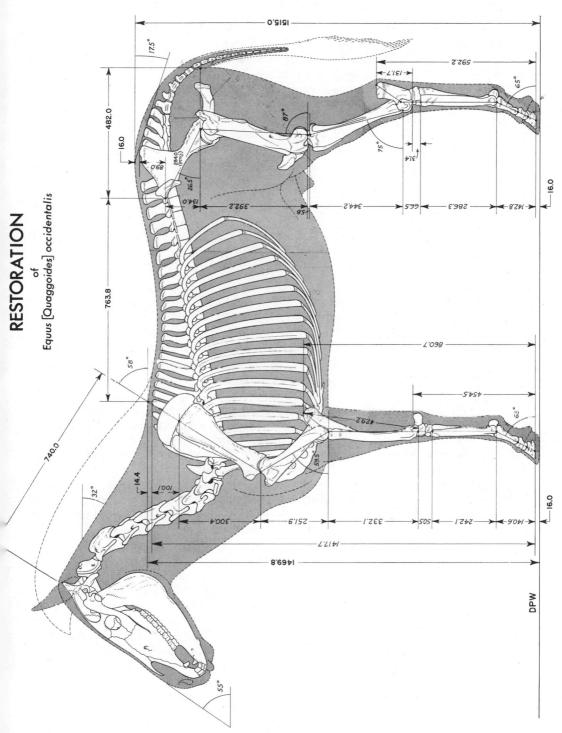

Fig. 248 Reconstruction, to exact scale, of the skeleton of a typical adult male specimen of the tar-pit quagga (*Equus occidentalis*) of Rancho La Brea. Only the principal dimensions are given. Measurements shown in heavy, vertical numbers are of restored *external* dimensions. x .07 nat. size.

same types. In relative ear length, the asses and the ass-like mountain zebra surpass all other species, although the broad-eared Grévy's zebra is a close third.

Numerous other proportions could be commented upon, but any and all comparisons may readily be made by consulting the figures listed in the table.

Wherever an absolute measurement is desired, it may be obtained simply by moving the decimal point in the ratio two places forward, then multiplying it by the shoulder height of the individual animal. For example, in a Standardbred stallion 15 hands (60 inches) high, the expected girth of chest would be 60 x 1.132, or 67.9 inches. If the height were in millimeters, the corresponding chest girth would be 1524 x 1.132, or 1725 mm. Thus, Table 29 may be used to obtain the absolute measurements of any of the 16 equine types listed, provided the height of the animal is known; and the measurements derived may be either in inches or millimeters. Body *weights* may be calculated on the general principle that, within a given breed or species, weight varies as the *cube* of the height. For instance, a horse 70 inches high, of the same body proportions as one 60 inches high, would be expected to weigh approximately

$$\frac{70 \times 70 \times 70}{60 \times 60 \times 60},$$

or 1.588, times as much as the 60-inch horse. Hence if the latter weighed 900 pounds, the 70-inch horse would weigh 1.588 x 900, or about 1430 pounds.

Two main procedures have been followed by the writer in making "conformation" drawings of equine species such as those shown in Figs. 241–248 inclusive. First, the known lengths of the bones of the skull, body, and limbs, along with their known typical inclinations, were used to make a restoration of each skeleton, after which the lengths of the dried bones were increased to their former "green" or living dimensions.* Then, the thickness of the skin, muscles, ligaments, and hoofs was added to the shoulder and croup heights of the restored skeleton. Secondly, the external widths and depths of the head, neck, body, and limbs were determined from numerous photographs of the various breeds and species, and correlated with dimensions of the skeleton. For instance, numerous straight profile photographs show the vertical width of the neck in Arabian horses to average .20 x the shoulder height in stallions and .189 x the shoulder height in mares. Similar ratios were established for the vertical depth of the chest, and the maximum fore-and-aft widths of the forearm, fore cannon, gaskin, and hind cannon. Once the relationship of these profile widths to the dimensions of the underlying bones was established for a number of diverse breeds of the domestic horse, it was a matter of similar procedure to establish them for such lesser-represented species as zebras, asses, and hemionids. Lateral widths, such as that of the shoulders and of the croup, were determined by relating shoulder width to chest girth and croup width to the known skeletal width of the pelvis. A great deal more had to be worked out than is here merely outlined; but the result, it is believed, is a series of equine conformation diagrams which for most measurements are probably 99 percent correct.

Despite the obvious external differences that prevail between such subgeneric forms as horses, asses, hemionids, and zebras, it is to the *measurements of the bones of the skeleton* that one must refer if definite and reliable morphologic distinctions are to be established. Moreover, it is not enough to lay a bone, say, of a zebra alongside the corresponding bone of a donkey and then say that no difference between the two can

---

* It was found that the average shrinkage of thoroughly dried bones from their original "green" lengths is about 1½ percent. Accordingly, in "restoring" the lengths of the bones, 1½ percent was added to the length of each dry bone as measured.

be detected. One must *relate the lengths of various limb bones one to the other,* as is done in Table 31, and then not just compare the resulting ratios, but *plot them on a graph,* as has been done, for example, in Fig. 224. Only by such a procedure may the structural similarities and dissimilarities of the various equine breeds, species, and subspecies be properly determined. In this connection it may be reemphasized that cranial (skull) measurements alone are insufficient; while the much-used measurements and grinding patterns of the cheek teeth are likely to lead to fallacious conclusions.

In Table 31 are listed the actual limb-bone measurements of a number of breeds of the domestic horse, two subspecies (one extinct) of the wild horse, five subspecies of onagers, three subspecies of asses, a mule, and seven forms of zebras or zebroids, one of which is the fossil Western quagga (*Equus occidentalis*). In the last column of this table are listed the estimated living shoulder heights in *inches* (averaging the two sexes). All other measurements in the table are in millimeters.

To refer to Table 32, it will at once be seen that the numbers of the *Hemionus* group differ markedly in certain of their skeletal proportions—particularly the lengths of the metacarpus and the metatarsus—from all the other subgeneric forms listed. This is shown especially in indices nos. 7, 9, 10, 11 and 12, as well as in the index of metacarpus width (no. 18) and index no. 20. Yet despite these typical and constant skeletal differences, along with external differences in body coloration, leg length, and hoof form, there are still some taxonomists who insist on putting the hemionids into the *same* subgeneric group as the domestic donkey and the African wild asses!

While certain other bones of the postcranial skeleton—such as the cervical, dorsal, and lumbar vertebrae, and the pelvis—are not considered in Table 31, their dimensions and their influence on the *external* measurements and proportions of the body have been used as a basis for the ratios B, C, G, Q, R^p, and S$'$ in Table 30.

To sum up, the conformation of the head, neck, body, and limbs in any skeletally well-documented species of *Equus* may be projected into the probable *living* dimensions and proportions of that species. In this Appendix this procedure has been applied to a sufficiently diverse series of equine forms to indicate its general suitability for determining the typical body measurements and outlines of any given species of horse, ass, hemionid, or zebra. Typical heights and weights of numerous breeds of the domestic horse are given in Table 13.

Table 33 lists some of the principal measurements of equine *skulls* that were measured by the writer during his researches at the California Institute of Technology, Pasadena, during the years 1946–1952 inclusive. In this connection it should be emphasized that skulls, even of the same breed or subspecies, cannot properly be compared as to size until they have been "corrected" or brought to the same age, nor in proportions until they have similarly been brought to a common overall (basilar or vertex) skull length.* The procedure for making these corrections is too involved to be explained here; but it is elucidated at length in the writer's technical paper on fossil and recent Equidae.

---

* A parallel to this "corrective" statistical procedure was enunciated earlier by the brilliant English criminologist, Charles Goring.[1] He showed that once the dimensions of the head in English convicts were corrected for the natural differences caused by age and general body size, there was less difference between the head-form of these criminals and that of a series of college students than there was between two groups of students who attended different universities. By this means, Goring dealt a death-blow to the views promulgated by Cesare Lombroso and other investigators who had attempted to show that criminals could be identified by physical characteristics which differed from those of noncriminals. The connection here is that zoologists who attempt to classify equine species by observed differences in the skull and teeth without first modifying those differences with respect to the age, sex, and general size of the animal, are, like the followers of the Lombroso school of criminology, apt to find "differences" where no real differences exist.

Table 31. Mean lengths of the limb bones in various examples of Equidae. Sexes *averaged* (wherever known), except in metacarpus caliber. Figures in parentheses are estimations.

| | | | Total lengths in fore limb, mm | | | | | | |
| | | | | | | | Phalanx | | |
Subgenus	Species, subspecies, or breed	Number of examples	Scapula	Humerus	Radius	Metacarpus	I	II	III (hoof)
Equus (caballus)	Average of 10 "warmblood" breeds	28	340	293	339	226	83	44	52
	Arabian	9	368	326	374	259	94	48	57
	Thoroughbred	3	398	349	404	273	98	51	59
	Shetland	5	253	214	252	158	60	32	36
	"Celtic"	2	326	276	320	213	(79)	(41)	(50)
	Fjord	1	(329)	284	333	218	78	(42)	(50)
	Draft	7	405	342	375	251	95	54	62
	Przevalsky's horse	13	319	264	316	220	82	43	50
	South Russian tarpan	1	(314)	271	316	208	75	38	51
Hemionus	Kulan	6	285	252	305	230	84	41	50
	Kiang	7	288	263	308	232	84	41	48
	Persian onager	1	280	243	295	218	74	35	43
	Ghorkhar	1	267	245	298	214	78	38	46
	Hemippus	3	241	211	251	192	69	36	36
Asinus	Domestic ass	27	240	215	256	172	66	33	32
	Nubian wild ass	1	252	234	279	182	68	33	32
	Somali wild ass	3	284	259	312	204	77	40	39
Dolichohippus	Grévy's zebra	5	353	291	335	233	86	47	46
Hippotigris	Mountain zebra	4	285	253	293	191	75	42	38
	Hartmann's zebra	3	312	274	310	206	79	45	43
Quaggoides	Chapman's zebra	9	299	269	303	216	81	43	45
	Grant's zebra	9	286	253	281	203	74	41	41
	Quagga	7	288	244	284	203	79	44	42
	E. occidentalis	17–112	362	314	352	253	96	52	53
Equus x Asinus	Mule (mare x ass)	4	325	277	328	214	82	43	45

| | Total lengths in hind limb, mm | | | | | | Metacarpus width at middle, mm and % | | | | Estimated living shoulder height, inches |
Femur	Tibia	Calcaneum	Metatarsus	Phalanx I	Phalanx II	Phalanx III (hoof)	Absolute, mm ♂	Absolute, mm ♀	Relative to length ♂	Relative to length ♀	
394	354	112	269	80	45	55	32.7	31.0	14.4	13.7	53.60
438	393	126	306	90	50	61	34.4	33.2	13.2	12.9	59.35
467	424	131	319	93	52	62	36.5	34.3	13.3	12.6	63.40
291	262	(84)	194	57	32	39	24.7	23.2	15.6	14.8	39.60
375	336	(106)	256	(75)	(43)	(54)	32.3	30.4	15.1	14.4	51.40
375)	340	(107)	257	75	(43)	(53)	32.6	30.8	15.0	14.3	52.00
438	395	138	291	92	55	66	42.8	40.2	17.1	16.1	63.90
361	326	103	260	77	44	54	32.3	30.1	14.6	13.8	50.20
372	338	103	252	71	39	53	32.6	30.7	15.7	14.9	49.40
339	323	103	272	77	41	51	28.7	26.9	12.4	11.7	48.40
346	328	103	271	76	40	49	29.5	27.6	12.6	11.9	49.20
323	310	93	252	67	36	44	28.1	26.3	12.8	12.1	46.30
321	305	(95)	252	71	38	46	(26.4)	(24.7)	(12.3)	(11.6)	46.10
279	263	85	223	65	36	37	22.6	21.1	11.7	11.0	40.20
288	268	78	203	61	32	33	23.5	22.7	13.6	13.2	39.50
315	296	86	218	65	33	33	(25.2)	(24.3)	(13.8)	(13.4)	42.13
353	331	98	241	71	40	40	28.4	27.4	13.9	13.5	47.40
397	352	118	269	82	48	49	33.4	32.4	14.3	13.9	54.10
352	312	97	215	71	42	39	28.1	26.7	14.7	14.0	45.67
374	339	105	233	75	44	42	31.9	29.7	15.4	14.4	49.30
369	325	111	246	77	43	47	32.3	31.1	14.9	14.4	48.80
347	309	102	230	70	41	43	30.6	29.5	15.0	14.6	45.85
354	307	103	235	74	44	45	30.8	29.7	15.1	14.6	45.85
437	388	134	292	91	53	56	41.0	38.6	16.2	15.4	57.87
366	344	108	256	78	43	47	32.1	30.4	15.0	14.3	51.84

Table 32. Limb-bone indices (derived from Table 31) adopted for specific and subgeneric differentiation in various examples of Equidae. For explanation, see text. Figures in parentheses are estimations.

Subgenus	Species, Subspecies, or breed	1 Humerus / Scapula	2 Scapula / Radius	3 Scapula / Tibia	4 Scapula / Vertex Skull	5 Radius / Femur	6 M^t / Scapula	7 M^c / Radius	8 M^c / M^t	9 M^t / Scapu
Equus (caballus)	Average of 10 "warmblood" breeds	86.2	100.2	95.6	64.4	86.1	66.6	66.7	84.1	79.2
	Arabian	88.6	98.5	93.6	68.1	85.4	70.4	69.3	84.5	83.2
	Thoroughbred	87.7	98.5	93.8	70.2	86.4	68.6	67.6	85.5	80.3
	Shetland	84.2	100.5	96.6	62.3	86.6	62.2	62.5	81.2	76.6
	"Celtic"	84.5	101.9	97.0	66.0	85.3	65.2	66.4	83.2	78.3
	Fjord	(86.3)	(98.8)	(96.9)	(61.2)	(88.9)	(65.7)	65.2	84.6	(78.0
	Draft	84.3	108.0	102.7	65.7	85.7	61.8	66.7	86.2	71.7
	Przevalsky's horse	82.7	100.8	97.8	60.4	87.5	69.0	69.6	84.6	81.6
	South Russian tarpan	(86.5)	(99.5)	(92.8)	(61.3)	84.9	(66.1)	65.7	82.3	(80.2
Hemionus	Kulan	88.4	93.4	88.1	55.4	89.8	80.8	75.4	84.7	95.4
	Kiang	91.2	93.5	87.4	56.2	89.0	80.6	75.3	85.7	94.0
	Persian onager	86.7	95.1	90.5	57.3	91.1	77.7	73.9	86.5	89.9
	Ghorkhar	92.0	89.3	87.3	55.7	92.8	80.3	71.7	84.9	94.6
	Hemippus	87.5	96.2	91.5	58.4	89.8	79.8	76.7	86.2	92.5
Asinus	Domestic ass	89.4	93.8	89.4	55.1	88.8	71.8	67.4	85.0	84.4
	Nubian wild ass	92.8	90.4	85.1	53.5	88.6	72.2	65.3	83.3	86.7
	Somali wild ass	91.3	90.7	85.8	54.0	88.5	72.0	65.3	84.6	85.6
Dolichohippus	Grévy's zebra	82.3	105.5	100.4	58.2	84.4	66.1	69.7	86.8	76.2
Hippotigris	Mountain zebra	88.9	97.2	91.1	55.2	83.1	67.0	65.1	88.5	75.6
	Hartmann's zebra	87.8	100.4	91.9	56.5	83.0	66.2	66.5	88.6	74.2
Quaggoides	Chapman's zebra	90.0	98.7	92.1	56.0	82.3	72.3	71.3	88.1	82.2
	Grant's zebra	88.5	101.7	92.5	57.1	81.0	71.1	72.3	88.4	80.2
	Quagga	84.8	101.3	93.8	57.5	80.2	70.8	71.7	86.6	81.2
	E. occidentalis	86.6	102.8	93.4	58.6	80.6	69.7	71.7	86.4	80.2
Equus x Asinus	Mule (mare x ass)	85.3	99.0	94.7	59.6	89.8	65.7	65.0	83.5	78.2

10	11	12	13	14	15	16	17	18	19	20
M^t	M^t	Calc.	Humerus	Fore Ph. III	Fore Ph. III width	Fore Ph. III	Hind Ph. III	Relative Metacarpus	Index 17	Index 11
Radius	Femur	M^t	R + M^c	Radius	length	Fore Ph. I	Tibia	minimum width	Index 9	Index 8
79.4	68.3	41.7	51.8	15.2	151.4	61.7	15.4	14.1	19.4	81.3
81.9	70.0	41.1	51.5	15.2	147.6	60.0	15.5	13.0	18.6	82.8
79.1	68.3	41.0	51.5	14.5	145.0	59.6	14.7	13.0	18.3	80.0
77.0	66.6	43.5	52.1	14.5	151.0	61.2	14.8	15.2	19.3	82.4
79.8	68.1	41.5	51.7	15.7	147.4	63.8	16.1	14.7	20.5	81.9
77.0	(68.8)	(41.5)	51.5	(15.1)	(150.1)	(64.1)	(15.6)	14.5	(20.0)	81.3
77.4	66.3	47.7	54.6	16.6	187.1	65.2	16.8	16.6	23.7	76.9
82.2	72.0	39.5	49.2	15.7	141.2	60.8	16.4	14.2	20.2	85.0
79.8	67.7	41.1	51.9	16.3	138.1	69.1	15.7	15.2	19.6	82.3
89.1	80.0	37.9	47.1	16.4	126.7	59.2	15.8	12.1	16.5	94.5
87.9	78.2	37.9	48.6	15.4	127.1	56.6	14.8	12.3	15.7	91.2
85.5	77.9	37.0	47.4	14.7	(131.7)	58.3	14.2	12.5	15.8	90.2
84.5	78.4	(37.8)	47.8	15.4	128.9	59.1	15.1	(12.0)	15.9	92.4
89.0	79.6	38.3	47.6	14.2	133.4	51.8	13.9	11.4	15.0	92.3
79.2	70.4	38.4	50.1	12.4	133.3	48.4	12.2	13.4	14.4	82.7
78.3	69.4	39.2	50.7	11.4	131.4	46.5	11.1	(13.6)	12.8	83.3
77.1	68.3	40.7	50.1	12.4	131.7	50.5	12.1	13.7	14.2	80.7
80.4	67.9	43.7	51.1	13.7	133.3	53.2	13.9	14.1	18.3	78.2
73.6	61.1	45.3	52.4	12.9	123.4	50.3	12.4	14.4	16.3	69.0
75.0	62.3	45.2	53.0	13.9	119.5	54.4	12.3	14.9	16.4	70.3
81.0	66.6	45.0	51.8	15.0	131.8	55.9	14.3	14.7	17.4	75.7
81.8	66.3	44.1	52.2	14.7	127.0	55.9	13.8	14.8	17.2	75.0
82.8	66.4	44.0	50.0	14.9	125.0	54.7	14.7	14.9	18.0	76.7
83.0	66.9	45.8	51.9	14.8	127.8	55.5	14.4	15.8	17.8	77.4
77.9	70.0	42.4	51.1	13.8	133.3	55.5	13.6	14.6	11.3	83.8

Table 33. Cranial and dental measurements of equine specimens measured by the author.
For diagram of skull showing measurements, see Fig. 25.

Subgenus	Breed or species	Museum and Cat. No.	Sex and est. age	Meas. No. 1 Basilar length	2 Vertex length	4 Mandible length	5 Frontal width	10 Muzzle width	11 Palate to Vomer	12 Vomer to Foramen Magnum
Horses (and mule)	Arabian	LA M 700	♂ 24	511	561	454	200	66	106	136
	Arabian	LA M1475	♀ 3	498	544	439	200	60	105	128
	Thoro.	LA M1485	♂ 10	503	555	450	223	66	101	133
	Shetland	LA M1483	♂ 25	384	425	347	164	65	74	99
	Unknown	CIT 0-6	♀ 7	519	578	466	227	74	108	128
	Unknown	CIT	♀ 15	536	586	475	216	70	116	136
	Unknown	CIT	♀ 2½	537	589	473	225	75	124	128
	Draft	LA M1079	♀ 18	570	637	515	232	76	118	145
	Draft	CIT	♀ 18	556	607	499	226	70	118	136
	Percheron	LA M1463	♂ 37	596	657	544	234	74	118	139
	Draft	CIT	♂ 5	613	668	545	256	82	133	151
	Draft mule	LA M1464	♀ 40	560	637	505	246	62	128	135
	Przevalsky	US 238111	♂ 8½	476	528	429	211	69	91	128
	Przevalsky	AM 90198	♂ 3¼	454	508	402	189	67	108	106
Hemionids	Kiang	US 84083	♂ 22	440	490	400	199	67	110	112
	Kiang	US 49493	♂ 14	452	500	407	202	67	117	111
	Kiang	US 84088	♀ 7	450	500	405	204	67	111	106
	Onager	AN 12586	♀ 12½	444	500	400	194	59	123	107
Asses	Donkey	LA M1478	♂ 6	441	508	402	204	62	119	93
	Donkey	CIT 0-5	♀ 22	402	458	358	182	56	104	96
	Nubian ass	AM 135017	♂ 25+	430	483	378	195	56	113	98
Zebras or Zebroids	Grévy's	LA M 67	♂ 12	(536)	602	473	196	67	140	130
	E. z. zebra	US 270125	♂ 14	467	526	416	204	70	111	111
	E. z. zebra	US 270514	♂ ? 3½	480	540	427	208	70	(120)	(115)
	Chapman's	CAS 8122	♀ 9	457	515	409	187	64	108	122
	Chapman's	CIT 0-130	♂ 8	460	515	410	192	61	107	114
	Grant's	CAS 45	♂ 8	437	495	389	196	67	94	118
	Grant's	CAS 41	♀ 10	444	491	393	184	69	110	104
	Grant's	CAS ?	♂ 9	438	498	393	182	62	110	100
	Grant's	CAS 40	♂ 18	444	496	393	191	62	95	117
	Grant's	CAS 44	♀ 10	458	513	406	188	62	108	113
	Grant's	LA M1315	♀ 5	448	507	404	193	66	(104)	(106)
	*Quagga	AN 6317	♂ 9	442	490	389	185	67	90	111
	*Quagga	PM 1623	♀ 22	467	510	413	191	71	101	112
	†E. occ.	LA 3500-3	? 3½	537	608	484	228	86	134	128
	†E. occ.	LA 3500-5	♂ 3½	550	618	488	245	83	143	125
	†E. occ.	LA 3500-6	♂ 8½	566	644	510	247	89	136	133
	†E. occ.	LA 3500-8	♂ 7½	547	613	493	231	76	(137)	(130)
	†E. occ.	LA 3500-15	? 3	533	605	483	226	83	132	131
	†E. occ.	LA 3500-21	♂ 3½	536	614	483	231	85	138	120
	†E. occ.	LA 3500-24	? 3½	538	615	484	241	84	123	142

LA = Los Angeles County Museum of Natural History.
CIT = California Institute of Technology.
US = United States National Museum.
CAS = California Academy of Sciences (San Francisco); (the numbers listed are Field numbers).
AM = American Museum of Natural History.
AN = Academy of Natural Sciences of Philadelphia.
PM = Peabody Museum, Yale University.
* = extinct.   ( ) = estimated.
† = fossil.

13	14	15	18	20	21	23	24	25
Diastema length	Upper Dental Series length	Anterior Ocular Line	Occiput Height from base of Mandible	Occiput to bottom of Occipital Condyles	Mandible Height to Condyles	Orbit diameter, horizontal	Orbit diameter, vertical	Upper Cheek Teeth, average width
115	152	412	290	106	232	65	54	22.5
105	177	393	296	102	237	65	55	21.0
108	173	381	311	103	250	63	59	27.3
70	124	296	197	78	162	48	46	19.8
107	179	403	335	114	260	65	61	28.5
112	176	410	320	100	239	65	54	28.5
107	189	411	318	116	243	63	57	24.5
125	183	449	349	119	280	66	59	28.5
124	177	437	325	120	266	66	58	27.5
132	185	470	335	107	273	67	57	28.5
122	(215)	476	368	122	282	74	65	28.5
127	162	447	345	126	274	61	50	28.3
92	167	375	275	101	219	59	52	25.0
85	172	362	249	91	198	65	52	23.2
77	145	359	253	96	202	62	56	24.4
76	152	356	266	98	212	61	57	23.2
79	154	362	262	95	211	59	57	24.5
70	160	360	250	90	201	62	55	24.1
70	163	345	255	95	206	50	50	24.2
83	133	313	247	91	194	51	51	22.9
67	142	327	259	96	206	45	48	24.4
109	169	(123)	298	107	234	61	59	27.1
94	147	371	280	99	212	55	56	24.5
86	167	378	316	105	241	64	53	23.0
108	(143)	365	(276)	100	212	62	58	22.1
95	151	358	310	111	237	59	52	23.8
85	138	346	285	108	217	61	56	21.1
93	141	343	279	100	211	58	52	21.9
82	151	346	274	102	218	56	54	23.3
102	137	347	281	107	227	55	52	22.1
100	145	351	307	101	245	61	54	22.5
98	147	356	300	104	225	63	58	21.7
94	147	352	272	100	212	60	54	23.5
90	144	365	285	100	228	58	54	24.3
87	200	419	337	128	250	65	57	27.2
96	192	432	326	129	248	66	57	27.8
107	196	442	319	126	252	64	58	29.8
94	199	433	324	128	251	65	57	26.8
97	(195)	413	314	125	247	65	58	26.2
106	204	429	328	126	246	61	53	26.2
88	(202)	418	319	134	(250)	74	66	27.4

Table 33 is presented primarily for the benefit of researchers interested in the measurements of equine skulls. Certain measurements (e.g., nos. 3, 6, 7, 8, 9, 16, 17, 19, and 22) have been omitted from the table for the reason that most of these measurements are not ordinarily taken, or may be of interest only to specialists. Measurement no. 16 is the Anterior Ocular Line (no. 15) *projected* into the mid-sagittal plane of the skull (that is, into measurement no. 15 as shown in Fig. 25, in straight *profile*). On the average, no. 16 is about .96 x no. 15, depending upon the ratio of Frontal Width (no. 5) to Anterior Ocular Line (no. 15). Cranial Length, projected (no. 17), is derived by subtracting measurement no. 16 from measurement no. 2 (Vertex Length).

Many interesting relationships, some of classifactory value, are evident from a perusal of Table 33. There is a great deal more to be learned than simply that draft horses have the largest skulls and Shetland ponies the smallest. Note, for instance, that Muzzle Width (measurement no. 10) in the Shetland is only one millimeter (.04 inches) less than in the generally much larger skull of the Thoroughbred; and that only in the two donkeys, the Nubian wild ass, and one Grant's zebra is the Frontal Width (no. 5) more than half the measurement of the Mandible Length (no. 4).

Back in 1892 the Russian zoologist, J. D. Tscherski, made the interesting discovery that in typical (caballine) horses the distance from Vomer to Foramen Magnum (here, measurement no. 12) was almost always greater than the distance from Palate to Vomer (here, measurement no. 11), while in donkeys the relationship of these two measurements was reversed (no. 11, here, being greater than no. 12). Table 33 bears out Tscherski's observation, and shows also that in the other subgeneric forms listed—the hemionids and zebras—either measurement 11 or measurement 12 may be the larger of the two.

Another interesting ratio is the average diameter of the orbit or eye-socket (average of measurements nos. 23 and 24) in relation to the main (basilar) length of the skull. In the Shetland pony this ratio is 15.9, while in the largest draft horse listed in the table it is only 11.3. This accords with the well-known fact that the eyes in small animals are relatively larger than those in larger forms of the same species; and it shows that the bony orbit around the eyeball is proportionate in size to the eye itself.

It should be noted that the cranial and dental measurements herein adopted as *typical* for the various equine species described have been derived from *all* sources of data on the subject—not merely the examples measured by the writer and listed (in part) in Table 33. As a means of comparison, Table 34 below lists the average basilar (Measurement no. 1) lengths of the skull corresponding with the respective examples of Equidae listed in Table 31.

As will be seen in Table 34, for most of the different breeds and species a larger number of skulls was available for measurement than were bones of the postcranial skeleton. Indeed, for the South Russian tarpan, the Fjord pony, the Persian and Indian onagers, and the Nubian wild ass only one set of limb-bone measurements has been recorded in each case. Accordingly, it cannot be said positively that the single example in each of these species represents an animal of average or typical size, although in the tarpan, at least, there is some evidence that this may be so.

The *vertex* length of the skull (measurement no. 2), as may be seen in Table 33, averages about 12 percent (1.120) longer than the basilar length. It indicates the extent to which the occipital crest extends backward beyond the occipital condyles (measurement no. 3). Additional comments on the significance of this cranial ratio are given in Chapter 5, where also there is a discussion of the relationship of tooth wear to age in the domestic horse.

The probable age of a horse, as every horseman knows, has from time immemorial been determined by opening the animal's mouth and noting the state of abrasion of the lower incisor teeth. But the writer believes that he was the first to show that in a horse's skull the approximate age may be determined also (within a given species or

Table 34. Basilar length of the skull (sexes combined and averaged).

Number of skulls measured	Breed or subspecies	Average Basilar length, mm
60	Average of 10 "warmblood" breeds	481.5
24	Arabian	493.7
5	Thoroughbred	518.6
1	Standardbred	526.0
7	Shetland	369.4
2	Celtic	452.0
1	Fjord	490.0
26	Draft	561.7
25	Przevalsky's horse	477.2
2	South Russian tarpan	466.0
33	Kulan	454.6
10	Kiang	456.0
1	Persian onager	434.5
1	Ghorkar	424.4
3	Hemippus	367.3
30	Domestic ass	384.2
6	Somali wild ass	458.8
25	Grévy's zebra	539.9
25	Mountain zebra	454.0
17	Hartmann's zebra	483.7
30	Chapman's zebra	473.3
16	Grant's zebra	444.8
12	Quagga	452.7
26	*E. occidentalis*	545.9
4	Mule	480.0

breed) by relating the length of the row of six upper molar-premolar teeth to the basilar length of the skull. As a horse grows older, the length of the tooth row in relation to the overall skull length becomes progressively less, at a rate which is proportionate to the *logarithm* of the age (see Chapter 5).

Another osteometric comparison by which the approximate age of a horse may be determined is simply to relate the length of the diastema in the upper jaw (measurement no. 13) to the length of the upper tooth-row (measurement no. 14). For as a horse wears down its grinding teeth with use, the tooth-row becomes shorter and the diastema longer. For example, in a domestic horse 5 years of age this index averages about 57.5, at 10 years 63.4, at 20 years 69.9, and at 40 years 77.0, the formula being:

$$\log \text{Age, years} = 71.2 \log \frac{\text{Diastema length}}{P^2 - M^3 \text{ length}} - 4.71$$

Accordingly, this index may be used as a supplementary means of determining a horse's age; or, in skulls where the incisor teeth are missing, as at least an approximation of the actual age. The index could be established also for donkeys, hemionids, and zebras, provided a sufficient number of skulls of various known ages could be measured in each of these subgeneric groups.

Living head length in all breeds and species has been derived from the formula:

Head length, mm = 1.06 Vertex Skull length, mm + 15.24

Thus, in the Arabian horse, for example, the living head length is 1.06 × 540.8 + 15.24, or 588.5 mm. The length in stallions is usually from 1 to 2 percent greater than in mares.

Workers with biological data are generally desirous of knowing not only the average or mean measurement of a character, but also the extent to which the character *varies or ranges* within a sizable population of its kind. In the genus *Equus,* or horse family, the degree of physical variability, while appreciable, is less than that which occurs in various other kinds of mammals—the primates, carnivores, and proboscidians (elephants), for example. Statisticians express the degree of variation by using two terms: Standard Deviation and Coefficient of Variation, respectively. The Standard Deviation is an *absolute* measure of the degree of variation below and above the average or mean value of a measurable character. It is derived by taking *the square root of the sum of the squares of the individual deviations from the mean, divided by the number of observations.* Expressed as a formula,

$$\text{S.D.} = \sqrt{\Sigma d^2 / N}$$

The Coefficient of Variation (C.V.), in turn, is a *relative* measure, derived by multiplying the Standard Deviation by 100 and dividing the product by the mean or average value of the character measured. Thus,

$$\text{C.V.} = \frac{100 \text{ S.D.}}{M}$$

Both the Standard Deviation and the Coefficient of Variation are standard measurements of variability, used universally by biologists, zoologists, and workers in all other scientific fields where variable material has to be accurately and systematically described.

As an illustration, man (in the United States) may be said to average 69 inches in height; and the Standard Deviation of this measurement is 2.76 inches. Hence the Coefficient of Variation is $\frac{100 \times 2.76}{69}$, or 4.00. In any distribution which follows what is known as the Normal Curve, the number of Standard Deviations (both below and above the mean value) in 1000 cases is 3.2414. Accordingly, in 1000 American men, selected at random, the expected range in height would be $\pm$ 3.2414 $\times$ 2.76 inches ($=$ 7.94 inches), or from about 61 inches to 77 inches. The assumption of 1000 cases as an adequate or representative range of a character, or measurement, is made on the basis that only one out of 1000 cases would be expected to lie *outside* $\pm$ 3.2414 Standard Deviations (and might be an altogether exceptional example in an otherwise normally ranging series).

In horses and their relatives, the Coefficient of Variation for most measurements of height (or long-bone length) is only 2.60, as compared with 4.00 in man. In 1000 cases (e.g., the so-called Standard Range), the *relative* degree of variation in such a measurement may be derived by multiplying the Coefficient of Variation by 3.2414 and adding the product to 100.00. Thus in 1000 horses, the shoulder or withers height would be expected to range $\pm$ 3.2414 $\times$ 2.60, or 8.42 $+$ 100; or $\pm$ $\times$ 1.0842. Therefore if the average height of a certain breed of horse, or other equine species, averages 50 inches, the *range* in height among 1000 specimens of that kind would be expected to be 50 $\pm$ $\times$ 1.0842, or from about 46 inches to 54 inches. This range, as calculated from the C.V. of the long bones of the skeleton, accords with the range in height of living horses, which is generally given as $\pm$ one "hand" (4 inches).

It should be added that the degree of variation in bones of the skeleton other than the long bones of the limbs (as, for example, the vertebrae and the pelvis) is not necessarily the same as the above. However, for the principal bones of the limbs, both fore and hind, along with the length of the skull,* the plus-or-minus range in 1000 cases may be taken as $\times$ 1.084. This degree of variability applies to all six subgenera of *Equus*.**

Before concluding this topic, the writer would like to refer briefly to the postcranial skeletons that he has measured, since these specimens constituted an important part of the data used to establish the typical limb-bone lengths assigned to the various species listed in Table 30. The skeletons measured were as follows (Table 34). All skeletons were measured either in the Vertebrate Paleontology Laboratory of the California Institute of Technology, Pasadena, or at the Los Angeles County Museum of Natural History, during the years 1947–1952, inclusive.

---

* *Within a given breed,* skull (or head) length varies to practically the same degree as long-bone length or shoulder height. However, when extremes of size are being compared—such as a Shetland pony and a draft horse—the range in head length is proportionately somewhat less than in shoulder height or long-bone length, and should be expected to vary at about .95 or .96 the rate of the latter.

** In bony *caliber,* or width, the greatest variation occurs in the minimum widths of the metacarpus and metatarsus, where the Coefficient of Variation may range as high as 7.10. This is mainly because of a sex difference in the minimum widths, in which stallions (for a given metapodial *length*) average from 1.06 to 1.07 larger (i.e., thicker) than mares. In general, however, the various width measurements of the limb bones have a C.V. that varies from about 3.00 to 4.50 (both sexes combined), with an average value of 3.75, or about half again the degree of variation that is typical of limb-bone *lengths*.

Table 35. Postcranial skeletons of equine specimens measured by the author.
(cf. Table 33)

Subgenus	Breed or species	Museum and Catalogue Number	Sex and estimated Age	Side of skeleton measured	Remarks	Estimated Shoulder Height mm	Estimated Living Height inches
Horses (Equus)	Arabian, "Deyr"	LA M 700	♂ 24	right		1471	57.91
	Arabian	LA M 1475	♀ 3	left		1503	59.17
	Arabian	UCAC ?	♀ c.5	av., r & l	skull lacking	1420	55.90
	Thoroughbred	LA M 1485	♂ 10	right		1608	63.31
	Shetland	LA M 1483	♂ 25	right & l		1044	41.10
	Percheron, "Blackie"	LA M 1463	♂ 37	right	skeleton	1676	65.98
	Draft	LA M 1079	♀ 18	left	mounted	1591	62.64
	Light Draft	LA M 699	♀ ?	(not noted)	metacarpal & foot bones lacking	1568	61.73
	Unknown	PM 108	♂ ? 12 days	av., r & l		1078	42.44
	Przevalsky's horse	AM 90198	♂ 3¼	av., r & l		1194	47.01
	Przevalsky's horse	US 238111	♂ 8½	av., r & l		1283	50.51
	Mule (draft)	LA M 1464	♀ 40	left		1610	63.39
Asses (Asinus)	Donkey	PM 1622	♀ 4½	av., r & l	Mc & foot bones lacking	1077	42.40
	Donkey	LA M 1478	♂ 6	left		1142	44.96
	Nubian wild ass	AM 135017	♂ 25+	av., r & l		1176	46.30
Hemionids (Hemionus)	Kulan	AM 57209	♂ 15	av., r & l	many small bones lacking	1237	48.70
	Kulan	AM 57211	♀ 13	av., r & l	many small bones lacking	1201	47.28
	Kiang	US 84081	♂ 2	av., r & l	pelvis & hoof pls. lacking	1199	47.20
	Kiang	US 84083	♂ 20	av., r & l	scap., pelvis & hoof pls. lacking	1214	47.80
	Kiang	US 49493	♂ aged	av., r & l	measured also by O. P. Hay, 1915	1246	49.06
	Kiang	US 84088	♀ 7	right	scap., pelvis & hoof pls. lacking	1237	48.70
	Persian onager	AN 12586	♀ 12½	av., r & l		1169	46.02
	Hemippus	PM 1637	♂ 8½	av., r & l		1030	40.55

Group		Specimen	Sex	Age	Side	Notes	No.	
Dolichohippus	Grévy's zebra	CAS Field 99	♀	4	(not noted)	scapula & foot lacking	1355	53.35
	Grévy's zebra	CAS Field 101	♂	10	(not noted)	phalanges lacking	1381	54.37
	Grévy's zebra	AM 82037	♀	6½	(not noted)	scapula lacking	1396	54.96
	Grévy's zebra	LA M 1598	♂	13+			1371	53.98
Plesippus	*Plesippus shoshonensis*	LA ———	♀	?	left	skeleton mounted (cf. measurements with Grévy's)	1411	55.55
Hippotigris	Mountain zebra	PM 1620	♂	1½	av., r & l		1109	43.66
	Mountain zebra	US 270514	♂	4	av., r & l	few bones only	1219	48.00
	Mountain zebra	US 270125	♂	aged	av., r & l		1146	45.12
	Chapman's zebra	LA M 1229	♂	2	av., r & l	skull & scapula lacking	1158	45.59
Burchelline zebras (*Quaggoides*)	Chapman's zebra	LA M 548	♂	3½	av., r & l		1235	48.62
	Grant's zebra	CAS Field 45	♂	8	av., r & l	phalanges lacking	1162	45.75
	Grant's zebra	CAS Field 41	♀	10	av., r & l	phalanges lacking	1144	45.04
	Grant's zebra	CAS Field 44	♀	10	av., r & l	phalanges lacking	1130	44.49
	Grant's zebra	CAS Field 40	♂	18	av., r & l	phalanges lacking	1188	46.77
	Quagga	AN 6317	♂	9	av., r & l		1131	44.53
	Quagga	PM 1623	♀	22	av., r & l	phalanges lacking	1182	46.54
	E. occidentalis (Western quagga)				av., r & l	(measured the equivalent of 28 unmounted skels.)	1470	57.87
(zebroid)	*E. conversidens*	CIT 3229	?		av., r & l	(measured 30 sets of unmounted bones)	1266	49.85
	leoni Stock	CIT 3230	?		av., r & l			

Someone, or some group of workers, should make an osteometric survey of *all* the equine specimens in *all* the natural history museums of the world. However, this would be a colossal task. In the meanwhile, it is hoped that the dimensional data presented herein will add materially to all which has been published heretofore.

---

b. The phylogeny of the genus *Equus*.

During the writer's study of fossil Equidae, it became evident that some attempt at a pictorial representation of the family tree of the horse tribe should be made, in order to show in a single view the manifold relationships of the various constituent subgenera in time and space.

Fig. 249 represents this attempt. Doubtless many paleontologists will question the validity of some of the conclusions drawn, but the writer will welcome constructive criticism. Possibly the most questioned point will be the writer's hypothesis that *E. occidentalis* was a possible ancestor of the Recent representatives (the Burchell's zebras and the quagga) of the subgenus *Quaggoides* in South and East Africa. However, a comparison of the skulls of these forms, and especially of the limb bones, makes such a conclusion quite warranted. A glance at the limb-bone indices charted in Fig. 224 shows a general correspondence of *E. occidentalis* with the other compared species in all 20 indices, and a *close* correspondence in no fewer than 18 of them—either with one, the other, or all three of the Recent zebras charted. As pointed out on p. 386, the probability of this correspondence being due to chance or coincidence is infinitesimally small. Indeed, in no other chartings of equine species, even those known to be closely related, can such remarkable affinity be demonstrated. This structural kinship of *E. occidentalis* with the Burchell's zebras and the quagga—as contrasted with a greater or lesser *lack* of relationship with other species of *Equus*—is, then, the basis for assuming herein a possible direct* descent of the Recent species of *Quaggoides* from *Equus* (*Quaggoides*) *occidentalis*.

Most of the other presumed lines of relationship and descent shown in Fig. 249 need no extended explanation here, since they have in effect been *dictated* by the known occurrences in time of many of the forms charted, and by the degree of similarity or dissimilarity shown in their respective cranial and limb-bone measurements and proportions.

Some of the lines—such as those of *E. stenonis, E. sanmeniensis, E. sivalensis,* and the European "coldblood" horses *E. mosbachensis, E. abeli,* and *E. germanicus*—are known, of course, only up to the time of their latest observed (unearthed) occurrence, which may long precede the actual time of their final existence. Accordingly, their effects, if any, on later and possibly related forms can only be surmised. Other forms, such as *Hesperohippus,* and O. P. Hay's several fossil subspecies of *E. caballus,* need additional postcranial material to aid in a more positive establishing of their relationships.

How many migrations across the Bering Strait land bridge from North America to Asia were made by members of the genus *Equus* will probably never be known. However, if such migrations could be made in one direction it would seem reasonable to suppose that they could be made in the opposite direction also. Hence, certain equine forms, originating in North America, could migrate not only to Asia, but beyond into Europe and even as far as the southern tip of Africa. Evolving further in the Old World, these

---

* Although transoceanic, via the land bridge across Bering Strait.

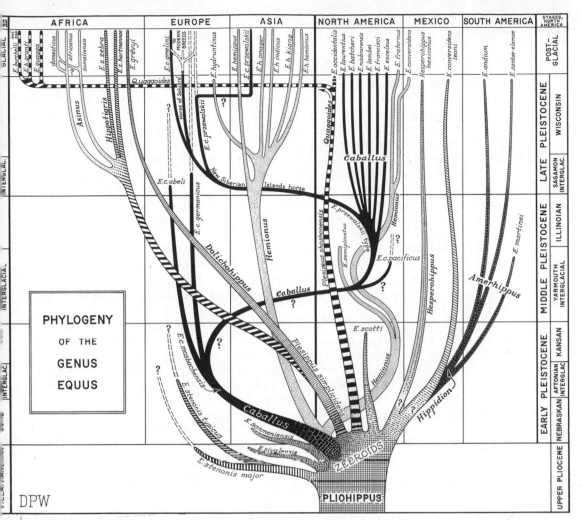

Fig. 249 Hypothetical family tree of the genus *Equus*. In this necessarily conjectural diagram no attempt is made to show forms other than those discussed, or mentioned, in the present volume. The hemispheric migrations of various types are not as yet systematically correlated with geologic time; accordingly, it is not known how many such back-and-forth migrations took place. For further explanation, see accompanying text.

forms could then migrate back to North America. Such migrations—if they occurred in both directions—could account for many as yet unexplained occurrences, as for example the appearance of a "coldblood" horse (*E. pacificus*) in North America (California) at a time when such draft-type horses were known to be flourishing in Europe. Certainly a generalized, perhaps larger form of the present-day Mongolian wild horse (*E. caballus przewalskii*) is known, through its skeletal remains, to have ranged, at one time or another during the Pleistocene, over most of Europe, the northern two-thirds of Asia, and across the Bering Strait land bridge into Alaska and the Yukon Territory. If Hay's *Equus niobrarensis,* which in all probability was a *horse,* could have been a still larger variant of *E. c. przewalskii,* it could have come into North America from Asia.

Likewise, *E. occidentalis,* before becoming extinct in the New World, could have migrated first into Asia and then into Africa, where some form of it could have given rise to the existing *Quaggoides* zebras there.

A concept similar to the latter was advanced by Dr. Paul McGrew (1944), who, however, expresses many points at variance with those of the present writer. For example, McGrew makes the true (caballine) horses descendants of *Astrohippus,* and declares that by Middle Pleistocene time the zebras had become extinct everywhere except in Africa. If this were true, it would become difficult to account for such probable zebrine or zebroid forms as the Mexican *Hesperohippus* and *E. conversidens leoni,* and the North American *Plesippus shoshonensis.* The fact is that of all fossil—or for that matter, living— Equidae recorded osteometrically in the literature, *E. occidentalis* is the best documented. This documentation reveals that an equine species exhibiting all the morphologic features of zebras—and enough of those of *Plesippus shoshonensis* to have descended either from it or from some more westerly variant of it—was flourishing, possibly in herds of thousands, over the grassy plains of the southwestern coastal area later to be named Rancho La Brea.

As to *Astrohippus* being the ancestor of the true horses (*Equus caballus* and subspecies)—as many paleontologists in addition to McGrew have assumed—it can be said that a plotting of the limb-bone indices of the well-represented species *Astrohippus stockii* shows divergences of such an unprecedented degree as to make any direct relationship with *E. caballus* unthinkable. If any existing subgenus could be descended from *Astrohippus,* it would be *Hemionus,* not *Equus**; but even in relation to *Hemionus* the small (shoulder height = C. 866 mm, or about 34 inches), slender-boned, extremely cursorial form *Astrohippus* exhibits such radical divergences in many of its indices as to make an affinity with the larger form highly unlikely. Here again is seen the fallacy of depending on dental characters alone—the only criteria used heretofore in the study of *Astrohippus*—as means of determining the relationships of either living or fossil forms of *Equus* and earlier Equidae.

While certain species of *Equus* have been proposed by other authors (and are listed as *caballus* in the accompanying family tree), these supposed species may in some cases be no more than regional subspecies or varieties. Hay's *E. hatcheri,* for example, could well be a large variant of *E. caballus* sp., and his *E. niobrarensis alaskae* (a form perhaps *specifically* distinct from his *E. niobrarensis*) an earlier variant of *E. c. przewalskii.* Gidley's *E. scotti,* from the Early Pleistocene of Texas, while generally regarded as a "true horse," presents in its skeletal proportions more characteristics of a zebrine than of a caballine nature. Hoffstetter (1952) places Branco's *E. andium* in a new subgenus, *Amerhippus,* a classification that would seem to be justified. Stock's (1948) *E. conversidens leoni* of Mexico should not be confused with Owen's (1869) *E. conversidens* sp., since the two forms are markedly dissimilar, the former showing some of the skeletal characters of both *Hippotigris* and *Quaggoides,* while Owen's species shows possible affinity with *Hemionus. E. excelus* Leidy is not sufficiently well represented by cranial and postcranial remains to permit of dependable specific classification. While such of the limb-bone proportions of *E. excelsus* as are known indicate caballine affinity, its teeth and its hoofs are more zebra-like in character. However, the dentition, as pointed out previously, is one of the least reliable criteria for morphologic identification in *Equus. E. sanmeniensis* Zdansky exhibits postcranial characters both of *Equus* and *Hemionus,* and probably

---

* In Fig. 241, the subgenus *Equus* is designated *Caballus,* in order to avoid its being confused with the entire genus, which is also *Equus.*

cannot, from its recorded remains, be identified any more closely than this. *E. sivalensis* (including *namadicus*) may turn out to be *subgeneric* variants akin to *Hemionus*. *Hesperohippus mexicanus* Hibbard, of which only the skull and teeth are known, is possibly of *generic,* rather than subgeneric, distinction. *Plesippus* represents a fossil North American genus of zebras, while *E. stenonis* is the Lower Pleistocene zebra of Europe. *E. hydruntinus,* the so-called "wild ass" of the Late Pleistocene of Europe, is shown by its limb-bone proportions to have been a hemionid (onager) rather than any form of *Asinus.*

But whatever the manifold variations of the numerous subgenera of *Equus* during the Pleistocene, it would appear safe to accept that they all descended from the generalized Upper Pliocene form *Pliohippus.* Indeed, some of the off-branchings of the genus *Equus,* all of which are shown in Fig. 249 as having occurred during the Pleistocene, may well have separated from the *Pliohippus* stem at earlier stages.

---

c. Baluchitherium, and the problem of size-limitation.

A great stir was created among zoologists and paleontologists by the discovery, in 1922, in central Mongolia, of the skeletal remains of an unprecedently large land mammal. It was determined that the animal was a giant hornless rhinoceros. Other finds of similar, but smaller, specimens had been made before in various localities in Asia; the first was in eastern Baluchistan. Hence the generic name adopted for the remains found there, and applied to other remains of the same type, was *Baluchitherium*. The animals themselves were called baluchitheres. The geologic locus of the species was determined as being the upper Oligocene, which would have been about 40 million years ago.

The reconstruction of the entire body of *Baluchitherium* proved to be a long and difficult job. At the American Museum of Natural History in New York City, a reconstruction on paper was made by Henry Fairfield Osborn and published in the *American Museum Novitates* (No. 78) for May 25, 1923. Osborn gave the animal a plausible shoulder height of 13 feet 4 inches. However, in the present writer's opinion— the result of long consideration of the subject—the animal is given a head that is too long for the skull, a neck that is too long for a rhinoceros, and a body the great vertical depth of which would result in a weight too great to be supported on the relatively tiny feet shown in Osborn's drawing. An earlier restoration had made the baluchithere 12 feet high at the shoulder, and in some respects depicted a more believable animal, since the neck was shorter, the feet substantially larger, and the limbs thicker. But it was stated that "The body outline in both restorations is highly conjectural." It would have had to be, since all that had actually been recovered of the specimen was a nearly complete skull, three neck vertebrae, and the bones of both the fore and the hind limbs, with the exception of a scapula. No pelvis, ribs, or post-cervical vertebrae were available.

A later restoration, made after many additional bones of smaller-sized baluchitheres had been unearthed in expeditions during 1922–1930, yielded (to those who interpreted the bones) a truly colossal mammal with an estimated shoulder height of no less than 17 feet 3 inches (one restoration even made it 17 feet 9 inches). In this restoration the missing bones of the largest-sized specimen—of which only two neck vertebrae and one metacarpal bone were secured—were "enlarged" by multiplying the corresponding bones of the smaller-sized specimens by factors ranging (among the smaller specimens) from 1.2 to 1.4. By application of this procedure, the reconstructed *Baluchitherium* with a height of 17 feet 3 inches was derived. That this height, and the implied body weight, were excessive, may be seen by a consideration of the following comparisons.

One of the most direct and valid comparisons is (1) to relate the size of the *foot bones* in various smaller hoofed mammals to the known bodyweights of the same specimens; (2) extrapolate the relationship to large graviportal (weight-bearing) types such as the hippopotamus and the elephant; and (3) thereby determine, within a reasonable range, the bodyweight "predicted" for *Baluchitherium*. The measurement used by the writer for this purpose is the side-to-side width across the upper row of the two layers of small bones of the carpus (or what corresponds to the bony width of the wrist in man). The resulting correlation is shown in Figure 250. It will be noted that the carpus width in *Baluchitherium* (specifically the Grade IV by 1.4) is 330 mm (13 inches), and the corresponding bodyweight, as shown by the graph, just over 20,000 pounds. For additional reasons, to follow, the weight here chosen for *Baluchitherium* is about 25,000 pounds. The figures for the Shetland, Thoroughbred, and draft horses shown on the graph represent the average (of stallion and mare) widths of the carpus and the average bodyweights for these breeds as listed elsewhere in this book.

A second way of estimating the probable bodyweight of a hoofed mammal of known, or estimated, height and length is to calculate the *surface area* of the animal as it appears in a straight, standing profile view, then convert the area to *volume*. This may be done by taking the *square root* of the area and cubing it, thereby converting the linear measurement into volume. This method, although constituting a rational approach to the problem, has not been seen elsewhere by the writer, and he introduces it herewith for what it may be worth. Using carefully measured scale drawings, here are some of the ratios derived for the species listed.

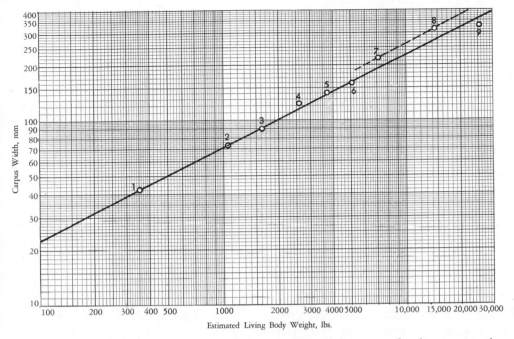

Fig. 250 Bodyweight in relation to carpus width in horses and other mammals of various sizes. 1 = Shetland pony, carpus width 42.4 mm, weight 354 pounds; 2 = Thoroughbred, 73.5 mm, 1066 pounds; 3 = draft horse, 90.5 mm, 1623 pounds; 4 = black rhinoceros, 125 mm, 2565 pounds; 5 = great Indian rhinoceros, 142 mm, 3700 pounds; 6 = hippopotamus, 160 mm, 5100 pounds; 7 = Indian elephant, 217 mm, 7100 pounds; 8 = African elephant "Jumbo," 318 mm, 14,560 pounds; 9 = Baluchitherium, 330 mm, 25,500 pounds. For details, see text. On graph, Bodyweight, pounds = .1975 Carpus Width^2.

Table 36. Relationships of profile area, volume, and bodyweight in various hoofed and graviportal mammals.

Breed or Species	Shoulder height, in.	Profile area, square inches	Volume,* cub. in.	Bodyweight, lbs.	Bodyweight / Volume
Horse, Shetland pony	39.6	1140	38,480	354	.0092
Horse, Arabian	59.35	2154	99,977	922	.0092
Horse, Thoroughbred	63.4	2486	123,980	1066	.0086
Horse, draft, av.	63.8	3001	172,660	1623	.0094
Rhinoceros, black	62.2	4148	267,190	2565	.0096
Rhinoceros, Indian	67.0	5217	376,900	3700	.0098
Rhinoceros, white	68.0	5475	405,100	3970	.0098
Elephant, African	132.0	12,900	1,466,000	14,660	.0100
Baluchitherium (est.)	160.0	19,150	2,656,800	25,500	.0096

* This "volume" is necessarily only relative. It has been derived, as explained, by taking the square root of the actual profile area (which in horses includes the *bony* tail and the projection of the ears beyond the body, but excludes the mane; and in rhinos and elephants includes the ears, such as project beyond the body, and the horns or tusks), then cubing it. The actual volume in cubic inches would be only about one-fourth of the amount listed, depending upon the specific gravity of the particular animal type.

Attention is called to the last column of figures in the above table. As any worker with biological data knows, it is very difficult to evolve formulas or ratios of relationship that closely apply to animals of widely different sizes. Yet here is a ratio that varies only 4 percent between a Shetland pony and *Baluchitherium*—an animal of some 70 *times* its bulk, and which accommodates also such huge quadrupeds as the elephant and the mammoth. There are several reasons why the Bodyweight/Volume ratio as determined from the area of a profile view of the animal *must* vary. One reason is because such a formula assumes a constant ratio of body *width* to body height and length, which does not hold true. The torso of an elephant or a rhinoceros is practically circular in cross-section, whereas that of a light-built running ungulate, such as an antelope, is oval-shaped (that is, much higher than it is wide). Even in a given type of animal, such as the horse, heavy individuals, such as occur in the various draft breeds, have a much "rounder" cross-section of body than does a Thoroughbred, an Arabian, or one of the other light breeds. Another factor which contributes to the small (.0086) ratio in the Thoroughbred is the "trained-down" condition of the animal when racing. All superfluous weight, including some muscle, is worked off the animal, so that in a sense the racing weight does not represent the "normal" weight. If in the Thoroughbred a factor of .0092 rather than .0086 be used (the former factor applying in the Arabian horse and the Shetland pony, and probably all other light breeds), the derived bodyweight is 1141 pounds. This is 75 pounds more than the "racing" weight listed. The extra 75 pounds could be added without the depth of chest or the general body profile changing materially, simply by reason of the animal's torso ("barrel") becoming *wider and rounder.*

Another factor that modifies the Bodyweight/Volume ratio is the weight of the four limbs in relation to the total bodyweight. If the limb length is relatively *long* (as for example in racehorses) the ratio becomes *smaller,* and vice versa. Indeed, in the hippopotamus, which is relatively extremely short-legged and huge-bodied, the ratio rises to .0130, which indicates a very high bodyweight in relation to profile area. If the weight in the hippopotamus were estimated even by the factor (.0100) applying to the African elephant, the bodyweight predicted would be only about 3900 pounds instead of the actual 5100 pounds. The reason for this is that in the elephant the weight of the four legs alone is about ¼ the weight of the entire body (including the limbs), whereas in the relatively long-bodied and short-limbed hippo the legs constitute only about 1/17 of the total weight. The higher-than-average ratio of .0100 in the African elephant doubtless results from the additional weight in this animal of its tusks, trunk, and huge ears.

A third, and more simple, factor directly relating to the weight of a four-footed animal—specifically, in this connection, a graviportal mammal—is the size of the animal's *feet,* either as measured direct or in the form of a clearly outlined track or impression in the ground. Here we are on safer ground (no pun intended!), since the size (area) of the sole of the foot is the only consideration, irrespective of the proportioning of the body and limbs.

Table 36 shows that several different types of graviportal animals each has a foot-size (supporting area of the sole) in direct ratio to its bodyweight. The amount supported is in each animal about *11 pounds per square inch* for each separate foot. It is interesting to note that in Figure 43 the supporting surface of the fore hoof in the Arabian horse is almost exactly circular and has an area of only about 18 square inches. Taking the bodyweight of an average-sized Arab as 922 pounds, it develops that the horse's hoof supports about 12¾ pounds per square inch, or nearly a sixth

(16 percent) more than in the multi-toed graviportal animals listed in Table 36. Here is an illustration of the extreme development and specialization of the foot of the horse as a compact, efficient weight-bearing structure.

Table 37. Supporting area of the foot in several graviportal mammals.

Species	Av. diameter of foot, in.	Circumference of foot, in.	Area of sole, sq. in.	Bodyweight, lbs.
Black rhinoceros	8.6	27	58	2565
White rhinoceros	10.8	34	90	3970
Hippopotamus	12.1	38	115	5100
African elephant	20.6	65	333	14,660
Baluchitherium (est.)	27.2	85	580	25,500

Although more could be written on the subject, it is not the writer's purpose to burden the lay reader with a plethora of mathematics on the size of animals only distantly related to the horse. Rather, the object here has been to demonstrate the *probability,* at least, that the Oligocene hornless rhinoceros named *Baluchitherium* could not have stood 17 feet 3 inches at the shoulder, as was once announced at the American Museum of Natural History and which has since been repeated in textbooks and articles the world over. (Some accounts even upped the height to 18 feet, as though a few inches more made no difference!).

For if Baluchitherium *did* stand 17 feet 3 inches, and had the body and limb proportions indicated in the gigantic plaque of the animal that was exhibited on one of the walls of the American Museum, it would have weighed approximately 53,000 pounds! This would have been almost as heavy as the largest of the herbivorous dinosaurs, such as *Brontosaurus,* which evidently did most of its walking while partly supported in water, and which in addition had foot-bones of extraordinary density and supporting strength.

It would appear that the feet of any mammal can *sustain* several times the weight that they are required to *move about with* in normal activity. A performing elephant, for example, may be able to balance and support its enormous weight for a moment on one foot. And in the bipedal human being, a professional strong-man has been known to support momentarily (on his shoulders, in a standing position) a load of approximately 2500 pounds.* In this performance, each of the man's feet bore about 1370 pounds, which was well over *ten times* the weight of his body alone. And in the weightlifting event known as the Back Lift, over 6000 pounds has been raised a fraction of an inch, which means that during the lift each foot was subjected to a pressure of over *3000 pounds.*

The essential consideration here is not what the foot of a man, or of a four-footed mammal, can support momentarily or briefly, but what the foot can *carry about through*

---

* For a review and discussion of this and other feats of lifting and supporting strength by human athletes, see the author's book, *The Super-Athletes* (South Brunswick (N.J.) and New York: A. S. Barnes & Co., Inc., 1970, 665 pp., illus.), pp. 170–182.

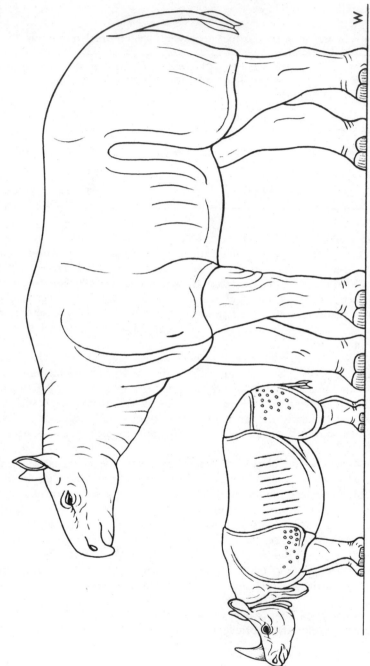

Fig. 251 *Baluchitherium grangeri* Osborn, as reconstructed by the author from Amer. Mus. skull No. 18652 and metacarpus III No. 21618 (the latter increased x 1.4). The shoulder height is 13 feet 4 inches, and the estimated bodyweight 25,500 pounds. For size-comparison, *Baluchitherium* is shown with a modern great Indian rhinoceros, standing 5 feet 7 inches at the shoulder and weighing 3700 pounds. x 1/45 natural size.

life as a normal "work-load." This is regulated, and evidenced, by the cross-sectional area of the foot-bones characteristic of a given type of mammal.

In any case, even by using the measurements of the largest foot-bones attributed to *Baluchitherium,* it would seem evident that this admittedly gigantic mammal did not much exceed a bodyweight of 25,000 pounds. The theoretical weight resulting from the writer's profile-area method is 25,500 pounds. The corresponding shoulder height is 13 feet 4 inches (the same as in Osborn's second restoration); but the feet and legs are much thicker than Osborn has them, in keeping with the enormous carpus width of 330 mm (13 inches). The resulting "restoration" of *Baluchitherium* by the writer is shown in Figure 251, in which the fossil animal is compared in size with an average-sized, present-day great Indian rhinoceros.

Note and Reference

1. Charles Goring, *The English Convict* (abridged edition). (London: 1919).

Selected Bibliography[*]
(nontechnical books only), with some annotations

Alexander, David. *A Sound of Horses.* Indianapolis: The Bobbs-Merrill Co., Inc., 1966. 317 pp., illus. ("The world of racing, from Eclipse to Kelso.")

Bailey, L. H. (Editor). *Cyclopedia of American Agriculture.* New York: The Macmillan Co., 1908. Vol. 3, Animals, 708 pp., illus. (On pages 415–507 and elsewhere in this important work are authoritative accounts of the various breeds of horses by such experts as Homer Davenport, Carl W. Gay, Frederick B. Mumford, John A. Craig, C. S. Plumb, and others.)

Barrier, G. See Goubaux, A.

Bloodgood, Lida Fleitmann, and Piero Santini. *The Horseman's Dictionary.* New York: E. P. Dutton & Co., Inc., 1964. 214 pp. (A comprehensive listing of horsemen's subjects, breeds, terms, etc., presented in alphabetical form.)

(numerous authors). *The Book of the Horse.* London: Paul Hamlyn, 1970. 152 pp., illus. (A beautiful, photographically illustrated book, dealing with various subjects, including show horses, racehorses, armor, hunters, horsemanship, and management.)

Brown, Lewis S. *Horse Anatomy.* New York: Bridgman Pubs., 1948. 80 pp., illus. (One of the best nontechnical books on the subject, beautifully illustrated by the author's line drawings, showing bones and muscles, proportions, gaits, etc.)

Brown, W. R. *The Horse of the Desert.* Derrydale Press, 1929. (A study of the Arabian horse.)

Dembeck, Hermann. *Animals and Men.* Translated from the German by Richard and Clara Winston. (New York: The Natural History Press, 1965). 390 pp., illus. (Contains a highly informative chapter on horses in history.)

Denhardt, Robert M. *The Horse of the Americas.* Freeport, Ill.: The Horseman's Book Shop, 1960. (A historical account, well illustrated, of all the breeds of horses native to North and South America.)

———. *Quarter Horses—a Story of Two Centuries.* Norman, Okla.: Univ. Oklahoma Press, 1967. 192 pp., illus. (A history of the Quarter Horse. Includes a comprehensive glossary and a bibliography of over 100 titles.)

De Trafford, Sir Humphrey. *The Horses of the British Empire.* 2 vols. London: Walter Southwood & Co., 1907. Vol. 1: 286 pp., 218 pls.; Vol. 2: 245 pp., 256 pls. (An outstanding work on British breeds of horses, profusely illustrated).

Dinsmore, Wayne, and John Hervey. *Our Equine Friends.* Chicago: Horse & Mule Asso. of America, Inc., 1944. 32 pp., illus. (A small but excellent brochure on 18 breeds of horses and ponies popular in the United States, by two outstanding authorities.)

---

[*] (See also Notes and References)

Disston, Harry. *Know About Horses.* New York: The Devin-Adair Co., 1961. 216 pp., illus. (This modest-sized book, illustrated by Jean Bowman, presents a surprising amount of information on horses, horsemanship, horse organizations, etc.)

Dobie, J. Frank. *The Mustangs.* Boston: Little, Brown & Co., 1952. 376 pp., illus. (A veritable mine of information on mustangs and all the other horses connected with them.)

Ensminger, M. E. *Light Horses.* Wash., D.C.: U.S. Gov't. Printing Office, 1958. 48 pp., illus. (15 breeds popular in the United States, described and depicted.)

————. *Horses and Horsemanship.* Danville, Illinois: The Interstate Printers, 1969. 907 pp., illus. Perhaps the most authoritative and comprehensive present-day guidebook on the care, production, and use of horses.

Flower, W. H. *The Horse—a Study in Natural History.* London: Kegan Paul & Co., Ltd., 1891. 196 pp., illus. (One of the first British books on the horse written during the last hundred years by an eminent authority on natural history.)

Géroudet, Paul. See Simon, Noel.

Goubaux, A., and G. Barrier. *The Exterior of the Horse.* Philadelphia: 1892. 916 pp., illus. One of the most thorough treatises on the conformation of horses, with excellent illustrations of changes in the teeth owing to age and wear.

Griffen, Jeff. *The Pony Book.* New York: Doubleday & Co., 1966. 287 pp., illus. (An account of most pony breeds, with emphasis on those currently popular in the United States.)

Hayes, Capt. M. H. *Points of the Horse* 5th ed. London, 1930. 595 pp., 658 figs. (A comprehensive survey, well illustrated, of living wild species of Equidae and domestic breeds of the horse. A more recent edition is now available.)

Hervey, John. *The American Trotter.* New York: Coward-McCann, Inc., 1947. 551 pp., illus. The definitive book on the subject, by an acknowledged authority on horses. See also under Dinsmore, Wayne.)

Howard, Robert West. *The Horse in America.* Chicago & New York: Follett Pub. Co., 1965. 299 pp., illus. (A scholarly review of the horse from prehistoric times to the present, with much additional information on the roles played by horses in American history. Many historic illustrations.)

Jepsen, Stanley M. *The Gentle Giants.* South Brunswick (N.J.) and New York: A. S. Barnes & Co., Inc., 1971. 160 pp., illus. (A comprehensive review of draft horses, with separate chapters devoted to the Belgian, Clydesdale, Percheron, Shire, and Suffolk breeds.)

Johnson, Patricia H. (see Osborne, Walter D.)

Knapp-Fisher, H. C. *Man and his Creatures.* London: George Routledge & Sons, Ltd., 1940. 236 pp., illus. (A concise, highly informative account of the horse, dog, elephant, camel, and cat.)

Lydekker, Richard. *The Horse and its Relatives.* London: George Allen & Co., Ltd., 1912. 286 pp., illus. (Although long out of print, this book is a "must" for all researchers on the subject. Lydekker in his day was one of the most popular and prolific of British writers on natural history.)

Montgomery, E. S. *The Thoroughbred.* South Brunswick (N.J.) and New York: A. S. Barnes & Co., Inc., 1971. 570 pp., illus. (An up-to-date history of the Thoroughbred in all aspects of its care and training.)

Muybridge, Edweard. *Animals in Motion.* (London: Chapman & Hall, 1899.) (A pioneering, classic work on the gaits of the horse, profusely illustrated with sequential photographs.)

Osborne, Walter D., and Patricia H. Johnson. *The Treasury of Horses.* New York: Golden Press, 1966. 251 pp., illus. (A beautifully illustrated book, with many photographs in full color.)

Phillips, Lance. *The Saddle Horse*. New York: A. S. Barnes & Co., Inc., 1964. 206 pp., illus. (A well-written and profusely-illustrated book on the American Saddle Horse —its origin, gaits, training and care.)

Pines, Philip A. *The Complete Book of Harness Racing*. New York: Grosset & Dunlap, 1970. 330 pp., illus.

Plumb, Charles S. *Types and Breeds of Farm Animals*. Boston: Ginn & Co., 1906. (Of the 563 pages of this book, the first 168 are devoted to an excellent discussion of the various breeds of horses and ponies. The book is valuable for historical references, but unfortunately has long been out of print.)

Pocock, R. I. In *Harmsworth Natural History, "The Horse Tribe."* 2: 786–800, London: Carmelite House, 1910. (An authoritative and remarkably comprehensive discussion of the horse and its relatives in only 15 pages. The entire *Harmsworth Natural History* consists of 3 volumes, and covers all the lower orders of animals as well as mammals.)

Ridgeway, William. *The Origin and Influence of the Thoroughbred Horse*. Cambridge: University Press, 1905, 538 pp., illus. (A classic memoir on the horse, its ancestors, and its existing wild relatives. An indispensable reference work for all students of the subject, whether or not they agree with the author's sometimes dogmatic views.)

Sanders, Alvin Howard. *History of the Percheron Horse*. Chicago: Breeder's Gazette, 1917. 602 pp., illus.

Scott, William B. *A History of Land Mammals in the Western Hemisphere*. New York: Macmillan, 1913. 693 pp., illus. (This well-written, profusely illustrated volume is indispensable to the study of fossil horses, et al.)

Self, Margaret Cabell. *The Horseman's Encyclopedia*. (New York: A. S. Barnes & Co., Inc., 1946). 519 pp., illus. (Lists and defines all the principal terms and subjects connected with domestic horses, horsemanship, stable management, etc.) A revised edition was published in 1963.

Simon, Noel, and Paul Géroudet. *Last Survivors*. New York: World Pub. Co., 1970. 275 pp., illus. (Lists and describes 48 species of animals in danger of extinction, including the Indian wild ass, the South American mountain tapir, and the Javan rhinoceros. Beautifully illustrated with full-color watercolor paintings.)

Simpson, George G. *Horses*. New York: Oxford Univ. Press, 1951. 236 pp., illus. (A general treatise on horses, zebras, et al, from the standpoint of an eminent paleontologist.)

Smith, Col. Hamilton. *Horses. Jardine's Naturalist's Library*, vol. 20. London; 1866. 352 pp., 30 plates. (An early but invaluable reference work on the history of the domestic horse and its wild relatives. It would appear that the 1866 edition is little if any different from the first edition, which was published in 1841.)

Speelman, Sanford R. *Breeds of Draft Horses*. Washington, D.C.: U.S. Govt. Printing Office, 1941. 16 pp., illus. (Six popular breeds of draft horses described in detail by an expert on the subject.)

———. *Breeds of Light Horses*. Washington, D.C.: U.S. Govt. Printing Office, 1941. 13 pp., illus. (9 Light breeds.)

Sullivan, George. *Harness Racing*. New York: Fleet Pub. Corp., 1964. 121 pp., illus. (A general review of the subject, including lists of world records in all classes up to 1962.)

Summerhays, R. S. *The Observer's Book of Horses and Ponies*. London: Frederick Warne & Co., Ltd., 1961. 256 pp., illus. (This little pocketbook is a true *multum in parvo* source of information, with 85 photographic illustrations and a description of 111 breeds of horses and ponies.)

—— — —. *Summerhays' Encyclopedia for Horsemen.* London and New York: Frederick Warne & Co., 1970. 385 pp., illus. (An extensive, informative dictionary-type book for horsemen, from a British expert's point of view.)

Vernon, Arthur. *History and Romance of the Horse.* Boston: Waverly House, 1939. (Interesting reading, but often inaccurate.)

Vesey-Fitzgerald, B., ed. *The Book of the Horse.* London and Brussels: Nicholson & Watson, 1946. (Well illustrated and informative, except for the first hundred or so pages, in which unwarranted conclusions are stated.)

Widmer, Jack. *The American Quarter Horse.* New York: Charles Scribner's Sons, 1959. 127 pp., illus. (An interesting and informative guide to this breed.)

Wyman, Walker D. *The Wild Horse of the West.* Lincoln, Neb.: Univ. of Nebraska Press, 1966. 348 pp., illus. (An excellent, fully referenced account of mustangs and other horses in the United States since the time of the Spanish explorers. Includes an extensive bibliography both of books and periodicals.)

Xenophon (*c.* 360 B.C.). *The Art of Horsemanship.* Translated by Morris H. Morgan. Boston: Little, Brown and Co., 1893. Illus.

NOTE: In addition to the foregoing general publications, and for the information of readers interested in the *evolution* of the horse, there are the guidebooks issued by the larger natural history museums in the United States, Great Britain, and continental Europe. These brochures, while modestly priced, in many cases give extra details about fossil horses, as well as other early mammals, that may not appear in larger books on the subject. An especially informative booklet in this respect is *The Ascent of Equus,* by Hildegarde Howard and the late Chester Stock, issued by the Los Angeles County Museum of Natural History. In this booklet, too, there is a valuable reference list of books, papers, and articles on horses both recent and fossil.

Authors who have contributed information (especially body measurements) on European and other breeds of domestic horses*

* This list, as will be noted, consists mainly of technical papers in German. These references have been added here mainly for the purpose of aiding other authors and students engaged in research on the bodily conformation of domestic horses of various breeds. Files of the leading German breed periodicals, such as the *Zeitschrift für Zuchtung, Zeitschrift für Tierzüchtung und Züchtungsbiologie,* and *Zeitschrift für Veterinarkunde,* may be found in the libraries of most agricultural colleges.

Breed	Author, Date, and Publication (Arranged Chronologically)
Anglo-Russian	Lesbre, F. X. 1894. *Etudes hippometriques.* Jour. Med. Veterinaire et de Zootechnie. (Lyons), pp. 14–24; 75–88; 150–156; 208–222.
Arabian	Bilek, F. 1914. *Über den Einfluss des Arabischen Blutes bei Kreuzungen mit bes. Hinsicht auf das Lipizzaner Pferd.* Jahrb. f. Wiss. und prakt. Tierzucht, IX Jahrg., Hannover.
	Kuffner, H. 1922. *Studien über das orientalische Pferd mit besonderer Berücksuchtigung seiner Zucht in Balbona.* Arb. Lehr. f. Tierzücht an der Hoch. f. Boden. in Wien, Vol. 1, pp. 151–192. (Cranial, dental, and external body measurements of Arab horses bred in Hungary).
	Stang, V., and D. Wirth. 1926. In: *Tierheilkunde and Tierzucht,* Vol. 1. Berlin. (Includes external body measurements of various breeds of the domestic horse).

Authors on European and other breeds (cont'd)

Breed	Author, Date, and Publication (Arranged Chronologically)
	Müller, —— von. 1933. *Die Bedeutung der Schulter fur die Beurteilung des Pferdes.* Zeitschr. f. Veterinarkunde, Vol. 45, pp. 175–185, 204–223, 255–264. The same, of "Brustmasse", pp. 321–350. (External measurements of the trunk and limbs in over 200 domestic horses of various breeds). Madroff, C. 1937. *Araberpferd und seine Zucht in den Donaulandern.* Zeitschr. f. Züch., Vol. 39, Sec. B, pp. 43–66. (External body measurements of purebred and halfbred Arab horses from the Balkan States). Team, C. B. 1949. Height, weight, chest girth and cannon girth of 25 Arabian stallions and 25 Arabian broodmares at the Kellogg Arabian Horse Ranch, Pomona, California. (Pers. comm. of 5-3-49). Willoughby, D. P. 1950. (Unpublished study). External body measurements of 3 stallions, 9 mares, and one foal (the latter both at 1½ days and 38 days) at the El Cortijo Arabian horse ranch of Donald and Charles McKenna, Claremont, California.
Belgian	Nathusius, S. von. 1891. *Unterschiede Zwischen der morgenlandischen und abendländischen Pferdegruppe.* Berlin. (External body measurements of nine different breeds of domestic horses). —— 1905. *Messungen an Hengsten, Stuten und Gebrauchspferden.* Berlin. (External body measurements of various breeds of domestic horses). Butz, Henseler, and Schottler. 1921. *Praktische Anleitung zum Messen von Pferden.* Anleitungen der Deutschen Gesellschaft f. Zuchtungskunde, Vol. 2. (External conformation of various domestic breeds). Boicoianu, C. 1932. *Studien über das belgische Pferd.* Zeitschr. f. Zucht., Vol. 23, pp. 25–54.
Coach	Grange, E. A. A. 1894. *The external conformation of the horse.* Michigan State Agric. Coll. Exper. Station Bull. 110, pp. 67–98. (Detailed measurements of 11 Roadster, 8 Coach, 6 General purpose, and 25 Draft horses exhibited at the Columbian Exposition, Chicago, and at the Michigan State Fair, 1893).
Criollo	Solanet, E. 1923. *El caballo Criollo.* Conf. Fac. Agron. Veter. Buenos Aires, 23 September, 1923. 35 pp., 9 figs. (History and physical characters of the Criollo horse). —— 1946. (An expanded version of the author's 1923 paper. 155 pp., 48 figs.).

Authors on European and other breeds (cont'd)

Breed	Author, Date, and Publication (Arranged Chronologically)
Danish-North Schleswig (draft)	Nathusius, S. von. 1891 and 1905. (See under Belgian). Butz, Henseler, and Schottler. 1921. (See under Belgian).
Draft (general)	Nathusius, S. von. 1891 and 1905. (See under Belgian). Grange, E. A. A. 1894. (See under Coach). Butz, Henseler, and Schottler. 1921. (See under Belgian). Rhoad, A. O. 1928. *A statistical study of pulling power in relation to conformation of draft horses.* Cornell Univ.: Master's thesis, February 1928, 35 pp., 11 graphs.
East Friesian (heavy Dutch carriage and farm horse)	Nathusius, S. von. 1891 and 1905. (See under Belgian). Butz, Henseler, and Schottler. 1921. (See under Belgian).
East Prussian (see also Trakehner)	Nathusius, S. von. 1891 and 1905. (See under Belgian). Voltz, W. 1913. *Über die Veranderung des Exterieurs während des Wachstums beim ostpreussischen Halbblutpferde.* Landwirt. Jahrb., Vol. 44, pp. 409–436. (External body measurements of East Prussian horses). Butz, Henseler, and Schottler. 1921. (See under Belgian). Schilke, F. 1922. *Biometrische Untersuchungen über das Wachstum der Trakehner Pferde.* Dissertation, Königsberg. Wiechert, F. 1927. *Messungen an ostpreussischen Kavalleriepferden und solchen mit besonderen Leistungen und die Beurteilung der Leistungsfähigkeit auf Grund der mechanischen Verhältnisse.* Arb. der D. G. för Zucht., No. 34. Schaper, Hannover. (Body measurements of East Prussian cavalry horses). Müller, —— von. 1933. *Die Bedeutung der Schulter für die Beurteilung des Pferdes.* Zeitschr. f. Veterinarkunde, Vol. 45, pp. 175–185, 204–223, 255–264. The same, of "Brustmasse", pp. 321–350. (External measurements of the trunk and limbs in over 200 domestic horses of various breeds). Alminas, K. 1939. *Zuchtungsbiologie Untersuchungen am litauisch-samogitischen "Zemaitukai" Pferd im Vergleich zu anderen Rassen.* Zeitschr. f. Tierzuch. und Zuchtungbiol., Vol. 43, pp. 273–349. (Comparative external conformations of various breeds of the domestic horse). Includes a bibliography of over 100 titles.
Finnish	Svanberg, V. 1928. *Beitrag zur Kenntnis der Rassenmerkmale des finnischen Pferdes.* Suomal. Tiede. Toimituksia, Ann. Acad. Sci. Fennicae, Vol. 27, Ser. A., No. 4, pp. 1–87, 2 pls. (Cranial and external body measurements of Finnish horses).
Gidran (Anglo-Arabian)	Madroff, C. 1936. *Das Gidranpferd und seine Zucht in Europa.* Zeitschr. f. Zücht., Vol. 36, Sec. B, pp. 169–184. (External body measurements of Gidran horses).

Authors on European and other breeds (cont'd)

Breed	Author, Date, and Publication (Arranged Chronologically)
Hanoverian	Nathusius, S. von. 1891 and 1905. (See under Belgian). Butz, Henseler, and Schottler. 1921. (See under Belgian). Nicolescu, J. 1923. *Messungen uber die Mechanik des Hannoverschen Pferdes im Vergleich zum Vollblut und Traber.* (In: Berliner Tierärztliche Wochenschrift, Vol. 39, pp. 74–77). Wöhler, H. 1927. *Variationsstatistische Untersuchungen an 200 hannoverschen Stutebuchstuten der Unterlbmarsch unter besonderer Berücksichtigung der Nelusko-Aldemann — 1 — Linie.* Dissert., Halle. (External body measurements of 200 Hanover broodmares). Stegen, H. 1929. *Die Entwicklung des hannoverschen Hengstfohlen in dem Hengstaufzuchtgestut Hunnesruck.* Züchskunde, Vol. 4, pp. 273–288. (External body measurements of Hanover colts). ———— 1929–30. *Die Entwicklung des hannoverschen Halbblutpferdes von der Geburt bis zum Abschluss des Wachstums.* Jour. f. Landwirtschaft., Vol. 77, pp. 139–190. (Growth of the Hanover horse). ———— 1931. (External body measurements of 53 Hanover stallions at 3½ years of age). Arch. f. Tierernarung v. Tierzucht., Vol. 6, pp. 612–635. Müller, ——— von. 1933. (See under East Prussian). Wagener, ———. 1934. (See under Alminas, K., 1939, East Prussian).
Holstein	Nathusius, S. von. 1891 and 1905. (See under Belgian). Butz, Henseler, and Schottler. 1921. (See under Belgian). Iwersen, E. 1926. *Die Körperentwicklung des holsteininischen marschpferdes von der Geburt bis zum Abschluss des Wachstums.* Züchtungskunde, Vol. 1, pp. 134–143. (Growth of the German horse of the Holstein breed).
Lipizzan	Madroff, C. 1935. *Das Lippizanerpferd und seine Zücht in Europa.* Zeitschr. f. Züch., Vol. 33, Sec. B, pp. 169–184. (External body measurements of Lipizzan horses).
Mecklenburg	Kruger, W. 1939. *Uber Wachstumsmessungen . . . der Trakehner Warmblut und Mecklenburger Kaltbludpferd.* Zeitschr. f. Tier. u. Zuch., Vol. 43, p. 145.
Mesohegyes (Hungarian)	Gregory, K. 1931. *Die Mässe von 280 Stuten aus Mezöhegyes, verarbeitet zu einem Beitrag für die Beurteilungslehre des Pferdes.* Arch. f. Tiernährung und Tierzucht, Vol. 6, Part 1, pp. 18–97. (External body measurements of 280 mares of the Hungarian "Furioso-North Star" breed).
Morgan	Dawson, W. M. 1948. Height, weight, and girth measurements of eight Morgan stallions and ten Morgan mares. (Pers. comm. from W. M. Dawson, Animal Husbandman, U. S. Dept. Agric., 10–27–48).
Nonius (Anglo-Norman from Hungary)	Lesbre, F. X. 1894. (See under Anglo-Russian). Madroff, C. 1936. *Das Noniuspferd und seine Zucht in Europa.* Zeitschr. f. Züch., Vol. 36, Sec. B, pp. 337–357. (External body measurements of Large Nonius and Small Nonius horses).
North Swedish (light draft)	Rosiö, B. 1928. *Die Bedeutung des Exterieurs und der Konstitution des Pferdes fur seine Leistungsfahigkeit.* Inaug. Diss., Berlin. (See also under East Prussian, Alminas, 1939).

Authors on European and other breeds (cont'd)

Breed	Author, Date, and Publication (Arranged Chronologically)
Norwegian	Marshall, F. H. A. 1905. *The horse in Norway.* Proc. Roy. Soc. Edinburgh, Vol. 26, pp. 22–32, 2 pls. Stejneger, L. 1904. *Den celtiske pony, tarpanen og fjordhesten.* Naturen, Vol. 28. (Reprinted in Smithson. Misc. Proc., Vol. 48, pp. 469 ff., 1907).
Oberlander (medium-draft, from Austrian Alps)	Kolbe, W. 1928. *Das Oberlander Pferd unter besonderer . . . Normanner, Clydesdaler und Clevelandstammes. Abhand.* des Inst. für Tier. und Molk, and der Univ. Leipzig, Vol. 15, pp. 1–87.
Oldenburg (heavy-type "warmblood")	Nathusius, S. von. 1891 and 1905. (See under Belgian). Butz, Henseler, and Schottler. 1921. (See under Belgian).
Orloff (Russian trotter)	Bantoiu, C. 1922. *Messungen an Trabern und die Beurteilung der Leistungfähigheit auf Grund der mechanischen Verhältnisse.* (In: Tierarztliche Rundschau, Vol. 28, p. 666). Afanassieff, S. 1930. *Der Untersuchung des Exterieurs, der Wachstumintensitat und der Korrelation zwischen Renngeschwindigkeit und Exterieur beim Traber.* Zeitschr. f. Zucht., Vol. 18, pp. 171–209. (Correlation between conformation and trotting ability in the Orloff). Alminas, K. 1939. (See under East Prussian).
Percheron	Grange, E. A. A. 1894. (See under Coach). Lesbre, F. X. 1894. (See under Anglo-Russian). Rhoad, A. O. 1928. (See under Draft). Trowbridge, E. A., and D. W. Chittenden. 1932. *Horses grown on limited grain rations.* Univ. Missouri. Agric. Exper. Sta. Bull. 316, 19 pp. (See also *Percheron News* for January 1939 and January 1942).
Pinzgauer (Austrian draft)	Weiss-Tessbach, A. 1923. *Studien über das Pferd des Pinzgaues.* Arb. d. Lehr. f. Tier. and der Hochschule f. Bodenkultur in Wien, Vol. 2, pp. 157–215.
Quarter Horse	Michaelis, H., and R. Denhardt. (1950?). *The Quarter Horse: why he is and what he is.* A typed copy of an unpublished article, furnished to the writer, including a table of the external body measurements (average) of four Quarter Horse stallions and four Quarter Horse mares. Cunningham, K., and S. H. Fowler. *A study of growth and development in the Quarter Horse.* Louisiana State Univ. Agric. Exper. Sta. Bull. No. 546, November 1961.
Rheinish-Belgian (heavy draft)	Müller, —— von. 1933. (See under East Prussian). Zimmermann, C. 1933. *Ein Beitrag zur Körperentwicklung der rheinishdeutschen Kaltblutpferde in Original zuchtgebeit.* Archiv f. Tierernahrung u. Tierzucht., Vol. 8, Part 4, pp. 497–542. (External body measurements of Rheinish draft horses).
Rheinish-Dutch (heavy draft)	Platen, J. 1925. *Die Abstammung der Stammtiere des rheinisch-deutschen Pferdes nebst kritschen Bemerkungen zur Zucht und Beurteilung des* rheinischen Kaltbluters. Dissertation, Hannover. Hering, A. 1925. *Ein Beitrag zur Kenntnis der Jugendentwicklung des rheinish-deutschen Kaltblutpferdes.* Diss. 1925, Gottingen. A.d.D.G. für Zuchtung, No. 27, Berlin.

Authors on European and other breeds (cont'd)

Breed	Author, Date, and Publication (Arranged Chronologically)
Shetland	Ullmann, G. 1939. *Entwicklung and Wachstum bei Shetlandponys.* Tierarztliche Rundschau, Vol. 45, No. 16, p. 312. (Weight and external body measurements of Shetland ponies from birth to the age of 48 days). Flade, J. E. 1959. *Shetlandponys.* Die Neue Brehm-Bucherei. Wittenberg: 79 pp., 45 figs., 32 tables. (Perhaps the best single work on the external body measurements of Shetland ponies).
Skyros (Greek island) pony	Dimitriadis, J. N. 1937. *Das Skyrospony. Ein Beitrag zum Studium der Pferde Griechenlands.* Zeitschr. f. Zucht., Vol. 37, Part B, pp. 343–385. (Body measurements of three mares, and skull measurements of three mares and three stallions).
Standardbred	Grange, E. A. A. 1894. (See under Coach. Grange calls his Standardbred horses "Roadsters"). Stratul, J. 1922. *Biometrische Untersuchungen an Vollblutpferden* . . . In: Tierarztliche Rundschau, Vol. 28, pp. 665–666. Radescu, T. 1923. *Biometrische Untersuchungen an Vollblutpferden* . . . In: Berliner Tierarztliche Wochenschrift, Vol. 39, pp. 490–492. Müller, —— von. 1933. (See under East Prussian). Alminas, K. 1939. (See under East Prussian). Hervey, J. 1941. *Champion stallions and their conformation.* The Harness Horse, Vol. 7, No. 7, December 10, 1941, p. 112. (External body measurements of five champion trotters). The latter measurements are listed here in Table 5.
Thoroughbred	Nathusius, S. von. 1891 and 1905. (See under Belgian). Lesbre, F. X. 1894. (See under Anglo-Russian). Butz, Henseler, and Schottler. 1921. (See under Belgian). Plischke, A. 1927. *Anatomische Körpermessungen am lebenen Vollblutpferde, ausgefuhrt nach der Messmethod von Schmaltz, unter vergleichsweiser Heranziehung des Trakehner Halbblutes.* Inaug. Dissert., Berlin, 40 pp. (External body measurements of Thoroughbreds compared with those of many other breeds). Müller, —— von. 1933. (See under East Prussian).
Trakehner (see also East Prussian)	Mieckley, ——. 1894. *Wagungen und Messungen von Fullen der Trakehner Fuchsherd in Guddin.* Archiv. f. Wiss. u. Prak. Thierheilkinde, Vol. 20, pp. 320–336. (Growth of the Trakehner horse). Gutsche, ——. 1914. In: *Messungen und Wagungen am Pferd,* by Dr. Reinhold Schmaltz, 1922. (External body measurements of various breeds of domestic horses). Brandes, H. 1926. *Der Einfluss der Vollblutpferdes auf die Herausbildung der ostpreussischen Halbblutzucht in bezug auf Körperform, Stärke und Leistung.* Zeitschr. f. Tierzucht. u. Zuchtungsbiol., Vol. 7, pp. 169–217. (External body measurements in Trakehner and Thoroughbred horses). Feige, E. 1927. *Über die Variation der Grosse ostpreussischer Halbblutpferde.* Zeitschr. f. Tier. u. Züch., Vol. 10, pp. 241–255. (External body measurements of 5840 East Prussian mares measured between 1887–1902). Müller, —— von. 1933. (See under East Prussian).

Authors on European and other breeds (cont'd)

Breed	Author, Date, and Publication (Arranged Chronologically)
	Horst, F. 1935. *Untersuchungen über den Einfluss des Korperbaus auf die Schrittlange des Pferdes.* Grevesmuhlen i. Mecklenburg. 44 pp. (Correlations of bone lengths and limb angles with length of stride in Trakehner horses). Kruger, W. 1939. (See under Mecklenburg).
Veglia Island (Austria) pony	Ogrizek, A. 1923. *Studie über die Abstammung des Insel-Veglia (Krk) Ponys.* Arbeit. der Lehrk. f. Tier. an der Hochschule f. Bodenkultur in Wien, Vol. 2, pp. 73–100. (External body measurements of seven stallions and one mare).
Zemaitukas (Lithuanian)	Alminas, K. 1939. (See under East Prussian).

Periodicals on the Horse

NOTE: Some breeder's or horsemen's magazines remain established for many years; others come and go, according to fluctuating popularity. The following list is accurate, it is believed, as of 1969. Information may sometimes be obtained by writing to the particular breed association involved, although associations, too, occasionally become inactive. The following list is confined to horses, rather than livestick generally.

Breed	Publication	Address
General	Chronicle of the Horse, The	Middleburg, Virginia. 22117.
	Hoofs and Horns	1750 Humboldt St., Denver, Colo. 80218.
	Horse and Rider	116 E. Badillo St., Covina, Calif. 91722.
	Horse Lover, The	Box 914, El Cerrito, Calif. 94530.
	Horseman	5314 Bingle Road, Houston, Texas. 77018.
	Horseman's Courier, The	57 So. Main St., Fairport, N.Y. 14450.
	Horsemen's Advisor, The	624 Payton Ave., Des Moines, Iowa. 50315.
	Horsemen's Journal	425- 13th St. N.W., Washington, D.C. 20004.
	Horsemen's Yankee Pedlar	Box 297, North Wilbraham, Mass. 01067.
	Horse Show	527 Madison Avenue, New York, N.Y. 10022.
	Horse World	Box 588, Lexington, Kentucky. 40501.
	Lariat, The	14239 N.E. Salmon Creek Ave., Vancouver, Wash. 98665.
	Maryland Horse, The	Box 4, Timonium, Maryland. 21093.
	National Horseman	933 Baxter Ave., Louisville, Kentucky. 40204.
	Northeast Horseman	Box 47, Hampden Highlands, Maine. 04445.
	Saddle and Bridle	8011 Clayton Road, St. Louis, Mo. 63117.
	Southern Horseman, The	Box 5735, Meridian, Mississippi. 39301.
	Trail Rider, The	Chatsworth, Georgia. 30705.
	Turf and Sport Digest	511-513 Oakland Ave., Baltimore, Md. 21212.
	Western Horseman, The	3850 N. Nevada Ave., Colorado Springs, Colo. 80901.
Appaloosa	Appaloosa News	Box 403, Moscow, Idaho. 83843.
Arabian	Arabian Horse News	Box 1009, Boulder, Colorado. 80302.
	Arabian Horse World	23 E. Main St., Springville, N.Y. 14141.
Hackney	Hackney Journal, The	Box 29, Columbus, Wisconsin. 53925.
Morgan	Morgan Horse Magazine	Box 149, Leominster, Massachusetts. 01453.
Paint	Paint Horse Newsletter, The	Box 12487, Fort Worth, Texas. 76116.
Palomino	Palomino Horses	Box 249, Mineral Wells, Texas. 76067.
Pinto	Pinto Horse, The	4315 Hilldale Road, San Diego, Calif. 92116.

Breed Associations and Registry Addresses (cont'd)

Breed or type	Association	Address
Ponies	American Shetland Pony Journal	Box 2339, West Lafayette, Indiana. 47906.
	Pony of Americas Magazine	Box 1447, Mason City, Iowa. 50401.
	Your Pony	1040 W. James St., Columbus, Wisc. 53925.
Quarter Horse	Quarter Horse Digest	Gann Valley, South Dakota. 57341.
	Quarter Horse Journal	Box 9105, Amarillo, Texas. 79105.
Spanish Mustang	Spanish Mustang News	1037 E. Lehigh Road, Mesa, Arizona. 85201.
Standardbred	Harness Horse, The	Telegraph Press Bldg., Harrisburg, Pa. 17101.
	Hoof Beats (Trotting Horses)	750 Michigan Ave., Columbus, Ohio. 43215.
	Standardbred Horse Review	21-300 Kennedy, Desert Hot Springs, Calif. 92240.
Tennessee Walking Horse	Voice of the Tennessee Walking Horse	Box 6009, Chattanooga, Tennessee. 37401.
Thoroughbred	Blood Horse, The	Box 4038, Lexington, Kentucky. 40504.
	Florida Horse, The	Box 699, Ocala, Florida. 32670.
	Thoroughbred of California, The	201 Colorado Place, Arcadia, Calif. 91006.
	Thoroughbred Record, The	Box 580, Lexington, Kentucky. 40501.
	Washington Horse, The	13470 Empire Way, Seattle, Wash. 98178.
Welsh Pony	Welsh News	1427 Hampshire St., Quincy, Illinois. 62301.

In addition to the above publications on light horses and ponies, some of the draft horse associations, such as the Percheron and the Belgian, issue periodic news reports on these heavy breeds.

Many excellent periodicals on horse breeding are published in Germany. Among them are these two, both published in Berlin:

Zeitschrift für Züchtung.

Zeitschrift für Tierzüchtung und Züchtungsbiologie, einschl. Tierernärung.

Breed Associations and Registry Addresses (as of mid-1971)*

Breed or type	Association	Address
American Albino Horse	American Albino Assn., Inc.	P.O. Box 79, Crabtree, Oregon. 97335.
American Cream Horse	American Cream Horse Assn.	Mrs. K. B. Topp, Hubbard, Iowa. 50122.
American Saddle Horse	American Saddle Horse Breeder's Assn., Inc.	929 South Fourth St., Louisville, Ky. 40203.
	American Saddlebred Pleasure Horse Assn.	801 South Court St., Scott City, Kan. 67871.
Andalusian	American Andalusian Assn.	Box 1290, Silver City, New Mex. 88061.
Appaloosa	Appaloosa Horse Club	P.O. Box 403, Moscow, Idaho. 83843.
Arabian	Arabian Horse Club Registry of America, Inc.	One Executive Park, 7801 E. Belleview Ave., Englewood, Colorado. 80110.
	Half-Arab and Anglo-Arab Registries	224 East Olive Avenue, Burbank, California. 91503.
	International Arabian Horse Assn.	224 East Olive Avenue, Burbank, California. 91503.
	Arabian Horse Racing Assn. of America	66 South Riverside Drive, Batavia, Ohio. 45103.
Belgian	Belgian Draft Horse Corp. of America	P.O. Box 335, Wabash, Indiana. 46992.
Buckskin	American Buckskin Registry Assn., Inc.	Box 1125, Anderson, Calif. 96007.
Chickasaw	National Chickasaw Horse Assn.	Clarinda, Iowa. 51632.
Cleveland Bay	Cleveland Bay Society of Amer.	White Post, Virginia. 22663.
Clydesdale	Clydesdale Breeders' Assn. of the United States	Chas W. Willhoit, Batavia, Iowa. 52533.
Cutting Horse	National Cutting Horse Assn.	P.O. Box 12155, Fort Worth, Texas. 76116.
Foxtrotting Horse	American Foxtrotting Horse Breed Assn., Inc.	Rt. 2, Box 160AA, Rogersville, Missouri. 65742.
	Missouri Foxtrotting Horse Assn.	Willow Springs, Missouri. 65793.
Galiceno	Galiceno Horse Breeders Assn., Inc.	111 E. Elm St., Tyler, Texas. 75701.
Gotland	American Gotland Horse Assn.	Box 181, R.R.2, Elkland, Mo. 65644.
Hackney	American Hackney Horse Society	527 Madison Ave., Room 725, New York, N.Y. 10022.
Hungarian Horse	Hungarian Horse Association	Bitteroot Stock Farm, Hamilton, Montana. 59840.
Morgan	American Morgan Horse Assn. Inc.	Box 265, Hamilton, N.Y. 13346.
Pinto-Paint	American Paint Horse Assn.	P.O. Box 12487, Fort Worth, Texas. 76116.
	Pinto Horse Assn. of America, Inc.	P.O. Box 1984, San Diego, Calif. 92103.
	Morocco Spotted Horse Co-operative Assn. of America, Inc.	Route 1, Ridott, Illinois. 61067.

* The great majority of these listings are through the courtesy of *The Western Horseman*.

Breed Associations and Registry Addresses (cont'd)

Breed or type	Association	Address
Palomino	Palomino Horse Breeders of America	P.O. Box 249, Mineral Wells, Texas. 76067.
	The Palomino Horse Association, Inc.	Box 446, Chatsworth, Calif. 91311.
Paso	American Paso Fino Horse Assn., Inc.	Arrott Building, 401 Wood St., Pittsburgh, Pa. 15222.
	American Assn. of Owners & Breeders of Peruvian Paso Horses	P.O. Box 371, Calabasas, Calif. 91302.
	Peruvian Paso Horse Registry of North America	P.O. Box 344, Guerneville, California. 95446.
	National Assn. of Paso Fino Horses of Puerto Rico	Aptdo. 253, Guavnabo, Puerto Rico. 00657.
Percheron	Percheron Horse Assn. of America	Route 1, Belmont, Ohio. 43718.
Quarter Horse	American Quarter Horse Association	P.O. Box 200, Amarillo, Texas. 79105.
	National Quarter Horse Registry, Inc.	Raywood, Texas. 77582.
	Original Half Quarter Horse Registry	Hubbard, Oregon. 97032.
	Standard Quarter Horse Association	4390 Fenton St., Denver, Colo. 80212.
Shire	American Shire Horse Association	Box 88, Lynden, Washington. 98264.
Spanish Mustang	Spanish Mustang Registry	Cayuse Ranch, Oshoto, Wyoming. 82724.
Standardbred	United States Trotting Association	750 Michigan Ave., Columbus, Ohio. 43215.
Suffolk	American Suffolk Horse Association	Box 88, Lynden, Washington. 98264.
Tennessee Walking Horse	Tennessee Walking Horse Breeders' & Exhibitor's Assn. of America	P.O. Box 87, Lewisburg, Tennessee. 37091.
Thoroughbred	American Thoroughbred Breeders & Owner's Assn.	1736 Alexandria Drive, P.O. Box 4038, Lexington, Kentucky. 40504.
	The Jockey Club	300 Park Ave., New York, N.Y. 10022.
	Thoroughbred Racing Assn. of the United States, Inc.	Suite 919, 220 East 42nd St., New York, N.Y. 10017.
Ysabella	Ysabella Saddle Horse Assn., Inc.	McKinzie Rancho, Route 2, Williamsport, Indiana. 47993.
Ponies	American Connemara Pony Society	R.R.2, Rochester, Illinois. 62563.
	American Quarter Pony Association	New Sharon, Iowa. 50207.
	American Walking Pony Association	Route 5, Box 88, Upper River Road, Macon, Georgia. 31201.
	American Shetland Pony Club	P.O. Box 2339, Route 52, North, West Lafayette, Indiana. 47906.

Breed Associations and Registry Addresses (cont'd)

Breed or type	Association	Address
Ponies (cont'd)	Cross-Bred Pony Registry	1108 Jackson St., Omaha, Neb. 68102.
	National Appaloosa Pony, Inc.	112 East Eighth St., P.O. Box 297, Rochester, Indiana. 46975.
	National Trotting Pony Assn., Inc.	575 Broadway, Hanover, Pa. 17331.
	Pony of the Americas Club, Inc.	P.O. Box 1447, Mason City, Iowa. 50401.
	Shetland Pony Identification Bureau, Inc.	1108 Jackson Street, Omaha, Nebraska. 68102.
	United States Trotting Pony Assn.	P.O. Box 1250, Lafayette, Indiana. 47902.
	Welsh Pony Society of America, Inc.	202 N. Church Street, West Chester, Pennsylvania. 19380.
Donkeys and Mules	American Donkey and Mule Society	Brier-Field Farms, Cloverport, Kentucky. 40111.
	Miniature Donkey Registry of the United States, Inc.	1108 Jackson Street, Omaha, Nebraska. 68102.
	Standard Jack and Jennet Registry of America	Route 7, Todds Road, Lexington, Kentucky. 40502.
	Horse and Mule Assn. of America	407 S. Dearborn St., Chicago, Ill.
Other	American Horse Shows Association	527 Madison Ave., New York, N.Y. 10022.
	American Indian Horse Registry, Inc.	P.O. Box 9192, Phoenix, Ariz. 85020.
	National Half-Walker Breeders' Assn	P.O. Box 442, Mansfield, Ohio. 44901.
	National Reining Horse Association	1290 Hine Road, Hamilton, Ohio. 45013.

Sources of Illustrations

NOTE: All drawings and photographs not otherwise credited are by the author.

Fig. 1. Div. of Geol. Sci., Calif. Inst. of Technology.

Fig. 13. L. Kreutzberg's *Wir Tiere*.

Fig. 26. Youatt, *The Horse*, 1880.

Fig. 27. Youatt, *The Horse*, 1880.

Fig. 29. British Museum (Natural History).

Fig. 31. H. F. Osborn's *The Titanotheres*, etc., 1929.

Fig. 33. Modified after Erich Thenius and Helmut Hofer, 1960.

Fig. 34. (source unknown).

Fig. 35. A. E. Brehm's *Life of Animals*, 1896.

Fig. 36. Zool. Soc. of Philadelphia.

Fig. 39. Capt. K. F. W. Dunn's *The Origin of the Horse*, 1928.

Fig. 40. W. B. Scott's *A History of Land Mammals in the Western Hemisphere*, 1913.

Fig. 42. Albrecht Dürer, illus., 1515 A.D.

Fig. 43. Joseph Wolf, illus.

Fig. 44. E. Ingersoll's *Life of Mammals*, 1917.

Fig. 45. (source unknown).

Fig. 46. Ed Nowak (Black Star).

Fig. 50. South African Tourist Corp.

Fig. 52. Redrawn from Herbert Lang, *The White Rhinoceros of the Belgian Congo*, 1920.

Fig. 53. Mainly after Abbe H. Breuil, 1924.

Fig. 54. Franz Roubal, in: O. Abel's *Das Reich der Tiere*, 1939, p. 112.

(cont'd)

Sources of Illustrations (cont'd)

Fig. 56. Bas-relief in British Museum.

Fig. 57. Metropolitan Museum of Art, New York.

Fig. 58. A. E. Champollion: *Monuments de l'Egypte et de la Nubie,* c. 1830.

Fig. 59. Bas-relief in British Museum.

Fig. 60. After original in British Museum.

Fig. 62. (source unknown).

Fig. 63. Ewing Galloway, New York.

Fig. 64. Louvre.

Fig. 65. New York City Hall.

Fig. 68. Brookgreen Gardens, Murrells Inlet, South Carolina.

Fig. 69. Brookgreen Gardens (as per No. 63).

Fig. 70. (unidentified).

Fig. 71. Walker Art Gallery, Liverpool.

Fig. 72. After a painting by John Elliott.

Fig. 73. A. Rowe, Nat. Park Service.

Figs. 76, 77, 78. New York Zool. Soc.

Fig. 79. After Hamilton Smith, 1866.

Fig. 80. A. E. Brehm's *Life of Animals,* 1896.

Fig. 81. M. Hilzheimer, 1935.

Fig. 82. Hellabrunn Zoo, Vienna.

Fig. 88. *Highlights for Children,* Honesdale, Pa.

Fig. 89. A. E. Brehm's *Life of Animals,* 1896.

Fig. 90. From Selby Stud brochure, 1937.

Fig. 91. G. F. Morris: *Portraitures of Horses.*

Fig. 92. Dr. & Mrs. R. W. Cosby.

Fig. 93. Henry W. Sheldon, Portland, Oregon.

Fig. 94. G. F. Morris: *Portraitures of Horses.*

Fig. 95. After a painting by George Stubbs.

Fig. 97. C. G. Wrangle's *Die Rassen des Pferdes,* 1908.

Fig. 98. Santa Anita (Calif.) Park Ass'n.

Fig. 99. Bert Thayer & Calumet Farm, Kentucky.

Fig. 100. Schreiber and Sons Photo, 1874.

Figs. 102, 103, 105. U.S. Trotting Ass'n, Columbus, Ohio.

Fig. 104. Cyclop. Amer. Agriculture, 1908.

Figs. 106, 107, 108. *The Harness Horse,* Harrisburg, Pa.

Fig. 109. U.S. Dept. Agric., Wash., D.C.

Fig. 110. G. F. Morris: *Portraitures of Horses.*

Fig. 111. The Morgan Horse Club, New York.

Fig. 112. Amer. Quarter Horse Ass'n.

Fig. 113. *The Cattleman,* Fort Worth, Texas.

Figs. 114, 115, 116. Raza Criolla, Buenos Aires.

Fig. 118. (not recorded).

Fig. 119. *Animal Life,* N.J.

Fig. 120. New York Zool. Society.

Fig. 121. Royal Agric. Society, London.

Fig. 122. R. Lydekker's *The Horse and its Relatives,* 1912.

Fig. 125. (source unknown).

Fig. 126. Mrs. Uhl, San Francisco.

Fig. 127. *National Horseman,* Louisville, Ky.

Fig. 128. From an old print.

Fig. 129. C. G. Wrangle (see No. 97).

Figs. 130, 131. U.S. Dept. Agric., Wash., D.C.

Fig. 122. After a painting by F. Jung.

Fig. 135. C. G. Wrangle (see No. 97).

Figs. 136, 137, 138. Percheron Horse Ass'n.

Fig. 139. W. K. Kellogg Institute.

Fig. 140. Bone, photo, Los Angeles.

Fig. 141. J. F. Abernathy; Clydesdale Breeders Ass'n. of the United States.

Fig. 142. Fred H. Bixby; photo by Bone, Los Angeles.

Fig. 143. Suffolk Horse Ass'n; photo by Strohmeyer & Carpenter, New York.

Fig. 144. Henry H. Sheldon, Portland, Oregon.

Fig. 148. After F. Smith: *Veterinary Physiology,* London, 1912.

Fig. 149. Hearst's Ranch; Preston Dyer photo.

Fig. 153. Double B Photo Shop, Wickenburg, Ariz.

Fig. 154. C. S. Howard.

Fig. 155. Robert E. Crowley.

Fig. 160. Clyde Brown, Chicago, Ill.

Fig. 161. H. H. Sheldon & *Highlights for Children,* Honesdale, Pa.

Fig. 162. Associated Press.

Fig. 163. Hearst's *American Weekly.*

Fig. 164. Chester Photo Service, Boston.

Fig. 165. Flagstaff, Ariz. Chamber of Commerce.

Fig. 169. New York Zoological Society.

Fig. 170. Tourist's Bureau, Naples, Italy.

(cont'd)

Sources of Illustrations (cont'd)

Fig. 171. After a wood engraving by Benno Adam.

Fig. 172. New York Zoological Society.

Fig. 173. Chicago Natural History Museum.

Figs. 174, 175. American Museum of Natural History.

Fig. 176. After a drawing by August Specht.

Fig. 177. R. Lydekker's *The Horse and its Relatives,* 1912.

Fig. 178. Oriental Institute, Univ. of Chicago.

Fig. 179. Museum of Fine Arts, Boston.

Fig. 180. New York Zoological Society.

Fig. 181. Tegetmeier & Sutherland, 1895.

Fig. 183. British Museum.

Fig. 184. Photo by author; courtesy Philadelphia Academy of Sciences.

Fig. 185. After a sketch by Walter Wilwerding.

Fig. 188. After Job Ludolphus, 1681.

Figs. 189, 190. Zoological Society of San Diego.

Figs. 191, 192. New York Zoological Society.

Fig. 193. California Academy of Sciences.

Fig. 194. George Edwards: *Gleanings of Natural History,* 1758.

Figs. 195, 196. New York Zoological Society.

Fig. 197. A. Griffini, 1913.

Fig. 198. A. Rzasnicki, 1931.

Fig. 199. Dixon photo, Cape Town.

Figs. 200, 201, 202. Angel Cabrera and the *Journal of Mammalogy.*

Fig. 203. Chicago Natural History Museum.

Fig. 204. South African Railways: P. W. Willis photo.

Fig. 206. Zoological Society of San Diego.

Figs. 207, 208, 209. (sources unknown).

Figs. 210, 211. So. African Rys.: P. W. Willis photo.

Fig. 212. Tegetmeier and Sutherland, 1895.

Fig. 213. George Edwards: *Gleanings of Natural History,* 1758.

Fig. 214. After S. Daniell, 1805.

Figs. 215, 216, 217. Zoological Society of London.

Fig. 218. South African Museum.

Fig. 219. Senckenburg Museum, Frankfurt, Germany.

Fig. 220. Photo by author, courtesy Peabody Museum, Yale University.

Fig. 221. British Museum (Natural History).

Fig. 222. Academy of Natural Sciences, Philadelphia.

Fig. 223. Tegetmeier and Sutherland, 1895, p. 42.

Fig. 225. Photo by Pirro Marconi.

Fig. 226. British Museum.

Fig. 227. After a painting by Alex. Wagner.

Fig. 228. Tegetmeier and Sutherland, 1895.

Fig. 229. (Zoo unidentified).

Figs. 230, 231. Bureau of Animal Industry, Wash., D.C.

Fig. 232. (Source unknown).

Fig. 233. George M. Ponton, photo.

Fig. 234. C. G. Good, photo.

Fig. 236. Danby Farm, Omaha, Nebraska.

Fig. 237. Anheuser-Busch, Inc.

Fig. 238. (Source unknown).

Fig. 239. Wide World.

Index

Name Index (of persons)

* name in footnote
( ) name in illustration
Exclusive of names listed on pages 000–000

Abel, O., 35
Adam, Benno, (310)
Afanassieff, S., 205, 453
Akeley, Carl, 313
Alexander, David, 167
Alexander the Great, 114, 121, 249
Allamand, Dr., 375
Allen, G. M., 365
Alminas, K., 226, 451
Ameghino, F., 35, 82
Amschler, W., 47, 48, 110
Andreewa, E., 135
Andrews, Roy Chapman, 317–18
Angel, J. Lawrence, 127
Antonius, Otto, 33, 35, 40, 43, 45, 46, 47, 48,
    77, 79, 129, 140, 140*, 142, 143, 146, 151,
    315, 316, 321, 324, 329, 330, 331, 350,
    358*, 377*, 397
Assurbanipal, King, 109, 110, (392)
Astley, Philip, 385
Astor, John Jacob, 174
Aubrey, "Little," 282
Azzaroli, A., 35

Bannikov, A. G., 133
Bantoiu, C., 453
Baum, H., 124
Beebe, C. William, 5, 22*, 27*
Benger, Thomas, 174
Bigalke, R., 351
Bilek, F., 449
Bill, Buffalo, 282
Blaine, G., 351
Bland, Jr., Theodore, 307*
Blanford, W. T., 316
Blumenbach, J. F., 25
Blundeville, Thomas, 165
Boddaert, P., 35
Boicoianu, C., 450
Bolton, G., 326
Bonaparte, Napoleon, (120), 121
Bonavia, Emmanuel, 149, 301, 303
Borisow, ——, 136
Bourdelle, E., 33, 43, 135*, 331, 340*
Bracho, Miguel E., 118
Branco, W., 438
Brandes, H., 454
Breakey, Donald R., 75
Breasted, J. H., 112
Brehm, Alfred Edmund, 164, 326

Brocklehurst, H. C., 312
Brody, Samuel, 66, 250
Brown, Earle, 402
Brown, Lewis S., 124, 259*
Buckley, T. E., 358
Buffon, G.L.L.de, 375
Burchell, W. J., 100, 352
Burmeister, H., 35
Busch, Jr., August, 407
Butz, ——, 450
Byerly, Captain, 166

Cabrera, Angel, 354–55, 358, 361, 363, 367,
    368, 382
Caesar, Julius, 249
Caldini, L. M., 25
Camphausen, W., 156, (157)
Carp, Bernard, 382
Carruthers, D., 316, 317, 330
Carter, ——, 400
Castle, W. E., 140, 149, 150, 151, 301, 303
Charles, Archduke, 192
Chittenden, D. W., 453
Clay, Henry, 307*, 392
Clive, Lord, 396
Columbus, Christopher, 117–18
Conners, R. J., 400
Cooke, H.B.S., 35, 382
Cope, E. D., 35, 44, (383), 404
Coronado, Francisco, 118
Cortez, Hernando, 118
Cosby, Dr. and Mrs. R. W., (161)
Cumberland, Duke of, 168
Cunningham, Kirby, 56, 66, 188, 190, 205, 453

Dallin, Cyrus, 119
Daniell, S., (373)
Darwin, Charles, 301
Dawson, W. M., 183, 205, 452
Denhardt, Robert, 301, 453
Denis, Armand, 396
De Romaszkan, Gregor, 284
De Soto, Fernando, 118
De Vaca, Cabeza, 118
De Winton, W. E., 364
Dimitriadis, J. N., 135, 454
Dittrich, H., 124
Dobie, J. Frank, 222, 282
Donnelly, Ignatius, 390

Duerst, J. U., 22, 35, 45, 46, 48, 79, 109, 140, 149
Dürer, Albrecht, (91), 92
Dowdall, R. C., 190

Edinburgh, Duke of, 133*, 150
Edwards, George, (345), (373), 375
Ellenberger, W., 124
Elliott, John, (126)
Ensminger, M. E., 205
Erastothenes, 112
Ericson, D. B., 43
Ernst, Mensen, 282
Estes, J. A., 166
Ewart, John Cossar, 44, 45, 46, 48, 137, 138, 139, 141, 149, 150, 167, 199, 203, 348, 382, 396
Ewing, M., 43

Falabella, J. C., 404
Fazl-Fein, F., 142
Feige, E., 454
Fieg, H., (170), (236)
Fisher, James, 133*, 150
Fitzinger, L., 35
Fitzsimons, F. W., 284
Flade, J. E., 202, 454
Flannery, "Doc," (182)
Fleming, V., (181)
Flower, William H., 64, 66
Forster, J. R., 137
Fowler, Stewart H., 56, 66, 188, 190, 205, 453
Franck, L., 123
Franco, Antonio, 294
Franco, Laurent, 294, (297)

Gee, E. P., 92, 328
George, H., 137, 138, 331
Gerrard, Edward, 377–78
Gidley, J. W., 35, 404
Gilbey, Walter, 232
Gmelin, J. F., 35, 137
Goodall, Daphne, Machin, 207
Good, C. G., 402
Goodwin, G.G., 325
Gordon, Colonel, 375
Gordon-Cumming, W., 101
Goring, Charles, 423*, 445
Grange, E. A. A., 205, 410–11, 450, 454
Grant, Ulysses S., 122
Gray, J. E., 35, 82, 306
Graziosi, P., 314
Gregory, Joseph T., 378
Gregory, K., 205, 452
Gregory, William King, 259*
Gremmel, Fred, 299, 303
Greve, C., 303, 304
Grévy, Jules, 335, 339
Grey, George, 376, (380)
Griffini, A., (348)
Gromova, Viera, 140, 142, 151, 314
Groves, C. P., 328
Grum-Grshimailo, 129
Gutsche, ——, 171, 454

Haag, William G., 48
Hablizl, C., 324
Haes, Frank, 377

Hagenbeck, Carl, 132, 133, 396
Hagmann, ——, 82
Hall, George, 283
Haller, Albrecht von, 25
Harris, W. C., 372
Hay, Oliver P., 35, 46, 48, 149, 434, 436
Hayes, Horace M., 64, 66, 385
Hayes, Mrs. H. M., (384)
Hayward, Wally, 282
Hazael, ——, 282
Heck, Heinz, 134, 151, 197
Heck, Lutz, 143, 151
Hedin, Sven, 317, 320
Heller, E., 35, 335, 337, 339, 340, 342, 343, 363, 364, 365
Henseler, ——, 450
Hervey, John, 454
Hibbard, C. W., 439
Hilzheimer, Max, 45, 48, 135, 140, 143, 150, 329, 331, 381, 382
Hofstetter, R., 438
Homer, 390
Hooijer, D. A., 93, 105
Hook, Raymond, 396, 398
Horst, F., 455
Houser, Homer, 406
Howard, Charles S., 270
Howard, Hildegarde, 449
Howard, Robert West, 112, 115*
Howell, A. Brazier, 259*

Isabella, Queen, 117
Iwersen, E., 452

Jackson, J. Wilfred, 48
James I, King, 117
Jefferson, Thomas, 121
Jerdon, ——, 316, 327–28
John, King, 232
Johnson, Mrs. James B., (182)
Johnston, Harry, 303
Jones, Robert E., 401
Jung, F., (228)

Kadny, I., 312*
Kellogg, W. K., 54, (239)
Kennelly, A. E., 268
Kibler, H. K., 66, 250
Kolbe, W., 453
Korschubei, Prince, 137
Kovalevsky, W., 35, 43
Kruger, W., 452
Kublai-Khan, 117
Kuffner, H., 449
Kupper, ——, 105
Kwaschain, S. N., 135

Lafayette, Marquis de, 392
Lamb, A. J. R., 257*, 262, 284
Lang, Ernst M., 105
Lavocat, R., 33, 43
Lee, Harry, 119
Lee, Robert E., 121
Leidy, Joseph, 35, 48, 385, (387)
Lemler, D., 280
Lesbre, F. X., 449
Lesson, R., 35
Leutemann, H., (401)

Leyder, ——, 239
Linnaeus, Carolus, 21, 33, 35, 140, 198, 306, 345
Lombroso, Cesare, 423*
Ludolphus, Job, (339)
Lundholm, Bengt, 46, 140, 381, 382
Lydekker, Richard, 33, 46, 66, 67, 71, 79, 98, 141, 142, 149, 198, (200), 312, 316, 320, 321, 325, 343, 346, 362
Lysippus, 114

McClellan, George B., 122
McCoy, Smith, 404
McGrew, Paul O., 314, 339*, 438
McKenna, Charles, 56
McKenna, Donald, 56
Madroff, Christo, 154-55, 171, 193, 196, 205, 450, 451, 452
Maharaja, of Cooch-Behar, 92*
Marsh, O. C., 44, 377-78
Marshall, F. H. A., 453
Matschie, P., 35, 316, 355, 363
Matthew, W. D., 35
Mazak, V., 328
Meade, George G., 122
Meinertzhagen, R., 96*, 105
Menelik, King, 335
Menke, Frank G., 167
Merriam, John C., 35, 385
Messonier, Jean L. E., (120)
Michaelis, Helen, 453
Mieckley, ——, 454
Milne, Lorus J. and Margery, 404*
Milne-Edwards, Alphonse, 335
Mockus, ——, 226
Mohammed, 116
Mohr, Erna, 134
Mootcroft, W., 35
Moraczewski, ——, 226
Morgan, E. D., 150
Morgan, Justin, 183
Morris, George Ford, 160, 166, 184
Motohashi, H., 320
Müller, —— von, 172, 450, 451

Napoleon, (120), 121
Nathusius, Simon von, 205, 450, 451, 452
Newell, Norman D., 48
Nehring, Alfred, 140, 146
Nicholls, Gov., 118
Nipher, Francis E., 272
Nissen, Jasper, 207
Nitsche, Max, 135*
Noack, T., 35
Norr, I., 248
Nott, Fortune, 359
Nye, N. C., 205

Ogrizek, A., 455
O'Kelly, Colonel, 168
Osborn, Henry Fairfield, 79, 439, 445
Oswell, W. C., 100*, 105
Oustalet, E., 35, 335
Owen, Richard, 28, 44, 438

Painter, K. V., 96
Palin, Sepp, (182)
Pallas, Peter Simon, 33, 129, 137, 316
Palmer, ——, 82

Palmer, Joe H., 166
Pavlow, M., 35
Peake, H. J., 307
Petrie, Flinders, 47, 112
Philip, Duke of Edinburgh, 150
Philonicus, 114
Platen, J., 453
Plinzner, M., (204)
Plischke, Alfred, 171, 454
Plumb, C. S., 115*, 167, 180, 205, 243, 307
Pocock, Reginald Innes, 30, 35, 46, 82*, 105, 149, 301, 303, 311, 313, 315, 316, 321, 326, 337, 343, 346, 366, 398
Poliakov, M., 128, 129, 137
Polo, Marco, 391
Pomel, A., 146
Ponton, A. E., 401, (402)
Powell Brothers, 120
Pownall, Harry, (180)
Pringle, Thomas, 384
Przevalsky, N. M., 21, 128, 129

Radde, G., 316
Radescu, T., 454
Rarey, Solomon, 385
Rau, G., 207, 211
Reichenau, W., 35, 146
Renshaw, Graham, 101, 337, 375, 375*, 381
Rhoad, A. O., 451
Ridgeway, William, 46, 66, 108, 109, 112, 115, 127, 137, 138, 139, 141, 142, 149, 165, 167, 243, 303*, 343, 350, 381, 382
Rieske, Bill, 401
Roberts, A., 366
Roe, Frank G., 118, 127
Roosevelt, Theodore, 337, 339, 340, 342, 363, 364, 365
Rosiö, B., 452
Roth, F. G. R., 184
Roubal, Franz, (108)
Rumjahcev, B. F., 45, 46, 48, 149
Rutimeyer, L., 35
Rytchkof, ——, 137
Rzasnicki, A., (349), 381

St. Bel, M., 167
St. Hilaire, I. G., 35
St. Leger, J., 368
Salensky, W., 134, 137, 138
Salisbury, G. W., 140, 300
Sandars, N. K., 106, 108, 127
Sanson, A., 66
Sartorious, ——, 160
Savage, M. W., 279
Savory, T., 390
Scharff, Robert F., 199
Schatiloff, I. N., 142
Schneider, E., (328)
Schottler, F., 450
Schreyer, Adolph, (159), 164
Schwartz, ——, 316
Schwarz, E., 35, 328, 382
Sclater, P. L., 345, 347*, 355, 363, 368
Scott, William B., 91, 105
Searle, A. G., 303
Sefve, I., 35
Selous, F. C., (360)
Sheridan, Philip H., 122

Sherman, William T., 122
Shortridge, G. C., 351, 372, (377)
Sisson, S., 79
Smith, Hamilton, 33, 35, 129, 133, 136, 138, 367, 381
Smith, Jonathan, 26
Smith, Sidney, 127
Soergel, W., 35
Solanet, E., 190, 450
Sorrell, ——, 343
Solomon, King, 116
Spain, King of, 392
Sparrman, Dr., 375
Specht, August, 212, (319)
Specht, Carl Gottlob, (170), 212
Specht, Friedrich, (138), 212
Sprott, Darrel B., 189
Stang, Valentin, 207, 211, 449
Stanton, H. R., 105
Stecher, Robert M., 66, 132
Steele, Dewey G., 170, 172*
Stegen, H., 452
Stegmann, ——, 46
Stehlin, H. G., 35, 314
Stejneger, L., 197, 453
Stirton, R. A., 35, 79
Stock, Chester, 17, 385, 438, 449
Strabo, 112
Stratul, J., 171
Stubbs, George, (126), (167), 168
Stuck, Franz von, 115
Svanberg, V., 205, 451

Tachard, G., 375
Team, C. B., 450
Teator, Earl, (207)
Tegetmeier, W. B., 132, 348
Trombe, ——, 135
Trowbridge, E. A., 66, 453
Trumbull, John, 121, 122*
Tscherski, J. D., 137, 140, 142, 430
Tschiffely, Aime F., 282

Ullmann, G., 202, 454
Upton, Roger D., 158*, 280
Urusoff, ——, 226

Vetulani, T., 46, 48, 147, 151
Victoria, Queen, 385
Volf, J., 134

Wagner, Alex, (394)
Ward, Rowland, 348, 95, 101
Warden, C. J., 255
Washington, George, 120, 121, (122), 307*, 392
Weiss-Tessbach, Adolf, 245, 453
Wellington, Duke of, 121
Wells, H. G., 31*
Wentworth, Lady, 158
Wettach, Fred, 285
Wheeler, Tex, 172
White, T. H., 249
Wiechert, F., 451
William the Conqueror, 116
Willoughby, David P., 35, 334*, 352, 450
Wilwerding, Walter J., (335)
Wirth, D., 449
Wöhler, H., 452
Woldrich, J. N., 35
Wollin, G., 43
Wooley, C. Leonard, 127
Woolf, G., (270)
Wooten, ——, (160)
Wrangle, C. G., 150
Wüst, E., 35, 146

Xenophon, 112–13

York, F., (374), 377, 378
Youatt, William, 163, 167, 280, 281

Zdansky, O., 438
Zebenka, ——, 226
Zeuner, F. E., 46, 48, 135
Zimmermann, C., 453

Name Index (of horses)

* name in footnote
( ) name in illustration
Generally exclusive of names in tables

Abdallah I (Thoroughbred), 174–75, (179)
Aberdeen (trotter), 175
Achilles (trotter), (179)
Adios Butler (pacer), 279
Albion d'Hor (Rheinish-Dutch draft), 244
Alexander Abdallah (trotter), 175
Arabella Matilda, 827 (donkey foal), 406
Assault (Thoroughbred), 249*, 273–74

Baby Gates (Morgan), 398
Baldy (charger), 122
Beau Boy (Suffolk), (244)
Bella (Hackney), 175
Bellfounder (trotter), 174, (179)

Bert (Quarter), 187
Big Bertha (pony foal), 405–6
Big Racket (Thoroughbred), 187
Billy Direct (pacer), (181), 279
Biskra (jumper), 285
Black Dan (charger), 122
Black Hawk (Morgan), 183
Black Jack (Thoroughbred), 283
Black Nick (Quarter), 188
Black Wolf (Quarter), 187
Blaze (trotter), (179)
Blenheim II (Thoroughbred), (173)
Bonaparte (Percheron), 120
Bossuet (Thoroughbred), (271)

Boughbrood Lady Grey (draft), 402
Bret Hanover (pacer), 279
Brownie (Thoroughbred), (271)
Brunette (mule), (395)
Bucephalus (of Alexander the Great), 114, 121*
Buckskin Joe (Quarter), 187
Bulle Rock (Thoroughbred), 274
Burgomaster (Thoroughbred), 274
Buster (draft), 292

Cactus (pony), 404
Calumet Evelyn (trotter and pacer), 279
Calypso (Percheron), (238)
Cap (draft), 291
Chandler (jumper), 288
Charles Kent Mare (trotter), 175, (179)
Cincinnati (charger), 122
Citation (Thoroughbred), 273
Civil Code (Thoroughbred), 274
Coaltown (Thoroughbred), 273
Colonel Clyde (Quarter), 187
Confidence (jumper), 285
Copenhagen (Thoroughbred), 121
Coriaci (Criollo), (190)
Count Fleet (Thoroughbred), 273
Cresceus (trotter), 175
Cricket (pony foal), 406
Crisp Horse (Suffolk), 243

Dad's Choice (Thoroughbred), (182)
Dan (Belgian), 291
Dan Patch (pacer), 279
Dan Waggoner (Quarter), 187
Darley Arabian, 166
Dee Dee (Quarter), 187
Denmark (Thoroughbred), 120
Dexter (trotter), 175
Dictator (trotter), 175
Diligence (Percheron), 120
Directum (trotter), 175
Dolly Spanker (Morgan), 183
Doncaster (Thoroughbred), (170)
Don Juan (Percheron), (237)
Douglas (charger), 121
Dr. Fager (Thoroughbred), 273
Driver (trotter), (179)
Dr. Le Gear (Percheron), 400
Dustwhirl (Thoroughbred), (173)
Dutchman (trotter), 278

Eclipse (Thoroughbred), 121, (167), 168
Electioneer (trotter), 175
Equipoise (Thoroughbred), 273
Ethan Allen (trotter), 183, (185)
Exterminator (Thoroughbred), 273

Flaebehhoppen (Knabstrup), 221
Flying Childers (Thoroughbred), (179), 281

Gallant Fox (Thoroughbred), 273
Gallant Prince (Shire), (242)
Gato (Criollo), 191
Gazelle (trotter), 175
General Washington (draft), 400
George Wilkes (trotter), (174), 183
Ghaniha (Arab), 263
Godolphin Barb, 166
Goldsmith Maid (trotter), 174, 276, 277, 279
Goliath (draft), 401

Gray Annie (Quarter), 187
Greatheart (jumper), 285, (288)
Grey Clyde 78 (Clydesdale), 120
Greyhound (trotter), (182), 276–79

Hambletonian 10 (trotter), 174–75, (179), 183
Hamburg Belle (trotter), 183
Hanover (Thoroughbred), (170)
Hans ("educated horse"), 255
Happy Medium (trotter), 175
Hard Twist (Quarter), 187
Harmon Baker Star (Quarter), 187
Harold (trotter), 175
Harvester, The (trotter), 175, 183
Heatherbloom (jumper), 285
Herod (Thoroughbred), 167, 168
Hiram (Belgian?), 400
Hobo (Quarter), 187
Huaso (jumper), 285

Imported Bellfounder (trotter), 174, (179)
Imported Messenger (Thoroughbred), 174, (179)
Indien de Biévène (Rheinish-Dutch), 244

Jane Hunt (Quarter), 187
Janus (Thoroughbred), 119
Jay Gould (trotter), 175
Jerry (Grevy's zebra), 398
Joe Hancock's Steeldust (Quarter), 187
Joe Reed II (Quarter), 187
John Burwell (Thoroughbred), 274
Juno (zebra x mare hybrid), 398
Justin Morgan (Morgan), 175, 183, (184)

Kelso (Thoroughbred), 270*, 274
Khaled (Arab), 155
King (draft), 291
King D. (pony), 280
King's Own (jumper), 285

Laddie (Clydesdale), 401
Lady Coolidge (Quarter), 187
Lady Suffolk (trotter), 278
Lady Wonder ("educated horse"), 255
Lee Axworthy (trotter), 175, 183
Leo (Quarter), 187
Lexington (Thoroughbred), 121, (122), 168
Limbo (Thoroughbred), 274, 403
Little Joe, Jr. (Quarter), 187
Lothar III (Rheinish-Dutch), 244
Lottery (jumper), 288
Lou Dillon (trotter), 276, 277
Lubber (draft), 401, (402)

Mambrino (trotter), 174–75, (179)
Mancha (Criollo), 191
Man o' War (Thoroughbred), 171, (172), 273, 278
Master Crump (jumper), 288
Matchem (Thoroughbred), 167, 168
Mesoud (Arab), 155
Messenger (Thoroughbred), 120, 174, (179), 278
Mount Joie III (jumper), 285
Mustafir (Arab), (289), 290

Nancy Hanks (trotter), 276, 277

Nebraska Queen (Shire), 402
Nelson (charger), 121
Nerva (Percheron), (238)
Nettie (trotter), 175
Nevele Pride (trotter), 276, 277
Nureddin (Arab), 155

Oklahoma Star (Quarter), 187
Omaha (Thoroughbred), 273
Orange Girl (trotter), 175
Oregon Wonder (long-maned), 407, (408)
Overall (jumper), 288

Paladere (French Coach), (227)
Pat (Suffolk), 400
Paul A.P.–19794 (Quarter), (196)
Pepper (Russian draft), 292
Peppy (Quarter), 187
Peter Manning (trotter), 277
Pluto XX (Lipizzan), (194)
Pyramus (Arab), 280

Ranger (Arab), 119
Recruit (Thoroughbred), 280
Rifage (Arab), (163)
Roamer (Thoroughbred), 273
Roan Dick (Quarter), 188
Rock (draft), 291, (292), (293)
Roquepine (trotter), 279
Roseben (Thoroughbred), 274
Roustabout (jumper), 288
Rowdy (Belgian), 291

Sahm (Arab), (161)
Salty (Quarter), 187
Salvator (Thoroughbred), 273
Sam (charger), 122
Sam (draft), 292
Seabiscuit (Thoroughbred), 171, (172), (270), 273

Secretariat (Thoroughbred), 273
Shark (Thoroughbred), 119
Sherman (Morgan), 183
Silver King (Quarter), 187
Sir Barton (Thoroughbred), 273
Sovereign 181 (Clydesdale), 120
Spencer Scott (trotter), 175
Steamin' Demon (trotter and pacer), 278
Steeldust's Cowboy (Quarter), 187
Stewart's Telegraph (Morgan), 188
Strathmore (trotter), 175
Strathore Guard 29109 (Clydesdale), (241)
Sugar-dumpling (pony), 404, (405)
Sysonby (Thoroughbred), 273

Texas (Belgian), 401
The Harvester (trotter), 175
Tiny Bit (pony), 203
Titan Hanover (trotter), 278
Tom (Belgian), 291, (292), (293)
Tom Thumb (pony), 404
Touraine (jumper), 288
Traveler (pony), 404
Traveller (charger), 121

Uhlan (trotter), 183, 277, 280

Volunteer (trotter), 175

Wait-a-Bit (Thoroughbred), 271
War Admiral (Thoroughbred), 273
Watson Hanover (trotting), (180)
Whirlaway (Thoroughbred), 273
Winchester (charger), 122
Windsor Lad (Thoroughbred), 249*
Wing Commander (Saddle Horse), (206)
Woven Web (Quarter), 187

Yankee (trotter), 278

Subject Index

* subject in footnote
( ) subject in illustration

abeli, Equus caballus, 148, 149, 232
Abel's horse, 148, 149, 232
Acchetta pony, 215
Acrocodia indica, 83, 84
Afghanistan, horses of, 210
Africa, horses of, 210; map of, (104), (338)
African wild asses, 311–14
Age-determination from teeth, 71–76, 432
Albinism, 301
Albino, American, 215
Alcock's Arabian, 166
Algeria, horses of, 210
Allen's rule, 305
"All-purpose" horse, 205
Amazons, 113, (115)
Amble (gait), 262
Amerhippus, 438
America, dates of horses in, 117–21; horses of, 209

American Albino, 215; Buckskin, 215; Cream, 215; Gotland pony, 215; jack and jennet, 307; Paint or Pinto, 215; Saddle Horse, 120, (123), 214
Anatomical description of existing Equidae, 37, 39, 40, 53; terms of horse, 53
Anau, "horse" of, 109
Anaze (Syrian) horse, 210
Ancestry, immediate, of horse, 44
Anchitherium, (34)
Andalusian horse, 192, 194, 215; jack, 307
andium, Equus, (65)
Anglo-Arab horse, 215
Anglo-Barb horse, 118
Anglo-Hungarian horse, 205
Anglo-Norman horse, 205, 215
Anglo-Russian horse, 449
"Annectent" zebra, 355
antiquorum, Equus burchelli, 367, 368, 372

Apollo, chariot of, 112
Appaloosa, 26, (211), 214
Arab, (123), (126), 205, 214, 449; ancestry of, 111–12; compared with Lipizzan, 194; feet of, compared with rhinoceros, 97; asserted distinctions in, 157; coat colors of, 162; differences from Thoroughbred, 168, 171; head of, 155–60; history and description of, 152–65; limbs of, 162; measurements of, (153), 413; measurements, comparative, of newborn and adult, 54; neck of, 160; racing records in, 280; tail of, 162; trunk of, 161; vertebrae of, 51; weight of, 155
Arabia, sub-breeds in, 210; first breeding of horse in, 116
Archaeohippus, (34), (38)
Ardennes (or Ardennais) horse, 215
Area of body, 441–42; of feet compared with body weight, 442–43
Art, horses in, 124
Asia, horses of, 210; map of, (129)
Ass, Andalusian, 307; Catalonian, 307; domestic, 306–11; Ethiopian wild, 314–15; Majorca, 306, 307; Maltese, 306; Nubian wild, 311; Somali wild, 313–14
Asinus asinus asinus, 306–11; *africanus,* 311–13; *somaliensis,* 313–14
Assyria, horses of, 111
Assyrian horse, head of, 109, 111
Astrohippus, 30*, (34), 316, 438
Augeron horse, 245
Australia, horses of, 210
Austria, horses of, 208 (*see also* Lipizzan)
Auvergne horse, 245

Back-breeding, 143
Baird's tapir, 82
Bald, 26
Bald face, (302)
Balearic pony, 215
Baluchithere and rhinoceros compared, (444)
Baluchitherium, 439–45, (444)
Bangtail, 26
Barb (or Berber) horse, (123), 215–16
Bareback riding, 294
Basuto pony, 215
Batak (or Deli) pony, 216
Bay coloration, 299, 300, 301
Bay roan, 300
Beberbeck horse, 216
Bedouins, (159)
Beetewk (or Bitjug) horse, 216
Belgian draft, 120, (124), 205, 239–40, 450
Belgium, horses of, 208
Bergmann's rule, 305
Bering Strait land bridge, 436*
Bhutia pony, 216
Bidet, 24
Black and white rhinoceroses compared, (99)
Black coloration, 299, 300
Black Forest draft, 216
Black horse of Flanders, 116, 218, 230, 236, 239, 244, 245
Black rhinoceros, 87, 95–98, (97), (99)
Black roan, 300
Blagdon (spotted horse), (211)
Blaze, (302)
Blood bay, 299

Blue roan, 300
Body area, volume, and weight, 441–42
Body build, 203, 205
Body build, index of, 188*, 203
Body measurements and proportions in various Equidae, 410–(21)
Body weight as estimated from carpus width, (441); from volume, (441); from foot bones, 440; general formula for, 177
Böhm's zebra, (335), 352, 363–65; coat patterns in, 355, 359
Bones of skeleton, 49–52; of limbs, growth of, 58; shrinkage in, 422*
Bontequagga, 352
Bosnian mountain horse, 216
Boulonnais draft, 216, 245
Brabançon (or Brabant) draft, 216, 245
Brain weight in relation to body weight in Equidae, (258), 259
Brandenburg semi-draft, 216
Brazilian tapir, 82, 83, 85
Breeds of horses (geographic), 208–10; number of, 212; light, in United States and elsewhere, 214, 215–16
Breton horse, 216, 245
Brisket, 53
Britain, horses of, 208; in Roman times, 116
Broad jumping, in horse, 286, 288
Bronco, 25, 296; buster, 25; busting, (296)
Brontosaurus, 443
Broodmare, 23
Broomtail, 26
Brown-black coloration, 300
Brown coloration, 300
Brownlow Turk, 166
Buckskin, American, 215
Buckskin dun, 300
Bulgaria, horses of, 208
burchelli, Equus, 352–62
Burchell's rhinoceros, 101
Burchell's zebra, 352–65; and mountain zebra, differences between, 361; coat patterns in, 355, 356, 359, 360; extinction of, 358; in harness, (371); proposed names for, 354
Burma horse, 210
Burmese (or Shan) pony, 216
Butea pony, 210
Byerly Turk, 165, 167

Caballine (definition of), 37
Caballus (= Equus), 33, 37, 198, 438
Caballus, meaning of, 21*
Calcaneum, (50)
Calico, 26, 301
Callosities. *See* Chestnuts, ergots
Caloric requirements, 249
Camargue horse, 216
Cameroons, horses of, 210
Canada, horses of, 209
Cannon, 53
Canter (gait), 260, 261
Cape mountain zebra. *See* Mountain zebra
Capriole, 193, (195)
Carpus, 49, (50)
Carpus width in relation to body weight, 441
Castor. *See* Chestnut
Catalonian jack, 307
Catskill Game Farm, 351*

Caucasus, first domestic horses in, 116
Caudal vertebrae, 49, (50), 51
Cavern paintings, prehistoric, 106, (107), 108
Cayuse, 25
Celtic pony, 196, 197, (198); hoofs of, 147
celticus, Equus caballus, 44
Center of gravity in the horse, 283–84
Ceratotherium simum, 98–103, (99), (102)
Cervical vertebrae, 49, (50), 52
Chalicotheres, (34)
Chalicotheriidae, (81)
chapmani, Equus. See Chapman's zebra
Chapman's zebra, (336), 352, (363–68); body measurements of, 413; body outline of, (420)
Charger, 23
Chariot, Egyptian war, 112; racing, 116, (117), 173
Cheetah, speed in, 266
Chestnut coloration, 299, 300
Chestnut roan, 300
Chestnuts (callosities), 53, 64
Chickasaw horse, 216
Chigetai. See Kulan
China, horses of, 210; first cavalry of, 116; first importation of horses, asses, and mules, 116
Chincoteague pony, 216
Chinese, taming of horse by, 116
Chubarry (spotted horse), 211
Circus horses, 294
Classification of the genus *Equus*, 33, 35; zoological, of the horse, 37
Claybank dun, 300
Clay family (trotters), 175
Cleveland Bay, (124), 205, (213), 214
Clydesdale, 120, (124), 240–41; x Shire cross, 240
Coach horse, 205, 212, (213), 217, (227), 450
Coat colors of horses, 299–305; of ponies, 197
Cob, 24, 217
Coefficient of variation, 432–33
Coffin bone, 53
"Coldblood", 116, 147, 148, 206, 232
Collier (or Pitter), 217
Colorado Ranger, 26, 217
Coloration of coat in horses, 299–305
Colors, basic, 140
Colt, 23; skull and teeth of, (74)
Comté (or Comtois), 217
Condylarthra, 28, 80, 81
Conestoga horse, 217
Connemara (or Hobbie), (123), 139, 197, 199
Conversano (lipizzan) family, 194
Coronet, 53, 304
Cranial and dental measurements taken by the author, 428–29
Cremello (coloration), 301
Criollo, 190–92, 205, 217, 450; measurements of, 191
Croatia, horses of, 209
Cro-Magnon man, 335
Cross-breeding, 139, 143, 203
Croup, 53; relative length of, 161; striping of, (349)
Croupade, 193
Czechoslovakia, horses of, 208

Dales pony, 197, 217
Damaraland zebra, 367–68, (369–71), 372; coat patterns in, 355–57

danielli, Equus quagga, 381
Daniell's quagga, (373)
Danish horse, 217
Danish-North Schleswig horse, 205, 451
Dappling, 301, 303
Dartmoor pony, 197
Date of extinction of horses in North America, 47
Dates in equine history (Old World), 115–17
"Dawn horses," 28
Dead heat, triple, (271)
Definitions of terms for horses, 23
Denmark, horses of, 208, 217
Dental Index, formula for, 432
Dental series, measurements of, 428–29
Dental series, upper, in various Equidae, (78)
Devonshire Pack Horse, (124)
Diana, (126)
Diastema, 71
Dicerorhinus sumatrensis, 94
Diceros bicornis, 87, (88), 95, 96, (97), (99)
Digestive tract in the horse, 251
Dispersion of the domestic horse, 122
Distaff side, 24
Diving horses, 294–95
Dobbin, 22
Dog, foot of, (89)
Dolichohippus, 35, 335–43, (336), (339–44)
Domestication of horse, first, 109, 110, 115
Domestic horse, anatomical description of, 40
Dongala horse, 210
Donkey (*see also* Ass, domestic), 306–11; body outline of, (417); domestication of, 116; differences from horse, 308–9; measurements of, 413; pelvis of, (61), (62); Sicilian, (307); x zebra hybrids, 396
Dorsal vertebrae, 49, (50), 51
Dow's tapir, 82
Draft horse (general), 451; body measurements of, 232, 413; body outline of, (231); most efficient size in, 234*, 293; origin of, 246
Dragon (= draft), 230*
Dun (coloration), 301
Dwarf horses of the Grand Canyon, 406
Dziggetai. See Kulan

East Friesian horse, 205, 451
East Friesland horse, (212)
East Prussian (Trakehner) horse, 205, 218, 451, 454–55
"Educated" horses, 255
Edwards's quagga, (373)
Egyptian horse and rider, statuette of (111)
Egyptian two-horse war chariot, (112)
Eohippus, 30, (31), (32), (34), (38), 82, (85), (88), 334; skeleton of, (29)
Epihippus, (34)
Equidae, dates of intercontinental migrations of, 47, 48; geologic and geographic distribution of, 39; brain weight in relation to bodyweight in, (258), 259; hoof form in various, 65; length of limb bones in, 424–25; proportions of skeleton in, 426–27
Equine giants, 400–404
Equine skeletons measured by the author, 434–35
Equus asinus, 306–15; *burchelli*, 352–62; *caballus abeli*, 148, (149); *caballus caballus*, 33, (34), 48, 438; *caballus germanicus*, 148; *caballus*

gmelini, 47, 136–46, (144); *caballus mosba-chensis,* 148; *caballus przewalskii,* 46, 47, 78, 128–35, (145), 437, 438; *caballus robustus,* 47, 48; *conversidens,* 438; *excelsus,* 438; *ferus,* 129; *giganteus,* 404; *grévyi,* 335–43, (336); *hatcheri,* 438; *hemionus hemionus,* 316–21, 390; *hemionus khur,* 327–28; *hemionus kiang,* 321–23; *hemionus onager,* 323–27; *namadicus,* 439; *niobrarensis,* 437, 438; *occidentalis,* 78, 385–86, (387), 438; *pacificus,* 48, 437; *san-meniensis,* 438; *sivalensis,* 439; *quagga,* 78, 372–84; *zebra,* (336), 345–50
Equus, classification of subgenera and species, 33, 35; family tree of, 437; phylogeny of, 436–39; evolution of, 30, (31); meaning of name, 21; subgenera compared, (62)
Ergots (callosities), 30, 53, 64, 164
Eruption time of teeth, (72), 73
Estonia, horses of, 208
Ethiopian wild ass, 314–15
European breeds of horses, measurements of, 171
Exmoor pony, 116, 197, 218
External anatomy of the horse, (41)
External measurements of the horse, how taken, (412)
External parts and regions of the horse, (42)

Family tree of the *Perissodactyla,* 81
Farm horse, ideal size of, 234*
Favory (Lipizzan) family, 194
Feather, 241
Feet of horse, tapir, and dog, compared, 89
Feet, white markings on, 304
Fell pony, 218
Feral horses, 25
ferus, Equus, 46, 129
Fetlock, 53
Fighting, by stallions, (125), 249
Finnish horse, 204, 205, 218, 451
Fjord (Norwegian) pony, 40, 197, 198–99, (200)
Flanders, black horse of, 230, 236, 239, 244, 245
Flemish horse, 116, 218
Foal, body proportions of, 54, (55); develop-ment of, 247
Foa's zebra, 355
Foot skeletons of tapir, rhinoceros, and horse, (88)
Forerunners of the horse, (31), (32), (34), (36), (38)
Forest horse, 44, 128, 146, 147–50, 242
French Coach horse, (124), 205
French draft horse, (124), 245
Friesian horse, 218
Frog, 63
Furioso-North Star horse, 218
Fuzztail, 26

Gaits, 259–62
Galiceno, 218
Gallop, 260–61
Gambia, horses of, 210
Garron, 208, 218, 220
Gaskin, 53
Gaucho, 116
Gelderland, 218
Gelding, 23
Genera of the Equidae, 39

Genet, 24
Geographic distribution of zebras, (338)
German Coach horse, (124), 205, 212
germanicus, Equus caballus, 148, 232
Germany, horses of, 208
Gestation, in horse, 247; in donkey, 397; in Grévy's zebra, 398
Get (produce), 23
Ghorkhar, 327
Giants, equine, 400–403
Gidran horse, 205, 219, 451
giganteus, Equus, 404
Ginete, 24, (123)
Gloger's rule, 305
gmelini, Equus caballus, 47, 136–46, (141)
Gotland pony, 219
Grade horse, 24
Granddam, 23
Grand National Steeplechase, 288
Grandsire, 23
Grant's zebra, (335), 352, 364, 365; measure-ments of, 413
"Great Horse," 230, 233, 239, 242
Great Indian rhinoceros, 90–92, (91)
Greek and Roman horses, 112, 113
Greek horse, 208
Grévy's zebra, 335–43, (336), (338–44); body outline of, (418); measurements of, 413
Grey (coloration), 299, 300
Greyhound and horse, speeds of, (264–66)
greyi, Equus quagga, (380), 381
Grey's quagga, (376), 381; skull of, (380)
Groningen, 219
Growth curves in various mammals, (57)
Growth of the limb bones in the horse, (58); in weight, 57
Grullo (coloration), 301
Gudebrandsdal horse, 44, 199, 219
Gulliver's Travels, 26

Hack, 219
Hackney horse, 120, (123), 214, 219
Hackney pony, (123), 219
Haflinger pony, 197, 219
Hal (trotting) family, 175
"Half-asses," 316–22
Halfbred, 24
Halfbred Arabian, 205
Hambletonian 10, pedigree of, (179)
Hanoverian horse, 212, 219, 452
hartmannae, Equus zebra, 350–52
Hartmann's (mountain) zebra, (347), 350–52; measurements of, 413
Head length, variability of, 414, 433*
Head of Arabian horse, (155), (156), 157, 158, 160
Head of Assyrian horse, 109, 111
Heads of black and white rhinoceroses, com-pared, 99
Heart, weight of in horse, 250
"Heat" (season) in mare, 247
Heavy ("coldblood") breeds, (124)
Height, how measured, 154*
Hemionus, Equus, 30, 33, 35, (129), 316–28
Hemippus, 329–32; skull of, (332)
Hesperohippus, 436, 438, 439
High jump in horse and man, comparison of, 286; stages of, (285), (287)

Highland pony, (123), 197, (201), 220
"High school" horses, 294, (295)
Hinny, 390, 391
Hipparion, 39
Hippidion, 39
Hippidium, (38)
Hippodrome, 22
Hippomorpha, 37
Hippotigris, (34), 35, 345–52, 352*, 438
Hittites, training of horses by, 116
Hobbie (or Connemara), 139, 199
Hoby, 22
Holland, horses of, 208
Holstein (German) horse, 220, 452
Hoofs, abnormal, 408, (409); of Celtic pony and horse of Solutré, 147; of horse, 60, (63), (65); of horse and donkey, compared, 63; of various Equidae, (65)
Horn dimensions in rhinoceroses, 96, 98
Horse, classification of, 37; draft, pulling ability in, 290–92; evolution of skull and feet in, (38); external measurements of, 412; gaits of, 259–62; head markings in, (302); intelligence of, 255–57; jumping ability in, 283–90; life history of, 247; muscles in, 251–54; nomenclature of, 21; origin of name of, 21–22; physiology of, 250; points of, (41), (42); stable management of, 248–50; of Solutré, 108, 109; weights of body parts, 251, 252
Horses, breeds of, geographical, 208–10; diving, 294–95; domestic, coat color in, 299–305; ancestral types of, 146; heights, weights, and body builds in, 205; "high school", 294, (295); in New World, first domestic, 117, 118; leading light breeds in the United States, 214; "Liberty", 294; optimum body weights in, 235; relative length of croup in, 161
Houyhnhnms, 26
Human skeleton, (51)
Hungarian horses, feral, (204)
Hungarian Shagya horse, 220
Hungary, horses of, 208
Huns, shod horses of the, 116
Hunter, 152, 220
Huzulen pony, 220
Hybrid, 24; in various Equidae, 395–99; donkey x zebra, 396; horse x zebra, 396
Hyksos ("shepherd kings"), 47, 112, 116
Hypohippus, 34, (38), 39
Hyracotherium, 28, 30, 39

Icelandic pony, 197, (198), 205, 208, 220
India, horses of, 210
Indian onager, 327–28
Indians, first horses of the, 118
Indochina, horses of, 210
Indonesia, horses of, 210
Iran, horses of, 210
Iraq, horses of, 210
Irish horse. *See* Connemara
Isabella (ysabella) coloration, 299

Jalda, 24
Japan, horses of, 210
Java horse, 210
Javan rhinoceros, (90), 93
Jockey Club, 166*
Jockey (name), 23

Jockeys, weights of, 165
Jumar (or *jumart*), 24
"Jungle jeep" (Army mule), 392
Jutland horse, 220

Kabarda (or Kabardin) horse, 220
Kathiawar horse, 221
Kellogg Percherons, (239)
Kentucky Derby, 273
Kiang, 321–23, (322)
Kladruby horse, 194, 221
Klepper pony, 221
Knabstrupper horse, (211)
Konik, 197, 221
Kruger National Park, (362)
Kulan, 129*, 316–21, (317–19); body outline of, (416); measurements of, 413

Large Nonius horse, 205
Lascaux Cave, paintings of horses in, 106
Latvia, horses of, 208
leoni, Equus conversidens, 438
"Leopard-spotted" horse, (211)
Lesser one-horned (Javan) rhinoceros, 93
"Liberty" horses, 221
Light ("warmblood") breeds, (123)
Limb bones, inclinations of, 233–34; indices of, in various Equidae, 426–27; measurements of, in various Equidae, 424–25
Limousin (hunter), 208, 221
Lindsay Arabian, 119
Lipizzan, 122, (124), 192–96, (193–95), 205, 452
Lithuanian horse, 208
Longevity in the horse, 248
lorenzi, Equus quagga, 381
Lundy pony, 221
Lung capacity in the horse, 250

Macassar horse, 210
Madagascar, horses of, 210
Majorca jack, 306, 307
Malay tapir, 83–85, (84)
Mallenders (chestnuts), 64
Maltese jack, 306
Mambrino (trotting) family, 175
Manada, 25
Manchurian horse, 210
Mandar horse, 210
Manipur pony, 221
Mare, 23
"Mark" in teeth, 71
Markham Arab, 117
Masure horse, 222
Measurement diagram of pelvis, (59)
Measurements, how averaged, 131*; metric, 365*; standard, of horse, (412)
Mecklenburg horse, 222, 452
Meniscotheridae, 80
Merychippus, (32), (34), (36), (38)
Mesohippus, (32), (34), (36), (38)
Mesopotamia, domestication of horses in, 116
Metacarpus. *See* Cannon, fore
Metacarpus, measurements of, 424–25, 433*
Metapodial width, variability of, 433*
Metatarsus (or hind cannon). *See* Metapodials, 49, (50)
Metric system, 365*

Mexico, horses of, 209
Mezohegyes horse, 205, 452
Milk teeth, 73, (74)
Miniature ponies, donkeys, and mules, 404–7
Miohippus, (34), (38)
Missouri fox-trotting horse, 222
Mongolian pony, 222; cross-breeding with Connemara, 139
Mongolian wild horse. *See* Przevalsky's horse
Mongols, war horses of, 117
Morgan horse, (123), 183–85, (184), 205, 214, 452
Morocco, horses of, 210
mosbachensis, Equus caballus, 148, 232
Mosbach horse (fossil), 148, 232
Mountain zebra, (336), 345–52, 361, (346), (348), (349); body outline of, (419); ridden under saddle, (384)
Mule, domestic, 390–95, (391–95); pregnancy in, 395
Mustang (or Bronco), 25, 121, (123), 222, 296
Mustanger, 25

Nag, 24
Names of horses, 21–27
Narragansett pacer, 174, 222
Neigh, 26
Newborn foal, body proportions of, 54, (55)
New Forest pony, 222
Nez Percé Indians, 26, (211), 214, 218
Nivernais (French) draft horse, 208, 245
Nomenclature of the horse, 21–27
Nonius (large and small), 205, 223, 452
Norfolk trotter, 174
Noric (Pinzgauer) horse, 223
Norische horse, 245
North Swedish horse, 452
Norwegian horse, 40, 223, 453
Nubian wild ass, 311–13, (312)

Oberlander horse, 245, 453
"Occidental" horse group, 123, 149
occidentalis, Equus. See Quaggoides
Occipital Index, 69
Oldenburg horse, 205, 212, 453
"Old English black horse" (Shire), 243
Onager, Indian, 327–29, (328); Persian, 323–27, (325); Syrian, 329–31, (330)
One-horned (Indian) rhinoceros, greater, 90–92
One-horned (Javan) rhinoceros, lesser, (90), 93
Oreana ("wild" horse), 26
"Oriental" horse group, 123, 149
Orloff trotter, 179–80, 181, 205, 209, 453
"Overweight" in horses, 236*
Oxen, pulling ability in, 292

Pacer, harness of, (178)
Pace (gait), 260
pacificus, Equus, caballus, 48, (437)
Pacing records, 276
Pacing time, formula for, 279*
Pad-nag, 24
Paint (coloration), 26, 300
Palfrey, 24
Palomino, 26, 152, 214, 223
Palomino-Pintados, 26
Parahippus, skull of, 36
Paso Fino, 209

Pastern, 53
Pelvis, 59–62; measurement diagram of, (59)
Percheron, 120, 122, 124, 236–37, (237–39), 245, 394, 404*, 453
Percherons, circus, 294
Perissodactyla, 37, (81)
Persian, 223
Persian onager, 323–27, (325)
Peru, horses of, 209
Peruvian Paso, 223
Pfalz-Zweibruck, 223
Phenacodus, 80
Phylogeny of the genus *Equus,* 436–39
Phylum, 37
Physiology of the horse, 250
Picardy horse, 245
Piebald (coloration), 26, 300
Pinchaque (Roulin's tapir), 82
Pintado, 26, 211
Pinto, 26, 224, 301
Pinzgauer (Austrian draft) horse, 208, 245, 453
Plantation Walking Horse, 214
Pleistocene period, age of, 147
Plesippus, 30*, (34), 334, 438
pli caballin, 77
Pliohippus, 30*, 31, 32, 33, (34), (36), 439
Points of a good horse, per Xenophon, 112–13
Points of the horse, (41), (42)
Poitou jack, 307; mule, (395)
Poll, 54
Polo, introduced into China, 116
Polo pony, 224
Pomeranian horse, 224
Ponies, breeds of, 196–97
Pony, 26; definition of, 40*
Pony of the Americas, 224
Pregnancy (gestation) in the horse, 247
Pregnancy in the mule, 395
Prehistoric paintings of horses, 107, 108
Produce (offspring), 26
Przevalsky's horse, 108, 128–35, (129), (130), (132), (133), (134), 147, 148, 303, 413, (415), (437)
przewalskii, Equus caballus, 46, 47 (*see also* Przevalsky's horse)
Pulling (draft) ability, 290–92
Pulse rate in the horse, 250
pumpelli, Equus, 45, 109
Purebred, 26

Quagga, 372–84; foal, (377); measurements of, 413; skull of, (379), (380), (383); Western, 385–86
quagga, Equus, (336), 372–84
Quaggoides (subgen. nov., Willoughby, 1966), 33, 345, 352–84, 352*, 385, 386, 387, (421), 436, (437), 438
Quarter Horse, 185–90, (186), (189), 205, 214, 266–67, 453; first breeding of, 119
"Quarter Pathers," 119

Racing records, 269, 275, 276, 280; effect of date on, 272
Rack (gait), 262
Rancho La Brea (fossil locality), 385–86, 387
Remuda, 25
Rheinish-Belgian draft horse, 453
Rheinish-Dutch draft horse, 244, 453

Rhinoceros, foot bones of, (88); Great Indian, 91–93. (90), (91), (444); Javan, 93; skull of Javan, (90); Sumatran, 94–95; black, 95–98, (97); foot of, 97; white, 98–103, (99), (102); distribution of white, (99), 104; horn dimensions in, 92; weight of newborn, 92
Rhinoceros and Baluchithere compared, (444)
Rhinoceroses, 87–105
Rhinoceros sondaicus, 87, (90), 93
Rhinoceros unicornis, (90), 91–93
Ridgeling, 23
Riding, bareback, 116, 294; of horse, first, 116
robustus, Equus caballus, 47
Roulin's tapir, 82
Running ability in the horse, 262–83, (263), (264), (265), (266), (267), (270), (271), (276)
Running (galloping) time, formula for, 272
Russia, horses of, 209
Russian Saddle Horse, 224

Sallenders (chestnuts), 64
Sardinian pony, 224
Schleswig horse, 224
Scythians, as horse tamers, 110, 138
Selene, horse of, (114)
selousii, Equus burchelli, 366–67
Selous's zebra, 352, 366–67; coat patterns in, 355, 357, (360)
Senegal, horses of, 210
Serbia, horses of, 209
Shetland pony, 199–203, (202); body outline of, (414); crossed with Shire, 203; crossed with Welsh pony, 139, 143; measurements of, 413; pelvis of, (61), (62)
Shire horse, 205, 206, 214, 232, 242–43, 404, 442, 454
Sire, 23
Skeleton of the horse, (50)
Skewbald (coloration), 26, 300
Skeletons measured by the author, 434–35
Skogruss (Gotland) pony, 224
Skull and teeth, equine, 67–79
Skull length (basilar) in various Equidae, 431; standard measurements of, in various Equidae, 428–29
Skulls, *Eohippus* to *Equus,* (31), (36), (38)
Skyros (Greek) pony, 224, 254
Sleep in the horse, 248
Solutré, horse bones at, 108; horse of, 243
Somaliland, horses of, 210
Somali wild ass, 313–14; measurements of, 413
South Africa, horses of, 210
South America, horses of, 209; horses first bred in, 119
South German draft horse, 224
South Russian tarpan. *See* Tarpan
Southwest Africa, horses of, 210
Spain, horses of, 209
Spanish horse, 224
Specific gravity in the horse, 252
Spiti pony, 225
Stallion, 23
Standardbred (harness) horse, (123), 173–79, (176), (178), 214, 225, 454; measurements of, 413
Standard Deviation, 432
Standard Range (1000 cases), 60*, (62)
Statistical measures, 432–33

Steed, 23
Steeplechase, Grand National, 288
stenonis, Equus, 148
"Steppe type," 44, 45
Stifle, 54
Stirrups, first in Europe, 116
Stomach, capacity of, 248*
Suckling, 23
Sudanese horse, 210
Suffolk (or Suffolk Punch) horse, 120, (124), 205, 243–44
Sumatran rhinoceros, 94–95
Supporting area of the feet (soles), 443
Surface anatomy of the horse, (41)
Surface area in the horse, 252
Sweating in the horse, 250
Sweden, horses of, 209
Switzerland, horses of, 209
Syrian (Anaze) horse, 210
Syrian onager, 329–32
Sythians, taming of horse by, 115

Tail male, 23
Tapir, Baird's, 82; Brazilian, 82, 83, 85, (86); Dow's, 82; Malay, 83–85, (84); Roulin's, 82
Tapirus terrestris, 82, 83, 85, (86), (88); *bairdi,* 82; *dowi,* 82; *roulini,* 82
Tarbenian horse, 225
Tarpan (= South Russian tarpan), 136–46, (138), (139), (141), (144), (228)
Temperature in the horse, 250
Tennessee Walking Horse, 214
Terms for horse, 21–27
Thoracic vertebrae, 49, (50), 51
Thoroughbred, 24, (123), 165, (166), (167), 168, (169), (170), 171, (172), (173), 205, 214, 273, 274, 442, 454; first in America, 119; measurements of, (169), 413; racing records in, 268–69
Tigre (spotted horse), 211
Timor pony, 225
Togo pony, 210
Tooth wear in the horse, (76)
Trakehner (East Prussian) horse, 205, 225, 451, 454–55
Tripolitania, horses of, 210
Trotter. *See* Standardbred
Trotters, data on, 278
Trotting records, 275–77
Trotting time, formula for, 277
trouessarti, Equus quagga, 381
Tunisia, horses of, 210
Turk, (123), 205, 225
Turkey, horses of, 210

Ukrainian steppe horse, 209

Vaquero, 25
Veglia (Austrian island) pony, 208, 455
Vertebrae, number of in various Equidae, 51
Viatka pony, 197, 225
Viking (Gotland) pony, 197
Virginia Saddle Horse (see American Saddle Horse)
Volume, area, and weight of body, 441–42

Ward's zebra, 348
"Warmblood," 206

Weanling, 23
Weight of limbs in relation to weight of body, 442
Weight of muscles in the horse, 251
Welsh mountain pony, (123), 197, 214, 226
Western quagga. *See Quaggoides*
Westfale (German) horse, 226
White rhinoceros, 98–103, (99), (102–4)
Wild horses in the Middle Ages, 114
Withers, 54; height, variability of, 433
"Wood-tarpan," 147
Woronesch (Russian draft) horse, 226
Württemberg horse, 226

Xenophon's description of a good horse, 112–13

Yellowish coat color. *See* Dun, 301
Yorkshire Coach horse, (124), 226
Yugoslavia, horses of. *See* Serbia and Croatia, 209

Zebra, Böhm's, (335), 355, (359), 363–65; Burchell's, (336), 352–65, (353), (356), (357), (359), (360), (362–64); Chapman's, (336), (363–71); Damaraland (*See* Chapman's); Grant's, (335), 364, 365; Grévy's, 335–43, (336–42); Hartmann's mountain, (347), 350–52; Mountain, 345–50, (344), (346), (348), (349), 361; body outline of, (419); Selous's, 355, (357), (360), 365, 366–67
zebra zebra, Equus. See Mountain zebra
zebra zebra hartmannae. See Hartmann's zebra
Zébret, 397
Zébrule, 397, (398)
Zébryde, 397, (397)
Zeeland (Friesian) horse, 208, 226
Zemaitukas (Lithuanian) horse, 197, 208, 226, 455
Zoological classification of the horse, 37